Family-Based Intervention for Child and Adolescent Mental Health

Family-Based Intervention for Child and Adolescent Mental Health

A Core Competencies Approach

Edited by

Jennifer L. Allen
University of Bath

David J. Hawes
University of Sydney

Cecilia A. Essau
University of Roehampton

CAMBRIDGE
UNIVERSITY PRESS

University Printing House, Cambridge CB2 8BS, United Kingdom

One Liberty Plaza, 20th Floor, New York, NY 10006, USA

477 Williamstown Road, Port Melbourne, VIC 3207, Australia

314–321, 3rd Floor, Plot 3, Splendor Forum, Jasola District Centre,
New Delhi – 110025, India

79 Anson Road, #06–04/06, Singapore 079906

Cambridge University Press is part of the University of Cambridge.

It furthers the University's mission by disseminating knowledge in the pursuit of
education, learning, and research at the highest international levels of excellence.

www.cambridge.org
Information on this title: www.cambridge.org/9781108706063
DOI: 10.1017/9781108682053

First published 2021

Printed in the United Kingdom by TJ Books Limited, Padstow Cornwall

A catalogue record for this publication is available from the British Library.

ISBN 978-1-108-70606-3 Paperback

Contents

Part IV Family Intervention for Children at Risk Due to Family Dysfunction or Past Adversity

Part V New Developments in Family-Based Intervention

Contributors

James F. Alexander
Functional Family Therapy, LLC, Seattle, Washington, USA, and Department of Psychology, University of Utah, Salt Lake City, Utah, USA

Jennifer L. Allen
Department of Psychology, University of Bath, Bath, United Kingdom

Emma A. Archibald
Robert S. and Grace W. Stone Primary Prevention Initiatives, Wellesley Centers for Women, Wellesley, Massachusetts, USA

Joan R. Asarnow
Semel Institute for Neuroscience and Human Behavior, University of California, Los Angeles, Los Angeles, California, USA

Rebecca F. Bertuccio
College of Education, Department of Educational Psychology, Counseling, and Special Education, Pennsylvania State University, University Park, Pennsylvania, USA

Kay Bunagan
Department of Psychology, Ateneo de Manila University, Manila, Philippines

Penny Corkum
Department of Psychology and Neuroscience, Dalhousie University, Halifax, NS, Canada

Mark R. Dadds
School of Psychology, University of Sydney, Sydney, NSW, Australia

Helena Draxler
Department of Social and Psychological Studies, Karlstad University, Karlstad, Sweden

Cecilia A. Essau
Department of Psychology, University of Roehampton, London, United Kingdom

Carri Fisher
School of Psychology, University of Sydney, Sydney, NSW, Australia

Elizabeth A. Fuller
MIND Institute, University of California, Davis, Davis, California, USA

Sarah H. Gladstone
Robert S. and Grace W. Stone Primary Prevention Initiatives, Wellesley Centers for Women, Wellesley, Massachusetts, USA

Tracy R. G. Gladstone
Robert S. and Grace W. Stone Primary Prevention Initiatives, Wellesley Centers for Women, Wellesley, Massachusetts, USA

Sasha Gorrell
Department of Psychiatry and Behavioral Sciences, University of California, San Francisco, San Francisco, California, USA

Sisi Guo
Semel Institute for Neuroscience and Human Behaviour, University of California, Los Angeles, Los Angeles, California, USA

Kyrill Gurtovenko
Department of Psychology, University of Washington, Seattle, Washington, USA

Cristin M. Hall
College of Education, Department of Educational Psychology, Counseling, and Special Education, Pennsylvania State University, University Park, Pennsylvania, USA

Sophie S. Havighurst
Mindful Centre for Training and Research in Developmental Health, Department of Psychiatry, University of Melbourne, Travancore, VIC, Australia

David J. Hawes
School of Psychology, University of Sydney, Sydney, NSW, Australia

Regina M. Hechanova
Department of Psychology, Ateneo de Manila University, Manila, Philippines

Jennifer Hudson
Department of Psychology, Centre for Emotional Health, Macquarie University, Sydney, NSW, Australia

Michelle Johnson
Department of Psychology and Neuroscience, Dalhousie University, Halifax, NS, Canada

Ernest N. Jouriles
Department of Psychology, Southern Methodist University, Dallas, Texas, USA

Lynn Fainsilber Katz
Department of Psychology, University of Washington, Seattle, Washington, USA

Christiane E. Kehoe
Mindful Centre for Training and Research in Developmental Health, Department of Psychiatry, University of Melbourne, Travancore, VIC, Australia

Elizabeth Keys
Department of Psychology and Neuroscience, Dalhousie University, Halifax, NS, Canada

Patrick LaCount
Center for Child Health, Behavior, and Development, Seattle Children's Research Institute, Seattle, Washington, USA

Daniel Le Grange
Benioff UCSF Professor in Children's Health, UCSF Weill Institute for Neurosciences, Department of

Psychiatry and Behavioral Sciences, University of California, San Francisco, San Francisco, USA, and Emeritus Professor of Psychiatry and Behavioral Neuroscience, The University of Chicago, Chicago, IL, USA

Patty Leijten
Faculty of Social and Behavioural Sciences, University of Amsterdam, Amsterdam, Netherlands

Renee McDonald
Department of Psychology, Southern Methodist University, Dallas, Texas, USA

Thomas H. Ollendick
Child Study Center, Department of Psychology, Virginia Polytechnic Institute and State University, Blackburg, Virginia, USA

Nicola Palfrey
Australian Child and Adolescent Trauma, Loss and Grief Network, Australian National University, Canberra, ACT, Australia

Dave S. Pasalich
Research School of Psychology, Australian National University, Canberra, ACT, Australia

Jocelyn Paul
Department of Psychology and Neuroscience, Dalhousie University, Halifax, NS, Canada

Tara S. Peris
Semel Institute for Neuroscience and Human Behaviour, University of California, Los Angeles, Los Angeles, California, USA

Caitlin Rancher
Department of Psychology, Southern Methodist University, Dallas, Texas, USA

Gabrielle Rigney
Appleton Institute, Central Queensland University, Wayville, South Australia

Michael S. Robbins
Functional Family Therapy, LLC, Seattle, Washington, USA, and Oregon Research Institute, Eugene, Oregon, USA

Sally J. Rogers
MIND Institute, University of California, Davis, Davis, California, USA

Satoko Sasagawa
Faculty of Psychology, Mejiro University, Tokyo, Japan

Margaret Sibley
Department of Psychiatry and Behavioral Sciences, University of Washington School of Medicine and Center for Child Health, Behavior, and Development and Seattle Children's Research Institute, Seattle, Washington, USA

Gemma Sicouri
Department of Psychology, Centre for Emotional Health, Macquarie University, Sydney, NSW, Australia

Caroline Swetlitz
Department of Psychological and Brain Sciences, Boston University, Boston, Massachusetts, USA

Chantal Ellis S. Tabo-Corpuz
Department of Psychology, Ateneo de Manila University, Manila, Philippines

Martha Tompson
Department of Psychological and Brain Sciences, Boston University, Boston, Massachusetts, USA

Lucy A. Tully
School of Psychology, University of Sydney, Sydney, NSW, Australia

Preface

Aims and Rationale for This Book

This book aims to outline (1) clinician skills, knowledge and attitudes forming the competencies that are core to the delivery of evidence-based family interventions (as opposed to a the traditional approach that focuses solely on the content that is delivered in such interventions) and (2) the adaptation of standardized intervention components for cases (including complex cases) that present with distinct needs in terms of co-morbid psychopathology and risk markers. To achieve these goals, the authors address questions such as (1) what do you consider to be the most important therapist competencies for achieving successful outcomes in the treatment presented in your chapter? (2) why are those competencies important when working with more severe/complex cases? (3) what aspects of those competencies are commonly misunderstood by new clinicians when beginning to deliver such therapy? and (4) what recommendations do you have for therapists wanting to develop those competencies?

Treatment protocols featured in this book reflect the shift towards the flexible delivery of family intervention of the last 20 years [1]. Treatment may be delivered in an individual or group family basis via different modalities, including traditional face-to-face treatment, bibliotherapy or the use of phone-assisted or internet-based technology (see Chapter 7). Modern family therapy for child and adolescent mental health problems no longer requires all family members to be present at all treatment sessions [2]. Instead, treatment may be parent focused, include parent-only sessions or include a mix of child-only, parent-only and family sessions. Family members who participate in treatment may include the child's biological or adoptive parents, foster or kinship carers and siblings or extended family members involved in the child's care. The role of parents in family intervention also differs across programmes. Parents may be viewed as a coach or co-therapist, providing motivation and support and helping to teach, plan and implement treatment strategies. Parents may be considered co-clients if they also have mental health difficulties [3].

This text focuses primarily on cognitive behavioural therapy (CBT) because of its strong evidence base, reflected in its status as a first-line recommended treatment in national guidelines published by the National Institute for Clinical Excellence (NICE) for many mental disorders in childhood and adolescence, including depression, anxiety and conduct problems [4–6]. We acknowledge that different therapeutic approaches to CBT also possess a solid evidence base or show great promise. This volume therefore includes systemic approaches to the treatment of eating disorders and conduct disorder in Part III, an attachment-based approach to working with kinship carers of children who have been maltreated in Part IV and emotion socialization-based approaches to family intervention in Part V. Finally, while family intervention for child and adolescent mental health problems has made great strides in recent decades, much work remains to be done to increase intervention reach and engagement, reduce dropout and improve treatment success rates for all families. As such, contributors acknowledge when their guidance is supported by an evidence base and when it is derived from their clinical experience.

Book Structure

This text is divided into five main parts. Part I focuses on the theoretical underpinnings of current family-based interventions for children and adolescents and the clinical competencies that are core to the delivery and implementation of such interventions. Part II addresses specific clinical competencies of core relevance to clinical practice with families of children and adolescents. Examples include engaging fathers and families from culturally diverse backgrounds and the rising application of technology to deliver family-based intervention. Parts III and IV address specific interventions that are informed by a core competencies perspective. Interventions presented in Part III will be those supported in the treatment and management of the major psychological disorders seen among children and adolescents, including anxiety, depression, attention deficit hyperactivity disorder, conduct disorder, autism spectrum disorder and eating disorders. Interventions presented in Part IV have been shown to benefit families at risk for the emergence of child and adolescent disorders due to contextual risk factors. These include interventions for families at risk for, or exposed to, child maltreatment, families affected by intimate partner violence and working with parents who suffer from anxiety or depression.

The chapters in Parts III and IV focus on specific intervention programmes, which will each be addressed in terms of theoretical foundations and the core competencies needed by therapists to effectively implement the programme, such as consultation with parents affected by their own mental health problems, engagement of fathers, liaison with key systems in the broader ecology of the child (e.g., schools, health or legal services), assessment methods, treatment planning, key treatment components and adaptations based on co-morbid disorders and markers for heterogeneous risk pathways. Chapters include case material to illustrate treatment principles and discuss barriers to treatment and problem-solving in relation to common difficulties. All chapters in Parts III–V make reference to the various competency domains identified in recent models of therapist competencies in the literature [7, 8]. Parts I and II do not include reference to these domains because of their focus on theory or knowledge specific to their set focus (e.g., engaging with families from diverse cultural backgrounds, use of phone-assisted or online technology) rather than the implementation of treatment programmes.

Conclusion

We hope that this book will help practitioners and trainers to understand the key competencies relating to the delivery of evidence-based family intervention programmes for child and adolescent mental health problems. We have encouraged contributors to portray complex cases involving co-morbid problems,

risk markers, events that cause disruptions to family and attachment relationships and cultural diversity to provide support for families with whom practitioners are likely to work in their real-world clinical practices. We believe that a core competencies–based approach assists practitioners to reflect on areas of strength and areas where they need further training and support and facilitates the uptake and quality of implementation of evidence-based family intervention.

References

1. Diamond G, Josephson A. Family-based treatment research: A 10-year update. *Journal of the American Academy of Child and Adolescent Psychiatry* 2005; **44**(9):872–87.

2. Josephson AM. Reinventing family therapy: Teaching family intervention as a new treatment modality. *Academic Psychiatry* 2008; **32**(5):405–13.

3. Hawes DJ, Allen J. Evidence-based parenting interventions: Current perspectives and clinical strategies. In: Hodes M, Gau S (eds.), *Positive Mental Health, Fighting Stigma and Promoting Resiliency for Children and Adolescents*. New York: Academic Press, 2016, pp. 185–204.

4. National Institute for Health and Care Excellence. Depression in children and young people: Identification and management. NICE Guideline No. NG134, 2019. Available at www.nice.org.uk/guidance/NG134.

5. National Institute for Health and Care Excellence. Anxiety disorders. Quality Standard QS53, 2014. Available at www.nice.org.uk/guidance/qs53/chapter/Quality-statement-2-Psychological-interventions.

6. National Institute for Health and Care Excellence. Antisocial behaviour and conduct disorders in children and young people: Recognition and management. Clinical Guideline No. CG158, 2013. Available at www.nice.org.uk/Guidance/CG158.

7. Sburlati ES, Schniering CA, Lyneham HJ, Rapee RM. A model of therapist competencies for the empirically supported cognitive behavioral treatment of child and adolescent anxiety and depressive disorders. *Clinical Child and Family Psychology Review* 2011; **14**(1):89–109.

8. Roth AD, Pilling S. Using an evidence-based methodology to identify the competences required to deliver effective cognitive and behavioural therapy for depression and anxiety disorders. *Behavioural and Cognitive Psychotherapy* 2008; **36**(2):129–47.

Chapter

A Core-Competency Perspective on Family-Based Intervention for Child and Adolescent Mental Health

Jennifer L. Allen, David J. Hawes and Cecilia A. Essau

Many fields of education have undergone a shift away from training models focused on traditional learning and assessment practices towards models that are competency based. In the field of clinical psychology, the competency-based movement has become particularly influential and has emphasized the need to support practitioners and trainees by identifying, teaching and assessing the competencies needed to effectively implement evidence-based practice in the treatment of mental health problems across the lifespan. *Competence* has been defined as 'the habitual and judicious use of communication, knowledge, technical skills, clinical reasoning, emotions, values, and reflection in the daily practice for the benefit of the individual and community served' and depends on 'habits of mind, including attentiveness, critical curiosity, self-awareness, and presence' [1, p. 227]. Competencies encompass specific skills, behaviours, attitudes, knowledge and personal factors that influence a professional's ability to execute evidence-based practice effectively in a range of areas, including assessment, case formulation and intervention [2, 3]. Competency-based education, training and assessment programmes have gained popularity in recent years because of the recognition that poor implementation of evidence-based practice (EBP) may be at least partly due to ineffective training approaches [4]. *Evidence-based practice* is defined as 'the integration of the best available research with clinical expertise, in the context of patient characteristics, culture, and preferences' [5, p. 1].

In recent decades, major advances have been made in the development and evaluation of evidence-based treatments for a wide range of mental health problems in children and adolescents, including depression [7] (see also Chapter 8), anxiety [6] (see also Chapter 9), conduct problems [8] (see also Chapter 10), attention deficit hyperactivity disorder (ADHD [9]; see also Chapter 11), autism spectrum disorder [11] (see also Chapter 13), eating disorders [10] (see also Chapter 14)

and sleep problems (e.g., see Chapter 15). Importantly, the most effective treatments for child and adolescent psychopathology are often family based, in that they emphasize the active involvement of family members beyond the referred individual. In this chapter, we use the term *family-based intervention* to refer to any treatment that involves two or more family members, with at least one parent considered an 'essential participant' [12, 13]. Family-based interventions feature heavily in guidelines regarding empirically supported treatments (ESTs) that have been published by professional bodies (e.g., Division 12 of the American Psychological Association, American Psychiatric Association), multidisciplinary research networks (e.g., Cochrane Collaboration), and government organizations (e.g., the UK National Institute for Health and Care Excellence [NICE]) in recent years. Empirically supported treatments are typically classified as such after being shown to be effective in treating particular disorders in randomized, controlled trials (RCTs) comparing a manualized treatment protocol to either an active or wait-list control condition [14, 15]. However, despite the growing number of ESTs that now exist, only a small proportion of children and adolescents in the general population receive these treatments, and this is understood to be due in large part to a lack of appropriately trained therapists [16].

Closing the Gap Between Science and Practice

In order to facilitate the regulation of teaching curricula for the training of mental health practitioners, Roth and Pilling [17] proposed a model of therapist competencies for delivering cognitive behaviour therapy (CBT) to adults with depression and anxiety disorders which has been particularly influential. The formulation of this model occurred as part of a large-scale initiative to increase the quality and dissemination of ESTs in England known as Improving Access to Psychological Therapies (IAPT). Since its commencement in 2008, IAPT has grown to treat more than 560,000 people each year. Outcomes are generally consistent with the evidence base, with roughly 50 per cent of adults recovering and another two-thirds showing reliable improvement [16]. This initiative was described as 'world-beating' in a *Nature* editorial (see [15]). Indeed, it represented a significant advancement for mental health practitioners in England, as prior to this adults suffering from anxiety and depression were offered medication as the sole treatment option [18].

In 2011, the Children and Young People's Improving Access to Psychological Therapies (CYP-IAPT) programme was launched. It differed from the adult version in that it set out to improve the quality of treatment in existing, as opposed to new, services in the health, social care, education or third-sector services. The programme insists on the use of manualized treatment protocols supported by positive outcomes in RCTs, and therapists must demonstrate that they possess the set of competencies required for effective implementation of these ESTs [15]. Staff at IAPT sites were trained in ESTs, including family CBT and parent training programmes, extending in the second year to systemic family therapy and interpersonal psychotherapy. The programme was systematically rolled out over a four-year period, with 70 per cent of all child and adolescent mental health services (CAMHS) reporting adhering to IAPT principles in a 2013 survey [15]. Positive outcomes include decreased waiting times, and more than half of surveyed clinicians reported using outcome data to inform therapy and often/always discussing outcome data with children and families, while 75 per cent reported usually/always engaging in shared decision-making with children and parents. Children and adolescents also reported that they felt empowered by their involvement in service delivery and that monitoring helped them to maintain focus during treatment. These positive outcomes highlight the potential of a core competencies base for the successful implementation of ESTs for families and their children in 'real-world' clinical practice.

Progress in the Conceptualization of Therapist Competencies

Competencies-based approaches have been adopted by clinical psychology training programmes in numerous countries in recent years, including Australia, Canada,

the United Kingdom and the United States, as means of disseminating ESTs [19–22]. Frameworks outlining practitioner competencies for working with child and adolescent populations in geographically specific service contexts have also been developed to promote the knowledge and skills of multidisciplinary workforces and enhance service provision (e.g., [23]). The clinical literature on core competencies and comprehensive models of these competencies have nonetheless focused largely on the evidence-based treatment of mental health problems in adults [17, 24, 25].

In response to the lack of such models focused on the psychological treatment of children and adolescents, Sburlati et al. [4] proposed a model of the core competencies involved in the delivery of CBT to children and adolescents with internalizing disorders. Whereas CBT programmes for anxiety and depression in children and adolescents are typically downward extensions of the adult treatments for these disorders, this model identified additional competencies of unique importance to the treatment of these disorders during childhood and adolescence. These additional competencies include knowledge of typical developmental processes across childhood and adolescence and the family factors implicated in the maintenance of these disorders as necessary for case formulation and treatment planning. An understanding of the unique legal and ethical requirements relating to the provision of therapy to children and adolescents was another competency identified. Additional competencies were those related to building positive therapeutic relationships with parents, the collaborative involvement of parents in treatment, and the ability to implement child/adolescent CBT-specific techniques that fall under the broad categories of general skills (e.g., friendship skills, dealing with bullying skills) and modifying the family environment (e.g., parent contingency management, family communication). Importantly, this model highlights the need for the continuous and flexible adaptation of treatment in response to emerging information regarding the needs of individual children and their families.

The model formulated by Sburlati et al. (4) grouped competencies into three domains: generic therapeutic competencies, CBT competencies, and specific CBT techniques. Generic therapeutic competencies are represented by four categories of competencies: 'practicing professionally', 'understanding of relevant child and adolescent characteristics', 'building a positive relationship' and 'conducting a thorough assessment'. Cognitive behavioural therapy competencies included understanding of CBT theory and research; devising, implementing and revising a CBT case formulation and treatment plan; and the collaborative conduct of CBT sessions; specific CBT techniques related to strategies aimed at changing maladaptive thoughts and behaviours associated with internalizing disorders, managing maladaptive mood and arousal, general skills training (e.g., problem solving, assertiveness) and modification of the family environment (e.g., parent intrusiveness and overprotection management, parental modelling of adaptive behaviour). At the time it was published, this model represented a critical step towards establishing a framework for competencies-based curricula in this area. Part of the important contribution of this model was to demonstrate that the clinical competencies necessary for the evidence-based treatment of internalizing problems in children and adolescents are distinct from those involved in the treatment of those problems in adults. It further demonstrated that such competencies may be somewhat specific to particular types of disorders and served to highlight the need to examine competencies for the treatment of specific mental health problems in their own right.

A Unified Model of Therapist Competencies for Family-Based Intervention

Despite the progress that has been made in formulating accounts of therapist competencies essential to the psychological treatment of child and adolescent psychopathology, there remains considerable scope to build on this work, particularly given ongoing advances in treatment. Although the model of Sburlati et al. [4] perhaps has been the most cited in the clinical psychology literature to date, the focus of that model was intentionally restricted in various ways. First, the forms of psychopathology addressed were limited to anxiety and depression, the treatment of which often differs in key ways from that of other problems. Moreover, the competencies that are required for the treatment of complex presentations of various disorders (e.g., comorbid disorders, disorders in the contexts of marked adversity) may diverge even further (see Chapters 10 and 19). Second, the model was intentionally focused specifically on competencies in the delivery of CBT. Although CBT forms the basis for many of the most well-established psychological treatments available for child and adolescent disorders in general, this is not

always the case. In the field of eating disorders, for example, the most well-established intervention for children and adolescents has been Maudsley family therapy, which is based on a family systems model (see Chapter 14). Likewise, recent progress has been made in the development of interventions that incorporate relationship-based processes related to emotion socialization and attachment (See Chapters 16, 18, 20 and 21). One model outside of CBT that has been addressed in more detail in the literature on therapist competencies is that of interpersonal psychotherapy (IPT) for adolescent depression, also based in part on attachment theory [26], but beyond this, there has been little else. Third, because evidence-based CBT interventions for anxiety and depression have typically been predominantly delivered directly to the individual child or adolescent, therapist competencies related to family-based intervention were a relatively minor focus of the model offered by Sburlati et al. [4].

We propose here that there is a key need for a model of therapist competencies for the evidence-based treatment of child and adolescent psychopathology that encompasses a broad spectrum of psychopathology and complex clinical presentations (e.g., internalizing, externalizing and neurodevelopmental disorders; children affected by severe adversities) as well as the various models of intervention that have received empirical support. Moreover, we argue that there is a need for an expanded account of family-based competencies, which have received only limited attention in the literature to date. In the following sections, we describe a new, unified model of therapist competencies for the family-based treatment of child and adolescent psychopathology that was developed specifically to address this need.

Development of the Current Model

The model presented herein emerged in large part through the process of designing and editing the volume in which it now appears. The previous adult and child/adolescent models were developed by Roth and Pilling [17] and by Sburlati et al. [4,26] using the Delphi technique, a method by which experts in a field are consulted to generate views that are then synthesized and used to establish a common consensus. Although the current model was not the product of a formal Delphi procedure, expert consultation of this kind was central to our method. In assembling the authors of this volume, care was taken to represent current evidence-based treatments for a broad range of child and adolescent disorders. Although the scope of these treatments is limited to those which are family based, inclusion was not otherwise limited based on the theoretical underpinnings of treatment models or theoretical orientations. The contributing authors were selected based on their expertise in the development and delivery of these interventions, and they were asked by the current editors to specifically address the therapist competencies of key importance to such delivery.

Specifically, all contributing authors were asked to identify the core competencies needed for the effective implementation of their manualized treatment protocols following the main categories outlined by Sburlati et al. [4]. These domains include (1) *generic therapeutic competencies* related to all forms of therapy (e.g., knowledge of development and psychopathology, including common co-morbidity; clinical engagement of children and families; assessment of child and adolescent mental health; culturally responsive practices with diverse populations), (2) *CBT- and other theory–based competencies* involved in child and adolescent mental health (e.g., understanding of maintaining factors and change mechanisms, including those concerning specific disorders or forms of co-morbidity; devising, implementing and revising case formulations and treatment plans; collaborative treatment processes; using CBT- or other theory-based strategies to conceptualize and manage inter-parental conflict when working with families), and (3) *specific evidence-based techniques* for the family

treatment of child and adolescent psychopathology (e.g., specific types of strategies for modifying family environment such as a 'behaviour correction routine' for parents).

The first editor reviewed each chapter and extracted the full list of therapist competencies identified by the authors as necessary for the successful implementation of their treatment protocol. After compiling a list of these competencies, an initial model was devised by mapping these identified competencies onto the competency domains emphasized in the model of Sburlati et al. [4]. This process was further informed by a review of existing frameworks of competencies for practitioners in child and adolescent mental health services (CAMHS) based on Australian government policy [23] and publicly available competency frameworks for child and adolescent mental health services by university-based clinical psychology doctoral training programmes [27] (see also www.ucl.ac.uk/CORE). In collaboration with the second and third editors, this model was then further modified and refined to reflect the characteristics of the competencies identified. Details of these modifications, as they relate to components that were retained, are outlined in the following sections.

Overview of the Current Model

The overall model of family-based competencies created through the method described is illustrated in Figure 1.1.

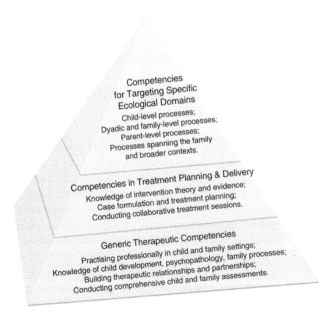

Figure 1.1 A unified model of therapist competencies for the family-based treatment of child and adolescent psychopathology

We refer to it as a *unified model* in that it integrates therapist competencies across child and adolescent disorders and treatments within a single framework. The structure of this model, like that of Sburlati et al. [4], is organized around three core competency domains. Before describing these in detail, it is worth noting how these domains relate to one another. The first domain consists of a foundational domain comprising *generic therapeutic competencies* that are fundamental to clinical practice across a broad range of child and family settings and support the optimal delivery of family-based interventions in general. The second domain, *competencies in treatment planning and delivery*, includes knowledge and abilities that establish the structure and context for delivering specific models of intervention and necessary to plan, implement and flexibly adapt evidence-based treatment components given the unique considerations and needs associated with specific clinical settings and specific families. The third domain, *competencies for targeting specific ecological domains*, relates to the therapists' ability to deliver the content of therapeutic components (e.g., psycho-education, exposure to reduce anxiety, skills training in parenting strategies) in a specific treatment plan. The conceptualization of this domain is informed by an ecological perspective on the various levels at which treatment targets within a family-based intervention may be situated (e.g., individual child/adolescent, dyadic relationships, family level), as soon described in more detail.

Generic Therapeutic Competencies

The competencies that make up this domain are categorized in relation to the four subdomains of practising professionally in child and family settings; knowledge of child development, psychopathology and family processes; building therapeutic relationships and partnerships; and conducting comprehensive child and family assessments (see Table 1.1). These competencies correspond largely to those specified by Sburlati et al. [4] yet are expanded upon in a number of key ways. First, with regard to practising professionally in child and family settings, our model includes the additional competency of understanding of the role, purpose and responsibilities of key disciplines and institutional systems (e.g., health, education, legal and child welfare services) involved in the care of children and families and supporting families to engage with such systems where appropriate. Such competencies are particularly relevant to complex cases and those involving child maltreatment and family violence (see Chapters 18 and 19).

Second, with regard to knowledge of child development, psychopathology and family processes, our model includes two additional competencies: age-appropriate parenting practices as associated with healthy child development and the determinants and origins of quality of parenting (e.g., parent psychopathology, parents' own developmental history) and the developmental psychopathology framework (e.g., ecological-transactional principles regarding the interplay between child characteristics and the family environment across development). This knowledge is particularly key to adapting family-based interventions according to child age and development and to informing interventions to prevent negative child outcomes following exposure to adversity in the family system (see Chapters 18, 19 and 21).

Third, our subdomain building therapeutic relationships and partnerships extends significantly beyond the corresponding subdomain (building a positive relationship) of Sburlati et al. [4] to include an understanding of the unique issues associated with engaging fathers and the ability to undertake father-inclusive practices (see Chapter 5); the ability to engage other family members (e.g., siblings), where appropriate, and to form partnerships with caregivers/stakeholders (e.g., teachers) involved in key assessment or treatment activities (see Chapter 10); and the ability to manage how information is shared and communicated across the family system. We further specify that a key aspect of engaging parents is the ability to jointly engage multiple parents/caregivers [28] and that building therapeutic relationships involves acknowledging the unique experiences, cultural values and expertise within families (see Chapter 6). Finally, our expanded subdomain of conducting comprehensive child and family assessments includes risk assessment not only in relation to self-harm/suicide [4] but the ability to screen for family safety/violence based on known risk factors such as parent anger and negative attributions about the child.

Competencies in Treatment Planning and Delivery

This domain, originally named 'CBT Competencies' by Sburlati et al. [4], was re-named based on the extended scope of the current model, which incorporates additional models of intervention. Subdomains include knowledge of intervention theory and evidence, case formulation and treatment planning, and conducting collaborative treatment sessions (see Table 1.2). More specific modifications to this domain relate, first, to the

Table 1.1 Generic Therapeutic Competencies

Practising Professionally in Child and Family Settings

Knowledge of and ability to operate within professional, ethical and legal codes of conduct relevant to working with diverse populations of children and adolescents and their families (e.g., providing a duty of care)

Possession of an open attitude towards psychotherapy research and an orientation towards evidence-based treatment

Engage in self-reflective practice to assess one's own levels of competence, process the potential impact of personal reactions (e.g., related to family of origin and cultural experiences) on clinical work with families and undertake professional training or supervision when required

Understanding of the role, purpose and responsibilities of key disciplines and institutional systems (e.g., health, education, legal and child welfare services) involved in the care of children and families and supporting families to engage with such systems where appropriate

Knowledge of Child Development, Psychopathology and Family Processes

Typical child development, cognitive, social and emotional developmental processes from childhood to adolescence and their relevance to therapy

Child or adolescent relevant individual differences (e.g., temperament, language impairment) and how these can impact on therapy

Environmental factors (e.g., socioeconomic status, family structure, education) and life events (e.g., bullying, trauma, life transitions) and how these can impact therapy

Diagnostic features of child and adolescent psychopathology and how co-morbid presentations (e.g., learning disorders, physical health conditions) can impact therapy

Age-appropriate parenting practices associated with healthy child development and the determinants and origins of quality of parenting (e.g., parent psychopathology, parents' own developmental history)

The developmental psychopathology framework (e.g., ecological-transactional principles regarding the interplay between child characteristics and the family environment across development)

Building Therapeutic Relationships and Partnerships

Ability to engage the child or adolescent through age-appropriate methods (e.g., interactive games, drawing, creative activities, humour, technology, language) and appropriate session pacing

Ability to engage parents, and form a therapeutic team with the multiple parents/caregivers who form the parental subsystem (or 'parenting team')

Understanding of the unique issues associated with engaging fathers and the ability to undertake father-inclusive practices

Ability to engage other family-members (e.g., siblings), where appropriate, and form partnerships with caregivers/

Table 1.1 (cont.)

Building Therapeutic Relationships and Partnerships

stakeholders (e.g., teachers) involved in key assessment or treatment activities

Ability to manage how information is shared and communicated across the family system

Ability to acknowledge the unique experiences, cultural values and expertise within families and instil hope and optimism for change

Conducting Comprehensive Child and Family Assessments

Ability to undertake an evidence-based, multi-method (e.g., self-report, observational), multi-informant (e.g., child, parent, teacher, allied health professional) clinical assessment of a presenting problem

Ability to integrate assessment reports from the child or adolescent, parents and other informants/professionals

Ability to determine clinical diagnoses with consideration of differential diagnosis

Ability to undertake a comprehensive assessment of the child's or adolescent's current functioning, family functioning, peer relationships, developmental history and stage and their suitability for the intervention

Ability to assess and manage risk of self-harm/suicide and child and family safety/violence based on known risk factors (e.g., parent anger, negative attributions about the child)

knowledge subdomain. Whereas Sburlati et al. [4] referred to the need for theoretical knowledge regarding 'family and other environmental factors', the current model further distinguishes this knowledge in terms of knowledge of parent-level factors (e.g., psychopathology, attributions) as they relate to risk and maintaining mechanisms for psychopathology, dyadic and family processes (e.g., parent-child attachment, interparental conflict and inconsistency, chaos) as they relate to risk and maintaining mechanisms for psychopathology, and other contextual factors (e.g., social isolation, deviant peer affiliation, parent-teacher conflict) as they relate to risk processes and therapy. These distinctions map onto those emphasized in current theories of family-based contributions to child and adolescent mental health (see Chapter 2) and are specified here given the importance of such theory to case formulation in family-based interventions. The presentation of these family-based risk processes may vary greatly in severity across distinct clinical settings and individual cases and at the extreme includes serious failures or disruptions in the

Table 1.2 Competencies in Treatment Planning and Delivery

Knowledge of Intervention Theory and Evidence

Theoretical underpinnings of evidence-based interventions for child and adolescent psychopathology (e.g., change process, indications and exclusions)

Child-level factors (e.g., individual differences, cognitions, behaviours) in explanatory models of psychopathology as they relate to risk and maintaining mechanisms

Parent-level factors (e.g., psychopathology, attributions) as they relate to risk and maintaining mechanisms for psychopathology

Dyadic and family processes (e.g., parent-child attachment, interparental conflict and inconsistency, chaos) as they relate to risk and maintaining mechanisms for psychopathology

Other contextual factors (e.g., social isolation, deviant peer affiliation, parent-teacher conflict) as they relate to risk processes and therapy

Case Formulation and Treatment Planning

Ability to use theory to devise a case formulation that accounts for child/adolescent symptoms/co-morbidity, developmental stage, individual differences, parent, family and social/contextual factors

Ability to design an evidence-based treatment plan that maps onto case formulation by selecting, sequencing and applying appropriate family-based intervention techniques at the appropriate dosage

Ability to communicate information regarding the nature of a disorder, case formulation and treatment plans, with family members (e.g., parents, children) and stakeholders (e.g., teachers) in accordance with their age and role in treatment

Ability to collaboratively negotiate treatment goals and the roles of family and stakeholders (e.g., teachers) in treatment

Ability to collaboratively negotiate the roles of family members (e.g., siblings, caregivers) and relevant stakeholders (e.g., teachers) in treatment

Ability to collect data on treatment progress and outcomes (e.g., self-monitoring) and revise case formulations, treatment plans and goals accordingly

Ability to plan for termination and long-term maintenance of gains following treatment

Conducting Collaborative Treatment Sessions

Ability to collaboratively set and adhere to session goals/agenda

Ability to communicate rationale for specific techniques and the involvement of specific family members/caregivers/stakeholders

Ability to deliver treatment components based on case formulation and characteristics of the child/parents/family, including cultural background, child and parent symptoms and family relationships

Ability to use active, experiential strategies to introduce and promote implementation of skills (e.g., role play, modelling, corrective feedback and reinforcement) and to monitor implementation and progress

Table 1.2 (cont.)

Conducting Collaborative Treatment Sessions

Ability to conduct sessions with developmental sensitivity (e.g., using age-appropriate worksheets, instruction, play-based activities and age-appropriate parenting strategies)

Ability to facilitate an appropriate level of in-session collaboration between child or adolescent, parents and therapist

Ability to promote family members' capacities to support each other as they implement therapeutic strategies between sessions (e.g., parents supporting a child's thought monitoring, mothers and fathers supporting each other to use parenting strategies)

Ability to collaboratively set, plan and review personally meaningful between-session activities

Ability to manage how information is shared across the family system

Ability to manage obstacles and resistance to change among family members

relationship between the child/adolescent and caregiver, as in the case of maltreatment or witnessing of interparental violence. The lasting impact of such adversity on children may include, among other things, difficulties forming close, trusting relationships with others, including foster or kinship carers, adoptive parents, peers and romantic partners (see Chapters 18 and 19). Working with families exposed to current or past adversities therefore often demands unique competencies encompassing attitudes, values, knowledge and skills on the part of the family practitioner.

Second, this expanded theoretical perspective is carried through also to competencies regarding case formulation and treatment planning, which include the ability to devise formulations that account for parent, family and social/contextual factors. Like Sburlati et al. [4], we refer to competencies here in relation to family members but extend this to include other stakeholders (e.g., teachers, other health professionals) who may have a significant role in the treatment plan for a child or adolescent (see Chapters 10, 18 and 19). As such, we make explicit reference to such stakeholders in relation to competencies concerning the ability to collaboratively negotiate treatment goals and the roles of family members and relevant stakeholders.

Third, with regard to competencies for conducting collaborative treatment sessions, the current model incorporates three additional competencies beyond those specified in the corresponding subdomain of Sburlati et al. [4]. Two of these competencies are based on an acknowledgement of the potential complexities associated with interventions involving multiple family members (the ability to promote family members' capacities to support each other as they implement therapeutic strategies between sessions, e.g., parents supporting a child's thought monitoring, mothers and fathers supporting each other in the use of parenting strategies, the ability to manage how information is shared across the family system). Incorporated also in this subdomain is the competency of managing obstacles and resistance to change among family members, which may be particularly challenging in the treatment of multi-problem families and may be dealt with using distinct theory-driven approaches in distinct models of intervention (see Chapter 10). The nature of these competencies may vary somewhat depending on the format of treatment, as reflected in emerging literature on the delivery of telehealth and e-health interventions with families (see Chapter 7).

Competencies for Targeting Specific Ecological Domains

This domain encompasses the knowledge and abilities required by therapists to deliver the specific content of therapeutic components within a family-based treatment plan and the broad range of clinical strategies that are used to address therapeutic targets to produce change in child and adolescent symptoms. The scope and organization of this domain are based on an ecological perspective on child and adolescent psychopathology and clinical intervention which emphasizes the multiple ecological domains or systems in which child development is embedded [29, 30]. According to this perspective, the mechanisms that maintain symptoms of psychopathology may occur across these domains, often implicating processes at the individual child level (e.g., biological characteristics, temperament, self-regulatory capacities, cognitive processes, the child's behavioural repertoire), as well as dyadic relationship processes (e.g., parent-child interactions, interparental conflict, child-peer social dynamics) and family-level processes (e.g., communication, chaos, dysfunctional boundaries). Risk pathways to psychopathology may be shaped by transactions between multiple levels of the child's ecology, and it is predicted that the nature and

strength of connections (e.g., relationships, communication) between the family and other settings (e.g., schools, neighbourhood communities) have the potential to buffer the effects of risk factors and promote resilience [29]. Such effects therefore implicate risk processes within specific ecological domains as well as those which span multiple domains. These multiple ecological levels are reflected in the respective subdomains that are differentiated in the current model (see Table 1.3).

As outlined by Hawes et al. in Chapter 2 and throughout this volume, the dyadic and family-level processes implicated in child and adolescent psychopathology have been conceptualized from a range of theoretical perspectives in current models of family-based intervention (e.g., learning contingencies, social information processing, attachment dynamics, emotion socialization) and targeted with a broad range of clinical components and processes. The specification of multiple theory-based subdomains related to the family environment in this model can be contrasted with the corresponding competency domain of Sburlati et al. [4], which addressed competencies for 'modifying the family environment' in more global terms.

The most common dyadic processes involve parenting skills and strategies focused on the parent-child dyad, which a therapist supports parents to acquire and implement through a range of potential approaches (e.g., psycho-education, role play, video-based materials, in vivo coaching) in sessions that may or may not also involve the referred child [31]. In the treatment of children with anxiety, for example, this may include skills for parental modelling of non-avoidant behaviours in response to fear-evoking cues (see Chapter 9). For young children with autism spectrum disorder (ASD), this may include teaching parents applied behaviour analysis strategies for promoting child development and skills related to social communication (e.g., expressive communication, social skills, imitation, adaptive functioning; see Chapter 13). In the example of adolescents with ADHD, parents may be supported to set up parent-teen contracts related to difficult behaviours and contexts and to regulate such contracts using autonomy-supporting behaviour management approaches (see Chapter 11). Other dyads in the family, including the parental relationship, may also be targeted. For example, parents of children with conduct problems may be provided with strategies not only for

Table 1.3 Competencies for Targeting Specific Ecological Domains

Child-Level Processes

Managing negative thoughts

Changing maladaptive behaviours

Managing maladaptive mood and arousal

Problem-solving skills

Interpersonal/social skills

Dyadic and Family-Level Processes

Parents supporting children to implement their own techniques

Parenting practices related to behavioural control in the parent-child relationship (e.g., limit setting, autonomy granting, monitoring and supervision, reinforcement of adaptive behaviour).

Parenting practices related to responsiveness and attachment in the parent-child relationship (e.g., warmth/sensitivity, rejection/intrusiveness, contingent responses to child cues).

Parent modelling of adaptive behaviour

Satisfaction, conflict and parental teamwork in the parents' own relationship

Family communication and problem-solving

Emotion socialization (e.g., discussion of the causes and meaning of emotions; minimizing or punitive reactions to negative emotions)

Dimensions of family functioning (e.g., chaos, subsystem boundaries, cohesion, flexibility, routines that support healthy child development; differential treatment of siblings)

Parent-Focused Processes

Parent psychopathology

Cognitive-affective processes (parent attributions, parent emotion regulation, confidence)

Parental knowledge of developmentally appropriate behaviour and effective parenting practices

Processes Spanning the Family and Broader Contexts

Parental social support

Transfer for care (e.g., referral pathways)

The ecological connectedness of the family (e.g., quality of relationships and communication between parents and individuals in other key settings, such as the school, neighbourhood and communities; structuring peer activities; home-to-school strategies)

promoting a child's age-appropriate behaviour and capacities for self-regulation but also partner-support strategies for improving teamwork, communication and satisfaction in the parents' own relationship (see Chapter 10).

Treatment components and processes focused on family-level mechanisms in families of youth with depression, for example, may include communication and problem-solving skills designed to replace maladaptive interactional patterns with adaptive interactions (see Chapter 8). Communication and problem-solving components are also often used to address family-level processes in the treatment of conduct problems (see Chapter 12), along with strategies for promoting positive relationships between siblings and setting limits on sibling conflict (see Chapter 10). In the example of anorexia nervosa, treatment may include strategies for establishing family meal routines that support a return to healthy eating behaviours, including the roles of specific family members and skills for parents to support their child and each other in this process (see Chapter 14).

Quality of parenting is understood to be influenced by a range of parent characteristics, including parent psychopathology, and cognitive affective processes, including parental attributions and emotional reactions to child cues [32]. Competencies concerning the delivery of components and strategies that target these characteristics are therefore often needed by family-based therapists, particularly when working with parents who themselves have severe psychological disorders (see Chapters 16 and 17). It is common in the treatment of a broad range of child and adolescent disorders for therapists to explicitly address skills and strategies for parents to use in regulating their own emotional reactions to their children (e.g., self-talk), at times for the purpose of reducing parent behaviours that inadvertently interfere with a child's attempts at implementing new therapeutic skills (see Chapter 11). In the family-based treatment of eating disorders, for example, a key emphasis is placed on helping parents to 'externalize the illness' such that they attribute illness behaviours not to the their child but instead to the eating disorder (see Chapter 14).

Finally, family-based interventions often require therapists to be competent in the implementation of treatment components, clinical strategies and programmes that span the family system and broader contexts (see Chapter 3). Included here are clinical strategies that address parental social support, ongoing referral pathways and transfer of care and the ecological connectedness of the family (e.g., quality of relationships and communication between parents and individuals in other key settings, such as the school, neighbourhood and communities; structuring peer activities). Child conduct problems, for example, may at times be associated with a breakdown in relationships between parents and teachers, thereby complicating attempts to reduce symptoms across these contexts. Treatment therefore may include strategies designed to improve communication between parents and teachers and school-to-home strategies for coordinating contingent consequences and reinforcement across these settings (see Chapter 10).

Implications and Limitations of the Current Model

One of the major challenges in categorizing therapist competencies into distinct domains is that the knowledge and abilities that make up these competencies are often overlapping to some extent or embedded within one another. For example, competencies for managing resistance to change among family members (subdomain of conducting collaborative treatment sessions) may rely in part on competencies for engaging in self-reflective practice related to one's personal reactions to family members' expressions of resistance (subdomain of practising professionally in child and family settings; see Chapter 10). Likewise, the ability to engage parents and form a therapeutic team with the multiple parents/caregivers may rely in part on the therapists' ability to acknowledge their unique experiences, cultural values and expertise and instil hope and optimism for change, both of which are part of building therapeutic relationships and partnerships. The range of competencies characterized within such frameworks therefore may vary as a function of how fine grained they are specified rather than reflecting absolute numbers of discrete competencies.

Although the approach used to create the current model included the initial (first three) processes involved in the Delphi research method, we recognized that this method was not used in full. As such, the current model did not benefit from the same breadth of review or repeated consultation with experts at multiple stages of model development that contributed to some previous models (e.g., [4, 17]). In addition, despite the aim of taking a broad-spectrum view of psychopathology, we recognize that some disorders that are low in frequency among children and adolescents (e.g., psychotic disorders) were not represented in the material on which the current

model was based, and we would welcome future research examining the current model through formal methods that incorporate additional checks and expert views pertaining to an even wider range of clinical populations.

As seen in this chapter and throughout this volume, the roles that family members play in current evidence-based treatments for child and adolescent psychopathology often differ markedly from that traditionally associated with the term *family therapy*. In contrast to traditional models that dictate that all family members participate in treatment sessions, current family-based models have demonstrated that improvements in child and family functioning are often best achieved through treatment components that are at times delivered to individuals or subsystems within the family system. In developing the current model, we have intentionally focused on aspects that most distinguish family-based intervention from treatment that is delivered to an individual child or adolescent exclusively.

The decision to address such individual treatment components in relatively less detail here should not be seen to minimize their importance. As noted earlier, our model highlights the need for therapists to be able to promote the capacity of parents to support their child or adolescent in implementing their own therapeutic activities and skills (e.g., parental modelling of cognitive restructuring skills to be used by a child, rewarding a child for engaging in vivo exposure homework) where relevant. For more information regarding therapist competencies related to such components, we refer readers to the work of Sburlati and colleagues [4, 26, 33].

Finally, we recognize that the evidence base for some of the interventions that informed this model are more established than others. Whereas previous approaches to mapping therapist competencies have at times applied inclusion criteria related to specific levels of evidence (e.g., number of published RCTs), the current model was informed in part by interventions for which evidence is emerging rather than well established. All interventions nonetheless build directly on established theory and evidence and reflect an emphasis on the scientific method over clinical wisdom. Details regarding the various levels of evidence presently available for these interventions can be found in the respective chapters of this volume, and as such evidence continues to grow through future research, the current model may move in new directions accordingly.

Conclusions and Future Directions

Models of therapist competencies have served multiple purposes in recent years, informing guidelines for the training and accreditation of mental health practitioners, as well as informing reflective practice among practitioners, and the development of resources to support training and professional development. It is our hope that this unified model of competencies for family-based intervention will likewise contribute to the field in these ways. It is nonetheless important to note that specific therapist competencies are only as beneficial as the treatments they are used to deliver, and the best evidence-based treatments currently available nonetheless produce clear benefit for only 60 to 70 per cent of children and adolescents [34, 35]. Inevitably, even therapists in possession of the full range of competencies outlined here will find that positive outcomes at times cannot be achieved.

In the last two decades, the field of family-based treatment has shifted from the question of what works best to what works best for whom, how, where, when and under what circumstances [36, 37]. This is reflected in policy and practice guidelines specifying which interventions are effective based on the characteristics of the disorder (e.g., severity, co-morbidity) and the child (e.g., age, developmental factors; see, e.g., [38]). There is a clear need, however, for further research into moderators and mediators of treatment effects in this field. Existing clinical trials have often failed to assess whether treatments were successful in modifying therapeutic targets related to parenting and family factors, making it difficult to determine how such targets relate to mechanisms of change [39]. Explicit tests of treatment mechanisms or mediators in research investigating these interventions remain limited to date and have focused on some variables (e.g., positive parenting practices) at the expense of others [40]. Research of this kind is a high priority because it stands to clarify which components of family-based interventions may account for treatment effects and thereby further inform models of the competencies needed for successful treatment delivery. The findings from such research may potentially point to competencies that should be given greater weight or added to accounts of these competencies.

Other pressing questions of the unique importance of family-based intervention relate to the optimal sequencing and combining of parent- and child-focused treatment components, as well as the optimal format (e.g., individual, group), modality (e.g., face-to-face, eHealth, telemental health), setting (e.g., community, home, school) and how best to deliver family-based intervention in the context of child and family adversity [12]. Other priorities for future research relate to various populations that have been largely neglected to date, including families who are immigrants, refugees, ethnic minorities and LGTBQ youth. Finally, despite the broad range of systems with which families of children with mental health problems come into contact (e.g., educational, health, social care and legal services), evidence and guidelines concerning the competencies by which practitioners may best facilitate access, support and advocacy across these systems remains particularly limited [12]. Our model of core competencies for family-based intervention is therefore expected to evolve as these research challenges are addressed and new evidence becomes available.

References

1. Epstein RM, Hundert EM. Defining and assessing professional competence. *Journal of the American Medical Association* 2002; **287**(2):226–35.

2. Kaslow NJ. Competencies in professional psychology. *American Psychologist* 2004; **59**(8):774.

3. Kaslow NJ, Borden KA, Collins Jr FL, et al. Competencies conference: Future directions in education and credentialing in professional psychology. *Journal of Clinical Psychology* 2004; **60**(7):699–712.

4. Sburlati ES, Schniering CA, Lyneham HJ, Rapee RM. A model of therapist competencies for the empirically supported cognitive behavioral treatment of child and adolescent anxiety and depressive disorders. *Clinical Child and Family Psychology Review* 2011; **14**(1):89–109.

5. American Psychological Association. Evidence-based practice in psychology. *American Psychologist* 2006; **61**(4):271–85.

6. Lebowitz ER, Marin C, Martino A, et al. Parent-based treatment as efficacious as cognitive-behavioral therapy for childhood anxiety: A randomized noninferiority study of supportive parenting for anxious childhood emotions. *Journal of the American Academy of Child and Adolescent Psychiatry* 2020; **59**(3):362–72.

7. Tompson MC, Sugar CA, Langer DA, Asarnow JR. A randomized clinical trial comparing family-focused treatment and individual supportive therapy for depression in childhood and early adolescence. *Journal*

of the American Academy of Child and Adolescent Psychiatry 2017; 56(6):515–23.

8. Leijten P, Gardner F, Melendez-Torres GJ, et al. Meta-analyses: Key parenting program components for disruptive child behavior. Journal of the American Academy of Child and Adolescent Psychiatry 2019; 58 (2):180–90.

9. Sibley MH, Rodriguez L, Coxe S, et al. Parent–teen group versus dyadic treatment for adolescent ADHD: What works for whom? Journal of Clinical Child and Adolescent Psychology 2019;16:1–17.

10. Lock J, Le Grange D. Family-based treatment: Where are we and where should we be going to improve recovery in child and adolescent eating disorders. Intnational Journal of Eating Disorders 2019; 52 (4):481–7.

11. Dawson G, Rogers S, Munson J, et al. Randomized, controlled trial of an intervention for toddlers with autism: The early start Denver model. Pediatrics 2010; 125(1):e17–23.

12. Diamond G, Josephson A. Family-based treatment research: A 10-year update. Journal of the American Academy of Child and Adolescent Psychiatry 2005; 44 (9):872–87.

13. Mack KN, Lebowitz ER, Silverman WK. Contemporary family psychotherapy: Behavioral and cognitive-behavioral theories. In: Fiese BH, Celano M, Deater-Deckard K, et al. (eds.), APA Handbook of Contemporary Family Psychology: Foundations, Methods, and Contemporary Issues across the Lifespan, Vol. 1. Washington, DC: American Psychological Association, 2019, pp. 57–73. Available at http://content.apa.org /books/16100–004.

14. Chambless DL, Hollon SD. Defining empirically supported therapies. Journal of Consulting and Clinical Psychology 1998; 66(1):7–18.

15. Fonagy P, Clark DM. Update on the improving access to psychological therapies programme in England: Commentary on . . . children and young people's improving access to psychological therapies. BJPsych Bulletin 2015; 39(5):248–51.

16. Clark DM. Realizing the mass public benefit of evidence-based psychological therapies: The IAPT program. Annual Review of Clinical Psychology 2018; 14:159–93.

17. Roth AD, Pilling S. A competence framework for the supervision of psychological therapies. University College London, 2015. Available at www.ucl.ac.uk/p als/sites/pals/files/background_document_supervi sion_competences_july_2015.pdf.

18. Clark DM. Implementing NICE guidelines for the psychological treatment of depression and anxiety disorders: The IAPT experience. International Review of Psychiatry 2011; 23(4):318–27.

19. Hunsley J, Barker K. Training for competency in professional psychology: A Canadian perspective. Australian Psychologist 2011; 46(2):142–5.

20. Knight BG. Training in professional psychology in the US: An increased focus on competency attainment. Australian Psychologist 2011; 46 (2):140–1.

21. Laidlaw K, Gillanders D. Clinical psychology training in the UK: Towards the attainment of competence. Australian Psychologist 2011; 46(2):146–50.

22. Pachana NA, Sofronoff K, Scott T, Helmes E. Attainment of competencies in clinical psychology training: Ways forward in the Australian context. Australian Psychologist 2011; 46(2):67–76.

23. MH-Kids, New South Wales, Ministry of Health. NSW Child and Adolescent Mental Health Services (CAMHS): Competency Framework. North Sydney, NSW, Australia.: NSW Ministry of Health, 2011.

24. Rodolfa E, Bent R, Eisman E, et al. A cube model for competency development: Implications for psychology educators and regulators. Professional Psychology: Research and Practice 2005; 36(4):347–54.

25. Snyder CR, Elliott TR. Twenty-first century graduate education in clinical psychology: A four level matrix model. Journal of Clinical Psychology 2005; 61 (9):1033–54.

26. Sburlati ES, Lyneham HJ, Mufson LH, Schniering CA. A model of therapist competencies for the empirically supported interpersonal psychotherapy for adolescent depression. Clinical Child and Family Psychology Review 2012; 15(2):93–112.

27. Roth AD, Calder F, Pilling S. A Competence Framework for Child and Adolescent Mental Health Services. Edinburgh: NHS Education for Scotland, 2011.

28. Piotrowska PJ, Tully LA, Lenroot R, et al. Mothers, fathers, and parental systems: A conceptual model of parental engagement in programmes for child mental health—Connect, Attend, Participate, Enact (CAPE). Clinical Child and Family Psychology Review 2017; 20 (2):146–61.

29. Bronfenbrenner, U. Ecology of the family as a context for human development: Research perspectives. Developmental Psychology 1986; 22(6):723–42.

30. Stormshak EA, Dishion TJ. An ecological approach to child and family clinical and counseling psychology. Clinical Child and Family Psychology Review 2002; 5 (3):197–215.

31. Hawes DJ, Allen J. Evidence-based parenting interventions: Current perspectives and clinical strategies. In: Positive Mental Health, Fighting

Stigma and Promoting Resiliency for Children and Adolescents. New York: Elsevier, 2016, pp. 185–204.

32. Taraban L, Shaw DS. Parenting in context: Revisiting Belsky's classic process of parenting model in early childhood. *Developmental Review* 2018; **48**:55–81.

33. Sburlati ES, Lyneham HJ, Schniering CA, Rapee RM. *Evidence-Based CBT for Anxiety and Depression in Children and Adolescents: A Competencies-Based Approach.* Hoboken, NJ: John Wiley & Sons, 2014.

34. James AC, James G, Cowdrey FA, et al. Cognitive behavioural therapy for anxiety disorders in children and adolescents. *Cochrane Database of Systemic Reviews* 2015; (2):CD004690. Available at http://doi.wiley.com/10.1002/14651858.CD004690.pub4 (accessed 9 June 2020).

35. Scott S, Dadds MR. Practitioner review: When parent training doesn't work: Theory-driven clinical strategies. *Journal of Child Psychology and Psychiatry* 2009; **50**(12):1441–50.

36. Stoltz S, Deković M, van Londen M, et al. What works for whom, how and under what circumstances? Testing moderated mediation of intervention effects on externalizing behavior in children. *Social Development* 2013; **22**(2):406–25.

37. Wei C, Kendall PC. Parental involvement: Contribution to childhood anxiety and its treatment. *Clinical Child and Family Psychology Review* 2014; **17**(4):319–39.

38. Fairchild G, Hawes DJ, Frick PJ, et al. Conduct disorder. *Nature Reviews Disease Primers* 2019; **5**(43):1–25.

39. Breinholst S, Esbjørn BH, Reinholdt-Dunne ML, Stallard P. CBT for the treatment of child anxiety disorders: A review of why parental involvement has not enhanced outcomes. *Journal of Anxiety Disorders* 2012; **26**(3):416–24.

40. Patel CC, Fairchild AJ, Prinz RJ. Potential mediators in parenting and family intervention: Quality of mediation analyses. *Clinical Child and Family Psychology Review* 2017; **20**(2):127–45.

The Role of the Family in Child and Adolescent Psychopathology

David J. Hawes, Jennifer L. Allen, Cecilia A. Essau and Carri Fisher

Therapist knowledge of psychological disorders, including their causes and maintaining mechanisms, is regarded as a core clinical competency in its own right. Moreover, among the competencies emphasized in the evidence-based treatment of children and adolescents, knowledge concerning the role of the family in psychopathology is particularly essential (e.g., [1]; see also Chapter 1). In this chapter we examine current theoretical perspectives on the role of the family in the major forms of psychopathology found among children and adolescents. The term *family*, as it is used here, refers to those individuals responsible for meeting the developmental needs of a child, whereas *parent* refers to primary caregivers who perform executive roles for a family. Our use of these terms recognizes the multiplicity of contemporary forms of family structure and the impact of contemporary social trends and reproductive technologies on family formation and structures. As such, the individuals represented by such terms potentially include biological parents and siblings (i.e., nuclear family), as well as those who assume family membership through legal processes of divorce, remarriage, custody change, foster care, adoption and informal arrangements (e.g., extended family members, live-in partners).

An Ecological Perspective on the Family

The family context has long been a primary focus of research into environmental contributions to child mental health. At the broadest level, these contributions have been examined in terms of cumulative risk. Early research, for example, found that children were more likely to exhibit conduct disorder when exposed to a greater range of adversity factors, including socioeconomic disadvantage, large family size, marital discord, maternal psychopathology, foster-care placement and parental criminality [2]. This reflects the ecological principle that adversities have a greater impact on child outcomes when they span multiple domains or systems than when they are limited to a single domain. Importantly, ecological theory also predicts that the nature and strength of connections (e.g., relationships, communication) between the family and other settings (e.g., schools, neighbourhood communities) have the potential to buffer the effects of risk factors and promote resilience [3].

Adverse environmental factors often co-occur in the population, and those related to maladaptive family functioning (e.g., parental mental illness, substance misuse, criminal behaviour, domestic violence, physical and sexual abuse, neglect) are particularly highly correlated [4]. Childhood adversities that are family based also predict later psychopathology more strongly than those which are not (e.g., socioeconomic disadvantage) [4]. Research into adverse childhood experiences (ACEs) has grown rapidly in recent years, with findings indicating that the overall number of such adversities experienced during childhood predicts not only the disorders typically associated with traumatic events but also the most prevalent forms of child and adult psychopathology, including anxiety, mood and disruptive behaviour disorders, along with various physical health problems [5].

Although such cumulative risk has become widely recognized, researchers have argued that in order to understand the mechanisms through which ACEs have an impact on mental health, there is a need for more fine-grained conceptualizations of adversity [5, 6]. McLaughlin et al. [7], for example, proposed that distinct clusters of adversities may produce similar mental health outcomes via distinct mechanisms, as suggested by evidence that deprivation-based adversities (e.g., parental neglect, poverty) affect neurodevelopment through the absence of stimulation, leading to excessive pruning of synapses in the central nervous system, whereas threat-based adversities (e.g., physical abuse) may affect neurodevelopment through changes in amygdala and hippocampal functioning, resulting in altered emotional development.

The features of the family environment implicated in child and adolescent psychopathology are not, however, limited to extreme forms of adversity. Variables related to functioning and stability at the family level often have been emphasized in the clinical literature. Influential conceptualizations of family functioning include Minuchin's model [8], in which the family is characterized as a system consisting of subsystems organized hierarchically (e.g., an executive parental subsystem, a child subsystem). These subsystems are defined by boundaries that determine who participates and how, and in healthy families, clear and appropriate boundaries enable these subsystems to perform their functions effectively and adapt to challenges successfully. Dysfunctional boundaries, however, may lie at either extreme of a dimension ranging from those which are enmeshed (e.g., diffuse, disregarding personal or psychological space) to disengaged (e.g., overly rigid, lacking feelings of loyalty and belonging). Elsewhere, family functioning has been conceptualized based on dimensions of cohesion (e.g., how the family balances emotional closeness versus separateness in their relationships), flexibility (e.g., how the family balances stability versus change in relationships and leadership) and communication (e.g., skills for listening and problem-solving) [9]. More recently, family-level risk processes have been conceptualized based on constructs related to instability, such as household chaos, as defined by high levels of confusion and agitation in the home, and a sense of rush, disorganization and time pressure in daily routines [10]. Evidence suggests that household chaos accounts for child mental health outcomes independent of quality of parenting and may serve as a context that exacerbates the effects of parental risk factors and poor parenting practices on child adjustment [11].

Parenting and the Parent-Child Relationship

The family-based variables theorized to play the most proximate role in child psychopathology relate to parenting and socialization processes based in the parent-child relationship. Some of the earliest and most influential accounts of these processes emphasized clusters or typologies of parenting, such as Baumrind's tripartite classification of parenting styles [12]. Research based on this model has found that the promotion of healthy child adjustment is most likely to occur through authoritative parenting, conceptualized as a balanced synthesis of two orthogonal dimensions – demandingness and responsiveness. Accordingly, such a parent is responsive to a child's needs but not indulgent and is firm but not rigid in setting limits on behaviour. In contrast, adverse outcomes have been associated with authoritarian (i.e., high demandingness with low responsiveness) and permissive (i.e., low demandingness with high responsiveness) parenting styles [13].

Darling and Steinberg [14] argued that the processes through which global parenting style influences child outcomes may be better understood by distinguishing between three related aspects of socialization in the family. The first comprises the values and goals towards which parenting is directed (e.g., beliefs regarding the importance of particular child behaviours, capacities and qualities). The second is the parenting practices that are used to achieve those goals (e.g., discipline methods to reduce misbehaviour; responses to enhance a loving relationship). Global parenting style is the third, as defined by the emotional climate or attitudes that parents express towards their child. From this perspective, parenting practices and parenting style are both seen to be influenced by parents' values and goals, but parenting practices are goal directed, whereas parenting style is not. Moreover, whereas parenting practices are predicted to have direct effects on specific child outcomes, parenting style is understood to serve more as a context that moderates the effects of such practices on child outcomes and influences a child's openness to parental socialization [14].

Control and Responsiveness

Although a broad range of variables has been invoked to describe and index quality of parenting and relationship processes, many of these can be grouped along two broad dimensions corresponding to control and responsiveness. The dimension of parental control encompasses methods and degrees of monitoring and limit setting on children's behaviour [15, 16]. Conceptualizations of this dimension have evolved considerably over time, with accounts shifting from a largely unitary construct to multiple forms of control including psychological control, whereby parents attempt to intrude on children's psychological and emotional processes through punitive practices such as love withdrawal and guilt induction (e.g., [17]). Theorists have also emphasized the distinction between these forms of control and those related to guidance and structure, including the extent to which parents communicate relations between actions and outcomes through clear and consistent guidelines, expectations and rules and provide children with predictable consequences and feedback regarding their actions [18].

The dimension of responsiveness concerns parent behaviours that convey affect towards a child and span the negative features of harsh discipline (e.g., hostility, criticism, rejection) through to supportive warmth and sensitivity. Included here is the caregiving that is predicted to account for the formation of a secure attachment between a child and caregiver, consisting of responses that are contingent on, and sensitive to, the signals through which a child's needs are expressed (e.g., [19]). A number of influential dyadic constructs have also been derived from attachment theory and operationalized in terms of emotional attunement (e.g., emotional availability) [20] and the coordination and temporal structure of rhythms and reciprocity in parent-child interactions (e.g., synchrony [21], mutually responsive orientation [22]). Although much research has focused on specific forms of control and responsiveness, the positive/ negative extremes of these dimensions have often been collapsed into composite variables reflecting positive (e.g., warmth, contingent rewarding of good behaviour) and negative (e.g., rejection, harsh and inconsistent discipline) parenting.

Emotion Socialization

There is now evidence that practices concerning parents' socialization of children's expression, understanding and regulation of emotion are important to consider alongside those traditionally emphasized in parenting research. Eisenberg, Cumberland and Spinrad [23] proposed that there are at least three key processes through which parents socialize their children to the world of emotions: reactions to their child's emotional displays, discussion of emotion and emotional expressiveness within the family. Parental emotion socialization behaviours have generally been conceptualized as either supportive (e.g., discussion of the causes and meaning of emotions, reactions that are

emotion focused, problem focused or encouraging of emotional expression) or non-supportive (e.g., avoidance of emotional discussion, minimizing or punitive reactions) [23]. Related to this are the emotion coaching processes through which parents teach children about the regulation and expression of emotions and the role of emotion in social contexts [24]. Emotion socialization during early childhood has been shown to influence later adjustment via effects on children's capacities for emotion regulation [25] and has been implicated in various forms of psychopathology. For example, non-supportive practices of this kind, particularly those in response to negative child emotion, were found to be significantly associated with current and prospective conduct problems in a recent meta-analysis of 49 studies [26].

Parenting, Development and Gene-Environment Interplay

The extent to which distinct parenting processes contribute to and protect against the emergence and amplification of psychopathology is understood to vary across development. Parental sensitivity and responsiveness are known to be particularly critical during infancy and early childhood [21]. Likewise, supportive emotion socialization practices have been associated most strongly with children's behavioural adjustment early in life [26]. Age-appropriate forms of parental control become increasingly important in setting limits on behaviour from the toddler years [27], and while sensitivity and responsiveness continue to shape outcomes across middle childhood and adolescence, autonomy granting and monitoring are thought to play an increasingly important role during this time [28, 29].

According to current developmental perspectives on parenting influences, child outcomes also reflect interactions and transactions between the family environment and individual differences at the child level. Although individual differences related to child temperament are known to have genetic and neurochemical underpinnings, it is now understood that such characteristics are only moderately heritable and are also influenced by socialization [30–32]. The family environment therefore may serve to potentiate the expression of biological vulnerabilities associated with risk for psychopathology, and dispositional risk factors that fall within the domains of temperament, social-cognitive style and intelligence have been described as entrained biosocial traits [33].

Entrainment refers to the role of environments in structuring neural pathways implicated in automatic overlearned response patterns [34]. Child characteristics such as response perseveration, behavioural inhibition and irritability may be shaped through thousands of interactions and routines within the family and broader social contexts across development [35]. Theories of these processes have proposed, for example, that the development and maintenance of self-regulation, a key aspect of temperament, are influenced by how parents manage the home environment and both scaffold and model appropriate behaviour and self-regulation for their children [36]. This is consistent with a bioecological perspective on child psychopathology, whereby the development of self-regulatory capacities is understood to be highly embedded in the multiple contexts or systems (e.g., family, school, peers) that are nested within the broader ecology of the child [37].

Researchers have hypothesized that genetic influences on a range of disorders operate through a relatively small number of dispositional risk factors, as seen in emerging trans-diagnostic models. Dadds and Frick [38], for example, recently proposed a model in which individual differences in major forms psychopathology are accounted for by early temperamental characteristics operationalized in terms of emotional attention (i.e., selectively attending to emotional cues produced by other people), responsiveness (i.e., behavioural responses to the emotional cues of other people) and learning (i.e., the propensity to show conditioned responses to stimuli associated with the emotional cues of others). The extent to which children develop excesses and deficits in these dispositional characteristics is predicted to explain distinct risk pathways to autism spectrum disorder, disruptive behaviour disorders, ADHD and anxiety disorders and to account for co-morbidity between these symptom domains. The authors further proposed that environmental factors (e.g., abusive parenting) may trigger, inhibit and interact with biological vulnerabilities underlying these characteristics during sensitive developmental periods. This may potentially occur via epigenetic mechanisms, whereby environments alter the functionality of genes associated with the neurodevelopmental systems of serotonin, dopamine, oxytocin and cortisol [38].

Individual differences in children's sensitivity to parenting practices have been a further focus of recent literature. Meta-analytic research examining studies of child adjustment has found that children with a more difficult (versus 'easy') temperament and infants with a temperament high in negative emotionality appear to be more vulnerable to negative parenting while also profiting more from positive parenting [39]. This is consistent with the differential susceptibility model, which asserts that children vary in their sensitivity to parenting and other environmental influences for better and for worse [40]. Elsewhere, support has been found for the diathesis-stress model, whereby individuals with particular characteristics are disproportionately affected by negative features of the environment (e.g., [41, 42]), as well as the vantage sensitivity hypothesis, which posits that some children may disproportionately benefit from environmental resources without being more adversely affected by negative environments [43]. On the basis of evidence to date, it has been proposed that certain child characteristics (e.g., social withdrawal) may operate as diatheses, increasing the risk for symptoms in the context of environmental stressors, whereas other characteristics (e.g., polymorphisms of *BDNF* and *COMT* genes) may operate as plasticity factors and thereby increase sensitivity to both positive and negative caregiving [44]. As these examples show, although biological factors have received growing attention in models of psychopathology, an emphasis on the family environment has endured.

Psychopathology and the Developing Child

Explanatory models of mental health disorders in recent decades have been influenced greatly by the principles of developmental psychopathology [45]. According to these principles, the transformations that occur as part of normative development are key to understanding the emergence and persistence of mental health disorders over time and the contributions of distinct social (e.g., family, peer) influences. Critically, the parent-child relationship is the primary context in which development unfolds and in which the earliest foundations for risk and resilience emerge. Based on the developmental profiles of the major forms of psychopathology that emerge in childhood and adolescence, disorders can be broadly classified as neurodevelopmental disorders, emotional/behavioural disorders and psychotic disorders [46].

The most prevalent of these disorders are emotional and behavioural disorders, encompassing common forms of internalizing problems (e.g., anxiety and mood disorders) and the externalizing disorders of oppositional defiant disorder (ODD) and conduct disorder (CD), otherwise known as the *disruptive behaviour disorders* or *conduct problems*. The genetic basis for most of these disorders is generally only moderate [46], and contributions from the family environmental are often emphasized in causal models. Neurodevelopmental disorders, which include ADHD, autism spectrum disorder (ASD) and tic disorders, are characterized by an onset early in life and atypical brain development [47]. Although the symptoms of these disorders are relatively stable across time and context, parenting and parental characteristics are nonetheless known to shape expression across development (e.g., [48, 49]). Psychotic disorders are viewed as a spectrum comprising schizophrenia and other disorders that involve prominent psychotic features (e.g., delusions, hallucinations, disorganized thinking). Included here are schizoaffective disorder, schizophreniform disorder and forms of bipolar disorder that include prominent psychotic features. Like the neurodevelopmental disorders, much of the risk for these disorders can be attributed to genetic factors [50]. Unlike the neurodevelopmental disorders, however, adolescent development is associated with a fundamental change in expression rather than a persistence or exacerbation of prepubertal symptoms. Again, despite the strong genetic basis of psychotic disorders, evidence indicates that family factors (e.g., low cohesion and support) may nonetheless influence symptom trajectories [51, 52].

Current Models of Emotional and Behavioural Disorders

The family-based variables associated with risk for child psychopathology number well beyond those already noted here, many of which show small to modest correlations with a broad range of symptoms. Less, however, is known about the actual mechanisms through which family-based factors confer risk. These mechanisms represent the processes through which parenting variables operate on the emergence, amplification and transformation of child dysfunction across development or protect against deviations from a healthy trajectory. Critically, they therefore point to treatment targets that can be predicted to translate into change in child symptoms. Here we examine current models of the disorders in which these mechanisms have been most strongly implicated and for which family-based interventions have been most established.

Externalizing Problems

The family-based mechanisms in current models of conduct problems have been specified more precisely that those of many other disorders, thanks in part to research that has emphasized the use of experimental and longitudinal methods in theory building [53]. The most established model of conduct problems is that of coercion theory, based on a social learning (operant conditioning) theory account of parent-child interactions [54]. Fundamental to coercion theory is the assumption that the frequency with which children engage in oppositional and aggressive behaviour and the amplification of this behaviour over time are linked to its functional value in the child's daily social environment. As such, the theory is concerned primarily with micro-social mechanisms in the moment-to-moment dynamics of relationships. Coercive dynamics based in the parent-child relationship are understood to be particularly proximal to child conduct problems, especially across early and middle childhood when the most chronic trajectories of antisocial behaviour are often initiated. The core dynamic of coercion is that conflict is resolved by emotional manipulation rather than by negotiation, with children and parents engaging in behaviours that may span low-level aversive behaviours (e.g., whining, complaining, nagging, scolding, threatening) through to acts of physical aggression, intimidation and hostile rejection.

A child's coercive behaviour may become highly functional in gaining social attention, desired outcomes and preferred activities (positive reinforcement). Negative reinforcement or escape conditioning is further understood to play a key role, with the theory predicting that these behaviours will be performed insofar as they are functional in escaping or avoiding punishment (e.g., deflecting a parents' command) or in terminating conflicts with others (e.g., hitting a sibling to stop them teasing). Initiated, such behaviour is more likely to be reciprocated by family members and to escalate through overlearned responses that may occur largely outside conscious awareness. These same learning mechanisms are understood to reinforce the harsh and inconsistent discipline that, in turn, models coercive and dysregulated behaviour and reinforces coercive child behaviour. As such, these parent-child interactions were conceptualized as escalating cycles of parent-child coercion that function as interlocking *reinforcement traps*. This reinforcement is bidirectional, or reciprocal, with children and parents continually shaping each other's behaviours [54].

In addition to specifying the processes through which parent-child contingencies play out on a moment-to-moment time scale, coercion theory also emphasizes the longer-term developmental time scale across which cascading risk processes are set in motion. Often first initiated during the toddler years, the longer that coercive cycles persist over time, the more rapidly they are likely to escalate, and the higher they are likely to push the upper amplitudes of family aggression. In addition, as children becomes increasingly skilled in the use of coercion, they become increasingly difficult to discipline. The more frustrating and exhausting parent-child interactions become for a parent, the more a parent is likely to avoid engaging with a child unless necessary. Given that healthy, age-appropriate child behaviours are less likely to require parental attention, these behaviours are likely to receive decreasing rates of positive reinforcement in day-to-day life, with such engagement becoming increasingly contingent on the child's misbehaviour. As conflict and discipline become the ways in which parent and child spend time together, the quality of their relationship suffers accordingly. The developing child enters school and additional social settings with social deficits that may generalize and initiate similar cycles of coercion with peers and other caregivers (e.g., teachers). It is predicted that parenting processes continue to shape antisocial trajectories across later childhood and adolescence but that the most proximal of these shift from those related to setting limits on behaviour in the home to those related to the regulation of children's peer activities in external settings (e.g., monitoring and supervision) [33].

Evidence regarding heterogeneity within clinical populations has further indicated that among different children, the same disruptive behaviour disorders may develop through risk pathways that involve somewhat distinct neurodevelopmental and family-based mechanisms [55]. Risk processes and related trajectories are known to covary somewhat with age of onset. Compared to an onset of ODD or CD early in childhood, onset in the adolescent years generally involved primarily rebellious (e.g., not physically aggressive) symptoms that are limited to adolescence and less likely to be related to family dysfunction (e.g., [56]). In addition, somewhat distinct parenting processes also appear to be implicated in distinct early-onset risk pathways. Most notably, it is possible to differentiate a particularly severe and chronic subgroup of early-onset youth with callous and unemotional traits or limited prosocial emotions (e.g., lack of remorse or guilt, callous-lack of empathy, shallow or deficient affect), whose conduct problems involve a greater genetic component, more significant neurodevelopmental underpinnings (e.g., amygdala dysfunction) and unique treatment needs [57, 58]. Compared to the conduct problems of children with normative levels of these traits, children with high callous-unemotional (CU) traits appear to be less proximally associated with negative parenting practices such as harsh/inconsistent discipline (e.g., [58a]). Additionally, there is evidence to suggest that a lack of parental warmth may be more robustly associated with the conduct problems of children with high levels of CU traits than those of children low in CU traits (e.g., [59, 60]; cf. [61]).

Internalizing Problems

Family-based contributions to internalizing problems are understood to include a number of trans-diagnostic risk processes common to both anxiety and mood disorders. The triadic model of these trans-diagnostic processes proposed by Schleider and Weisz [62] emphasizes the potential for parent and family factors to shape the proximal child-level risk processes that underlie anxiety and depression, particularly cognitive processes. These cognitive processes include attentional biases (e.g., hypervigilance to threatening stimuli, difficulty disengaging from negative emotional content), negative attributional styles (e.g., attributing negative life events to internal, stable, global causes), maladaptive implicit theories (e.g., beliefs that difficulties are a product of one's fundamental flaws) and poor emotion regulation skills (e.g., difficulties modulating internal states and physiological processes for the purpose of achieving goals). The child-level risk processes that may be shaped as such also include insecure attachment styles, which themselves reflect maladaptive competencies for regulating fear and distress [63]. It is predicted that these child processes may be shaped by multiple parent-level factors (e.g., parental psychopathology, interparental conflict) and parent-child or dyadic-level factors (e.g., parenting style, parental modelling, parental feedback, sibling relationship quality), which are themselves shaped by family-level factors (e.g., family chaos, differential treatment of siblings, dimensions including enmeshment and cohesion), all of which may amplify one another [62].

In addition to those risk processes shared among internalizing disorders, research has also indicated key distinctions concerning the role of the family in pathways to anxiety versus depression. Most notably, parental overprotection and control appear to be more consistently associated with the anxiety disorders, whereas parental rejection and lack of warmth appear to be more strongly associated with depression [64, 65]. Given that anxiety and depression occur at considerably higher rates among parents of children with internalizing problems than in the wider population, it has often been unclear whether particular family processes operate as risk mechanisms independent of the genetic vulnerabilities shared by parents and their children. Theoretical accounts of such mechanisms have nonetheless informed a number of evidence-based treatments for these disorders, particularly in the field of child and adolescent anxiety (see Chapter 9).

Anxiety Disorders

In current models of anxiety, family environmental influences are understood to confer risk through interactions and transactions with temperament characteristics consisting of withdrawal and behavioural inhibition and an avoidant style of coping with perceived threat [66]. Early aspects of the parent-child relationship are thought to modify and shape this temperamental style, which, in turn, elicits parenting responses that further contribute to the child's avoidance [67]. This may play out in an *anxious-coercive cycle* in which fearful children solicit attention, comfort and protection from their parents during novel situations, which, in turn, functions to reinforce children's avoidance and dependence on parents [68]. Avoidance itself further functions to maintain anxiety in various ways, such as removing opportunities to disconfirm negative beliefs and preventing inhibitory learning and fear extinction [69].

Parents of children with anxiety disorders have been found to excessively restrict their children's behaviour and engagement with situations based on

anticipation of potential threat, and this overprotection is thought to increase anxiety by contributing to children's beliefs that the world is a dangerous place [66]. Similarly, a critical parent may reinforce beliefs that the children are not capable of coping with or controlling potential risks in the world. Additionally, parents who themselves have anxiety may overcontrol their children's environment because of fears for the safety of their child, inadvertently reducing opportunities for normative exposure to occur [70–72]. Children's avoidance may also be promoted inadvertently by a failure to encourage or reinforce approach to novelty, as well as parenting behaviours that actually reinforce avoidance. Compared to parents of non-anxious children, parents of anxious children are more likely to reciprocate avoidant interpretations of social situations expressed by their children and to agree with their children's avoidant plans. This, in turn, has been associated with increases in avoidance among anxious children following the discussion of social situations with their parents [73].

According to accounts of the environmental processes involved in the transmission of anxiety and avoidance from parents to children, fears may be acquired without direct exposure to threatening stimuli through vicarious learning [74]. This may occur via nonverbal learning pathways involving the observation of others' reactions to ambiguous stimuli (i.e., vicarious/observational learning or modelling). Examples of this include social referencing early in development, whereby infants use caregivers' reactions to guide their own reactions to novel stimuli [75]. This may also occur via instruction learning or the verbal communication of fear-related information by parents to children (e.g., emphasizing threat and danger when describing objects and experiences) [76, 77]. Children with an inhibited temperament may, however, be particularly open to incorporating these messages [78]. A child's avoidance and inhibition may also increase the likelihood of experiencing negative life events, such as bullying, which interact with the child's vulnerabilities to further contribute to the emergence and maintenance of anxiety [79].

Mood Disorders

Despite the many known risk factors for mood disorders in childhood and adolescence, evidence regarding the mechanisms implicated in their onset and maintenance remains particularly limited. Based on the common course of these disorders in relation to pubertal timing and adolescent development, literature on the pathogenesis of depression has emphasized hormonal and maturational processes that may alter individual sensitivity to stressors and biological risk mechanisms associated with changes to the neuroendocrine system and brain structure and function [47]. Parenting and family-level processes are nonetheless thought to play a critical role [80]. Parental conflict, characterized by high levels of hostility and negative affectivity towards children, has been found to predict the onset of youth depression [81], whereas unsupportive parenting has been associated with trajectories of depressive symptoms among children and adolescents that remain high or increase over time [82].

A parent's own mood disorder may influence these parenting processes [83]. The intergenerational transmission of depression also may be explained by the negative cognitive style underlying a parent's own depression and the increased levels of marital conflict among parents with mood disorders (e.g., [84, 85]). Negative parenting may lead to depression through its contributions to negative cognitive biases among children and adolescents, who then interpret family interactions more negatively than they actually are [84]. This, in turn, may lead to further negative family interactions, creating a negative-feedback loop that maintains depressive symptoms [86]. Based on neuroscientific evidence regarding the effects of parenting on the developing brain, emerging theory has also posited that particular affective parenting processes (e.g., frequent expressions of aggression, lack of positivity) may contribute directly and indirectly to depression via their role in shaping the strategies by which adolescents regulate their emotions [87].

Origins and Determinants of Parenting

A comprehensive understanding of the role of the family in child and adolescent psychopathology includes an awareness of the factors that influence quality of parenting. In Belsky's [88] influential model, it was proposed that parenting is multiply determined by various characteristics of the parent, the child and the family's social context, and much support for these influences has since accumulated [89].

Parent Characteristics

Among the parent characteristics that are theorized to contribute to poor quality of parenting, the strongest

evidence has been seen for parent psychopathology, particularly maternal depression [83], and similar associations have been reported for fathers [90]. Relatedly, emerging neurobiological evidence has indicated that characteristics of the maternal oxytocin system may underlie both depression and sensitive parenting among mothers of infants [91]. Likewise, personality research has shown that high levels of neuroticism have been negatively associated with warm parenting, and high levels of conscientiousness with increased warmth [92, 93]. Research into the intergenerational transmission of parenting practices has also supported the prediction that such practices are shaped by the developmental history of caregiving that parents receive in their own family of origin [94]. Taraban and Shaw [89] recently proposed an expanded account of these parent characteristics, which included parental self-efficacy, as reflected in the expectation caregivers hold about their ability to parent successfully [95]; parenting knowledge (e.g., awareness of effective and age-appropriate discipline practices [96]; and processes related to attributional biases and emotional flooding, as follows.

Biases in parents' dispositional attributions about their children have been implicated in risk pathways to both internalizing and externalizing problems [97, 98] and have been predicted to have particularly strong effects on parent emotion and behaviour when a child's actions are attributed to characteristics that are stable, global and internal to the child (e.g., under the child's control) [99]. A related body of research has emphasized social information-processing biases concerning parents' attention to (i.e., encoding) and interpretation of (i.e., appraisal) child cues (e.g., [100]). Such biases may lead to emotional flooding, which occurs when one relationship partner perceives the other's negative affect to be increasingly unpredictable and overwhelming. This is thought to lead to emotional (escape) conditioning involving hypervigilance to others' negative affect [101]. The flooded individual then appraises ambiguous cues as threatening or frustrating, in turn, making the individual more prone to arousal. This flooding disrupts the higher-order cognitive processes required for problem-solving, thereby compromising the individual's capacity to respond adaptively during conflict. Snyder et al. [102] proposed that flooding may be a mechanism through which child anger compromises parents' capacity to effectively problem-solve discipline scenarios, resulting in a reliance on overlearned strategies. This is consistent with research showing that maternal anger organizes and directs behaviour towards coercion and away from strategies that reduce child arousal [103]. In support of this, Mence et al. [104] found that flooding predicted hostile discipline among parents of children with conduct problems, particularly when parents exhibited negative biases in the appraisal of their children's emotional cues.

Characteristics of the Social Context

Quality of parenting may be explained in part by characteristics of the broader social context in which the parent-child relationship is nested, particularly those related to sources of stress and social support. For the most part, research has found that high levels of satisfaction in the parents' own relationship (e.g., affection, effective communication) are associated with warm, sensitive parenting, whereas interparental conflict (e.g., withdrawal, verbal and physical aggression) has been related to negative parenting practices [89, 105]. Beyond the parents' own relationship, parent social isolation has also been associated with a range of parenting problems, including child abuse and neglect, and considerable research has demonstrated beneficial effects of social support on quality of parenting. Nonetheless, social support does not function in the same way for all parents, and although such support may provide an important buffer against the negative effects of broader social stressors, such benefits may be mitigated when environmental stressors are particularly severe or when the providers of support also serve as sources of stress or encourage negative parenting practices [106, 107].

Child Characteristics

Quality of parenting may be adversely influenced by a range of child characteristics, including the symptoms through which child and adolescent psychopathology is expressed. As outlined already, explanatory models of internalizing and externalizing problems often emphasize transactional cycles in which the symptoms of a problem (e.g., aggressive and defiant behaviour, anxious and avoidant behaviour) function to elicit the very parenting processes that are problem maintaining. Indeed, the evocative child-driven effects of internalizing and externalizing symptoms on parenting practices may often be more pronounced than the parent-to-child effects on those symptoms [108]. It is further assumed that individual differences associated with child

temperament may predispose families to initiating such cycles [27], and there is evidence that child temperament and parenting influence one another through similar dynamics. This includes longitudinal evidence of bidirectional associations between negative emotionality in early childhood and harsh parenting [109]. There is also some evidence that the relationship between negative emotionality and parenting may be moderated by socioeconomic status (SES), with meta-analytic evidence suggesting that higher levels of negative emotionality may elicit less supportive parenting among low-SES families but more supportive parenting among high-SES families [110].

Parenting, Mental Health and Cross-Cultural Evidence

The cultural context in which parenting occurs has received growing recognition in recent years, and growing research has investigated the extent to which findings regarding child psychopathology can be generalized across countries and cultures. It is noteworthy that the prevalence and persistence of mental health disorders appear to be highly stable across cultures and ethnicity, with differences generally accounted for by social adversity factors. For example, in a meta-analysis of studies conducted in 27 countries in every region of the world from 1985 to 2012, it was found that prevalence rates of child and adolescent disorders were associated neither with geographic location nor year of data collection [111]. Likewise, research into parenting influences has for the most part emphasized cross-cultural similarities. For example, internalizing and externalizing symptoms have been found to show associations with variables including parental control, warmth and rejection that are highly comparable across families sampled from nine countries [108, 112].

At the same time, evidence suggests that the child outcomes associated with parental discipline may vary depending on how normative (either perceived or actual) that discipline is within a particular culture. For example, a study of children aged 8 to 12 years across six countries found that parental yelling and corporal punishment were less strongly associated with child anxiety and aggression in countries where such discipline was perceived by children to be normative compared to those in which it was not [113]. Interestingly, research examining parental warmth has also found that it may moderate the influences of corporal punishment on child anxiety and aggression in ways that are somewhat culturally specific. For example, Lansford et al. [114] found that while high levels of parental warmth protected against the detrimental effects of corporal punishment on child anxiety among samples from Colombia and Naples, the combination of high levels of warmth and corporal punishment among children from other regions (e.g., China, America) was associated with increases in anxiety over time. These findings suggest that parenting processes shape child outcomes in remarkably similar ways across diverse populations of families while pointing to complex questions that may be answered only with further research into cross-cultural differences.

Conclusions: Theory and Practice

Theoretical accounts of psychological disorders among children and adolescents have evolved significantly in recent years, and considerable progress has been made in characterizing the role of the family environment in risk pathways. Despite the broad range of factors that have been associated with risk for these disorders, those which play the most proximal role are often based in the parent-child relationship, as reflected in the parenting processes targeted in current evidence-based interventions. It is noteworthy, however, that evidence regarding the precise mechanisms through which family and parenting processes confer risk and maintain problems remains limited for many disorders. Ongoing research is needed to understand these mechanisms and to translate emerging risk models into family-based interventions that may improve on existing treatments.

Some key points regarding the role of theory in clinical practice warrant clarification in light of the literature reviewed here. First, it is important not to dismiss the potential importance of a family-based intervention for children and adolescents whose problems are thought to be explained largely by neurodevelopmental rather than family-based processes. Although family-based interventions would not be predicted to eliminate the core symptoms of disorders such as ADHD or ASD, they may nonetheless improve overall functioning significantly and potentially reduce symptom severity when delivered early in development (e.g., [115, 116]). Second, although family-based interventions for many child and adolescent problems focus on parenting processes as primary mechanisms of change, it is often necessary to understand and address broader aspects of the family system in order to target parenting effectively. For example, attempts to engage mothers and fathers in parenting interventions may fail when clinical engagement strategies ignore systemic issues such as discord in the parents' own relationship [117]. Finally, family therapists are likely to acquire, and draw on, considerable theoretical knowledge regarding child psychopathology and the family, yet this knowledge is not the exclusive domain of the therapist. A key role of the therapist in current evidence-based interventions is to empower parents and family members by educating them about the science of child mental health. We firmly believe that therapists should be willing to openly share such theory and to acknowledge the limitations of current scientific explanations.

References

1. Sburlati ES, et al. A model of therapist competencies for the empirically supported cognitive behavioral treatment of child and adolescent anxiety and depressive disorders. *Clinical Child and Family Psychology Review* 2011; **14**(1):89–109.

2. Rutter ML, Hersov SD. Family, area, and school influences in the genesis of conduct disorder. In: Hersov LA, Berger AL, Shaffer D (eds.), *Aggression and Anti-social Behavior in Childhood and Adolescence*. London: Pergamon Press, 1978, pp. 95–113.

3. Bronfenbrenner U. Ecology of the family as a context for human development: Research perspectives. *Developmental Psychology* 1986; **22**(6):723–42.

4. Kessler RC, et al. Childhood adversities and adult psychopathology in the WHO World Mental Health Surveys. *British Journal of Psychiatry* 2010; **197** (5):378–85.

5. Lacey RE, Minnis H. Practitioner review: Twenty years of research with adverse childhood experience scores: Advantages, disadvantages and applications to practice. *Journal of Child Psychology and Psychiatry* 2020; **61**(2):116–30.

6. Siddaway AP. Adverse childhood experiences research: Commonalities with similar, arguably identical, literatures and the need for integration. *British Journal of Psychiatry* 2019, 1–2.

7. McLaughlin KA, Sheridan MA, Lambert HK. Childhood adversity and neural development: Deprivation and threat as distinct dimensions of early experience. *Neuroscience and Biobehavioral Reviews* 2014; **47**:578–91.

8. Minuchin S. *Families and Family Therapy*. Cambridge, MA: Harvard University Press, 1974, pp. viii, 268.

9. Olson DH. Circumplex model of marital and family systems. *Journal of Family Therapy* 2000; **22**(2):144–67.

10. Dumas JE, et al. Home chaos: Sociodemographic, parenting, interactional, and child correlates. *Journal of Clinical Child and Adolescent Psychology* 2005; **34** (1):93–104.

11. Coldwell J, Pike A, Dunn J. Household chaos: Links with parenting and child behaviour. *Journal of Child Psychology and Psychiatry* 2006; **47** (11):1116–22.

12. Baumrind D. Current patterns of parental authority. *Developmental Psychology* 1971; **4**(1 pt. 2):1.

13. Larzelere RE, Morris ASE, Harrist AW. *Authoritative Parenting: Synthesizing Nurturance and Discipline for Optimal Child Development*. Washington, DC: American Psychological Association, 2013.

14. Darling N, Steinberg L. Parenting style as context: An integrative model. *Psychological Bulletin* 1993; **113** (3):487.

15. Schaefer ES. A configurational analysis of children's reports of parent behavior. *Journal of Consulting Psychology* 1965; **29**(6):552.

16. Steinberg L. Autonomy, conflict, and harmony in the family relationship. In Feldman SS, Elliott GR (eds.), *At the Threshold: The Developing Adolescent*. Cambridge, MA: Harvard University Press, 1990, pp. 255–76.

17. Soenens B, Vansteenkiste M. A theoretical upgrade of the concept of parental psychological control: Proposing new insights on the basis of self-determination theory. *Developmental Review* 2010; **30**(1):74–99.

18. Grolnick WS, Pomerantz EM. Issues and challenges in studying parental control: Toward a new conceptualization. *Child Development Perspectives* 2009; 3(3):165–70.

19. Ainsworth MD, et al. *Patterns of Attachment*. Hillsdale, NJ: Erlbaum, 1978.

20. Biringen Z, Easterbrooks MA. Emotional availability: Concept, research, and window on developmental psychopathology. *Development and Psychopathology* 2012; **24**(1):1–8.

21. Feldman R. Parent-infant synchrony and the construction of shared timing; physiological precursors, developmental outcomes, and risk conditions. *Journal of Child Psychology and Psychiatry* 2007; **48**(3–4):329–54.

22. Aksan N, Kochanska G, Ortmann MR. Mutually responsive orientation between parents and their young children: Toward methodological advances in the science of relationships. *Developmental Psychology* 2006; **42**(5):833.

23. Eisenberg N, Cumberland A, Spinrad TL. Parental socialization of emotion. *Psychological Inquiry* 1998; **9** (4):241–73.

24. Katz LF, Maliken AC, Stettler NM. Parental meta-emotion philosophy: A review of research and theoretical framework. *Child Development Perspectives* 2012; **6**(4):417–22.

25. Perry NB, et al. Maternal socialization of child emotion and adolescent adjustment: Indirect effects through emotion regulation. *Developmental Psychology* 2020; **56**(3):541–52.

26. Johnson AM, et al. Emotion socialization and child conduct problems: A comprehensive review and meta-analysis. *Clinical Psychology Review* 2017; **54**:65–80.

27. Patterson GR. The early development of coercive family process. In: *Antisocial Behavior in Children and Adolescents: A Developmental Analysis and Model for Intervention*. Washington, DC: American Psychological Association, 2002, pp. 25–44.

28. Kobak R, et al. Adapting to the changing needs of adolescents: Parenting practices and challenges to sensitive attunement. *Current Opinion in Psychology* 2017; **15**:137–42.

29. Hawes DJ, Tully LA Parent discipline and socialization in middle childhood. In: Hupp S, Jewell, JD (eds.), *Encyclopedia of Child and Adolescent Development*. Hoboken, NJ: Wiley-Blackwell, 2019, pp. 1–10.

30. Cloninger CR, et al. The complex genetics and biology of human temperament: A review of traditional concepts in relation to new molecular findings. *Translational Psychiatry* 2019; **9**(1):290.

31. Nigg JT. Temperament and developmental psychopathology. *Journal of Child Psychology and Psychiatry* 2006; **47**(3–4):395–422.

32. Kiff CJ, Lengua LJ, Zalewski M. Nature and nurturing: Parenting in the context of child temperament. *Clinical Child and Family Psychology Review* 2011; **14** (3):251–301.

33. Dishion TJ, Patterson GR The development and ecology of antisocial behaviour. In: Cicchetti D, Cohen DJ (eds.), *Developmental Psychopathology*, Vol. 3: *Risk, Disorder, and Adaptation*. Hoboken, NJ: Wiley, 2006, pp. 503–41.

34. Lewis MD. The promise of dynamic systems approaches for an integrated account of human development. *Child Development* 2000; **71**(1):36–43.

35. Steinberg L, Avenevoli S. The role of context in the development of psychopathology: A conceptual framework and some speculative propositions. *Child Development* 2000; **71**(1):66–74.

36. Deater-Deckard K. Family matters: Intergenerational and interpersonal processes of executive function and attentive behavior. *Current Directions in Psychological Science* 2014; **23**(3):230–6.

37. Bronfenbrenner U, Ceci SJ. Nature-nuture reconceptualised in developmental perspective: A bioecological model. *Psychological Review* 1994; **101** (4):568–86.

38. Dadds MR, Frick PJ. Toward a transdiagnostic model of common and unique processes leading to the major disorders of childhood: The REAL model of attention, responsiveness and learning. *Behavior Research and Therapy* 2019; **119**:103410.

39. Slagt M, et al. Differences in sensitivity to parenting depending on child temperament: A meta-analysis. *Psychological Bulletin* 2016; **142**(10):1068–110.

40. Belsky J, Pluess M. Beyond diathesis stress: differential susceptibility to environmental influences. *Psychological Bulletin* 2009; **135** (6):885–908.

41. Hastings PD, et al. Dispositional and environmental predictors of the development of internalizing problems in childhood: Testing a multilevel model. *Journal of Abnormal Child Psychology* 2015; **43** (5):831–45.

42. Davies P, Cicchetti D, Hentges RF. Maternal unresponsiveness and child disruptive problems: The interplay of uninhibited temperament and dopamine transporter genes. *Child Development* 2015; **86** (1):63–79.

43. Pluess M, Belsky J. Vantage sensitivity: Individual differences in response to positive experiences. *Psychological Bulletin* 2013; **139**(4):901–16.

44. Rabinowitz JA, Drabick DA. Do children fare for better and for worse? Associations among child features and parenting with child competence and symptoms. *Developmental Review* 2017; **45**:1–30.

45. Cicchetti D, Toth SL. The past achievements and future promises of developmental psychopathology: The coming of age of a discipline. *Journal of Child Psychology and Psychiatry* 2009; **50**(1–2):16–25.

46. Pine DS, Fox NA. Childhood antecedents and risk for adult mental disorders. *Annual Review of Psychology* 2015; **66**:459–85.

47. Thapar A, Cooper M, Rutter M. *Neurodevelopmental disorders*. Lancet Psychiatry 2017; **4**(4):339–46.

48. Hawes DJ, et al. Parenting practices and prospective levels of hyperactivity/inattention across early- and middle-childhood. *Journal of Psychopathology and Behavioral Assessment* 2013; **35**(3):273–82.

49. Nikolas MA, Momany AM. DRD4 variants moderate the impact of parental characteristics on child attention-deficit hyperactivity disorder: Exploratory evidence from a multiplex family design. *Journal of Abnormal Child Psychology* 2017; **45**(3):429–42.

50. Bacanu SA, Kendler KS. Extracting actionable information from genome scans. *Genetic Epidemiology* 2013; **37**(1):48–59.

51. Koutra K, et al. Impaired family functioning in psychosis and its relevance to relapse: A two-year follow-up study. *Comprehensive Psychiatry* 2015; **62**:1–12.

52. Schlosser DA, et al. Predicting the longitudinal effects of the family environment on prodromal symptoms and functioning in patients at-risk for psychosis. *Schizophrenia Research* 2010; **118**(1–3):69–75.

53. Patterson GR, Reid JB, Eddy JM. A brief history of the Oregon model. In: Reid JB, Patterson GR, Snyder J (eds.), *Antisocial Behavior in Children and Adolescents: A Developmental Analysis and Model for Intervention*. Washington, DC: American Psychological Association, 2002, pp. 3–20.

54. Patterson GR. *Coercion theory: The study of change.* In: Dishion TJ, Snyder JJ (eds.), *Oxford Library of Psychology. The Oxford Handbook of Coercive Relationship Dynamics*. Oxford, UK: Oxford University Press, 2015, pp. 7–22.

55. Fairchild G, et al. Conduct disorder. *Nature Reviews Disease Primers* 2019; **5**(1):43.

56. Silberg J, Moore AA, Rutter M. Age of onset and the subclassification of conduct/dissocial disorder. *Journal of Child Psychology and Psychiatry* 2015; **56** (7):826–33.

57. Frick PJ, et al. Can callous-unemotional traits enhance the understanding, diagnosis, and treatment of serious conduct problems in children and adolescents? A comprehensive review. *Psychological Bulletin* 2014; **140**(1):1–57.

58. Hawes DJ, Price MJ, Dadds MR. Callous-unemotional traits and the treatment of conduct problems in childhood and adolescence: A comprehensive review. *Clinical Child and Family Psychology Review* 2014; **17**(3).

58a. Imm Sng K, Hawes DJ, Raine A, et al. Callous unemotional traits and the relationship between aggressive parenting practices and conduct problems in Singaporean families. *Child Abuse and Neglect* 2018; **81**:225–34.

59. Kochanska G, et al. Children's callous-unemotional traits moderate links between their positive relationships with parents at preschool age and externalizing behavior problems at early school age. *Journal of Child Psychology and Psychiatry* 2013; **54** (11):1251–60.

60. Pasalich DS, et al. Do callous-unemotional traits moderate the relative importance of parental coercion versus warmth in child conduct problems? An

observational study. *Journal of Child Psychology and Psychiatry* 2011; **52**(12):1308–15.

61. O'Connor TG, et al. Sensitivity to parenting in adolescents with callous/unemotional traits: Observational and experimental findings. *Journal of Abnormal Psychology* 2016; **125**(4):502–13.

62. Schleider JL, Weisz JR. Family process and youth internalizing problems: A triadic model of etiology and intervention. *Development and Psychopathology* 2017; **29**(1):273–301.

63. Sroufe LA, et al. Implications of attachment theory for developmental psychopathology. *Development and Psychopathology* 1999; **11**(1):1–13.

64. Beesdo K, et al. Incidence and risk patterns of anxiety and depressive disorders and categorization of generalized anxiety disorder. *Archives of General Psychiatry* 2010; **67**(1):47–57.

65. Rapee RM. Family factors in the development and management of anxiety disorders. *Clinical Child and Family Psychology Review* 2012; **15**(1):69–80.

66. Rapee RM, Schniering CA, Hudson JL. Anxiety disorders during childhood and adolescence: Origins and treatment. *Annual Review of Clinical Psychology* 2009; **5**:311–41.

67. Chorpita BF, Barlow DH. The development of anxiety: The role of control in the early environment. *Psychological Bulletin* 1998; **124**(1):3–21.

68. Dadds MR, Roth JH. Family processes in the development of anxiety problems. In: Vasey MW, Dadds MR (eds.), *The Developmental Psychopathology of Anxiety*. Oxford, UK: Oxford University Press, 2001, pp. 278–303.

69. Craske MG, Hermans D, Vervliet B. State-of-the-art and future directions for extinction as a translational model for fear and anxiety. *Philosophical Transactions of the Royal Society B: Biological Sciences* 2018; **373** (1742):20170025.

70. Van Der Bruggen CO, Stams GJJ, Bögels SM. Research review: The relation between child and parent anxiety and parental control: A meta-analytic review. *Journal of Child Psychology and Psychiatry* 2008; **49**(12):1257–69.

71. McLeod BD, Wood JJ, Weisz JR. Examining the association between parenting and childhood anxiety: A meta-analysis. *Clinical Psychology Review* 2007; **27** (2):155–72.

72. Möller EL, et al. Associations between maternal and paternal parenting behaviors, anxiety and its precursors in early childhood: A meta-analysis. *Clinical Psychology Review* 2016; **45**:17–33.

73. Dadds MR, et al. Family process and child anxiety and aggression: An observational analysis. *Journal of Abnormal Child Psychology* 1996; **24**(6):715–34.

74. Askew C, Field AP. The vicarious learning pathway to fear 40 years on. *Clinical Psychology Review* 2008; **28** (7):1249–65.

75. Aktar E, et al. The interplay between expressed parental anxiety and infant behavioural inhibition predicts infant avoidance in a social referencing paradigm. *Journal of Child Psychology and Psychiatry* 2013; **54**(2):144–56.

76. Muris P, Field AP. The role of verbal threat information in the development of childhood fear: 'Beware the Jabberwock!' *Clinical Child and Family Psychology Review* 2010; **13**(2):129–50.

77. Percy R, et al. Parents' verbal communication and childhood anxiety: A systematic review. *Clinical Child and Family Psychology Review* 2016; **19**(1):55–75.

78. Field AP. The behavioral inhibition system and the verbal information pathway to children's fears. *Journal of Abnormal Psychology* 2006; **115**(4):742–52.

79. Allen JL, Rapee RM, Sandberg S. Severe life events and chronic adversities as antecedents to anxiety in children: A matched control study. *Journal of Abnormal Child Psychology* 2008; **36**(7):1047–56.

80. Restifo K, Bögels S. Family processes in the development of youth depression: Translating the evidence to treatment. *Clinical Psychology Review* 2009; **29**(4):294–316.

81. Griffith JM, et al. Parenting and youth onset of depression across three years: Examining the influence of observed parenting on child and adolescent depressive outcomes. *Journal of Abnormal Child Psychology* 2019; **47**(12):1969–80.

82. Shore L, et al. Review: Longitudinal trajectories of child and adolescent depressive symptoms and their predictors: A systematic review and meta-analysis. *Child and Adolescent Mental Health* 2018; **23**(2):107–20.

83. Lovejoy MC, et al. Maternal depression and parenting behavior: A meta-analytic review. *Clinical Psychology Review* 2000; **20**(5):561–92.

84. Alloy LB, et al. Role of parenting and maltreatment histories in unipolar and bipolar mood disorders: Mediation by cognitive vulnerability to depression. *Clinical Child and Family Psychology Review* 2006; 9 (1):23–64.

85. Cummings ME, Keller PS, Davies PT. Towards a family process model of maternal and paternal depressive symptoms: Exploring multiple relations with child and family functioning. *Journal of Child Psychology and Psychiatry* 2005; **46**(5):479–89.

86. Sheeber L, Hops H, Davis B. *Family processes in adolescent depression. Clinical Child and Family Psychology Review* 2001; **4**(1):19–35.

87. Schwartz OS, et al. Affective parenting behaviors, adolescent depression, and brain development:

A review of findings from the Oregon Adolescent Development Study. *Child Development Perspectives* 2017; **11**(2):90–6.

88. Belsky J. *The determinants of parenting: A process model. Child Development* 1984; **55**(1):83–96.

89. Taraban L, Shaw DS. Parenting in context: Revisiting Belsky's classic process of parenting model in early childhood. *Developmental Review* 2018; **48**:55–81.

90. Wilson S, Durbin CE. Effects of paternal depression on fathers' parenting behaviors: A meta-analytic review. *Clinical Psychology Review* 2010; **30** (2):167–80.

91. Feldman R, et al. Sensitive parenting is associated with plasma oxytocin and polymorphisms in the *OXTR* and *CD38* genes. *Biological Psychiatry* 2012; **72**(3):175–81.

92. Prinzie P, et al. The relations between parents' big five personality factors and parenting: A meta-analytic review. *Journal of Personality and Social Psychology* 2009; **97**(2):351–62.

93. Bornstein MH, Hahn C-S, Haynes OM. *Maternal personality, parenting cognitions, and parenting practices. Developmental Psychology* 2011; **47** (3):658–75.

94. Capaldi DM, et al. Continuity of parenting practices across generations in an at-risk sample: A prospective comparison of direct and mediated associations. *Journal of Abnormal Child Psychology* 2003; **31**(2):127–42.

95. Jones TL, Prinz RJ. Potential roles of parental self-efficacy in parent and child adjustment: A review. *Clinical Psychology Review* 2005; **25**(3):341–63.

96. Kirkman JJL, Dadds MR, Hawes DJ. Development and validation of the knowledge of parenting strategies scale: Measuring effective parenting strategies. *Journal of Child and Family Studies* 2018; **27**(10):3200–17.

97. Chen M, et al. Parent and adolescent depressive symptoms: The role of parental attributions. *Journal of Abnormal Child Psychology* 2009; **37**(1):119–30.

98. Johnston C, Ohan JL. The importance of parental attributions in families of children with attention-deficit/hyperactivity and disruptive behavior disorders. *Clinical Child and Family Psychology Review* 2005; **8**(3):167–82.

99. Dix T. Attributing dispositions to children: An interactional analysis of attribution in socialization. *Personality and Social Psychology Bulletin* 1993; **19** (5):633–43.

100. Lorber MF, O'Leary SG, Kendziora KT. Mothers' overreactive discipline and their encoding and appraisals of toddler behavior. *Journal of Abnormal Child Psychology* 2003; **31**(5):485–94.

101. Gottman JM. A theory of marital dissolution and stability. *Journal of Family Psychology* 1993; **7** (1):57–75.

102. Snyder J, et al. Escalation and reinforcement in mother-child conflict: Social processes associated with the development of physical aggression. *Development and Psychopathology* 1994; **6** (2):305–21.

103. Dix T. The affective organization of parenting: Adaptive and maladaptative processes. *Psychological Bulletin* 1991; **110**(1):3–25.

104. Mence M, et al. Emotional flooding and hostile discipline in the families of toddlers with disruptive behavior problems. *Journal of Family Psychology* 2014; **28**(1):12–21.

105. Harold GT, Sellers R. Annual research review: Interparental conflict and youth psychopathology: An evidence review and practice focused update. *Journal of Child Psychology and Psychiatry* 2018; **59** (4):374–402.

106. Ceballo R, McLoyd VC. Social support and parenting in poor, dangerous neighborhoods. *Child Development* 2002; **73**(4):1310–21.

107. Thompson RA. Social support and child protection: Lessons learned and learning. *Child Abuse and Neglect* 2015; **41**:19–29.

108. Rothenberg WA, et al. Examining effects of mother and father warmth and control on child externalizing and internalizing problems from age 8 to 13 in nine countries. *Development and Psychopathology* 2019; 1–25.

109. Scaramella LV, et al. Parenting and children's distress reactivity during toddlerhood: An examination of direction of effects. *Social Development* 2008; **17**(3):578–95.

110. Paulussen-Hoogeboom MC, et al. Child negative emotionality and parenting from infancy to preschool: A meta-analytic review. *Developmental Psychology* 2007; **43**(2):438.

111. Polanczyk GV, et al. Annual research review: A meta-analysis of the worldwide prevalence of mental disorders in children and adolescents. *Journal of Child Psychology and Psychiatry* 2015; **56** (3):345–65.

112. Putnick DL, et al. Perceived mother and father acceptance-rejection predict four unique aspects of child adjustment across nine countries. *Journal of Child Psychology and Psychiatry* 2015; **56**(8):923–32.

113. Gershoff ET, et al. Parent discipline practices in an international sample: Associations with child behaviors and moderation by perceived normativeness. *Child Development* 2010; **81** (2):487–502.

114. Lansford JE, et al. Corporal punishment, maternal warmth, and child adjustment: A longitudinal study in eight countries. *Journal of Clinical Child and Adolescent Psychology* 2014; **43**(4):670–85.

115. Faraone SV, et al. Attention-deficit/hyperactivity disorder. *Nature Reviews Disease Primers* 2015; **1**:15020.

116. French L, Kennedy EMM. Annual research review: Early intervention for infants and young children with, or at-risk of, autism spectrum disorder: A systematic review. *Journal of Child Psychology and Psychiatry* 2018; **59**(4):444–56.

117. Piotrowska PJ, et al. Mothers, fathers, and parental systems: A conceptual model of parental engagement in programmes for child mental health–Connect, attend, participate, enact (CAPE). *Clinical Child and Family Psychology Review* 2017; **20** (2):146–61.

Implementation of Family-Based Intervention
Current Status and Future Directions

Satoko Sasagawa, Cecilia A. Essau and Thomas H. Ollendick

Remarkable advances have been achieved in the treatment of social, emotional and behavioural problems in childhood and adolescence in the past few decades. Evidence-based treatments have been established in the multifarious fields concerning youth mental health [1, 2], and the promotion of the scientist-practitioner model has clearly served to heighten the quality of services being provided within local settings. Continued efforts are being made to spread these treatments, and the field is now shifting towards better implementation and dissemination of evidence-based childhood and adolescent intervention programmes [3].

Family-based intervention is one treatment option that has been subject to extensive research and can be used to support children and their families from as early as the prenatal period (e.g., [4]) through to late adolescence (e.g., [5]). In this research, the family is viewed as the most influential and malleable context for promoting long-lasting behavioural and emotional adjustment among children and youth; accordingly, these interventions aim to provide education to families, improve the quality of family relationships and teach key family management skills [6]. Parents learn skills such as those used to monitor and manage child behaviour, and familial changes in domains such as conflict negotiation, problem-solving and improved positive affect are accomplished. Systematic reviews and meta-analyses have found family-based interventions to be effective at preventing or reducing a wide range of psychosocial problems, including externalizing and disruptive behaviour problems [7, 8], attention deficit hyperactivity disorder [9], conduct disorder [10], anxiety disorders [11] and eating disorders [12].

While the effectiveness of various family-based interventions has been well established, the dissemination and implementation of such interventions still remain a task to be accomplished. Previous studies in

implementation science have acknowledged the many barriers related to the diffusion of evidence-based practices (e.g., [1, 13, 14]. Furthermore, there are factors specific to family-based intervention which further complicate this implementation. One such factor is parent engagement. Many previous studies have highlighted the importance of parent engagement, but optimal levels of engagement have nevertheless been difficult to achieve [15]. Recruitment rates for family-based prevention programmes have been found to range from 3 to 35 per cent, and even when parents are successfully recruited, many family-based programmes have high dropout rates [16]. Importantly, a number of studies have reported successful instances of large-scale implementation despite the many challenges associated with family-based programmes. In this chapter, we review the scientific evidence regarding implementation research in the field of family-based intervention for child and adolescent mental health and aim to clarify the challenges and future directions associated with its advancement.

Implementation Framework

Implementation is defined as 'a specified set of activities designed to put into practice an activity or programme of known dimensions' [17, p. 5]. It is now widely recognized that no matter how effective or engaging a given intervention is, the diffusion of scientific findings to human services does not happen automatically. Numerous frameworks to promote active implementation efforts have been proposed. An extensive review of implementation frameworks is provided by Tabak et al. [18], whereas Albers et al. [19] provide a broad review of the frameworks used within the area of child, youth and family services. They also identified eight distinct implementation frameworks that served as the theoretical underpinnings for the 33 articles included in their review: (1)

the active implementation framework (AIF) [20], (2) the availability, responsiveness and continuity organizational and community (ARC) intervention model [21], (3) the community development team (CDT) [22], (4) the consolidated framework for implementation research (CFIR) [23], (5) the exploration, preparation, implementation and sustainment (EPIS) model [24], (6) getting to outcomes (GTO) [25], (7) the interactive systems framework (ISF) [26] and (8) the practical, robust implementation and sustainability model (PRISM) [27].

The AIF was developed by the National Implementation Research Network based on the Fixsen et al. [17] monograph synthesizing implementation research findings across a range of fields. The main aim of this framework is to guide implementation processes in human services. The ARC model was designed to support the improvement of social and mental health services for children at the organizational and community levels and has been used to facilitate the implementation of multisystemic therapy [5]. The CDT approach is an implementation strategy established by the California Institute of Mental Health. It aims to build peer-to-peer networks of adopters in mental health services to provide an environment where implementation barriers can be problem-solved together. Within this model, the bidirectional partnerships between researchers and communities are stressed. The CFIR is a meta-theoretical framework that is based on an extensive review of multiple implementation theories. It incorporates not only intervention-related factors but also contextual factors (inner and outer settings) and characteristics of the participating individuals and implementation process, thereby offering a pragmatic framework for approaching the complex, interacting, multilevel and transient states of implementation. The EPIS model was developed for use in public-sector service systems and assumes a staged process. The underlying proposition is that the influential feature of the organization changes depending on the implementation phase. The GTO approach was developed by the National Center for the Advancement of Prevention as a guide to help practitioners plan, implement and evaluate their programmes. Applicable to a wide range of fields, including treatment, prevention and education, the main purpose of the framework is to develop a comprehensive and systematic approach to *accountability* (defined as 'the inclusion of critical

elements of programme planning, implementation, and evaluation in order to achieve results' [25, p. 389]. The ISF is a community-centred model that consists of three systems: prevention synthesis and translation, prevention support and prevention delivery. It emphasizes the continuity between distilling information about innovations and translating it into user-friendly formats, providing support and building capacity for the adoption of innovations, and the actual implementation process. The PRISM approach is used to evaluate how a healthcare programme or intervention interacts with the recipients to influence programme adoption, implementation, maintenance, reach and effectiveness. An emphasis is placed on the sustainability of the intervention.

Although somewhat similar in scope, each of the preceding models stress different aspects of the implementation process and is applied to distinct levels of implementation (e.g., individual, organizational, community or system level); thus, researchers can adopt the individual model that is most applicable to their research setting. One of the most frequently used model is the EPIS model [28, 29]. The reason for its high adoption rate is the fact that the EPIS model is simple, generic and can depict the influence of both outer and inner contexts across the different stages of implementation. By contrast, there is a general consensus regarding which factors need to be addressed for effective implementation and in what temporal order implementation proceeds. Indeed, Albers et al. [19] note that while each of the models included in their review differs in its level of operationalization and universal applicability, common factors such as implementation stages, key influences (i.e., competencies, organizational factors and leadership), stakeholders and capacity (e.g., individuals or teams providing implementation-specific knowledge and skills) emerge. Consequently, efforts to extract the basic components of the various implementation models are currently being made.

An example of a review which aimed to identify the essential implementation components is provided by Meyers, Durlak and Wandersman [30]. The authors included 25 implementation frameworks from previous studies and established the four phases and 14 steps that are associated with quality implementation (see Table 3.1). Although the frameworks included in the review do not solely target family-based interventions, a majority of the models

Table 3.1 Four Implementation Phases and 14 Critical Steps Associated with Quality Implementation

Phase one: Initial considerations regarding the host setting
Assessment strategies;
1. Conducting a needs and resources assessment
2. Conducting a fit assessment
3. Conducting a capacity/readiness assessment
Decisions about adaptation:
4. Possibility for adaptation
Capacity-building strategies:
5. Obtaining explicit buy-in from critical stakeholders and fostering a supportive community/organizational climate
6. Building general/organizational capacity
7. Staff recruitment/maintenance
8. Effective pre-innovation staff training
Phase two: Creating a structure for implementation
Structural features for implementation:
9. Creating implementation teams
10. Developing an implementation plan
Phase three: Ongoing structure once implementation begins
Ongoing implementation support strategies:
11. Technical assistance/coaching/supervision
12. Process evaluation
13. Supportive feedback mechanism
Phase four: Improving future applications
14. Learning from experience

Source: Meyers et al. [30, p. 468].

identified in Albers et al. [19] were included. The review depicts the implementation process as a staged series of linking steps, including assessment, collaboration/negotiation, monitoring and reflection. Dynamic interplay between the four phases is assumed, and specific questions that need to be clarified in each of the steps are provided in detail. The synthesized model is referred to as the *quality implementation framework* (QIF), which provides a guideline when examining and evaluating the implementation process of a particular programme. It is noteworthy that 10 of the 14 steps must be addressed before implementation begins, suggesting that when developing a new programme, careful planning before launching is necessary. The QIF is exemplary of how

theoretical models can serve as a guideline in promoting real-life implementation of specific programmes.

Research on the Implementation of Family-Based Interventions

Although comprehensive theoretical models exist, data regarding implementation of family-based interventions remain fairly limited. Because implementation often involves studying innovations in real-world settings, rigorous experimental designs encompassing all the possible influential variables are not possible to accomplish [30]. Thus, established methods in treatment effectiveness studies (e.g., randomized, controlled trials) are not always the absolute approach within this field, and various methodological proposals have been made to date. Mixed-methods studies, which collect both quantitative and qualitative data, are emerging as an alternative to better integrate complex findings into a more complete and comprehensive picture (e.g., [31]). An overview of research and evaluation designs is provided in a paper by Brown et al. [32].

One of the factors studied most extensively in relation to the implementation of family-based interventions is treatment fidelity. Also called *treatment integrity, fidelity* is defined as the 'degree to which an intervention is delivered as intended' [33]. Fidelity comprises (1) treatment adherence, or the extent to which prescribed strategies and content were delivered as intended, and (2) therapist competence, which represents how skilfully and responsively the therapist was able to deliver both the prescribed content and the relational components [34, 35]. Fidelity, by definition, is the internal validity of the intervention, and since evidence accumulated in favour of the intervention is specific to that particular set of procedures, increasing fidelity generally is associated with better outcomes. However, there is continued debate as to whether certain levels of flexibility in procedure can maximize operating effectiveness, thereby promoting the implementation process overall.

A number of family-based studies have indicated that higher treatment adherence indeed produces better outcomes. For example, an early study by Henggeler et al. [36] found that outcomes for violent and chronic juvenile offenders and their families were considerably more favourable when adherence fidelity to multisystemic therapy (MST) was high. Similarly, Schoenwald et al. [37] demonstrated that higher levels of adherence to MST predicted better long-term out-comes. Houge et al. [38] and Huey et al. [39] also report that higher levels of adherence are related to positive programme effects.

Other studies have found mixed results. For example, a study by Byrnes et al. [40] examined the relationship between programme fidelity (i.e., adherence and quality of implementation) and family satisfaction and participation in the Strengthening Families Programme (SFP) [41]. Interestingly, higher adherence scores were related to higher satisfaction only in the youth data; the opposite was found for parent data, where, surprisingly, higher adherence scores were associated with lower satisfaction. The authors attributed this difference to the distinctive format between the two groups – the parent sessions involved much more discussion and tightly timed activities compared to the youth sessions. For the health educators to obtain high adherence scores, implementation of all programme activities was necessary, which presumably limited free discussion and flexibility in time schedules. Such delivery challenges may have accounted for the reduced dissatisfaction with the programme.

Durlak and DuPre [42] reviewed studies related to prevention and health promotion programmes for children and adolescents. Here implementation dosage (i.e., quantity, intervention strength), quality (i.e., how well different programme components have been conducted) and programme reach (i.e., participation rates, programme scope) were examined in addition to fidelity. Results showed that levels of implementation, regardless of which aspect was measured, affected outcomes. Accordingly, the authors maintained that assessment of implementation is an absolute necessity in programme evaluations, and psychometrically sound assessment strategies based on operational definitions of relevant constructs need to be developed and used. While the studies included in this review were not limited to family-based programmes and the results need to be replicated within this context, it is highly probable that the same results would be applicable.

Akin et al. [43] compared the implementation process of two family programmes, SFP and Celebrating Families! (CF!) [44], in a state-wide project. A unique aspect of this study was that the former programme was successfully implemented in all five sites of the project, whereas the latter was delivered at only one of the intended sites and was then discontinued. The study aimed to clarify what supports and barriers contributed to the successful implementation of one programme and a failure in another. Semi-structured phone interviews with site coordinators and agency practitioners were used to collect data for this purpose. High-quality training, coaching and fidelity monitoring, funding and flexibility of the programme were found to be key factors in promoting the implementation of a particular programme. The authors concluded that the largest difference between the successful and non-successful implementation was staff training. Specifically, the participants felt positively about implementing SFP regardless of initial staffing challenges and scheduling difficulties, while more ambivalent or negative responses were evident for the CF! These differences illustrate that high-quality training and high staff involvement, in interaction with other implementation factors, have a powerful impact on intervention outcomes.

A similar interview methodology was used by Sanders, Prinz and Shapiro [45] for the Triple P-Positive Parenting Programme [46]. The authors aimed to determine facilitators and barriers of continued programme use by means of a large-scale interview study. A total of 650 multidisciplinary service providers were contacted six months after receiving programme training, of which 611 participated in a 20-minute telephone interview. As a result, predictors of continued programme use included being trained in Group Triple P, receiving positive feedback from parents, exposure to only minor or moderate workplace barriers, seeing observable changes in children or families and consultation with other Triple P practitioners. Inhibitors were low confidence in parent consultation work and use of Triple P, difficulty incorporating Triple P into everyday work and low workplace support. These findings were replicated in a more recent study by Asgary-Eden and Lee [47] and echo the importance of training reported by Akin et al. [43].

Another study that highlights the importance of quality training has been reported by Stern et al. [48]. In this study, treatment adherence and barriers/facilitators to the implementation of the Incredible Years programme [49] were examined using both quantitative (e.g., adherence checklist) and qualitative (e.g., audiotapes of supervision) data. The authors reported high levels of treatment adherence and identified the following factors as key contributors to adherence: training and structure of the programme, emphasis on accountability and ongoing session monitoring and supervision and group leader qualities. However, one major limitation of this study is that correlational analysis between treatment adherence and the potential barriers/facilitators was not provided.

In other research, Seng, Prinz and Sanders [50] investigated the relationship between training and other implementation factors. Specifically, the relationship between training completion and individual service provider characteristics, barriers to programme use and subsequent implementation of Triple P were examined. Interestingly, individual-level variables such as level of education, training adequacy, self-efficacy and training satisfaction did not predict training completion. The differences emerged in organizational variables, potential barriers regarding workplace characteristics (e.g., caseload and other responsibilities), issues related to provider/programme fit (e.g., clash with theoretical orientation or preferred treatment approach) and challenges in programme management (e.g., difficulty coordinating with other practitioners involved with family) were rated significantly higher by non-completers than completers of the programme training. These results suggest that while programme training is essential for the adoption of a particular intervention, other contextual factors can accelerate or hinder the maintenance of a new attempt. Similar results have been reported by Zazzali et al. [51] in a pilot study of the implementation of functional family therapy (FFT). It was concluded that the programme fitting with the mission of the organization and the organization having a strong interest in evidence-based treatments were associated with the adoption of FFT. Once a decision to adopt FFT was made, the degree to which the programme fit with organizational characteristics (e.g., available resource sets, organizational structure and culture) influenced the ease with which it was implemented.

While the preceding studies focused on the adoption phase of family-based programmes, the question of how to maintain such practices in the long run is also important. It has been documented that many programmes are discontinued after external funding ends [52]; hence, intervention sustainability is an important avenue to explore. Scheirer and Dearing [53, p. 2060] define *sustainability* as 'the continued use of programme components and activities for the continued achievement of desirable programme and population outcomes' and offer practical advice on measurement variables and research designs. Sustainability is often understood as a process variable, but Scheirer and Dearing [53] maintain that for research purposes, it is better conceptualized as a set of measurable outcome variables. Their review outlines alignment, compatibility or convergence of the programme; problem recognition in the external environment; and internal organizational variables as a facilitator of sustainability in general. In other words, for a programme to be successfully continued after external funding ends, the notions that there is a problem to be solved, that the programme can provide a solution to the problem and that the organization possesses the resources to support the programme need to be articulated and shared. Given this orientation, the question of whether and to what extent sustainability is desirable is raised. Sustainability research should be encouraged in order to avoid premature abandonment of potentially beneficial programmes; however, programme efficacy, which is a prerequisite for programmes to be sustained, is often ambiguous or unproven at the time of decision-making. The dilemma can be construed as a controversy over how much adaptation or modification can be made to programme components while still defining the intervention as 'sustained'.

Meanwhile, explicit measurement tools of sustainability are being developed. For example, Luke et al. [54] proposed the Programme Sustainability Assessment Tool (PSAT) and applied it to state- and community-level chronic disease programmes. The instrument is versatile and applicable to a wide range of fields, including family-based interventions. Such standardized assessment tools with sound reliability and validity provide promising theory-driven methods for sustainability research.

Future Directions for the Field

Assessment of implementation is a fundamental issue and a practice that needs to be further established to advance the field of child and adolescent mental health. As Durlak and DuPre [42] note, implementation data are analysed either categorically, by creating groups of providers who differ in their level of implementation (e.g., examining statistical differences between low and high implementation groups) or by assessing implementation in a continuous fashion (e.g., by using percentages to assess the level of dosage or fidelity achieved and examining its correlation with outcome variables). The primary methods of assessing implementation have been provider self-reports and independent behavioural observations. Although such methods have been useful, developing consensus on the terminology and operational definitions of relevant constructs and sound methodology for measurement need to be further achieved.

An example of a study in which methodological innovation augmented the identification of implementation factors is presented by Crowley et al. [55]. In this study, propensity and marginal structural models were used to improve the precision level of causal inferences involving implementation factors which cannot be easily randomized. The sample was collected from the PROmoting School-university-community Partnerships to Enhance Resilience (PROSPER) study [56], which is a community-randomized trial of an innovative approach for delivery of substance use prevention programmes. Within this framework, all families were offered the Strengthening Families Programme, and 17 per cent of the families enrolled. One year after, all the youth received preventive interventions within the school setting. Findings illustrate the capacity of this approach to successfully account for confounders that influence enrolment and attendance, enabling a more accurate estimation of causal relations. As illustrated in this example, measurement methodologies can greatly inform theoretical perspectives on implementation processes in family-based intervention.

Although treatment fidelity and quality training have emerged as important factors in research investigating successful implementation, a dearth of studies has examined other factors which may potentially influence the implementation process. In particular, factors unique to family-based programmes need to be pursued. A starting point may be factors that are known to be treatment moderators, including socioeconomic status [57], method of treatment delivery [58, 59] and levels of engagement in an intervention [60]. For example, Cotter et al. [61] investigated the effect of delivery format (i.e., parent-only one- to two-day workshop, parent/adolescent five-week group, parent-only five-week group and parent/adolescent online sessions) on the effectiveness of the Parenting Wisely programme. The authors noted that while all delivery formats yielded positive changes, group delivery over five weeks was superior to the other formats. The study was followed up over a six-month period [62], and the parent-only intensive workshop group was shown to be less effective than other formats, including online delivery.

Intervention engagement also has been examined as a moderator variable in this programme of research. Smokowski et al. [63] reported on structural, attitudinal and interpersonal barriers in engaging parents in multiple violence prevention programmes across a rural and urban implementation setting. Common barriers identified across the two settings included scheduling concerns/parent time management concerns, engagement difficulties, access to bilingual services and lack of relationships with service providers. While preliminary in nature, these qualitative studies provide the first step in clarifying factors influencing implementation. Further clarification is nonetheless needed through more sophisticated research designs and replication across samples.

Conclusion

Research into the implementation and dissemination of family-based interventions for child and adolescent mental health has been shaped by theoretical models that originated in a wide range of fields spanning health services, medicine and organizational research. Some studies in the field (e.g., [29]) have predicated a particular model, whereas others have synthesized the universal findings of individual models into a higher-order framework, as with the QIF [30]. These frameworks are useful in identifying the basic steps to implementation and common barriers encountered in each phase. Moreover, evidence indicates that by addressing these barriers before launching a particular intervention, quality implementation and sustainability may be maximized.

The strongest evidence for processes that promote effective implementation has been seen for processes that ensure the fidelity of a programme. Although research results to date have been mixed, the most common finding has been that higher treatment adherence is related to better implementation. While a certain degree of flexibility is favourable in the implementation process, this does not mean that fidelity needs to be compromised. Durlak and DuPre [42] maintain that 'the fidelity-adaptation debate is framed inappropriately in either-or terms'. Forehand et al. [64], in their commentary on the Triple P study by Mazzucchelli and Sanders [65] highlight how flexibility can be a feature that actually facilitates adherence. These views are endorsed by service providers themselves as well; for example, Chung, Mikesell and Miklovitz [66], through a survey of service providers and administers who participated in a workshop on family-focused therapy, reported that while the key characteristic perceived by providers to enhance the feasibility and acceptability of evidence-based programmes was flexibility, the providers also believed that training elements essential to implement evidence-based programmes effectively were precise, step-by-step guidelines and supervisory feedback. Such results suggest that providers are willing to accept manualized treatments on the whole, and the prime focus for researchers should be to offer guidance on the right mix of fidelity and adaptation. Providing cost-effective supervision should be another priority; having someone outside the immediate treatment structure monitor fidelity will enable practitioners to track whether and how much they are aligned with the recommended intervention method. At the same time, the assurance that excessive deviance will be monitored and amended to maximize programme effectiveness should enable practitioners to creatively experiment with adaptation issues; lack of supervisory guidance gives the practitioner no choice but to follow the immediate manual. Schoenwald, Sheidow and Chapman [67] showed that supervisor focus on adherence predicts therapist adherence, which results in better youth outcomes in MST; such findings provide a model case example of appropriate supervision promoting positive intervention outcomes via implementation-related factors.

Schoenwald et al. [68] describe and discuss the adaptation of the MST supervision model to a new service setting, referred to as the *Links service model*. In this model, an intervention team is comprised of a mental health provider, a parent advocate and a key opinion-leader teacher. The team facilitates training and provides extensive consultation to teachers and parents of the referred children throughout the implementation process of the programme. This study demonstrated that as with theoretical models for implementation, models for supervision can be adapted for application across a wide range of intervention fields. While the Links model assumes an extensive supervisory framework consisting of agency supervision, school supervision and team supervision, use of information technology and other supplementary methods may be a promising way to disseminate quality supervision cost-effectively [69].

Across all stages of implementation, measurement issues are an important challenge to consider. For example, adoption, implementation and sustainment are often conceptualized as continuous processes in current theoretical models (e.g., [27]). However, in regards to data collection, the measurement of these phases often involves distinct procedures. Implementation research suffers from imprecision in the measurement of various constructs [42], and ambiguity in the measurement methods generally used throughout these stages often adds to inconsistency in the evaluation process. While quantitative measures are being developed (e.g., [54]), the field heavily relies on qualitative (e.g., [70]) or mixed methods (e.g., [71]). Noticeable gaps exist in this research, especially that focusing on the sustainability stage; qualitative research is important in refining hypothesis, understanding the relationships between sustainability drivers and developing strategies to promote sustainment [72]. At the same, rigorous quantitative methods of evaluation (i.e., prospective and experimental designs) are needed to test such hypotheses and specify causal relationship. New methodologies are being developed and applied to a wide range of both quantitative and qualitative data [32] as part of a new trend that stands to promote innovative research in these areas.

Finally, a key challenge in implementing family-based interventions concerns the diverse contexts in which they are often delivered. Field of delivery is wide ranging and can involve multiple contexts based in the community, schools and family (e.g., the PROSPER project [56]). As a result, more than one external context typically needs to be taken into consideration, and interplay between such contexts should be carefully assessed and examined where relevant. The identification of potential barriers can become much more complex under such circumstances, and causal relations can become much more intricate to specify. These barriers to treatment, conceived as potential moderators to change by us, are important factors to pursue. Individual and ecological characteristics such as cultural background, age group, gender and the presence of parental psychopathology, as well as organizational/environmental characteristics such as programme delivery, need to be addressed. Although much work remains to be done, a solid foray into the implementation and dissemination of family-based interventions among international researchers appears to be prospering.

References

1. Ollendick TH, White SW, White BA (eds.). *The Oxford Handbook of Clinical Child and Adolescent Psychology.* Oxford, UK: Oxford University Press, 2018.

2. Weisz JR, Sandler IN, Durlak JA, Anton BS. Promoting and protecting youth mental health through evidence-based prevention and treatment. *American Psychologist* 2005; **60**:628–48.

3. Southam-Gerow MA, Rodriguez A, Chorpita BF, Daleiden EL. Dissemination and implementation of evidence based treatments for youth: Challenges and recommendations. *Professional Psychology: Research and Practice* 2012; **43**:527–34.

4. Feinberg ME, Kan ML. Establishing family foundations: Intervention effects on coparenting, parent/infant well-being, and parent-child relations. *Journal of Family Psychology* 2008; 22:253–63.

5. Henggeler SW, Borduin CM. *Family Therapy and Beyond: A Multisystemic Approach to Treating the Behavior Problems of Children and Adolescents.* Pacific Grove, CA: Brooks/Cole, 1990.

6. Van Ryzin MJ, Fosco GM. Family-based approaches to prevention: The state of the field. In: Van Ryzin MJ, Kumpfer KL, Fosco GM, Greenberg MT (eds.), *Family-Based Prevention Programs for Children and Adolescents: Theory, Research, and Large-Scale Dissemination.* New York: Taylor & Francis, 2016, pp. 1–19.

7. Eyberg SM, Nelson M, Boggs SR. Evidence-based psychosocial treatments for children and adolescents with disruptive behaviour. *Journal of Clinical Child and Adolescent Psychology* 2008; **37**:215–37.

8. Kazdin AE. Practitioner review: Psychosocial treatments for conduct disorder in children. *Journal of Child Psychology and Psychiatry* 2006; **38**:161–78.

9. Pelham Jr WE, Fabiano GA. Evidence-based psychosocial treatments for attention-deficit/hyperactivity disorder. *Journal of Clinical Child and Adolescent Psychology* 2008; **37**:184–214.

10. Woolfenden SR, Williams K, Peat JK. Family and parenting interventions for conduct disorder and delinquency: A meta-analysis of randomised controlled trials. *Archives of Diseases in Childhood* 2002; **86**:251–6.

11. Ginsburg GS, Schlossberg MC. Family-based treatment of childhood anxiety disorders. *International Review of Psychiatry* 2002; **14**:143–54.

12. Couturier J, Kimber M, Szatmari P. Efficacy of family-based treatment for adolescents with eating disorders: A systematic review and meta-analysis. *International Journal of Eating Disorders* 2012; **46**:3–11.

13. Mendez JL, Carpenter JL, LaForett DR, Cohen J. Parental engagement and barriers to participation in a community-based preventive intervention. *American Journal of Community Psychology* 2009; **44**, 1–14.

14. Pagoto SL, Spring B, Coups EJ, et al. Barriers and facilitators of evidence-based practice perceived by behavioural science health professionals. *Journal of Clinical Psychology* 2007; **63**:695–705.

15. Heinrichs N, Bertram H, Kuschel A, Hahlweg K. Parent recruitment and retention in a universal prevention program for child behaviour and emotional problems: Barriers to research and program participation. *Prevention Science* 2005; 6:275–86.

16. Chacko A, Jensen SA, Lowry LS, et al. Engagement in behavioural parent training: Review of the literature and implications for practice. *Clinical Child and Family Psychology Review* 2016; **19**:204–15.

17. Fixsen DL, Naoom SF, Blase KA, et al. *Implementation Research: A Synthesis of the Literature* (FMHI Publication No.231). Tampa, FL: University of South Florida, Louis de la Parte Florida Mental Health Institute, National Implementation Research Network, 2005.

18. Tabak RG, Khoong EC, Chambers D, Brownson RC. Bridging research and practice: Models for dissemination and implementation research. *American Journal of Preventive Medicine* 2012; **43**: 337–350.

19. Albers B, Mildon R, Lyon AR, Shlonsky A. Implementation frameworks in child, youth and family services: Results from a scoping review. *Children and Youth Services Review* 2017; **81**:101–16.

20. Metz A, Bartley L. Active implementation frameworks for program success. *Zero to Three* 2012; **32**:11–18.

21. Glisson C, Schoenwald SK. The ARC organizational and community intervention strategy for implementing evidence-based children's mental health treatments. *Mental Health Services Research* 2005; 7:243–59.

22. Saldana L, Chamberlain P. Supporting implementation: The role of community development teams to build infrastructure. *American Journal of Community Psychology* 2012; **50**:334–46.

23. Damschroder LJ, Aron DC, Keith RE, et al. Fostering implementation of health services research findings into practice: A consolidated framework for advancing implementation science. *Implementation Science* 2009; **4**:50.

24. Aarons GA, Hurlburt M, Horwitz SM. Advancing a conceptual model of evidence-based practice

implementation in public service sectors. *Administration and Policy in Mental Health* 2011; **38**:4–23.

25. Wandersman A, Imm P, Chinman M, Kaftarian S. Getting to outcomes: A results-based approach to accountability. *Evaluation and Program Planning* 2000; **23**:389–95.

26. Wandersman A, Duffy J, Flaspohler P, et al. Bridging the gap between prevention research and practice: The interactive systems framework for dissemination and implementation. *American Journal of Community Psychology* 2008; **41**:171–81.

27. Feldstein AC, Glasgow RE. A practical, robust implementation and sustainability model (PRISM) for integrating research findings into practice. *Joint Commission Journal of Quality and Patient Safety* 2008; **34**:228–43.

28. Kotte A, Hill KA, Mah AC, et al. Facilitators and barriers of implementing a measurement feedback system in public youth mental health. *Administration and Policy in Mental Health and Mental Health Services Research* 2016; **43**:861–78.

29. Novins DK, Green AE, Legha RK, Aarons GA. Dissemination and implementation of evidence-based practices for child and adolescent mental health: A systematic review. *Journal of the American Academy of Child and Adolescent Psychiatry* 2013; **52**:1009–25.

30. Meyers DC, Durlak JA, Wandersman A. The quality implementation framework: A synthesis of critical steps in the implementation process. *American Journal of Community Psychology* 2012; **50**:462–80.

31. Green AE, Fettes DL, Aarons GA. A concept mapping approach to guide and understand dissemination and implementation. *Journal of Behavioural Health Services and Research* 2012; **39**:362–73.

32. Brown CH, Curran G, Palinkas LA, et al. An overview of research and evaluation designs for dissemination and implementation. *Annual Review of Public Health* 2017; **38**:1–22.

33. Perepletchikova F, Treat TA, Kazdin AE. Treatment integrity in psychotherapy research: Analysis of studies and examination of the associated factors. *Journal of Consulting and Clinical Psychology* 2007; **75**:829–41.

34. Cox JR, Martinez RG, Southam-Gerow MA. Treatment integrity in psychotherapy research and implications for the delivery of quality mental health services. *Journal of Consulting and Clinical Psychology* 2019; **87**:221–33.

35. McLeod BD, Southam-Gerow MA, Weisz JR. Conceptual and methodological issues in treatment integrity measurement. *School Psychology Review* 2009; **38**:541–6.

36. Henggeler SW, Melton GW, Brondino MJ, et al. Multisystemic therapy with violent and chronic juvenile offenders and their families: The role of treatment fidelity in successful dissemination. *Journal of Consulting and Clinical Psychology* 1997; **65**:821–33.

37. Schoenwald SK, Chapman JE, Sheidow AJ, Carter RE. Long-term youth criminal outcomes in MST transport: The impact of therapist adherence and organizational climate and structure. *Journal of Clinical Child and Adolescent Psychology* 2009; **38**:91–105.

38. Houge A, Henderson CE, Dauber S, et al. Treatment adherence, competence, and outcome in individual and family therapy for adolescent behavior problems. *Journal of Consulting and Clinical Psychology* 2008; **76**:544–55.

39. Huey Jr SJ, Henggeler SW, Brondino MJ, Pickrel SG. Mechanisms of change in multisystemic therapy: Reducing delinquent behavior through therapist adherence and improved family and peer functioning. *Journal of Consulting and Clinical Psychology* 2000; **68**:451–67.

40. Byrnes HF, Miller BA, Aalborg AE, et al. Implementation fidelity in adolescent family-based prevention programs: Relationship to family engagement. *Health Education Research* 2010; **25**:531–41.

41. Kumpfer KL, Molgaard V, Spoth R. The strengthening families program for the prevention of delinquency and drug use. In: Peters RD, McMahon RJ (eds.), *Preventing Childhood Disorders, Substance Abuse, and Delinquency* (Banff International Behavioral Science Series, Vol. 3). Thousand Oaks, CA: Sage Publications, 1996, pp. 241–67.

42. Durlak JA, DuPre EP. Implementation matters: A review of research on the influence of implementation on program outcomes and factors affecting implementation. *American Journal of Community Psychology* 2008; **41**:327–50.

43. Akin BA, Brook J, Lloyd MH, et al. A study in contrasts: Supports and barriers to successful implementation of two evidence-based parenting interventions in child welfare. *Child Abuse and Neglect* 2016; **57**:30–40.

44. Brook J, Akin BA, Lloyd MH, Yan Y. Family drug court, targeted parent training, and family reunification: Did this enhanced service strategy make a difference? *Juvenile and Family Court Journal* 2015; **66**:35–52.

45. Sanders MR, Prinz RJ, Shapiro CJ. Predicting utilization of evidence-based parenting interventions with organizational, service-provider and client variables. *Administration and Policy in Mental Health* 2009; **36**:133–43.

46. Sanders MR. Triple P-Positive Parenting Program: Towards an empirically validated multilevel parenting and family support strategy for the prevention of behavior and emotional problems in children. *Clinical Child and Family Psychology Review* 1999; **2**:71–90.

47. Asgary-Eden V, Lee CM. Implementing an evidence-based parenting program in community agencies: What helps and what gets in the way? *Administration and Policy in Mental Health and Mental Health Services Research* 2012; **39**:478–88.

48. Stern SB, Alaggia R, Watson K, Morton TR. Implementing an evidence-based parenting program with adherence in the real world of community practice. *Research on Social Work Practice* 2008; **18**:543–54.

49. Webster-Stratton C. The incredible years: Parents, teachers, and children training series. *Residential Treatment for Children and Youth* 2001; **18**:31–45.

50. Seng AC, Prinz RJ, Sanders MR. The role of training variables in effective dissemination of evidence-based parenting interventions. *International Journal of Mental Health Promotion* 2006; **8**:20–8.

51. Zazzali JL, Sherbourne C, Hoagwood KE, et al. The adoption and implementation of an evidence based practice in child and family mental health services organizations: A pilot study of functional family therapy in New York State. *Administration and Policy in Mental Health* 2008; **35**:38–49.

52. Shediac-Rizkallah MC, Bone LR. Planning for the sustainability of community-based health programs: Conceptual frameworks and future directions for research, practice and policy. *Health Education Research* 1998; **13**:87–108.

53. Scheirer MA. Dearing JW. An agenda for research on the sustainability of public health programs. *American Journal of Public Health* 2011; **101**:2059–67.

54. Luke DA, Calhoun A, Robichaux CB, et al. The program sustainability assessment tool: A new instrument for public health programs. *Preventing Chronic Disease* 2014; **11**:E12.

55. Crowley DM, Coffman DL, Feinberg ME, et al. Evaluating the impact of implementation factors on family-based prevention programming: Methods for strengthening causal inference. *Prevention Science* 2014;**15**(2):246–55.

56. Spoth R, Greenberg M, Bierman K, Redmond C. PROSPER community-university partnership model for public education systems: Capacity-building for evidence-based, competence-building prevention. *Prevention Science* 2004; **5**:31–39.

57. Lundahl B, Risser HJ, Lovejoy C. A meta-analysis of parent training: Moderators and follow-up effects. *Clinical Psychology Review* 2006; **26**:86–104.

58. Maughan DR, Christiansen E, Jenson WR, et al. Behavioral parent training as a treatment for externalizing behaviors and disruptive behavior disorders: A meta-analysis. *School Psychology Review* 2005; **34**:267–86.

59. Thompson-Hollands J, Edson A, Tompson MC, Comer JS. Family involvement in the psychological treatment of obsessive-compulsive disorder: A meta-analysis. *Journal of Family Psychology* 2014; **28**:287–98.

60. Stormshak EA, Connell AM, Véronneau MH, et al. An ecological approach to promoting early adolescent mental health and social adaptation: Family-centered intervention in public middle schools. *Child Development* 2011; **82**(1):209–25.

61. Cotter KL, Bacallao M, Smokowski PR, Robertson CIB. Parenting interventions implementation science: How delivery format impacts the Parenting Wisely program. *Research on Social Work Practice* 2013; **23**:639–50.

62. Stalker KC, Rose RA, Bacallao M, Smokowski PR. Parenting Wisely six months later: How implementation delivery impacts program effects at follow-up. *Journal of Primary Prevention* 2018; **39**:129–53.

63. Smokowski P, Corona R, Bacallao M, et al. Addressing barriers to recruitment and retention in the implementation of parenting programs: Lessons learned for effective program delivery in rural and urban areas. *Journal of Child and Family Studies* 2018; **27**:2925–42.

64. Forehand R, Dorsey S, Jones DJ, et al. Adherence and flexibility: They can (and do) coexist! *Clinical Psychology Research and Practice* 2010; **17**:258–64.

65. Mazzucchelli TG, Sanders MR. Facilitating practitioner flexibility within an empirically supported intervention: Lessons from a system of parenting support. *Clinical Psychology Research and Practice* 2010; **17**:238–52.

66. Chung B, Mikesell L, Miklovitz D. Flexibility and structure may enhance implementation of family-focused therapy in community mental health settings. *Community Mental Health Journal* 2014; **50**:787–91.

67. Schoenwald SK, Sheidow AJ, Chapman JE. Clinical supervision in treatment transport: Effects on

adherence and outcomes. *Journal of Consulting and Clinical Psychology* 2009; **77**:410–21.

68. Schoenwald SK, Mehta TG, Frazier SL, Shernoff ES. Clinical supervision in effectiveness and implementation research. *Clinical Psychology Research and Practice* 2013; **20**:44–59.

69. McHugh RK, Barlow DH. Training in evidence-based psychological interventions. In: McHugh RK, Barlow DH (eds.), *Dissemination and Implementation of Evidence-Based Psychological Interventions*. New York: Oxford University Press, 2012, pp. 43–58.

70. Furlong M, Gilloway S. Barriers and facilitators to implementing evidence-based parenting programs in disadvantaged settings: A qualitative study. *Journal of Child and Family Studies* 2015; **24**:1809–18.

71. Proctor E, Luke D, Calhoun A, et al. Sustainability of evidence-based healthcare: Research agenda, methodological services, and infrastructure support. *Implementation Science* 2015; **10**:88.

72. Stirman SW, Kimberly J, Calloway A, et al. The sustainability of new programs and innovations: A review of the empirical literature and recommendations for future research. *Implementation Science* 2012; **7**:17.

Chapter 4

Effective Components of Parenting Programmes for Children's Conduct Problems

Patty Leijten

Conduct problems in early and middle childhood are characterized by argumentative defiant behaviour, vindictiveness, an angry or irritable mood and aggression [1]. These problems compromise children's well-being and relationships with parents and peers [2]. If left untreated, conduct problems can seriously deteriorate children's psychological, social, academic and physical development [3, 4].

The origins of children's conduct problems lie in child characteristics (e.g., temperament and executive functioning [5, 6]), environmental characteristics (e.g., family dynamics, neighbourhood [7, 8]) and interactions between child and environmental characteristics [9, 10]. Children with conduct problems typically find it more difficult to regulate their emotions and behaviours and often interpret others' behaviour as angry or hostile [11]. Distortions in the parent-child relationship, dysfunctional parental cognitions and attributions (e.g., compromised sense of self-efficacy or blaming the child for misbehaviour) and parental emotional and suboptimal reactions to children's conduct problems can inadvertently increase children's conduct problems [12–15]. The latter typically take the form of cycles of coercive parent-child interactions [16].

Coercive cycles may begin when the child acts with resistance or anger to the parent's directives, eliciting anger in the parent which exacerbates the child's resistance or anger. If the parent disengages to stop the child's anger, this serves as a reinforcement to both the parent's and the child's behaviour: the parent learns to give up when the child's behaviour becomes aversive, and the child learns that aversion results in getting one's way (i.e., through operant learning [17]). If the parent, alternatively, forces the child to comply through verbal or physical violence or by threatening with violence, this too is likely to increase both the parent's and the child's aversive behaviour: the parent learns to use violence to direct the child's behaviour, and the child learns to use violence to get one's way

(i.e., through modelling and reinforcement [18]). These reinforcement processes create a feedback cycle where parent-child interactions become more difficult to manage, maintaining and increasing conduct problems over time [19].

Parenting Programmes as a Key Intervention Strategy

Because of the key role parenting plays in how children's conduct problems develop, parenting programmes are the key strategy to prevent and reduce children's conduct problems [20]. Most established programmes are based on relationship perspectives [21, 22] and operant or social learning theory [17, 18], designed to improve the parent-child relationship and break patterns of coercive parent-child interaction. This dual focus was conceived by Constance Hanf [22a] in the second half of the twentieth century, and is now used in the majority of empirically supported parenting programmes for children's conduct problems (see Kaehler, Jacobs and Jones [23] for an overview).

Programmes typically consist of manualized treatment protocols that explain how therapists can increase parents' understanding of what they can expect from their child (e.g., psycho-education about child developmental stages), encourage adaptive cognitions (e.g., parental self-efficacy) and suggest adaptive parenting strategies (e.g., involvement, positive reinforcement and non-physical discipline). Change is achieved through the use of established behaviour change techniques (e.g., modelling and role play [24]). Parenting programmes can be delivered either in a clinical setting or at home, individually or in groups.

In terms of their evidence base, parenting programmes for children's conduct problems are among the more 'mature' family-based interventions. Around 200 randomized trials and dozens of meta-analyses have evaluated their effectiveness, typically showing robust small to medium effects on children's observed and parent-reported conduct problems [20, 25, 26]. In addition, parenting programme effects are robust across countries [27], and gains tend to be sustained in the months and years after programmes have ended [28].

However, because many programmes are complex and costly to implement, few are actually taken to scale – therefore, most families affected by children's conduct problems cannot access empirically supported programmes [29]. Recent developments in identifying the effective components of parenting programmes hold promise to fill the gap between available complex evidence-based programmes and the need for effective, low-cost programmes that are easy to implement. If we can identify what components parenting programmes should include and what components are ineffective or superfluous in light of other components, this will allow for 'leaner' programmes that are less complex and costly to implement. In addition, identifying the effective components of parenting programmes improves our understanding of the specific aspects of parenting that matter most for children's conduct problems, refining theories on the development of conduct problems and guiding our efforts to optimize intervention strategies.

Identifying Effective Parenting Programme Components

Components are discrete aspects of parenting programmes that are expected to contribute uniquely to reductions in children's conduct problems. Components can reflect programme content (i.e., parenting techniques taught), delivery methods (i.e., the way parenting techniques are taught, such as through modelling or role play) and programme structure (i.e., the broader setting of the programme, such as individual versus group delivery, and programme duration). Alternative terms for programme components include *kernels* [30] and *elements of therapeutic change* [31].

Common research strategies to identify effective parenting programme components include (1) associations between the presence of components and programme effects on children's conduct problems (i.e., correlational evidence, for example, in a meta-analysis that compares the effects of programmes that have different components [25, 32]) and (2) effects of experimentally manipulated components on

children's conduct problems (i.e., causal evidence, for example, in a focused experimental study, sometimes called *micro-trials* [33, 34] or *additive or dismantling trials* [35]). In a micro-trial, families are randomized to receive either one discrete intervention component or no components; in an additive or dismantling trial, families are randomized to receive a full intervention package either with or without the target component.

These two types of research strategies (i.e., studying associations between components and programme effects and studying the effects of experimentally manipulated components) are complementary. Studying associations is less rigorous – it does not allow for causal inferences because it relies on associations between the presence of components and programme effect sizes. It therefore cannot rule out the possibility that any difference in effect sizes associated with the presence of target components are actually caused by other characteristics that programmes with the target component share [36]. However, it provides a solid first test of the merit of discrete parenting programme components: if a component is essential for programme success, programmes with this component should outperform programmes without this component. In addition, more research on this type of evidence exists, meaning that we can draw from a larger and more diverse parenting programme literature. Studying experimentally manipulated components is more rigorous and therefore provides more conclusive evidence. Yet, fewer studies fall into this category, and they come with their own limitations, such as the often limited statistical power of additive and dismantling trials [37]. More details on the relative strengths and limitations of different types of evidence can be found in a review of research strategies to identify the effective components of psychotherapy [38]. This review also includes some other research strategies, such as expert opinion and listing the components that empirically supported programmes have in common [39], not addressed in this chapter because they are less rigorous than the two types of evidence discussed here. However, these other strategies can be helpful to catalogue the components included in parenting programmes as a first step towards developing an overview of potentially important programme components and to generate research questions on what components may be less or more effective.

In this chapter, I will discuss what we know about whether parenting programmes with a range of differing components that yield, on average, larger effects than parenting programmes without the component (i.e., correlational evidence) and what we know about the unique effects of the component (i.e., causal evidence). The overview of components is not meant to be exclusive but provides the first overview of literature on the empirical support of frequently used parenting programme components for reducing conduct problems in children.

Content Components

Theoretical Orientation

Parenting programmes can be distinguished in terms of their theoretical orientation, typically behavioural, relational and/or cognitive. Behavioural parenting programmes teach parents techniques based on learning-theory perspectives to redirect their child's behaviour, including positive reinforcement (e.g., praise and rewards) and negative consequences (e.g., planned ignoring and time-out). Relational programmes teach parents how they can improve their relationship with their child through sensitive and responsive parenting and effective communication. Cognitive programmes strive to change parenting practices through altered parental cognitions, such as parents' sense of competence (i.e., self-efficacy) and parents' attributions for child behaviour (e.g., the extent to which parents hold themselves or their children responsible for problematic child behaviour). Most parenting programmes draw from multiple perspectives. For example, many established programmes are based on the *Hanf model*, combining behavioural and relationship orientations, teaching parents first relationship building and then behaviour management skills [23]. That said, programmes vary in how much emphasis they place on each orientation, and some explicitly distance themselves from some, often the dominant behavioural, orientations [40, 41].

Evidence is conflicting regarding whether the theoretical orientation of programmes makes a difference in terms of parenting programme effects on children's conduct problems. Individual trials suggest that each type of programme is effective [41–43], but the evidence for relational and cognitive approaches is thinner than that for behavioural programmes in terms of the number of rigorous programme evaluation trials. Most meta-analyses that compare the effectiveness of two or more orientations do not suggest any differences in effectiveness between programmes based on different orientations [44, 45]. However, when we examined the possible additive or synergistic effects of combining multiple theoretical orientations in one programme, our meta-analysis suggests combining behavioural and relational orientations in one programme outperforms more purely behavioural orientations in treatment settings, though not in prevention settings [46].

The most stringent test, direct head-to-head comparisons of behavioural programmes and relational programmes, in some cases suggests that behavioural programmes outperform relational programmes [47], whereas other tests do not suggest differential effects [48]. Findings by Högström et al. [49], who compared four different programmes, suggest that the effects of behavioural programmes are more immediate, whereas the effects of relational programmes continue to evolve over time. In a recent meta-analysis, my colleagues and I tested whether these 'sleeper effects' of relational approaches were present above and beyond behavioural approaches and across trials and programmes, but this was not the case [46].

Psycho-education

Many parenting programmes include psycho-educational components, informing parents about typical and atypical child development and about how parents and children shape each other's behaviour. Little research has been conducted on whether explicit psycho-education is an essential component of parenting programmes for children's conduct problems. One difficulty in studying the value of psycho-education is that while it may sometimes be an explicit separate programme component, it is often woven into other components, for example, as part of explaining the pros and cons of certain parenting techniques. Two meta-analyses, one by Kaminski et al. [32] and one by me and my colleagues [25], show that parenting programmes with explicit attention to psycho-education are not more (or less) effective in reducing children's conduct problems than parenting programmes without explicit attention to psycho-education.

Some parenting programmes focus primarily on psycho-education. These programmes typically include a limited number of sessions (e.g., two or three) that can be attended by a large group of parents (e.g., the Triple P seminar series). Because they are less costly, these programmes are often offered in regions with fewer resources for mental health support. Individual trials suggest that seminar programmes can be effective for reducing parent-reported conduct problems in children [50, 51]. The dominant clinical view, however, is that guidance with practising and implementing new parenting techniques is needed for achieving sustained change in parent-child interactions and children's conduct problems, especially when problems are more severe [52].

Rewards and Praise

Many parenting programmes, in particular those adopting a more behavioural approach, encourage parents to use rewards and praise as positive reinforcement to promote appropriate child behaviour. The premise underlying this approach, based on learning-theory principles, is that rewarding children (verbally, socially or tangibly) for prosocial and compliant behaviour, and not for disruptive behaviour, increases their prosocial and compliant behaviour and reduces their disruptive behaviour. Indeed, two meta-analyses show that parenting programmes that teach parents to use rewards and praise are, on average, more effective for reducing children's conduct problems than parenting programmes that do not teach parents these techniques [25, 32], especially in cases were children's conduct problems are more severe [25]. Looking at causal evidence of the unique contributions of praise to children's conduct problems, the literature is more mixed. Although several experimental studies have shown that praise increases child compliance [53, 54], reviews and meta-analyses indicate that the overall evidence is inconsistent [34, 55].

While this chapter focuses on children's conduct problems specifically, the broader literature on the consequences of praise for other child developmental outcomes seems too important to ignore. There is a vast literature showing that specific forms of praise, such as praise focused on the child's personal abilities ('you're so smart!') and inflated praise ('that's an incredibly wonderful painting!') negatively impact children's emotions (e.g., person praise increases the shame children experience when they fail), motivation (e.g., choosing easier tasks over difficult tasks) and behaviour (e.g., less persistence in academic tasks) [56–8]. Similarly, rewarding children for prosocial behaviour that is intrinsically motivating for them backfires – it reduces, rather than increases,

prosocial behaviour [59, 60]. These findings show that while praise and rewards have traditionally been associated with positive child development – in terms of reduced risk for conduct problems – they are a complex phenomenon that affects children in many different ways, both positive and negative (see Brummelman [61] for recent comprehensive reviews on the effects of praise).

Although it may seem difficult to draw conclusions from such a complex and diverse literature about whether praise and rewards are 'effective components', the pattern that seems to emerge is that for reducing children's noncompliance, especially in cases where noncompliance is more severe, praise and rewards can be effective. However, in the general population, and for outcomes other than noncompliance specifically (e.g., for health promotion and general wellbeing), caution is warranted in relying on praise and rewards to direct children's behaviour.

Time-Out and Planned Ignoring

Time-out and planned ignoring are often taught in behavioural parenting programmes. In a time-out procedure, parents prevent the child from receiving reinforcement for disruptive behaviour [62] and encourage the child to self-regulate his or her emotions [63]. This is typically done by removing the child from the situation where disruptive behaviour occurred for either a set amount of time (e.g., two or three minutes) or the time it takes for children to calm down. In a planned ignoring procedure, parents ignore low-level disruptive, attention-seeking or demanding child behaviour by not paying attention to it.

There is sound evidence that time-out procedures reduce children's disruptive behaviour. One meta-analysis shows that parenting programmes that teach parents to use time-out are, on average, more effective for reducing children's conduct problems than parenting programmes that do not teach parents time-out [32]; another suggests that this is the case for programmes targeting children with more severe conduct problems specifically [25]. In addition, a range of experimental studies on the unique causal effects of time-out indicates their effectiveness for improving children's conduct problems [34, 64–6]. Of all the components of parenting programmes for children's conduct problems, time-out is probably the most well studied, including studies on the relative effectiveness of different time-out procedures [66–8].

The evidence for the effectiveness of planned ignoring is thinner. One of the meta-analyses linking different components to programme effect sizes did not examine planned ignoring as a separate component [32]; another meta-analysis found no evidence that programmes that teach parents to selectively ignore disruptive behaviours are more effective than programmes that do not [25]. Experimental studies suggest that planned ignoring is effective for reducing noncompliance [69], and a meta-analysis of experimental trials confirms the effectiveness of ignore for reducing noncompliance and conduct problems more generally [34]. However, the number of experiments on planned ignoring is substantially lower than the number of experiments on time-out.

Although the evidence for the effectiveness of time-out in reducing children's conduct problems is substantial, so is the criticism levelled at this component. The main criticism is that time-out procedures break the attachment bond between parents and children by communicating to the child that the parent is not available to the child for support and soothing [70]. There is no empirical evidence for iatrogenic or harmful effects of time-out [71]. That said, time-outs are known to be difficult to implement correctly, and incorrect implementation of time-out is associated with parents' perceptions of their ineffectiveness [72]. For a more detailed discussion of time-out, I refer readers to a recent overview by Dadds and Tully [73].

Giving Clear Instructions

A sometimes less visible but key component of many parenting programmes is to guide parents in giving children clear instructions. The premise underlying this component is that children must first process verbal information they receive from parents before deciding whether or not to comply [74]. The way instructions are given can therefore greatly influence children's interpretation and subsequent behaviour. Most programmes encourage parents to give positive, direct commands: instructions that clearly state the specific behaviour that is expected of the child. Indirect commands, in contrast, are suggestions (e.g., 'why don't we clear up your toys'), polite commands or commands stated in a question form (e.g., 'could you clear up your toys, please?') or state the behaviour that is not expected from the child (e.g., 'please don't make such a mess').

None of the meta-analyses that studied direct commands suggest that including direct commands as a programme component more effectively reduces children's conduct problems [25, 32]. Some experimental research suggests that preschoolers understand direct commands better than indirect commands but that this difference disappears in kindergarten [75]. Although limited in number, available studies that manipulated parental instructions suggest that teaching parents to give clear instructions reduces children's noncompliance [76].

Child-Led Play

Virtually all parenting programmes focus at least to some extent on improving the parent-child relationship. Many programmes encourage parents to spend quality time together with their children, to be involved in their children's activities and to monitor their whereabouts. Some programmes, however, adopt specific techniques to improve the parent-child relationship. One of these is child-led play, also known as *the child's game*.

The Kaminski meta-analysis [32] did not test child-led play as a separate component. Our recent meta-analysis did [25], and it found that programmes that encourage parents to use child-led play in addition to basic behaviour management techniques were not more effective overall but more effective in cases where children have already developed conduct problems. The authors speculate that the parent-child relationship in these families may be more distressed and that this might be why this component seems to work well for these families. In prevention settings, where most children have not yet developed conduct problems, including child-led play as a parenting programme component did not have additional merit for reducing children's conduct problems [25].

Findings from experimental studies on the causal effects of child-led play on child compliance are mixed. Some studies suggest that child-led play improves child compliance [77, 78]; others suggest that this is the case for children with more severe conduct problems only [79]. One study that compared child-led play to limit setting and discipline (e.g., planned ignoring) found that the latter was more effective for reducing children's conduct problems [80]. Together these results seem to suggest that child-led play can be an effective component, particularly when children's conduct problems are more severe and perhaps especially when combined with behaviour management.

Promoting Children's Social, Cognitive and/or Academic Skills

Many children with conduct problems experience difficulties in their social relationships (e.g., with peers), cognitive development (e.g., executive functioning) and academic development (e.g., school achievement), and these difficulties can contribute to the development of their conduct problems [81, 82]. It is not surprising, therefore, that some parenting programmes teach parents techniques to manage their child's conduct problems at home, as well as techniques to support their child's broader development.

There is no evidence to suggest that parenting programmes that invest in enhancing children's social, cognitive and academic development are more effective for reducing children's conduct problems than parenting programmes that do not invest in these additional domains [25, 32]. Whether more comprehensive programmes produce additional benefits for child development more broadly is unknown, but they are not superior to more focused parenting programmes in reducing children's conduct problems specifically. If anything, the meta-analysis by Kaminski et al. [32] suggests that programmes with a broader focus are inferior to more targeted programmes. It might be that the broader approach to child development comes at the cost of sufficient emphasis on key parenting strategies to reduce children's conduct problems.

Delivery Components

While there is a rich literature on the most effective techniques to change people's behaviour (e.g., to increase a healthy lifestyle), few of these techniques have been evaluated in the context of parenting programmes for children with conduct problems. In this section, we discuss key techniques often used in parenting programmes for children's conduct problems for which at least some studies have been conducted. For more general reviews on effective behaviour change techniques, I refer readers to other work [83].

Practice with Child During Sessions

Parenting programmes differ from each other in the extent to which only parents themselves attend the sessions or whether parents attend (parts of) the sessions together with their child. Having parents practise with their child (e.g., using bug-in-ear coaching) allows parents to learn new skills in interaction with their child, potentially making the transition to implementing new skills at home easier. This premise is in line with the general educational literature on the importance of learning in context [84]. The seminal meta-analysis by Kaminski et al. [32] showed that parenting programmes where parents practised with their own child during sessions yielded larger effects on children's conduct problems than parenting programmes were parents did not practise with their own child during sessions. Most trials on programmes where parents practise with their child, however, came from the same programme (parent-child interaction therapy [85]), potentially limiting the generalizability of this finding to other programmes, and were based on relatively few and small trials. That said, the finding by Kaminski et al. [32] suggests that practising with children during sessions may be an effective parenting programme component. Experimental research where parents are randomized to either practice skills with their child during programme sessions versus only practising at home is lacking.

Role Play

Practising skills, as opposed to only discussing them, is known to enhance skill development [86]. Practising parenting skills using role play is therefore a key part of many parenting programmes for children's conduct problems. However, the seminal meta-analysis by Kaminski et al. [32] showed that parenting programmes where parents practised skills using role play were not more (or less) effective than parenting programmes that use other teaching methods.

Findings from experimental studies on the merits of role play are inconsistent. Some studies suggest that role play is not more (or less) effective than other teaching methods (e.g., a video modelling the technique) [87], whereas other studies suggest that at least some parents benefit more from modelling and role play than from readings and discussions [88]. In sum, there is some but inconsistent empirical evidence that role play is an important component of parenting programmes for children's conduct problems.

Video Modelling and Video Feedback

Videos are used in different ways in parenting programmes for children's conduct problems. Some programmes use video vignettes to model different parenting strategies to families (e.g., Incredible Years parenting programme [89]); other programmes use videos to provide parents with individualized feedback on their interactions with their child (e.g., Video-feedback Intervention to Promote Positive Parenting and Sensitive Discipline [90]). The meta-analysis by Kaminski et al. [32] showed that parenting programmes that use video modelling (and/or in-person modelling) are not more (or less) effective than parenting programmes that do not use video modelling. They did not test whether the use of video feedback is associated with programme effectiveness.

Findings from experimental studies suggest that video modelling is an effective method, and more effective than written materials, for teaching parenting skills [91, 92]. However, the evidence is not unequivocal: some studies suggest that video modelling is not superior to written materials for teaching parenting skills [87]. In one study, the effectiveness of a group discussion programme with video modelling was compared to the same group discussion programme without video modelling [93]. Although differences in programme effects were small, adding video modelling seemed to enhance programme effectiveness on some outcomes related to children's conduct problems. Another study added individualized video feedback to the Incredible Years video modelling programme and found that this enhanced parents' behaviour change (no effects on children's conduct problems were assessed) [94]. These findings suggest that both video modelling and video feedback can uniquely contribute to parenting programme effects.

Homework

Because regular practice enhances skills development [86], many parenting programmes for children's conduct problems ask parents to work on assignments at home in between sessions. Some trials suggest that adherence to homework assignments predicts how much families benefit from the programme [95, 96], although it remains unclear whether homework contributes to programme effectiveness or whether it is a marker of parental engagement or experience of initial success. In their meta-analysis comparing programmes with versus without homework assignments, Kaminski et al. [32] did not find evidence that parenting programmes with homework assignments are more effective. Experimental studies that manipulate the implementation of homework assignments in parenting programmes for children's conduct problems, to my knowledge, do not exist.

Structure Components

Programme Duration

There is evidence to suggest that shorter parenting programmes outperform longer programmes. While not studied exhaustively for programmes to reduce children's conduct problems, we see this finding consistently in related fields, such as in parenting programmes to increase parental sensitivity in infancy and early childhood [97], parenting programmes to reduce child maltreatment [98] and video-feedback programmes to improve parenting behaviour more generally [99]. For children with conduct problems specifically, the evidence suggests that brief programmes (i.e., fewer than eight sessions) can be effective [100].

One perhaps intuitively appealing explanation for findings that 'less is more' is that longer programmes typically target more severe cases. Therefore, it is important to note that the most consistent moderator of parenting programme effectiveness is conduct problem severity: children with more severe problems at baseline tend to benefit more than children with less severe difficulties [101]. This implies that even if programme duration was confounded with problem severity in analyses relating programme duration to programme effects, this would contribute to the likelihood of finding results indicating that longer programmes outperform shorter programmes. Yet most meta-analyses suggest otherwise.

Trials that randomize families to receive either shorter or longer programmes, and can therefore rule out any alternative explanations for the findings from meta-regressions comparing parenting programme effects across trials, are scarce. Available comparative trials suggest the non-superiority of shorter (or longer) programmes: abbreviated programmes yield, on average, effects that are not different from those of the original version of the same programmes [102, 103]. In addition to these trials being scarce, they tend to be statistically underpowered, with sample sizes too small to detect small effects between treatment conditions. In sum, the minimal or optimal number of sessions is unknown, but empirical findings strongly challenge the assumption that 'more is better' and encourage the use of 'lean' programmes.

Group vs. Individual Delivery

Evidence that either group or individually delivered programmes are more effective is inconsistent. An influential meta-analysis by Lundahl et al. [44]

showed that individually delivered programmes yielded larger effects on children's conduct problems. Also, some individual trials suggest that some parents may prefer individual programmes [104]. However, most trials that directly test group and individually delivered versions of the same programme against each other show no advantage of individually delivered programmes over group programmes [93, 105–7], and some suggest advantages of group programmes over individually delivered programmes [108, 109]. Thus there is no consistent evidence that either individual or group delivery is more effective.

Self-Directed and Online Delivery

Although most parenting programmes are delivered by a trained therapist, some programmes are developed as self-directed programmes using a booklet or, increasingly, a website or app. Meta-analyses of online programmes with no or limited therapist contact suggest that they reduce parent-reported conduct problems in children [110, 111]. Head-to-head comparisons, where parents are randomized to receive either a self-directed or therapist-assisted or therapist-led programme, suggest that self-directed programmes are in general inferior to therapist-led programmes – families benefit less from programmes when no or less therapist contact is involved [112–14]. Although differences in effectiveness tend to be small, the available evidence suggests that therapist contact increases the effects of parenting programmes for children's conduct problems.

Next Steps

There is a growing interest in research on the effective components of parenting programmes for children's conduct problems. This interest fits emerging trends to develop and implement lean programmes that can be easily accessed, either in person or online, and stepped-care models that require insight into how to vary the content and intensity of care needed for families facing different levels of child conduct problems [115]. To a certain extent, research on effective parenting programme components can help guide these trends. It can inform policymakers and practitioners on programme components that seem to drive programme effectiveness and those which could perhaps be safely eliminated. At the same time, research on effective parenting programme

components faces several challenges. One of these is the likely complex interplay between components in exerting programme effects. Until now, most research on parenting programme components has focused on their individual effects, not their additive or synergistic effects. Alternative study designs are needed for this, such as experimental studies that test all relevant combinations of programme components against each other (i.e., factorial experiments) [116, 117]. An additional challenge is that much as in any psychological therapy, parenting programme effects are in part driven by non-specific programme characteristics, such as therapist-client alliance and placebo effects [118]. Research on effective parenting programme components needs to find a way to integrate the seemingly divided research lines on *effective components* and *non-specific elements*. Building a more precise intervention science that integrates a range of research strategies to identify effective parenting programme components is needed to better understand and overcome these challenges.

References

1. American Psychiatric Association. *Diagnostic and Statistical Manual of Mental Disorders*, 5th ed. Washington, DC: APA, 2013.

2. Moffitt TE, Scott S. Conduct disorders of childhood and adolescence. In: Rutter M, Bishop D, Pine D, et al. (eds.), *Rutter's Child and Adolescent Psychiatry*. Oxford, UK: Blackwell, 2008, pp. 543–64.

3. Campbell SB, Shaw DS, Gilliom M. Early externalizing behavior problems: Toddlers and preschoolers at risk for later maladjustment. Developmental Psychopatholgy 2000; **12**:467–88.

4. Odgers CL, Moffitt TE, Broadbent JM, et al. Female and male antisocial trajectories: From childhood origins to adult outcomes. Developmental Psychopathology 2008; **20**:673–716.

5. Frick PJ, Morris AS. Temperament and developmental pathways to conduct problems. *Journal of Clinical Child and Adolescent Psychology* 2004; **33**:54–68.

6. Ogilvie JM, Stewart AL, Chan RC, Shum DH. Neuropsychological measures of executive function and antisocial behavior: A meta-analysis. *Criminology* 2011; **49**:1063–107.

7. Stormshak EA, Bierman KL, McMahon RJ, Lengua LJ. Parenting practices and child disruptive behavior problems in early elementary school. *Journal of Clinical Child Psychology* 2000: **29**;17–29.

8. Ingoldsby EM, Shaw DS. Neighborhood contextual factors and early-starting antisocial pathways. *Clinical Child and Family Psychology Review* 2002: **5**:21–55.

9. Mesman J, Stoel R, Bakermans-Kranenburg MJ, et al. Predicting growth curves of early childhood externalizing problems: Differential susceptibility of children with difficult temperament. *Journal of Abnormal Child Psychology* 2009; **37**:625–36.

10. Sulik MJ, Blair C, Mills-Koonce R, et al. Early parenting and the development of externalizing behavior problems: Longitudinal mediation through children's executive function. *Child Development* 2015; **86**:1588–603.

11. Crick NR, Dodge KA. Social information-processing mechanisms in reactive and proactive aggression. *Child Development* 1996: **67**:993–1002.

12. Bowlby J. *Attachment and Loss: Separation, Anxiety and Anger*, Vol. **2**. New York: Basic Books, 1973.

13. Bretherton I, Munholland KA. Internal working models in attachment relationships: Elaborating a central construct in attachment theory. In: Cassidy J, Shaver PR (eds.), *Handbook of Attachment: Theory, Research, and Clinical Applications*. New York: Guilford Press, 2008, pp. 102–27.

14. Bandura A. Self-efficacy: Toward a unifying theory of behavioral change. *Psychological Review* 1977; **84**:191–215.

15. Jones TL, Prinz RJ. Potential roles of parental self-efficacy in parent and child adjustment: A review. Clinical Psychological Review 2005; **25**:341–63.

16. Patterson GR. *Coercive Family Process*. Eugene, OR: Castalia, 1982.

17. Skinner BF. Are theories of learning necessary? *Psychological Review* 1950; **57**:193–216.

18. Bandura A, Walters RH. *Social Learning and Personality Development*. New York: Holt, Rinehart and Winston, 1963.

19. Smith JD, Dishion TJ, Shaw DS, et al. Coercive family process and early-onset conduct problems from age 2 to school entry. *Development and Psychopathology* 2014; **26**:917–32.

20. Weisz JR, Kazdin AE. *Evidence-Based Psychotherapies for Children and Adolescents*. New York: Guildford Press, 2017.

21. Cassidy J, Shaver PR. *Handbook of Attachment: Theory, Research, and Clinical Applications*. New York: Guilford Press, 2008.

22. Maccoby EE, Martin JA. Socialization in the context of the family: Parent-child interaction. In: Mussen PH, Hetherington EM (eds.), *Handbook of Child Psychology*, Vol. 4: *Socialization, Personality,*

and Social Development. New York: Wiley, 1983, pp. 1–101.

23. Hanf C. A collaborative treatment procedure for altering the interpersonal, environmental, and attitudinal contingencies that maintain problem behaviors in parent-child interaction. Working paper, University of Oregon Medical School, Portland, 1969.

24. Kaehler LA, Jacobs M, Jones DJ. Distilling common history and practice elements to inform dissemination: Hanf-model BPT programmes as an example. *Clinical Child and Family Psychology Review* 2016; **19**:236–58.

25. Abraham C, Michie S. A taxonomy of behavior change techniques used in interventions. *Health Psychology* 2008; **27**:379–87.

26. Leijten P, Gardner F, Melendez-Torres GJ, et al. Meta-analyses: Key parenting programme components for disruptive child behavior. *Journal of the American Academy of Child and Adolescent Psychiatry* 2019; **58**:180–90.

27. Menting AT, Orobio de Castro BO, Matthys W. Effectiveness of the Incredible Years parent training to modify disruptive and prosocial child behavior: A meta-analytic review. *Clinical Psychological Review* 2013; **33**:901–13.

28. Leijten P, Melendez-Torres GJ, Knerr W, Gardner F. Transported versus homegrown parenting interventions for reducing disruptive child behavior: A multilevel meta-regression study. *Journal of the American Academy of Child and Adolescent Psychiatry* 2016; **55**:610–17.

29. Van Aar J, Leijten P, Orobio de Castro B, Overbeek G. Sustained, fade-out or sleeper effects? A multilevel meta-analysis of parenting interventions for disruptive child behavior. *Clinical Psychological Review* 2017; **51**:153–63.

30. Merikangas KR, He JP, Brody D, et al. Prevalence and treatment of mental disorders among US children in the 2001–2004 NHANES. *Pediatrics* 2010; **125**:75–81.

31. Embry DD, Biglan A. Evidence-based kernels: Fundamental units of behavioral influence. *Clinical Child and Family Psychology Review* 2008; **11**:75–113.

32. Institute of Medicine. *Psychosocial Interventions for Mental and Substance Use Disorders: A Framework for Establishing Evidence-Based Standards*. Washington, DC:National Academies Press, 2015. https://doi.org/10.17226/19013.

33. Kaminski JW, Valle LA, Filene JH, Boyle CL. A meta-analytic review of components associated with parent training programme effectiveness. *Journal of Abnormal Child Psychology* 2008; **36**:567–89.

34. Leijten P, Dishion TJ, Thomaes S, et al. Bringing parenting interventions back to the future: How randomized controlled microtrials may benefit parenting intervention efficacy. *Clinical Psychology: Science and Practice* 2015; **22**:47–57.

35. Leijten P, Gardner F, Melendez-Torres GJ, et al. Parenting behaviors that shape child compliance: A multilevel meta-analysis. *PloS One* 2018; **13**: e0204929.

36. Sanders MR, Pidgeon AM, Gravestock F, et al. Does parental attributional retraining and anger management enhance the effects of the Triple P – Positive Parenting Programme with parents at risk of child maltreatment?. *Behavioral Therapy* 2004; **35**:513–35.

37. Lipsey MW. Those confounded moderators in meta-analysis: Good, bad, and ugly. *Annals of the American Academy of Political and Social Science* 2003; **587**:69–81.

38. Cuijpers P, Cristea IA, Karyotaki E, et al. Component studies of psychological treatments of adult depression: A systematic review and meta-analysis. *Psychotherapy Research* 2019; **29**:15–29.

39. Leijten P, Weisz JR, Gardner F. Discerning active ingredients of psychological therapy: A scoping review. *Clinical Psychological Science*. In press.

40. Garland AF, Hawley KM, Brookman-Frazee L, Hurlbut MS. Identifying common elements of evidence-based psychosocial treatments for children's disruptive behavior problems. *Journal of the American Academy of Child and Adolescent Psychiatry* 2008; **47**:505–14.

41. Kirby JN. The role of mindfulness and compassion in enhancing nurturing family environments. *Clinical Psychology: Science and Practice* 2016; **23**:142–57.

42. Havighurst SS, Wilson KR, Harley AE, et al. Tuning in to kids: Improving emotion socialization practices in parents of preschool children – Findings from a community trial. *Journal of Child Psychology and Psychiatry* 2010; **51**:1342–50.

43. Ogden T, Hagen, KA. Treatment effectiveness of parent management training in Norway: A randomized controlled trial of children with conduct problems. *Journal of Consulting and Clinical Psychology* 2008; **76**:607–21.

44. Mouton B, Loop L, Stiévenart M, Roskam I. Confident parents for easier children: A parental self-efficacy programme to improve young children's behavior. *Education Sciences* 2018; **8**:134–52.

45. Lundahl B, Risser HJ, Lovejoy MC. A meta-analysis of parent training: Moderators and follow-up effects. *Clinical Psychological Review* 2006; **26**:86–104.

46. Mouton B, Loop L, Stievenart M, Roskam I. Parenting programmes to reduce young children's externalizing behavior: A meta-analytic review of their behavioral or cognitive orientation. *Child and Family Behavior Therapy* 2018; **40**:115–47.

47. Leijten P, Melendez-Torres GJ, Gardner F, et al. Are relationship enhancement and behavior management the 'Golden Couple' for reducing disruptive child behavior? Two meta-analyses. *Child Development* 2018; **89**:1970–82.

48. Pinsker M, Geoffroy K. A comparison of parent effectiveness training and behavior modification parent training. *Family Relations* 1981; **30**:61–8.

49. Stattin H, Enebrink P, Özdemir M, Giannotta F. A national evaluation of parenting programmes in Sweden: The short-term effects using an RCT effectiveness design. *Journal of Consulting and Clinical Psychology* 2015; **83**:1069–84.

50. Högström J, Olofsson V, Özdemir M, et al. Two-year findings from a national effectiveness trial: Effectiveness of behavioral and non-behavioral parenting programmes. *Journal of Abnormal Child Psychology* 2017; **45**:527–42.

51. Jordans MJ, Tol WA, Ndayisaba A, Komproe IH. A controlled evaluation of a brief parenting psychoeducation intervention in Burundi. *Social Psychiatry and Psychiatric Epidemiology* 2013; **48**:1851–59.

52. Sumargi A, Sofronoff K, Morawska A. A randomized-controlled trial of the Triple P – Positive Parenting Programme seminar series with Indonesian parents. *Child Psychiatry and Human Development* 2015; **46**:749–61.

53. Forgatch MS, Bullock BM, Patterson GR, Steiner H. From theory to practice: Increasing effective parenting through role play. The Oregon Model of Parent Management Training (PMTO). In: Steiner H, Chang K, Lock J, Wilson J (eds.), *Handbook of Mental Health Interventions in Children and Adolescents: An Integrated Development Approach*. San Francisco: Jossey-Bass, 2004, pp. 782–813.

54. Leijten P, Thomaes S, Orobio de Castro B, et al. What good is labeling what's good? A field experimental investigation of parental labeled praise and disruptive child behavior. *Behaviour Research and Therapy* 2016; **83**:134–41.

55. Bernhardt AJ, Forehand R. The effects of labeled and unlabeled praise upon lower and middle class children. *Journal of Experimental Child Psychology* 1975; **19**:536–43.

56. Owen DJ, Slep AM, Heyman RE. The effect of praise, positive nonverbal response, reprimand, and negative nonverbal response on child compliance:

A systematic review. *Clinical Child and Family Psychology Review* 2012;**15**:364–85.

57. Kamins ML, Dweck CS. Person versus process praise and criticism: Implications for contingent self-worth and coping. *Developmental Psychology* 1999; **35**:835–47.

58. Henderlong J, Lepper MR. The effects of praise on children's intrinsic motivation: A review and synthesis. *Psychological Bulletin* 2002; **128**:774–95.

59. Brummelman E, Thomaes S, Orobio de Castro B, et al. 'That's not just beautiful – that's incredibly beautiful!' The adverse impact of inflated praise on children with low self-esteem. *Psychological Science* 2014; **25**:728–35.

60. Lepper MR, Greene D, Nisbett RE. Undermining children's intrinsic interest with extrinsic reward: A test of the 'overjustification' hypothesis. *Journal of Personality and Social Psychology* 1973; **28**:129–37.

61. Warneken F, Tomasello M. Extrinsic rewards undermine altruistic tendencies in 20-month-olds. *Developmental Psychology* 2008; **44**:1785–8.

62. Brummelman E (ed.). *Psychological Perspectives on Praise.* Abingdon, UK: Routledge, 2020.

63. MacDonough TS, Forehand R. Response-contingent time-out: Important parameters in behavior modification with children. *Journal of Behavior Therapy and Experimental Psychiatry* 1973; **4**:231–6.

64. Joshi PT, Capozzoli JA, Coyle JT. Use of a quiet room on an inpatient unit. *Journal of the American Academy of Child and Adolescent Psychiatry* 1988; **27**:642–4.

65. Olson RL, Roberts MW. Alternative treatments for sibling aggression. *Behavioral Therapy* 1987; **18**:243–50.

66. Gardner HL, Forehand R, Roberts M. Time-out with children. *Journal of Abnormal Child Psychology* 1976; **4**:277–88.

67. Roberts MW. Enforcing chair timeouts with room timeouts. *Behavior Modification* 1988; **12**:353–70.

68. Bean AW, Roberts MW. The effect of time-out release contingencies on changes in child noncompliance. *Journal of Abnormal Child Psychology* 1981; **9**:95–105.

69. Hamilton SB, MacQuiddy SL. Self-administered behavioral parent training: Enhancement of treatment efficacy using a time-out signal seat. *Journal of Clinical Child and Adolescent Psychology* 1984; **13**:61–9.

70. Reid MJ, Walter AL, O'leary SG. Treatment of young children's bedtime refusal and nighttime wakings: A comparison of 'standard' and graduated ignoring procedures. *Journal of Abnormal Child Psychology* 1999; **27**:5–16.

71. Siegel D, Bryson TP. 'Time-outs' are hurting your child. *Time* (September 23, 2014). Available at http://time.com/3404701/disciplinetime-out-is-not-good.

72. Quetsch L, Wallace N, Herschell A, McNeil C. Weighing in on the time-out controversy: An empirical perspective. *Clinical Psychology* 2015; **68**:4–19.

73. Riley AR, Wagner DV, Tudor ME, et al. A survey of parents' perceptions and use of time-out compared to empirical evidence. *Academic Pediatrics* 2017; **17**:168–75.

74. Dadds MR, Tully LA. What is it to discipline a child: What should it be? A reanalysis of time-out from the perspective of child mental health, attachment, and trauma. *American Psychologist* 2019; **74**(7):794–808.

75. Kalb LM, Loeber R. Child disobedience and noncompliance: A review. *Pediatrics* 2003; **111**:641–52.

76. Roberts MW, McMahon RJ, Forehand R, Humphreys L. The effect of parental instruction-giving on child compliance. *Behavioral Therapy* 1978; **9**:793–8.

77. Elrod MM. Children's understanding of indirect requests. *Journal of General Psychology* 1987; **148**:63–70.

78. Parpal M, Maccoby EE. Maternal responsiveness and subsequent child compliance. *Child Development* 1985; **56**:1326–34.

79. Wahler RG, Meginnis KL. Strengthening child compliance through positive parenting practices: What works?. *Journal of Clinical Child Psychology* 1997; **26**:433–40.

80. Kotler JS, McMahon RJ. Compliance and noncompliance in anxious, aggressive, and socially competent children: The impact of the child's game on child and maternal behavior. *Behavioral Therapy* 2004; **35**:495–512.

81. Eisenstadt TH, Eyberg S, McNeil CB, et al. Parent-child interaction therapy with behavior problem children: Relative effectiveness of two stages and overall treatment outcome. *Journal of Clinical Child Psychology* 1993; **22**:42–51.

82. Hinshaw SP. Externalizing behavior problems and academic underachievement in childhood and adolescence: Causal relationships and underlying mechanisms. *Psychology Bulletin* 1992; **111**:127–55.

83. Clark C, Prior M, Kinsella G. The relationship between executive function abilities, adaptive behaviour, and academic achievement in children with externalising behaviour problems. *Journal of Child Psychology and Psychiatry* 2002; **43**:785–96.

84. Abraham C, Michie S. A taxonomy of behavior change techniques used in interventions. *Health Psychology* 2008; **27**:379–87.

85. Hattie J, Biggs J, Purdie N. Effects of learning skills interventions on student learning: A meta-analysis. *Review of Educational Research* 1996; **66**:99–136.

86. Zisser A, Eyberg S. Parent-child interaction therapy and the treatment of disruptive behaviors. In: Weisz J, Kazdin A (eds.), *Evidence-Based Psychotherapies for Children and Adolescents*. New York: Guilford Press, 2010, pp. 179–93.

87. Biggs J. What the student does: Teaching for enhanced learning. *Higher Education Research and Development* 1999; **18**:57–75.

88. O'Dell SL, Krug WW, Patterson JN, Faustman WO. An assessment of methods for training parents in the use of time-out. *Journal of Behavior Therapy and Experimental Psychiatry* 1980; **11**:21–25.

89. Knapp PA, Deluty RH. Relative effectiveness of two behavioral parent training programmes. *Journal of Clinical Child Psychology* 1989; **18**:314–22.

90. Webster-Stratton C, Reid M. The Incredible Years parents, teachers, and children training series: A multifacted treatment approach for children with conduct disorders. In: Weisz J, Kazdin A (eds.), *Evidence-Based Psychotherapies for Children and Adolescents*. New York: Guilford Press, 2010, pp. 194–210.

91. Bakermans-Kranenburg MJ, Van IJzendoorn MH, Mesman J, et al. Effects of an attachment-based intervention on daily cortisol moderated by dopamine receptor D_4: A randomized control trial on 1- to 3-year-olds screened for externalizing behavior. *Development and Psychopathology* 2008; **20**:805–20.

92. Flanagan S, Adams HE, Forehand, R. A comparison of four instructional techniques for teaching parents to use time-out. *Behavioral Therapy* 1979; **10**:94–102.

93. O'Dell SL, Mahoney ND, Horton WG, Turner PE. Media-assisted parent training: Alternative models. *Behavioral Therapy* 1979; **10**:103–10.

94. Webster-Stratton C, Kolpacoff M, Hollinsworth T. Self-administered videotape therapy for families with conduct-problem children: Comparison with two cost-effective treatments and a control group. *Journal of Consulting and Clinical Psychology* 1988; **56**:558–66.

95. Phaneuf L, McIntyre LL. Effects of individualized video feedback combined with group parent training on inappropriate maternal behavior. *Journal of Applied Behavior Analysis* 2007; **40**:737–41.

96. Clarke AT, Marshall SA, Mautone JA, et al. Parent attendance and homework adherence predict response to a family-school intervention for children with ADHD. *Journal of Clinical Child and Adolescent Psychology* 2015; **44**:58–67.

97. Högström J, Enebrink P, Melin B, Ghaderi A. Eighteen-month follow-up of internet-based parent management training for children with conduct problems and the relation of homework compliance to outcome. *Child Psychiatry and Human Development* 2015; **46**:577–88.

98. Bakermans-Kranenburg MJ, Van IJzendoorn MH, Juffer F. Less is more: Meta-analyses of sensitivity and attachment interventions in early childhood. *Psychology Bulletin* 2003; **129**:195–215.

99. Van der Put CE, Assink M, Gubbels J, van Solinge NFB. Identifying effective components of child maltreatment interventions: A meta-analysis. *Clinical Child and Family Psychology Review* 2018; **21**:171–202.

100. Fukkink RG. Video feedback in widescreen: A meta-analysis of family programmes. *Clinical Psychological Review* 2008; **28**:904–16.

101. Tully LA, Hunt C. Brief parenting interventions for children at risk of externalizing behavior problems: A systematic review. *Journal of Child and Family Studies* 2016; **25**:705–19.

102. Leijten P, Raaijmakers MAJ, Wijngaards L, et al. Understanding who benefits from parenting interventions for children's conduct problems: An integrative data analysis. *Prevention Science* 2018; **19**:579–88.

103. Nixon RD, Sweeney L, Erickson DB, Touyz SW. Parent–child interaction therapy: One-and two-year follow-up of standard and abbreviated treatments for oppositional preschoolers. *Journal of Abnormal Child Psychology* 2004; **32**:263–71.

104. Berkovits MD, O'Brien KA, Carter CG, Eyberg SM. Early identification and intervention for behavior problems in primary care: A comparison of two abbreviated versions of parent-child interaction therapy. *Behavioral Therapy* 2010; **41**:375–87.

105. Eyberg SM, Matarazzo RG. Training parents as therapists: A comparison between individual parent-child interaction training and parent group didactic training. *Journal of Clinical Psychology* 1980; **36**:492–9.

106. Niec LN, Barnett ML, Prewett M, Shanley Chatham JR. Group parent-child interaction therapy: A randomized control trial for the treatment of conduct problems in young children. *Journal of Consulting and Clinical Psychology* 2016; **84**:682–98.

107. Sutton C. Training parents to manage difficult children: A comparison of methods. *Behavioural and Cognitive Psychotherapy* 1992; **20**:115–39.

108. Dretzke J, Davenport C, Frew E, et al. The clinical effectiveness of different parenting programmes for children with conduct problems: A systematic review of randomised controlled trials. *Child and Adolescent Psychiatry and Mental Health* 2009; 3:7–16.

109. Webster-Stratton C. Long-term follow-up of families with young conduct problem children: From preschool to grade school. *Journal of Clinical Child Psychology* 1990; **19**:144–9.

110. Pevsner R. Group parent training versus individual family therapy: An outcome study. *Journal of Behavior Therapy and Experimental Psychiatry* 1982; **13**:119–22.

111. Thongseiratch T, Leijten P, Melendez-Torres GJ. Online parent programmes for children's behavioral problems: A meta-analytic review. *European Child and Adolescent Psychiatry* 2020. https://doi.org/10.1007/s00787-020-01472-0

112. MacDonell KW, Prinz RJ. A review of technology-based youth and family–focused interventions. *Clinical Child and Family Psychology Review* 2017; **20**:185–200.

113. Sanders MR, Markie-Dadds C, Tully LA, Bor W. The Triple P – Positive Parenting Programme: A comparison of enhanced, standard, and self-directed behavioral family intervention for parents of children with early onset conduct problems. *Journal of Consulting and Clinical Psychology* 2000; **68**:624–40.

114. Morawska A, Sanders MR. Self-administered behavioral family intervention for parents of toddlers: I. Efficacy. *Journal of Consulting and Clinical Psychology* 2006; **74**:10–19.

115. Kling Å, Forster M, Sundell K, Melin L. A randomized controlled effectiveness trial of parent management training with varying degrees of therapist support. *Behavioral Therapy* 2010; **41**:530–42.

116. Stein MA. Editorial: Is less parent training 'not inferior' to more? *Journal of the American Academy of Child and Adolescent Psychiatry* 2019; **58**:565–6.

117. Fisher RA. *Statistical Methods for Research Workers.* Edinburgh: Oliver & Boyd, 1925.

118. Schlam TR, Fiore MC, Smith SS, et al. Comparative effectiveness of intervention components for producing long-term abstinence from smoking: A factorial screening experiment. *Addiction* 2016; **111**:142–55.

119. Messer SB, Wampold BE. Let's face facts: Common factors are more potent than specific therapy ingredients. *Clinical Psychology: Science and Practice* 2002; **9**:21–5.

Chapter 5

Engaging Fathers in Family-Based Interventions for Child Mental Health

Lucy A. Tully, David J. Hawes and Mark R. Dadds

Many evidence-based interventions for child and adolescent mental health problems rely on the engagement of parents, often to modify risk and protective factors in the family environment. As outlined in this chapter, however, clinical services have traditionally approached such engagement with a predominant focus on mothers, whereas fathers have often been overlooked or excluded. The under-representation of fathers in interventions for child mental health has been highlighted in research concerning the treatment of a range of problems, including externalizing problems (e.g., disruptive and aggressive behaviour [1, 2]), internalizing problems (e.g., anxiety [3]) and neurodevelopmental disorders such as attention deficit hyperactivity disorder (ADHD) [4] and autism spectrum disorder (ASD) [5]. Mothers and fathers have a profound influence on a child's development and mental health, and together form a complex and dynamic subsystem within the broader system of the family. When an intervention focuses on mothers as the sole agents of change, risk and protective factors may inadvertently be modified in only part of the parental system, thereby potentially reducing the overall effectiveness of treatment. Conversely, focusing jointly on mothers and fathers in such interventions stands to enhance outcomes for children in both the short term [6] and the longer term [7]. Thus, enhancing the clinical engagement of fathers has the potential to improve treatment effectiveness and can be considered a process of critical importance to interventions that are family based in any way.

In this chapter we examine therapist competencies related to the engagement of fathers in family-based interventions. Attention is given to the importance of fathers to child development and psychopathology, the importance of engaging both parents in clinical assessment and interventions, common barriers to engaging fathers, and a range of process strategies that clinicians can enact to enhance the engagement of fathers. Our use of the term *father* here refers to any male caregiver and includes biological, adoptive, step, kinship and foster caregivers. The term *core parenting team* is used to describe the primary caregivers who are responsible for caregiving on a day-to-day basis. Although the term *engagement* has been defined in many ways, here we use the term as conceptualized in the CAPE model of clinical engagement [8], which defines engagement across the stages of connecting (enrolment in an intervention), attending (presence at intervention sessions), participating (active participation in sessions) and enacting (implementing the intervention strategies). It should be noted that while we focus here on the benefits of engaging fathers, the engagement of a father (or mother) may at times be contraindicated because of issues related to domestic and family violence, substance use or mental health difficulties. The information that clinicians should consider when making decisions about whether to engage fathers in interventions, and how clinicians can identify who is part of the core parenting team and should be engaged in interventions, are discussed later in this chapter.

Importance of Fathers to Child Mental Health

Fathers are an important influence on the wellbeing and mental health of children. Although the role of fathers varies widely across differing cultural and social groups, fathers are more involved in caregiving than ever before. Research examining the influence of fathers on children has been predominantly focused on father involvement in the lives of their children, with findings indicating that father involvement confers positive effects for children's wellbeing and mental health. For example, evidence from a systematic review of 24 longitudinal studies found that positive father involvement (e.g., interacting with their child and having a role in childcare) reduced the frequency of behaviour problems in boys and psychological problems in girls [9]. Despite a significant growth in research concerning fathers and child development over the past few decades, there remains a clear lack of evidence regarding the specific influence of fathers on child outcomes. In reviewing evidence on the influence of fathers and fathering on child psychopathology, Barker, Iles and Ramchandani [10] noted that while numerous studies have examined the influence of a range of parenting dimensions and parent factors on child psychopathology, few have examined such influences among fathers specifically. Research into differential effects for mothers versus fathers in relation to risk and protective factors for child psychopathology has also been lacking.

Research to date has generally found that mothers and fathers show considerable similarities across different dimensions of parenting (e.g., parenting skills, beliefs and behaviours), and children appear to be similarly affected by paternal and maternal parenting styles [11]. For example, a review of research studies concluded that the influence of fathers' parenting on young children's anxiety is at least as important as that of mothers [12]. Children are also equally affected by paternal as well as maternal psychopathology. For example, systematic reviews of the effects of depression in fathers have found that it is associated with decreased positive and increased negative parenting [13] and is also associated with an increased risk of externalizing and internalizing problems in children [14]. The relationship between fathers' depression and parenting is similar to that found in mothers (14). Fathers are also a key part of the co-parenting team, and substantial research demonstrates that positive co-parenting interactions (e.g., support, agreement over childrearing) are significantly associated with positive child adjustment [15]. Overall, available research suggests that fathers are just as important as mothers in terms of conferring risk and protective influences on child mental health. Despite this, research and interventions focusing on child mental health and wellbeing continue to focus largely on mothers [16].

Father Engagement in Services for Child Mental Health

Very little research has quantified the actual rates at which fathers engage with child mental health services despite many researchers concluding that fathers are under-represented in a range of parent-focused interventions for child mental health [2–5, 16]. Most of the research that has examined levels of father engagement has focused on initial engagement. That is, the connection or attendance phases rather than participation levels or enactment of key intervention strategies [8]. Furthermore, most research has focused on father engagement in interventions within a research context rather than clinical services delivered in community contexts. In any case, research findings to date suggest that rates of father engagement are low. For example, one review found that fathers comprised only around 20 per cent of participants connecting (enrolling in) an intervention for child externalizing problems [1].

To address this gap in research, we recently conducted the first study to benchmark rates of father engagement across a range of services for child mental health [17]. The aim of this benchmarking study, which included 10 Australian services, was to quantify father attendance in terms of the rates at which mothers and fathers instigated referrals to the service and attended parent-focused sessions. In cases where the referral to the service was parent instigated, mothers referred their child in 87 per cent of cases versus 13 per cent father referral [17]. In terms of rates of attendance at sessions, fathers attended, on average, 48 per cent of parent sessions, which was significantly lower than mothers, who attended 92 per cent of sessions. Though the rates of father attendance identified were somewhat higher than found in previous research, it is likely that services with a greater propensity towards father-inclusive practice may be over-represented among those choosing to participate in such a study [17]. Based on available evidence, it appears that mothers are both the primary instigators of help seeking for child mental health problems and the key recipients of parent-focused interventions. Given that children achieve better short- [6] and long-term outcomes [7] from parent-focused interventions when fathers participate in interventions, the lower participation rates of fathers relative to mothers represents an area for immediate action.

Importance of Engaging Fathers in the Clinical Assessment of Children

The inclusion of fathers as well as mothers in clinical assessment procedures enables clinicians to form a more comprehensive account of a child's presenting problem. By involving the complete core parenting team in the assessment, clinicians can obtain information from both parents about child symptoms and the history of the problem, along with details regarding a range of child, parent, and family factors related to problem onset and maintenance, as well as barriers to treatment [18]. This may include, for example, the unique perspectives of individual parents; each parent's family history of mental health problems; parenting behaviours and attributions; specific parent-child relationships; individual parent mental health, social support and family-of-origin history; unique perspectives on the structure and dynamics of the family system; the quality of the co-parenting relationship and parents' readiness for change. Obtaining and integrating such information from both parents has the potential to significantly inform differential diagnosis, case conceptualization and treatment planning (e.g., sequence, length, focus and timing of treatment).

The comprehensive assessment of child mental health problems involves the collection and integration of information from a variety of sources and informants, including interviews with parents (as well as children, teachers and significant others), completion of standardized questionnaires by parents (and other relevant informants) and also potentially structured observation of parent-child and family interactions. Clinicians should aim to involve both mothers and fathers in all aspects of the assessment process and not assume that information gathered from one parent will necessarily apply or be relevant to the other parent [19]. Parents may have differing perspectives on child presenting problems, as reflected in divergent answers to interview questions and responses to standardized questionnaire measures, and these differences may be informative in their own right.

Although mothers and fathers generally show higher levels of agreement on standardized measures of child mental health than do other reporters, such as parents and children or parents and teachers [20], discrepancies are common and have been investigated in research. A meta-analytic review of mother-father discrepancies on standardized measures found that mothers tend to report slightly more externalizing behaviour problems in school-aged children than do fathers [21]. Studies have also found that mothers report more internalizing problems in preschool children than fathers [22] and more symptoms of inattention in children diagnosed with ADHD [23]. There

may be a number of reasons for these mother-father discrepancies, such as differences in perceptions of the child's problems, differences in time spent with children (e.g., mothers spending more time with children than fathers) or actual differences in children's interactions with both parents [21].

When discrepancies emerge between mothers and fathers in reports on child presenting problems or questionnaire ratings it can be helpful for clinicians to acknowledge and normalize these differing views [24]. Clinicians can also explore these discrepancies with parents, as parents' own understanding of these differences may hold important clinical information and may be relevant for the clinician's diagnosis and formulation of the child's presenting problems. It is important for clinicians to explore whether parents' differing attributions for the causes of their child's difficulties explains the discrepant reports. Attributions may include ideas that a child's behaviour is intentional and under the child's control, is deliberately designed to upset the parent, is a sign of serious mental problems or is in some way a punishment the parent deserves [25]. Clinicians should also explore parent perceptions around whether they think the child's problems warrant treatment [26]. Discrepancies between parents may hinder participation in intervention, particularly when parents hold differing view about whether treatment is needed. At the end of the assessment, clinicians should aim to integrate assessment findings to facilitate a shared understanding with parents about the nature of the child's presenting problems and likely maintaining factors, and this may require a careful integration of discrepant reports from parents (along with other informants, such as teachers and children) [27].

Overall, it is clear that there are many benefits to involving both parents in the assessment of child mental health problems in terms of ensuring a comprehensive assessment, an accurate diagnosis, and a thorough case conceptualization and treatment plan. Involvement of the core parenting team also allows treatment goals to be set for both parents in relation to both their child's mental health and their own parenting, co-parenting or wellbeing. The involvement of only one parent in the assessment may miss important information which may reduce the accuracy of diagnosis and case formulation and result in ineffective treatment planning, which together may attenuate the effectiveness of the intervention. Thus, an important clinician competency is the ability

Table 5.1 Therapist Competencies for Engaging Fathers in Assessment and Intervention for Child Mental Health Problems

Domain	Therapist Competency
Assessment	Ability to identify which caregivers are part of the core parenting team and should therefore be engaged in the assessment and intervention
	Ability to undertake a comprehensive assessment with fathers and mothers (and other key reporters) and integrate their assessment reports
	Ability to positively engage with fathers by inviting them to participate in assessment and treatment
	Ability to identify, discuss and problem-solve barriers to father engagement with each family
Intervention	Ability to develop a treatment plan that integrates assessed risk factors for both fathers and mothers
	Ability to review ongoing treatment progress with fathers and mothers and make changes to the treatment plan as needed
	Ability to foster and maintain a positive therapeutic alliance with both fathers and mothers
	Ability to effectively manage conflict between parents

to undertake a comprehensive assessment with fathers and mothers (and other key reporters) and to integrate their assessment reports (see Table 5.1).

Importance of Engaging Fathers in Interventions for Child Mental Health

The core parenting team should be engaged in interventions for child mental health problems to systematically address risk and protective factors for both parents individually and as a team. The targets of an intervention will likely vary depending on the child's presenting problem, the parent/family risk and protective factors formulated to maintain the child's problems, the preferences of the parents and the theoretical orientation of the intervention. However, key targets of parent-focused interventions for child mental health problems include parenting practices and the co-parenting relationship.

Many interventions for child mental health focus on reducing negative parenting behaviours, improving positive parenting, and strengthening the parent-child relationship. For example, interventions for child externalizing problems often focus on modifying harsh or coercive parenting, whereas interventions for child anxiety focus on reducing overprotective parenting and critical/rejecting parenting [27]. Research has also highlighted that there may be considerable overlap among the parenting processes that are common to trajectories of both externalizing and internalizing problems [28]. The involvement of the core parenting team enables both parents individually and as a team to improve their parenting skills, which may improve child outcomes. A meta-analytic review found that the engagement of mothers and fathers in interventions for child externalizing behaviour was associated with improved parenting practices, along with improved child outcomes [6]. Interventions that involve active skills training provide an opportunity for parents to learn and rehearse new parenting skills and receive feedback from clinicians. Active skills training is a hallmark of interventions based on social-learning theory, which are the most evidence-based interventions for treating child externalizing behaviour problems [29]. The involvement of the core parenting team provides an opportunity for both parents to modify their parenting, which may increase consistency in the implementation of the new skills across the parental system and, in turn, enhance the effectiveness of the intervention.

Another important focus in interventions for child mental health that is often overlooked is strengthening the co-parenting relationship. The term *co-parenting* has been used to describe aspects of the couple relationship, such as interparental cooperation, agreement on child rearing, interparental conflict and triangulation (where *triangulation* refers to the coalition formed between one parent and a child) and involvement of the child in parental conflicts [15]. Family systems theory describes the overlapping but independent child, parent and extended family subsystems and emphasizes the importance of the executive (co-parenting) subsystem in regulating family interactions and creating a positive family climate [30]. Importantly, research has found that quality of co-parenting is significantly associated with children's psychological adjustment, including internalizing and externalizing symptoms [15], suggesting that it is an important target in interventions to improve child mental health.

Clinical assessment may identify difficulties in the co-parenting relationship such as low agreement over discipline or high levels of unresolved conflict, and these may be targets for change in an intervention. Treatment may include strategies to improve the quality of the parents' relationship as partners and co-parents, and some interventions may even include adjunctive modules that focus on enhancing co-parenting across a number of sessions. A few studies have examined whether the addition of an adjunctive co-parenting component can enhance the outcomes of an intervention for child externalizing behaviour. These studies have found positive effects of adjunctive co-parenting components in terms of improvements in parental communication and problem-solving [31] and outcomes for children [32–34]. However, there is also evidence of improvements in co-parenting from standard parenting interventions alone [35]. Regardless of whether co-parenting is targeted directly or indirectly in interventions for child mental health, the engagement of both parents in the intervention appears necessary to bring about such change.

Beyond parenting skills and the co-parenting relationship, there may be a range of parent risk and protective factors targeted in an intervention, such as parental mental health problems [36] and parental attributions for child behaviour [37]. Regardless of the targets of the intervention, the inclusion of both fathers and mothers enables risk and protective factors to be addressed systematically across the parental system. The engagement of both parents not only increases the likelihood of positive outcomes for parents and children but also avoids any unintended negative outcomes that may come from engaging only one parent in the intervention. For example, a qualitative study of participants in a parenting intervention for child externalizing problems found that mothers reported that implementing the new parenting strategies alone caused interparental discrepancies in parenting, resulting in parental conflict [38]. Thus, a key competency is the ability to develop a treatment plan that addresses risk processes across both fathers and mothers.

The involvement of the core parenting team also enables clinician monitoring of treatment progress, as well as evaluation of intervention outcomes for both parents. This is particularly important as there is evidence to suggest that fathers may receive fewer benefits from interventions for child mental health than mothers. Meta-analyses have demonstrated smaller effect sizes for changes in fathers' ratings of parenting and child behaviour compared with mothers' ratings [1, 39], although it should be noted

that many studies do not report on outcome measures separately for mothers and fathers [16]. Because of the lack of research, the reasons for the smaller benefits for fathers versus mothers are largely unknown. One possibility is that interventions for child mental health have been developed for, and empirically tested with, mothers, and thus they may not adequately meet the needs of fathers [40]. More research is needed to better understand fathers' needs and preferences regarding parent-focused interventions for child mental health. However, it is clear that tracking intervention progress and outcomes for the parenting team is critical to ensure that both parents are meeting their goals and receiving benefits from the intervention. Thus, a key clinician competency is the ability to review ongoing treatment progress with fathers and mothers and revise the treatment plan as needed.

Barriers to the Clinical Engagement of Fathers

There is a range of barriers that may prevent fathers from engaging in interventions for child mental health. These barriers are likely to be specific to each father and family; however, clinicians' knowledge and awareness of these barriers may be helpful in identifying strategies to overcome them. Researchers have hypothesized that there is likely to be a range of interrelated factors that may act as barriers to the engagement of fathers (particularly in relation to the connecting and attending phases of engagement). While there is a lack of research that has investigated barriers to father engagement, researchers have suggested that these may include practical factors, personal factors, family factors, practitioner factors and organizational factors [41, 42].

Practical factors that act as barriers to father engagement include the cost of an intervention, difficulties with transportation, childcare availability, lack of time to attend the intervention and work commitments. Surveys that have assessed fathers' and clinicians' perspectives have found that practical factors appear to be the primary barriers to father engagement in interventions. The most commonly endorsed barriers by fathers include the cost of the service and work commitments [41, 42], and the most commonly endorsed barriers by clinicians include fathers' work commitments and lack of time [43]. In order to address these practical barriers, it is important that clinicians provide flexible delivery options and a range of intervention delivery modalities (e.g., face-to-face, online) to make it easier for fathers to attend. The provision of low- or no-cost interventions may also be important for overcoming financial barriers to fathers' engagement in interventions.

Personal factors may act as barriers to father engagement in interventions for child mental health and may include fathers' unhelpful attitudes or beliefs about interventions or low motivation to engage in interventions. Findings of a research study highlighted that there may be differences between mothers and fathers in motivation to participate in interventions and readiness for change. A study of parents participating in an intervention for child externalizing behaviour problems found that mothers were significantly more likely to rate themselves as ready for change than fathers, despite both mothers and fathers rating their child as having clinical levels of externalizing problems and parenting stress [44]. Mothers reported more motivation to change their parenting, felt more capable of changing and placed more importance on treatment than fathers, whereas fathers were more defensive about the need for treatment. Thus, there may be parent sex differences in motivation and readiness for change in relation to child mental health, although further research on this topic is required. This finding highlights the importance of clinicians assessing readiness for change of both parents and matching intervention strategies to the stage of change.

Family factors may also present a barrier to the engagement of fathers with a service. Family factors may include the quality of the interparental relationship, the presence of conflict or violence, and mothers not actively encouraging father engagement. The term *maternal gatekeeping* was first used to describe mothers' behaviour – either encouraging or discouraging – towards father involvement in domestic or child-care responsibilities [45], but it has also been used to describe the extent to which mothers may facilitate the participation of fathers in interventions [46]. There is a lack of research on this topic, but a survey of clinicians found that almost one-third reported that they believed that mothers did not encourage fathers to participate in interventions for child mental health [47]. It is not possible to know whether the clinicians had specific knowledge about mothers actively discouraging fathers from

participating or simply assumed that this was the case, and further research on this topic is needed. However, where a mother attends an intervention alone, it is important for clinicians to explore maternal attitudes and beliefs towards father engagement to determine whether this poses a potential barrier to father engagement.

Clinician factors that may act as barriers to father engagement include low levels of confidence and skills to engage fathers and unhelpful attitudes regarding the importance of father engagement. A survey of clinicians found that while the majority viewed father engagement as important to improving child outcomes of the intervention, one-third reported low levels of confidence in working with fathers [47]. Clinicians had the lowest levels of confidence in relation to working with fathers who had been violent, working with fathers with substance use issues, and dealing with resistance from fathers. These therefore appear to be specific topics in which clinicians may require additional training in order to increase their confidence. Participation in general training programmes on the topic of father engagement strategies may also enhance clinicians' confidence and skills. Research has found that clinicians' reporting of participation in training on father engagement was positively associated with high levels of competencies (including confidence and skills) in engaging fathers [47]. In addition, a training programme on father engagement was associated with significant improvements in clinicians' competencies from pre- to post-training [48]. These findings suggest the need for increased availability of training programmes to enhance clinicians' skills and competencies in relation to father engagement.

Organizational factors that may present barriers to father engagement in interventions include inflexible session times, lack of father-inclusive policies and practices and low commitment to involving fathers. Many researchers have highlighted that policy frameworks for family-based interventions often assume a *deficit model* of fathering, whereby fathers are regarded as deficient in their skills and knowledge about child wellbeing [16]. Organizational support for father-inclusive practices appears to be important for ensuring high rates of father engagement in interventions. Studies have found clinician ratings of organizational support to be a key predictor of higher father engagement rates [47]. In relation to flexible working hours, a survey of practitioners found that only 40 per cent reported that their organizations frequently provided sessions outside working hours [47]. Although flexibility in session times may be important for engaging fathers, providing services outside working hours may not be feasible for all organizations. In addition, few interventions or services routinely collect data on rates of father engagement [17], and this is recommended as a key practice to monitor rates of father engagement over time and evaluate any strategies implemented to increase father engagement [47, 49].

It is clear that there is a range of barriers to engaging fathers in interventions for child mental health and that it is a key clinician competency to be able to identify, discuss and problem-solve barriers to father engagement with families. A review of interventions to increase parental engagement in mental health services found that interventions in which clinicians worked with the family to address practical barriers (e.g., limited time, transportation problems) and personal barriers (e.g., resistance, beliefs about the treatment process) were effective in improving engagement in early sessions [50]. This review also found that long-term gains in parental engagement and retention were most likely to be seen in interventions that integrated motivational interviewing, family systems approaches and strategies for enhancing family support and coping. Although these interventions were not specific to fathers, they may offer promising strategies or approaches for enhancing the engagement of fathers. Research on barriers to father engagement has focused on the connection and attendance phases of engagement, but there may be barriers to engagement throughout an intervention, such as barriers to the enactment of intervention strategies in the home. Thus, clinicians should identify and address barriers to father engagement throughout the delivery of an intervention.

Strategies for Promoting the Engagement of Fathers

In previous work by our team we proposed a number of strategies to promote the engagement of fathers across all stages of clinical intervention, from the connection phase to the enactment of intervention strategies. These strategies were developed in part through a programme of research that investigated approaches to enhancing the engagement of Australian fathers in parenting interventions at the national level [18] and

the promotion of related practitioner competencies through a dedicated training programme [48]. An evaluation of this training programme, in face-to-face and online delivery formats, found that both formats were associated with significant improvements in practitioner reports of their competencies for engaging fathers, with improvements maintained at a three-month follow-up [48]. The strategies addressed in this section include setting up a father-inclusive environment, identifying the core parenting team and making decisions about engaging fathers, encouraging father attendance, actively engaging fathers in interventions, and using a flexible approach to engaging fathers. Although some of these strategies assume that interventions are delivered to families individually rather than in group-based formats, many can be adapted to group-based delivery of interventions.

Setting up a Father-Inclusive Environment. It has been noted that many interventions for child well-being may be perceived by fathers as being mother focused and not appropriate for them. If fathers perceive that the physical environment is mother focused, they may be less likely to attend the service. Some of the suggestions for setting up a father-friendly environment have included displaying and using resources (e.g., posters, leaflets, brochures) which depict images of fathers as well as mothers in the service or setting in which the intervention in delivered [49, 51]. Clinicians should also advertise and promote that the intervention is for fathers as well as mothers. Where interventions can be provided outside standard working hours, such as on weeknights or even on weekends, it may make it easier for fathers to attend. Providing childcare onsite will also help encourage father attendance where childcare is a barrier for both parents attending the service.

In order to encourage father attendance, it is important for clinicians to be welcoming of fathers and to actively encourage father attendance and participation throughout assessment and intervention. Some studies have found that fathers hold the belief that services for children and families are only suitable for mothers [52] so it is important to address this misunderstanding by setting an expectation that fathers routinely attend the service and by actively encouraging father attendance. In other words, clinicians should communicate to families that fathers are 'core business' [53] and are as essential to the process of change as mothers. Discussion about the importance of father involvement should be done as early as possible in the engagement process, such as when a family is first referred to the intervention or at initial intake to the service.

Identifying the Core Parenting Team and Making Decisions About Engaging Fathers. Prior to engaging parents in assessment or intervention for child mental health, it is important for clinicians to determine the structure of the family and identify who forms part of the core parenting team [18]. In other words, clinicians should identify the caregivers who are responsible for providing the majority of the caregiving to the child and who are important to engage in the assessment and intervention. Families may have complex structures, and there may be a number of father (and mother) figures who undertake regular caregiving for the child. For some families, the core parenting team may include more than two caregivers, and it may be beneficial to involve all caregivers in the intervention. However, engaging more than two primary caregivers may be too complex or practically challenging for some interventions (e.g., because of limited space in consultation rooms). Discussions around which caregivers form part of the core parenting team and are important to engage in the intervention should occur as early as possible, such as when the family first contacts the service or a family is first referred. A key competency here is the ability to identify which caregivers are part of the core parenting team.

In families where there has been separation or divorce, decisions about whether or not to engage the father in the intervention should be discussed with the mother (or the father, in cases where the referring parent is the father). It may be important for clinicians to discuss with the referring parent their preferences regarding the engagement of the co-parent, current custody arrangements and court proceedings, the quality of the co-parenting relationship (e.g., communication, levels of conflict), aspects of the parent-child relationship (e.g., amount of time each parent spends with child, perceived quality of relationship) and any potential safety concerns associated with engaging the father (or mother). Parents who are separated or divorced or currently undergoing separation and who have high levels of conflict can still be engaged in interventions where they agree to a moratorium on conflict to allow them to jointly focus on the intervention for their child. For some separating couples, however, the timing of the intervention for their child's mental health problems may not be ideal, and clinicians can explore with parents the option of delaying the intervention until a later date following the separation, when couple issues are more likely to have been resolved.

Following discussions with the referring parent, there may be some instances where the engagement of the father (or mother) in the intervention is contraindicated. This may include, for example, parents who are violent, using substances, or engaging in antisocial behaviour. There is no one-size-fits-all approach for which caregivers should be engaged in interventions, and clinicians should base such decisions on a thorough assessment, preferences of the referring parent and their own clinical judgement. However, unless there are clear reasons to not include a father in an intervention, every effort should be made to engage fathers, as the involvement of the core parenting team is likely to enhance the immediate and long-term effectiveness of the intervention.

Inviting Fathers to Attend the Intervention. Fathers should be encouraged to attend the assessment and intervention from the very first communication with the family. Fathers can be directly invited to participate or invited indirectly through their partner. Direct communication with a father is usually preferable, and in some circumstances this may involve asking for the mother's permission to contact the father by telephone to directly invite him to be involved. Speaking directly to the father may be particularly important where a mother expresses uncertainly about father involvement because of barriers such as fathers' work commitments, lack of time or even fathers' lack of interest in the intervention. Fathers are more likely to attend when they feel that their parenting role is valued and their involvement is important. A direct approach enables clinicians to establish rapport with fathers and identify issues and barriers relevant to them, and this may increase the likelihood that the father engages in an intervention. During an initial discussion with fathers it can be helpful for clinicians to provide information about the intervention and answer questions; emphasize the unique knowledge and expertise that a father has in caring for their child; emphasize that the intervention is more likely to be effective if the core parenting team participates; discuss barriers that may prevent fathers from attending and respond to these discussions with empathy and understanding, and problem-solve barriers to attendance.

A direct approach to father engagement is always the preferred course of action. However, a direct approach may not always be possible for reason such as lack of availability of the father or mothers expressing a reluctance for direct communication to occur. As an alternative, clinicians may engage fathers indirectly through mothers. Where the mother makes the referral or initially engages in an intervention alone, it is important to discuss the benefits of having the core parenting team attend treatment together, since mothers have the potential to encourage and also discourage father engagement. It may be helpful for clinicians to elicit mothers' attitudes towards father engagement, emphasize the importance of father engagement to the success of the intervention, explore mothers' willingness to facilitate father engagement, prompt mothers to invite fathers to attend the intervention, and support mothers to problem-solve barriers to father attendance. Regardless of the specific strategies used to engage fathers, a key competency is to positively engage fathers by inviting fathers to participate in assessment and treatment.

Actively Engaging Fathers During the Intervention. Once fathers have connected with a service (initial attendance), it is important for clinicians to use active engagement strategies in session that are likely to encourage the participation of fathers in sessions and their ongoing involvement in the intervention. Clinicians can create a therapeutic team approach for working with parents during the intervention [25]. In establishing this team approach, clinicians can explain that each member has expert roles, and together the team will develop a plan for how the team will work, which may include rules, as well as strategies for managing any barriers or obstacles. Clinicians may prompt parents to suggest rules that they believe will be helpful for the team in working collaboratively (e.g., one parent speaking at a time, use of 'I' statements, commenting on own behaviour rather than partner's behaviour).

When working with the parenting team, it is important to seek input from both parents equally and use active listening skills with both parents. There may be a tendency for one parent to speak more than the other, but it is important to try to provide equal time to both parents and to ensure that both parents' perspectives are taken into account. Specific efforts may be needed to engage a disengaged parent in a session by inviting them to comment on the topic of discussion, exploring their perspective or

experience with curiosity and empathy, and use of active listening skills to check for understanding. Even when a parent expresses distressing experiences or controversial views, it is important that clinicians remain neutral and empathic and explore each parent's story. All aspects of the intervention should be discussed with both parents, and where active skills training is conducted in sessions, both parents should be equally involved in the rehearsal of strategies. Discussions around goals for treatment and setting of homework tasks should also be undertaken with both parents. Thus, a key clinician competency is the ability to foster and maintain a positive therapeutic alliance with both fathers and mothers.

Where both parents attend sessions together, there may be instances where there is disagreement or conflict between parents during a session. Setting up rules at the commencement of the intervention will help to manage any conflict or disagreement between parents. It is important for clinicians to acknowledge and normalize disagreements between mothers and fathers and remain impartial and avoid siding with one parent wherever possible. Having both parents attend together provides an opportunity to discuss and potentially resolve disagreements, which may strengthen the co-parenting relationship. A key clinician competency is therefore the ability to effectively manage conflict between parents.

Using a Flexible Approach to Engaging Fathers. Despite the best efforts of clinicians to engage both parents, only one parent may be able to attend the assessment and intervention. However, clinicians can use a flexible approach to engage both parents even when they cannot be physically present in sessions. This may include, for example, engaging fathers in sessions with the mother via telephone, having a separate session (via telephone or in person) with the father, or alternating attendance at weekly sessions between mothers and fathers where only one parent can attend a session each week. Clinicians may also explore the potential to audio- or video-record sessions with the mother for the father to listen to at a later time.

A flexible approach to father engagement may also involve offering participation in interventions via a range of delivery formats. Research has found that fathers prefer to participate in less intensive interventions such as internet-based interventions and brief interventions rather than more intensive individual or group interventions [41]. It is not surprising to find that less intensive interventions are preferred by fathers, as light-touch interventions make fewer demands on parent time and are likely to address practical barriers to engagement such as lack of time, work commitments and child care. There is increasing research to demonstrate the effectiveness of internet-based interventions for child mental health [54] and also emerging evidence on the effectiveness of brief interventions of fewer than eight sessions in duration [55]. In addition to exploring parent preferences for intervention delivery format, parent preferences and expectations regarding the focus of the intervention should also be explored. One study found that that a group parenting intervention for child externalizing problems that incorporated father-relevant content resulted in high levels of session attendance and programme satisfaction for both parents, and significant improvements in fathers' and mother's reports of child behaviour, parenting, and interparental conflict [56]. However, this study did not compare interventions with and without father-relevant content to determine whether the additional content led to improvements in engagement or outcomes for fathers.

Even with a flexible approach to engagement, there will be times when fathers are simply unable to participate directly in an intervention. It is important that clinicians do not assume that a non-attending father is disinterested or disengaged [19]. In instances where both parents cannot participate, clinicians can use an indirect approach to engaging both parents in the intervention, whereby the attending parent communicates the information and skills learned in the intervention to their partner or co-parent [8]. A qualitative study found that fathers' indirect engagement in an intervention was effective in changing parenting practices (child outcomes were not examined), but this was only for couples who reported high relationship satisfaction [57]. Thus, indirect participation may be effective for some families. There are many ways in which clinicians can facilitate indirect involvement of fathers in interventions, including discussing with the mother how information will be communicated to the father, encouraging the mother to prompt the father to enact intervention strategies at home, and prompting the mother to record questions from the father and discuss these in session with the clinician, with mother then providing feedback to the father. In sum, clinicians should use a flexible approach to

engaging fathers in interventions for child mental health by offering different delivery modalities as well as different options for direct and indirect participation in order to maximize the likelihood of positive intervention effects.

Father Engagement: A Clinical Case Study

Matthew was six-year-old child of separated parents (Fiona and Joe) who lived for part of the week with his mother (four days) and part with his father (three days) in separate households. Fiona had self-referred because of problems with Matthew's behaviour (e.g., daily noncompliance and argumentativeness, temper tantrums and aggression during tantrums) at home and at school. In the clinician's initial telephone contact with Fiona it was established that despite being separated for almost one year, parenting decisions remained shared by both parents, and Fiona identified Joe as an important part of Matthew's parenting team. The clinician provided Fiona with information about the importance of involving both parents to the success of treatment and asked for Fiona's preferences about including Joe. Fiona reported that she believed that it was important for Joe to be involved in Matthew's treatment but that he was unlikely to attend because he did not view Matthew's behaviour as a problem. She also explained that Joe worked in a highly stressful job and did not have time to attend the programme. In addition, Fiona described regular conflict between Joe and herself over how to manage Matthew's behaviour and reported that Joe often told her that she was 'too tough', whereas she felt that Joe was 'too soft' on Matthew. The clinician requested permission to telephone Joe directly in order to tell him about the clinic and invite him to attend, which Fiona agreed to.

The clinician's judgement was that Joe's involvement in both assessment and treatment appeared critical, given the shared care arrangements of Matthew, the seemingly divergent approaches to discipline, and the contradictory perspectives on Matthew's behaviour within the parenting team. Prior to the first face-to-face assessment session, the clinician contacted Joe to directly invite him to attend. On the telephone, Joe told the clinician that he did not have time to participate because of work demands. He also asserted that Matthew's behaviour was not a problem for him and that it was Fiona who needed help with her parenting. Rather than attempting to immediately problem-solve the barriers to Joe's availability, the clinician expressed empathy regarding the work demands described. The clinician listened to, and reflected on, Joe's perspective regarding Matthew's behaviour and normalized the differences in Joe's and Fiona's perspectives. The clinician also described the approach of the clinic, including the focus on evidence-based treatment and support for the parenting team. The importance of Joe's expertise and involvement to treatment success was emphasized. The clinician highlighted the scope for flexibility and presented Joe with a range of options for different ways that he could participate in treatment. The clinician also emphasized the importance of Joe attending the initial assessment in order to understand both parents' perspectives on Matthew's behaviour. It was agreed that Joe would discuss his involvement with Fiona that evening and that the clinician would follow up the next day. After speaking with Fiona, Joe subsequently agreed to attend. He said that he would take some time off work in order to attend the initial assessment interview in person with Fiona, after which time he would potentially telephone into sessions if they were scheduled during his lunch break.

During the initial assessment interview, Fiona reported that Matthew had daily tantrums, aggression and noncompliance, and that she would frequently yell and threaten Matthew and occasionally spank him. Joe reported that Matthew would occasionally engage in tantrums (once every two weeks) and non-compliance (every second day) and that he would respond to those behaviours by comforting or talking to Matthew or completing the task for him (e.g., dressing him if he refused to dress himself). Joe and Fiona reported that they tried to have a family dinner together every fortnight but that this was usually not a positive experience because of Matthew's behaviour, which would provoke arguments between his parents. Conflict over parenting often escalated into screaming matches in front of Matthew, according to his parents. Joe blamed this conflict on Fiona's 'aggressive' parenting (e.g., yelling, smacking). Fiona complained that Joe left all discipline to her and believed that Matthew regarded his father as the 'fun' parent, while her own relationship with Matthew was deteriorating.

By meeting both parents face-to-face for the first time together in this interview, the clinician avoided

giving the impression that she might already have sided with the mother before even meeting the father, thereby maximizing the chances of forming a positive therapeutic relationship with both. The clinician formed a therapeutic team with both parents and negotiated ground rules for working together. At various points, Joe expressed blame towards Fiona (e.g., 'It's all your fault') regarding Matthew's behaviour. The clinician managed this by staying neutral, reminding the parents of the ground rules that the team had set earlier (e.g., to focus on one's own behaviour). However, rather than discouraging Joe from expressing negativity, the therapist expressed curiosity about his feelings and 'spoke to his story' in order to understand his perspective. Joe was then able to explain how he felt when Fiona engaged in yelling and spanking because of memories from his own childhood. Specifically, Joe described feelings of anger, saying that his own parents had used harsh discipline with him growing up and that he was determined to parent differently. Likewise, Fiona had the opportunity to share her fears about Matthew rejecting her if he saw her as the disciplinarian in the family. By enabling the parents to openly express this information, which had never previously been communicated to each other, the parents were able to form a new shared understanding of each other's experiences and emotions.

Joe participated in subsequent sessions via telephone, beginning with a review of assessment findings and collaborative discussion of formulation, goals and treatment planning. The clinician hypothesized that Fiona's and Joe's use of ineffective and inconsistent parenting practices, including Joe's accidental reinforcement of Matthew's misbehaviour (e.g., responding to tantrums with cuddles and withdrawing instructions) and Fiona's modelling of aggression and emotional dysregulation (e.g., yelling and smacking), were serving to maintain Matthew's problem behaviours. The clinician further hypothesized that Matthew's exposure to his parents' overt conflict was contributing to his behaviour via modelling. Both parents agreed that they wanted to be able to parent as a team and to find a consistent approach to disciplining Matthew.

Treatment proceeded with initial components focused on positive parenting strategies for encouraging good behaviour through warmth and positive reinforcement, and limit setting for misbehaviour through calm, non-aggressive consequences. An emphasis was placed on maximizing consistency between both parents and using these practices to enhance each parent's relationship with Matthew. Subsequent components focused on improving practices within the parenting team concerning mutual support and effective communication. Significant improvements in the presenting problem were observed following the implementation of these strategies and related improvements in parental teamwork.

Conclusions

Interventions for child mental health often involve parents in some or all phases. Among services for child and adolescent mental health, interventions that involve parents are often delivered mainly to mothers, whereas fathers are under-represented. The participation of fathers as well as mothers allows for a thorough approach to assessment, diagnosis, case formulation, and treatment planning. Evidence suggests that the inclusion of fathers as well as mothers can enhance the effectiveness of an intervention in terms of benefits for children, making it important to maximize the engagement of fathers. There is a range of barriers that prevent fathers from engaging in interventions, and clinicians should identify and problem-solve these barriers with fathers and families. As outlined here, clinicians can nonetheless enact a number of strategies to increase the engagement of fathers, including strategies for setting up a father-inclusive environment, identifying the core parenting team and making decisions about engaging fathers, inviting fathers to attend interventions, engaging fathers during interventions, and using a flexible approach to increase the engagement of fathers. Furthermore, we would argue that clinicians should monitor rates of father engagement in interventions to ensure that both parents actively participate and derive optimal benefits from their involvement. Given the lack of research on father engagement in interventions for child mental health, particularly in relation to strategies for enhancing rates of father engagement, this is an important target for future research.

References

1. Fletcher R, Freeman E, Matthey S. The impact of behavioural parent training on fathers' parenting: A meta-analysis of the Triple P – Positive Parenting Program. *Fathering: A Journal of Theory, Research, and Practice about Men as Fathers* 2011; **9**(3):291–312.

2. Tiano JD, McNeil CB. The inclusion of fathers in behavioral parent training: A critical evaluation. *Child and Family Behavior Therapy* 2005; **27**(4):1–28.

3. Bögels S, Phares V. Fathers' role in the etiology, prevention and treatment of child anxiety: A review and new model. *Clinical Psychology Review* 2008; **28**(4):539–58.

4. Fabiano GA. Father participation in behavioral parent training for ADHD: Review and recommendations for increasing inclusion and engagement. *Journal of Family Psychology* 2007; **21**(4):683–93.

5. Flippin M, Crais ER. The need for more effective father involvement in early autism intervention: A systematic review and recommendations. *Journal of Early Intervention* 2011; **33**(1):24–50.

6. Lundahl BW, Tollefson D, Risser H, Lovejoy M. A meta-analysis of father involvement in parent training. *Research on Social Work Practice* 2008; **18**(2):97–106.

7. Bagner DM, Eyberg SM. Father involvement in parent training: When does it matter? *Journal of Clinical Child and Adolescent Psychology* 2003; **32**(4):599–605.

8. Piotrowska PJ, Tully LA, Lenroot R, et al. Mothers, fathers, and parental systems: A conceptual model of parental engagement in programmes for child mental health – Connect, Attend, Participate, Enact (CAPE). *Clinical Child and Family Psychology Review* 2017; **20**(2):146–61.

9. Sarkadi A, Kristiansson R, Oberklaid F, Bremberg S. Fathers' involvement and children's developmental outcomes: A systematic review of longitudinal studies. *Acta Paediatrica* 2008; **97**(2):153–8.

10. Barker B, Iles JE, Ramchandani PG. Fathers, fathering and child psychopathology. *Current Opinion in Psychology* 2017; **15**:87–92.

11. Fagan J, Day R, Lamb ME, Cabrera NJ. Should researchers conceptualize differently the dimensions of parenting for fathers and mothers? *Journal of Family Theory and Review* 2014; **6**(4):390–405.

12. Möller EL, Nikolić M, Majdandžić M, Bögels SM. Associations between maternal and paternal parenting behaviors, anxiety and its precursors in early childhood: A meta-analysis. *Clinical Psychology Review* 2016; **45**:17–33.

13. Wilson S, Durbin CE. Effects of paternal depression on fathers' parenting behaviors: A meta-analytic review. *Clinical Psychology Review* 2010; **30**(2):167–80.

14. Sweeney S, MacBeth A. The effects of paternal depression on child and adolescent outcomes: a systematic review. *Journal of Affective Disorders* 2016; **205**:44–59.

15. Teubert D, Pinquart M. The association between coparenting and child adjustment: A meta-analysis. *Parenting: Science and Practice* 2010; **10**(4):286–307.

16. Panter-Brick C, Burgess A, Eggerman M, et al. Practitioner review: Engaging fathers: Recommendations for a game change in parenting interventions based on a systematic review of the global evidence. *Journal of Child Psychology and Psychiatry* 2014; **55**(11):1187–212.

17. Dadds MR, Collins DA, Doyle FL, et al. A benchmarking study of father involvement in Australian child mental health services. *PloS One* 2018; **13**(8):e0203113.

18. Hawes DJ, Dadds MR. Parent and family assessment strategies. In: McLeod BD, Jensen-Doss A, Ollendick T (eds.), *Handbook of Child and Adolescent Diagnostic and Behavioral Assessment*. New York: Guilford Press, 2013, pp. 316–47.

19. Lechowicz ME, Jiang Y, Tully LA, et al. Enhancing father engagement in parenting programs: Translating research into practice recommendations. *Australian Psychologist* 2019; **54**(2):83–9.

20. Achenbach TM, McConaughy SH, Howell CT. Child/ adolescent behavioral and emotional problems: Implications of cross-informant correlations for situational specificity. *Psychological Bulletin* 1987; **101** (2):213–32.

21. Duhig AM, Renk K, Epstein MK, Phares VJCPS, Practice: Interparental agreement on internalizing, externalizing, and total behavior problems: A meta-analysis. *Clinical Psychology Science and Practice* 2000; **7**(4):435–53.

22. Mascendaro PM, Herman KC, Webster-Stratton C. Parent discrepancies in ratings of young children's co-occurring internalizing symptoms. *School Psychology Quarterly* 2012; **27**(3):134–43.

23. Mayfield AR, Parke EM, Barchard KA, et al. Equivalence of mother and father ratings of ADHD in children. *Child Neuropsychology* 2018; **24**(2):166–83.

24. Fabiano GA. Father participation in behavioral parent training for ADHD: Review and recommendations for increasing inclusion and engagement. *Journal of Family Psychology* 2007; **21** (4):683–93.

25. Dadds MR, Hawes DJ. *Integrated Family Intervention for Child Conduct Problems: A Behaviour-Attachment-Systems Intervention for Parents*. Queensland: Australian Academic Press, 2006.

26. De Los Reyes A, Kazdin AE. Informant discrepancies in the assessment of childhood psychopathology: A critical review, theoretical framework, and recommendations for further study. *Psychological Bulletin* 2005; **131**(4):483–509.

27. Hawes DJ, Allen J. Evidence-based parenting interventions: Current perspectives and clinical strategies. In: *Positive Mental Health, Fighting Stigma and Promoting Resiliency for Children and Adolescents*. New York: Elsevier, 2016, pp. 185–204.

28. Levy F, Hawes DJ, Johns A. Externalizing and internalizing comorbidity. In: Kaufman E, Crowell SE, Stepp SD, et al. (eds.), *Oxford Handbook of Externalizing Spectrum Disorders*. Oxford, UK: Oxford University Press, 2015, pp. 443–99.

29. Kaminski JW, Claussen AH. Evidence base update for psychosocial treatments for disruptive behaviors in children. *Journal of Clinical Child and Adolescent Psychology*. 2017; **46**(4):1–23.

30. Minuchin P. Families and individual development: Provocations from the field of family therapy. *Child Development* 1985; **56**(2):289–302.

31. Webster-Stratton C. Randomized trial of two parent-training programs for families with conduct-disordered children. *Journal of Consulting and Clinical Psychology* 1984; **52**(4):666–78.

32. Dadds MR, Sanders MR, Behrens BC, James JE. Marital discord and child behavior problems: A description of family interactions during treatment. *Journal of Clinical Child Psychology* 1987; **16** (3):192–203.

33. Dadds MR, Schwartz S, Sanders MRJJ, Psychology C. Marital discord and treatment outcome in behavioral treatment of child conduct disorders. *Journal of Consulting and Clinical Psychology* 1987; **55**(3):396–403.

34. Griest DL, Forehand R, Rogers T, et al. Effects of parent enhancement therapy on the treatment outcome and generalization of a parent training program. *Behaviour Research and Therapy* 1982; **20** (5):429–36.

35. Sanders MR, Kirby JN, Tellegen CL, Day JJ. The Triple P – Positive Parenting Program: A systematic review and meta-analysis of a multi-level system of parenting support. *Clinical Psychology Review* 2014; **34**(4):337–57.

36. Gunlicks ML, Weissman MM. Change in child psychopathology with improvement in parental depression: A systematic review. *Journal of the American Academy of Child and Adolescent Psychiatry* 2008; **47**(4):379–89.

37. Sawrikar V, Dadds M. What role for parental attributions in parenting interventions for child conduct problems? Advances from research into practice. *Clinical Child and Family Psychology Review* 2018; **21**(1):41–56.

38. Mockford C, Barlow J. Parenting programmes: Some unintended consequences. *Primary Health Care Research and Development* 2004; **5**(3):219–27.

39. Sanders MR, Dittman CK, Farruggia SP, Keown LJ. A comparison of online versus workbook delivery of a self-help positive parenting program. *Journal of Primary Prevention* 2014; **35**(3):125–33.

40. Helfenbaum-Kun ED, Ortiz C. Parent-training groups for fathers of head start children: A pilot study of their feasibility and impact on child behavior and intra-familial relationships. *Child and Family Behavior Therapy* 2007; **29**(2):47–64.

41. Tully LA, Piotrowska PJ, Collins DA, et al. Optimising child outcomes from parenting interventions: Fathers' experiences, preferences and barriers to participation. *BMC Public Health* 2017; **17** (1):550.

42. Frank TJ, Keown LJ, Dittman CK, Sanders MR. Using father preference data to increase father engagement in evidence-based parenting programs. *Journal of Child and Family Studies* 2015; **24**(4):937–47.

43. Tully L, Collins DA, Piotrowska PJ, et al. Examining practitioner competencies, organizational support and barriers to engaging fathers in parenting interventions. *Child Psychiatry and Human Development* 2018; **49**(1):109–22.

44. Niec, L. N., Barnett, M. L., Gering, C. L., et al. Differences in mothers' and fathers' readiness for change in parent training. *Child and Family Behavior Therapy* 2015; **37**(3):224–35.

45. Allen SM, Hawkins AJ. Maternal gatekeeping: Mothers' beliefs and behaviors that inhibit greater father involvement in family work. *Journal of Marriage and the Family* 1999; **61**(1):199–212.

46. Glynn L, Dale M. Engaging dads: Enhancing support for fathers through parenting programmes. *Aotearoa New Zealand Social Work* 2015; **27**(1–2):59–72.

47. Tully L, Collins D, Piotrowska P, et al. Examining practitioner competencies, organizational support and barriers to engaging fathers in parenting interventions. *Child Psychiatry and Human Development* 2018; **49**(1):109–22.

48. Burn M, Tully L, Jiang Y, et al. Evaluating practitioner training to improve competencies and organizational practices for engaging fathers in parenting interventions. *Child Psychiatry and Human Development* 2019; **50**(2):230–44.

49. Fletcher R, May C, St George J, et al. *Engaging Fathers: Evidence Review*. Canberra: Australian Research Alliance for Children and Youth (ARACY), 2014.

50. Ingoldsby EM. Review of interventions to improve family engagement and retention in parent and child mental health programs. *Journal of Child and Family Studies* 2010; **19**(5):629–45.

51. Palm G, Fagan J, Care: Father involvement in early childhood programs: Review of the literature. *Early Child Development and Care* 2008; **178**(7–8):745–59.

52. Sicouri G, Tully L, Collins D, et al. Toward father-friendly parenting interventions: A qualitative study. *Australian and New Zealand Journal of Family Therapy* 2018; **39**(2):218–31.

53. Zanoni L, Warburton W, Bussey K, McMaugh A. Fathers as 'core business' in child welfare practice and research: An interdisciplinary review. *Children and Youth Services Review* 2013; **35**(7):1055–70.

54. Nieuwboer CC, Fukkink RG, Hermanns JM. Online programs as tools to improve parenting: A meta-analytic review. *Children and Youth Services Review* 2013; **35**(11):1823–9.

55. Tully LA, Hunt C. Brief parenting interventions for children at risk of externalizing behavior problems: A systematic review. *Journal of Child and Family Studies* 2016; **25**(3):705–19.

56. Frank TJ, Keown LJ, Sanders MR. Enhancing father engagement and interparental teamwork in an evidence-based parenting intervention: A randomized-controlled trial of outcomes and processes. *Behavior Therapy* 2015; **46**(6):749–63.

57. Huntington C, Vetere A. Coparents and parenting programmes: Do both parents need to attend? *Journal of Family Therapy* 2015; **38**(3):409–34.

6

Cultural Diversity and Family-Based Interventions

Regina M. Hechanova, Chantal Ellis S. Tabo-Corpuz and Kay Bunagan

Family-based interventions can help children and adolescents with their psychosocial needs and improve health and wellbeing related to a broad range of issues, including mental health, risky behaviours of adolescents, and postdisaster trauma. Family interventions also have the potential to change the dynamics of family relations and strengthen the recovery capital of individuals at risk. However, the effectiveness of family-based interventions often depends on a number of factors, and an important consideration is culture. Global migration has increased diversity in populations. However, healthcare systems often do not recognize racial and ethnic disparities and needs. Given this, understanding of cultural difference and working effectively in different cultural contests are core principles in community-based systems of care for children [1]. In this chapter, we examine how culture can influence family interventions for child and adolescent mental health.

Recognition of Mental Health Problems

Culture can shape openness to interventions by influencing what people recognize and acknowledge as problems that need to be addressed. Cultural norms on substance use, parenting behaviour, risky behaviour, sexual relationships and marriage, for example, can determine what is considered problematic or not. For example, in some countries marriage at 13 years is acceptable, whereas in other countries it may be considered shocking. In the United States, alcohol is not sold to anyone younger than 21 years, but some European countries allow 15-year-olds to purchase alcohol [2].

A study by Napoles-Springer at al. [3] reports that troubling behaviours of minority children and adolescents are more often identified by the school or the court than by their parents. One explanation given for this is that minority families have a higher threshold

for disruptive behaviours and tend not to seek professional intervention until the situation becomes unmanageable. Yeh et al. [4] likewise affirm that children and adolescents of ethnic and racial minorities are referred to health treatment from involuntary sources and that their self-referral rates are lower than those of their peers.

Access to Information and Resources

Awareness is a key factor in participating in interventions. A lack of awareness of the harmful effects of a behaviour such as substance abuse [5], of the possible solutions to the problem [6], and of existing programmes to address the problem [7] may hinder individuals from seeking help. By contrast, there are people who are aware that clinical services exist but lack the means or resources to access them. These resources could pertain to financial constraints [5, 8, 9] and/or transportation [9, 10]. Especially when interventions are conducted in developing countries, resources such as equipment needed for an intensive home-based behavioural intervention for children in the autism spectrum [11], printed information and educational materials [12] and even something as basic as a telephone to contact authorities for abused women facing domestic violence [9] are unavailable. In developing countries, the lack of physical space for family interventions, whether in a school setting [13] or at home [14], is a commonly cited barrier.

Openness to Help Seeking

Personal Factors Affecting Help-Seeking Behavior. Confounding this lack of awareness are personal factors. Generally, parents would like to think that their children are developing healthily, and seeking help would bring shame or guilt because it would mean that there is a problem in their family [8] or that they have failed as parents [8, 15]. This may be exacerbated in societies with extended families who are involved in family decisions. For example, parents might feel concern and worry about a problem behaviour, but a grandmother or an aunt would say otherwise, thus lowering the chances for the family to seek help [8].

For orphans and vulnerable children, some abusers instil fear, discouraging them from seeking help [16]. Women who face violence may feel that counselling interventions are not needed or useful for them, so they do not accept the help that is offered to them (e.g., police assistance, counselling and medical care). They may accept their situation as normative and not serious enough to warrant the intervention [9].

Developmental Factors Affecting Help-Seeking Behaviour. Peer acceptance and conformity are of outmost importance for adolescents. Thus, they may fear being judged or criticized by others and may choose to keep silent about what difficulties they are going through [9]. In a study on a family drug intervention, about two-thirds (or 72 per cent) of the adolescents who were suspected or observed to use drugs resisted interventions provided for them [17]. A study on college students revealed that they were fearful of unpacking emotional experiences, thus preventing them from seeking help [18].

In instances where adolescents open up about their experiences, they disclose to their peers rather than to their family [19]. Factors that hinder disclosing to their family include their perception of their parents' openness, satisfaction with family relationships and family cohesion. In general, adolescents are not likely to share their problems even if they have problematic families making it difficult to implement family interventions [19].

Cultural Beliefs. Beyond awareness and access, societal norms can shape help-seeking behaviour. In Nigeria, for example, interviews and focus-group discussions with community workers who worked with orphans and vulnerable children across 15 organizations in 6 different areas revealed that some cultural beliefs and practices shape the acceptability of interventions [16]. The cultural belief that children should always respect and follow their elders may prevent them from speaking out. The belief that children are not educated or informed enough to question their elders' decisions may also make it difficult for vulnerable children to get out of abusive and oppressive situations. Interventions against child labour may be more difficult in cultures where children are expected to work to help their families survive. Child

protection interventions likewise may be particularly challenging in societies that consider disciplining children as a family matter and solely the family's responsibility, making external help difficult to accept [16].

Stigma and Shame. Culture also may become a barrier to participation in child and adolescent mental health services because of the presence of stigma. Several studies support this, naming stigma as one of the reasons that prevents people from participating in interventions [5, 8, 9, 20, 21]. Stigmatization can come from the public or from one's self and may consequently affect help-seeking behaviour [22].

Being labelled as different or an outcast makes people think twice before seeking help [23]. Participating in mental health interventions may also be seen as a personal failure [5], making participants feel shame about their experience [9]. For example, in Nigeria, those who provide interventions for orphans and vulnerable children are called *shame-givers* because approaching a family would bring shame when other people would know about it [16]. Studies likewise show that Asians, in general, are reluctant to see therapists because they are generally hesitant to open up to strangers, they do not want to tarnish their dignity or damage their family's reputation, and they are concerned that they will be seen as crazy [24].

Lack of Social Support

Interventions that aim to enhance the lifestyle of a person often require solid social support for changes to be maintained [25]. This is especially so in collectivist cultures where people derive their strength from significant others and from external resources [24]. Perceived lack of social support was among the barriers for Latino clients to access specialty treatment for substance use disorders (SUDs) [5]. Pinedo, Zemore and Rogers [5] report that persons who use drugs worry that seeking treatment would be confirmation for families that they had a problem with substances and that their families would not approve of them undergoing treatment.

Beyond stigma or shame, culture also may shape the amount of social isolation that, in turn, can influence help-seeking behaviour [8]. People who are isolated have no one to encourage and support them to seek help and join interventions, as in the case of abused women [9]. In cultures where violence against women and children is tolerated, victims may also worry that participating in clinical services for mental health issues would further isolate them, particularly from their families [5].

Acceptance of Service Providers

Studies also suggest that some ethnicities are sensitive to their service provider's backgrounds. Latinos, for example, are more open to receiving SUD treatment from providers who have similar experiences or who empathize with their experiences [5]. Cambodian participants are also cautious about whom to trust because of their political history [26, 27]. According to Wong and Mock, as cited in Kumpfer et al. [28], interventions that require reflecting and sharing of personal feelings would be difficult for cultures that would rather take the wisdom of the elderly than have to reflect how they feel about situations.

Intervention providers who are of a different ethnicity from participants can also pose a problem to prospective clients because they may perceive an imbalance of power. The report of the Surgeon General of the US Department of Health and Services in 2001 [29] suggests a differential treatment for mental health concerns between African-American and Caucasian populations. The history of slavery, segregation and discrimination against African Americans facilitates their resistance against and distrust of the oppressors, putting them at a disadvantage in terms of mental health care. Poverty likewise limits access to health insurance. Even when the number of African-American individuals and families who need mental health care is significantly higher than the majority, they are less likely to do so [30]. Another major concern is racial bias or discrimination in how services are provided for minorities. Despite the need to address mental health concerns, it is unlikely that minorities will access mental health services because those from low socioeconomic status have high levels of distrust of mental health professionals [31], especially Caucasian professionals [32]. Because of the differential treatment of African-American and Caucasian children with emotional and behavioural problems, African-American parents choose not to enrol their children in interventions for fear that they will be taken away from them [20, 30]. Generally, both African-American and Hispanic cultures tend to distrust professionals in the medical and mental health fields [31]. Parents from the minority group are less likely to accept help from

formal mental health providers than Caucasian families [33, 34] and would only consider this option as a last resort [35]. For minority adolescents, it is often external agencies such as schools and social services that refer those with mental health needs to the proper service provider via coercive means [30]. In general, minorities tend to participate less in intervention services than dominant ethnicities [36].

Acceptance of Interventions

Beyond acceptance of service providers, culture also shapes people's conceptualization of what kind of help they need and what interventions they may be more open to. Culture influences people's perception of what the problem is, or even the existence of a problem itself [37]. Specific elements of one's culture influence families' decisions to participate in interventions. In this section, we discuss the roles of spirituality, emotional expression, language and time in the decision to accept mental health interventions.

Spirituality

Faith is an important coping mechanism in some cultures [24]. Studies on women and the elderly suggest that interventions that include aspects of religion and spirituality are more acceptable to low-income rural women and rural elderly individuals who associate spirituality and religiosity with wellness [38, 39]. In these cultures, non-spiritual interventions (i.e., psychological, medical) may be difficult to implement because prayers and other spiritual practices are key aspects of coping for many ethnic minorities [37]. Thus, in cultures where religion is important, consulting and involving the religious community when implementing programmes may be important to encourage participation, even when interventions are not primarily spiritual [10, 20].

Emotional Expression

Cultures differ in emotional expression [40], and this may affect the acceptability of interventions. In Western cultures, people express their physical or social pain by sharing their thoughts and feelings. The talk-therapy approach is widely accepted in Western culture [24]. By contrast, in some East Asian and Latin cultures, talking about or sharing one's problems with others is frowned upon [5, 14] or discouraged [41]. In these cultures, distracting oneself, rather than talking about the experience or seeking comfort from others, is the primary mode for coping [24]. Thus, interventions that require sharing one's thoughts and feelings may meet resistance.

The culture of silence and emotional suppression may be particularly salient for family interventions. In cultures where emotional expression is frowned upon, people may believe that sharing information about their family problems may tarnish their reputation as a family [24]. Thus, non-disclosure may be seen as a form of maintaining relationships and preserving interpersonal harmony [40].

Language

Language can also be a barrier for families to access interventions, especially if the languages of the service provider and participant are different [42]. In such cases, communication between the two parties can be difficult, hindering the effectiveness and extent and quality of participation in any intervention [36]. There is also an imbalance of power if only one parent knows how to speak the same language as the service provider. The parent who does not know the language well may receive no, little or even incorrect information from the service provider. If the parent who speaks the language well is biased against joining interventions, it will not be possible for the other parent to participate [8].

Time

Some interventions are time consuming, and thus, time may become a barrier for participation if the sessions are too long [21] and interfere with participants' schedules [43]. Families may be willing to join interventions but may be hard pressed to do so when the time spent for the intervention can be devoted to something else [14]. For example, in competitive and fast-paced environments such as Hong Kong, both parents and children are already busy with their day-to-day tasks, such as household chores, homework and extracurricular activities, and may view interventions that interferes with their busy life as burdensome [14].

Sometimes the issue of time also may simply be a matter of conflict in schedules because people have different working hours, and therefore, their availability for interventions varies [7, 10]. Some interventions that adopt a lifestyle-like approach (i.e., one has to actively change one's lifestyle in order for the intervention to take effect) may require time-consuming preparation [6] and implementation [11]. Even schools that have attempted to implement school-

based interventions have a difficult time trying to fit them into tight class schedules [12].

More creative ways to provide interventions are needed for families to overcome these barriers [44]. Providers of interventions and related services should be mindful not only of the programme content but also of the implementation process and the implications for families' resources to encourage family involvement in such programmes [34].

Engaging with Diverse Ethnic and Cultural Groups

Given the many cultural factors that may influence awareness related to mental health, help-seeking behaviour and treatment, there are a number of strategies that can be used when engaging different ethnic and cultural groups in family-based interventions. In this section, we discuss critical factors to enable community engagement with diverse ethnic and cultural groups. We begin with the importance of identifying barriers to access and focus on the value of information sharing, referral pathways and building social support. We also highlight the value of cultural adaptation, building trust relationships and building cross-cultural competence. Finally, we focus on the importance of harnessing resources and using multidisciplinary teams.

Identifying Barriers to Access

The American Academy of Child and Adolescent Psychiatry (AACAP) Diversity and Culture Committee identified a number of principles to ensure cultural competence in the practice of child and adolescent psychiatry [45]. The first principle is that clinicians should identify barriers that may prevent culturally diverse families from accessing mental health services. They cite barriers such as financial needs, lack of insurance, poorly understood procedures and lack of linguistic support.

Assessment

Migration brings about a number of stressors, including disruption and separation from family, traumatic journeys, exposure to crime and violence and victimization. Studies suggest that children who experience parental separation or losses have a higher risk for developing depression, conduct disorders and SUDs [1]. Similarly, adolescent victims of war have elevated rates of post-traumatic stress disorder (PTSD), conduct disorder and aggressive and sexual behaviour, SUD and depression [46]. In addition, adolescents from migrant families may face issues of marginalization, acculturation stress and intergenerational acculturation conflict that can put them at higher risk for SUDs, mental health issues and conduct disorders [45]. The AACAP suggests that treatment of immigrant, refugee and inner-city minority children must address their exposure to trauma and acculturation stressors [45].

Information Sharing and Language

Awareness of information about developmental indicators and available programmes affects access to those programmes by culturally and linguistic diverse (CALD) parents [47]. Parents from CALD backgrounds appear to need more access to information that could increase how much they use health services, especially for their children's developmental needs [8]. The lack of available or accessible information to these families was cited as one of the barriers that prevent them from tapping available health services. Parents need to have knowledge about available services, as well as information about children's development. Access to information ensures more access to culturally appropriate services.

However, AACAP also identifies linguistic barriers as critical because many immigrants are not fluent in English and thus may be unable to participate in treatment. The AACAP also suggests that a lack of appropriate linguistic ability and interpreter support has been associated with misdiagnoses and adverse clinical outcomes. The organization suggests that evaluation and intervention should be conducted in the language in which children and families are proficient [45]. CALD parents tend to go to doctors who speak their language or come from the same culture, and this is also likely to apply to providers of family interventions for child and adolescent mental health. Interpreters also may help parents acquire more information and access to services [8].

Referral Pathways

Related to this, complex, out-of-reach or underutilized referral systems have been found to be barriers to access for children with developmental needs from culturally diverse backgrounds, particularly those with limited English proficiency [8]. Gatekeepers of these referral systems, such as general practitioners, may not pick up on cues that children from these families may need developmental attention. Streamlined, accessible and clear referral pathways ensure that more children and families are aware of these services, and know how to avail themselves of these programmes [8].

Building Social Support

Beyond referral pathways, intervention effectiveness increases with social support provided by families, friends and other professionals because there is a collective effort in addressing the problem [11, 25]. Extended family networks can be tapped because they may encourage developmental surveillance and enable family members to avail themselves of early childhood interventions [8]. This is also emphasized by the AACAP, which suggests that mental health workers should make efforts to include family members and key members of extended families such as grandparents or elders in assessment, treatment planning and treatment [45].

Cultural Adaptation

As suggested by the AACAP, a culturally competent approach in working with children and their families requires incorporating their beliefs, values, attitudes and cultural rituals within the treatment [45]. There is robust evidence that culturally adapted family interventions result in more favourable outcomes for more diverse populations [28, 48–50]. African-American families dealing with cancer developed better communication patterns after undergoing a programme that was culturally adapted [49]. Caribbean-African participants and their families in the United Kingdom who participated in a culturally adapted family intervention programme for families living with schizophrenia also showed promising outcomes [50]. Cultural adaptations of the Strengthening Families Programme (SFP) had higher retention rates when compared with the generic version for African Americans, Hispanics, Asian/Pacific Islanders and Native American families [28]. A meta-analysis of research on individual treatments such as depression reported that cultural adaptations led to better outcomes, even when only the implementation of the programme, and not the content, has been modified for diverse populations [51]. Finally, a parenting programme adapted for Latino populations revealed greater parental engagement [52].

Building Trusting Relationships and Cultural Competence of Community Interventionists. A study on Latinos' use of SUD treatment found that one barrier to seeking help is the perception that practitioners do not know the culture and experience of clients [5]. Conversely, a study on the cultural adaptation of family interventions for treating schizophrenia found that families seek service providers who know their child's difficulties and culture [50]. Having multicultural workers with an understanding of CALD families' situation and culture is a crucial part of community engagement [8]. Parents respond to multicultural workers who are able to nurture trust and establish relationships. They note, however, that it is not necessary that service providers come from the same culture, as long as the families feel respected [8].

Given this, an important strategy for the effective delivery of family interventions is building the cultural competence of providers. Familiarizing oneself with participants' cultural practices and establishing good rapport with them before implementing the programme are good ways facilitators can address these cultural and ethnic barriers that affect participation [53]. Conversely, a principle advocated by the AACAP is that health workers should be cognizant of their own cultural biases that may interfere with their judgement and treatment of clients. Studies show that stereotyping and biases can lead to unequal treatment [45].

Cultural competence also requires understanding cultural differences in developmental progression, idiomatic expressions of distress and presentation of symptoms. Distress is expressed differently across cultures. For example, among Latinos of Caribbean origin, *ataques de nervios* (a reaction combining anxiety, agitation and dissociation) can be confused with a psychotic reaction. Among Afro-Caribbeans, *falling out* (an expression of emotional stress that includes sudden acute paralysis and dissociation) may be confused with catatonia [45].

Another important component of cultural competence is understanding how to deal with the resistance of families from diverse cultural backgrounds. Given the reluctance towards help seeking and the stigma towards mental health often seen among such families, a client-centred approach may work best when dealing with resistance. Woolfenden et al. [8] suggest that parents should be allowed the chance to observe

and identify child mental health issues themselves. When they are unable to do so, clinicians may inform families directly, but in a sensitive way. They describe these interactions with family as needing to be 'fluid, open-ended and tentative' [8]. Citing the arrogance that health professionals sometimes have as 'experts', Wolff [53] calls for the need for giving community members choice and dealing with them with tact, tolerance and humility.

Harnessing Resources within the Community

The AACAP also advocates the importance of treating culturally diverse clients in familiar settings within their communities whenever possible [45]. This is because financial constraints are real barriers to accessing services for families [8]. In developing economies, resources for mental health are limited, and costs for private services are prohibitive. Funds for public programmes also compete with other programmes for acute conditions that seem more urgent. Towards this end, another key strategy is using community members in delivering interventions. McKleroy et al. [54] indicated that an important but least used model in community-based interventions is that of the community as agent. This means using community resources and institutions (i.e., religious people, family members, school personnel, human resource management personnel, community leaders, local healers, etc.) as providers of interventions. Wolff [53] likewise advocates the importance of empowering community members into self-help, mutual help and natural helping networks. He recounts that in the case of domestic violence, the natural ecological system of communities from police, hospitals, churches and even hairdressers was tapped to locate and help clients.

Using Multidisciplinary Team–Based Approaches

Given the many competencies required in delivering family-based interventions, the task often may be too challenging for just one person and thus require a team-based approach. A study in the United Kingdom reported that a factor that facilitates favourable outcomes from family intervention programmes is using a multidisciplinary team approach in the various aspects of implementation, such as training, supervision and obtaining organizational commitment [55]. Wolff [53] suggests that bringing together practitioners from multiple disciplines not only enables different perspectives but creates a collaborative process that models respect for diversity.

Summary

Family-based interventions for child and adolescent mental health may be particularly challenging to deliver in certain cultures. Cultures where violence against children is normalized or where mental illness is stigmatized may deter recognition of a problem and openness to help seeking. Social norms that discourage emotional expression and the desire to avoid bringing shame on one's family may also discourage both parents and children from seeking help. Culture may also shape the amount of social support available to families of children with mental health problems and acceptance of help from service providers. Spirituality, emotional expression, literacy and time constraints can also influence clients' acceptance of various aspects of interventions.

Despite these barriers, studies also suggest that family interventions may be successful when communities are engaged in planning, designing and implementing interventions and when trust and relationships are built. Information sharing, strengthening referral pathways, harnessing resources and using a multidisciplinary and team approach to implementing interventions are other ways to connect families and service providers. A critical element in implementing interventions is building the cultural competence of community-based practitioners who are working with children and their families. However, an even more sustainable approach would be to use community actors as intervention providers. This ensures not only that interventions are informed by knowledge of relevant cultural factors and practices but also that having trained community facilitators is likely to enable the sustainability of family-based interventions.

References

1. Pumariega AJ, Rothe E. Leaving no children or families outside: The challenges of immigration. *American Journal of Orthopsychiatry* 2010; **80**(4):505.

2. Room R. Drinking and coming of age in a cross-cultural perspective. In: Bonnie RJ, O'Connell ME (eds.), *Reducing Underage Drinking: A Collective Responsibility*. Washington, DC: National Research Council, Institute of Medicine of the National Academies, 2014, pp. 654–7.

3. Napoles-Springer A, Santavo J, Houston K, et al. Patient's perceptions of cultural factors affecting the quality of their medical encounters. *Health Expectations* 2005; **8**:4–17.

4. Yeh M, Cabe K, Hurlburt M, et al. Referral sources, diagnoses, and service types of youth in public outpatient mental health care: A focus on ethnic minorities. *Journal of Behavioral Health Services and Research* 2002; **29**:45–60.

5. Pinedo M, Zemore S, Rogers S. Understanding barriers to specialty substance abuse treatment among Latinos. *Journal of Substance Abuse Treatment* 2018; **94**:1–8.

6. Musaiger AO, Al-Mannai M, Tayyem R, et al. Perceived barriers to healthy eating and physical activity among adolescents in seven Arab countries: A cross-cultural study. *Scientific World Journal* 2013.

7. Santiago CD, Fuller AK, Lennon JM, Kataoka SH. Parent perspectives from participating in a family component for CBITS: Acceptability of a culturally informed school-based program. *Psychological Trauma* 2016; **8**(3):325.

8. Woolfenden S, Posada N, Krchnakova R, et al. Equitable access to developmental surveillance and early intervention: Understanding the barriers for children from culturally and linguistically diverse (CALD) backgrounds. *Health Expectations* 2014; **18**(6):3286–301.

9. Fugate M, Landis L, Riordan K, et al. Barriers to domestic violence help seeking. *Violence Against Women* 2005; **11**(3):290–310.

10. Mendez JL, Carpenter JL, LaForett DR, Cohen JS. Parental engagement and barriers to participation in a community-based preventive intervention. *American Journal of Community Psychology* 2009; **44**(1–2):1–4.

11. Johnson E, Hastings RP. Facilitating factors and barriers to the implementation of intensive home-based behavioural intervention for young children with autism. *Child: Care, Health and Development* 2002; **28**(2):123.

12. Aston C, Graves Jr S. Challenges and barriers to implementing a school-based Afrocentric intervention in urban schools: A pilot study of the sisters of Nia cultural program. *School Psychology Forum and Research Practice* 2016; **10**(2):165–76.

13. Langley AK, Nadeem E, Kataoka SH, et al. Evidence-based mental health programs in schools: Barriers and facilitators of successful implementation. *School Mental Health* 2010; **2**(3):105–13.

14. Chu JT, Ho HC, Mui M, et al. Happy Family Kitchen II: Participants' perspectives of a community-based

family intervention. *Journal of Child and Family Studies* 2018; **27**(5):1629–39.

15. Lau A, Takeuchi D. Cultural factors in help-seeking for child behavior problems: Value orientation, affective responding, and severity appraisals among Chinese-American parents. *Journal of Community Psychology* 2001; **29**(6):675–92.

16. Adebayo KO, Ogunbanwo AO. 'Children without a family should come out!': Sociocultural barriers affecting the implementation of interventions among orphans and vulnerable children in Nigeria. *Vulnerable Children and Youth Studies* 2017; **12**(4):375–83.

17. Szapocznik J, Perez-Vidal A, Brickman AL, et al. Engaging adolescent drug abusers and their families in treatment: A strategic structural systems approach. *Journal of Consulting and Clinical Psychology* 1988; **56**(4):552.

18. Komiya N, Good GE, Sherrod NB. Emotional openness as a predictor of college students' attitudes toward seeking psychological help. *Journal of Counseling Psychology* 2000; **47**(1):138.

19. Papini DR, Farmer FF, Clark SM, et al. Early adolescent age and gender differences in patterns of emotional self-disclosure to parents and friends. *Adolescence* 1990; **25**(100):959.

20. Breland-Noble AM, Bell C, Nicolas G. Family first: The development of an evidence-based family intervention for increasing participation in psychiatric clinical care and research in depressed African American adolescents. *Family Process* 2006; **45**(2):153–69.

21. Howard BN, Van Dorn R, Myers BJ, et al. Barriers and facilitators to implementing an evidence-based woman-focused intervention in South African health services. *BMC Health Services Research* 2017; **17**(1):746.

22. Eisenberg D, Downs MF, Golberstein E, Zivin K. Stigma and help seeking for mental health among college students. *Medical Care Research and Review* 2009; **66**(5):522–41.

23. Barney LJ, Griffiths KM, Jorm AF, Christensen H. Stigma about depression and its impact on help-seeking intentions. *Australian and New Zealand Journal of Psychiatry* 2006; **40**(1):51–4.

24. Hechanova R, Waelde L. The influence of culture on disaster mental health and psychosocial support interventions in Southeast Asia. *Mental Health Religion Cult* 2017; **20**(1):31–44.

25. McCloskey J, Flenniken D. Overcoming cultural barriers to diabetes control: A qualitative study of southwestern New Mexico Hispanics. *Journal of Cultural Diversity* 2010; **17**(3):241–6.

26. Rozée PD, Van Boemel G. The psychological effects of war trauma and abuse on older Cambodian refugee women. *Women and Therapy* 1990; **8**(4):2350.

27. Strober SB. Social work interventions to alleviate Cambodian refugee psychological distress. *International Social Work* 1994; **37**(1):23–35.

28. Kumpfer KL, Alvarado R, Smith P, Bellamy N. Cultural sensitivity and adaptation in family-based prevention interventions. *Prevention Science* 2002; **3**(3).

29. US Department of Health and Human Services (US). Mental health: Culture, race, and ethnicity. Supplement to mental health: A report of the Surgeon General. Rockville, MD: US Department of Health and Human Services, Public Health Services, Office of Surgeon General, 2001.

30. Takeuchi DT, Bui KVT, Kim L. The referral of minority adolescents to community mental health centers. *Journal of Health and Social Behavior* 1993; **34**(2):153–64.

31. Armstrong K, Ravenell KL, McMurphy S, Putt M. Racial/ethnic differences in physician distrust in the United States. *American Journal of Public Health* 2007; **97**(7):1283–9.

32. Wallerstein N, Duran B. Community-based participatory research contributions to intervention research: The intersection of science and practice to improve health equity. *American Journal of Public Health* 2010; **100**(S1):S40–6.

33. McMiller WP, Weisz JR. Help-seeking preceding mental health clinic intake among African-America, Latino, and Caucasian youths. *J Am Acad Child Adolesc Psychiatry* 1996; 35(8):1086–94.

34. Baker CN, Arnold DH, Meagher S. Enrollment and attendance in a parent training prevention program for conduct problems. *Prevention Science* 2011; **12**(2):126–38.

35. Lin KM, Inui T, Kleinman A, Womack W. Sociocultural determinants of help-seeking behaviors of patients with mental illness. *Journal of Nervous and Mental Disease* 1982; **170**:78–85.

36. Murthy VH, Krumholz HM, Gross CP. Participation in cancer clinical trials. *Journal of the American Medical Association* 2004; **291**(22):2720.

37. Cheung FK, Snowden LR. Community mental health and ethnic minority populations. *Community Mental Health Journal* 1990; **26**(3):277–91.

38. Gill CS, Minton CAB, Myers JE. Spirituality and religiosity: Factors affecting wellness among low-income, rural women. *Journal of Counseling and Development* 2010; **88**(3):293–302.

39. Yoon DP. Factors affecting subjective well-being for rural elderly individuals: The importance of spirituality, religiousness, and social support. *Journal*

of Religious and Spiritual Social Work 2006; **25**(2): 59–75.

40. Kim HS, Sherman DK. 'Express yourself': Culture and the effect of self-expression on choice. *Journal of Personality and Social Psychology* 2007; **92**(1):1.

41. Atkins D, Uskul AK, Cooper NR. Culture shapes empathic responses to physical and social pain. *Emotion* 2016; **16**(5):587–601.

42. Yu SM, Huang ZJ, Schwalberg RH, Nyman RM. Parental English proficiency and children's health services access. *American Journal of Public Health* 2006; **96**(8):1449–55.

43. Spoth R, Redmond C, Hockaday C, Shin CY. Barriers to participation in family skills preventive interventions and their evaluations: A replication and extension. *Family Relations* 1996; **45**(3):246–54.

44. Coatsworth JD, Duncan LG, Pantin H, Szapocznik J. Patterns of retention in a preventive intervention with ethnic minority families. *Journal of Primary Prevention* 2006; **27**(2):171–93.

45. Pumariega AJ, Rothe E, Mian A, et al. Practice parameter for cultural competence in child and adolescent psychiatric practice. *Journal of the American Academy of Child and Adolescent Psychiatry* 2013; **52**(10):1101–15.

46. Lustig SL, Kia-Keating M, Knight WH, et al. Review of child and adolescent refugee mental health. *Journal of the American Academy of Child and Adolescent Psychiatry* 2004; **43**(1):24–36.

47. Garg P, Tinh M, Ha J, et al. Explaining culturally and linguistically diverse (CALD) parents' access of healthcare services for developmental surveillance and anticipatory guidance: Qualitative findings from the 'Watch Me Grow' study. *BMC Health Services Research* 2017; **17**(1):228.

48. Berry K, Haddock G. The implementation of the NICE guidelines for schizophrenia: Barriers to the implementation of psychological interventions and recommendations for the future. *Psychology and Psychotherapy* 2008; **81**(4):419–36.

49. Davey MP, Kissil K, Lynch L, et al. A cultural adapted family intervention for African American families coping with parental cancer: Outcomes of pilot study. *Psychooncology* 2013; **22**:1572–80.

50. Edge D, Degnan A, Cotterill S, et al. Culturally adapted family intervention (CaFI) for African-Caribbean people diagnosed with schizophrenia and their families: A mixed-methods feasibility study of development, implementation and acceptability. *Health Services and Delivery Research* 2018; **6**(32).

51. Chowdhary N, Jotheeswaran A, Nadkami A, et al. The methods and outcomes of cultural adaptations of psychological treatments for depressive disorders: A systematic review. *Psychological Medicine* 2013; **44**(6):1131–46.

52. Dumas JE, Arriaga X, Begle AM, Longoria Z. 'When will your program be available in Spanish?': Adapting an early parenting intervention for Latino families. *Cognitive Behavioral Practice* 2010; **17**(2):176–87.

53. Wolff T. Community psychology practice: Expanding the impact of psychology's work. *American Psychologist* 2014; **69**(8):803.

54. McKleroy K, Norton B, Kegler M, et al. Community-based interventions. *American Journal of Public Health* 2003; **93**(4):529–33.

55. Bucci S, Berry K, Barrowclough C, Haddock G. Family interventions in psychosis: A review of the evidence and barriers to implementation. *Australian Psychologist* 2016; **51**(1):62–8.

Chapter 7

Delivering Family-Based Interventions Using Phone-Assisted and Internet-Based Technology

Cristin M. Hall and Rebecca F. Bertuccio

Real-Life Challenges: Finding Solutions

The Jones family has a 16-year-old daughter who is severely depressed and frequently cuts herself. Yet the Jones family lives in a rural community where the nearest mental health clinic that serves children and youth is more than 50 miles away. They have difficulty with being able to afford transportation costs and finding sufficient childcare for their younger children to take their teenage daughter for treatment.

The Sanchez family needs parent training because of severe externalizing behaviour problems (e.g., hitting, biting and tantrums) for their four-year-old son. The Sanchezes do not have local providers that offer mental health services in Spanish, although they have been encouraged to 'make do' with the English-speaking service providers despite it being nearly impossible for them to communicate effectively in English on personal topics such as their family dynamics.

The Keenan family has been referred for counselling services after school personnel recommended them for their nine-year-old daughter, who is displaying separation anxiety that is interfering with her academic progress, but they hesitate to be seen at any psychiatric or mental health clinic in their town because they are afraid of what neighbours or other community members may think of their parenting or that there may be rumours about their daughter being 'crazy'.

The Miller family is having difficulty with finding care for their two children with autism spectrum disorder (ASD) because Mr Miller is an active-duty military service member and the family frequently move (on average, every two years). With every move, they are at the bottom of a six- to eight-month waiting list for services such as applied behaviour analysis (ABA) and respite care and must

complete yet another intake process and explain the histories of both children. They have experienced vast differences in the quality and availability of services in various locations.

Although all these families have seemingly different challenges, including diversity in their cultural identities, referral concerns (e.g., ASD, anxiety, depression, problematic behaviours) and needs (e.g., transportation, childcare, care continuity, concerns with stigma), all these families could potentially benefit from an emerging delivery model of care, specifically *telemental health* (TMH) services. TMH services can be conceptualized in several ways, and other terms may be used interchangeably, such as *eHealth*, *telemedicine*, and *telepsychiatry*; for the purposes of this chapter, the term TMH will be used, given that the term expansively may include parent training, individual and family therapy, medication monitoring, parent psycho-education and coaching and consultation between professionals.

Terms, Definitions and Overview

TMH includes the use of *synchronous communication*, where families and practitioners work together in real time using a video-chat interface over the Internet. There are other forms of 'virtual therapy', including cell phone text-based interventions [1], online text instant messaging interventions [2] and phone-assisted therapy [2], but given the burgeoning expansion of access to the Internet, the decrease in hardware costs, increases in relative security and a closer approximation to face-to-face interaction, online video-chat interfaces will primarily be discussed in this chapter. It is also important to consider how TMH sessions may be used, including the setting and how it is integrated (or not) with face-to-face services.

TMH services may be provided in *supervised* or *unsupervised* settings. Supervised settings are those which occur in a location where there are medical personnel, mental health professionals or other staff that can be with the client receiving services in person, such as at a regional telemedicine centre where the client still goes to an office to receive services while the telehealth provider is in another location. Unsupervised settings are those which include the client's home or other setting where no personnel are available who can assist in the event of an emergency. Both settings may be used, and considerations for safety and logistics (which will be discussed later in this chapter) in each setting are different. Sometimes, when thinking about TMH, it is assumed that TMH will be the only or primary modality of services. For rural or other remote populations, it is possible that their primary care will be received remotely using TMH. In other instances, however, TMH can be used as a supplemental intervention. For example, the Jones family (whose 16-year-old daughter is displaying self-harm behaviours) may have monthly in-person visits with their provider and then receive supplemental TMH services in the interim at their home. A hybrid arrangement such as the one just described may help to assuage the family's burden of transportation and childcare but also may allow for regular in-person visits in which the practitioner may more closely examine evidence of cutting and so forth.

Many practitioners, even those with years of clinical experience and who recognize the potential of TMH, are hesitant to actually use of TMH in their practices. Questions arise such as the following: Is it really just as good as in-person sessions? What if I have technical problems? How can I be sure that it is really safe for the families that I am serving? Are there legal or ethical concerns? How do I even start something like TMH, or why would I attempt to start a TMH practice?

We explore all these questions in this chapter. First, we present a discussion of the origins of TMH and the populations in which it appears to best serve. Practitioners will have a better understanding of how TMH may be useful in their practices and will gain a sense of basic technology and logistics considerations (e.g., network requirements, security and hardware). Second, a brief review of the research about TMH will be examined. Understanding the basic research findings and limitations of the evidence base may help to assuage concerns about whether or not TMH is helpful to families and may help individuals identify the kinds of referral issues for which TMH may be best indicated.

Third, ethical considerations such as privacy, informed consent, safety planning and backup considerations (e.g., use of telephone or other 'lower tech' solutions when connections are lost) will be discussed for TMH. Practitioners who have an understanding of the guidelines for TMH practice will be better prepared for providing safe and quality care to families. Finally, relationship building and rapport for TMH will be described in terms of how to overcome technology interface issues that may interrupt family-based practice and how technology-based interfaces may actually be more beneficial to families under certain circumstances. Despite fears surrounding how technology may thwart a positive therapeutic relationship, there is evidence to suggest that with some planning and careful attention, any challenges can be largely overcome [3].

History of TMH and Applications to Family-Based Interventions

The idea of providing services remotely is not new to the dawn of the Internet. Given that the need for mental health and medical services for populations that are transient, isolated or require specialist care has long been a concern, other ways of providing distance intervention have been used for many years. Some authors trace the very beginnings of remote service provision to the use of smoke signals many thousands of years ago to warn neighbouring villages of the spread of disease [4]. Beyond smoke signals, regional medical centres with helicopter transport, ambulatory services, travelling physicians and telephone consults between professionals were also used to some degree before the advent of video teleconferencing (VTC). We are greatly beyond the use of mail, telephone and facsimile sharing of records at this point. The use of regional telemedicine centres in which people use dedicated VTC systems before the wide-ranging availability of video streaming from cameras over the Internet was a major thrust for psychiatric and medical consultations for rural populations and emergency and disaster responses for decades [5].

'Tele' methods of providing services and consultations between professionals are one way to think about how the Internet has changed the landscape of mental health services, yet there are other implications that are important to consider. Many professionals rely on the Internet as an invaluable resource to find information quickly and at low to no cost. In addition, many parents of children with special needs or mental health problems, as well as adults with medical and mental health needs of their own, have turned to the Internet to both find information and share their experiences [6]. Though professionals are grateful for their access to information, many who work in allied mental health fields and education have reservations about the information that parents and other stakeholders are finding online in terms of its accuracy and relative quality [7]. Despite concerns related to online information seeking and support, it cannot be excluded as an important facet of how the Internet has broken down some important barriers that once required access to a library, interactions with friends and family or reliance on information received directly from professionals. Access to the Internet has levelled the playing field (e.g., decreased stigma, provided more reach for large advocacy organizations such as Autism Speaks) but has also muddied the waters in the case of misinformation being shared and accessed (e.g., 'anti-vaxxer' movements in ASD, alternative therapies with limited or no empirical support offered for fees). Furthermore, the Internet is a double-edged sword of sorts. With the aid of the Internet, nations of people now have access to various networks of support, communities of practice and expertise, scholarly resources, expert consultation services and other services in ways that were once unimaginable, but an abundance of information and resources exist on the Internet that must be consumed cautiously because they may miscommunicate information or advertise false claims.

TMH services were likely never envisioned to supplant or suppress face-to-face service delivery (at least not intentionally), and it is unlikely that TMH models will ever do so. Countries such as the United States have unique challenges related to providing TMH. Specifically, licensing and credentialing requirements are under the purview of individual states, which makes interstate practice difficult in some circumstances without violating regulations. New policies are underway to try to grant reciprocity in credentials across states for TMH services, yet it is unclear when the licensing barrier will be resolved. Further, in the United States, private insurance companies (e.g., Highmark®, Aetna®) make decisions about when, and if, they will pay for telephone or internet-delivered services, and therefore, individuals who seek TMH services may have to pay out-of-pocket, making

them, potentially, prohibitively expensive. Given the ongoing policy and payment challenges in the United States, it is difficult to imagine how, in this context, TMH would ever take the place of in-person services, nor should it.

Responsible use of TMH practices, however, implies using the 'right tool for the right job'. For families that are struggling with geographic isolation, frequent moves or limited service availability, TMH may be the best alternative to no treatment at all for the family or child [8]. For situations in which specialist intervention is required for disorders that necessitate more specific or sophisticated treatment, such as eating disorders, TMH may connect general practitioners with specialists, or specialists may provide needed specific treatment remotely [9]. In general, the most promising practices in TMH have not included novel developments of treatment models but rather adapted evidence-based models of intervention (i.e., validated in face-to-face service provision trials) to virtual delivery mechanisms such as TMH.

Evidence Base for TMH Practice

TMH practice for family and individual therapeutic services has been studied in many trials over the last 15 years [10]. Although some of the studies are less rigorous in their methodological design [11, 12] given the exploratory and pilot nature of the research as it has emerged, there has been an increase in randomized trials of TMH services, and the results have been promising [13]. Comer and Myers [14, p. 297] recently posed the insight that 'the question should not be simply *whether* telemental health strategies are supported, but rather *when, under what circumstances*, and *for whom* telemental health formats may be most indicated'. In general, it seems that providing support using the Internet is superior to no-treatment conditions and comparable to (and sometimes more ecologically valid than) clinic-based treatment [14].

Although an exhaustive review of TMH and its related interventions (e.g., online parent psychoeducation, text-supported interventions and prevention programmes) is beyond the scope of this chapter, a brief review of the state of evidence will be considered. Several systematic reviews have been published over the last decade that support promising results of family-based TMH, yet all have indicated that larger-scale and more rigorous trials are needed to advance the field. More rigorous findings related to the effectiveness of TMH have been largely gleaned from the literature on TMH applications for adult mental disorders [13]. As an overview of the current findings about family-based TMH, Goldstein and Myers [13] found in their review that there were four randomized trials to date with children and adolescents, including studies of attention deficit hyperactivity disorder (ADHD), depression, parent skills training and externalizing behavioural disorders. In all four of these studies, Goldstein and Myers [13] reported that findings were positive, and the use of TMH was shown to be effective.

The American Telemedicine Association (ATA) conducted a large-scale review of findings related to all TMH services that included various populations of interest and service models, such as geriatrics, incarcerated persons and marital and family therapies, and also included diagnostics, medication prescription and management, as well as therapeutic interventions (e.g., talk therapies, parent training) [15]. In the review, the ATA coded studies based on a rating system of video application quality and clinical confidence recommendations. Although this review is becoming somewhat dated, notable findings include that rapport with and adjustment to the TMH interface are swift and comparable to the level of personal interaction in in-person settings. Interestingly, the ATA also learned that some clients found that the TMH interface actually better facilitated the therapeutic process by providing a level of privacy and remoteness that made participation in services more comfortable, specifically for post-traumatic stress, eating disorders and agoraphobia.

Specific to services geared towards children and adolescents, the review also found that TMH had been successful in a variety of settings and with various populations. The Telemental Health Standards and Guidelines Working Group reported that TMH for children and adolescents has demonstrated effectiveness with health centres, physicians' offices, schools, day care and private practice [15]. Findings for persons who are members of minority populations, including Indigenous peoples, have also been effectively served using TMH. More recently published studies seem to be consistent with the previous report indicating that TMH can be used successfully to treat adolescent anxiety [16] and ADHD [17] and children with obsessive-compulsive disorder (OCD)[18].

Promising findings indicating efficacy at ameliorating symptoms does not seem to negate continued concerns about safety of the delivery of TMH services

in settings such as homes. For example, some practitioners still wonder if they will be able to adequately ensure confidentiality of the services they provide over the Internet or manage lethality risk (e.g., violence, suicidal ideation) when at a distance from those they serve. In their review of nine studies of safety for TMH being delivered in unsupervised settings, Luxon and Mishkind [19] found that safety was adequately addressed. Findings from the review indicated that two-thirds of the published studies did explicitly address safety planning and took steps to prevent and anticipate such instances occurring [19]. It is reassuring to note that of the studies that were reviewed, only two groups of researchers had to implement their safety plans in emergency situations, which were quickly resolved. Procedures and guidelines regarding safety planning and prevention in both supervised and unsupervised settings will be reviewed in the section covering ethical guidelines and recommendations.

The use of TMH does not have to necessarily require practitioners to reinvent the proverbial wheel. Best practices in your area of expertise, including the use of evidence-based interventions, should always be the standard to have the best chance at success in using TMH. Essentially, TMH practices are slightly adapted versions of the operations and interventions that are typically conducted in person. The adaptation of previously validated interventions, PCIT, Applied Behaviour Analysis, the Early Start Denver Model, and the Family Check-Up such as parent-child interaction therapy (PCIT), for example, has been studied in several trials. The interested reader should review the article by Comer et al. [20] in which they detail the steps taken to adapt their clinic-based intervention model for PCIT for online delivery. Adaptations of applied behaviour analysis for autism [21], the early-start Denver model [22] and the family check-up [23] have all been studied for use with TMH interfaces. The study and development of Internet-delivered versions of face-to-face best practices constitute the continued movement in the field at large but still could benefit from larger-scale study.

Ethical Practice of TMH

As with any form of mental health service provision (regardless of the mode of transmission), practitioners should be concerned with providing all services in accordance with best practices and the highest ethical standards to avoid iatrogenic effects. Although most researchers who publish in the field of TMH mention that the same standards as typically followed in face-to-face practice should be followed, such as the ethical standards set forth by the Declaration of Helsinki and professional regulatory bodies (e.g., state or national boards of medicine or psychology), additional standards that are specifically tailored to telepractice have been created to help guide this burgeoning field. Examples of standards for telepractice that will be reviewed here include those from both the American Psychiatric Association (APA) and the ATA [24], the Joint Task Force for the Development of Telepsychology Guidelines for Psychologists [25], [26]. Readers are encouraged to review these guidelines independently after reading the overview presented in this chapter and to think of them as an 'overlay' of guidelines superimposed over and above other ethical and legal guidelines to which they would adhere in face-to-face service provision.

When comparing the face-to-face and telepractice sets of standards, common areas that are addressed are confidentiality, informed consent, clear delineation of roles and responsibilities, regulatory issues (e.g., compliance with regulations across state lines, if applicable) and safety planning. Guidance provided by the ATA includes a blueprint for how TMH services should be appropriately established; in other words, there are important recommendations and information regarding the best way to start a telepractice, including technological and administrative considerations. Specifically, the ATA sets forth the idea that telepractice should only be started after a needs assessment is conducted for an agency or group, including specification of the programme scope, services to be given, information about the population to be served, technology and staffing needs, safety plans, training needs for personnel and an evaluation and sustainability plan [26]. TMH therefore should never be conducted without a careful consideration of the *who, what, when, where, why* and *how* of the programme before it is established. Practitioners and agencies would do best in terms of efficiency, effectiveness and safety of their TMH practice if they are clear on the goals and intentions for that practice before considering launching such a programme.

Both the APA and the ATA are clear that considering the legal and regulatory realities of TMH is absolutely necessary [24]. In particular, practitioners of TMH need to adequately address the following:

- Am I appropriately credentialed in the location in which I practice and the locations where I reach clients?
- Is it permissible for me to provide these services both where I am and to the location that I am delivering?

Issues related to the legality and acceptability of TMH practice are strongly associated with challenges that include insurance company reimbursement for services. Although this is not directly related to *whether or not* services are lawful, it does relate to business practices that may make such services billable and sustainable.

The APA and ATA are both candid about practising within the scope of one's competence [24]. Practitioners who hesitate to use computer interfaces for TMH services or who have reservations about TMH in general are most likely wise in their discretion. Having the appropriate clinical training to work with clients and families in person is not necessarily sufficient for delivering TMH. Practitioners who deliver TMH are strongly encouraged to participate in continuing education and professional development that is specific to considerations of ethical and effective TMH service provision in order to facilitate preparedness in the discipline of TMH. Readers are encouraged to visit the American Telemedicine Association Learning Center (http://learn.americantelemed.org/diweb/start) to access online learning materials to better understand the nuances of TMH. Necessary but not sufficient TMH training includes content related to appropriate documentation, informed consent, technology basics, ethical considerations, safety planning and rapport building.

Many practitioners are aware that the Internet is less than secure. Data are being stored with every click that a person uses on social media, search engines, online shopping sites and other on-screen applications, thus making mental health professionals understandably wary of conducting something as sensitive and personal as family-based services over the Internet. Both sets of guidelines for the APA and the ATA are direct in that it is the responsibility of the mental health practitioner to have a working knowledge of and take steps to provide adequate security when delivering TMH. Security includes encryption of the video streaming (so that online eavesdropping is unlikely) as well as adequate data encryption, storage and disposal in the event of giving assessments, documentation of session notes, arranging appointments, storing information about the client and other safety-related considerations. Using an interface that is commercially available, such as Skype® or Zoom®, is not adequate or appropriate for conducting TMH.

In the United States, the Health Insurance Portability and Accountability Act of 1996 (HIPAA) is the guiding policy standard for the sharing, storage and disposal of protected health information for both medicine and mental health services [27]. HIPAA-compliant online telemedicine interfaces are available that include online appointment scheduling, secure video streaming and secure document sharing (e.g., Chiron Health). HIPAA-compliant data storage for electronic progress notes is also available. In any setting, be sure that whatever interfaces you use for transmission or storage of data are compliant with safety and encryption standards for your location. Some of these technologies offer services from laptop computers as well as mobile devices such as tablets or smartphones, which may make access easier. It is not necessary for every TMH practitioner to be a computer programmer, but it is necessary that they understand whether or not the technology they select is adequate to fulfil privacy and security standards for their jurisdiction.

Informed consent is not a new standard for mental health services, but both the APA and the ATA outline special considerations for obtaining informed consent from persons seeking TMH services [24]. There are two aspects to think about when ensuring informed consent for TMH, including (1) laws regarding verbal and written consent and (2) potential clients fully understanding the risks of participation in TMH. First, if you are conducting TMH in an unsupervised setting and you have not received electronic signatures for informed consent, you may be tempted to simply read through an informed consent document and gain verbal consent from clients while on the video-chat interface. While verbal consent may be lawful and permissible in some circumstances and in some jurisdictions, it is not universally accepted. Be sure that you are aware of whether or not verbal consent is sufficient before you use it as a method. There are electronic document-signing applications, such as DocuSign, that may be able to assist with written forms of consent, but even electronic signatures may or may not be permissible given the law in your location. Second, it is important that you outline all the potential risks (and steps you have taken to

Table 7.1 Required and Verified Information for all TMH Sessions

1. Name and credentials of the provider and the name of the patient

2. The location(s) of the patient during the session

3. Immediate contact information for both the provider and the patient (phone, text message or email) and contact information for all relevant support people, both professional and family

4. Expectations about contact between sessions should be discussed and verified with the patient, including a discussion of emergency management between sessions.

Source: Adapted from *Best Practices in Videoconferencing-Based Telemental Health* (April 2018). American Psychiatric Association. American Telemedicine Association.

minimize them through technology or other means) for participating in TMH. Each client should understand that their information and conversations may not be guaranteed to be private. Mental health professionals also need to be mindful of the cognitive ability, cultural considerations, fluency and familiarity with technology and other individual family factors that may impede obtaining true informed consent.

Emergencies, unfortunately, are not uncommon in providing mental health services (in person or remotely delivered), and therefore, the ATA specifically outlines ways to best safeguard clients in the event of emergencies during TMH. An old saying suggests that 'an ounce of prevention is worth a pound of cure', and this adage is especially relevant to safety considerations in TMH. Before beginning any TMH session, the ATA states that certain information must be recorded (see Table 7.1). The ATA further notes that at the outset of a session, all persons present should be identified to all others.

Emergency management may depend on the setting of the TMH session. In supervised settings, the ATA recommends that emergency protocols be established such that all staff are aware of their role in managing emergencies and how to manage after-hours emergency situations. In clinically unsupervised settings (e.g., the patient's home or other non-clinical setting), providers are directed to know about emergency services in the immediate area where the person is receiving services and be prepared to contact the client's local police, emergency room or crisis teams. Information about local resources should be at the ready for the professional at the outset of each session. The ATA also recommends the designation of a *patient support person* (PSP) who may be a family member, friend or community member chosen by the client who can be with the client in the event of an emergency and can assist. Providers should have the information for the PSP in case that individual needs to be called on in an emergency.

The APA and ATA guidelines also reference considerations relevant to rapport, boundaries and cultural competence [24]; these topics will be discussed in relation to the following section on TMH and relationship building. Overall, as mental health professionals consider the use of TMH after having reviewed the summary on some of the special legal and ethical considerations, it may seem too daunting to attempt TMH. However, given the ways in which TMH may support access to much-needed services to those who are otherwise left without professional intervention, it is worth considering engaging in professional development to be able to provide TMH services, even as a supplemental service. Practitioners are encouraged to remember that conducting TMH does not require a law degree or a background in computer engineering, in addition to being a skilled clinician; it simply requires a new 'out of the box' way of thinking about logistics, ethics, regulations and technology to be able to add to the cache of skills already at your disposal.

TMH and Relationship Building

Despite concerns about whether or not good therapeutic relationships can be developed in the context of TMH, it seems that there is evidence that supports that it is comparable to therapeutic alliances with face-to-face services for adult, child and adolescent and family-oriented services [10]. Clinicians may ask such questions as 'How can video-chat be the same if it is difficult to hear or see their face(s)?' Although it is arguably not 'the same' as in-person services, TMH can be comparable in terms of the perceptions that the client has regarding the bond of trust their may have with the clinician [9]. In addition, sometimes in-home TMH provides a level of ecological validity and a window into the real worlds of clients that are not possible in clinic-based intervention. Being able to see the toys, bedrooms, living rooms and overall experiences of families where they eat, sleep and live is critical and only replaceable with home visiting, which can be prohibitively expensive. Furthermore, being able to

Table 7.2 Technology Checklist for Clinicians and Families

1. A computing device in the therapist's office (tablet, desktop/laptop computer)

2. A computing device in the family/client's home (tablet, desktop/laptop computer)

3. Webcam, microphone at both sites (may be built into the computing device or be separate pieces of equipment)

4. Web-conferencing application to allow for logging in from anywhere (both therapist and family/client) with sufficient encryption and security standards

provide services related to referral issues, such as parent training and managing problematic child behaviours or tantrums, sometimes works very well in TMH, given that the clinician can coach the parent right in their own home [20]. This section covers the technological, logistical and clinical microskills integration necessary for developing TMH skills.

Adequate audio and camera quality go hand-in-hand with both the software interface you are using (e.g., Chiron Health or other streaming service) and the bandwidth of the internet connection. All these factors related to the hardware, software and transmission capability will have a direct effect on the degree to which you can establish rapport (if TMH is not acting as a supplement to face-to-face sessions) and maintain the flow within sessions. Several researchers and experts in the field have recommended various standards for getting the best out of your TMH sessions [20]. See Table 7.2 for an example of a technology checklist for a starting place for setup.

There are advantages to current computing devices that have built-in cameras and microphones, but built-in audio and visual devices may impede the quality of video and sound transmission. Ultimately, it depends on the purpose of the intervention and interaction. If the intervention includes PCIT or other interventions where parents and children interact and need feedback from the clinician in real time, the use of a computer or tablet camera may limit the viewing field for the clinician; in this kind of scenario, cameras and microphones that are separate from the device being used for the TMH services may be a better fit because they can be placed more strategically for the purposes of the intervention. However, if the therapy is largely 'sit and talk', where the client(s) can simply sit in front of a screen, a built-in camera and microphone may be sufficient.

Sometimes clinicians and families may find that they have difficulty with transmission of video in the form of video or audio delays, being disconnected, not being able to adequately see or hear and other disruptions. In these cases, there may be several explanations for the problem, and they will certainly interfere with the clinician's ability to connect meaningfully with the family as they troubleshoot the technology. Problems may include insufficient bandwidth in the internet connection to support the video streaming, slow processing on the computing device or other challenges. It is important for clinicians to practise using their interface with test persons who use different devices in various locations to have a sense of what might work best when actually working with families. In the event that problems arise during practice sessions, having adequate technical assistance at the ready (either by phone, in person or online) to try to fix any problems or professional advice on how to prevent and correct such problems is critical to deal with in advance.

In addition to practising using the technology with test persons, even proficient TMH providers will conduct a trial run with each family or client before starting any interviews, therapy or assessments. It is important for clinicians to think about doing the following:

- Create a 'how-to' sheet that explains how-to log onto or access the video-streaming interface. The how-to sheet should include screen shots, simple written instructions and the clinician's phone number in case clients or families need to be talked through the procedure the first time.
- Use the telephone as a backup plan. If the connection is lost in a session or as clients or families are beginning their initial session, being able to speak with the clinician as they set up will aid continuity or clarify if transmission is lost.
- During the trial run with a client or family, it is critical that practitioners
  - Check that the client/family feels comfortable using the interface,
  - Answer any questions about how the interface works,
  - Understand and practise appropriate security and encryption procedures,
  - Be able to see or hear adequately,
  - Have the necessary phone numbers they need for backup,
  - Have a plan in place in case a connection is lost,
  - Understand how scheduling and between-session contact will be handled, and

- Ensure that they have adequate privacy in their home to complete sessions.

Rapport building with families in many ways is the same online as it is in person. Use of microskills [28], including verbal and nonverbal behaviours that show that you are listening and are open with your clients, can still be done on an online interface. Similar to the way in which beginning practitioners learn how to intentionally listen with their whole body, when embarking on TMH endeavours, special attention must be given to your own facial expressions, body posture and use of words (and silence) as ways to convey that you understand the experience of the person(s) on the screen in front of you. Examining and paying attention to the affect of clients, including their facial expressions, tone, volume and pacing of speech, body language and the correspondence between their face, body, and words is possible in online interactions as well. Although listening (especially in a video-streaming context) is still largely the same skill set as it is in person, there are some considerations related to the addition of the technological 'wall' that should be managed. Sometimes simply 'naming' the strangeness of the technology addition can be helpful. Asking questions such as the following can help to investigate how the client is feeling about the interface to assist with normalizing any discomfort: 'How much experience do you have with using video-chat like this? How does it feel to be talking about personal topics with me while on a computer/phone/tablet?' Following up with reflections about feelings and explaining some of the differences from face-to-face interactions may help as well. For instance, replying with, 'Yes, I can understand that maybe it feels a bit strange. You may notice that our eye contact does not match up the same way as in person. I am looking at your face on the screen. Feel free to stop me if the picture or audio quality is making it hard for us to talk.'

Comfort with Technology. People will largely vary in their level of comfort with using technology, and assumptions must not be made based on a client's age, ethnicity or cultural background regarding the degree of comfort that he or she may feel. It may be easy to assume that older individuals, those that live in poverty or those with less formal education may be less comfortable with technology interfaces, yet this is not necessarily true. Given the ranging levels of engagement with technology in everyday personal life and professional settings, it is difficult to know which families or clients may be uneasy with talking over a video-chat interface. This is why it is critical to conduct a trial run of sessions, provide written information and offer a phone number as a backup plan. Furthermore, it is important to simply investigate (with kindness) the degree of comfort that a family or client may have. Clinicians would do well to address the topic of comfort with TMH at the beginning of the professional relationship by saying something such as, 'Not everyone feels very comfortable with using technology. How do you feel about using the computer/online system to receive mental health services?' It is important then to follow up with clients, equipped with strategies and supports in place to help increase comfort, in case they are needed. Providing additional practice sessions, deciding to hold a session in person to get to know one another first (if possible) or staying on the phone at the beginning of all sessions until the client is more comfortable may help. Remember that the discomfort may not simply be about 'clicking' the right parts of the screen; it may also be related to seeing oneself on camera, fears about security or other issues that may be discussed to build trust.

Minimizing Distractions. If TMH services are being provided in a person's home rather than at a regional centre or office, distractions are bound to be a concern [29]. Neighbours visiting, phone calls or text messages, children in the home needing help or pets can all wreak havoc on a session provided via TMH. In order to support the best possible relationship between a practitioner and a client or family, preparing for and eliminating (as much as possible) these potential interruptions are important. Clinicians are encouraged to include instructions or helpful tips to families at the outset of TMH that include the following:

- Post 'Do Not Disturb' signs on the front door of the home or videoconferencing location and the door of the room in which the session is occurring.
- Turn off (or turn to vibrate or airplane mode) cell phones before the session.
- Provide snacks, a video to watch, an activity or even a family member or friend to play with the children in the home during sessions.
- If children are to participate in the sessions, ensure that they have a chance to become familiar with the interface, are fed and rested, have used the bathroom and are ready to participate before the session.

Visual Field. When summarizing the checklist of technology needs, some aspects of the visual field were considered in terms of how well the clinician may see the family or client. Although the visual field from the practitioner to the family is important, be thoughtful about the visual field from your office to the client or family. Your space should be professional, tidy and in line with how you would typically see a person in a clinic or professional office. Your dress and demeanour should be consistent with your in-person practice as well to maintain appropriate boundaries and to demonstrate that while you may be providing services from your home and clients are not coming to your office, you are still a well-trained professional who can help. As part of setting up your initial practice in TMH, you should critically look at what clients can see from their vantage point and consider whether it is consistent with the image you would portray in a face-to-face interaction. Lighting, wall hangings, decor and ambient noise (e.g., air conditioner, traffic, other people) should all be considered before beginning your TMH practice.

Eye Gaze. When a person sits in front of you in a room, eye contact is easy to maintain and observe. In video interfaces, it can be more challenging to make eye contact and interpret a lack of eye contact. Specifically, when practitioners and families use cameras that are built into their computing device, sometimes the angle of the camera makes it such that the receiver of the video sees that the person appears to be looking in a slightly different direction. This may be because it is difficult, if not impractical, for the person to gaze into the camera, giving the illusion of looking at the receiver. Sometimes when people are using a video interface, they are also distracted by seeing the simultaneous image of their own face on the screen and tend to look at themselves rather than at the clinician or camera. In these instances, it is important not to 'over-interpret' a seeming lack of eye contact because it may be an artefact of the interface setup. During a practice session, it would be helpful for a clinician to normalize any challenges with eye gaze and simply say something such as, 'With the way the cameras are working, it looks as if we aren't looking directly at each other, which may seem awkward. I am looking at your image on the screen as you speak rather than the camera. Let me know if that ever feels strange for you.'

Voice Inflection and Pacing. It is not uncommon for it to take some time for people to acclimate to the flow of the online interface in conversation. Clients and families who have used such tools as Facetime or Skype® to talk to family and friends may be more comfortable and familiar with what the experience is like and will likely need less support and orientation. For families or clients who have not communicated in this way, or if there are other challenges that make pacing awkward, reassurance and guidance from clinicians may be helpful. For example, a clinician may say, 'It seems that we have a little bit of a delay/feedback noise here that's distracting. Let's see if we can get that to settle a bit.' Also, your voice inflection may be more difficult to discern over a computer, and clients may have to speak more loudly or clearly if audio quality is compromised. Remember to sort through what issues of pacing or tone of voice are related to perhaps the therapeutic interaction and what is related to the technology. A check-in such as 'You sound a little quiet today. Is that the connection, or are you feeling down?' can be useful.

Checking In. In the discussion of rapport building and other issues, we have frequently used the check-in for understanding as a way to cope with or overcome the technology 'wall'. Checking in is a critical skill in face-to-face interactions but is perhaps even more important in technology-based delivery. Just as message and meaning can be lost in written communication, video streaming is not without its problems, as we have outlined. It cannot be overstated how important it is for you, as the clinician, to help establish and maintain trust by being comfortable, prepared to use the technology and frequently seeing how the people you serve are understanding, interacting and feeling. Check-ins can be related to the quality of the interaction from a technology standpoint or in terms of trust and therapeutic alliance. Crum and Comer [29] have recommended the use of a more formal metric of alliance, such as the Working Alliance Inventory [30] or other measures to periodically see how trust and alliance are established or maintained throughout family-based TMH. If it is challenging at all to tell how the relationship is going in TMH services, verbal and more formalized measures can help you to navigate a course correction if needed.

Getting Creative with Engagement. If you are inclined to be creative in your interactions, especially with children, there are many ways to leverage the computer interface to add elements of play and fun into your practice. Comer et al. [18] described how they used free applications such as Google Drawing so that children participating in a TMH intervention for OCD could drag, click and interact with the screen as a way to practise various skills that were taught in the intervention. Not all clinicians feel equipped to take on the addition of interactive games, yet if you are interested in adding more elements with which the client is able to engage in a more active way, it could be a helpful addition to your TMH practice.

Concluding Remarks

In sum, TMH services are an instrumental alternative or supplement for those who may have limited access, logistical or geographical constraints or personal reservations related to in-person mental health supports. In light of the novel coronavirus in 2020, the use of TMH has become a necessity for many practitioners and their clients, perhaps forever changing the landscape of service provision. For many clients or families facing such issues, TMH services may be the solution, given the ease with which it can reach clients and approximate in-person services. In fact, there is evidence to suggest that there is significant promise in TMH practice with individuals from a wide range of backgrounds, ages and developmental levels – no matter the medium through which it is delivered. Though there are several ethical, legal and relationship-building considerations that must be addressed prior to delving into the TMH discipline, many guidelines, standards and protocols are available that may help to settle any concerns or hesitations that new TMH practitioners may have, many of which are included in this chapter. To make a lasting contribution to the field and to help meet individuals' needs on a more widespread level, practitioners are encouraged to adapt, share and deliver their unique areas of expertise through a TMH model.

References

1. Hall AK, Cole-Lewis H, Berhnardt JM. Mobile text messaging for health: A systematic review of reviews. *Annual Review of Public Health* 2015; **36**:393–415.

2. Elleven RK, Allen J. Applying technology to online counseling: Suggestions for the beginning e-therapist. *Journal of Instructional Psychology* 2004; **31**:223–7.

3. Sucala M, Schnur JB, Constantino MJ, et al. The therapeutic relationship in e-therapy for mental health: A systematic review. *Journal of Medical Internet Research* 2012; **14**:1–13.

4. Waller M, Stotler C. Telemedicine: A primer. *Current Allergy and Asthma Reports* 2018; **18**(10):1–9.

5. Xiong W, Bair A, Sandrock C, et al. Implementing telemedicine in medical emergency response: Concept of operation for a regional telemedicine hub. *Journal of Medical Systems* 2012; **36**:1651–60.

6. Hall CM, Culler ED, Frank-Webb A. Online dissemination of resources and services for parents of children with autism spectrum disorders (ASDs): A systematic review of evidence. *Review Journal of Autism and Developmental Disorders* 2016; **3**:273–85.

7. Christensen H, Griffiths K. The internet and mental health literacy. *Australian and New Zealand Journal of Psychiatry* 2000; **34**:975–9.

8. Adams SM, Rice MJ, Jones SL, et al. Telemental health: Standards, reimbursement, and interstate practice. *Journal of the American Psychiatric Nurses Association* 2018; **24**:295–305.

9. Grady B, Myers KM, Nelson E, et al. Evidence-based practice for telemental health. *Telemedicine and e-Health* 2011; **17**:131–48.

10. Hilty DM, Ferrer DC, Parish MB, et al. The effectiveness of telemental health: A 2013 review. *Telemedicine and e-Health* 2013; **19**:444–54.

11. Hall CM, Bierman KL. Technology-assisted interventions for parents of young children: Emerging practices, current research, and future directions. *Early Childhood Research Quarterly* 2015; **33**:21–32.

12. Gros DF, Morland LA, Green CJ, et al. Delivery of evidence-based psychotherapy via video telehealth. *Journal of Psychopathology and Behavioral Assessment* 2013; **35**:506–21.

13. Goldstein F, Myers K. Telemental health: A new collaboration for pediatricians and child psychiatrists. *Pediatric Annals* 2014; **43**:79–84.

14. Comer JS, Myers K. Future directions in the use of telemental health to improve the accessibility and quality of children's mental health services. *Journal of Child and Adolescent Psychopharmacology* 2016; **26**:296–300.

15. Telemental Health Standards and Guidelines Working Group. Evidence-based practice for telemental health. *Telemedicine and e-Health* 2011; **17**:131–48.

16. Carpenter AL, Pincus DB, Furr JM, et al. Working from home: An initial pilot examination of videoconferencing-based cognitive behavioral therapy for anxious youth delivered to the home setting. *Behavior Therapy* 2018; **49**:917–30.

17. Sibley MH, Comer JS, Gonzalez J. Delivering parent-teen therapy for ADH through videoconferencing: A preliminary investigation. *Journal of Psychopathology and Behavioral Assessment* 2017; **39**:467–85.

18. Comer JS, Furr JM, Kerns CE, et al. Internet-delivered, family-based treatment for early-onset OCD: A pilot randomized trial. *Journal of Consulting and Clinical Psychology* 2017; **85**:909–17.

19. Luxton DD, Sirotin AP, Mishkind MC. Safety of telemental healthcare delivered to clinically unsupervised settings: A systematic review. *Telemedicine and e-Health* 2010; **16**:705–11.

20. Comer JS, Furr JM, Cooper-Vince C, et al. Rational and considerations for the internet-based delivery of parent-child interaction therapy. *Cognitive and Behavioral Practice* 2015; **22**:302–16.

21. Lindgren S, Wacker D, Suess A, et al. Telehealth and autism: Treating challenging behavior at lower cost. *Pediatrics* 2016; **137**:S167–75.

22. Vismara LA, McCormick CEB, Wagner AL, et al. Telehealth parent training in the early start Denver model: Results from a randomized controlled study. *Focus on Autism and Other Developmental Disabilities* 2016; **33**:67–79.

23. Hall CM. Parent consultation and transitional care for military families of children with autism: A teleconsultation implementation project. *Journal of Educational and Psychological Consultation* 2018; **28**:368–81.

24. American Psychiatric Association and American Telemedicine Association. *Best Practices in Videoconferencing-Based Telemental Health.* Washington, DC: American Psychiatric Association, 2018, pp. 1–10.

25. Joint Task Force for the Development of Telepsychology Guidelines for Psychologists. Guidelines for the practice of telepsychology. *American Psychologist* 2013; **68**:791–800.

26. American Telemedicine Association. *Core Operational Guidelines for Telehealth Services Involving Provider-Patient Interaction.* Washington, DC: American Telemedicine Association, 2014, pp. 1–14.

27. Health Insurance Portability and Accountability Act of 1996, Public Law No. 104–191, §110 Stat. 1936.

28. Ivey AE, Ivey MB, Zalaquett CP. *Intentional Interviewing and Counseling: Facilitating Client Development in a Multicultural Society*, 8th ed. Boston: Cengage Learning, 2014.

29. Crum KI, Comer JS. Using synchronous videoconferencing to deliver family-based mental health scare. *Journal of Child and Adolescent Psychopharmacology* 2016; **26**:229–34.

30. Horvath AO, Greenberg LS. Development and validation of the Working Alliance Inventory. *Journal of Counseling Psychology* 1989; **36**:223–33.

A Family-Based Approach to the Treatment of Youth Depression

Martha C. Tompson, Caroline Swetlitz and Joan R. Asarnow

Depression during childhood and adolescence has a powerful negative impact on youth development and adjustment [1]. Depression in youth impairs social adjustment and overall functioning, has high chronicity and recurrence and results in considerable personal and overall societal costs [2–5]. Youth depression manifests in a highly interpersonal context, fuelled by and contributing to interpersonal stress. Negative interpersonal transactions increase the risk for depressive symptomology and powerfully and negatively impact interpersonal transactions, leading to a vicious cycle of stress and symptoms [6]. Within this framework, treatments for depression must address the interpersonal context – one in which families play a central role. In this chapter, we have five objectives. First, we provide a conceptual model for understanding the role of families in the development and maintenance of depressive disorders in youth, emphasizing the ways that family involvement in treatment has the potential to reduce symptoms and risk of relapse. Second, we provide a concise outline of family-based interventions to be implemented in such a model. Third, using case descriptions, we illustrate case formulation within this model. Fourth, we describe core competencies required of clinicians in implementing such a family-based approach to youth depression. Finally, we describe common challenges in the implementation of family-focused treatment for childhood depression (FFT-CD) and strategies for addressing these challenges. Throughout this discussion, we highlight the critical role of developmental factors that may bear on the applicability and structure of family-focused treatment models for preadolescent and adolescent youth.

Conceptual Model Underlying FFT-CD

A number of theoretical models have influenced the development of FFT-CD, including vulnerability-stress models [7], interpersonal theories [8, 9] and cognitive behavioural approaches [10]. These models,

along with studies of both family processes in middle childhood through adolescence [11, 12] and factors impacting the emergence of youth depression [13], have contributed to FFT-CD. The FFT-CD model was developed specifically for youth during middle childhood and into emerging adolescence, considering both the stress context and particular developmental characteristics.

Stress Context

Through a vulnerability-stress lens, depression in youth is viewed as a biopsychosocial phenomenon. Biological (e.g., genetic factors) and environmental vulnerabilities (e.g., poverty, early loss experiences) contribute to the risk and onset of depression, and both vulnerability and stress are acted upon and shaped by negative cognitive processes and environmental stressors to contribute to depression course and outcome. Parental depression, a significant risk factor for youth depression, represents both a potential genetic and environmental vulnerability [14], and depressive episodes in parents and children may be linked, with depression in one triggering depression in the other [15]. Attributes of the child, including difficult temperament, presence of early emerging forms of psychopathology (e.g., anxiety, attention deficit hyperactivity disorder) and cognitive differences (e.g., learning disorders and autism spectrum disorder), may share underlying vulnerabilities with depression but also may contribute to ongoing personal and interpersonal stress throughout childhood and beyond. Through an interpersonal lens, symptoms and stress interact in a bidirectional fashion. The emergence of depressive symptoms, including, in particular, irritability, anhedonia and social withdrawal, contributes to further interpersonal stress; this stress further fuels a downward spiral of intensifying symptoms and stress [16]. Given the central role of families during middle childhood and early adolescence, they may be particularly likely to be swept up in these negative interpersonal processes. Through a cognitive behavioural lens, this accelerating downward spiral contributes to increasingly negative thoughts and perceptions of the self and the world and reduces engagement in potentially pleasurable activities and positive interpersonal interactions. Thus, depressive symptoms become maintained by an environment to which the symptoms contribute, and so on.

FFT-CD was specifically designed to work with families to reduce the downward spiral of depressive symptoms and interpersonal transactions and to build and enhance 'upward spirals' of positive, supportive feelings and behaviours [17]. Through this process, parents and children are provided with support and skills for addressing the negative interactions associated with depression and for building emotion regulation processes within a family context. FFT-CD integrates psycho-education, relationship enhancement, communication skills and problem-solving specifically focused on increasing adaptive and decreasing maladaptive interactional processes.

Developmental Adaptation

In considering the developmental needs of youth and the importance of attending to both the durability and generalization of change across settings, we incorporated four primary features. First, recognizing that youth during the middle and late childhood and early adolescent periods may be reticent to discuss problems, we introduced interventions gradually. Using handouts, we review concepts, provide hypothetical examples and only then apply these to actual family/interpersonal situations. For example, in teaching communication, we start with listening to non-emotional topics (e.g., instructions for a particular activity), move to emotional topics about another child's experience (e.g., how another child feels when failing a test or having a nice surprise) and finally address the child's own emotional experience (e.g., a specific positive or negative event).

Second, family tools/strategies are often presented initially as games played within family sessions. For example, we use a communication training exercise where one family member draws a written prompt from an envelope and the other practices active listening. The prompt may be 'describe how to make a peanut butter and jelly sandwich'. As one member describes, in some detail, how this is done, the other engages the steps listed on the 'active listening'

handout – making eye contact, listening carefully, asking questions and summarizing. We have found that this gradual approach engages depressed youth and families in the process of practising new skills and creating positive interactions. Given the preference of depressed school-aged youth for behaviourally focused, as opposed to cognitively focused, cognitive behavioural therapy (CBT) interventions, we have incorporated active behavioural strategies in FFT-CD.

Third, during middle childhood and emerging adolescence, youth are more cognitively limited than during later adolescence and adulthood; for this reason, our approach involves incorporating more concrete ways of communicating positively. Using an approach employed in other treatments [18, 19], we use colourful poker chips or 'thank-you chips/notes' throughout the treatment to provide positive feedback both during and outside sessions. Initially, the therapist models using the thank-you chips/notes to give positive feedback. Family members are then encouraged to use them to give positive feedback and express appreciation during sessions. We have found that this intervention often can lead to playful, warm interactions between family members. With younger children, family members are each sent home with some thank-you chips to use for between-session 'homework' to increase positive parent-youth interactions throughout the week. Unlike a 'token economy', where the objective is to earn rewards, the goal is not to accrue thank-you chips but rather to give them all away – increasing generalization of both positive feedback and noticing positive behaviour/ interactions. As youth get older and/or with more practice, we may replace the chips with colourful sticky 'thank-you notes' on which family members can write brief words of appreciation, valuing and positive remarks [19].

Fourth and lastly, skills are broken down into small pieces to promote mastery. For example, giving positive feedback (a core communication skill) is divided into identifying/noticing positive behaviour ('catching upward spirals') and providing verbal feedback ('keeping upward spirals going'). These features increase the developmental specificity and utility of this intervention model.

FFT-CD Overview

In order to evaluate the child's mental health symptoms and functional problems, strengths and stressors within the family and broader environment and areas to be targeted in treatment, a thorough evaluation of the child, parent(s) and family functioning is conducted prior to the beginning of treatment. In the initial evaluations, the clinician assesses family values, cohesiveness and attitudes, paying careful attention to whether and in what ways family members converge in their perceptions of the family environment. Current levels of conflict and ongoing stressors are also assessed in order to contextualize symptoms. In our research and clinics, we have typically used measures such as the Schedule for Affective Disorders and Schizophrenia for Children and Adolescents (K-SADS [20]) to establish youth diagnosis, sections of the Structured Clinical Interview for *Diagnostic and Statistical Manual of Mental Disorders*, 5th ed. (SCID [21]) to establish parental depression diagnosis and other questionnaires to assess youth functioning (e.g., Social Adjustment Scale for Children and Adolescents [22]) and stress and protective influences in the social environment (e.g., the Family Environment Scale [23] for self-reports of family cohesion, expressiveness and conflict; the Issues Checklist [24] to assess the frequency and specific areas of parent-child conflict; the Parenting Stress Index [25] to assess parent and family life stress).

In the sessions following the initial evaluation (the 'education about depression' module), the therapist meets with the parent(s) and child individually to provide information about the causes and correlates of depression and offer individualized feedback about how these factors manifest in their family. In meeting with the parents, the clinician offers psycho-education about depression and, in doing so, both supports the role of parents as models for their children and empowers parents to help their child. It is also helpful to emphasize the role of stress in perpetuating family difficulties and child symptoms and discuss that the goal of treatment is to help the family cope with stress, not to 'fix' the child. The individual child meeting begins with a discussion of feelings, allowing the therapist to gauge the child's ability to identify and communicate emotions. The therapist then leads the child through a discussion about the interplay between thoughts, feelings, and actions, emphasizing that treatment will focus on the association between our moods and our interactions within the context of the family. Ultimately, both parents and child come away from these initial sessions with an understanding that mood and interpersonal relationships are mutually influencing and that we can impact depression by working on relationships.

After these initial individual meetings, all remaining sessions will include the parent(s) and child together. The first of the joint sessions serves to consolidate and review information about the interpersonal model of depression and rationale for treatment. The therapist underscores the idea that by working as a team to reduce stress and enhance support, the family can combat depression together. The idea of upward spirals (that positive interpersonal interactions contribute to positive emotions, further fuelling positive interpersonal interactions) and downward spirals (that negative interpersonal communication contributes to negative emotions, further fuelling negative interactions) is introduced. The family is encouraged to offer examples of these concepts, and the therapist emphasizes the role of both upward and downward spirals in perpetuating and treating depression. We have found that the concept of these spirals is an easy one for both parents and children to grasp and provides a strong rationale and framework for treatment.

Typically, after the initial psycho-educational sessions, the remaining sessions maintain a regular structure. After a brief meeting with the child to assess changes in depressive symptoms, the parents join the session. The therapist and family discuss highlights and problems that occurred since the last session and review the assigned skill practice from the preceding week. After this, the therapist presents a new concept or skill. The idea that familial interactional spirals are linked to moods is central to treatment, and each new concept is introduced within the context of these patterns. After orienting the family to the new concept/skill, the therapist guides the family in practising and applying what they have learned through role plays, games, discussions and problem-solving exercises. Finally, the therapist assigns at-home skill practice for the next session to encourage generalization of skills and concepts to the home environment.

After the 'education about depression' module, the therapist and family spend three to four sessions focusing on enhancing communication skills. The overarching goal of this module is to increase the child's assertiveness skills, decrease depressive withdrawal and irritability and encourage the development of empathy between family members. The therapist explains how offering positive feedback to family members makes that person feel good and keeps upward spirals going. Family members practise exchanging positive feedback by using thank-you chips or notes provided by the therapist. The parent(s) and child are encouraged to give thank-you chips/notes to other family members when someone has done something that they liked or made them feel good both in treatment and at home. Active listening is also introduced as a strategy for keeping upward spirals going. The parent(s) and child practise listening carefully, asking clarifying questions and attending to others' thoughts and feelings. Finally, the therapist guides the family in communicating about things they did not like and offering negative feedback. This is presented as a strategy for stopping the progression of downward spirals. Specific guidelines for negative feedback are designed to increase the transmission of specific behavioural information and reduce more generalized and harsh criticism. The family begins to practise offering negative feedback with hypothetical examples first before moving on to examples from their own family experiences, again beginning with non-threatening examples (e.g., dirty shoes on the carpet) and eventually proceeding to more personally relevant, affectively charged examples (e.g., homework isn't completed).

The next module is covered over the course of two to three sessions and focuses on behavioural activation within the family. In CBT approaches, behavioural activation strategies are used to increase engagement in pleasurable activities to enhance mood and decrease depressive symptoms. In FFT-CD, the chief aim of these sessions is to increase reinforcers in the child's environment through positive family interactions; thus, unlike in traditional CBT approaches, the family is brought in to support and provide a context for behavioural activation. Family members are asked to write down one fun activity that they like to do. The therapist explains that doing enjoyable activities together is another way of initiating/maintaining upward spirals and reversing downward spirals. The therapist then leads the family through a role-playing exercise wherein each member practices asking for what they want, focusing on formulating specific requests and communicating why this request is important to them. At-home practice for this week includes planning and implementing several enjoyable activities for the family to do together. The therapist highlights the importance of selecting activities that are feasible, anticipates and problem-solves potential barriers to engaging in the activities and emphasizes the relationship between family engagement in enjoyable activities and improvements in mood. We have also found it helpful for families to specify activities that can be useful in promoting wellness on a regular basis (e.g., regular enjoyable activities) and those which can be used when negative moods are already in play (e.g., when getting home from school in a bad mood).

The last skill-based module focuses on problem-solving skills and strategies over the course of three to four sessions. This module is divided into two portions – identifying problems and solving problems. The purpose of the former module is to guide the family in developing problem identification skills, practising self-monitoring emotions and reframing problems as choices/opportunities to problem-solve. The therapist stresses that everyone has problems but explains how unsolved problems can lead to downward spirals. Each family member is asked to generate examples of problems outside the family environment. Once the family has demonstrated an understanding of general problem-solving, each member is asked to define a few specific problems within the family environment. At this point, the therapist introduces the idea of monitoring mood states by taking one's 'emotional temperature'. The clinician explains how problems are especially difficult to solve when people are upset and that attempting to do so often contributes to downward spirals. At-home practice involves identifying problems in the family and making sure to use the feeling thermometer to monitor moods and recognize when high distress could lead to accelerating downward spirals rather than the desired upward spirals.

The second portion of this module focuses on problem solving – practising conflict resolution skills, empowering the family in their efforts to solve problems, and encouraging flexibility in the problem-solving process. In these sessions, the clinician presents a step-by-step model for problem solving. The model highlights the importance of family agreement on the problem at hand, full family engagement in brainstorming possible solutions, discussing each option as a group, agreeing on a solution as a team and reviewing/troubleshooting after the solution has been implemented. The therapist guides the family in solving a problem using this model and assigns family problem-solving for at-home practice.

Throughout treatment, therapists seek to identify 'core' downward spirals. Often the conflicts families have repeat in regular ways. For example, conflicts may predictably occur around homework, sibling interactions, chores, computer use and so on. These regular conflicts become essential targets for both communication and problem-solving. By identifying regular processes, we can assist families in identifying high-risk situations.

Finally, the family and clinician spend one to two sessions consolidating treatment gains, considering relapse-prevention strategies and preparing for treatment termination. This typically includes additional practice in problem-solving and encouraging skill generalization. Often the practice in problem-solving centres on the issue of the family concluding treatment and missing the weekly opportunity to strengthen relationships and address problems with the support of a therapist. The therapist works with the family to develop a relapse-prevention plan that includes attention to early signs of depression relapse or recurrence, anticipation of future stressors (e.g., school starting after summer vacation) and strategies for addressing these challenges effectively. The therapist offers the idea of implementing weekly family meetings as one possible solution to this problem. In the last session, the child receives a booklet that contains all the handouts that have been used over the course of treatment and is given the opportunity to decorate and personalize it. The clinician explains how this book can be used as a reference in the future when issues emerge. It is helpful to guide the family through anticipating future stressors and engage in anticipatory problem-solving.

FFT-CD treatment modules, goals and strategies are outlined in Table 8.1. Following this, two composite cases (based on case material from several families) are provided that illustrate implementation of FFT-CD.

Table 8.1 FFT-CD Treatment Outline

Module	Primary goals	Strategies
Understanding **depression** (three sessions)	Get to know family	• Individual feedback with parents and child • Normalizing • Individual child/family conceptualization
	Present interpersonal model of depression	• Interactions impact mood, vice versa • To improve mood, change interactions • Reframe problem as interpersonal
	Outline upward and downward spirals	• Present examples • Family generates examples • Lay out rationale and major goals (increase upward and decrease downward spirals)
Families **talking together** (three or four sessions)	Increase positive feedback	• Present rationale: It starts upward spirals • Give tokens as signs of appreciation • Practise 'saying what you liked' • Home practice: 'Keep upward spirals going'
	Promote active listening	• Present rationale: It keeps upward spirals going • Practise active listening • Family games and practice
	Improve negative feedback skills	• Present rationale: It stops downward spirals • Practise 'saying what you didn't like' • Family games and practice
Things we do affect how we feel (two to three sessions)	Identify pleasurable events/ activities	• Generate lists for each family member • Rate enjoyability of each activity • Include activities with family, friends, self
	Promote assertiveness	• Asking can start upward spirals • Practise 'asking for what you want'
	Plan enjoyable family and individual activities	• Emphasize 'doable' activities • Make certain all members have input

Table 8.1 (cont.)

Module	Primary goals	Strategies
We can solve problems together (three to four sessions)	Enhance problem identification	• A problem is a 'choice' • Normalize
	Institute mood monitoring	• Review 'emotional temperature' • Present and generate examples
	Present problem-solving model	• Define the problem • Brainstorm • Evaluate choices • Choose a solution and carry it out • Evaluate and revise solutions
	Solve family problems	• Pick a solvable problem • Work on each step of the model • Be specific (the devil is in the details!)
Saying **goodbye** (one to two sessions)	Promote skill generalization	• Present colourful handbook of handouts • Briefly review concepts/relate back to model • Praise efforts
	Empower family to continue process	• Review child/family progress • Praise progress • Acknowledge steps still to take • Problem-solve ways to keep progress going • Suggest a family meeting
	Plan for the future	• Anticipate potential stressors • Plan for possible booster sessions

Case Description Illustrating Model

Noah: Building Parent and Child Strengths

Noah is an eight-year-old white third-grade boy living with his parents and younger sisters. Noah endorsed no symptoms of any kind and was disengaged during the initial feedback session, answering most questions with 'I don't know'. Conversely, his parents reported significant depressed mood, anhedonia, sleep disturbance, irritability, low self-esteem and suicidal thoughts. Additionally, Noah's oppositionality emerged as a significant issue. His parents expressed concern about his tendency to lie, throw temper tantrums, steal from his siblings and exhibit blatant noncompliance. Physical punishment had been used in the past, but not currently, to manage his difficult behaviour. The clinician emphasized that Noah's oppositionality would also be a focus of treatment and discussed the need to enhance parenting skills known to be helpful in managing problematic behaviour.

Despite Noah's hesitation to engage in the first session, he was receptive to the interpersonal model presented by the clinician during the 'education about depression' module. The entire family seemed to enjoy using thank-you chips and quickly began incorporating them into their daily routine. Family members reported that this practice was already resulting in more upward and fewer downward spirals. Although Noah was able to engage in positive exercises and role-play negative feedback with hypothetical examples, he had a difficult time voicing dissatisfaction and admitting anger. Noah often expressed his anger by disengaging from the situation. In one particularly challenging session, Noah's father brought up a downward spiral that had emerged around Noah's refusal to attend his music class. Noah became quite angry, refusing to participate in the discussion and stating that he did not want to come to treatment anymore.

Following this session, the therapist held an over-the-phone session with Noah's parents to discuss behavioural issues and parenting strategies for managing difficult behaviour. For example, the clinician encouraged Noah's parents not to engage with Noah when he is entering a downward spiral (i.e., active ignoring). The clinician also suggested increasing one-on-one time, continuing praise and creating clear choices for challenging situations. Although phone coaching is not a regular part of FFT-CD, this case illustrates how, within the general framework, additional in-person and on-phone sessions can be integrated to address the downward spirals associated with particular co-morbidities.

In the next session, the therapist acknowledged the difficult session the week before and told Noah that this session would focus on scheduling fun activities, which Noah was pleased to hear. The therapist met briefly and separately with Noah's parents to review what was discussed in the over-the-phone ancillary session and review progress. Noah's parents reported that the increased one-on-one time seemed to help and that Noah's behaviour was mostly better. The therapist praised the parents' efforts to incorporate these new practices.

It was in the 'problem-solving' module that Noah's mood and behavioural issues began to improve significantly. The therapist introduced problem-solving strategies using non-emotional examples. Noah soon began employing these new skills at home. Noah's mother reported that he had initiated productive problem-solving discussions about studying for tests, whether to visit extended family and what to have for dinner. Noah and his mother were able to successfully work together to resolve these conflicts.

Noah's depression emerged within the context of poor interpersonal skills. Noah benefitted from learning communication and problem-solving strategies and having a designated place to practise them. Noah also exhibited symptom reductions once his parents were equipped with strategies to teach him these skills and effectively reinforce positive behaviour rather than focus on punishing negative behaviour. Although occasional issues with noncompliance persisted at the end of treatment, Noah's parents reported that Noah's mood was significantly better and that the severity of his behavioural problems was reduced. They also reported enhancements in the quality of Noah's social interactions inside and outside the family as well as improved academic performance. Noah's downward spiral is portrayed in Figure 8.1.

Leah: Rebuilding the Mother-Child Relationship

Leah is a 12-year-old Latina seventh-grade girl who presented with depressed mood, low self-esteem, suicidal ideation and sleep disturbances. She lived with her mother and three younger siblings. Leah's mother and grandmother had a history of depression. However, Leah's mother was remarkably resilient. Although born into poverty and giving birth to Leah in high school, she was fully employed, maintained strong relationships with family and friends and was effectively raising her three children alone. Although

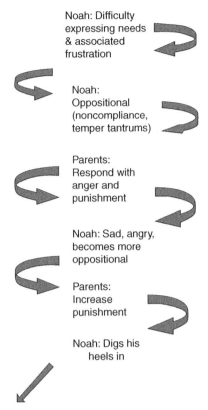

Figure 8.1 Noah's downward spiral

Leah's mother worked hard to provide for Leah and her siblings, finances remained a major source of familial stress. Although loving, Leah's father was inconsistently involved in her life. Leah, a bright girl and exceptional student, found refuge from these difficult circumstances in school. Although Leah and her mother had once been very close, their relationship had eroded in the wake of these environmental stressors. Leah's mother expressed a longing to become close with her daughter again.

Although Leah was open to participating in treatment, she doubted that her relationship with her mother would improve. She felt constantly criticized by her mother and tended to withdraw as a result. When Leah isolated herself, her mother would attempt to engage Leah by becoming harsh or intrusive with her, causing Leah to pull away even more. For example, Leah's mother would initiate discussion about sexuality. This was a principal concern of Leah's mother given her own unplanned pregnancy as a teenager. Leah was not comfortable discussing this topic with her mother and would withdraw when it was brought up. While this downward spiral was readily identified by Leah and her mother during the 'education about depression' module, neither Leah nor her mother was able to offer examples of upward spirals.

Leah's initial resistance to treatment and tendency to withdraw continued into the beginning stages of the second treatment module ('communication training'). When asked to give her mother some positive feedback, Leah withdrew and refused to role-play. The clinician responded to this by demonstrating ways that Leah could reinforce others' positive behaviour and tried role-playing with Leah's mother. Similarly, Leah's mother became upset and used harsh language upon hearing negative feedback from Leah, prompting Leah to withdraw. The clinician helped Leah and her mother identify this as the beginning of a downward spiral, and Leah's mother said that she would try to be mindful about her tone and levels of irritability when stressed.

Nonetheless, it was during this phase of treatment that treatment gains were first observed. Leah and her mother seemed to bond over the use of thank-you notes and used humour to playfully ease tension around communication exercises at home. As Leah and her mother began to notice and acknowledge the small positives in their relationship, Leah's depressive symptoms began to subside. Leah began to spend more time outside her room and was finally able to acknowledge positive interactions with her mother.

The clinician decided to spend less time on the 'fun activities scheduling' module because of the emergence of a significant environmental stressor. Leah's family had to move out of their apartment, and Leah would have to switch schools as a result. This was devastating to Leah because school was a source of comfort and solace for her. Instead, the clinician introduced the 'problem-solving' module and employed problem-solving strategies around finding an affordable apartment within the same school district. While there were obvious benefits to this solution, there were also downsides – in order to stay in the district, Leah's mother would need to work more hours and would have less time to spend with Leah. The clinician emphasized this as well. Interestingly, even with this stressor, Leah's depression symptoms continued to decrease. The clinician returned to the 'fun activities scheduling' module to continue stopping downward spirals and starting upward spirals.

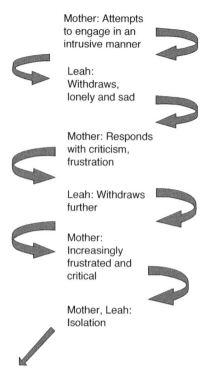

Figure 8.2 Leah's downward spiral

By the end of treatment, both Leah and her mother reported feeling more supported by the other, and Leah's depressive symptoms showed significant reductions. In one of their final sessions, Leah revealed to her mother that she was struggling with her sexual orientation. To this, Leah's mother expressed her unconditional and loving support. Given that conversations concerning sexuality were once a major source of tension between Leah and her mother, this interaction was an important milestone both in their relationship and in Leah's course of treatment. While Leah's depression emerged in the absence of pre-existing psychopathology, it manifested during a period of elevated strain in a family struggling to break out of poverty. This stressful environment contributed to the erosion of a once-supportive mother-daughter relationship – one that eventually became a stressor in itself. In this case, it was evident that enhancing communication between Leah and her mother was core to her symptom improvements. At discharge, Leah presented as a confident and capable early adolescent. Leah's downward spiral is presented in Figure 8.2.

Core Competencies in a Family-Based Approach

Core competencies in implementing FFT-CD include both foundational and functional competencies. *Foundational* competencies include an understanding of family processes and family lifespan, bi-directionality in parent-child interactions and interpersonal models of depression. FFT-CD therapists need to recognize the role individuals take within a family system and how these roles are shaped and reinforced through family interactions. Foundational competencies include the adoption of a particular stance, implementation of core family therapy skills and application of the interpersonal model. These are detailed next.

Stance

The therapeutic stance in this family-based approach shares both similar and unique features with other family-based and CBT approaches. This stance is active and structuring. The therapist continually guides the family, intervening to reduce conflict and increase positive interaction and exploring family transactions and looking for solutions. Maintaining a sense of optimism throughout treatment, the therapist empowers the family by focusing on strengths and existing resources. The family is viewed as the expert on what works for them; the therapist provides information and skills but views the family as most knowledgeable about themselves and defers to this experience. Particularly during the initial sessions, the therapist conveys that 'I have ideas about ways to help you through this tough time, but every family is different. I will never know your family (or your child) as well as you do, and you'll need to let me know what does and doesn't work for your particular family. You are the experts; I'm here to help you figure it out.' This is an inquisitive and problem-focused stance, one in which the therapist continually gathers information from the family and uses this information to frame and resolve issues. Although the focus is on skills building, a secondary goal is changing attributions to help the family gain a more positive but realistic perspective, focusing on strengths while emphasizing areas for improvement. The therapist is flexible while not becoming sidetracked. Although the modules proceed in a typical order, rearrangement can occur to respond to particular family needs. For example, although therapy typically begins with communication training, problem-solving can become the focus when particular symptoms (e.g., suicidality) or family issues (e.g., severe conflict) require immediate attention.

Principal Techniques

Primary techniques employed include circular questioning, reframing and normalizing. In using circular questioning, the therapist strives to get each person's view of the situation. An open-ended approach is best. Example questions include 'then what did he do?', 'what happened when your mom said no?', 'how do you remember it?'. By focusing on specific behaviours, the therapist helps the family move away from global criticisms (e.g., 'he's so selfish'). In using reframing, the therapist restates complaints in a way that emphasizes the positive and recognizes the underlying values and positive emotions within the family. For example, in a family with lots of conflict, reframing might include 'sounds like expressing feelings is something you value as a family'. As another example, when a family reports that the father yelled when the child was late arriving home, reframing might include, 'wow, it sounds like you were really worried about (child); your dad really cares about your safety'. In using normalizing, the therapist conveys that the family is often doing its best to try to address complex situations and that the reactions of members are understandable: 'Families these days are so busy that it's hard to remember to . . .' or 'balancing homework and sports is hard for kids'. Normalizing recognizes the real challenges families face, conveys positive regard for the family and its efforts and helps members to see their difficulties as normal challenges to be overcome.

Application of Techniques During Specific Treatment Modules

During the first module ('education about depression'), this therapeutic stance is used to join with families and to convey an understanding of their unique yet understandable concerns. Normalizing is used in three primary ways. First, normalizing is used to offer information about the nature of depression and to help families see that their experience is comprehensible. For example, 'irritability is often something that we see in children with depression, but it's one of the things that makes depression really hard to deal with at times'. This reframing emphasizes that (1) irritability is not wilful and defiant but rather a common and expectable concomitant of depression and (2) their reactions are understandable. Second, it is normal to need to practise skills and try new strategies. For example, 'it sounds like some of the things that used to work with her aren't working so well anymore; it's hard as children become teens, and many parents aren't sure what to do'. Third, every family has positive and negative interactions (upward and downward spirals); our goal is to help the family change the relative frequency of those interactions and to experience more control in shaping them. For example, 'I can hear that you have had some really great times with him, lots of fun, and at the same time you can have some big conflicts. This is such a challenge with kids becoming teenagers, especially when they are struggling with depression too.' Relatedly, reframing is used to present the model and rationale for the family approach, explaining that although depression has many causes, it is best addressed by families working together incrementally. The therapist validates the frequent parental feelings of hopelessness, self-blame and frustration while also acknowledging previous efforts and emphasizing parent strengths. The therapist conveys that 'although it might not feel like it right now, you are the most important person (people) in your child's life and have the power to help your child; my job is to help you use that power'.

In second through fifth modules, a new set of therapist competencies comes to centre stage – modelling and scaffolding/directing. When implementing the treatment with depressed children, a gradual approach is essential. Skills such as giving positive feedback and active listening are gradually introduced, with the therapist modelling with a family member, having a family member demonstrate (with the therapist playing another family member's role), and then having family members work on these skills with one another. Not surprisingly, we have found that it is much more effective to show/demonstrate skills and concepts to children as opposed to telling them (behavioural versus cognitive). Praising all efforts (even small ones), using respectful humour and focusing on specific feedback are essential. The therapist scaffolds and directs, guiding families towards the implementation of these skills, troubleshooting along the way, reinforcing, starting with easier skills/topics, and moving gently to more difficult ones as families members gain confidence. Anticipating barriers (to good communication, behavioural activation, and problem solving)

normalizes difficulties and frames these as expected and navigable opportunities to problem-solve and fine-tune.

Common Challenges in FFT-CD

Comorbidity

Anxiety disorders and externalizing disorders, such as ADHD are highly comorbid with paediatric depression. In many cases, comorbidity fuels the negative interactional processes (i.e., downward spirals) that are targeted by family-focused treatment. For example, in children with comorbid ADHD and depression, difficulties around homework or following instructions are a common source of family conflict. This familial conflict drives downward spirals and contributes to the onset and maintenance of depressive symptoms. Similarly, conflicts around school avoidance in families with anxious children often fuel downward spirals, leading to the emergence or exacerbation of depression. In both of these cases, it can be helpful to conceptualize comorbidity within an interpersonal framework by focusing on the implications of the comorbidity (i.e., family conflict and criticism around the comorbid symptoms).

Conflict related to comorbidity is often addressed in the problem-solving module. Here, the therapist has the opportunity to help the family understand the nature of conflicts related to comorbid symptoms by framing them within the context of downward spirals. The therapist should emphasize that by using problem-solving skills and strategies to address comorbidity-related issues and avoiding downward spirals, depressive symptoms will improve as well.

It is also appropriate to integrate other evidence-based interventions into family-focused treatment to address comorbidity. For example, graded exposure can be implemented as a strategy for addressing comorbid anxiety. In the case of comorbid ADHD or oppositional defiant disorder (e.g., Noah) supplementary sessions can be incorporated to discuss parent management skills. The therapist might frame these exposures and/or supplementary parent management sessions as a proactive strategy for reducing family conflict related to specific behaviours and avoiding downward spirals.

Siblings

Although most sessions involve the parent(s) and the target child, the decision to incorporate siblings in family interventions will depend in part on the siblings' age. Very young siblings are sometimes integrated into the session if childcare cannot be coordinated. Otherwise, parents might choose to alternate turns attending sessions and watching the other children. In this case, it is important that the therapist emphasizes the importance of communicating information reviewed in each session with the non-attending parent.

Incorporating siblings into some sessions is particularly useful when downward spirals involve sibling conflict or competition. Teasing is an especially common precursor to downward spirals, as it often begins as light-hearted and can quickly escalate to full-blown conflict.

Problem-solving around this issue might involve recognizing/anticipating when teasing begins to transform into a negative interaction and having a strategy for when this happens. Some families have designated a time-out signal for these instances, which means that everyone must go to their rooms and calm down before things can escalate. It is also helpful to engage in some brief psycho-education with siblings about how moods affect interactions and vice versa.

If the decision is made to incorporate siblings into session, it is critical that the proband is not placed in the 'identified patient' role. Discussions should focus on interactional and relational difficulties between the siblings and avoid assigning any undue blame to the proband. One way to approach this is to discuss each sibling's role in the conflict in a playful and light-hearted way, highlighting that everyone has a part to play in the generation of downward spirals. The therapist might then guide a problem-solving discussion about what each family member could do differently to avoid conflict.

Parental Mood Disorder

Children with depression are at heightened risk for having a parent with a mood disorder. Bottom-up studies of family aggregation indicate that youth with depressive disorders are particularly likely to have parents with mood disorders [14]. Both unipolar and bipolar depression in parents can create challenges in family treatment. The FFT-CD model facilitates psycho-education for the full family on depression, depression treatments and strategies for recovery. This approach allows parents who may be struggling with their own depression or depression in a spouse/partner to learn about depression, the

influence of interpersonal stress on moods and coping and strategies for managing depression. By focusing on downward and upward spirals, we can also help parents identify how their own mood-related challenges contribute to family stress, which further impacts both their own and their child's mood symptoms. In providing more personalized information about depression and including cognitive behavioural strategies (e.g., behavioural activation), parents have some exposure to depression treatment through the FFT-CD model. When additional individual or medication treatments are thought to merit consideration, parents are referred to other treatment providers. As has been frequently noted in literature on parent depression, treatment referrals for parents do not often result in parents obtaining care [26–29]. By offering depression treatment in a family context in FFT-CD, parents receive some exposure to depression treatment components. Furthermore, the therapeutic alliance that develops with the FFT-CD clinician combined with weekly treatment contacts may encourage and support treatment seeking in parents when needed and facilitate parents receiving needed treatments. Additionally, FFT-CD sessions can include parent-only sessions. Such sessions provide an opportunity to problem-solve issues around accessing treatment (e.g., brainstorming solutions for potential logistical obstacles). Additionally, participation in the family sessions may help parents recognize the deleterious impact of their mood disorder on the family and child, increasing their receptiveness to seeking help.

Conclusion

Youth depression is powerfully influenced by the social context, and families are core to this context. A comprehensive intervention strategy may involve numerous pieces, including medication, psychotherapy, and school-based interventions. FFT-CD provides a framework for the integration of more complex and comprehensive approaches and provides a number of distinct advantages. First, FFT-CD addresses common interpersonal stressors in youth with depression. The focus on identifying both helpful and unhelpful interpersonal processes and enhancing both communication and problem-solving skills can be used to increase social support and decrease stress. Both directly and indirectly, problem-solving can extend beyond the family to assist children in solving interpersonal problems in school and peer situations.

Effective problem-solving about external stressors can also increase the child's trust in and the parent's confidence in the family as a reliable and helpful resource. Second, it is flexible in its implementation and can address a wide range of family structures, stresses and strengths. Third, its broad framework can incorporate additional interventions aimed at common co-morbidities and challenges.

Although circular questioning, normalizing and reframing are all essential competencies in implementing FFT-CD, the overarching competency is the ability of therapists to tailor the intervention to the specific needs of families. The upward and downward spirals may differ greatly in individual cases, and the competent therapist is able to see these patterns and to convey them in a compassionate, caring, collaborative and respectful manner to families. This competency is greatly challenged by the heterogeneity of, not only depressive disorders, but of family structures, strengths and needs. In more complex cases, the use of these skills may be particularly difficult but essential, as families may be more sensitive to long histories of blame, assumptions and misunderstanding. As therapists, we come into the development of the downward spirals at different points – particular patterns may be concretized over time, and some may be recently emerging. We have found that by emphasizing positives and enhancing communication at the outset, we can often build resiliency to allow more effective and impactful problem-solving. One of the biggest challenges for therapists is to recognize the powerful impact of children's depressive symptoms on parents.

Some recommendations for therapists attempting to develop these competencies:

1. FFT-CD case conceptualizations attend to the child within the context of his or her family environment and broader social ecological context. A key skill is to develop this social ecological case conceptualization and a builds and mobilizes family strengths to promote recovery and functional improvement.

2. Practise engaging families in active but structured interactions and role-plays. This is an intervention that requires a structuring approach.

3. Remember that families, particularly more complex ones, often have a history of disappointment with service providers; this is not a treatment that is about blaming families but rather based on building strengths.

In a large two-site randomized, controlled trial, FFT-CD demonstrated greater and more rapid depression treatment response than individual supportive therapy for youth (aged 7 to 14) with depressive disorders, with roughly 80 per cent of youths showing a positive treatment response at the end of treatment. Further, parents receiving FFT-CD reported greater knowledge and efficacy in being able to solve family problems and manage symptoms. Longer-term one-year follow-up data indicate that 76 per cent of youths receiving FFT-CD showed depression remission, with youths in the comparator individual supportive therapy also recovering by the one-year follow-up. However, there was a hint that FFT-CD may lead to greater protection from depression recurrence and future suicide attempts [1]. These data, in conjunction with the research literature indicating that depression tends to run in families and that treatments with strong family components appear to have the greatest benefits for reducing suicide attempt risk [30], underscore the potential of FFT-CD and other family-focused approaches for mobilizing family strengths and supports to promote recovery and address the needs of children and families.

References

1. Tompson MC, Sugar CA, Langer DA, Asarnow JR. A randomized clinical trial comparing family-focused treatment and individual supportive therapy for depression in childhood and early adolescence. *Journal of the American Academy of Child and Adolescent Psychiatry* 2017; **56**(6):515–23.

2. Birmaher B, Williamson DE, Dahl RE, et al. Clinical presentation and course of depression in youth: Does onset in childhood differ from onset in adolescence? *Journal of the American Academy of Child and Adolescent Psychiatry* 2004; **43**(1):63–70.

3. Kovacs M. Presentation and course of major depressive disorder during childhood and later years of the life span. *Journal of the American Academy of Child and Adolescent Psychiatry* 1996; **35**(6):705–15.

4. Kovacs M, Obrosky S, George C. The course of major depressive disorder from childhood to young adulthood: Recovery and recurrence in a longitudinal observational study. *Journal of Affective Disorders* 2016; **203**:374–81.

5. Lynch FL, Clarke GN. Estimating the economic burden of depression in children and adolescents. *American Journal of Preventive Medicine* 2006; **31**(6):143–51.

6. Rudolph KD, Hammen C, Burge D, et al. Toward an interpersonal life-stress model of depression: The developmental context of stress generation. *Development and Psychopathology* 2000; **12**(2):215–34.

7. Hankin BL, Abela JR, eds. *Development of Psychopathology: A Vulnerability-Stress Perspective.* Thousand Oaks, CA: SAGE Publishing, 2005.

8. Hammen C, Shih J. Depression and interpersonal processes. In: Gotlib IH, Hammen CL (eds.), *Handbook of Depression*, vol. **3**. New York: Guilford Press, 2014, pp. 277–95.

9. Rudolph KD, Flynn M, Abaied JL. A developmental perspective on interpersonal theories of youth depression. In: Abela JRZ, Hankin BL (eds.), *Handbook of Depression in Children and Adolescents.* New York: Guilford Press, 2008, pp. 79–102.

10. Tompson MC, Boger KD, Asarnow JR. Enhancing the developmental appropriateness of treatment for depression in youth: Integrating the family in treatment. *Child and Adolescent Psychiatric Clinics of North America* 2012; **21**(2):345–84.

11. Ladd GW. Peer relationships and social competence during early and middle childhood. *Annual Review of Psychology* 1999; **50**(1):333–59.

12. Steinberg L. We know some things: Parent–adolescent relationships in retrospect and prospect. *Journal of Research on Adolescence* 2001; **11**(1):1–9.

13. Beardslee WR, Gladstone TR, O'Connor EE. Developmental risk of depression: Experience matters. *Child and Adolescent Psychiatric Clinics* 2012; **21**(2):261–78.

14. Tompson MC, Asarnow JR, Mintz J, Cantwell DP. Parental depression risk: Comparing youth with depression, attention deficit hyperactivity disorder and community controls. *Journal of Psychology and Psychotherapy* 2015; **5**(4):1.

15. Hammen C, Burge D, Adrian C. Timing of mother and child depression in a longitudinal study of children at risk. *Journal of Consulting and Clinical Psychology* 1991; **59**(2):341–5.

16. Chan PT, Doan SN, Tompson MC. Stress generation in a developmental context: The role of youth depressive symptoms, maternal depression, the parent–child relationship, and family stress. *Journal of Family Psychology* 2014; **28**(1):32–41.

17. Tompson MC, Langer DA, Hughes JL, Asarnow JR. Family-focused treatment for childhood depression: Model and case illustrations. *Cognitive and Behavioral Practice* 2017; **24**(3):269–87.

18. Rotheram-Borus MJ, Goldstein AM, Elkavich AS. Treatment of suicidality: A family intervention for adolescent suicide attempters. In: Hofmann SG, Tompson MC (eds.), *Treating Chronic and Severe Mental Disorders: A Handbook of Empirically Supported Interventions.* New York: Guilford Press, 2002, pp. 191–212.

19. Asarnow JR, Hughes JL, Babeva KN, Sugar CA. Cognitive-behavioral family treatment for suicide attempt prevention: a randomized controlled trial. *Journal of the American Academy of Child and Adolescent Psychiatry* 2017; **56**(6):506–14.

20. Kaufman J, Birmaher B, Brent D, et al. Schedule for affective disorders and schizophrenia for school-age children-present and lifetime version (K-SADS-PL): Initial reliability and validity data. *Journal of the American Academy of Child and Adolescent Psychiatry* 1997; **36**(7):980–8.

21. First MB, Williams JB, Karg RS, Spitzer RL. *Structured Clinical Interview for DSM-5 Disorders*, Clinician Version (SCID-5-CV). Washington, DC: American Psychiatric Association, 2015.

22. Weissman MM, Orvaschel H, Padian N. Children's symptom and social functioning: Self-report scales. *Journal of Nervous and Mental Disorders* 1980; **168**:736–40.

23. Moos RH, Moos BS. *Family Environment Scale Manual.* Sunnyvale, CA: Consulting Psychologists Press, 1994.

24. Robin AL, Weiss JG. Criterion-related validity of behavioral and self-report measures of problem-solving communication-skills in distressed and non-distressed parent-adolescent dyads. *Behavioral Assessment* 1980; **2**(4):339–52.

25. Abidin RR. Parenting Stress Index: A measure of the parent–child system. In Zalaquett CP, Wood RJ (eds.), *Evaluating Stress: A Book of Resources.* Lanham, MD: Scarecrow Education, 1997, pp. 277–91.

26. Bauer NS, Ofner S, Pottenger A, Carroll AE, Downs SM. Follow-up of mothers with suspected postpartum depression from pediatrics clinics. *Frontiers in Pediatrics* 2017; **5**:212.

27. Canty HR, Sauter A, Zuckerman K, Cobian M, Grigsby T. Mothers' perspectives on follow-up for postpartum depression screening in primary care. *Journal of Developmental and Behavioral Pediatrics* 2019; **40**(2):139–43.

28. McGarry J, Kim H, Sheng X, Egger M, Baksh L. Postpartum depression and help-seeking behavior. *Journal of Midwifery and Women's Health* 2009; **54**(1):50–6.

29. Featherstone B, Broadhurst K. Engaging parents and carers with family support services: What can be learned from research on help-seeking?. *Child and Family Social Work* 2003; **8**(4):341–50.

30. Ougrin D, Tranah T, Stahl D, Moran P, Asarnow JR. Therapeutic interventions for suicide attempts and self-harm in adolescents: systematic review and meta-analysis. *Journal of the American Academy of Child and Adolescent Psychiatry* 2015; **54**(2):97–107.

Chapter

9

A Family-Based CBT Approach to the Treatment of Anxiety Disorders in Children and Adolescents

Gemma Sicouri and Jennifer Hudson

Anxiety disorders are the most common mental health problems that children and adolescents experience in Western countries, with approximately 10 to 20 per cent of youth affected [1–3]. Although everyone experiences anxiety, children and adolescents with anxiety disorders experience excessive and pervasive fear, worry or nervousness that can have a negative impact on their lives [4, 5]. Left untreated or treated ineffectively, anxiety disorders can persist into adulthood [6] and develop into depression, substance abuse and/or suicidality in later life [7–9].

Cognitive behavioural therapy (CBT) is the most empirically supported treatment for anxiety disorders in children and adolescents [10–12]. A clinician wishing to effectively implement CBT for youth anxiety disorders needs competence across general therapeutic and CBT-specific domains. A clinician also needs to consider the role of family environment factors in maintaining such disorders and the potential importance of targeting such factors. Parents are typically involved in CBT for youth with anxiety disorders, but the extent and nature of parental involvement may vary across treatment protocols. Moreover, as addressed in the material that follows, the clinical decision to involve parents in such therapy may depend on a number of factors, such as the child's age and developmental stage.

The aim of this chapter is to describe the clinical competencies required to implement CBT for anxiety disorders in children and adolescents. First, we introduce the theoretical framework that underpins current CBT treatment protocols for anxiety. This includes the factors that, according to current research and theory, play a proximal role in the development and maintenance of youth anxiety disorders. Second, we describe the clinical competencies required to implement this treatment. Third, we highlight some of the common obstacles to successful intervention and strategies for overcoming them.

Theoretical Foundations of CBT for Anxiety

What Is Anxiety?

Anxiety itself is a normal emotion. It is an innate reaction to a real or perceived threat that triggers the fear circuitry of the brain, otherwise known as the 'flight or fight' response. Excessive or unwarranted fear or worry may be associated with physiological symptoms such as shortness of breath, heart palpitations, muscle tensions, headaches and stomach aches [5]. However, a child with an anxiety disorder experiences this reaction in certain environments that is excessive compared to typically developing children of a similar age. Importantly, the child avoids certain environments that elicit fear and may engage in specific behaviours to increase safety (e.g., reassurance seeking or avoiding eye contact). The key factors differentiating normal versus abnormal anxiety are the extent to which fears and worries are enduring (e.g., typically at least six months) and the extent to which they interfere with the child's and/or the family's functioning. Persistent fears that have an impact on day-to-day functioning, such as attending school, making and keeping friendships or participating in age-appropriate activities, may indicate a diagnosable problem, and treatment may be warranted.

According to categorical systems of diagnosis (e.g., *Diagnostic Statistical Manual*, 5th Edition [DSM-V] [5] and *International Classifications of Diseases* [ICID-10] [13]), there are eight types of anxiety disorders that young people experience. The most common youth anxiety disorders are separation anxiety disorder, social anxiety disorder, generalized anxiety disorder and specific phobia [4,14]. Less common disorders in youth include selective mutism, agoraphobia and panic disorder. The key factor distinguishing these disorders is the content of the fear and worry. For example, children with social anxiety disorder worry about what others think of them, whereas children with separation anxiety disorder typically worry about something bad happening to them or a parent. Children with generalized anxiety tend to worry about a range of events or activities (e.g., work or school performance), whereas children with specific phobias worry about a circumscribed object or situation (e.g., insects or getting an injection). Despite this categorization of anxiety disorders, research has highlighted that a number of common risk and maintenance factors underpin all anxiety disorders [14]. These are highlighted in the cognitive behavioural models of childhood anxiety that have been translated into effective interventions, outlined next.

A Theoretical Framework

Cognitive behavioural models of childhood anxiety highlight the interactions between an individual's cognitive processes, emotional experiences and behavioural responses in the development and maintenance of anxiety disorders [15–17]. In contrast to adult models of anxiety, these models emphasize the role and influence of the family in childhood anxiety. Although various disorder-specific models of child and adolescent anxiety have emerged, the models of child anxiety often emphasize risk mechanisms that are transdiagnostic rather than differentiating between specific anxiety disorders.

Internal Factors

Temperament and Avoidant Coping

Avoidant coping is a core feature of anxiety disorders and marks temperamental styles that typically precede anxiety disorders. Extensive evidence has shown that a fearful or inhibited temperament early in life increases the likelihood of developing anxiety disorders later in life [18, 19]. An inhibited temperament has been shown to confer vulnerability for anxiety disorders in general but particularly social anxiety disorder [20]. Behavioural avoidance is a key feature of anxiety disorders and serves to maintain anxiety by reducing opportunities for a child to acquire accurate information pertaining to threat and to develop coping capacities in feared situations.

Emotion Lability

Individual differences in physiological arousal and poor emotion regulation also play a role in anxiety

across the lifespan and are likely to be core maintaining processes. In one landmark study, infants who were more emotionally and physically aroused at three months of age were more likely to become inhibited children by age two [21]. Negative affectivity has also been shown to be associated with anxiety in children and adolescents and changes in anxiety over a seven-month period [22]. Children with anxiety disorders who present for treatment have been shown not only to have difficulty regulating fear and worry but also to demonstrate a more general deficit in the regulation and understanding of a range of emotions [23–5].

Cognitive Bias

Cognitive bias plays an integral role in the maintenance of anxiety during childhood and adulthood [26, 27]. In particular, children with anxiety disorders are more likely to display excessive attention to threat, biases towards interpreting ambiguous information in a threat-congruent manner and high levels of automatic thoughts related to threat [28, 29]. Further, children with anxiety disorders are more likely to respond to threatening information in an avoidant manner [30]. These cognitive processes maintain a sense of threat for the young person, which directly increases their experience of anxiety.

Environmental Factors

Life Events

Anxious children tend to experience a greater number of negative events in their lives than children without anxiety disorders [31, 32]. This difference is a result of both *dependent* life events and *independent* life events. Dependent life events are those which could potentially be a product of the child's own behaviours (e.g., an argument with a friend) and which are more likely to be a result of the child having an anxiety disorder. A cycle develops whereby negative life events may trigger or exacerbate anxiety which, in turn, is likely to lead to further negative dependent life events. Children with anxiety also experience a greater number of negative independent life events (i.e., events and circumstances not associated with the child's behaviours [33]), which may precede the onset of anxiety disorders. For example, children with anxiety disorders are more likely to come from families with a lower socioeconomic status and higher rates of separation or divorce [34]. Specific events that have been associated with anxiety disorders include sexual and physical abuse, teasing and peer victimization [35, 36].

Family Factors

Anxiety runs in families. Having an anxious parent places a child at risk of developing an anxiety disorder [37, 38]. The mechanisms by which this transmission occurs are likely the result of both genetic heritability and specific familial environments that may increase the child's chances of developing an anxiety disorder (e.g., a controlling parenting style, anxious modelling, transmission of threat information and avoidant coping) [14, 39]. Twin studies of anxiety in children and adults suggest a moderate degree of heritability, with approximately 30 to 40 per cent of variance in anxiety symptoms accounted for by genetic factors [39, 40].

Parenting. Two styles of parenting have been primarily associated with anxiety disorders in children: control (overprotection, overinvolvement) and rejection (negative, critical parenting). A controlling parenting style broadly refers to the excessive regulation of children's activities and routines, encouragement of the child's dependence on parents and instructions to children about how to think and feel [41]. Rejection involves a low level of parental warmth, approval and responsiveness [42, 43]. Control has been more strongly linked to the development of anxiety disorders than rejection [44–7]. There is also some evidence to suggest that parental control may be elicited by the child's anxiety or anxious vulnerability [48]. For example, a child who is anxious may elicit more help and reassurance from the parent. In turn, a parent who helps or who provides reassurance to the child reduces the child's ability to learn accurate threat and coping information about the situation, which maintains and may further exacerbate the child's anxiety. There is some preliminary evidence that parental reassurance during an anxiety-provoking situation only serves to increase child fear [49].

Parental Modelling/Conditioning. Anxiety in children may develop or be maintained through a child's observation of their parents' statements, behaviours and attitudes [16, 50, 51]. A parent acting in fearful and inhibited ways can provide the child with information relevant to a specific or generalized threat or the value of avoidant coping. For example, maternal facial expressions of fear and disgust demonstrated increased avoidant behaviour in young infants [52]. Similarly, maternal modelling of anxious

versus non-anxious responses to a stranger predicted infants' subsequent expression of fear and avoidant response to the same unfamiliar adult [53, 54].

Key Features of Clinical Competencies in Treating Anxiety Disorders in Children and Adolescents

In this section, we describe the key features of clinical competencies required to effectively implement evidence-based CBT for youth with anxiety disorders. In line with the model of clinician competencies outlined in Chapter 1 and other literature [55], these competencies are classified into three broad domains: (1) generic therapeutic competencies, (2) CBT-based competencies and (3) specific CBT techniques. The importance of these competencies as they relate to parental involvement in such therapy is highlighted where relevant.

Generic Competencies

Conducting a Competent and Thorough Assessment

A competent and thorough assessment of youth anxiety disorders requires clinicians to adopt an evidence-based multi-method (e.g., structured or semi-structured interview, self-report, observational) and multi-informant (e.g., child, parent, teacher) assessment of the disorder [56, 57]. The clinician should also integrate these multifaceted assessment methods to determine a clinical diagnosis, with consideration of differential diagnosis. This is particularly important given the high level of co-morbidity that exists with anxiety disorders in children and adolescents [58].

A range of assessment tools exists to assess anxiety disorders. Structured or semi-structured interviews are considered the 'gold standard' of assessment for youth anxiety disorders [59]. One semi-structured interview that is commonly used is the Anxiety Disorders Interview Schedule for Children for DSM-IV (ADIS C/P – IV) [60], which is designed to assess the presence of an anxiety disorder based on DSM criteria using both parent- and child-report interviews. The ADIS has excellent psychometric properties [61, 62] and is commonly used in research ratings. Conducting the ADIS requires significant time commitment and trained raters.

Questionnaire methods are cost- and time-efficient tools to gain information on a child's current symptoms and to track changes in symptoms over time. However, they do not provide enough information to make a diagnosis in isolation. Commonly used self- and parent-report questionnaire measures to assess anxiety symptoms include the Multidimensional Anxiety Scale for Children (MASC) [63] and the Spence Children's Anxiety Scale (SCAS) [64]. A child's score can be compared to normative data and provide some indication of the severity of the anxiety compared to peers. In addition to measures of symptom severity, questionnaire measures such as the Child Anxiety Life Interference Scale (CALIS) [65] can also be used to determine the impact of the symptoms on the child as well as the family. Behavioural observations can also provide useful assessment data on levels and features of a child's anxiety, as well as the family's response to the child, particularly when structured around threat-related contexts (e.g., behavioural approach tasks) [66].

A thorough and competent assessment requires a broader assessment of the onset, development and context of anxiety symptoms, as well as information regarding the child's or adolescent's developmental, medical, school and social history and family psychiatric history. Given the possible role of the family in maintaining anxiety disorders, a competent assessment should also consider the broader family factors which may be maintaining the disorder, including the level of family functioning, the parent-child relationship and parenting behaviours theorized to play a role in youth anxiety (e.g., control). Family variables can be assessed using both formal assessment measures [67] and as part of a clinical interview.

Children and adolescents with anxiety disorders are at increased risk of self-harm and suicide [68]; therefore, it is essential that such risk is assessed routinely throughout treatment as appropriate. A clinician must also take into consideration relevant legislation and ethical requirements around mandatory reporting where child safety is an issue.

Understanding Relevant Child and Adolescent Characteristics

It is essential that clinicians have knowledge informed by current literature about the general patterns of development in children and adolescents across cognitive, social and emotional domains. In addition, knowledge of the clinical importance of family environmental factors (e.g., parenting, family structure and relationships), life events (e.g., trauma, bullying), individual differences (e.g., developmental history,

family culture) and co-morbidity is also required for the purposes of case formulation and treatment planning.

Building a Positive Therapeutic Relationship

Integral to treatment for youth anxiety is a positive therapeutic alliance between the clinician and the family. A *positive alliance* is defined as a combination of an emotional bond between clinician and client, collaboration on techniques and agreement on goals and tasks of treatment [69]. A positive relationship of this kind is associated with advantageous treatment outcomes across treatments for youth mental health disorders and youth anxiety in particular [70, 71]. It promotes positive outcomes by increasing a child's and parents' engagement in therapy and helps to facilitate a child's willingness to engage in critical components of CBT, such as exposure tasks and skills building [72].

When working with children, rapport-building behaviours that elicit information, provide emotional validation and support and explore the child's subjective feelings may help to develop an affective bond [73]. The use of interactive games, toys and drawing may also be helpful to engage and develop a positive rapport with the child.

When working with adolescents, engaging them through conversations on topics of interest such as their hobbies and peer group activities may be important [74]. As children get older, they have an increased need for autonomy. It is therefore essential that clinicians give young people an increasing say in establishing tasks, treatment goals and homework assignments in order to increase their motivation and treatment engagement.

When working with parents, treatment engagement and motivation can be facilitated by explaining the parents' role in treatment and emphasizing how their involvement will help to achieve the treatment goals. It is recommended to agree on tasks and goals in the early sessions and set realistic treatment expectations discussed to engage parents and prevent premature termination of treatment. During the initial assessment, or during treatment without the child present, it is also important to provide parents with a space to discuss concerns about their child, as well as their own fears and anxieties about helping their child face challenging situations (e.g., in exposure tasks). These behaviours can help to develop the therapeutic relationship between the therapist and parents and encourage parents to engage in the therapeutic process.

Practising Professionally

A clinician should have an up-to-date knowledge of the professional, ethical and legal guidelines relevant to working with youth and their families. This includes additional skills and knowledge related to working with youth, including the limits of confidentiality and duty of care. Supervision is also a key component of effective practice [75], and clinicians should have an ability to critically evaluate and make use of research which informs current practice. Finally, clinicians should be able to engage in self-reflective practice to assess their own levels of competence and undertake additional professional training or supervision when required.

CBT Competencies

Devising, Implementing and Revising a CBT Case Formulation and Treatment Plan

Following a thorough and competent assessment, the clinician should develop a case formulation that describes the causal and maintaining factors of the child's anxiety disorder. A case formulation is specific to a child's particular problem but will draw upon knowledge of cognitive, behavioural and environmental factors which tend to maintain youth anxiety in line with cognitive behavioural models (see the section 'Theoretical Foundations of CBT for Anxiety'). Importantly, the case formulation is flexible and should be updated to reflect new information as it arises [76].

Drawing upon the case formulation, a treatment plan which aims to intervene on the identified maintaining factors can then be developed. The treatment plan should select appropriate and sequenced CBT techniques that account for the social, emotional and cognitive capacity of the young person. The decision to include parents in treatment is also an important consideration, considered in the next section. Decision-making regarding the selection of specific treatment components and the duration of treatment delivery is also important to the treatment plan. Evidence-based protocols that target anxiety disorders typically range between 10 and 16 sessions. Although the specific length (or dosage) of a treatment plan ideally would be determined by the child's success in acquiring and performing the respective skills, it is often influenced by factors such as the financial capacity of the family and organizational or funding limits. Nevertheless,

treatment planning regarding dosage should consider the anticipated time that it will take a child to learn and apply a skill based on the child's developmental capacity and/or the parents' capacity.

Potential obstacles to treatment and areas of risk (e.g., suicidality) should be considered as part of the treatment plan. Appropriate techniques to deal with potential obstacles (e.g., resistance, noncompliance in homework tasks, a parent's unwillingness to assist) should be identified, drawing upon relevant theory and research, and when necessary, supervision should be obtained. The case formulation and treatment plan should be communicated with both the child and parents in age-appropriate language. As well aiding the family's understanding of anxiety and the particular presenting problem, a key part of this communication is to instil hope in the family that change is possible and to convey confidence in the treatment plan proposed. Following this, the treatment goals should be discussed and negotiated among the clinician, parents and child. The clinician should review the case formulation and treatment plan at regular intervals (e.g., every six weeks in a weekly treatment programme), and these reviews should also be communicated to the family as part of treatment.

Parental Involvement in CBT for Child and Adolescent Anxiety

One important consideration during the treatment planning stage is whether the parents should be involved in CBT treatment for their child's anxiety. The reason for including parents is primarily that it might help the child be more engaged in the treatment and may also change the parents' attitudes towards their child's problem and their own ability to handle it. Parents seeking help for their child's anxiety often struggle to know the best way to manage their child's anxiety and are presenting for treatment so that they can better assist their child. Another reason to include the parents in the treatment is the notion that anxiety runs in families and that parents with anxiety disorders might involuntarily elicit anxiety in their children through reinforcement and modelling [30]. The evidence for the enhanced benefits of including parents in CBT treatment for child anxiety is mixed, and a recent meta-analysis suggests that including parents in treatment does not improve treatment effects for child anxiety compared to CBT for the child alone [77]. These results are based on a small and heterogeneous set of studies in which the level and type of parental involvement vary across treatments and in which the sample of parents varied significantly (e.g., level of psychopathology, parent-child relationship). In practice, parents have always, more or less systematically, taken part in the treatment of their children [78]. For example, parents usually initiate therapeutic contact and are usually important for implementing components of treatment at home, particularly for younger clients (e.g., exposures). The evidence suggests, however, that involvement of parents is not an essential ingredient for change. Further, some practice guidelines recommend parent involvement for particular anxiety disorders (e.g., social anxiety disorder, obsessive compulsive disorder [OCD]) [79, 80]. Therefore, a few guiding principles are recommended when deciding on the extent and type of parental involvement in CBT for child and adolescent anxiety.

The first consideration as to whether to involve parents in treatment is the age or stage of development of the child. If the child has reached the stage of seeking independence from parents, then it seems suitable that a parent is less involved in treatment as adolescents can understand and practise treatment components on their own. In contrast, a younger child who still depends on his or her parents is likely to require more input from parents, particularly around practising key components of treatment at home (e.g., exposures). The second consideration is the level of family functioning (or whether the parent-child relationship is problematic) and the parents' own levels of psychopathology. This would determine whether some parents need additional intervention. For example, parents with psychological disorders or parents who have difficulties in parenting associated with child anxiety (e.g., overprotection or anxious modelling) may need additional intervention to improve treatment effects. Indeed, studies have shown that parental psychopathology tends to attenuate CBT treatment outcomes for child anxiety [81], and therefore – in the absence of effective treatment for the parents' own anxiety or parenting difficulties – including parents in treatment may hinder the child's treatment. This is because parents are more likely to intervene during anxiety-provoking situations for their child when he or she displays negative emotions or distress [82]. Finally, the level of parental involvement also may be determined by factors outside the therapist's control, such as the parents' willingness and ability to be involved in treatment [83].

Collaboratively Conducting Treatment Sessions

Collaboration is a key feature of CBT for youth with anxiety disorders. It has been associated with less attrition, positive treatment outcomes and a more positive therapeutic relationship [72, 84]. It also helps to maintain client motivation and contributes to skill acquisition and implementation [84]. Activities that build collaboration with children and adolescents include jointly setting treatment goals or session agendas and eliciting and responding to feedback about the child's or adolescent's current mood and life events. Jointly planning and reviewing personally meaningful homework are also important to increase the chances of treatment success [85].

Collaboration also means being flexible and adapting the use of CBT techniques to address the client's unique presentation, needs or preferences and cultural background [83]. This means that the young person's developmental stage and the level of parental involvement should be taken in to account when considering the appropriate level of in-session collaboration. For example, children with lower levels of cognitive and social capacity will be less likely to collaborate early on in treatment, whereas children with more advanced capacities may be more willing and/or able to collaborate in treatment [74, 86]. If parents are involved in treatment, a clinician can collaborate with the parents by helping them develop skills to coach and/or support their child. Coaching could involve helping the child complete tasks and providing reinforcement and/or an opportunity for skills practice out of session [87].

Competency in Specific CBT Techniques

CBT aims to teach children and adolescents skills to reduce anxiety symptoms to manageable levels and prevent interference in day-to-day functioning. CBT techniques address maintaining factors outlined earlier in child anxiety, including cognitive bias and behavioural avoidance. Skills to identify, regulate and manage anxiety, as well as social skills training, also may be included. When parents are involved in CBT treatment, specific techniques to modify parenting factors associated with child anxiety (such as parental control or the overprovision of reassurance) and support for the parents are typically provided.

One empirically supported CBT treatment for anxious youth is the *Cool Kids Anxiety Program* [10, 88, 89]. This Program is designed for children aged 7 to 17 years with anxiety disorders or experiencing elevated anxiety symptoms, and it can be delivered in multiple formats (e.g., individual or group format). It usually runs for 10 sessions and has received empirical support in randomized, controlled trials across community, clinical and school settings [87–89]. Components include cognitive restructuring, gradual exposure, response prevention and, when needed, additional skills training in areas such as assertiveness, problem-solving and relaxation. Parent management techniques are also included in the programme, and parents are encouraged to actively help their child through the programme. For adolescents, parents take more of a supportive than active role. Each component is designed to address one of the key factors that research suggests maintain problematic anxiety. This section will describe the CBT techniques included in the Cool Kids Anxiety Program through the use of a case example.

Case Study

A case example is used to describe the specific CBT techniques employed in the Cool Kids Anxiety Program. Mia is an 11-year-old girl who is described by her parents as shy, has few friends and does not talk in class or in front of new people. Her parents are concerned that she is not developing close friendships and that she will fall behind academically as a result of an increasing focus on group projects at primary school. She has also experienced teasing from her peers in the past. Her social fears are impacting the family's ability to do activities outside the home as she refuses to go to new places or try new activities as a result of her fear of talking to unfamiliar people.

Mia is the oldest child of Robert and Ruth. She has a younger brother. Ruth describes a longstanding history of anxiety in the family. She reported that she has a tendency to worry, particularly in regard to her children's wellbeing and her work, and she reported previous episodes of low mood. She reported that she has never received treatment or medication for these difficulties. She also reported that she is constantly providing Mia with reassurance about her fears and worries and that she finds it both distressing and frustrating to witness her daughter's anxiety. Robert has a very time-consuming and stressful job which involves long periods of extensive travel. The parents said that they have few social supports as they have recently moved, but they have a happy marriage and enjoy spending time together as a family. No risk issues were reported by Mia or her parents.

Mia and her parents were invited to take part in the Cool Kids Anxiety Program, and Mia and her parents agreed to attend to learn skills to manage Mia's worries. Mia's and her parents' goals for treatment were for Mia to be able to speak in class and meet new people, as well as for the family to go on social outings and enjoy time outside the family home.

Case Formulation

Following the initial assessment, a case formulation was developed by the clinician to guide the selection of treatment components. The following case formulation was briefly discussed with the family, and the components of CBT to address the factors maintaining Mia's anxiety were introduced.

Mia worries a great deal about what others think of her, and her anxiety is triggered in situations where she may be negatively evaluated by others. Mia was described as having always been shy, so a biological and temperamental predisposition may underpin her current difficulties. Her experience of having few friends and being bullied and teased in the past may also have contributed to her current anxiety. To alleviate her anxiety, Mia avoids social situations where she may be negatively evaluated, such as speaking in class or engaging in new situations involving unfamiliar others. In turn, this reinforces her beliefs that she cannot cope in these situations. Mia's mother often provides Mia with reassurance, and the family have stopped going out to social events to prevent Mia from feeling anxious in situations involving unfamiliar others. In turn, these behaviours have reinforced Mia's belief that she cannot cope in social situations.

The main components of CBT treatment to address Mia's difficulties were to target her beliefs that she was not able to cope in social situations through cognitive restructuring (detective thinking) and to gradually expose her to these situations. In addition, Mia was taught problem-solving and assertiveness skills to increase her confidence in managing her anxiety and dealing with social situations, including potential teasing and bullying. Mia's parents were also provided with skills and encouragement to reinforce Mia's non-anxious behaviour, reduce reassurance and provide Mia with opportunities to practise her new skills.

Managing Maladaptive Mood and Arousal

Mia was given information about anxiety and introduced to the worry scale. The worry scale is a scale that rates the intensity of the worry/fear between 0 (very relaxed) and 10 (extremely worried). Mia was asked to record situations in which she feels anxious, including information on (1) the situation, (2) the thoughts she is having by asking herself 'what do you think will happen?', 'what bad thing am I expecting?' or 'what could go wrong' and (3) the intensity of the worry/fear using the worry scale (0–10) and her behaviour (what she does). Mia also was guided to identify bodily responses to anxiety (e.g., stomach aches, heart racing, trembling hands) to alert herself to the fact that she is feeling anxious. Mia was provided with additional relaxation techniques, including controlled breathing and progressive muscle relaxation, to use when she is aware that she is feeling anxious.

Cognitive Restructuring/Detective Thinking

Starting on a small worry, Mia was asked to collect evidence in situations to work out whether her thinking is realistic and helpful. Evidence was collected by asking such questions as, 'what are the facts?', 'what else could happen?', 'what has happened when I worried about this before?' and 'what has happened to other people?'. Mia was also prompted to answer questions around the consequences of her worry; such as 'how bad would it be if it happened?' and 'how could I cope?'. Finally, Mia was asked to come up with a realistic or alternative thought that summarized the discovered evidence (e.g., 'most likely, people will not even notice'). She was then asked to provide her worry rating and compare it to her original worry rating for the same worry. Mia used 'detective thinking' on a number of her worries. An example of one of Mia's completed detective thinking worksheets on having to read aloud in class is shown in Figure 9.1.

Exposure

Mia and her parents learned that to overcome fears, they must face their fears in a gradual way. They learned that the goal of exposure is to reduce physiological arousal

Event — I have to read cloud in class

Thought Rating 0–10 [8] I 'll get my words muddled up and everyone will lough at me

Evidence
Alternative outcomes (facts, other possibilities, how likely, history or other people)

- I 'm good at reading and I read to my brother all the time
- I have read cloud in class once before and I didn't mess up my words and no-one loughed at me
- I haven't noticed anyone lough when other people read in class

Realistic consequences (how bad, disaster or not, can I cope, how long will it last, do others survive)

- If people do lough at me it might be because I said something furry
- If I mess up a few words most people won't notice

Realistic Thought

Rating 0–10 [3] Even if I do mess up a few words, most people won't notice and they are unlikely to lough at me

Figure 9.1 Mia's detective thinking worksheet on having to read aloud in class

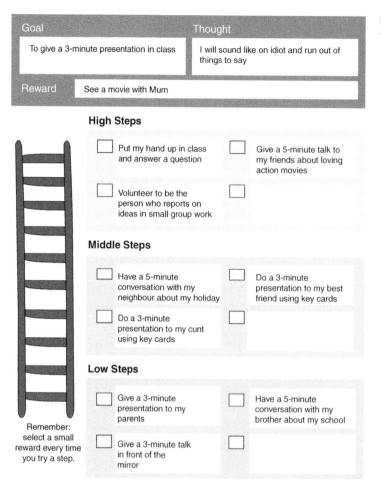

Figure 9.2 Mia's stepladder about giving a presentation in class

and change unhelpful behaviours (e.g., avoidance) to the feared stimulus. Undertaking exposures also provided them with evidence for detective thinking tasks. The family designed 'stepladders' together, beginning with small fears and increasing to bigger fears. The steps were designed to be practical and repeated frequently. The more difficult steps on the stepladders included exposure to cost. That is, Mia was encouraged to deliberately make mistakes or do silly things in front of increasingly difficult situations. Mia was encouraged to stay in the situation long enough to experience a decrease in her anxiety and to learn that what she thought was going to happen was less likely than she anticipated. Mia was encouraged to use detective thinking before engaging in an exposure task and reflect after the task what information she learned. Mia and her parents were encouraged to frequently engage in and conduct exposures between and in sessions. An example of one of Mia's stepladders about giving a presentation in class is shown in Figure 9.2.

General Skills Training

In addition to detective thinking and exposure tasks, Mia and her parents were taught problem-solving and assertiveness skills. Problem-solving is a skill used to help children generate and choose adaptive responses rather than limited and avoidant responses. Problem-solving skills were provided to increase Mia's confidence and autonomy in managing her anxiety and to help her make everyday decisions. First, Mia was asked to identify a specific problem/situation (e.g., does not know how to do a homework task) and, second, think of a number of possible solutions (e.g., try to understand the task, ask the teacher to clarify the task, ask peers to clarify the task). The third step involved Mia thinking of the possible short- and long-term consequences of each solution and, fourthly, identify the pros and cons of each solution, Finally, the most preferred solution was chosen. Mia was also taught assertiveness skills to deal with potential teasing and bullying. Specific strategies were to respond in a confident way (e.g., eye contact) and to show that the teasing does not bother her (e.g., ignoring, providing confident remarks). Mia was asked to role-play these skills and coached in session in order to master these skills in a safe and supportive environment.

Modifying the Family Environment

Mia's parents were invited to take part in treatment for two main reasons. First, Mia still depended on her parents and their input in treatment sessions, as well as their support for homework tasks. Second, their own behaviours (by their own admission) were having an impact on Mia's anxiety, and the therapist thought that targeting them in treatment would be beneficial for both Mia and her family. Therefore, Mia's parents were taught how their own responses to Mia were unintentionally helping to maintain Mia's anxiety. In particular, they were taught that providing reassurance or too much assistance may increase Mia's anxiety because Mia is prevented from learning accurate information about the situation and her ability to cope with it. Given that Mia's mother is anxious herself, Ruth was also encouraged to consider how her own anxiety may impact her parenting choices. Ruth was encouraged to use the same strategies – particularly cognitive restructuring and exposure – to manage her own anxiety. This not only provided Mia's mother with an opportunity to face her own real-world fears, but it also helped to model non-anxious and brave behaviours to Mia.

Second, Mia's parents were encouraged to provide Mia with positive reinforcement for non-anxious behaviours through the use of tangible (e.g., stickers, special outings) and intangible (e.g., praise, attention) rewards to their child, particularly for engaging in exposure tasks. Mia's parents were asked to record their responses to Mia's anxiety in order to increase their awareness of their responses and to attempt to alter them when necessary. Finally, they were asked to model adaptive and non-avoidant behaviours during treatment. This was implemented both in session (e.g., doing a presentation in session) and between sessions. Modelling cognitive restructuring skills before engaging in exposures can also be helpful for both the parents and child.

Summary of Treatment Outcome

Mia made positive improvements during the course of therapy. By the end of treatment, Mia was able to

effectively identify and challenge her thoughts around social situations. Initially, she found this task quite difficult, especially when challenging her bigger worries, but she responded well to encouragement and prompting. Mia exposed herself to a number of social situations which she initially feared. For example, she answered questions in class, and she joined in on group activities and went to a friend's house by herself. Mia often used problem-solving to decide about how to deal with situations which might make her feel anxious. Mia's parents reduced their reassurance and worked hard to reward and praise Mia's non-anxious behaviour. In particular, Mia's mother found that working on Mia's anxiety and learning new skills not only increased her empathy for her daughter but also motivated her to seek treatment for her own difficulties. As a family, they went out to new places (such as a new restaurant), and while this was not as regular as they would like, they were pleased with the progress. Future treatment should focus on continuing to expose Mia to a range of social situations (e.g., joining a new activity or going to a party) and encourage the use of assertive communication skills in these situations (e.g., saying what she thinks and contributing to discussions).

Empirical Evidence for CBT

Numerous controlled-outcome studies have demonstrated the effectiveness of CBT for children and adolescents with anxiety disorders [12, 90], and CBT is recommended as the treatment of choice for children and young people with anxiety disorders in clinical guidelines around the world [79, 80]. Research studies have shown that different forms of CBT (e.g., group versus individual) are promising treatments for child and adolescent anxiety disorders, but research is mixed for the effects of parental involvement in children's treatment. For example, a meta-analysis that directly compared CBT for child anxiety with and without parental involvement ($n=16$) found no significant differences between the two groups on treatment outcome [77]. This concurs with other reviews which found that child-only treatment was significantly better or equivalent to parental-involved treatment [91-3]. Another meta-analysis evaluated whether type of parental involvement was a potential moderator in CBT outcomes for children [94]. Results showed that children in the two conditions with active parental involvement (e.g., reducing controlling parenting behaviour) had fewer anxiety diagnoses at follow-up than the low-involvement group. However, reviews are limited by the fact that the authors aggregated findings across a heterogeneous set of studies – all with varying levels and types of parental involvement in treatment, as well as heterogeneous samples of parents – thus further research is needed to determine whether and how parents should be involved in treatment. For example, it seems likely that the impact of parental involvement in treatment varies with the child's age, with the inclusion of parents expected to decrease as children get older. Similarly, it seems likely that targeting specific parenting behaviours or difficulties in treatment is likely to be more beneficial for families that exhibit these difficulties – rather than those which do not. In sum, CBT is the treatment of choice for anxiety disorders in children and adolescence, and the decision to include parents in treatment is currently guided by the developmental stage of the child and individual case formulation.

Common Obstacles to Competent Practice and Strategies to Overcome Them

The effective treatment of child and adolescent anxiety can easily be undermined or sidetracked by a range of obstacles. Moreover, clinicians working in real-world settings have been known to modify or shorten the treatment protocols evaluated in research trials, often at the expense of the most effective components of the treatment (e.g., gradual exposure) [95–97]. This section describes common obstacles that may arise during the family-based treatment of anxiety and the therapist competencies needed to overcome them.

Lack of Response to Treatment

A lack of a response to treatment may arise because the child and/or parents lack motivation to implement treatment, lack belief in the utility of treatment or a lack of effective collaboration between parents and child or adolescent or between client and clinician. Unlike adults, children and young people seeking treatment are not necessarily in agreement about attending and may be brought to treatment by caregivers against their will. This might create resistance and hinder treatment progress or lead to premature termination of treatment. Therefore, it is important to assess motivational levels early on in treatment and address motivational issues as they arise. Strategies include the use of motivational enhancement

techniques [98], such as questions around how anxiety is disabling and may warrant change and the pros and cons of change versus staying the same. A lack of belief in the utility of treatment could be addressed by providing an age-appropriate rationale for the treatment and spending time collaboratively establishing goals of treatment with the child. This may help to build the child's self-efficacy and create positive expectations about treatment.

A lack of treatment response may also occur because of a child or parent's non-adherence to treatment tasks and goals (e.g., non-completion of homework, refusal to complete exposure tasks or missing appointments). Identifying these behaviours – a form of behavioural avoidance – and incorporating them into the formulation can help the clinician to assess their impact on treatment and identify ways to address them. Following this, the clinician should discuss these behaviours with the parents and/or child in the context of the overall goals of treatment (i.e., acknowledging how they may be impacting treatment progress) and collaboratively discuss appropriate ways to address the behaviours. In addition, explicitly stating the importance and value of both the parents' and child's involvement and skills practice may help to increase their motivation and treatment engagement.

Discrepancy Between Child and Parents

Disagreement between a child and his or her parent(s) is a common obstacle faced by many clinicians working with families. For example, parents and a child may have different perspectives on the presenting problem, or conflict may have arisen depending on who has brought the child to treatment. Parents may believe that the problem lies with the child and may anticipate limited involvement in treatment, whereas children may view their parents or other key relationships as the problem and may resent being the focus of treatment. In these situations, the clinician is encouraged to work towards consensus using both communication and negotiation techniques. Ultimately, the clinician must help the child and parents come to a compromise that enables the child to feel in charge of the treatment while also not rejecting parental involvement and input. Keeping parents in the 'loop' and agreeing with the family on how this is done constitutes one way to manage disagreement between them. In all cases, the clinician should avoid taking sides with either parents or child and try to make decisions within the professional guidelines and responsibilities towards the child.

Disagreement between the parents/child and clinician may also occur. For example, there may be disagreement on the conceptualization of problem; parents may view their child as having disruptive behaviour, whereas a clinician may view the behaviour as part of the anxiety. Again, using general therapeutic and CBT-specific competencies of alliance building and collaboration is so important to work towards a consensus. Building and maintaining a positive relationship with parents may be helped by having separate sessions or time set aside during the session to listen and validate parents' concerns, as well as providing them with additional psychoeducation about anxiety and the treatment approach (e.g., understanding how anxiety may manifest in a variety of ways). This can also be an opportunity to build therapeutic alliance by building parents' expertise in skills and getting their knowledge and insight into their child's difficulties and progress.

Nature of Anxiety and Impact on Treatment

The nature of anxiety disorders may present particular obstacles for clinicians. For example, children with anxiety are likely to be inhibited, so alliance building may take time or be difficult to gauge during treatment. Therefore, it is important that clinicians assign time to build a strong rapport with the child and then also regularly 'check in' with the child and/or adolescent as well as parents to assess the progress and quality of the alliance.

Exposure (and response prevention) is a critical component of CBT and can be extremely emotionally demanding and challenging for children with anxiety disorders. Given that children with anxiety are likely to have difficulty regulating emotions, it may be important to introduce and practise relaxation skills before starting exposure tasks. Enough time must also be set aside in treatment to provide in-depth and age-appropriate rationale for the tasks to build a child's and parents' motivation to engage in this component of treatment. Similarly, working on building a positive alliance before conducting exposure tasks is also important to maximize child involvement. Within the context of an established positive alliance, exposures do not have a negative impact on the therapeutic relationship [99]. Exposures are also extremely challenging for parents and therapists because the steps are designed to elicit anxiety in the child. Novice therapists can find this difficult and can be tempted to avoid delivering effective exposures. However, the

absence of challenging exposures is associated with poorer treatment outcomes [95], and thus, this should be a focus of supervision if the therapist is finding this aspect of therapy delivery difficult.

Particular obstacles to treatment may arise as a function of the type of anxiety disorder experienced by the child, but these obstacles may also provide an opportunity for treatment. For example, children with social anxiety disorder may find interaction with the therapist challenging and may avoid treatment if these interactions are too anxiety provoking or challenging for them. However, interactions with the clinician may provide an opportunity for exposure and help the child overcome his or her social anxiety. Therefore, the clinician should take particular care to build rapport with the child and build his or her confidence and self-efficacy in attending and taking part in treatment.

Children with social anxiety may also have a social desirability bias and want to 'please' the clinician (e.g., completing written homework tasks 'perfectly'); therefore, the clinician should use sessions to role-play mini-exposures for these clients, for example, by making mistakes and 'stuffing up' in interactions. Rigid styles of thinking and a low tolerance for uncertainty are also typical in children with OCD and generalized anxiety disorder; therefore, explicitly structuring sessions in a predictable way helps these children to focus on content in session rather than worrying about what will happen next. CBT is particularly good for this because it incorporates structure as part of therapy (e.g., agenda setting and homework). However, if a child is overly fixated on adhering to session agendas or home-working compliance, then adapting these parts of CBT as a type of exposure task may be helpful.

Issues Around Modifying Family Environment Factors

Consistency between parents in implementing the strategies will result in more rapid change. To this end, it is more ideal, where possible, for all parents involved in the child's care to attend the therapy sessions. In some cases, this will not be possible; for example, when there are high levels of conflict between parents, separate sessions for each parent may be required. Ideally, the parents will work together, in a consistent manner, to support the child in facing anxiety-provoking situations.

Parents who are anxious may inadvertently interfere with treatment by negatively reinforcing escape behaviours or by encouraging avoidance by 'rescuing' the child from challenging tasks. Parents may also feel stigma, guilt or shame about attending therapy with their child. Therefore, it is essential that the clinician identifies and normalizes parents' feelings and behaviours and addresses them within the context of a positive therapeutic alliance. The therapist could also provide the parents with strategies for coping with their own anxiety or difficulty watching their child face distressing situations, problem-solve how to overcome practical barriers to engaging in skills practice or recommend that the parents seek their own treatment to deal with difficult emotions.

Clinicians should aim to be courageous and confident leaders and lead by example by creating an atmosphere that is upbeat, engaging and motivating. The use of liberal positive reinforcement for both children and parents is also recommended to increase a family's motivation. The use of clinician modelling around exposure tasks (e.g., supporting a child during an exposure) may also be particularly helpful, as well as 'coaching' parents in session. Planning exposure tasks, including when and where they are conducted and how to overcome potential barriers to practise, is also important to avert issues around non-compliance. Finally, welcoming feedback from families about skills practice and treatment progress and acknowledging instances where therapy may have moved too quickly are also important in order to adapt and modify the treatment plan (e.g., by breaking exposure tasks into more manageable steps).

Co-morbidity and Individual Differences

Anxiety disorders in youth rarely occur in isolation and often co-occur with related disorders (e.g., a co-morbid anxiety disorder, depression, attention deficit hyperactivity disorder, chronic illness). Co-morbidity is typically associated with greater severity and impairment for the child, and CBT may need to be adapted to treat these co-morbidities. Most treatment protocols focus treatment on the primary anxiety disorder (i.e., most interfering), and this usually results in the reduction of co-morbid anxiety disorders [100]. However, the presence of co-morbidity does not seem to be associated with poorer treatment outcome [101, 102]. There are also an increasing number of protocols that have been developed for anxiety and specific co-morbidities: anxiety and depression [103], anxiety and attention deficit hyperactivity disorder [104], anxiety and asthma [105]. In

cases where evidence-based guidelines do not exist for specific patterns of co-morbidity, clinicians should balance fidelity to treatment protocols with choosing and sequencing CBT techniques on an individual basis and add appropriate evidence-based treatment components or modules that explicitly address the specific co-morbidity [15, 106, 107]. For example, if a child has disruptive behaviour difficulties which are distinct from his or her anxiety, it may be necessary to treat aspects of the disruptive behaviour that may impact anxiety treatment before targeting the anxiety. Treating elements of anxiety and related disorders via such a modular approach has also been shown to increase treatment uptake [108].

Other factors that may impact treatment approach is the family's ethnicity or culture. For example, there is some evidence that particular ethnic groups have higher rates of internalizing disorders [109] and have higher rates of attrition from treatment [110]. Further, symptom expression may vary across cultures, and/or a family's belief about the origins of the disorder may affect both treatment compliance and outcome [111]. Similarly, particular cultures may prohibit or encourage certain beliefs, emotions and behaviours, and attempts by the clinician to increase or minimize these factors may lead to a poor therapeutic alliance and poor treatment outcome. The bulk of the treatment protocols that have been developed have been developed primarily in Caucasian populations, and thus it is important to be aware of the possible limitations of our evidence-based approaches to all cultures. Thus, clinicians should educate themselves about the client's culture and be aware of the various cultural beliefs and practices that may impact the child and parents in treatment progress.

Developmental Considerations

When treatment is not developmentally appropriate, then it is likely that the child will disengage from treatment, and progress in CBT will be limited. In addition to gaining knowledge about child and adolescent general patterns of development (see the section 'Key Features of Clinical Competencies in Treating Anxiety Disorders in Children and Adolescents') and using treatments that have age-appropriate evidence (e.g., Cool Kids Anxiety Program), it is essential that clinicians keep up-to-date on developmental literature to adapt evidence-based CBT for particular age groups or developmental capacities. For example, treatment materials and examples could be adapted according to the age and language ability (e.g., reading ability) of the child, as well as the language used in therapy and relevant exposure tasks. In addition, the cognitive capacity of the child needs to be accounted for before conducting in CBT, or tasks such as cognitive restructuring may be ineffective. It is generally considered that when children reach seven years of age, they have the cognitive capacity to engage in cognitive restructuring tasks [112], but the tasks need to be adapted according to the individual cognitive capacity of the child. Components of treatment that can be modified as part of developmentally appropriate care include language, materials and examples provided; the use of rewards; and changes in therapy space (e.g., provision of toys to build alliance in younger children). Difficulties arising because of developmental differences can be overcome to some extent if there is a thorough assessment and case formulation.

Consideration of informed consent and decision-making capacity is also important because clinicians need to balance ethical responsibility and confidentiality. Intensive and appropriate supervisions from clinicians who have expertise in relevant age groups is also essential when working with youth populations. The extent of parental involvement also needs to be sensitive to the child's developmental level. Younger children will be more dependent on parents than older children, particularly around planning and implementing exposures. Therefore, clinicians need to balance the degree of parent involvement and client autonomy in accordance with the developmental level of each child.

Conclusion

This chapter highlights the key competencies required by clinicians to deliver effective evidence-based CBT for youth with anxiety disorders and their families. To summarize, there are a number of both generic and specific competencies that are important for a clinician to master. The first of the generic competencies includes the ability to conduct a competent and thorough assessment before treatment as well as adequate monitoring of client outcomes during and after treatment to track progress. Given the high levels of co-morbidity and increased suicide risk in youth with anxiety disorders, clinicians also need to be competent in conducting risk assessments throughout the therapy process. Other generic competencies include

understanding relevant child and adolescent characteristics, building a positive relationship and practising professionally.

As discussed throughout this chapter, specific competencies relevant to the delivery of CBT for youth anxiety disorders relate to the ability to develop, implement and revise CBT case formulations and work collaboratively with the child and family within sessions. Perhaps the most important and pertinent specific competencies for delivering treatment relate to the ability to competently deliver key CBT strategies such as cognitive restructuring, gradual exposure (including response prevention) and parent training that addresses the key maintaining factors. Owing to a lack of studies evaluating the essential ingredients for effective treatment, we encourage therapists to receive adequate training in the delivery of evidence-based packages that include these core components. There are a number of training programmes available around the world (e.g., Cool Kids Anxiety Program; www.mq.edu.au/CEH). Importantly, there is currently insufficient evidence to recommend training in and delivery of other psychological treatments for anxiety disorders such as mindfulness or acceptance and commitment therapy. Until other psychological therapies have been proven to be more effective than existing psychological treatments, there is limited value in investing in retraining therapists in treatments that are not based on the CBT core competencies outlined herein.

The specific competencies outlined in this chapter are particularly important for overcoming common obstacles encountered when working with youth with anxiety and their families. Specifically, clinicians need to consider the role of the family and other environmental factors that play in maintaining the child's symptoms. When devising and implementing the treatment plan, the clinician should ensure that these maintenance factors are adequately addressed in therapy, including making an informed clinical decision around whether to involve parents in treatment. Finally, at all stages of evidence-based assessment and treatment, the therapist needs to be aware of and consider the child's developmental needs to ensure that the tasks are appropriately matched to the child's reading skill, cognitive ability and emotional maturity. By mastering the generic and specific core competencies outlined in this chapter, clinicians will be more likely to deliver effective treatment, thereby reducing the life interference that results from anxiety disorders in children and adolescents.

References

1. Beesdo K, Knappe S, Pine DS. Anxiety and anxiety disorders in children and adolescents: Developmental issues and implications for DSM-V. *Psychiatric Clinics* 2009; **32**(3):483–524.

2. Costello EJ, Mustillo S, Erkanli A, et al. Prevalence and development of psychiatric disorders in childhood and adolescence. *Archives of General Psychiatry* 2003; **60**(8):837–44.

3. Merikangas K, He J-P, Burstein M, et al. Lifetime prevalence of mental disorders in U.S. adolescents: Results from the National Comorbidity Survey Replication–Adolescent Supplement (NCS-A). *Journal of the American Academy of Child and Adolescent Psychiatry* 2010; **49**(10):980–9.

4. American Psychological Association. *Diagnostic and Statistical Manual of Mental Disorders*, 5th ed. Arlington, VA: American Psychiatric Publishing, 2013.

5. American Psychological Association. Diagnostic and Statistical Manual of Mental Disorders, 5th ed. Arlington, VA: American Psychiatric Publishing, 2013.

6. Kessler RC, Berglund P, Demler O, et al. Lifetime prevalence and age-of-onset distributions of DSM-IV disorders in the National Comorbidity Survey replication. *JAMA Psychiatry* 2005; **62**(6):593–602.

7. Angold A, Costello EJ, Erkanli A. Comorbidity. *Journal of Child Psychology and Psychiatry and Allied Disciplines* 1999; **40**(1):57–87.

8. Brent DA. Risk factors for adolescent suicide and suicidal behavior: Mental and substance abuse disorders, family environmental factors, and life stress. *Suicide and Life-Threatening Behavior* 1995; **25**(S1):52–63.

9. Rudd MD, Berman AL, Joiner TE, et al. Warning signs for suicide: Theory, research, and clinical applications. *Suicide and Life-Threatening Behavior* 2006; **36**(3):255–62.

10. Hudson JL, Rapee RM, Deveney C, et al. Cognitive-behavioral treatment versus an active control for children and adolescents with anxiety disorders: A randomized trial. *Journal of the American Academy of Child and Adolescent Psychiatry* 2009; **48**(5):533–44.

11. Kendall PC, Hudson JL, Gosch E, et al. Cognitive-behavioral therapy for anxiety disordered youth: A randomized clinical trial evaluating child and family modalities. *Journal of Consulting and Clinical Psychology* 2008; **76**(2):282–97.

12. James AC, James G, Cowdrey FA, et al. Cognitive behavioural therapy for anxiety disorders in children and adolescents. *Cochrane Database of Systematic Reviews* 2015; (2):1–90.

13. World Health Organization. *The ICD-10 Classification of Mental and Behavioural Disorders: Clinical Descriptions and Diagnostic Guidelines*: Geneva: WHO, 1992.

14. Rapee RM, Schniering CA, Hudson JL. Anxiety disorders during childhood and adolescence: Origins and treatment. *Annual Review of Clinical Psychology* 2009; **5**:311–41.

15. Chorpita BF, Taylor AA, Francis SE, et al. Efficacy of modular cognitive behavior therapy for childhood anxiety disorders. *Behavior Therapy* 2004; **35**(2):263–87.

16. Hudson JL, Rapee RM. From anxious temperament to disorder: An etiological model. In: Heimberg RG, Turk CL, Mennin DS (eds.), *Generalized Anxiety Disorder: Advances in Research and Practice*. New York: Guilford Press, 2004, pp. 51–74.

17. Manassis K, Bradley SJ. The development of childhood anxiety disorders: Toward an integrated model. *Journal of Applied Developmental Psychology* 1994; **15**(3):345–66.

18. Chronis-Tuscano A, Degnan KA, Pine DS, et al. Stable early maternal report of behavioral inhibition predicts lifetime social anxiety disorder in adolescence. *Journal of the American Academy of Child and Adolescent Psychiatry* 2009; **48**(9):928–35.

19. Hudson JL, Murayama K, Meteyard L, et al. Early childhood predictors of anxiety in early adolescence. *Journal of Abnormal Child Psychology* 2019; **47**(7):1121–33.

20. Hirshfeld-Becker DR, Biederman J, Henin A, et al. Behavioral inhibition in preschool children at risk is a specific predictor of middle childhood social anxiety: A five-year follow-up. *Journal of Developmental and Behavioral Pediatrics* 2007; **28**(3):225–33.

21. Kagan J, Snidman N. Temperamental factors in human development. *American Psychologist* 1991; **46**(8):856–62.

22. Lonigan CJ, Phillips BM, Hooe ES. Relations of positive and negative affectivity to anxiety and depression in children: Evidence from a latent variable longitudinal study. *Journal of Consulting and Clinical Psychology* 2003; **71**(3):465–81.

23. Hurrell KE, Hudson JL, Schniering CA. Parental reactions to children's negative emotions: Relationships with emotion regulation in children with an anxiety disorder. *Journal of Anxiety Disorders* 2015; **29**:72–82.

24. Southam-Gerow MA, Kendall PC. A preliminary study of the emotion understanding of youths referred for treatment of anxiety disorders. *Journal of Clinical Child Psychology* 2000; **29**(3):319–27.

25. Suveg C, Zeman J. Emotion regulation in children with anxiety disorders. *Journal of Clinical Child and Adolescent Psychology* 2004; **33**(4):750–9.

26. Vasey MW, MacLeod C. Information-processing factors in childhood anxiety: A review and developmental perspective. In: Vasey MW, Dadds MR (eds.), *The Developmental Psychopathology of Anxiety*. Oxford, UK: Oxford University Press, 2001, pp. 253–77.

27. Ehrenreich JT, Gross AM. Biased attentional behavior in childhood anxiety: A review of theory and current empirical investigation. *Clinical Psychology Review* 2002; **22**(7):991–1008.

28. Klein AM, Rapee RM, Hudson JL, et al. Content-specific interpretation biases in clinically anxious children. *Behaviour Research and Therapy*. 2019; **121**:103452.

29. Waters AM, Craske MG. Towards a cognitive-learning formulation of youth anxiety: A narrative review of theory and evidence and implications for treatment. *Clinical Psychology Review* 2016; **50**:50–66.

30. Barrett PM, Rapee RM, Dadds MM, Ryan SM. Family enhancement of cognitive style in anxious and aggressive children. *Journal of Abnormal Child Psychology* 1996; **24**(2):187–203.

31. Allen JL, Rapee RM. Are reported differences in life events for anxious children and controls due to comorbid disorders? *Journal of Anxiety Disorders* 2009; **23**(4):511–18.

32. Goodyer IM, Altham PM. Lifetime exit events and recent social and family adversities in anxious and depressed school-age children and adolescents–I. *Journal of Affective Disorders* 1991; **21**(4):219–28.

33. Eley TC, Stevenson J. Specific life events and chronic experiences differentially associated with depression and anxiety in young twins. *Journal of Abnormal Child Psychology* 2000; **28**(4):383–94.

34. Lawrence D, Johnson S, Hafekost J, et al. *The Mental Health of Children and Adolescents: Report on the Second Australian Child and Adolescent Survey of Mental Health and Wellbeing*. Canberra: Australian Department of Health, 2015.

35. Storch EA, Masia-Warner C. The relationship of peer victimization to social anxiety and loneliness in adolescent females. *Journal of Adolescence* 2004; **27**(3):351–62.

36. Hudson JL. Interparental conflict, violence and psychopathology. In: Hudson J, Rapee R (eds.), *Psychopathology and the Family*. New York: Elsevier, 2005, pp. 53–69.

37. Johnson JG, Cohen P, Kasen S, Brook JS. Parental concordance and offspring risk for anxiety, conduct, depressive, and substance use disorders. *Psychopathology* 2008; **41**(2):124–8.

38. Last CG, Hersen M, Kazdin A, et al. Anxiety disorders in children and their families. *JAMA Psychiatry* 1991; **48**(10):928–34.

39. Eley TC, Bolton D, O'Connor TG, et al. A twin study of anxiety-related behaviours in pre-school children. *Journal of Child Psychology and Psychiatry* 2003; **44**(7):945–60.

40. Hettema JM, Neale MC, Kendler KS. A review and meta-analysis of the genetic epidemiology of anxiety disorders. *American Journal of Psychiatry* 2001; **158**(10):1568–78.

41. Barber BK. Parental psychological control: Revisiting a neglected construct. *Child Development* 1996; **67**(6):3296–319.

42. Clark KE, Ladd GW. Connectedness and autonomy support in parent–child relationships: Links to children's socioemotional orientation and peer relationships. *Developmental Psychology* 2000; **36**(4):485–98.

43. Maccoby EE. *The Role of Parents in the Socialization of Children: An Historical Overview*. Washington, DC: American Psychological Association, 1994, pp. 589–615.

44. Wood JJ, McLeod BD, Sigman M, et al. Parenting and childhood anxiety: Theory, empirical findings, and future directions. *Journal of Child Psychology and Psychiatry* 2003; **44**(1):134–51.

45. McLeod BD, Wood JJ, Weisz JR. Examining the association between parenting and childhood anxiety: A meta-analysis. *Clinical Psychology Review* 2007; **27**(2):155–72.

46. McLeod BD, Wood JJ, Avny SB. Parenting and child anxiety disorders. In: McKay D, Storch EA (eds.), *Handbook of Child and Adolescent Anxiety Disorders*. New York: Springer, 2011, pp. 213–28.

47. Rapee RM. Potential role of childrearing practices in the development of anxiety and depression. *Clinical Psychology Review* 1997; **17**(1):47–67.

48. Hudson JL, Doyle AM, Gar N. Child and maternal influence on parenting behavior in clinically anxious children. *Journal of Clinical Child and Adolescent Psychology* 2009; **38**(2):256–62.

49. McMurtry CM, Chambers CT, McGrath PJ, Asp E. When 'don't worry' communicates fear: Children's perceptions of parental reassurance and distraction during a painful medical procedure. *Pain* 2010; **150**(1):52–8.

50. Bögels SM, Brechman-Toussaint ML. Family issues in child anxiety: Attachment, family functioning, parental rearing and beliefs. *Clinical Psychology Review* 2006; **26**(7):834–56.

51. Chorpita BF, Barlow DH. The development of anxiety: The role of control in the early environment. *Psychological Bulletin* 1998; **124**(1):3–21.

52. Gerull FC, Rapee RM. Mother knows best: Effects of maternal modelling on the acquisition of fear and avoidance behaviour in toddlers. *Behaviour Research and Therapy* 2002; **40**(3):279–87.

53. de Rosnay M, Cooper PJ, Tsigaras N, Murray L. Transmission of social anxiety from mother to infant: An experimental study using a social referencing paradigm. *Behaviour Research and Therapy* 2006; **44**(8):1165–75.

54. Murray L, Creswell C, Cooper PJ. The development of anxiety disorders in childhood: An integrative review. *Psychological Medicine* 2009; **39**(9):1413–23.

55. Sburlati ES, Schniering CA, Lyneham HJ, Rapee RM. A model of therapist competencies for the empirically supported cognitive behavioral treatment of child and adolescent anxiety and depressive disorders. *Clinical Child and Family Psychology Review* 2011; **14**(1):89–109.

56. Kazdin AE. Psychotherapy for children and adolescents. *Annual Review of Psychology* 2003; **54**(1):253–76.

57. Silverman WK, Ollendick TH. Evidence-based assessment of anxiety and its disorders in children and adolescents. *Journal of Clinical Child and Adolescent Psychology* 2005; **34**(3):380–411.

58. Costello EJ, Angold A, Keeler GP. Adolescent outcomes of childhood disorders: The consequences of severity and impairment. *Journal of the American Academy of Child and Adolescent Psychiatry* 1999; **38**(2):121–8.

59. Morris TLGLA. Assessment and treatment of childhood anxiety disorders. In: Vandecreek L (ed.), *Innovations in Clinical Practice: A Source Book*, vol. **20**. Sarasota, FL.: Professional Resource Press, 2002, pp. 76–86.

60. Silverman WK, Albano AM. *Anxiety Disorders Interview Schedule for DSM-IV*. Boulder, CO: Graywind Publications, 1996.

61. Lyneham HJ, Abbott MJ, Rapee RM. Interrater reliability of the anxiety disorders interview schedule for DSM-IV: Child and parent version. *Journal of the American Academy of Child and Adolescent Psychiatry* 2007; **46**(6):731–6.

62. Wood JJ, Piacentini JC, Bergman RL, et al. Concurrent validity of the anxiety disorders section of the anxiety disorders interview schedule for DSM-IV: Child and parent versions. *Journal of Clinical Child and Adolescent Psychology* 2002; **31**(3):335–42.

63. March JS, Sullivan K, Parker J. Test-retest reliability of the multidimensional anxiety scale for children. *Journal of Anxiety Disorders* 1999; **13**(4):349–58.

64. Spence SH. A measure of anxiety symptoms among children. *Behaviour Research and Therapy* 1998; **36**(5):545–66.

65. Lyneham HJ, Sburlati ES, Abbott MJ, et al. Psychometric properties of the Child Anxiety Life Interference Scale (CALIS). *Journal of Anxiety Disorders* 2013; **27**(7):711–19.

66. Ollendick TH, Lewis KM, Cowart MJW, Davis T. Prediction of child performance on a parent–child behavioral approach test with animal phobic children. *Behavior Modification* 2012; **36**(4):509–24.

67. Ginsburg GS, Siqueland L, Masia-Warner C, Hedtke KA. Anxiety disorders in children: Family matters. *Cognitive and Behavioral Practice* 2004; **11**(1):28–43.

68. Dougherty DM, Mathias CW, Marsh-Richard DM, et al. Impulsivity and clinical symptoms among adolescents with non-suicidal self-injury with or without attempted suicide. *Psychiatry Research* 2009; **169**(1):22–7.

69. Brown RC, Parker KM, McLeod BD, Southam-Gerow MA. Building a positive therapeutic relationship with the child or adolescent and parent. In: Sburlati ES, Lyneham HJ, Schniering CA, Rapee RM (eds.), *Evidence-Based CBT for Anxiety and Depression in Children and Adolescents: A Competencies-Based Approach*. Chichester, UK: Wiley Blackwell, 2014, pp. 63–78.

70. Hawley KM, Weisz JR. Youth versus parent working alliance in usual clinical care: Distinctive associations with retention, satisfaction, and treatment outcome. *Journal of Clinical Child and Adolescent Psychology* 2005; **34**(1):117–28.

71. Hudson JL, Kendall PC, Chu BC, et al. Child involvement, alliance, and therapist flexibility: Process variables in cognitive-behavioural therapy for anxiety disorders in childhood. *Behaviour Research and Therapy* 2014; **52**:1–8.

72. Chu BC, Kendall PC. Positive association of child involvement and treatment outcome within a manual-based cognitive-behavioral treatment for children with anxiety. *Journal of Consulting and Clinical Psychology* 2004; **72**(5):821–9.

73. Karver MS, Handelsman JB, Fields S, Bickman L. Meta-analysis of therapeutic relationship variables in youth and family therapy: The evidence for different relationship variables in the child and adolescent treatment outcome literature. *Clinical Psychology Review* 2006; **26**(1):50–65.

74. Sauter FM, Heyne D, Michiel Westenberg P. Cognitive behavior therapy for anxious adolescents: developmental influences on treatment design and delivery. *Clinical Child and Family Psychology Review* 2009; **12**(4):310–35.

75. Beidas RS, Kendall PC. Training therapists in evidence-based practice: a critical review of studies from a systems-contextual perspective. *Clinical Psychology: Science and Practice* 2010; **17**(1):1–30.

76. Lyneham HJ. Case formulation and treatment planning for anxiety and depression in children and adolescents. In: Sburlati ES, Lyneham HJ, Schniering CA, Rapee RM (eds.), *Evidence-Based CBT for Anxiety and Depression in Children and Adolescents: A Competencies-Based Approach.* Chichester, UK: Wiley Blackwell, 2014, pp. 114–27.

77. Thulin U, Svirsky L, Serlachius E, et al. The effect of parent involvement in the treatment of anxiety disorders in children: A meta-analysis. *Cognitive Behaviour Therapy* 2014; **43**(3):185–200.

78. Morris RJ, Kratochwill TR. Childhood fears and phobias. In: Moms J, Kratochwill TR (eds.), *The Practice of Child Therapy.* Boston: Allyn & Bacon, 1998.

79. National Collaborating Centre for Mental Health (NCCfMH) (ed.). *Social Anxiety Disorder: Recognition, Assessment and Treatment.* London: British Psychological Society, 2013.

80. National Collaborating Centre for Mental Health (NCCfMH) (ed.). *Obsessive-Compulsive Disorder: Core Interventions in the Treatment of Obsessive-Compulsive Disorder and Body Dysmorphic Disorder.* London: British Psychological Society, 2006.

81. Creswell C, Willetts L, Murray L, et al. Treatment of child anxiety: An exploratory study of the role of maternal anxiety and behaviours in treatment outcome. *Clinical Psychology and Psychotherapy* 2008; **15**(1):38–44.

82. Hudson JL, Comer JS, Kendall PC. Parental responses to positive and negative emotions in anxious and nonanxious children. *Journal of Clinical Child and Adolescent Psychology* 2008; **37**(2):303–13.

83. Kendall PC, Beidas RS. Smoothing the trail for dissemination of evidence-based practices for youth: Flexibility within fidelity. *Professional Psychology: Research and Practice* 2007; **38**(1):13–20.

84. Creed TA, Kendall PC. Therapist alliance-building behavior within a cognitive-behavioral treatment for anxiety in youth. *Journal of Consulting and Clinical Psychology* 2005; **73**(3):498–505.

85. Hudson JL, Kendall PC. Showing you can do it: Homework in therapy for children and adolescents with anxiety disorders. *Journal of Clinical Psychology* 2002; **58**(5):525–34.

86. Cartwright-Hatton S, Murray J. Cognitive therapy with children and families: Treating internalizing disorders. *Behavioural and Cognitive Psychotherapy* 2008; **36**(6):749–56.

87. Rapee RM, Abbott MJ, Lyneham HJ. Bibliotherapy for children with anxiety disorders using written materials for parents: A randomized controlled trial. *Journal of Consulting and Clinical Psychology* 2006; **74**(3):436–44.

88. Rapee RM, Lyneham HJ, Wuthrich V, et al. Comparison of stepped care delivery against a single, empirically validated cognitive-behavioral therapy program for youth with anxiety: A randomized clinical trial. *Journal of the American Academy of Child and Adolescent Psychiatry* 2017; **56**(10):841–8.

89. Mifsud C, Rapee RM. Early intervention for childhood anxiety in a school setting: Outcomes for an economically disadvantaged population. *Journal of the American Academy of Child and Adolescent Psychiatry* 2005; **44**(10):996–1004.

90. Cartwright-Hatton S, Roberts C, Chitsabesan P, et al. Systematic review of the efficacy of cognitive behaviour therapies for childhood and adolescent anxiety disorders. *British Journal of Clinical Psychology* 2004; **43**(4):421–36.

91. Barmish AJ, Kendall PC. Should parents be co-clients in cognitive-behavioral therapy for anxious youth? *Journal of Clinical Child and Adolescent Psychology* 2005; **34**(3):569–81.

92. Reynolds S, Wilson C, Austin J, Hooper L. Effects of psychotherapy for anxiety in children and adolescents: A meta-analytic review. *Clinical Psychology Reviews* 2012; **32**(4):251–62.

93. Silverman WK, Kurtines WM, Jaccard J, Pina AA. Directionality of change in youth anxiety treatment involving parents: an initial examination. *Journal of Consulting and Clinical Psychology* 2009; **77**(3):474–85.

94. Manassis K, Lee TC, Bennett K, et al. Types of parental involvement in CBT with anxious youth: A preliminary meta-analysis. *Journal of Consulting and Clinical Psychology* 2014; **82**(6):1163–72.

95. Peris TS, Compton SN, Kendall PC, et al. Trajectories of change in youth anxiety during cognitive-behavior therapy. *Journal of Consulting and Clinical Psychology* 2015; **83**(2):239–52.

96. Vande Voort JL, Svecova J, Jacobson AB, Whiteside SP. A retrospective examination of the similarity between clinical practice and manualized treatment for childhood anxiety disorders. *Cognitive and Behavioral Practice* 2010; **17**(3):322–8.

97. Whiteside SPH, Sattler A, Ale CM, et al. The use of exposure therapy for child anxiety disorders in a medical center. *Professional Psychology: Research and Practice* 2016; **47**(3):206–14.

117

98. Miller WR, Rollnick S. *Motivational Interviewing: Helping People Change*. New York: Guilford Press, 2012.

99. Kendall PC, Comer JS, Marker CD, et al. In-session exposure tasks and therapeutic alliance across the treatment of childhood anxiety disorders. *Journal of Consulting and Clinical Psychology* 2009; **77**(3):517–25.

100. Kendall PC, Brady EU, Verduin TL. Comorbidity in childhood anxiety disorders and treatment outcome. *Journal of the American Academy of Child and Adolescent Psychiatry* 2001; **40**(7):787–94.

101. Ollendick TH, Jarrett MA, Grills-Taquechel AE, et al. Comorbidity as a predictor and moderator of treatment outcome in youth with anxiety, affective, attention deficit/hyperactivity disorder, and oppositional/conduct disorders. *Clinical Psychology Review* 2008; **28**(8):1447–71.

102. Hudson JL, Keers R, Roberts S, Coleman JR, Breen G, Arendt K, et al. Clinical predictors of response to cognitive-behavioral therapy in pediatric anxiety disorders: the Genes for Treatment (GxT) study. *American Academy of Child and Adolescent Psychiatry Journal* 2015; **54**(6):454–63.

103. Ehrenreich-May J, Rosenfield D, Queen AH, et al. An initial waitlist-controlled trial of the unified protocol for the treatment of emotional disorders in adolescents. *Journal of Anxiety Disorders* 2017; **46**:46–55.

104. Sciberras E, Mulraney M, Anderson V, et al. Managing anxiety in children with ADHD using cognitive-behavioral therapy: a pilot randomized controlled trial. *Journal of Attention Disorders* 2018; **22**(5):515–20.

105. Sicouri G, Sharpe L, Hudson JL, et al. A case series evaluation of a pilot group cognitive behavioural treatment for children with asthma and anxiety. *Behaviour Change* 2017; **34**(1):35–47.

106. Chorpita BF, Becker KD, Daleiden EL. Understanding the common elements of evidence-based practice: Misconceptions and clinical examples. *Journal of the American Academy of Child and Adolescent Psychiatry* 2007; **46**(5):647–52.

107. Chorpita BF, Daleiden EL, Weisz JR. Identifying and selecting the common elements of evidence based interventions: A distillation and matching model. *Mental Health Services Research* 2005; **7**(1):5–20.

108. Garland AF, Hawley KM, Brookman-Frazee L, Hurlburt MS. Identifying common elements of evidence-based psychosocial treatments for children's disruptive behavior problems. *Journal of the American Academy of Child and Adolescent Psychiatry* 2008; **47**(5):505–14.

109. Twenge JM, Nolen-Hoeksema S. Age, gender, race, socioeconomic status, and birth cohort difference on the children's depression inventory: A meta-analysis. *Journal of Abnormal Psychology* 2002; **111**(4):578–88.

110. Gonzalez A, Weersing VR, Warnick EM, et al. Predictors of treatment attrition among an outpatient clinic sample of youths with clinically significant anxiety. *Administration and Policy in Mental Health and Mental Health Services Research* 2011; **38**(5):356–67.

111. Ishikawa S-I, Kikuta K, Sakai M, et al. A randomized controlled trial of a bidirectional cultural adaptation of cognitive behavior therapy for children and adolescents with anxiety disorders. *Behaviour Research and Therapy* 2019; **120**:103432.

112. Stallard P. Cognitive behaviour therapy with prepubertal children. In: Graham P (ed.), *Cognitive Behaviour Therapy for Children and Families*. Cambridge, UK: Cambridge University Press, 2004, pp. 121–35.

Case Complexity and Resistance to Change in the Treatment of Child Conduct Problems

David J. Hawes and Mark R. Dadds

Manuals detailing evidence-based interventions for child conduct problems (CPs) have become so abundant in recent years that such treatment is now among the most well documented in all mental health. Clinicians nonetheless face the daunting task of delivering these interventions to children whose CPs are often embedded in a range of other problems and with parents who may want very different things from treatment. At such times, successful outcomes can rely on clinical competencies beyond those which have often been the focus of training resources in the area. In our view, therapist competencies for responding to case complexity and difficulties often described in terms of resistance to change are particularly core to the treatment of CPs. In this chapter, we outline these competencies and present recommendations for approaching these aspects of clinical practice.

Integrated Family Intervention

The interventions for CPs that have received the strongest empirical support can be seen as variations on the same fundamental model, wherein family-based risk mechanisms are conceptualized and targeted with parenting strategies based on social learning theory (SLT) [1–3]. The packaging of these treatments into manualized programmes was instrumental to the growth in dissemination of evidence-based interventions for CPs towards the end of the twentieth century and enabled rigorous research into these interventions to be conducted on a large scale. Research has highlighted that the effects produced by these packaged programmes are highly comparable (see, e.g., [4]) and has pointed to common elements shared among programmes that are understood to serve as the 'active ingredients' for change in child CPs [5, 6]. These include a central focus on increasing parental warmth and positive reinforcement of desirable child behaviour followed by discipline-focused components that emphasize clear and consistent limit-

setting (e.g., effective child instructions, non-aggressive consequences such as brief time-out) and reduce parental responses that inadvertently reinforce escalations in misbehaviour. Skills training for parents typically emphasizes active methods such as in-session modelling by therapists, role-play rehearsal and homework [2, 7]. These elements can be seen in the structure and content of integrated family intervention (IFI) for child conduct problems [8], which in recent years has formed the basis for much of the research conducted at the Child Behaviour Research Clinic (CBRC) at the University of Sydney. IFI consists of three major phases that span the initial contacts with a family through to termination, and focus respectively, on (1) initial assessment, engagement and treatment planning, (2) skills training targeting parent-child dynamics of proximal importance to the child's symptoms and (3) strategies targeting systemic issues in the family and ecology of the child for the purpose of maximizing and maintaining treatment gains (see Table 10.1).

Research at the CBRC has been concerned largely with improving the effectiveness of treatment for child CPs, and in the context of this work, IFI has served as a foundation intervention upon which novel adaptations have been tested in various trials (e.g., [9, 10]). It has also been adapted for eHealth delivery in one form that incorporates therapist assistance [11, 12] and another that is entirely self-guided [13]. For most referrals, however, IFI is delivered individually, with families over a period of approximately eight weeks following a comprehensive assessment.

Responding to Complexity in the Treatment of Child CPs

In the broader field of mental health, there has been growing interest in approaches to the treatment of complex cases, despite limited consensus as to how such complexity is defined or characterized [14–16].

Table 10.1 Overview of Integrated Family Intervention

Phase	Major components	Core competencies
1. Assessment, engagement, treatment planning (sessions 1–3)	Clinical engagement of parents Assessment of the child and family Review assessment results with parents to form a shared formulation of the presenting problem and broader family system Establish a treatment plan based on shared goals	Skills for forming a therapeutic team with parents (e.g., identifying and inviting in members of the child's 'parenting team'; father-inclusive practices; managing in-session conflict between parents; non-judgemental validation of parent emotion and attributions) Parent-centred assessment skills (e.g., assessing sensitive parent/family issues beyond the child issue); skills for multi-method (e.g., interview, observation, standardized checklist) and multi-informant (e.g., mother, father, teacher) assessment Case formulation skills informed by the integration of distinct theoretical perspectives (e.g., interplay between social learning and attachment dynamics in family relationships) Parent-centred treatment planning (e.g., promoting an optimistic narrative; empowering parents to be active in decision-making by openly sharing evidence-based information)
2. Treatment components targeting parent-child processes (sessions 4–7)	Parenting strategies for encouraging age-appropriate child behaviour and self-regulation (e.g., positive reinforcement; modelling of emotional skills) and setting limits on problem disruptive/aggressive behaviour (e.g., age-appropriate instructions; brief time-out) Adapting and generalizing parenting strategies to distinct contexts in the home (e.g., with siblings, bed time) and community (e.g., shopping, socializing); family rules.	Skills-training practices based on active learning (e.g., role-play and performance feedback; communication of abstract concepts; use of humour; attending to parent emotion and attributions); shaping parents' implementation of child-focused strategies to ensure that positive reinforcement is meaningful to children on an attachment level (e.g., rewards based in the parent-child relationship) and that limit-setting does not activate attachment dynamics (e.g., it is free from rejection; independent of parent-child emotional engagement); reflective practice competencies for responding to a lack of change; empowering parents to improve boundaries and routines with other caregivers; monitoring change in child, parent, and family targets and updating goals accordingly.
3. Treatment components targeting the broader family system (sessions 8–10)	Select modules including Partner-support strategies (e.g., couples communication and problem-solving; maintaining an intimate relationship) Cognitive coping skills (e.g., for parental mood and anxiety); family time management Parent anger management; family problem-solving skills; pleasant events and social support.	Establishing goals that prioritize attention to the parent/family needs of most importance to the child outcomes; engaging additional family members (e.g., older children) and caregivers (e.g., across separated households) in skills-focused sessions where appropriate Distinguishing between needs that can be addressed within this phase of treatment versus those which warrant longer-term goals or additional referrals

For children with CPs, a broad range of factors can be seen to contribute to complexity in so far as they have the potential to complicate treatment. These factors relate largely to six domains, which we propose can be considered key dimensions of case complexity (see Table 10.2). These dimensions reflect complexity arising from (1) the topography of the child's CPs (e.g., range and severity of problem behaviours, settings in which symptoms occur [17]), (2) developmental and dispositional factors (e.g., language impairments, forms of temperament such as negative reactivity, fearlessness, callous and unemotional traits [18]), (3) co-morbid child psychopathology (e.g., internalizing disorders, neurodevelopmental disorders [19]), (4) quality of parenting (e.g., harsh or inconsistent discipline, skill deficits in age-appropriate caregiving; see Chapter 2), (5) parent characteristics (e.g., personality and mental health, parental attributions [20]) and (6) the family system and social environment (e.g., interparental conflict, lack of social support, financial disadvantage, cultural beliefs [21]).

The risk factors implicated in the causes of a child's CPs often 'spill over' into clinical settings in ways that disrupt the very treatment of these problems. For example, conflict in the parents' own relationship

Table 10.2 Key Dimensions of Case Complexity Among Children Referred for Conduct Problems

Complexity Arising from . . .	Common Examples	Principles for Treatment Planning and Delivery
1. The topography of the CPs	The range and severity of problem behaviours/symptoms the settings in which symptoms occur (e.g., home, school, with peers), each of which may implicate distinct risk mechanisms and distinct barriers to treatment)	Engage key stakeholders (e.g., teachers) from relevant contexts starting early in treatment while ensuring that this does not detract from the primary focus on the family context; empower parents to manage relationships and communication with other stakeholders while providing clinical recommendations directly when necessary.
2. Developmental and dispositional child factors	Language impairments; negative reactivity; poor effortful control; callous and unemotional traits.	Adapt core treatment content based on the capacities of the individual child, along with adjunctive components to target additional needs where appropriate (e.g., emotion recognition training for children with CU traits)
3. Co-morbid child psychopathology	Internalizing disorders (e.g., separation anxiety disorder; generalized anxiety disorder); neuro-developmental disorders (e.g., ADHD, ASD)	Because of the potential for CPs to interfere with the treatment of other problems, focus specifically on co-morbid disorders only after first reducing CPs while integrating parenting strategies for co-morbid disorders into those focused on CPs where possible
4. Quality of parenting	High levels of harsh and inconsistent discipline; lack of warmth/sensitivity; skill deficits in age-appropriate caregiving practices (e.g., unsupportive emotion socialization)	Attempt to target parenting only once a sufficient understanding (formulation) of parenting difficulties and shared goals has been achieved. Ensure that parents' implementation of core child-focused parenting strategies is sufficient before proceeding further in treatment
5. Parent characteristics	Parental personality and mental health (e.g., depression, substance use); cognitive-affective processes (e.g., negative attributions, emotional flooding).	Openly explore and acknowledge parent attributions during initial assessment and engagement; openly discuss parent emotions and attributions during skills training in child-focused strategies and incorporate related skills (e.g., self-talk) where relevant; jointly plan for longer-term mental health goals and support (e.g., referrals) prior to termination.
6. The family social environment	Family structure and dysfunction (e.g., interparental conflict; interference from extended family); parental social and economic adversity (e.g., lack of social support; financial disadvantage); cultural beliefs (e.g., values about parenting roles/functions at odds with evidence-based treatment).	Assess issues openly and establish shared goals with parents during initial treatment planning; encourage parents to call a moratorium on any conflict in their own relationship that may interfere with their implementation of child-focused strategies; parents are predicted to be most amenable to working on such conflict later in treatment following some improvement in the child problem; empower parents to improve their own relationships, boundaries and routines with other caregivers (e.g., scheduling dedicated skills training to target these issues where needed)

may be both a causal variable and interfere with a therapist's attempts to engage parents before treatment even begins. Parents' own mental health, or biases in cognitive-affective processes stemming from family-of-origin experiences, may create unanticipated challenges for parents as they attempt to implement new family-based strategies [20]. Furthermore, socioeconomic disadvantage and parent psychopathology have both been associated with apparent expressions of resistance to change among parents during treatment for CPs [22]. Importantly, case complexity also has the potential to subvert and derail the effective treatment of CPs via its impact on therapists. We have seen many therapists become overwhelmed by

such aspects of a case and deem various evidence-based approaches unsuitable in the absence of a compelling rationale. In this way, the complex needs of a case may at times shift the focus of treatment only further away from the very approaches that are most likely to meet those needs. A basic assumption underlying IFI is that complex presentations require interventions that are not only intensive but also formulation driven. As such, IFI is best understood not as a standardized programme to be delivered 'off the shelf' but as a model for designing evidence-based treatment plans on a case-by-case basis. One implication of this is that while the delivery of treatment is focused predominantly on parents, the scope of treatment extends beyond parenting practices. This is seen in an emphasis on initial engagement strategies that are sensitive to issues in the broader ecology of the child and family and the integration of treatment components targeting the broader family system and additional contexts.

Competencies for Formulation-Driven Practice

A therapist's capacity to use theory as a clinical tool is fundamental to the treatment of highly complex cases. The theoretical base underpinning IFI integrates SLT with a focus on attachment processes, parental attributions and family structure. This integrated perspective provides possible solutions to a number of the common difficulties that parents and therapists experience in interventions for CPs. In IFI, this integrated use of cognate theories informs each phase of treatment, guiding clinical engagement, assessment, treatment planning and skills training as follows.

Social Learning Theory. According to accounts of CPs based on SLT, the frequency and persistence of a child's oppositional and aggressive behaviour can be explained largely by its functional value in the child's daily social environment. The most well-developed account is *coercion theory*, which specifies how learning mechanisms based in the parent-child relationship are particularly proximal influences on CPs across early and middle childhood and often generalize to relationships with peers and other caregivers (e.g., teachers) across development [23]. This includes the modelling of negative behaviour by family members and escalating cycles of parent-child negativity based on operant (escape-avoidance) mechanisms. These cycles function as 'reinforcement traps' that inadvertently reward both parents' and children's use of aversive control tactics (e.g., whining, nagging, shouting, hitting) while extinguishing positive family interactions. The central reinforcement of children's problem behaviours provided by families is understood to occur during family conflict episodes, with the critical factor being the relative rate at which a child's coercive behaviour is reinforced [24]. That is, among the broad array of behaviours that a child performs in response to the aversive behaviour of others, are coercive behaviours reinforced more frequently than adaptive behaviours? Negative reinforcement or escape conditioning is a lynchpin, with child behaviours performed in so far as they are functional in escaping or avoiding punishment (e.g., deflecting a parents' command) or in

terminating conflict with others (e.g., hitting a sibling to stop them teasing). Because the daily repetition of these routines leads children to become increasingly skilled in the use of coercion, they become increasingly difficult to discipline. Moreover, these cycles elicit and reinforce harsh and inconsistent discipline practices that allow parents to avoid or escape from escalations in children's aversive behaviour in the short term but that inadvertently provide modelling and accidental rewards for that behaviour and lead to the ongoing escalation of coercive cycles in the long term.

For families trapped in such cycles, conflict escalates more and more rapidly and reaches higher and higher amplitudes over time. At the same time, the more frustrating and exhausting parent-child interactions become for parents, the more they are likely to avoid engaging with a child unless necessary. Given that healthy, age-appropriate child behaviours demand less parental attention, these behaviours receive decreasing rates of positive reinforcement in day-to-day life, and parental engagement becomes increasingly contingent on the child's misbehaviour. Misbehaviour and discipline become the ways that parent and child spend time together, and the quality of their relationship suffers accordingly.

In IFI, these mechanisms are targeted in two core components involving parenting strategies designed to shut down cycles of coercion and reverse the effects that CPs have on family life. The first 'reward' component focuses on encouraging good behaviour through strategies to increase positive reinforcement of age-appropriate child behaviour. Here parents select specific, observable target behaviours that they would like to see the child engaging in more often (e.g., speaking with a calm voice, playing independently, following instructions) and provide immediate rewarding responses contingent on the performance of these behaviours. These responses include descriptive praise and tangible rewards, but priority is given to rewards that are based in the parent-child relationship and emphasize emotional connection (e.g., physical affection, shared parent-child time), for reasons soon discussed (see 'Attachment Theory'). Parents are encouraged to alternate unpredictably between these different responses based on the enhanced effects of variable reinforcement schedules. The second 'limit-setting' component focuses on responses to misbehaviour and includes strategies for giving clear instructions to children and applying consistent, non-coercive consequences (e.g., time-out). These strategies form a predictable behaviour correction routine that acts as a circuit breaker for escalating cycles of coercion in large part by preventing misbehaviour from eliciting responses from parents that inadvertently reinforce problem behaviours further. In contrast to the reward strategies used to target-specific pre-selected behaviours, this routine is applied uniformly to all misbehaviours that may potentially escalate, thereby reducing the cognitive demands on parents to problem-solve specific consequences in the moment and enabling effective limit-setting skills to become the parent's new over-learned response at such times.

Structural Theory. Minuchin's [25] model of structural dynamics characterizes the family system as consisting of overlapping but independent subsystems (e.g., parents, children, extended family). These subsystems are organized hierarchically, and boundaries determine who participates in each and how. According to this theory, a healthy family structure is organized with parents forming an executive subsystem that holds the highest level of power, and this subsystem is capable of solving family problems through effective teamwork and leadership. Moreover, this structure benefits from clear boundaries that prevent other subsystems (e.g., grandparents, children) from interfering with parenting functions and enables parents to maintain a healthy intimate relationship independent of their caregiving roles. Although there is little evidence that structural dynamics are direct causal variables for CPs, these dynamics may nonetheless contribute to them indirectly. In families of children with CPs, the boundaries between parent and child subsystems often become unclear, the parents' relationship becomes conflicted and extended family get drawn into ineffective attempts to manage the child's behaviour (e.g., [26, 27]). Such structural dysfunction can in turn increase vulnerability to other risk mechanisms, including cycles of parent-child coercion, in the family system.

Based on this theory, we predict that parenting interventions for CPs are most likely to produce systemic change when delivered to the family in partnership with the full executive subsystem as opposed to individual members of it. It is further predicted that when the structure of the executive subsystem is dysfunctional, clinical processes that serve to strengthen it will, in turn, serve to enhance the impact of such interventions on the child and family. Accordingly, the first major aim of the therapist in IFI is to join with the executive subsystem or 'parenting team' of the family to form a therapeutic team. This is facilitated by a parent-centred interview scheduled for the first assessment session and attended by the full parenting team without children or other family members. The parenting team may take many forms, often comprising step-parents or separated biological parents who live apart but co-parent closely. This requires the therapist to be able to identify the members of this parenting team during initial (e.g., telephone) contacts. Effective strategies for engaging fathers are essential, as are skills for responding to in-session conflict between parents [28, 29]; (see also Chapter 5). Other competencies here concern skills in the assessment of parent and family relationships (e.g., intimacy, conflict) and consultation processes that enable the therapeutic team to form a shared perception of such issues and their relevance to the child problem (see [30]). Finally, therapists must be able to target problems within the parenting team, when indicated, by integrating related skills training in partner-support strategies (e.g., couples communication and problem-solving) into treatment [31].

Attribution Theory. Parents' dispositional attributions about their child and the meaning of the presenting problem represent a critical aspect of the parent-child relationship and may be subject to biases that contribute to the parenting problem [32]. This may include beliefs that a child's negative behaviour is designed to deliberately upset the parent, is a sign of serious mental illness or is inherited from other (disliked) family members (e.g., an abusive ex-spouse). Parents may also see it as a sign of their own failings or as a punishment they deserve. These attributions may be loaded with intense emotion, including guilt, shame or explosive anger, that 'floods' the parent when activated. A defining characteristic of this emotional flooding is that it disrupts the higher-order cognitive processes required for problem-solving, thereby compromising the individual's capacity to respond adaptively in conflict situations [33, 34].

Therapist competencies related to this assessment of parent attributions are not only essential to case formulation but critical to the initial engagement process. The therapist approaches this assessment with the aim of helping parents voice these largely unspoken thoughts. This can be done using direct, open-ended questions (e.g., 'How would you describe your feelings toward Oscar?') that progress to close-ended questions oriented towards the parents' emotions (e.g., 'How did you feel the last time he really tried to hurt you?', 'In those moments when you are really struggling, how bad does it get?', 'What is the worst thought that you have had at that time?', 'What is your greatest fear about his behaviour?', 'In your darkest moments, what do you think is happening with him?'). Simply verbalizing these attributions may help parents to begin reprocessing irrational cognitions that have not passed beyond implicit levels, gaining an improved perspective on ideas that have been too confronting to put into words. The formation of a strong therapeutic relationship in this treatment can depend on a therapist's capacity to openly explore these attributions and provide validation by listening to disclosures non-judgmentally and empathically no matter how controversial.

Attempts to challenge parents' cognitions early in treatment risk undermining the engagement process and are best deferred until the therapeutic relationship has been established and active treatment is underway. Moreover, although evidence suggests that maladaptive attributions often improve in response to change in child behaviour during treatment, there is limited evidence that the outcomes of such treatment are enhanced by targeting such attributions directly. [32]. Therapist competencies for responding to parent attributions and related emotions are essential nonetheless in IFI. Noteworthy shifts in parent affect during skills-training, especially during role-plays or when recalling between-session events, cue the therapist to explore the parents' internal reactions (e.g., 'What was running through your mind just then?'; 'What was happening for you in that moment?'; 'What was it about that time in particular that really got to you?'). The effective therapist acknowledges and validates the parents' reactions, normalizes challenges associated with implementing new strategies, and utilizes opportunities to introduce skills (e.g., self-talk, distress tolerance skills) with which parents can self-regulate reactions that interfere with their use of effective parenting strategies.

Attachment Theory. Children with insecure attachments to caregivers are at an increased risk for CPs, and this appears to be in part because such insecurity interferes with the healthy development of self-regulatory capacities [35]. Evidence also supports the view that attachment processes may contribute to

CPs in concert with learning based mechanisms [36]. Likewise, the importance of attachment theory in IFI lies in the effects that coercive cycles can be seen to have on attachment dynamics in the family and the role that attachment dynamics often appear to play in fuelling coercive cycles. Applications of attachment theory to child CPs have highlighted that when developmentally appropriate behaviours and expressions of affect are not effective in eliciting proximal contact with a caregiver, the child may develop maladaptive strategies to serve this function [37]. Although the harsh and rejecting reactions of parents trapped in coercive cycles differ wildly from the sensitive (e.g., warm and emotionally attuned) responses that sustain a secure attachment, they may nonetheless provide a child with his or her most immediate and intense moments of closeness with a caregiver. In IFI it is predicted that oppositional and aggressive behaviours will persist so long as they function as the child's most reliable strategy for eliciting such contingent contact with an attachment figure, despite the damage done to the quality of the attachment relationship as this continues [8].

Importantly, the more that parental reactions threaten a child's attachment security, the more an insecurely attached child may escalate problem behaviours in an attempt to re-establish caregiver proximity. As demonstrated in early experimental research (e.g., [38]), this can seem counterintuitive and at odds with learning theory, which might predict that such children should behave as to avoid or escape from the harsh and punitive reactions elicited by their actions. It is not unusual for the paradoxical nature of these dynamics to be echoed in the therapy room by exasperated parents as they confide that 'it is almost like he wants me to hit him'. As is commonly seen, the child's attempts to force greater physical and emotional engagement with a parent through continued oppositional and aggressive behaviour amounts to further escalations in mutual parent-child coercion. Parents whose time, energy and emotions are dominated by attempts to manage oppositional and defiant behaviour are often left spending little time engaging with children when such behaviour is not occurring. Misbehaviour and discipline therefore often become the times at which children are most likely to share close physical contact with parents and reciprocated expressions of emotion. In this way, the family interactions that accompany misbehaviour commonly become rich in the parent-child dynamics that activate a child's attachment system and in IFI are referred to accordingly as 'attachment rich'. Conversely, the remainder of family life becomes increasingly devoid of such dynamics, or 'attachment neutral'. Based on this perspective, a core aim of the treatment components that target parent-child inter-actions in IFI is to reverse this by removing emotional dynamics from discipline and returning them back to the rest of family life.

Our conceptualization of attachment and reinforce-ment as synergistic change processes is shown in Figure 10.1. As applied to limit-setting for misbehav-iour, it is predicted that the behavioural strategy of time-out, for example, will fail or aggravate problems if its implementation is attachment rich (e.g., parents are emotional or express subtle cues of rejection). Conversely, when parents implement time-out calmly, consistently, and without such cues, they are enacting the fundamental attachment process of age-appropriate separation and rapprochement. Through attachment-secure discipline of this kind the child learns that time can be spent apart without threat to the attachment relationship, and time-out is predicted to improve behaviour and self-regulation, particularly among chil-dren with an insecure attachment [39].

A Treatment Planning Case Study. Conner was a seven-year-old boy whose mother self-referred to the CBRC following an unsuccessful parenting group programme. Clinical assessment commenced with

a parent-centred (child-free) interview in which the therapist joined with Conner's mother (Violet) and father (Russell) to form a therapeutic team. Structured family observations, a child interview, a teacher inter-view and multi-informant checklist reports followed. Assessment results indicated clinically severe symp-toms of oppositional defiant disorder (ODD) and separation anxiety disorder (SAD) across home and school (e.g., multiple school suspensions due to peer aggression, more than 50 absence days in the past year due to anxiety-related school refusal). Hypothesized predisposing factors in Conner's early development included an insecure attachment (e.g., excessive clingi-ness in novel situations) and extreme temperamental reactivity. While screening found no immediate risk to family safety, significant interparental conflict was identified along with maternal depression and anxiety arising from family-of-origin trauma (violence and sexual abuse). Ongoing conflict was also occurring between Violet and her mother-in-law (Conner's grandmother), in whose house the family were cur-rently living because of financial hardship.

Hypotheses regarding problem maintenance emphasized ineffective approaches to managing and coping with Conner's behaviour by his parents as well as his teacher. The school had instituted a behaviour support plan that restricted his classroom interactions with peers and isolated him during recess, following

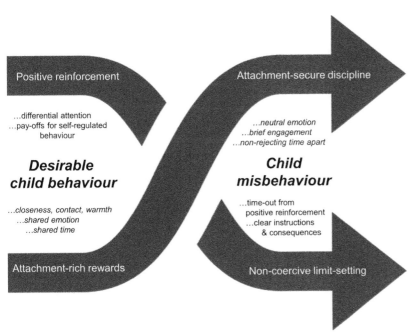

Figure 10.1 Parenting responses to desirable (age-appropriate) child behaviour versus misbehaviour: attachment and reinforcement as synergistic processes

Positive reinforcement

Attachment-secure discipline

...differential attention
...pay-offs for self-regulated behaviour

...neutral emotion
...brief engagement
...non-rejecting time apart

Desirable child behaviour

Child misbehaviour

...closeness, contact, warmth
...shared emotion
...shared time

...time-out from positive reinforcement
...clear instructions & consequences

Attachment-rich rewards

Non-coercive limit-setting

an escalation in his aggressive behaviour with teachers and peers and a one-off incident involving sexual exploration with a peer six months prior. The parent-teacher relationship had also broken down across this period, leading to poor communication and mutual blame. In the home, escalating cycles of parent-child coercion were seen to provide inadvertent reinforcement for Conner's dysregulated outbursts and aggression. These cycles were further compounded by problematic parental attributions, attachment dynamics and family structural dynamics as follows. For Violet, Conner's lengthy tantrums triggered intrusive memories of violence in her own family of origin, provoking an overwhelming urge to escape (e.g., sometimes locking herself in her bedroom or the backyard). Conner would become increasing emotional in response to his mother's distress. She, in turn, would feel intense guilt associated with thoughts of 'I am a terrible mother for causing my child the kind of pain that my parents caused me' and would then hold him physically until he calmed down. A similar dynamic occurred in situations requiring Conner to separate from his mother (e.g., school drop-offs), often resulting in his demands to stay with her being accommodated. Russell expressed frustration and disappointment that he and his son lacked the kind of positive relationship he had shared with his own father and was consequently spending less and less time with Conner. He would typically involve himself in discipline only to insist on the need for harsher punishment following tantrums, and volatile arguments about discipline would ensue involving both parents and the grandmother.

Assessment was followed by collaborative formulation and treatment planning focused on the simple narrative that Conner's skills for self-soothing were stuck at an earlier age and that the behaviours he had developed as substitute skills were now preventing his parents and teachers from helping him to develop more mature competencies. Key parent and systemic issues were discussed openly, and it was proposed that treatment would be likely to fail once again if they were ignored. This included discussion of whether Violent and Russell would be able to call a moratorium on conflict in their own relationship at least for three weeks in order to focus on implementing new child-focused strategies as a team, which they agreed to. The rationale for this was that first reducing the severity of the child's CPs would free the parents up to then work on other issues (e.g., their own relationship and mental health).

Because of the prominence of problems in the school context, the therapist engaged Conner's teacher early in treatment while ensuring that this did not detract from the primary focus on the home. The therapist informed the teacher by phone that Conner's parents were commencing an intervention that was expected to significantly improve his behaviour, and she was asked to report any improvements she noticed to them. This call was also used to clarify the school's policies regarding disruptive/aggressive behaviour and to recommend that the school revise its existing behaviour support plan where possible to allow Conner increased participation in peer activities. Later, following the introduction of positive reinforcement and limit-setting strategies in the home, the therapist supported Conner's parents to establish a system of school-to-home reinforcement and consequences with the teacher and briefly addressed the parents' skills for communicating effectively with the school when advocating for their child.

While working through the parenting strategies that form the core CP-focused components of IFI, particular attention was given to how Violet could be supported to overcome the emotional distress that had served as a barrier to her effective use of such strategies in the past (e.g., praise reminding her that she was not shown such warmth by her own parents, the sound of Conner crying in time-out evoking Violet's memories of childhood violence). The parents were encouraged to raise questions and concerns regarding strategies such as time-out, which in IFI are understood to serve particularly beneficial functions for a child such as Conner, promoting age-appropriate self-regulatory skills among children who are overly reliant on caregivers for co-regulation because of anxiety or an insecure attachment [39]. Parent role plays were used in part to facilitate habituation of Violet's aversive arousal during discipline and to introduce distress tolerance skills (e.g., self-talk). In addition to targeting reinforcement mechanisms, these core strategies were further used to break down problematic family structures. For example, it was hypothesized that the parents' own arguments were inadvertently reinforcing to Connor, given that his parents were otherwise interacting less and less. By having Connor's parents team up to reward him, his desirable/regulated behaviours instead became functional in bringing his parents together. In other families, such an approach might be used to break down problematic structures involving siblings (e.g., promoting a child team by rewarding all siblings for one child's prosocial behaviour).

Because of the severe separation anxiety in the presenting problem, parenting strategies for child anxiety (e.g., parental modelling of self-regulation in emotional situations, positive reinforcement of non-avoidant behaviours) were woven into the CP strategies. Components focused exclusively on anxiety were, however, scheduled to follow those aimed at reducing CPs, given the potential for CPs to interfere with the treatment of other problems. Specifically, parent-child separation was subsequently targeted as a high-risk situation using CBT anxiety strategies (e.g., parent-implemented graduated exposure). Play dates with peers were also included as a high-risk situation at this time in order to target Conner's aggressive behaviour. In the final phase of treatment, dysfunctional communication and problem-solving in the parenting team were targeted through skills training in partner-support strategies. This included practices for maintaining a loving relationship independent of their lives as parents (e.g., date nights) and managing influences that may serve to undermine the parenting team (e.g., establishing discipline boundaries with Conner's grandmother). Longer-term goals and referral planning concerning maternal depression/anxiety were also addressed at this time.

Understanding Resistance to Change

By the time many parents of children with CPs meet with a therapist, they may have invested considerable time and money to access treatment and often feel in desperate need of the help they seek. This serves in no way, however, to guarantee that parents will act on the treatment recommendations they eventually receive. The concept of resistance to change has a long history in psychotherapy, and in early family therapy models was conceptualized as attempts to prevent disruptions to homeostasis in the family system [40]. Current models reflect a decided shift away from conceptualizations of resistance that place blame on clients, and have focused instead on concepts such as discord in the therapeutic relationship [47]. Based on research into parent training for CPs, Patterson and Chamberlain [41] conceptualized parental resistance as avoidance. This account emphasizes the negative emotions that parents of such children often bring with them to treatment, stemming from a metaphorical 'history of 10,000 defeats' in the arena of discipline. It is predicted that these emotions underlie parents' avoidance of future discipline encounters despite the new

approaches to discipline presented in treatment. The attributions that accompany these emotions are likely to form a family story that explains why the child is antisocial and does not respond to discipline, and this was predicted to further drive resistance to the extent that it diverges from the therapist's point of view.

Using observational data from therapy sessions, these researchers showed that high levels of resistant behaviour essentially operate to 'turn off' the therapist. That is, they reduce caring and empathic responses and time spent focused on evidence-based treatment material while increasing therapists' use of confrontation and dislike for these clients [41]. These counter-therapeutic responses were predicted to play a key role in maintaining resistance by feeding back into such behaviour from parents. In line with this perspective, resistance to change in IFI is conceptualized not as a trait of some parents but rather as a process that is based on the dynamics of the therapeutic team and that may be driven by both parents and therapists. It is further assumed that it can hold information about a family's needs that may be essential to therapy. We therefore think of resistance not as a problem but as an important communication from parents [8].

Clinical Competencies for Promoting Family Change

It is well recognized that attempts to change client behaviour through direct confrontation are likely to fail, and observational research with parents has supported this conclusion [42]. Clinical recommendations for overcoming resistance in the treatment of CPs have centred largely around two themes. First, the therapeutic relationship has been emphasized as playing a key role in facilitating behaviour change. Accordingly, initial engagement practices for establishing a strong therapeutic relationship at the outset of treatment are understood to be of primary importance [43]. Likewise, when faced with a lack of change in parent behaviour mid-treatment, headway may come from considering 'what kind of interaction would move your relationship with this parent in a positive direction?' [44]. A second theme concerns practices that target the change process directly. Webster-Stratton, Herbert and Ollendick [45], for example, recommended problem-solving barriers to change using the force-field analysis method (see [46]). This involves helping parents identify facilitative/helping forces for change (e.g., existing strengths in parenting skills, available social support), restraining/hindering forces for change (e.g., depression, marital conflict), followed by strategies for strengthening existing facilitative forces, adding new facilitative forces, and reducing or removing restraining forces. Other such approaches include motivational interviewing practices [47], which have been integrated into parenting interventions for CPs in various ways (e.g., [48, 49]). Research has provided some support for this yet has also produced mixed findings, highlighting the need for further research into such integration (e.g., [50]).

A Reflective Practice Process Model

The delivery of IFI in the CBRC is guided by a number of principles designed to promote a shared therapeutic agenda and empower parents in the change process. This approach reflects the themes already outlined and draws heavily on principles and practices from the broader field of family therapy. The process strategies involved are initiated from the earliest contacts with a family and build on one another as needed throughout treatment. Much like parenting strategies that serve to reverse the effects of child behaviours on parents, this approach is concerned largely with pre-empting and reversing the effects of parental behaviours on therapists. As such, therapists' reflections on their own responses to parents are central to the competencies involved.

1. **Expect a Struggle for Change.** The parent behaviours that have been used to operationalize resistance in observational research are not limited to rare cases or even those which respond poorly to treatment. These behaviours include parent expressions of 'I can't' (e.g., statements of defensiveness, hopelessness, blame, side-tracking), parent expressions of 'I won't' (e.g., statements that challenge the therapist's competence or express disagreement or complaints) and noncompliance with prescribed home-based activities between sessions [54]. Research has found that the successful treatment of CPs is often characterized by an increase in these behaviours from the initial to middle phases of treatment and then decrease during the closing phases. Moreover, the total absence of any such increases across the first half of treatment has been associated with poor outcomes, leading researchers to suggest that for parents and therapists, the struggle and working-

through of this are important parts of the core treatment process [41, 51]. An enduring struggle that does not resolve, however, is associated with particularly poor outcomes and may be important to pre-empt using strategies built into routine treatment with all cases. Such strategies can be found in phase 1 of IFI. First and foremost are those used during initial assessment and engagement to join with the executive subsystem of the family. As discussed earlier, these strategies are designed to establish a strong therapeutic alliance between the therapist and parents, creating a therapeutic team based on empathy, collaboration and shared empowerment.

Second, based on evidence that various risk factors for CPs are also risk factors for the aforementioned parent behaviours, initial assessment data on these factors may alert therapists to proceed with caution. Indeed, in addition to formulating hypotheses about the role that risk factors have played in driving the child's CPs, it is valuable at this early stage to also predict whether, and how, risk factors may drive later difficulties regarding parent implementation in a specific case. Parent psychopathology (e.g., depression, parental antisocial behaviour), socioeconomic disadvantage, and particularly poor discipline practices, have been found to predict the persistence of high levels of such parent behaviour across treatment for CPs [41, 51]. We believe that the assessment of negative attributions may also be informative here, based on our recent findings that child outcomes three months following treatment were predicted by pre-treatment attributions of both mothers and fathers [52]. For procedures regarding the clinical assessment of such attributions, we refer readers to Hawes and Dadds [30] and Sawrikar et al. [53].

Third, during collaborative treatment planning, it can be valuable to forecast and normalize the struggle of change and openly discuss its importance to treatment goals. Parents should also be invited to openly share any doubts, discomfort and objections they may later have during treatment (e.g., 'It's important to know about the things that can stop this kind of treatment from working. One of the main things is just not giving new strategies a proper chance. It's normal for new strategies to sometimes look like they are not working at first. It's also normal to go through some trial and error to fine-tune strategies based on the individual child. Please always tell me about what's not working well so we can really get these strategies working for you').

2. **Recognize the Signs of a Struggle.** Our capacity to respond to dynamics that undermine the change process relies in part on our capacity to recognize them. We think of this as 'tuning in' to the cues by which they may be expressed. Important resistance cues include the *parent behaviours* seen in expressions of 'I can't' and 'I won't', but also parent behaviours that may be less overt. Some parents for example, take a perfunctory approach to the core components of treatment under the misapprehension that the 'real' solutions of therapy are yet to be revealed. A therapist might be alerted to this by repeated requests for 'something more' or 'something else' (e.g., individual therapy for the child).

Other cues may arise from the effects of parent behaviour on the therapist. These cues, based in the therapists' own behaviour, cognition and affect, may be more challenging to detect as are largely internal and accessible to the therapist only via self-reflection. In our experience, these may be particularly important for recognizing dynamics that are more ambiguous or have already begun to undermine treatment gains, as follows.

Therapist Affect. The treatment of CPs can be a highly emotional experience for parents and therapists alike. A therapist's own negative affect may at times mobilize responses that enhance the therapeutic alliance. For example, a therapist who shares his or her own anxiety about how a child has responded to newly introduced strategies in the home may convey empathy and normalize the experience of the parent in doing so. However, the negative affect and related 'counter-transference' elicited by parent expressions of 'I can't/won't' can involve feelings of dislike that erode this alliance. An affective response of this kind, even subtle, may therefore serve as an important warning sign.

Therapist Behaviour. Expressions of 'I can't/won't' may elicit increases in various confrontational responses by therapists in session (e.g., expressions of disapproval, irritation, sarcasm, disbelief), and the self-monitoring of such behaviour by therapists can therefore be helpful in recognizing a counter-therapeutic process.

Therapists' attention to any decreases in their use of active-learning activities in session (e.g., role-plays, modelling) may do likewise. Therapists may also be alerted to such a process when observing themselves repeating the same explanations of treatment material more than usual ('feeling like a broken record').

Therapist Cognition. Reflecting on the decision-making processes used to revise an intervention mid-treatment may further alert therapists. Most telling is decision-making that reflects the spread of anxiety and avoidance from the parent to the therapist. It can be useful for therapists to critically question whether their treatment planning, particularly changes in direction or the removal of challenging components, is indeed based on a valid reformulation of the case and justified by evidence-based guidelines. If not, it may potentially reflect a parallel process whereby therapists inadvertently collude with ('buy into') a parent's avoidance of treatment strategies that require the parent to take on child misbehaviour in limit-setting confrontations (see [39]).

3. **Thank Parents for Dissenting.** When parents verbalize doubts, objections, complaints or ambivalence about treatment, the immediate response we recommend is to thank them for doing so (e.g., 'I'm really glad that you didn't just keep that to yourself – thank you for telling me'). While it may seem counter-intuitive to welcome this, such open communication is far preferable to obstructive behaviour or inaction. Moreover, we predict that parents who feel encouraged and supported to express their honest concerns will be more receptive to a therapist's subsequent attempts to understand any issues underlying an impasse.

4. **Name (Reframe) Resistance.** When a problem in the therapeutic relationship is implicit and unspoken in nature, these characteristics may enable it to go unchecked. By naming it, a therapist brings it into the open, making it something that can be examined together with parents. This does not mean using the term *resistance*, which carries critical and accusatory connotations and may only aggravate defensiveness. Rather, this naming is a process of reframing whereby a problem is relabelled to promote alternative approaches to understanding and acting on it. The strategic use of reframing has

a long history in family therapy [55], where it is typically applied to the presenting problems of the family (e.g., [56]). It can also serve to explicitly name resistance in terms that invite cooperative and constructive action from parents.

Using this approach, a parent's lack of change is described using language that is neutral, non-judgemental and identifies it as an issue based not within the parent but the therapeutic team. It may simply be reframed as 'we're stuck' (e.g., 'In my experience, when these strategies are working for parents they really know it. . . . they see big differences in child behaviour . . . feel much more in control . . . are happier at home, and I am worried that this is not happening for you. I think we've gotten stuck talking about these strategies and still need to find a way to really get them working'). The idea of resistance as important communication from the parent may also be incorporated (e.g., 'I've learned that when things are not changing it can sometimes mean that we've missed something important . . . or maybe that I haven't done a good enough job explaining something').

5. **Pause Skills Training.** By conceptualizing resistance as something based in the dynamics and interactions of the therapeutic team, we assume that it will persist as long as those dynamics remain unchanged. A key step towards interrupting and remediating these dynamics is to temporarily suspend skills-training activities. The therapist might highlight the need for this by forecasting the treatment failure that is anticipated based on the current rate of progress (e.g., 'I think what we need to do is actually stop what we have been working on and look more at the bigger picture. Otherwise, I can see us getting to the end of treatment and finding that his behaviour is exactly the same as it was to begin with'). While the responsibility for resolving problematic issues is shared by the therapist and parents, it is the therapist alone who is responsible for creating a space to address these issues. By initiating this 'pause', the therapist gives the therapeutic team permission and time to jointly reflect on the progress of treatment. Once an impasse has been recognized, taking steps to pause and acknowledge it can nonetheless be intimidating, and therapists may need to self-regulate impulses to avoid or deny the impasse they face.

6. **Empower Parents to Decide the Future of Treatment.** Given that parents of children with CPs commonly experience powerlessness in family life, it stands to reason that this may play out in the family-based treatment of these problems. This can often be seen is in the expectations that parents hold for therapy, which may place undue responsibility for change on the therapist. Once the therapeutic team agrees that they are 'stuck', the most valuable process strategies are often those which shift the balance of power from therapist to parents and correct these expectations.

Depending on the nature of the scenario, two approaches are often beneficial here. The first involves engaging parents in structured problem-solving, which may be most useful when parents perceive various barriers to their implementation of strategies in the home. Rather than proposing solutions to these barriers, the therapist guides parents to draw on their own expertise (e.g., knowledge of their child, family, personal strengths), modelling and scaffolding the process of problem-solving using questions corresponding to key steps: defining the problem, brainstorming solutions, selecting the most appropriate solution and preparing to implement the solution. Motivational interviewing practices may further facilitate this process (e.g., promoting parent feelings of self-efficacy by breaking goals down into achievable small steps, addressing the pros and cons of different courses of action).

Such problem-solving may be sufficient for the most common expressions of 'I can't', but in cases of greater ambivalence or unwillingness to follow the recommendations of the therapist (e.g., 'I won't'), a second line of questioning may be more successful. This emphasizes what have been referred to in the family therapy literature as *reflexive questions* (see [57]). Various types of reflexive questions (e.g., future-oriented questions, observer-perspective questions) are used in family therapy to encourage individuals to become observers of their own behaviour and mobilize behaviour change based on new awareness. Observer-perspective questions may lead to insights about challenges associated with specific treatment components (e.g., 'What is the difference between the times when these strategies have worked well compared to the times when they haven't?'). Future-oriented questions can be used to compel parents to face the significant implications that current circumstances may have for the future (e.g., 'If things continued without improving any further, what would that mean for your family in a few years when he becomes a teenager?'). The therapist might also use such questions to introduce hypothetical possibilities in a process of co-creating a future together with the family (e.g., 'It took us some trial and error to get this strategy working to change his uncooperative behaviour, and it sounds like if we could just get it working for his aggressive behaviour as well, that would open up a whole new world of having friends over and a proper social life with other families'). Reflexive questions can serve to generate hypotheses about family issues that may need to be taken into account or viewed differently within the therapeutic team for change to occur (e.g., 'I am wondering if there are things that I may have not understood properly about the problem or what happened when you used these strategies at home').

Reflexive questions such as these can play a key role in generating the 'news of difference' that according to various models of family therapy is a necessary impetus for systemic change to occur. The therapist, listening to a parent's description of an issue that may be impacting on treatment, elaborates on this description and in doing so incorporates new perspectives on it. It is predicted that parents will be most open to working with a therapist to overcome challenges in treatment after receiving news that it is possible for treatment to make accommodations for a particular issue and approach it in ways that were not previously considered. Using this approach, the therapist validates negative emotions while introducing new information that enables the parent to feel positive about the future of treatment (e.g., 'I can see why you would start to feel hopeless – each time you tried the strategy, his behaviour seemed to get worse. It may sound strange, but this can sometimes be a sign that it's actually starting to work').

In the current model, these exchanges occur while active treatment remains paused. The role of the therapist here is to empower parents to take action to resume treatment and indeed to decide if treatment resumes at all. To do this, the therapist

refrains from proposing any course of action on behalf of the therapeutic team or applying any pressure to the parents' decision-making. Rather, the therapist implicitly steps back and hands control to the parents, inviting them to step forward and take the lead. This process itself can convey impactful news of difference to parents, about therapy and what it can look like without a power struggle. Note that the emotions and impulses that therapists experience here can easily undermine this process and therefore warrant careful self-reflection. For example, an overwhelmed therapist may secretly wish for a family to drop out and inadvertently cue them for such an outcome. At the other extreme, a therapist may fear drop-out and view it as a personal failure. Such fear is problematic when it causes therapists to avoid the open discussion of difficult but important issues and when it prevents therapists from allowing parents the freedom to make their own decisions about participating in treatment. It is therefore important that therapists are able self-regulate such reactions and feel comfortable openly discussing the freedom that parents have to choose whether or not treatment continues. On occasion, paradoxical suggestions that encourage parents to consider drop-out as an option might serve to further highlight this. This must nonetheless be coupled with a stance that communicates an acceptance of parents and an optimism for treatment regardless of the difficulties experienced.

The therapist can further empower parents in this process by sharing evidence-based information about child CPs and their treatment. For this purpose the therapeutic team is conceptualized as comprising three independent subsystems: the parenting team, the therapist and science. This model highlights that while mental health professionals are in the privileged position of having been trained in the science of child CPs, they do not have exclusive ownership over it. It is the responsibility of the therapist to enable parents to access this science. The therapist gives a voice to this silent member of the team and in doing so may be called on to communicate relevant research findings in terms suited to the parents' level of education and existing knowledge. The aim is not to assert the therapist's expertise but to support parents to ask their own questions and draw their own interpretations of the independent evidence base that is available to inform treatment.

This may extend to supporting parents to use the scientific method to test assumptions regarding treatment. Such an approach was used with the father of a seven-year-old boy referred for ODD and ASD, who was engaging in acts of cruelty towards family members and pets. This father believed that new parenting strategies would be futile because cruelty was his son's ASD special interest, maintained only by the pleasure he derived from it. Rather than challenging the father's interpretation, the therapist set up a behavioural experiment with him. It was planned that the father would react to the child's behaviour in various ways during a video-recorded interaction. The child was observed to consistently glance at his father after speaking or acting with cruelty and increased such behaviour when the father enacted planned ignoring. Based on this evidence, the father was able to reinterpret the causes of this behaviour and became amenable to a parenting intervention.

7. **Reset the Shared Therapeutic Agenda.** Once parents are ready to resume active skills training, it is also necessary to establish that the therapeutic team is ready to move forward based on a shared therapeutic agenda. It is not enough that parents are motivated to continue therapy or that damage to the therapeutic relationship may have been repaired. What matters is that parents and therapists also agree on the goals and activities for the remainder of treatment and that this plan maps onto the case formulation. This process of updating the therapeutic agenda can, however, be complicated by the impact that case complexity and poor progress often have on treatment planning. At these times it can be difficult to determine whether a lack of change involves a skill deficit (i.e., parents have not yet acquired a skill) or a performance deficit (i.e., a skill exists but is not being applied). It can be useful to consider whether the current formulation of a case is sufficiently clear on this distinction, given that the goals and treatment activities indicated for a parent who is struggling to acquire a skill (e.g., corrective feedback focused on specific steps) might differ considerably from those indicated for a parent who is struggling to perform that skill (e.g., exploration of attributional processes triggered when using it with the child).

Another common example is seen when the early components/modules of treatment have failed to produce change in a child's behaviour, and the seemingly complex needs of the case compel the therapist to move onto a range of advanced/additional treatment components. Indeed, the early components of such treatment (e.g., strategies for rewarding good behaviour and setting limits on misbehaviour) can appear simplistic to parents and therapists alike. What is often overlooked, however, are the core shifts in family dynamics that these components are designed to initiate. That is, these components are fundamentally concerned with parents being able to connect positively with their child regardless of the child's behaviour, and parents being able to stop CPs from provoking reactions that feed back into those problems. More advanced components focused on additional issues in the family system (e.g., parent mental health, marital discord or issues arising from a history of trauma) may offer limited benefit until these fundamental shifts have first been achieved. When the complex needs of a family become apparent, or when the core components of treatment fail to produce change, it is easy for therapists to fall into the trap of overreaching, whereby more and more is added to treatment only to find that nothing is working. In our experience, it is often far more beneficial to narrow the focus of treatment and return to the unfinished business of the core treatment components before moving beyond them.

Conclusions

It is no coincidence that issues related to case complexity are commonplace in the treatment of child CPs. The risk factors implicated in the causes of CPs are many, and the struggle for change faced by families of children with CPs inevitably extends to the therapy room. Among the most important competencies for responding to such issues are those which support the formulation-driven delivery of evidence-based treatments for CPs and enable therapists to adapt manualised programmes while maximizing treatment integrity. As outlined here, complexity also has potential to derail treatment via a therapist's own reactions, including reactions outside of immediate awareness. For this reason, competencies that enable a therapist to promote change and reset shared therapeutic goals through reflective practice are also considered particularly core. With this chapter we hope to have highlighted the central importance of such competencies to the treatment of child CPs and the attention they deserve in clinical training and professional development.

References

1. Comer JS, Chow C, Chan PT, et al. Psychosocial treatment efficacy for disruptive behavior problems in very young children: A meta-analytic examination. *Journal of the American Academy of Child and Adolescent Psychiatry* 2013; **52**(1):26–36.

2. Kaminski JW, Claussen AH. Evidence base update for psychosocial treatments for disruptive behaviors in children. *Journal of Clinical Child and Adolescent Psychology* 2017; **46**(4):477–99.

3. Pilling S, Gould N, Wittington C, et al. Recognition, intervention, and management of antisocial behaviour and conduct disorders in children and young people: Summary of NICE-SCIE guidance. *British Medical Journal* 2013; **346**:f1298.

4. Lindsay G, Strand S, Davis H. A comparison of the effectiveness of three parenting programmes in improving parenting skills, parent mental-well being and children's behaviour when implemented on a large scale in community settings in 18 English local authorities: The parenting early intervention pathfinder (PEIP). *BMC Public Health* 2011; **11**:962.

5. Kaehler LA, Jacobs M, Jones DJ. Distilling common history and practice elements to inform dissemination: Hanf-model BPT programs as an example. *Clinical Child and Family Psychology Review* 2016; **19** (3):236–58.

6. Kaminski JW, Anne Valle L, Filene JH, Boyle C. A meta-analytic review of components associated with parent training program effectiveness. *Journal of Abnormal Child Psychology* 2008; **36**(4):567–89.

7. Garland AF, Hawley CM, Brookman-Frazee L, Hurlburt M. Identifying common elements of evidence-based psychosocial treatments for children's disruptive behavior problems. *Journal of the American Academy of Child and Adolescent Psychiatry* 2008; **47**(5):505–14.

8. Dadds M, Hawes D. *Integrated Family Intervention for Child Conduct Problems: A Behaviour-Attachment-Systems Intervention for Parents.* Bowen Hills, QLD, Australia: Australian Academic Press, 2006, pp. viii, 136.

9. Dadds MR, Cauchi AJ, Wimalaweera S, et al. Outcomes, moderators, and mediators of empathic-emotion recognition training for complex conduct problems in childhood. *Psychiatry Research* 2012; **199**(3):201–7.

10. Dadds MR, English T, Wimalaweera S, et al. Can reciprocated parent-child eye gaze and emotional engagement enhance treatment for children with conduct problems and callous-unemotional traits: A proof-of-concept trial. *Journal of Child Psychology and Psychiatry* 2019; **60**(6):676–85.

11. Kirkman JJ, Hawes DJ, Dadds MR. An open trial for an e-health treatment for child behavior disorders II: outcomes and clinical implications. *Evidence-Based Practice in Child and Adolescent Mental Health* 2016; **1**(4):213–29.

12. Dadds MR, Thai C, Mendoza Diaz A, et al. Therapist-assisted online treatment for child conduct problems in rural families: Two randomized controlled trials. *Journal of Consulting and Clinical Psychology* 2019; **87** (8):706–19.

13. Piotrowska PJ, Tully LA, Collins DAJ, et al. ParentWorks: Evaluation of an online, father-inclusive, universal parenting intervention to reduce child conduct problems. *Child Psychiatry and Human Development* 2020; **51**:503–13.

14. Delgadillo J, Huey D, Bennett H, McMillan D. Case complexity as a guide for psychological treatment selection. *Journal of Consulting and Clinical Psychology* 2017; **85**(9):835–53.

15. Ruscio AM. Holohan DR. Applying empirically supported treatments to complex cases: Ethical, empirical, and practical considerations. *Clinical Psychology: Science and Practice* 2006; **13**(2):146–62.

16. Tarrier N, Johnson J. *Case Formulation in Cognitive Behaviour Therapy: The Treatment of Challenging and Complex Cases.* London: Routledge, 2015.

17. Tung I, Lee SS. Context-specific associations between harsh parenting and peer rejection on child conduct problems at home and school. *Journal of Clinical Child and Adolescent Psychology* 2018; **47**(4):642–54.

18. Fonagy P, Luyten P. Conduct problems in youth and the RDoC approach: A developmental, evolutionary-based view. *Clinical Psychology Review* 2018; **64**:57–76.

19. Levy F, Hawes DJ, Johns A. Externalizing and internalizing comorbidity. In: *The Oxford Handbook of Externalizing Spectrum Disorders.* New York: Oxford University Press, 2016, pp. 443–60.

20. Taraban L, Shaw DS. Parenting in context: Revisiting Belsky's classic process of parenting model in early childhood. *Developmental Review* 2018; **48**:55–81.

21. Miller GE, Prinz RJ. Enhancement of social learning family interventions for childhood conduct disorder. *Psychology Bulletin* 1990; **108**(2):291–307.

22. Patterson GR, Chamberlain P. A functional analysis of resistance during parent training therapy. *Clinical Psychology: Science and Practice* 1994; **1**(1):53–70.

23. Patterson GR. Coercion theory. In: Dishion T, Snyder J (eds.), *The Study of Change*. Oxford, UK: Oxford University Press, 2015.

24. Snyder J, Stoolmiller M. Reinforcement and coercion mechanisms in the development of antisocial behavior: The family. In: *Antisocial Behavior in Children and Adolescents: A Developmental Analysis and Model for Intervention*. Washington, DC: American Psychological Association, 2002, pp. 65–100.

25. Minuchin S. *Families and Family Therapy*. Cambridge, MA: Harvard University Press, 1974, pp. viii, 268.

26. Green SM, Loeber R, Lahey BB. Child psychopathology and deviant family hierarchies. *Journal of Child and Family Studies* 1992; **1**(4):341–9.

27. Shaw DS, Criss M, Schonberg M, Beck J. The development of family hierarchies and their relation to children's conduct problems. *Development and Psychopathology* 2004; **16**(3):483–500.

28. Burn M, Tully LA, Jiang Y, et al. Evaluating practitioner training to improve competencies and organizational practices for engaging fathers in parenting interventions; *Child Psychiatry and Human Development* 2019; **50**(2):230–44.

29. Piotrowska PJ, Tully LA, Lenroot R, et al. Mothers, fathers, and parental systems: A conceptual model of parental engagement in programmes for child mental health – connect, attend, participate, enact (CAPE). *Clinical Child and Family Psychology Review* 2017; **20**(2):146–61.

30. Hawes DJ, Dadds MR. Parent and family assessment strategies. In: McLeod BD, Jensen-Doss A, Ollendick T (eds.), *Diagnostic and Behavioral Assessment in Children and Adolescents: A Clinical Guide*. New York: Guilford Press, 2013, pp. 316–47.

31. Dadds MR. Concurrent treatment of marital and child behaviour problems in behavioural family therapy. *Behaviour Change* 1992; **9**(3):139–48.

32. Sawrikar V, Dadds M. What role for parental attributions in parenting interventions for child conduct problems? Advances from research into practice. *Clinical Child and Family Psychology Review* 2018; **21**(1):41–56.

33. Mence M, Hawes DJ, Wedgwood L, Morgan S, Barnett B, Kohlhoff J, Hunt C. Emotional flooding and hostile discipline in the families of toddlers with disruptive behavior problems. *Journal of Family Psychology* 2014; **28**(1):12–21.

34. Snyder J, Edwards P, McGraw K, Kilgore K, Holton, A. Escalation and reinforcement in mother-child conflict: Social processes associated with the development of physical aggression. *Development and Psychopathology* 1994; **6**(2):305–21.

35. Fearon RP, Bakermans-Kranenburg MJ, van Ijzendoorn MH, Lapsley AM, Roisman GI. The significance of insecure attachment and disorganization in the development of children's externalizing behavior: A meta-analytic study. *Child Development* 2010; **81**(2):435–56.

36. Kochanska G, Barry RA, Stellern SA, O'Bleness JJ. Early attachment organization moderates the parent-child mutually coercive pathway to children's antisocial conduct. *Child Development* 2009; **80**(4):1288–300.

37. Greenberg MT, Speltz ML, Deklyen M. The role of attachment in the early development of disruptive behavior problems. *Development and Psychopathology* 1993; **5**(1–2):191–213.

38. Harlow HF, Harlow MK. Psychopathology in monkeys. In: Kimmel HD (ed.), *Experimental Psychopathology: Recent Research and Theory*. New York: Academic Press, 1972, pp. 203–29.

39. Dadds MR, Tully LA. What is it to discipline a child: What should it be? A reanalysis of time-out from the perspective of child mental health, attachment, and trauma. *American Psychologist* 2019; **74**(7):794–808.

40. Beutler LE, Moleiro C, Talebi H. Resistance in psychotherapy: What conclusions are supported by research? *Journal of Clinical Psychology* 2002; **58**(2):207–17.

41. Patterson GR, Chamberlain P. A functional analysis of resistance during parent training therapy. *Clinical Psychology: Science and Practice* 1994; **1**(1):53–70.

42. Patterson GR, Forgatch MS. Therapist behavior as a determinant for client noncompliance: A paradox for the behavior modifier. *Journal of Consulting and Clinical Psychology* 1985; **53**(6):846–51.

43. Scott S, Dadds MR. Practitioner review: When parent training doesn't work: Theory-driven clinical strategies. *Journal of Child Psychology and Psychiatry* 2009; **50**(12):1441–50.

44. Cavell TA. *Working with Parents of Aggressive Children: A Practitioner's Guide*. Washington, DC: American Psychological Association, 2000.

45. Webster-Stratton C, Herbert M, Ollendick TH. *Troubled Families Problem Children: Working with Parents. A Collaborative Process*. New York: Wiley, 1994.

46. Gottman JM, Leiblum SR. *How to Do Psychotherapy and How to Evaluate It: A Manual for Beginners*. New York: Holt, Rinehart & Winston, 1974.

47. Miller WR, Rollnick S. *Motivational Interviewing: Helping People Change*. New York: Guilford Press 2012.

48. N'zi AM, Lucash RE, Clionsky LN, Eyberg SM. Enhancing parent–child interaction therapy with motivational interviewing techniques. *Cognitive and Behavioral Practice* 2017; **24**(2):131–41.

49. Tully LA, Piotrowska PJ, Collins D, et al. Study protocol: Evaluation of an online, father-inclusive, universal parenting intervention to reduce child externalising behaviours and improve parenting practices. *BMC Psychology* 2017; **5**(21):11.

50. Webb HJ, Thomas R, McGregor L, et al. An evaluation of parent–child interaction therapy with and without motivational enhancement to reduce attrition. *Journal of Clinical Child and Adolescent Psychology* 2017; **46**(4):537–50.

51. Stoolmiller M, Duncan T, Bank L, Patterson G. Some problems and solutions in the study of change: Significant patterns in client resistance. *Journal of Consulting and Clinical Psychology* 1993; **61**(6):920.

52. Sawrikar V, Hawes DJ, Moul C, Dadds MR. How do mothers' parental attributions affect child outcomes from a positive parenting intervention? A mediation

study. In: *Child Psychiatry and Human Development.* 2019, pp. 1–12.

53. Sawrikar V, Mendoza Diaz A, Moul C, et al. Why is this happening? A brief measure of parental attributions assessing parents' intentionality, permanence, and dispositional attributions of their child with conduct problems. *Child Psychiatry and Human Development* 2019; **50**(3):362–73.

54. Chamberlain P, Patterson G, Reid J, et al. *Observation of client resistance. Behavior Therapy* 1984; **15** (2):144–55.

55. White LJ, Rosenthal D. Reframing in family therapy: Past, present, and future perspectives. *Family Science Review* 1989; **2**(3):237–48.

56. Robbins MS, Alexander JF, Newell RM, Turner CW. The immediate effect of reframing on client attitude in family therapy. *Journal of Family Psychology* 1996; **10**(1):28–34.

57. Tomm K. Interventive interviewing: II. Reflexive questioning as a means to enable self-healing. *Family Process* 1987; **26**(2):167–83.

Chapter 11

Enhancing Engagement and Motivation with Adolescents with ADHD and Their Parents

The Supporting Teens' Autonomy Daily (STAND) Model

Margaret H. Sibley and Patrick A. LaCount

Like most adolescents with attention deficit hyperactivity disorder (ADHD), 14-year-old Andy did not self-refer for therapy. His mom brought him in the door – he shuffled in reluctantly, uninterested in change and wary of a therapist who knew nothing about his life. Mrs. Edwards was eager for change because her original dreams for Andy were desperately dwindling. She brought Andy to therapy because she was stuck. And she was stuck because parenting an adolescent with ADHD involves a lot of dilemmas – dilemmas with no clear answers. When parents like Mrs. Edwards escort their teen to treatment, they often have high hopes that the magic of therapy will spark long-term change in the teen's attitude, work ethic, and behaviour. They often do not expect that they will be called on as an active participant and that their own change process will be central to the success of their teen. Thus, when Andy and Mrs. Edwards arrived for treatment, they shared one thing in common: both believed it was the other who needed to change. This is a disastrous combination for successful parent-teen therapy – a process that requires buy-in from both participants. It is no wonder that early family therapy models for teens with ADHD saw very high rates of conflict, disinterest and premature termination [1].

Over the last 10 years, our team worked to break this stalemate by leveraging a diverse set of therapy engagement strategies. In this chapter, we will introduce our population (teens with ADHD and their parents), model (Supporting Teens' Autonomy Daily) and mindset when approaching the treatment of teens with ADHD [2]. We hope that readers will use our experiences as a springboard for their own engagement-based approaches. The strategies presented herein can be applied to a range of clients who, like many of our families, are not sure that they want to be there, do not believe that they have the capacity to change, and struggle to turn intentions into action.

Being a Teen with ADHD

To create engagement, therapists must first cultivate deep understanding of a client's worldview. To do so, we must understand the neurodiverse brains of adolescents with ADHD. Teens with ADHD are often mischaracterized as possessing a defect in character – laziness, self-indulgence, indifference to others – but the truth is that many of their difficulties are biologically rooted [3]. As a result, ADHD is chronic, and its symptoms are very challenging to overcome. Individuals with ADHD possess neurocognitive deficits in two major brain circuits [4, 5]. The first is a 'cool' executive function (EF) deficit associated with mesocortical dopamine circuits and impairments in cognitive control. These functions include lower-order EFs such as working memory and inhibitory control, as well as higher-order EFs such as cognitive flexibility, metacognition, and planning. The second is a 'hot' rewards-processing deficit associated with cortical-striatal dopamine loops and difficulties with delay discounting, delay aversion, risky decision-making and motivation. The cool circuits typically correlate with inattentive symptoms, whereas the hot circuits often correlate with hyperactive/impulsive symptoms. Thus, adolescents with ADHD may experience dysfunction in one or both circuits with individual differences in how these deficits manifest [4, 5].

When an individual with these difficulties enters adolescence, life can get really hard. The adolescent brain has its own challenges. In general, adolescents experience heightened difficulties suppressing disadvantageous responses to immediately rewarding stimuli. This inability to delay gratification is associated with impulsive behaviours in adolescence [6]. Adolescents also experience a peak in sensation seeking characterized by a preference for low-probability high payouts over gradual low payouts that maximize long-term gain [7]. This urge is posited to underlie risk behaviours that are temporarily exhibited in adolescence [8]. Thus, the brain of an adolescent with ADHD struggles with symptoms such as forgetfulness, self-motivation and decision-making, and these difficulties are further compounded by adolescent neurobiology. Teens with ADHD may need to repeatedly learn from mistakes to eventually modify their behaviour [9, 10]. In the words of Mrs. Edwards, 'Andy has to get banged up or hurt to finally get serious about something' [11]. Unfortunately, Andy's world is not always forgiving.

Adolescence is characterized by increased academic demands, including heavier workloads, less guidance from teachers and new expectations for self-regulated learning [12, 13]. Successful mastery of adolescent academics requires precisely the EF skills and motivation that teens with ADHD characteristically lack. If the cognitive load demanded by adolescent life surpasses one's abilities, an adolescent with ADHD may experience greater impairments than in childhood. Similarly, adolescent social environments are increasingly complex, and teens with ADHD experience elevated rates of social rejection and bullying, fewer friendships and difficulties in romantic relationships [14–16]. In the family setting, parent-teen conflict is particularly elevated in youth with ADHD, which also impacts parenting stress [1, 17]. These failures create a world of negative feedback, and many adolescents with ADHD feel demoralized, defensive and misunderstood – over time, these experiences may be detrimental to their self-concept [18].

Thus, like most teens with ADHD, Andy entered therapy with low motivation to change (characteristic motivation deficits), low self-concept (years of negative feedback) and difficulty executing goal-directed behaviours (characteristic EF deficits). These challenges can inhibit the desire for success, goal pursuit and consistent practice of therapy skills outside of session. In this context, Mrs. Edwards' engagement

in therapy becomes crucial. As part of STAND, she will be engaged to apply behavioural strategies that reinforce teen engagement and skill practice [2]. As we trained parents in these skills, we learned that they also faced substantial barriers to making parenting changes.

Parenting a Teen with ADHD

As the transition to young adulthood loomed, Andy was not growing out of his ADHD, as his paediatrician hoped [19]. In fact, a lot of things seemed to be getting worse. Motivation for schoolwork was at an all-time low. Ambition for college was non-existent. On some days, household and school responsibilities were neglected in favour of video games, social media and online message boards. On other days, homework pressed on into the early morning. Andy was aggravated by Mrs. Edwards' attempts to talk about these issues, and Mrs. Edwards felt that every neglected task was an argument about to erupt. She worriedly looked into the future and saw a big question mark. Meanwhile, Andy resisted all help. As the clock ticked, the dilemmas of parenting Andy became increasingly stressful for Mrs. Edwards.

- How much should she assist versus let him stumble?
- Should she let him learn from the natural consequences of poor choices, even if it means serious penalties such as course failure or not being accepted to university?
- Should she stick to her rules when it can trigger rage, family stress and emotional shutdown?
- Everyone kept telling her to pick your battles, but which battles were worth picking?
- How late should Andy stay up doing homework – are grades more important than sleep?
- Should she encourage Andy to pursue gifted programmes, which may be more engaging for him but drain him to keep up?
- Are electronics just a big distraction, or are they an important lifeline to the outside world?
- How can she restrict inappropriate internet use when Andy needs his electronic devices for homework and basic communication?
- And at the end of the day, how are her actions influencing how Andy feels about himself?

No one talks about how difficult it is to parent a teenager with ADHD. Adolescence is a time of exciting firsts – driver's licences, romances, leadership positions, parties and college acceptances. In Andy's house, though, these celebrations were often replaced with worry, disappointment and indifference. Mrs. Edwards desperately wanted to help but felt out of answers. Nothing seemed to work.

Searching for solutions, parents like Mrs. Edwards often consult doctors, therapists, teachers and tutors. These professionals may provide advice that parents perceive as unrealistic. Careful monitoring of homework time and electronics use is often recommended, but many parents get home late, leaving hours of unsupervised time after school. Furthermore, family routines are not always consistent. Behavioural strategies, such as rewards systems, are often recommended but rarely gain traction. Parents feel that nothing seems to motivate the teen – even taking everything away. When medication is recommended, many teens say that they do not like the way it makes them feel [20]. Others do not want friends to find out. Not surprisingly, medication use drops by over 50 per cent from childhood to adolescence [21]. All in all, it can feel like every strategy works for a few weeks and then things return to old patterns. From this perspective, many parents of teens with ADHD enter therapy exhausted, sceptical and lost for solutions.

Overview of STAND

The development of outpatient therapy models for adolescent ADHD lagged behind school-based and intensive day-treatment models [22–24]. Until recently, there were no evidence-based family-focused treatments for adolescents with ADHD [25]. Family-based treatments are well suited for the treatment of adolescent ADHD. For one, the family context allows parent-teen conflict to be addressed – a majority of which stems from homework problems and difficulty with daily routines [26]. Furthermore, many parents of teens with ADHD interfere with youth autonomy development or disengage completely from parenting – remediation of maladaptive parenting behaviours is prime for a family therapy setting [27]. Finally, parents are ideal partners in behaviour therapy because they are uniquely positioned to oversee contingency management approaches. In light of these advantages, the first author of this chapter (MHS) decided to develop STAND as a family-based treatment for adolescent ADHD. In 2009, she began this pursuit as her dissertation at the State University of New York at Buffalo.

The initial concept was simple: pair evidence-based EF skills modules from school interventions with parent-implemented contingency management to reinforce teen skill use at home [22, 28]. We piloted this model with a handful of families at a university psychology clinic. Engaging parents and teens with ADHD in weekly therapy was anything but simple. As reported previously [29], key issues included

- Parents and teens failing to practise weekly strategies at home;
- Inconsistent parent and teen schedules that prevented consistent contingency management programmes;
- Challenges regulating electronics, which are both effective rewards and an activity that many parents wish to limit;
- Teens providing inaccurate reports of their functioning at school or with peers;
- Parents who were not satisfied with the slow, gradual change that is characteristic of treating a chronic condition (such as ADHD);
- Parents who used therapy time to complain about, blame and criticize the teen;
- Disconnect between what family members said they wanted to work on and what appeared to be the true presenting problems; and
- Parental beliefs that evidence-based strategies are ineffective because past experience did not produce long-term success.

During this pilot work, we also intuited parenting patterns that we would later identify empirically. In a sample of 299 parents of adolescents with ADHD, we detected four parenting profiles: *parental control* (18.7 per cent), *parent-teen collaboration* (20.4 per cent), *homework assistance* (20.4 per cent) and *uninvolved* (40.5 per cent) [27]. The parental control group micromanaged all aspects of academics. This pattern was most prevalent in young teenagers with ADHD and parents with somatic anxiety. The homework assistance group limited their involvement to intensive homework help – even to the point of completing assignments for the teen. This style was associated with parental mental health difficulties and severe adolescent inattention symptoms. The uninvolved group reported offering almost no academic support and was associated with higher levels of teen oppositional behaviour, older teens and higher levels of parental depression. Finally, the adaptive parent-teen collaborative group used pre-emptive behavioural strategies to motivate teen success and often helped with planning rather than completion of academic work. This group was also associated with the lowest levels of teen and parent mental health symptoms. Thus, as STAND evolved, a clear objective became helping parents overcome maladaptive parenting – moving them towards the parent-teen collaborative style [27].

In our pilot study, we observed that population-specific barriers were hampering treatment response. Therefore, the next iteration of STAND took an engagement-focused approach. This iteration of STAND combined evidence-based treatment components (i.e., cool compensatory EF strategies, hot contingency management strategies) with novel components that addressed observed population-specific barriers, drawing heavily from motivational interviewing (MI) [30]. In its current version, STAND is a 10-session psychosocial treatment for adolescent ADHD that engages the parent and teen simultaneously in weekly one-hour treatment sessions [2, 31–5] (see Table 11.1). Typically, the primary

Table 11.1 STAND Content (for Dyadic and Group Models)

Skill	Dyadic Session	Group Session
Goal-setting	2	3
Active listening and I statements	3	7
Contingency management	4	2
Writing down homework	Selected (5–6)	4
Book bag organization	Selected (5–6)	4
Homework plan	Selected (5–6)	5
Time management	Selected (5–6)	5
Study skills	Selected (5–6)	5
Note-taking	Selected (5–6)	8
Problem-Solving	Selected (5–6)	2
Communicating with teachers	7	8
Setting a daily routine	8	6
Parent-teen contracting	4–9	7

Note: Selected sessions in dyadic STAND represent skill modules selected by dyads based on client preferences. In group STAND, all families receive didactic instruction in all skill modules.

caregiver (rather than both parents) is engaged in treatment to maintain a balance of power (one parent, one adolescent) in the therapy room. STAND infuses skills-based treatment with engagement strategies directed at parents and teens, pairing motivational components with carefully guided practice of contingency management and teen EF skills. STAND also takes a developmentally tailored approach, training parents how to monitor and reinforce of school performance in secondary school settings, largely through widely used online grade books. STAND is organized into engagement, skills and planning modules, and engagement strategies are blended into all phases [2]. Three published randomized, controlled trials of STAND indicate a range of significant acute effects on ADHD symptoms, teen use of organization skills strategies, parent-teen use of contingency management, homework time behaviour, parenting stress and grade-point average [31, 33, 35].

Engagement Phase

The first four STAND sessions cultivate parent and teen engagement prior to skills training. STAND's manual offers a sequential ordering of engagement modules [2]. However, we encourage reordering, lengthening or truncating activities to tailor treatment to families [36]. In fact, one of the most important aspects of an engagement-based approach is emphasis on *tailoring* – a sure-fire way to lose parent and teen interest is to demonstrate that your treatment approach does not fit their unique needs. Manual-based treatments that impose rigid structures can undermine treatment credibility. Flexible modular approaches (like STAND) increasingly show promise of enhancing evidence-based treatment for children and adolescents with a range of presenting difficulties [37, 38]. To promote generalization of STAND strategies to other treatments and populations, this chapter will organize strategies by their function rather than by their typical sequence [2].

Strengthen Values. Values are a motivational factor that influence behaviour and can be differentiated by type and strength [39, 40]. Values are stable goals that guide behaviour across contexts and time [41]. Values cultivation can facilitate long-term therapy gains. Strong personal values are a factor that protects against mental health problems in adolescents, and parenting values are a strong predictor of parental behaviour [42, 43]. When working with Andy and

Mrs. Edwards, a primary goal was to strengthen their pre-existing values (i.e., being allowed to have more freedom, raising an independent son) to cast therapy participation as a values-consistent action. A secondary goal was to seed dissatisfaction with values-inconsistent living. This approach, which is central to MI, includes presenting families with a values inventory, asking them to select their top values and describe their importance [30]. By listening to this story telling, the therapist can connect with family members on a personal level, helping them live in harmony with core ideals. MI-consistent communication strategies can help clients visualize the link between therapeutic change and a values-consistent life. Once values crystallize, the therapist returns to them weekly, threading these themes into unfolding therapy and practice activities.

Strength-Based Approach. Parents and teens with ADHD may hold negative self-beliefs that undermine their faith in treatment [44–47]. These beliefs stem from years of negative environmental feedback [48–50]. In addition, there is no evidence that childhood treatments for ADHD produce effects that last into adolescence [21]. Thus, parents and teens may be sceptical about the efficacy of adolescent treatments. Strength-based approaches build self-efficacy and optimism in treatment [51, 52]. In STAND, strength-based assessment feedback is integrated into early sessions. Parents and teens reflect on each other's positive attributes and share how strengths might contribute to long-term success. In these discussions, parents and teens identify environments that promote success and intrinsic motivation (i.e., effort because the work is enjoyable). Thus, strengths also are leveraged to make choices about the teen's daily environment. When teens with ADHD are in enjoyable environments that make them feel successful, they are more likely to engage [53]. As part of a strength-based approach, the therapist can affirm all positive steps taken by the parent and teen in therapy, no matter how small [30].

Non-Judgemental Discussions. Unconditional positive regard is a long-standing element of supportive therapy [54]. It may be a particularly critical engagement strategy for teens with ADHD and their parents, who may expect judgement from others. In STAND, parents and teens define their own difficulties. Using an MI-consistent elicit-provide-elicit approach, therapists use tools that list impairments associated with ADHD and ask teens to self-identify

presenting problems [30]. Similarly, parents are asked to share the extent to which they relate to common parenting traps (e.g., doing homework for the teen, avoiding checking the teen's report card). With elicit-provide-elicit, the therapist first *elicits* how the client views their challenges, *provides* information on common experiences of similar others and *elicits* the client's reaction to this shared information [30]. Therapists use parent and teen language when describing presenting problems. Normalization of difficulties communicates acceptance of the teen and parent despite challenges. This approach is designed to reduce defensiveness when discussing difficulties.

Attention to Ambivalence and the Change Process. The MI tradition teaches that long-term behaviour change can be hard for anyone [30]. For successful change to occur, the client both must desire *and* must believe in their ability achieve change. Strengthening desire involves cultivating an emotional connection with reasons for change and abandoning the status quo [30]. It also means experiencing urgency – the belief that without change *now*, quality of life will worsen (or will never improve). When these necessary psychological conditions for change are present, verbal commitment to behaviour change may occur, but action may be delayed. Many individuals experience ambivalence about change – feeling two ways about a potential decision or set of actions. For example, Mrs. Edwards wished to reduce intrusive homework assistance because it was preventing Andy's autonomy development. Yet, she hesitated with this goal because of worries that reduced parental support might result in school failure [11]. Visually, the change process can be depicted on a continuum (though movement across this continuum is not always linear):

$$\text{Desire} \rightarrow \text{self} - \text{efficacy} \rightarrow \text{strong reasons} \rightarrow$$
$$\text{urgency} \rightarrow \text{verbal commitment} \rightarrow \text{action}$$

Many evidence-based behaviour therapies start the change process by eliciting verbal commitment, ignoring important cognitive restructuring around desire, self-efficacy, reasons, and urgency. MI-consistent approaches acknowledge the internal change process that precedes successful behaviour change. These therapies support clients to resolve ambivalence so that therapist-proposed actions are met with client eagerness. Many rich strategies to promote internal change are outside this chapter's scope. Receiving training in MI is an excellent way to develop these therapeutic skills [30]. STAND therapists are encouraged to attend at least a two-day basic MI training (which our team typically blends into a three-day STAND training) so that STAND is delivered to its full potential.

Andy and Mrs. Edwards completed several tasks in STAND to promote their internal change process. These included (1) writing about one's successful self, three years in the future, and (2) writing a letter from one's successful future self to the present self, offering advice. They also created change cards – colour-coded note cards that prioritize desired changes. Completing these exercises allowed the therapist to explore Andy's and Mrs. Edwards' change language related to improving academic effort and parental limit setting.

Self-Selected, Gradually Advancing Therapy Homework. Therapy homework is a critical element of evidence-based treatments [55]. In STAND, therapy homework is the cornerstone of skill generalization. Homework in STAND builds on engagement practices. Although basic procedures for weekly therapy homework can be recommended by the therapist, ultimately, parents and teens are free to decline. If they wish to complete homework, parents and teens work with the therapist to tailor the assignment to their interest level, personal routine and therapy goals. In fact, therapy homework is not referred to as *homework* in STAND – which may have a negative connotation for teens who were referred for academic problems. Instead, it is referred to as *practice*. Because many families in community settings do not complete therapy homework, home practice gradually advances across the weeks of STAND [56, 57]. The first activity Andy and Mrs. Edwards completed was to simply discuss their long-term goals – which escalated to written brainstorming of strategies, completing family outings and, finally, daily practice of the new skills they were learning (i.e., recording assignments in a planner, keeping an organized bedroom, making video games contingent on work completion). Promoting choice in practice activities allows parents and teens to examine personal reasons for skill use (beyond 'because the therapist asked me to'). It also allows them to choose aspects of STAND that feel most relevant. Slowly increasing the content of therapy homework allows families to gradually welcome these activities and develop self-efficacy about its completion.

Personal Goal-Setting. Many evidence-based treatments ask parents and teachers to identify a child's treatment targets. However, in STAND, Andy set his own goals (i.e., turning in more homework, convincing his mother that he could handle less supervision). The therapist ensured that Andy's goals were personally meaningful and aligned with his values (e.g., less parental oversight). By the same token, Mrs. Edwards set values-based parenting goals (rather than goals for Andy). There is evidence that goal-setting interventions improve self-regulation in adolescents with ADHD [58]. Goals offer concrete outcomes for treatment that are personally meaningful and allow the family to continually reassess progress. Because goal-directed actions are particularly challenging for youth with ADHD [59, 60], goal-setting tasks also model a compensatory strategy for EF deficits.

Collaborative, Modular, Menu-Based Approach. Recognizing the heterogeneity of youth with psychiatric disorders, modular approaches offer benefits that include (1) allowing treatment content to follow an unfolding case conceptualization, (2) promoting family-specific treatment plans and (3) empowering parents and teens to take an active role in treatment planning [37]. Using the elicit-provide-elicit framework [30], STAND includes a treatment menu listing a range of therapy skills that are evidence based for adolescent ADHD (i.e., organization skills, problem-solving strategies, study skills, time management strategies, planning approaches). Therapists first elicit from family members the skills they are hoping to learn, provide a menu listing options for skills training and elicit family member preferences for skill learning. Using a collaborative framework, the therapist can provide feedback on family choices and help parents and teens negotiate divergent opinions. The menu is presented early in session, linked to values and goals, and can be revisited as treatment priorities refine.

Emphasis on Parent-Teen Communication. Because parent-teen conflict is a known barrier to treatment for adolescents with ADHD, a plan for managing these difficulties is addressed upfront [1, 61]. An entire session is devoted to discussing the parent-teen relationship. Andy and Mrs. Edwards were asked to reflect on the meaning of partnership and what they value in their relationship. They identified argument triggers (e.g., Andy forgetting to clean up after himself) and brainstormed strategies to prevent and recover from escalated conflicts. The therapist introduced two ubiquitous communication strategies, *I statements* and *reflective listening*, that can be called on in future sessions if conflicts arise [62]. To promote generalization, Andy and Mrs. Edwards were asked to plan a one-on-one activity during the next week to practise their positive communication skills and discuss progress on goals. This content is situated in the engagement phase to prevent parent-teen conflict from derailing therapy. In fact, some families require multiple parent-teen communication sessions before advancing to subsequent content.

Behaviour Management with Autonomy Support. Successful parent-teen contracting takes a lot of work. It involves parent comprehension of behavioural principles, teen openness to limit-setting, parent willingness to reduce intrusive support behaviours and monitoring teen behaviour under logistically challenging circumstances. Autonomy-support behaviour management approaches inhabit the terrain between parental over-control and full extension of teen freedoms. Parental expectations should be viewed as fair by the teen. Requested incentives and consequences should be natural and effective motivators rather than excessive or overindulgent rewards. Because launching a successful parent-teen contract requires trial and error, we believe that honing these skills must precede skills training for presenting problems (i.e., EF difficulties, academic problems). A successful parent-teen contract can cultivate a brand of extrinsic motivation that leads to rapid gains in therapeutic engagement. However, unsuccessful contracts can reinforce negative beliefs about treatment or the teen. Thus, developmentally inappropriate behavioural strategies can promote therapy disengagement and dropout among teens with ADHD. Parents and teens should show basic competence in simple contracts (i.e., minor chores around the house, easily achievable behavioural goals) before applying this framework to presenting problems.

Use of Natural, Daily Incentives. When selected rewards are unrealistic for the parent to administer, unappealing to the teen or too long term, contingency management programmes are likely to be ineffective. Thus, contingency management based in long-term, tangible or monetary rewards can sabotage engagement. Poor contingency management can reinforce existing parental beliefs that the teen does not respond to behavioural treatment. In contrast, basing contingency management in the teen's natural environment is a face-valid approach that is often easier to administer. Using natural incentives also appeals to parental

values about justice (i.e., 'I shouldn't be rewarding him for something he should be expected to do at this age'). Examples of natural, daily incentive programmes include reserving electronics use until all homework is completed, making use of the car contingent upon respectful behaviour to parents and providing videogame time if one's room passes a weekly inspection. These natural, daily programmes are sustainable and realistic for families to implement, supporting treatment credibility.

Managing Impatience. Laying engagement groundwork takes time and delays direct work on therapy targets. Some dyads may experience early target behaviour gains anyway; others may express impatience with the delay in reaching STAND's face-valid skills phase. If unmanaged, this exasperation could presumably contribute to premature dropout. Thus, therapists are encouraged to frame the goal of adolescent ADHD treatment as building a foundation for successful transition to adulthood rather than immediately extinguishing crises. The engagement phase offers critical foundational skills that will increase the likelihood of success in later phases of therapy and life. Impatience can be acknowledged, normalized and monitored with candid conversations that ultimately surrender to family choice. If a dyad strongly wishes to front load skills training in STAND (at the cost of engagement activities), an engagement-centric approach would honour this autonomy.

Skills Phase

Engagement practices continue throughout the skills phase. These include blended MI strategies, reinforcement of goals and values, promoting parent and teen choice and assigning and reviewing home practice using engagement-centric paradigms.

Reinforcing Goals and Values. Each week, Andy and Mrs. Edwards reflected on how recent actions supported their goals and values. This practice reinforces intentions and ensures that progress is personally meaningful. Their therapist started each session with a five-minute strength-based conversation – affirming even small steps that support personal goals. Skills sessions deliberately began with this positive conversation to help Andy and Mrs. Edwards acknowledge each other's efforts. Despite positive steps in therapy, negative incidents commonly continue throughout STAND. Parents may become frustrated or sceptical of treatment when progress is seesawing rather than transformative. Eliciting positive conversations prevents sessions from taking a negative tone.

Promoting Parent and Teen Choice. There are so many creative and interesting ways to apply STAND's basic EF skills. Parents and teens often come up with unique adaptations that exceed basic applications in the manual [2]. Parents and teens are encouraged to make each therapy skill their own. For example, the STAND manual contains basic content on active studying and its application to flashcards and note-taking from text. Additional family-constructed study tools can spin off these concepts. When promoting parent and teen choice, therapists communicate that parents and teens are experts on the family's unique context. The skills phase includes brainstorming how to use skills in ways that fit with the teen's daily life. If the parent or teen make questionable selections rather than imposing an alternative, the therapist can promote an experimental mindset. If the parent and teen try the idea for a week and take careful notes, they collect their own evidence on the approach's effectiveness.

Skill Practice as Information Gathering Rather than Permanent Change. When family members are ambivalent about a new therapy skill, pushing skill adoption may be counter-therapeutic. Consistent with MI, the therapist can frame practice activities as exercises that collect data on the utility of potential habits [30]. This approach acknowledges that not all skills are a good fit. Emphasizing the teen's personal control in skill selection also increases openness to trying new skills. Doing so also promotes home practice.

Imaginal Practice and Implementation Intentions. Parent-teen contracts clarify expectations about skill practice. However, a well-designed parent-teen contract is necessary but not sufficient to promote success. Skill practice is constantly threatened by logistical barriers. Unforeseen scenarios arise that fall outside the initial agreement. Many families abandon contracts at the first sign of a hiccup, reinforcing the belief that behavioural strategies are ineffective. *Imaginal practice* is a practical in-session activity that prepares families for barriers that may emerge. It can occur immediately following contract completion. After Andy and Mrs. Edwards contracted to have phone use be contingent on homework completion, the therapist asked them to walk through executing the contract – both for when the Andy appropriately practices the skills and for when he does not. As part

of this activity, the therapist warmly peppered Andy and Mrs. Edwards with scenarios that might derail the contract. This strengthens and normalizes problem-solving (i.e., what happens if Andy forgets his phone at school, preventing you from taking it away?; what happens if your mother doesn't give you the privilege, even though you earned it?). By preparing for a range of scenarios, atypical days and weeks become a part of the plan instead of a barrier to strategy use. Through imaginal practice, Andy and Mrs. Edwards developed several implementation intentions – if-then plans that support successful execution of contracts under a variety of circumstances (e.g., *if* I forget to write down my homework, *then* I will contact a classmate to find out what I missed) [63, 64].

Reinforcing Successful Practice. Progress in STAND is often inconsistent. Parents may over-focus on treatment-resistant behaviours, failing to acknowledge small steps and efforts along the way. When small successes occur, the therapist has an opportunity to capitalize – reinforcing strengths, self-efficacy, optimism and the connection between hard work and achieving one's goals. Doing so can be artfully accomplished through MI [30]. Reflecting on successful practice can deepen parent and teen language about long-term change. MI can be used to reinforce statements about desire to continue new habits, the ability to successfully implement skills, the connection between goals and skill use and commitment to continued use. Therapists can use MI skills such as change-oriented open-ended questions, complex therapeutic reflections, affirmations and summaries to strengthen parent and teen change language. Meanwhile, counter-change language can be sidestepped to reduce emphasis on barriers or reasons to desist the new skill. At the end of a conversation about success, the therapist can pose a simple but powerful question to the parent and teen: 'based on your experience this week, what do you think you'll do long-term?' This communicates that decisions about change are up to the family rather than the therapist.

Unsuccessful Practice as Wisdom Gained. Practice of therapy skills outside of session is rarely seamless. Even when Andy successfully applied a skill four out of five days, Mrs. Edwards tended to focus on the single failure. When therapists sense a parent's urge to complain, he or she can pre-emptively begin with a conversation about successes – no matter how small. Each minute clocked discussing small successes becomes a powerful tool to offset the impact of impending negative talk. When the time comes to discuss problems, the therapist's reaction is critical. The therapist asked Mrs. Edwards to describe an unsuccessful day one moment at a time. Doing so helped Mrs. Edwards gain insight about how her parenting behaviours contributed to Andy's low motivation to practise skills. The therapist can offer therapeutic reflections to crystallize these insights. He or she can also reflect that privilege removal reflects a parenting success, not a defective contract. In this context, therapeutic reflections can reframe failures as valuable learning experiences (i.e., 'this week you learned that you will have to physically check his planner and can't take his word for it; that will be useful going forward'). Therapeutic reflections can also shield the teen from parental shaming. By reframing parent criticisms rather than confronting the parent's point of view, therapist neutrality is maintained (e.g., 'you are starting to realize that it's hard for him to self-motivate, and we may need to support him better in this process'). Modelling neutral problem-solving rather than blaming and shaming can expose the parent to adaptive communication styles. Therapists can close conversations about failure with forward-focused questions such as 'based on what you learned this week, how would you modify this plan to make it stronger?'

Attention to Interfering Parental Behaviours. As is common, Mrs. Edwards' interfering parenting behaviours became apparent midway through the skills phase. Her anxiety-driven assistance often prevented Andy from independently completing work and experiencing the natural consequences of his inaction. Other parents experience parental disorganization and time management difficulties, preventing consistency in behavioural contracts. If the therapist ignores maladaptive parenting behaviours, treatment will be largely ineffective (reinforcing parental scepticism). On the other hand, confronting a parent about their need to change can risk full disengagement – especially when parental behaviours are fear-driven or stable traits. Andy's therapist supported Mrs. Edwards to self-identify interfering parental behaviours and set goals for reducing them. This approach creates a parallel therapeutic process that is steeped in empathy and supports parental change.

Planning Phase

The planning phase creates long-term plans for turning parent and teen therapy skills into habits. These sessions emphasize integrating skills into the daily routine and reflecting on changes that occurred during STAND.

Trial-and-Error Is Expected. One major message of the planning phase is that trial-and-error is to be expected. Long-term behaviour change is challenging to achieve and takes time. When family members expect initial failures, they are more likely to stay optimistic and persist with the process. As part of this message, parents and teens are encouraged to envision life after therapy and brainstorm ways to reinitiate trial and error should new challenges arise. Trial and error also mean waiting to form opinions until *after* trying a strategy.

Consolidated Learning. At the end of STAND, Andy and Mrs. Edwards wrote a letter to a future family, sharing what was learned and advice on how to be successful in therapy. This activity is designed to strengthen family members' commitment to continued skill practice after termination. It also consolidates parent and teen self-exploration that occurred during therapy, increasing awareness of how each participant contributes to family success.

STAND Mind-set

ADHD is a chronic disorder that persists through adulthood in a majority of paediatric cases [19]. Thus, a goal of treatment is to equip families with a mind-set that promotes long-term success. Sometimes long-term success is pursued at a cost to short-term functioning. For example, in the developmentally appropriate transfer from parent-managed academics to self-managed academics, teens may struggle to demonstrate autonomy. This can produce a temporary drop in grade-point average (GPA). Increasing rules and consequences at home may have a long-term effect of reducing teen negative behaviours at a short-term cost to escalating parent-teen conflict [65]. In some ways, these are negative side effects of STAND – much like appetite suppression and sleep disruption can be side effects of stimulant medication [66]. However, if these side effects can be tolerated, the long-term payoff to families may be tremendous. Thus, the STAND mind-set is that some therapeutic changes hurt, and others will not pay off for years – but make them anyway. The STAND mind-set also accepts that some families are not ready to make the changes they desire – it is okay to need more time. If we plant the seeds known to promote self-motivation and success and consistently water them, eventually they are likely to grow.

Delivering STAND as a Group

Group STAND evolved as a cost-effective model with benefits that include (1) promoting self-confidence through peer encouragement, (2) idea sharing and normalization of difficulties by hearing the experiences of similar others and (3) enhancing one's social support system [2, 67]. In this model, parents and teens attend a combined therapy group for an initial meeting to review progress, sit in separate groups to discuss therapy skills and then return to the combined group to participate in a practice activity. Research on group STAND suggests that this model increases parent implementation of behavioural strategies, promotes teen use of organization skills and reduces missing homework assignments [32]. Group STAND's effects are commensurate with the effects of dyadic STAND. However, the group model is less effective when parent-teen conflict is high, parents have elevated ADHD symptoms or parents experience depression [35]. We hypothesize that the individualized engagement strategies in dyadic STAND are better at promoting change in families with higher adversities.

Limitations of STAND

Adolescents with ADHD and their parents are a challenging population to treat. Their difficulties are chronic, and their behaviour patterns are often ingrained. STAND is not a panacea. Although our research suggests that STAND produces medium- to large short-term changes on organization skills, ADHD symptoms, parenting stress and parent behavioural strategy use, it shows smaller immediate effects on functional indices such as GPA [31, 33]. Long-term follow-up of our STAND studies is planned but has not yet occurred. Thus, we do not yet know the long-term impact of receiving STAND. As is typically the case for evidence-based interventions, we also have evidence that STAND is less effective when delivered in community contexts (compared to university clinics) [68, 69]. A recent study suggests that *licenced* clinicians in community contexts successfully delivered STAND to clients, but the *unlicenced* workforce struggled to implement this treatment. Trainees successfully implemented STAND in our university clinic. However, junior clinicians, who made up most of our community mental health workforce, may need enhanced training and coaching to deliver STAND [69]. The families served in these contexts face higher barriers, and their

therapists may have lower levels of training – making mastery of STAND engagement strategies challenging without augmented support.

From a process perspective, there are some engagement barriers that we are still trying to address. It is challenging to balance a family's immediate crisis with the long-term change process – the former often requires an immediate solution at the expense of the latter. For example, a large parent-delivered incentive for success may produce immediate behavioural change but fails to promote the process of self-motivation – an important long-term skill for individuals with ADHD. Our provisional approach is to clarify these dilemmas with parents and allow their personal values to steer the course of treatment. However, this still remains a challenging process issue for clinicians. Sometimes a family has a limited capacity to change in the current moment. We learned to slow down the course of treatment for these families, but it can be unclear how to proceed when nothing seems to work. Another area for STAND development is promoting long-term change by planning the transition to adulthood. This content is desired by the families but not yet developed. Finally, it is hard to deliver STAND without support, training and practice. The strongest STAND therapist will be MI proficient, display familiarity with population-specific issues, and be able to make in situ decisions about which engagement strategy a family needs at a given moment. Simplistic family-based approaches that solely focus on skills training are not sufficient for adolescents with ADHD [1]. An adage suggests that sometimes complex problems can be solved with simple solutions, but in truth, some complex problems still require multifaceted approaches. We would love to find ways to simplify STAND's elements and are open to input in this regard. We also view our work as a torch to be passed to all clinicians who work with families – from our starting point, we hope that each of you can evolve your own personalized brand of STAND to improve the lives of families.

Because there may be side effects to STAND (i.e., temporary increases in parent-teen conflict, temporary reductions in GPA), a skilled professional is needed to usher families through these challenges. Premature dropout in the midst of these disruptions can be dangerous – reinforcing teen negative behaviours or leaving parents with insufficient skills to manage exacerbated symptoms [65]. Thus, it is critical that

STAND clinicians have adequate skills to manage these difficulties and that parents and teens are informed that functioning can sometimes worsen before it improves.

Training in STAND Engagement Strategies

As a therapist, it is challenging to master the engagement strategies discussed in this chapter. As a result, we provide some suggestions for training and self-study. With respect to formal training, MI training is provided by individuals in the Motivational Interviewing Network of Trainers (MINT; www.motivationalinterviewing.org). Worldwide trainings are listed on the MINT website. Typically, a three-day beginner course provides a basic introduction to strategies, but research suggests that achieving MI fluidity may require three to four sessions of post-training coaching [88]. This can be achieved through engaging a one-on-one coach or attending an advanced MI workshop. For STAND-specific application of MI and non-MI engagement strategies listed herein, our STAND training team is comprised of three MINT trainers with language fluency in English, Spanish and Portuguese. Our team regularly provides trainings (both scheduled and upon request) to promote dissemination. Recommended readings for self-study include the third edition of the seminal MI text and the STAND manual [2, 30]. Video seminars on how to apply STAND's engagement strategies are also available online (https://vimeo.com/ondemand/standvideotrainingseries). Self-study can also involve audio recording therapy sessions and reviewing your own progress – noting when engagement strategies were successfully and unsuccessfully applied and creating personalize goals for your own therapist behaviours. This practice is enhanced by partnering with a colleague who shares similar learning goals.

The Next 10 Years

At the time this chapter was written, STAND celebrated its tenth birthday. As we look forward to its continued evolution, our team has set the following strategic directions for the next 10 years. We hope that improving this engagement-focused approach will increase quality of life for parent and teens with ADHD.

Preparing for Young Adulthood. The transition to young adulthood is a time of profound change, during which adolescents adjust to independence from parents, navigating unstructured environments, maintaining healthy adult relationships, achieving financial self-sufficiency and managing demanding academic curricula and/or vocations [89]. Because young adulthood demands self-regulation and provides fewer external supports, many encounter difficulties – especially individuals with ADHD, itself a disorder of self-regulation.

Although the transition to young adulthood is associated with a reduction of ADHD *symptoms*, it is also associated with increasing *impairment* [90, 91]. Teens transitioning to young adulthood often struggle to meet demands and experience greater difficulties despite receiving comprehensive treatment in childhood and often adolescence [90]. Thus, the success of STAND hinges on its ability to prepare teens for this vulnerable time.

Adjustment during young adulthood can have enduring ramifications [92]. The long-term risks for those with ADHD adjusting to young adulthood underscore the importance of engaging in mental health services. However, the opposite often occurs, and there is almost complete disengagement from services in emerging adulthood [93, 94]. Because of the high rate of engagement and parent-teen collaborative nature of the treatment model, we believe that STAND is ideal for preparing individuals and families for the transition to young adulthood.

Within the framework of STAND, clinicians can provide anticipatory guidance about the transition to young adulthood, such as (1) planning for academic, vocational and living environments that optimize functioning, (2) helping parents taper supports, and (3) strengthening protective factors (e.g., academic supports) that can attenuate difficulties in the face of increasing self-regulatory demands (for discussion, see LaCount et al. [95]). Further, STAND's framework allows teens to practise adult-expected behaviours while parents supervise and provide feedback. Indeed, many parents do not anticipate the restriction of their ability to monitor or support their child when they turn 18 years of age. At this point, health professionals and professors in many countries are legally restricted from disclosing any information about the young adult (e.g., U.S. Health Insurance Portability and Accountability Act of 1996, Family Educational Rights and Privacy Act of 1974). Thus, parent education may be an important part of transition-focused STAND modules. In light of the decline in treatment utilization among young adults with ADHD, we believe that clinicians should prioritize improving future use and access to mental health services in young adulthood, including identification of adult mental health providers, questions about the logistics of accessing health care and planning institutional supports.

After reaching the legal age of adulthood, fewer young adults receive services from health providers who specialize in working with children. At the same time, adult health providers may be less comfortable managing the care of young adults. Although those attending university have access to health services, comprehensive services are often available while school is not in session (e.g., winter break). Planning for the transition to the adult health system, such as establishing care with an adult mental health provider *before* transitioning to young adulthood, can facilitate improved adjustment.

In addition to adjusting to an adult model of health care, many suddenly have poor access to health services because of insurance coverage issues in young adulthood. For example, the likelihood of being insured is more than halved after the age of 18 in the United States [96, 97]. Because health services expenses are twice as high as for those without ADHD, obtaining health insurance and anticipating health-care-related expenses improves health-care access and engagement in young adulthood [98].

Associated with the transition period is a loss of institutional supports. Patients entering the workforce may qualify for vocational accommodations. Similarly, postsecondary students may be able to access student support services and receive standardized testing accommodations. Of note, clinicians should familiarize themselves with the documentation required for patients to qualify for accommodations or services (for a detailed review, see Gordon et al. [99]).

Adapting to Community Contexts. Despite the promise of STAND, very few adolescents with ADHD receive therapy in their communities [100]. When youth with ADHD receive community-based services, they are typically pharmacological [101]. Although stimulant medications provide effective *symptom* reduction for teens with ADHD, they are less effective than adolescent psychosocial treatments with regards to reducing ADHD-related *impairments* [25]. Community mental health services offer an important opportunity to increase access to effective therapies such as STAND. The health-care sector allocates sufficient public and/or commercial resources to treat most

adolescents with mental health problems [102]. Furthermore, ADHD is the most common diagnosis among youth presenting in community mental health settings [38, 103]. The engagement problems associated with adolescent ADHD may be compounded in community mental health settings, where retention in services is lower than in specialty clinics [104, 105]. Our current outreach efforts include partnering with community mental health agencies to adapt STAND to this setting. Initial results suggest that after training and supervision in STAND, therapists are more likely than their colleagues to employ engagement-focused approaches with adolescents with ADHD [106]. Furthermore, STAND-trained therapists viewed the treatment as less demanding than usual care interventions and were likely to recommend the approach to colleagues. Despite these positive signals, STAND produced much lower responses to treatment than in past university clinic trials [87]. Thus, our team continues to partner with the community mental health workforce to learn how we can adapt this treatment to better suit their setting.

References

1. Barkley RA, Edwards G, Laneri M, et al. The efficacy of problem-solving communication training alone, behavior management training alone, and their combination for parent–adolescent conflict in teenagers with ADHD and ODD. *Journal of Consulting and Clinical Psychology* 2001; **69**:926–41.

2. Sibley MN. *Parent-Teen Therapy for Executive Function Deficits and ADHD: Building Skills and Motivation.* New York: Guilford Press, 2016.

3. Thapar A, Cooper M, Eyre O, et al. Practitioner review: what have we learnt about the causes of ADHD?. *Journal of Child Psychology and Psychiatry* 2013; **54**:3–16.

4. Castellanos FX, Sonuga-Barke EJ, Milham MP, et al. Characterizing cognition in ADHD: Beyond executive dysfunction. *Trends in Cognitive Sciences* 2006; **10**:117–23.

5. Sonuga-Barke EJ. The dual pathway model of AD/HD: An elaboration of neuro-developmental characteristics. *Neuroscience and Biobehavioral Reviews* 2003; **27**:593–604.

6. Casey BJ, Jones RM, Hare TA. The adolescent brain. *Annals of the New York Academy of Sciences* 2008; **1124**:111–26.

7. Steinberg L, Albert D, Cauffman E, et al. Age differences in sensation seeking and impulsivity as indexed by behavior and self-report: evidence for a dual systems model. *Developmental Psychology* 2008; **44**:1764–78.

8. Steinberg LA. Social neuroscience perspective on adolescent risk-taking. *Developmental Review* 2008; **28**:78–106.

9. Humphreys KL, Lee SS. Risk taking and sensitivity to punishment in children with ADHD, ODD, ADHD + ODD, and controls. *Journal of Psychopathology and Behavioral Assessment* 2011; **33**:299–307.

10. Iaboni F, Douglas VI, Baker AG. Effects of reward and response costs on inhibition in ADHD children. *Journal of Abnormal Psychology* 1995; **104**:232–40.

11. Sibley MH, Yeguez CE. Managing ADHD at the post-secondary transition: A qualitative study of parent and young adult perspectives. *School Mental Health* 2018; **10**:352–71.

12. Eccles JS. Schools, academic motivation, and stage-environment fit. In: *Handbook of Adolescent Psychology*, vol. **2**. 2004, pp. 125–53.

13. Zimmerman BJ. Becoming a self-regulated learner: An overview. *Theory into Practice* 2002; **41**:64–70.

14. Steinberg L, Morris AS. Adolescent development. *Annual Review of Psychology* 2001; **52**:83–110.

15. Bagwell CL, Molina BS, Pelham WE, et al. Attention-deficit hyperactivity disorder and problems in peer relations: Predictions from childhood to adolescence. *Journal of the American Academy of Child and Adolescent Psychiatry* 2001; **40**:1285–92.

16. Rokeach A, Wiener J. The romantic relationships of adolescents with ADHD. *Journal of Attention Disorders* 2018; **22**:35–45.

17. Evans SW, Sibley MH, Serpell ZN. Changes in caregiver strain over time in young adolescents with ADHD: The role of oppositional and delinquent behavior. *Journal of Attention Disorders* 2009; **12**:516–24.

18. Houck G, Kendall J, Miller A, et al. Self-concept in children and adolescents with attention deficit hyperactivity disorder. *Journal of Pediatric Nursing* 2011; **26**:239–47.

19. Barkley RA, Murphy KR, Fischer M. *ADHD in Adults: What the Science Says.* New York: Guilford Press, 2010.

20. Brinkman WB, Simon JO, Epstein, JN. Reasons why children and adolescents with attention-deficit /hyperactivity disorder stop and restart taking medicine. *Academic Pediatrics* 2017.

21. Molina BS, Hinshaw SP, Swanson JM, et al. The MTA at 8 years: Prospective follow-up of children treated for combined-type ADHD in a multisite study. *Journal of the American Academy of Child and Adolescent Psychiatry* 2009; **48**:484–500.

22. Evans SW, Axelrod J, Langberg JM. Efficacy of a school-based treatment program for middle school youth with ADHD: Pilot data. *Behavior Modification* 2004; **28**:528–47.

23. Langberg JM, Epstein JN, Becker SP, et al. Evaluation of the homework, organization, and planning skills (HOPS) intervention for middle school students with ADHD as implemented by school mental health providers. *School Psychology Review* 2012; **41**:342–64.

24. Smith BH, Pelham WE, Gnagy E, et al. The reliability, validity, and unique contributions of self-report by adolescents receiving treatment for attention-deficit/ hyperactivity disorder. *Journal of Consulting and Clinical Psychology* 2000; **68**:489–99.

25. Sibley MH, Kuriyan AB, Evans SW, et al. Pharmacological and psychosocial treatments for adolescents with ADHD: An updated systematic review of the literature. *Clinical Psychology Review* 2014; **34**:218–32.

26. Garcia AM, Medina D, Sibley MH. Conflict between parents and adolescents with ADHD: Situational triggers and the role of comorbidity. *Journal of Child and Family Studies* 2019; **28**(12):3338–45.

27. Sibley MH, Campez M, Perez A, et al. Parent management of organization, time management, and planning deficits among adolescents with ADHD. *Journal of Psychopathology and Behavioral Assessment* 2016; **38**:216–28.

28. Patterson GR, Forgatch M. *Parents and Adolescents Living Together, Part 1: The Basics.* Eugene, OR: Castalia, 1987.

29. Sibley MH. Supporting autonomy development in teens with ADHD: How professionals can help. *ADHD Report* 2017; **25**:1–7.

30. Miller WR, Rollnick S. *Motivational Interviewing: Helping People Change.* New York: Guilford Press, 2013.

31. Sibley MH, Pelham WE, Derefinko KD, et al. A pilot trial of Supporting Teens' Academic Needs Daily (STAND): A parent-adolescent collaborative intervention for ADHD. *Journal of Psychopathology and Behavioral Assessment* 2013; **35**:436–49.

32. Sibley MH, Altszuler AR, Ross JM, et al. A group-based parent-teen collaborative intervention for high school students with ADHD. *Cognitive and Behavioral Practice* 2014; **21**:32–42.

33. Sibley MH, Graziano PA, Kuriyan AB, et al. Parent-teen behavior therapy + motivational interviewing for adolescents with ADHD. *Journal of Consulting and Clinical Psychology* 2016; **84**:699–712.

34. Sibley MH, Comer J, Gonzalez J. Delivering parent-teen therapy for ADHD through videoconferencing: A preliminary investigation. *Journal of Psychopathology and Behavioral Assessment* 2017; **39**:477–85.

35. Sibley MH, Rodriguez LM, Coxe SJ, et al. Parent-teen group versus dyadic treatment for adolescent ADHD: What works for whom? *Journal of Clinical Child and Adolescent Psychology* 2019.

36. Lau A, Barnett M, Stadnick N, et al. Therapist report of adaptations to delivery of evidence-based practices within a system-driven reform of publicly funded children's mental health services. *Journal of Consulting and Clinical Psychology* 2017; **85**:664–75.

37. Chorpita BF, Daleiden EL, Park AL, et al. Child STEPs in California: A cluster randomized effectiveness trial comparing modular treatment with community implemented treatment for youth with anxiety, depression, conduct problems, or traumatic stress. *Journal of Consulting and Clinical Psychology* 2017; **85**:13–25.

38. Weisz JR, Chorpita BF, Palinkas LA, et al. Testing standard and modular designs for psychotherapy treating depression, anxiety, and conduct problems in youth: A randomized effectiveness trial. *Archives of General Psychiatry* 2012; **69**:274–82.

39. Bardi A, Schwartz SH. Values and behavior: Strength and structure of relations. *Personality and Social Psychology Bulletin* 2003; **29**:1207–20.

40. Schwartz SH. An overview of the Schwartz theory of basic values. *Online Readings in Psychology and Culture* 2012; **2**:11.

41. Rokeach M. *The Nature of Human Values*. New York: Free Press, 1973.

42. Olsson CA, Bond L, Burns JM, et al. Adolescent resilience: A concept analysis. *Journal of Adolescence* 2003; **26**:1–11.

43. Bornstein MH. Cultural approaches to parenting. *Parenting* 2012; **12**:212–21.

44. Jiang Y, Gurm M, Johnston C. Child impairment and parenting self-efficacy in relation to mothers' views of ADHD treatments. *Journal of Attention Disorders* 2014; **18**:532–41.

45. Newark PE, Elsässer M, Stieglitz RD. Self-esteem, self-efficacy, and resources in adults with ADHD. *Journal of Attention Disorders* 2016; **20**:279–90.

46. Philipsen A, Richter H, Peters J, et al. Structured group psychotherapy in adults with attention deficit hyperactivity disorder: Results of an open multicentre study. *Journal of Nervous and Mental Disease* 2007; **195**:1013–19.

47. Ramsay JR, Rostain AL. Adult ADHD research: Current status and future directions. *Journal of Attention Disorders* 2008; **11**(6):624–7.

48. Johnston C, Mash EJ. Families of children with attention-deficit/hyperactivity disorder: Review and recommendations for future research. *Clinical Child and Family Psychology Review* 2001; **4**:183–207.

49. Nelson JR, Roberts ML. Ongoing reciprocal teacher-student interactions involving disruptive behaviors in general education classrooms. *Journal of Emotional and Behavioral Disorders* 2000; **8**:27–37.

50. Hoza B. Peer functioning in children with ADHD. *Journal of Pediatric Psychology* 2007; **32**:655–63.

51. Cox KF. Investigating the impact of strength-based assessment on youth with emotional or behavioral disorders. *Journal of Child and Family Studies* 2006; **15**:278–92.

52. Lee MY, Greene GJ, Hsu KS, et al. Utilizing family strengths and resilience: Integrative family and systems treatment with children and adolescents with severe emotional and behavioral problems. *Family Process* 2009; **48**:395–416.

53. Martin AJ. Improving the achievement, motivation, and engagement of students with ADHD: The role of personal best goals and other growth-based approaches. *Journal of Psychologists and Counsellors in Schools* 2013; **23**:143–55.

54. Rogers CR. The necessary and sufficient conditions of therapeutic personality change. *Journal of Consulting Psychology* 1957; **21**:95–103.

55. Kazantzis N, Whittington C, Dattilio F. Meta-analysis of homework effects in cognitive and behavioral therapy: A replication and extension. *Clinical Psychology: Science and Practice* 2010; **17**:144–56.

56. Brookman-Frazee L, Garland AF, Taylor R, et al. Therapists' attitudes towards psychotherapeutic strategies in community-based psychotherapy with children with disruptive behaviour problems. *Administration and Policy in Mental Health and Mental Health Services Research* 2009; **36**:1–12.

57. Garland AF, Brookman-Frazee L, Hurlburt MS, et al. Mental health care for children with disruptive behavior problems: A view inside therapists' offices. *Psychiatric Services* 2010; **61**:788–95.

58. Gawrilow C, Morgenroth K, Schultz R, et al. Mental contrasting with implementation intentions enhances self-regulation of goal pursuit in schoolchildren at risk for ADHD. *Motivation and Emotion* 2013; **37**:134–45.

59. Hoza B, Waschbusch DA, Owens JS, et al. Academic task persistence of normally achieving ADHD and control boys: Self-evaluations, and attributions. *Journal of Consulting and Clinical Psychology* 2001; **69**:271.

60. Nyman A, Taskinen T, Grönroos M, et al. Elements of working memory as predictors of goal-setting skills in children with attention-deficit/hyperactivity

disorder. *Journal of Learning Disabilities* 2010; **43**:553–62.

61. Edwards G, Barkley RA, Laneri M, et al. Parent-adolescent conflict in teenagers with ADHD and ODD. *Journal of Abnormal Child Psychology* 2001; **29**:557–72.

62. Barkley RA, Robin AL. *Defiant Teens: A Clinician's Manual for Assessment and Family Intervention.* New York: Guilford Press, 2014.

63. Gollwitzer PM. Implementation intentions: Strong effects of simple plans. *American Psychologist* 1999; **54**:493–503.

64. Ramsay JR. 'Turning intentions into actions' CBT for adult ADHD focused on implementation. *Clinical Case Studies* 2016; **15**:179–97.

65. Barkley RA. Adverse events associated with behavior management training for families experiencing parent–ADHD teen conflict. *ADHD Report* 2018; **26**:1–5.

66. Barkley RA. Focus on the side effects of psychosocial treatments for children and teens with ADHD: A special issue. *ADHD Report* 2018; **26**:1–4.

67. Connors GJ, Donovan DM, DiClemente CC. *Substance Abuse and the Stages of Change: Selecting and Planning Interventions.* New York: Guilford Press, 2001.

86. Weisz JR, Ugueto AM, Cheron DM, et al. Evidence-based youth psychotherapy in the mental health ecosystem. *Journal of Clinical Child and Adolescent Psychology* 2013; **42**:274–86.

87. Sibley MH, Graziano PA, Bickman L, et al. Implementing parent-teen motivational interviewing plus behavior therapy for ADHD in community mental health. *Prevention Science* 2020; **26**:1–11.

88. Schwalbe CS, Oh HY, Zweben A. Sustaining motivational interviewing: A meta-analysis of training studies. *Addiction* 2014; **109**:1287–94.

89. Arnett JJ. Emerging adulthood: A theory of development from the late teens through the twenties. *American Psychologist* 2000; **55**:469–80.

90. Swanson JM, Arnold LE, Molina BS, et al. Young adult outcomes in the follow-up of the multimodal treatment study of attention-deficit/hyperactivity disorder: Symptom persistence, source discrepancy, and height suppression. *Journal of Child Psychology and Psychiatry* 2017; **58**:663–78.

91. Howard AL, Strickland N, Murray DW, et al. Progression of impairment in adolescents with ADHD through the transition out of high school: Contributions of parent involvement and college attendance. *Journal of Abnormal Psychology* 2016; **125**:233–47.

92. Schulenberg JE, Sameroff AJ, Cicchetti D. The transition to adulthood as a critical juncture in the course of psychopathology and mental health. *Development and Psychopathology* 2004; **16**:799–806.

93 McCarthy S, Asherson P, Coghill D, et al. Attention-deficit hyperactivity disorder: Treatment discontinuation in adolescents and young adults. *British Journal of Psychiatry* 2009; **194**:273–77.

94. Turgay A, Goodman DW, Asherson P, et al. Lifespan persistence of ADHD: The life transition model and its application. *Journal of Clinical Psychiatry* 2009; **73**:192–201.

95. LaCount PA, Hartung CM, Canu WH, et al. Interventions for transitioning adolescents with ADHD to emerging adulthood: Developmental context and empirically-supported treatment principles. *Evidence-Based Practice in Child and Adolescent Mental Health* 2019; **4**(2):170–86.

96. Newacheck PW, Park MJ, Brindis CB, et al. Trends in private and public health insurance for adolescents. *Journal of the American Medical Association* 2004; **291**:1231–7.

97. White PH. Access to health care: Health insurance considerations for young adults with special health care needs/disabilities. *Pediatrics* 2002; **110**:1328–35.

98. Nigg JT. Attention-deficit/hyperactivity disorder and adverse health outcomes. *Clinical Psychology Review* 2013; **33**:215–28.

99. Gordon M, Lewandowski LJ, Lovett BJ. Assessment and management of ADHD in educational and workplace settings in the context of ADA accommodations. In: Barkley RA (ed.), *Attention-Deficit Hyperactivity Disorder: A Handbook for Diagnosis and Treatment*, 4th ed. New York: Guilford Press, 2014.

100. Bussing R, Zima BT, Mason DM, et al. Receiving treatment for attention-deficit hyperactivity disorder: Do the perspectives of adolescents matter? *Journal of Adolescent Health* 2011; **49**:7–14.

101. Epstein JN, Kelleher KJ, Baum R, et al. Variability in ADHD care in community-based pediatrics. *Pediatrics* 2014; **134**:1136–43.

102. US Census Bureau. *CPS ASEC Health Insurance Historical Tables*, 2000–2015. Available at www.census.gov/topics/health/healthinsurance/data/tables.2017.html.

103. Accurso EC, Taylor RM, Garland AF. Evidence-based practices addressed in community-based children's mental health clinical supervision. *Training and Education in Professional Psychology* 2011; **5**:88–96.

104. Southam-Gerow MA, Chorpita BF, Miller LM, et al. Are children with anxiety disorders privately

referred to a university clinic like those referred from the public mental health system? *Administration and Policy in Mental Health and Mental Health Services Research* 2008; **35**:168–80.

105.   Southam-Gerow MA, Weisz JR, Kendall PC. Youth with anxiety disorders in research and service clinics: Examining client differences and similarities.

Journal of Clinical Child and Adolescent Psychology 2003; **32**:375–85.

106.   Sibley MH, Graziano PA, Bickman L, et al. Implementing parent-teen motivational interviewing plus behavior therapy for ADHD in community mental health. *Prevention Science* 2020; **26**:1–11.

Functional Family Therapy for Antisocial Behaviour in Adolescents

12

Michael S. Robbins and James F. Alexander

Functional family therapy (FFT) is a well-established treatment for helping troubled youth and their families [1, 2]. FFT offers a comprehensive framework for understanding adolescent behaviour problems that is quite unique. This framework provides the context for integrating and linking behavioural and cognitive intervention strategies to the specific familial and ecological characteristics of each family. At the heart of FFT is the assumption that all behaviour is motivated to achieve a relational goal or 'function' (e.g., contact or distance) and that rather than trying to alter the underlying relational goals, therapists can achieve more powerful and lasting changes by providing healthy ways for family members to achieve their relational goals.

For almost five decades, FFT has evolved from the experiences and results of clinical research, critical review, clinical training of diverse professionals and dissemination across populations, cultures and treatment contexts [3]. From the early 1970s, basic and process research has informed the evolution of the model. This research has helped to refine theory. For example, early conceptualizations of FFT were primarily behavioural and systemic [4–6]. However, based on the results of research with delinquent adolescents and their families (see later), FFT was expanded to include cognitive elements to address the pervasive and destructive negative attributions that were common in these families. Ultimately, FFT evolved into a complex family therapy approach that systematically integrates family systems theory and cognitive behavioural therapy (CBT) strategies to provide state-of-the-science interventions to address referral problems and risk and protective factors in one of the most recalcitrant clinical populations: adolescents with externalizing disorders.

The purpose of this chapter is to provide an overview of the philosophy and components of FFT. Using the framework informed by research on core competencies in CBT for youth with internalizing disorders

developed by Sburlati et al. [7], we describe prior research into the FFT model, the phase-based nature of the FFT model and specific strategies that FFT uses to address youth externalizing problems. In doing so, we present how FFT systematically matches a wide range of specific interventions to the unique and special qualities of each youth, family, culture and treatment system.

Brief History of the Development of FFT as an Evidence-Based Intervention

The first published articles on FFT established the efficacy of the approach with adolescents exhibiting delinquent behaviour problems [4, 5], and subsequent research replicated the efficacy of FFT across sites and settings [8]. FFT has also been established as an efficacious treatment for adolescent substance use disorders [9]. Moreover, evidence has been found for the preventive effects of FFT for siblings of problem youth [10] and for the long-term effectiveness of the intervention into early adulthood [11]. More recently, extensive research has documented the effectiveness of FFT in real-world settings [3], with gang-involved youth [12, 13] and as an alternative to incarceration [14].

The evolution of FFT has been continuously informed by rigorous research, and much of this research has placed a core value on understanding the process of change. This focus on examining both processes and outcomes has meant that FFT has remained informed by and at the cutting edge of research on core competencies in family therapy. For example, with respect to general therapeutic competencies described by Sburlati et al. [7], early research on FFT demonstrated that therapist interpersonal/relational characteristics (e.g., warm, respectful, non-judgemental) were integrally related to clinical outcomes in FFT [4], which was striking because the treatment model was primarily behavioural based and systemic. Later, an in-session process study further demonstrated the importance of general therapist competencies by identifying how alliances are linked to dropout in FFT [15]. This study showed that it was not the overall level of alliance with the therapist that was important but rather how skilled the therapist was in maintaining balanced alliances with parents and delinquent youth that was associated with treatment retention.

Sburlati et al. [7] also noted that a core feature of effective treatment is the competent implementation of CBT techniques. One of the techniques highlighted in this work is cognitive restructuring, as designed to alter the automatic processing of negative thoughts. FFT is a front-loaded intervention that uses extensive strategies for addressing negative attributions, particularly early in therapy when family members typically exhibit high rates of negativity, blame, and hopelessness (see 'Motivation Phase' later). The articulation of these strategies has been informed by extensive basic and process research. Early non-clinical studies showed that families with delinquent adolescents interacted quite differently than families that did not have a delinquent adolescent. For example, families with a delinquent adolescent were more negative and were more likely to reciprocate negativity [16, 17] than the families that did not have a delinquent youth. However, research also showed that the expression of negativity was quite malleable to manipulations of family members' attributional set. For example, if a task was set up to be cooperative, no differences were observed between the two groups of families, whereas when the task was set up to be competitive, the expression of negativity escalated in the delinquent families while it remained constant in non-delinquent families [18]. Two other studies demonstrated how non-clinical manipulations of family members' attributions were associated with reductions in family members' blaming attributions [19, 20]. For example, offering a reframe or creating a cooperative set (as opposed to a competitive set) was directly related to less negative or blaming between family members. Similarly, within the clinical context, Robbins et al. [21, 22] demonstrated the immediate impact of therapist reframing interventions (e.g., statements that offer benign or positive reasons for a negative behaviour) on family members' expressed negativity.

Taken together, the data provide support for reattribution techniques, which are explicitly focused on expanding the families frame to include a more

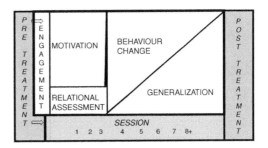

Figure 12.1 Phases of treatment in the FFT model

workable frame where family members are willing to try out new behaviours. These observational studies have been critical in influencing the development or articulation of specific intervention strategies and for creating a motivational context (e.g., less negative, relationship-oriented, hopeful) conducive to adaptive and supportive family behaviours.

In the sections that follow, we provide an overview of the FFT model. Throughout this chapter, we provide information about specific areas that correspond to the areas of core therapeutic competencies suggested by Sburlati et al. [7].

Clinical Model Overview

FFT consists of five major phases in addition to pre-treatment and post-treatment activities (see Figure 12.1): (1) Engagement, (2) Motivation, (3) Relational assessment, (4) Behaviour change and (5) Generalization [23].

Pre-Treatment Preparation

Prior to seeing or contacting the family, therapists engage in linking with referral sources, gathering information about the youth and family and preparing/planning for the initial contact. The therapist, upon receipt of a referral, first contacts the referral source(s) to acknowledge receipt of the referral and to solicit all information (including impressionistic as well as formal assessments) available. In the case of formal legal involvement (e.g., juvenile justice, child welfare), the therapist also clarifies system expectations and requirements as well as issues of confidentiality. In situations where the therapist might not have experience with the culture or other characteristics of the referral, he or she will contact additional resources within or outside the treatment system to become better informed. The goal of these activities is to be fully ready to assist the youth and family, to anticipate potential barriers and to use strengths to create a positive initial impression and experience for family members.

Engagement Phase

The engagement phase begins prior to first contact and includes any activity that is intended to facilitate the family's willingness to attend early sessions. Engagement involves creating an initial positive reaction to the therapist. A key part of this is family members' experience of the therapist as a credible helper. Initially, therapists may know very little about the family. As such, early activities can include 'superficial' but important activities such as wearing clothes that seem appropriate for family members and 'matching' their language to families with regards to ethnicity, gender and developmental stage. Therapists must be culturally competent and work to help family members feel comfortable and respected. Many of the early contacts with family members occur via telephone, so therapists can listen for potential problems such as transportation difficulties, distrust of and resistance to treatment and confusion about the referral and/or treatment goals. Thus, the engagement phase is less characterized by a formal set of therapeutic techniques than it is by an attitude on the part of FFT therapists that families should be shown as much respect as possible and be made to feel comfortable during the initiation of the process of intervention.

FFT therapists should take advantage of any sources of information about the family to understand as much as possible about the context in which intervention is to occur. For the FFT therapist, an important initial question becomes, 'Is there information available that might facilitate cultural sensitivity, enlighten me about multisystem pressures (e.g., poverty) and resources and might suggest individual constraints (e.g., learning disability, illiteracy) that must be considered?' From a core competencies perspective, effective negotiation of the engagement phase requires therapists to establish credibility through their professionalism, warmth, knowledge of contextual issues and sensitivity to cultural and developmental variability.

Motivation Phase

As direct contact with the referred youth and parent figure(s) is initiated in the first session, FFT therapists quickly move from relatively superficial engagement strategies to more powerful motivational interventions. The primary objective of the motivation phase of intervention is to create a context within which family members are willing to change their behaviours. Family members are helped to experience a reduction in anger and blame, coupled with an increase in hopefulness. Decreasing negativity is essential in this early phase of intervention, prior to initiating formal behaviour change techniques, because family members' intense negative emotions can preclude them from making a realistic commitment to change.

FFT addresses the motivation phase risk factors for dropout by undertaking two major domains of activity: changing focus and changing meaning. Change focus techniques include (1) divert and interrupt, (2) point process, (3) sequencing and (4) strength-based relational statements. Change meaning techniques include (1) relabelling, (2) theme hints, (3) reframing and (4) creating themes. As noted earlier, the techniques of the motivation phase are supported through extensive process research. And a central feature of these techniques involves the disruption of negative attributions within highly conflicted family patterns. Interventions systematically focus on being relational, strength based and respect based.

Change Focus Techniques

Change focus interventions are intended to disrupt negativity by shifting, stopping or redirecting communications. Change focus interventions are relatively simple interventions to implement, and they are often used when the therapist is still getting a sense of how to effectively intervene with the family but recognizes the need to address quickly the negative behaviours in the session.

Divert and Interrupt. Therapists *divert* family negativity when they intercept a negative statement made by a family member instead of allowing the family member to whom it was directed to answer. Therapists *interrupt* family negativity when they say or do something which prevents a family member who is making a negative or defensive speech act to complete a blaming statement. In our prior research, diverting and interrupting require an active and involved therapist who is highly attuned to the meaning and nature of interactions in the family. As such, these interventions are used in a manner that is sensitive to the current interactions and – although they may involve interfering or speaking over family members – are delivered in a manner that is respectful and accepting of the family.

Pointing Process. As therapists observe and attend to each family members' perception of within-family and extra-family interactions, they can comment on the process of how family members relate to each other. This is especially important with respect to interactions that are characterized by negativity and blaming. By employing a pointing process, therapists are able to make explicit the inter-relatedness of family members' feelings, thoughts and behaviours. This serves to defuse negativity by shifting the focus from the specific content being discussed to the underlying relational aspects that underlie but are often hidden from family members in the current moment.

Sequencing. Sequencing behaviour or circular questioning is a method used to assess what happens and who does what within a family with regards to the specifics of a presenting problem. Because information is drawn out in a sequence and in a circular fashion, it is easier to see or visualize the context in which behaviour occurs. For example, the therapist might ask each caregiver where they are at, what they are doing and how they react when their son is out past curfew. Information can be gathered about how they reach out (or not) to their son via texts or calls, whether the parents speak to each other while their son is out and how the son responds (or not). Such sequencing might also be done to determine what happens when the son comes home (e.g., mother yells, son calls her name, father comes out of bedroom and son and father fight).

Sequencing interventions create depth of knowledge about all the family members involved in a presenting problem, including the action each took. The purpose of sequencing in the motivation phase is to help family members to understand that their behaviours are connected. When used in a relationally focused and non-blaming way, the focus of sequencing is not narrowly on the presenting problem or other problems but more inclusively on family members' interactions. That is, the focus is not only on the content or problem that occurred but more inclusively on family relationships and the meaning of relationships and behaviours to individual family members. Sequencing reveals family patterns which lead to either positive or negative familial outcomes.

Selectively Attend to the Positive. These are statements that acknowledge or highlight positive behaviours or interactions that therapists observe in the session and/or that family members report about outside the session. Family members have become stuck in rigid patterns that are characterized by negativity and conflict. Positive behaviours are ignored or dismissed. Selectively attending to positive statements helps reduce negativity and blame by systematically noting complex behaviours/interactions that are both positive and that do not fit the attributions or emotions in the current interaction climate in the session. The intent of these statements is *not* to convince the family that things are positive, *nor* is it to challenge their current viewpoint; rather, these statements help shift the focus to other, relevant aspects of family members' experiences. For example, a mother is describing how angry she is at her daughter for not attending her son's graduation because the son had been violent towards the daughter several months ago. Daughter and son had not spoken for months. When mother asked daughter to go, she was able to get her in the car, but the daughter refused to get out when they arrived at the auditorium. Rather than simply acknowledging mother's fury at daughter, the therapist attended to the positive by noting, 'You [mother] saw this as a chance to bring your family back together again.'

Strength-Based Relational Statements. Strength-based relational statements include interventions that ascribe a positive (even noble) attribution about one person's efforts towards another person. These include seeing the positive side of apparently negative relational patterns. For example (to parent and child who are beginning to argue loudly with each other): 'OK – I'm going to jump in here for a second. You both are angry right now, and pretty much yelling. I'm sure that at times you or someone else wants you to stop yelling. But for now, I want to note that you seem to be at least on the same page . . . no one seems to be holding back much, and both of you are honest in expressing your anger. Lots of families tend to go underground with their anger . . . but with you two, I can trust that you will bring it out and deal with it directly. That gives me something to work with that often I don't have. Now, I wonder.' This strength-based relational focus pervades FFT interventions. Even simple acknowledgements of family members are expected to convey a strength-based relational focus. For example, instead of acknowledging a mother's anger about her daughter's truancy by simply stating, 'I can hear how angry you are', therapists may rather state, 'Your exasperation is even more difficult for you because you have such high expect-ations and ideas for how she can excel in school.' Both interventions serve to acknowledge mother's anger, but the latter goes further by highlighting the strength-based aspects in the mother's anger.

Change Meaning Techniques

Like change focus interventions, change meaning techniques are intended to disrupt negativity and unproductive family interactions. However, change meaning techniques involve attempts to change how the family members understand the motivations of themselves and each other. The goal of change mean-ing techniques is not simple cognitive change but rather the creation of the opportunity (or possibility) of a different, more positive and hopeful, frame. Thus, these techniques are not intended to simply challenge 'maladaptive' cognitions or provide an interpretation. Rather, the focus is on providing a non-blaming, even positive perspective about behaviours that create an opportunity in the session for family members to experience one another in a new way.

Relabelling. The therapist relabels by reflecting to family members a similar but less harmful explan-ation for a behaviour for the purpose of shifting some of the negative intensity in the meaning of that behaviour. Consider a teenage son's complaint about his mother arising in an early session, 'As soon as I walked in the door, she just went off on me!', and the therapist's response of, 'So she let you know right off the bat that she had an issue with you.' While these statements may seem quite similar, 'she just went off' conjures up a more intense image than 'she let you know right off that she had an issue with you'. This relabel also added a 'softer' relational component ('she ... with you') rather than the more attacker–victim tone of 'she ... on you'. Relabels set a tone that is less negative and provide the therapist with more positive avenues to pursue. They also represent an intervention style that families generally experience in more positive ways than therapist interventions that amplify the negativity with which they already struggle. In addition, they do not involve any element of blaming or suggestion that the behaviours will need to change.

Theme Hints. Theme hints are brief statements that imply an alternative meaning for the attributions or behaviours of family members. Theme hints are dis-tinct from relabels in that they offer a different per-spective or new meaning. In response to a negative

statement made by a family member, the therapist might state, 'I get the sense that there is a lot of loss in this family.' An alternative to anger is presented (loss) but is not necessarily developed in that moment. These hints of something unique are important to help family members experience themselves differ-ently. Just as important, these hints are also helpful for therapists to begin to develop their own traction in the session by starting the process of developing new perspectives in the session.

Reframing. Reframing is generally described as a 'technique', and although its elements may differ across therapy models, the process of reframing seems to transcend most family-based intervention models. Many in fact consider it a *core technique* for all family therapy approaches. As defined by Paul Watzlawick et al. [24], reframing involves changing the conceptual setting or viewpoint in which a situation in experienced and putting it in a different frame which thereby changes the meaning ascribed to the original experience [24]. Reframing is not only a technique; it is also an attitude, a perspective and a belief system that helps FFT ther-apists facilitate positive change even when all the technical elements of a reframe cannot be presented.

Reframes, as defined in FFT, involve two compo-nents of the change meaning process: (1) acknow-ledgement of the negative and (2) proposal of a possible alternative (and perhaps benign or even 'noble but misguided') motive. These components add significantly to the therapist's ability to impact upon family negativity while maintaining an overall non-blaming relationship with all family members. Reframes include a clear acknowledgement of the negative aspects of a behaviour (thereby supporting those who are negatively impacted by the behaviours in question). This acknowledgement does not include an agreement with the family member. Rather, the focus of the acknowledgement is to establish that the therapist is attuned to and understanding of the rele-vance of the negative behaviour or problem to the family member. After the acknowledgement, therap-ists then offer an alternative and possibly more benign *motive* for the behaviour.

In our experience, the most powerful reframes acknowledge negative behaviour but rather than offering an alternative neutral or benign *motive* for the behaviour (e.g., mother's frustration), the hypothesized motive is labelled as 'noble' in its intent. Usually the noble intentions are seen as 'misguided', but they are nonetheless well intended. In FFT, therapists attempt to find nobility or dignity in the actions of all family members. For example, a daughter who runs away rather than fight with a depressed mother may be viewed as *protecting* the mother from having to deal with more problems, or a mother who states that she 'does not want to be a parent anymore' may be viewed as wanting the best for her child, even if it means losing the child. The focus of such statements is to move beyond the narrow, blaming attributions that often drive family conflict to a more open and hopeful attributional view where there is dignity in family members' behaviours or motives. It does not mean that negative behaviour is excused or minimized. Therapists acknowledge the negative aspects of interactions and note the devastating impact family members have on one another. However, the focus of what drives such behaviours is expanded to include more positive, strength-based and relationally focused reasons. As we move from relabelling to reframing with noble intent, the complexity and level of inference increase. We are not concerned that we do not 'know' if family members' motives are 'truly' positive or noble in order to suggest that they might be. In fact, hopeless families often are surprised and feel more supported when therapists seem willing to 'see the strength and possible nobility' in them, even when it is not apparent.

Creating Themes. To generate *behavioural* themes, therapists identify sequences of several problem family member interactions in which all the negative elements are identified but reframed (or at least relabelled). This focus has the advantage of helping create a family (versus individual) focus, and because all members are subject to reframing, the therapist can identify negative interactions and yet still 'come across' as seeing the possible benign intent of each member. In this way, the therapist avoids taking sides with family members and prevents defensiveness that typically occurs when only an individual's negative behaviour is the focus. *Relational* themes are so called because they switch the focus to relationships rather than the narrower focus of behavioural themes. Of course, in relational themes, specific behaviours may be noted, but often they are not. Instead, relational patterns, and how they have been *experienced*, become the major focus. And while relational themes maintain the basic elements of reframes (acknowledge negative, reframe intent or meaning in more benign, if not noble, terms), they often seem more like stories

and even myths than specific sequences of negative behaviours. Coupled with our core generic principles of matching and respectfulness, our powerful change meaning techniques help families move quickly to being open and responsive to techniques that change behaviour (in both the short and long term).

Relational Assessment Phase
Assessment occurs at multiple levels in FFT. Therapists are always focused on understanding the nature of the current referral and the associated risk and protective factors. The most critical assessment that orients the nature of all subsequent behaviour change efforts is the assessment of relational functions.

By the time FFT receives referrals for dysfunctional behaviours, the relational patterns expressed in families are usually well established. FFT therapists look for these stable patterns, first assessing the relational functions involved for each family member. These relational functions represent *inferred* internal motivations of family members based on overtly expressed patterns within the family. Thus, FFT assumes that all behaviour is motivated, but assessing the internal motivations can only be accurately identified by attending to observed behavioural outcomes or patterns. Thus, although family members are considered to relate to one another based on their own inferred internal motivations, the focus is not on the inferred internal process but rather on the resulting patterns that emerge from family interactions.

FFT does not attempt to change the relational function itself, but we do change the *cognitive, physiological, emotional,* and *behavioural strategies* in which the youth or parent engages to meet relational functions. For example, if a child acts out to get attention, FFT does not work hard to eliminate children's need for attention! Instead, we change the *means* through which this attention is elicited. This, of course, usually requires dealing with the rest of the system(s) involved with the youth, because comfort or attention may only be (or at least seem to be) available through maladaptive behavioural patterns.

Relational Connection: Contact/Closeness versus Distance/Autonomy/Independence. The first and most salient category is the degree of interpersonal *connectivity* that is expressed in the behaviour patterns that directly or indirectly impact another person (or persons) in the family (and other systems). The degree of connection can range from close and highly interconnected to distant and quite independent or autonomous. These dimensional anchors are not considered to be fixed and invariant points on a dimension; they are instead the central tendency (or apparent default mode or average) behavioural pattern that best characterizes the ongoing relationship. Imagine a couple in an ongoing relationship: they are not *always* close or *always* distant or *always* a mixture of both. In general; however, couples can be distinguished in terms of whether their pattern is generally close and connected, generally distant and autonomous or generally variable. Whatever the behavioural pattern is over time, FFT's intervention philosophy, that is, 'the respectful acceptance of the diversity that all family members bring', is what we identify as relational functions. All three of the aforementioned relational states can be adaptive, and all three can be maladaptive. The problem is not what the relational function is, but how it is expressed and met.

Relational Hierarchy. Relational hierarchy reflects the pattern of relative influence parents and youth have over each other in terms of controlling each other's behaviour. With adolescent conduct problems, it is common to use such phrases as 'She [or he] is out of control'. However, FFT examines more than the behaviour patterns of one individual. Instead, we examine the relative balance of control and power rather than simply isolating our focus on whether or not the parent can control the youth. When we broaden our focus to look at the relative balance of power, it is not uncommon to find that sometimes a youth is able to exert more control over a parent's behaviour than vice versa. In other families, the youth, although acting out, is not able to control the parental behaviour any more than the parent can control the youth! Thus, the power differential is more one of balance than of one or the other in control. Interventions that fail to examine the relative balance of the interpersonal control in these relationships often fail repeatedly if all they attempt to do is to increase the control the parent has over the youth.

Of course, parents often experience the power issue as the most salient in raising adolescents. However, FFT asserts that primarily what parents want is a sense of being able to control (if not help) their youth. As a result, when therapists provide alternative ways to influence youth, hierarchy itself becomes less salient. In fact, many parents are quite pleased when their kids begin to comply because the

relationship with the youth has been repaired, and the youth now *wants* to maintain a positive and less conflictual relational pattern with the parent(s). Power and consequences are important and have their role, but often they are more difficult to change, and certainly they are less positive than relational changes that motivate youth to comply and develop positive behaviours.

Unlike the concept of personality, which presumes a core and consistent underlying motivational structure in people across contexts, FFT assessment of functions often identifies important differences in motivation within one person. The FFT therapist understands, for example, that the motivational needs of a parent with different children can be markedly different. As a result, child behaviours that would be comfortable for the parent with respect to the 'close' child could be quite unacceptable with respect to the 'distanced' child (or vice versa). Thus, prescriptions for good parenting cannot be homogeneous because the behaviours through which effective parenting is carried out will differ depending on the child and parent in question.

Finally, the assessment of relational functions is essential if therapists want to ensure rapid compliance with change interventions. Prescribing tasks or change strategies for one family member with respect to another member will elicit considerable resistance if the prescriptions are implicitly or explicitly inconsistent with the family members' functions. As an empowerment model, FFT offers a more relational and less oppositional or coercive intervention philosophy for change.

Behavioural Change Phase

FFT uses several broad classes of techniques for behaviour change. The first class is represented by *general family interaction–focused interventions*, such as communication training, problem-solving and conflict-management techniques. Some version of these techniques is used with almost all families, and they represent skill development which is useful to family members when they interact but also generalize nicely to other extra-family systems (school, work, friendships). The second class of techniques represents problem-specific techniques which may apply to some people and families but not others, including (1) 'internal' coping techniques for people with anger impulse problems and cravings, (2) techniques for overcoming challenges unique to some families, such as a single parent with a physical disability which precludes the use of many parenting strategies, and (3) techniques specific to a particular problem (such as substance use, depression, anxiety). For example, with substance-using youth, FFT commonly employs strategies that include identifying triggers, coping with urges and cravings and decision-balance exercises. Or, when working with depressed youth, strategies might include introducing challenging provocative thoughts or managing negative mood in family sessions. FFT borrows heavily from the extant CBT literature to introduce strategies that have been shown to be effective for a specific referral problem or risk factor. These techniques are delivered in conjoint sessions with family members in a manner that is developmentally and culturally appropriate and that matches the family's relational functions.

Next, we describe several common strategies that are used in FFT. This list is not exhaustive. Rather, the examples that follow provide a sample of the range of strategies that therapists are expected to be proficient in when working with families. Therapists are more like general practitioners than specialists. As such, an FFT therapist is always expanding his or her strategies based on experience and knowledge of the clinical research literature. For example, over the past decade, therapists have increasingly integrated trauma-focused CBT techniques into their behaviour change plans as well as including emerging research on mindfulness. The inclusion of strategies is always matched to the specific needs of a family.

Specific Elements of Behaviour Change

Communication Training. Communication training is commonly used in FFT. In some families, the training represents a focus on a true skill deficit; family members do not know the basics of interpersonal communication. However, in many other families, members know how to communicate but, in the current context, are unwilling or unable to communicate in an effective manner. With family members who truly are characterized by skill deficits, emphasis is on explaining and practising the positive elements of communication listed next. When the problem is one of performance rather than ability, emphasis is placed on reattribution (e.g., reframing) interventions and providing constant reminders of the rationale behind effective communication.

The most common examples of communication training in FFT are not unique to the model but rather are core elements of effective communication. Examples include source responsibility (e.g., 'I' statements), source directness (e.g., clearly noting who is being addressed), brevity, concreteness and behavioural specificity, congruent (e.g., tone and content match), present alternatives (e.g., giving a youth multiple options), active listening and impact statements (e.g., a clear presentation of what someone wants, feels or thinks).

Basic Parenting and Family Principles/ Techniques

The established techniques of positive reinforcement/ praise, negative reinforcement, selectively ignoring, distracting, clear limit-setting with consistent follow-through and a reasonable number of limits, parent-child special time and parental monitoring of activities are applied when deemed appropriate during the behaviour change phase of FFT. On their own, parent management techniques appear to be more effective with younger rather than older adolescents. Because FFT is a systemic model and all family members are included in therapy, choosing and relaying these techniques to family members must be done in a sensitive and flexible way. This is because of the fact that the educational descriptions of reinforcement principles that are sometimes used in parent training are likely to come across as manipulative to an adolescent who is in the session. Thus, they should be rethought/ rephrased by the therapist prior to presentation in the family setting. In general, the use of these basic parenting principles is encouraged in FFT through incorporation into the more systemic and collaborative techniques of response cost and contracting. Therapists should keep these principles in mind, but their application is more commonly conducted through more systemic means than classic parent training.

Contracting. Contracting involves having family members identify specific things they would like other family members to do in exchange for interactions/behaviours or tangible rewards. This procedure is especially important with adolescents (as opposed to children). In fact, other than basic communication training, contracting is the parent-youth interaction/influence technique that is most commonly used by FFT therapists because it is systemic (e.g., involves considering the idea of reinforcement/ reward for all members of a system or subsystem), it can be initiated inside the therapeutic environment and it can be adapted for use with youth at almost all developmental levels. Contracting should initially be conducted within the therapy session because therapists need to do a number of things to make early contracting as positive an experience as possible.

Therapists also need to monitor contracts to make certain that they are attainable based on the functional relationship needs of each participant. Finally, therapists need to monitor the in-session contracting process to maintain the decreased negativity attained during the motivation phase. To this end, therapists often refer back to specific reframes and themes that were particularly helpful in creating positive attributions in family members during the motivation phase. If communication training was conducted earlier in the behaviour change phase, the therapist will also model and remind the family members to use communication techniques during their in-session contracting discussions.

Response Cost Techniques. Especially effective with children and preadolescents, the specific approach to reward and punishment identified by Webster-Stratton and Herbert as response-cost techniques provide a framework that helps parents learn how to set clear penalties (typically loss of privileges/current rewards) for inappropriate child behaviours or failures to perform [25]. Expected behaviours and penalties should be fair and clearly stated – and augmented by visual aids whenever possible.

Using Technical Aids

A number of technical aids are frequently used to facilitate behaviour change in FFT. Examples of technical aids include (1) recordings of sessions or therapist handouts for the family to take home and review, (2) reminder cards, notes, charts, message centres on refrigerators, pictures, corny sayings and symbols to remind family members about the behaviour in question, (3) school-home feedback report sheets with detailed tasks and timelines and (4) answering machines, texting, and cell phones.

Problem-Solving

Behaviour change techniques often follow a very specific sequence for resolving problems. First, therapists help to focus on a specific problem to be addressed. In this process, the therapist helps family members to punctuate the nature of the problem and who it

involves and narrows the focus to a manageable goal that can be accomplished in the session. Second, therapists help family members to use the principles of communication described earlier to help family members clarify desired outcomes and agree/negotiate to accomplish the task. Therapists actively anticipate ways in which problem-solving attempts can be derailed and provide relational-based, non-blaming interventions to maintain a positive working context. At the conclusion of problem-solving, therapists help family members to review the process of problem-solving and to discuss any agreements or plans that were resolved.

Domain-Specific Activities

Therapists are expected to use strategies that have been shown to be effective for specific referral problems and/or risk factors. Over time, research has provided strong support for CBT strategies for a range of problems, such as depression, anxiety and substance use. Much of this research is in the public domain and is readily available to the provider community. In FFT, it is common for therapists to pull from this literature to include a range of CBT strategies. For example, for families with a history of violent interpersonal relationships, FFT behaviour change strategies may include challenging pro-violent beliefs, strategies for fighting fair and emotion regulation exercises. Whereas, for a depressed youth or parent, treatment may integrate some version of the antecedent-behaviour-consequence (ABC) model or the stimulus-organism-response-consequence (SORC) model, challenging provocative thoughts, managing negative mood, or disrupting downward cognitive spirals.

Summary of Behaviour Change

Therapists need to be very creative and energetic with respect to providing specific and concrete resources for families as they enter the change process. We do not want to send families (many of whom have only limited resources and low motivation for change) out of sessions with little more than suggestions about how to change behaviour. Instead, we are in some ways controlling (or educational) to ensure that family members are given very clear information and directions during behaviour change.

The preceding examples represent the more common techniques used by FFT therapists. As evident from this description, therapists need to have a solid grounding in child and adolescent development, the clinical research literature on effective change interventions and the ability to develop new skills via structured tasks in the session. In FFT, just about any structured activity can represent a useful technique *as long as the behaviours they create and maintain are consistent with relational functions.* FFT therapists have used a wide range of CBT techniques, trauma and experiential techniques and already established cultural practices as contexts for FFT behaviour change. Once they become comfortable with the core construct of matching to relational functions, FFT therapists have found that almost limitless techniques are available in the clinical literature that may be applied during this phase of FFT intervention.

Generalization Phase

Families are involved in a vast array of social, legal, cultural, economic, community and other systems. FFT recognizes the multisystemic influences on youth and family, and the model incorporates specific principles that govern the inclusion (as well as exclusion) of these systems in the treatment planning process. Unlike generic treatment planning, which sometimes wraps services around families and family members with little consideration of family dynamics, FFT focuses on each individual family's interpersonal and systemic needs when considering adjunctive support services. In addition, before ideas with face validity are presented, that is, specific change plans involving community resources to advance a treatment plan, it is necessary for a therapeutic alliance to exist. The family also must view these ideas as valid, and the specific parameters of the community resource must be based on an understanding of the functional aspect of family behaviour. For example, job training for a 16-year-old male may be viewed as valuable in that it increases protective factors, supports emancipation and provides necessary skill building. However, participation in such a programme may not be supported by the mother if it replaces the father's role with his son and in doing so contributes to the father further disengaging from the family. Often situations such as this are associated with low support by key family members (e.g., mother becomes too busy or forgets to drive the son to the job training site on the third day). According to FFT, this noncompliance is predictable if the son's previously disruptive behaviour functioned to pull the father into parenting and, more important, into supporting

the mother. However, if taking her son to the job training programme is coupled with increased support and involvement from the father to the mother, then she will be likely to facilitate the increased system involvement of job training. Again, this example stands as a reminder that the phases of FFT are developmental, synergistic, and dependent on one another.

FFT extends or exports family functioning into a variety of community systems, which helps the family as well as the community. This reflects our belief that facilitating and managing appropriate links to adjunctive services often (or usually) must be developed for the treatment effects to be generalized outside the treatment context and sustained over time. In accomplishing such linkage, the FFT therapist helps anchor the family and family members to a larger supportive community.

We also believe that if this is done without consideration of the family relational functions, these efforts will fail. Because of this, successful intervention cannot begin with this phase of intervention. To simply wrap services around a family or family member without considering the impact on family functioning is to risk destabilizing an already precarious family process. Thus, the accomplishments of the generalization phase are predicated on successful handling of therapist-family *core therapy processes* described earlier and summarized again next.

Case Example

Kennet is a 15-year-old boy referred for treatment for fighting peers and threatening to stab his teacher. Kennet lives with his mother and younger sister (age 13). Mother works two jobs (cashier and security guard). Kennet has a history of involvement with the police and behavioural problems at school. During the intake session, his mother described multiple interventions that Kennet and the family had received over time, including contact with case managers and counsellors dating back to when Kennet was five years old. Kennet's father was incarcerated nine years ago, and he has had no contact with the family since that time.

The therapist received the referral directly from the police and was given detailed information about the current referral, vague references to prior illegal/disruptive behaviours and very little information about the family except for how to contact mother. The first engagement contacts involved multiple unanswered phone calls to mother. When the mother answered the fifth call, she was very busy at work. The therapist introduced herself, indicated how she had received mother's number and asked if she was aware that her family had been referred to the therapist. The mother had some awareness but was not clear about what was expected. They agreed to speak later that afternoon when the mother was on break. During the second conversation, the therapist focused on connecting with the mother around her busy schedule and around the commitment it takes to provide for her family as a single mother. The therapist used the phrase 'carrying the weight of the world on her shoulders', and she noted that it sounded like the mother was exhausted and isolated. Although the call was brief, the therapist was able to establish credibility with the mother (e.g., the mother felt like this was someone who could understand and help her) and to find a reasonable time to meet in three days with her family. The mother also gave the therapist Kennet's mobile number and agreed to let him know that the therapist would be calling.

Kennet answered his mobile on the first call. He was quiet and answered questions with brief, typically one- or two-word answers. He said that he was aware of why he had been referred, but he provided no indication about his view about the referral or what prompted it. The therapist did not push the notion of helping him. Instead, she noted that it must feel bad to always have people telling him where he needs to be and what he needs to do all the time. This sent him a non-blaming acknowledgement that established her understanding of his current situation. He did not affirm or disagree with the statement. The therapist asked if there was anyone that he was worried or concerned about. He thought for a bit and then responded with an 'I don't know.' However, again, the therapist presented herself in a non-blaming manner, and this time she was able to expand the focus into a potential strength- and relationship-based manner (e.g., he might be worried or concerned about his family). Kennet agreed to meet at the time that his mother had suggested.

All three family members were present when the therapist arrived at their apartment for the first session. The apartment was small but clean and organized. The mother and sister had their own rooms, but Kennet slept on the living room couch. His clothes and belongings were in storage bins along one wall. There was a small kitchen and one bathroom which they all shared. The mother noted that they had been living in this apartment for about 10 years, which seemed to correspond to the timeframe for her ex-husbands arrest and subsequent incarceration (this was confirmed at a later session). Given the family's history of prior contact with social services, the therapist moved quickly to ask the family about their understanding of why they were referred for family services. The mother immediately responded, and her tone shifted from relaxed to tense. Her explanation initially started with facts around the fight and threat that prompted the referral to the fact that this has been going on for a very long time. As the session progressed, the content became increasingly personal and blaming. For example, she stated, 'There is something wrong with him ... something evil' and 'He is just like his father.' It did not take long for Kennet to jump in and argue with his mother. Initially, he rolled his eyes and muttered, 'What a bunch of <expletive>', but then he become more verbal and direct. For example, he said that his mother was 'useless' and that she only cared about herself. The younger sister was quiet but was tracking all the interactions. She would laugh in a knowing/confirming manner when Kennet would make a comment about his mother.

The therapist was very active during the initial sessions with the family. She was careful to give the family space to speak their mind, but she frequently interrupted statements and diverted the flow of communication. For example, the mother was able to provide a detailed and complex history of the numerous problems that she had with Kennet, and she would launch into long dialogues about this history. Rather than simply acknowledge her through active listening (which would have resulted in increased blame and negativity), the therapist would interrupt with strength-based statements (e.g., 'You have some strong expectations of your kids' or 'It sounds like you take your role as a mother very seriously and you refuse to give up on your kids') and then divert the flow to other family members. With respect to the latter, for example, the therapist would say to Kennet, 'I get the sense that you don't see the refusing to give up part. All you see is the anger and disappointment'). Or, to the daughter, she would divert and point process with statements like 'You seem to have an interesting role as observer. In some ways, you are fortunate because you get to stay out of the fighting, but it is clear you know what is going on and you feel it deeply. It seems that the angrier your brother gets, the more connected you get to the process between them. For you, it might come out as a laugh.' Such statements served to disrupt negativity and blame and establish a relational focus. It is important to note that such statements are also powerful ways to connect or build relationships with family members. In FFT, developing balanced alliances is not about small talk or validation. Building alliances is done by tracking interactions and focusing on what is meaningful and relevant to family members in their relationships with one another.

As the therapist spent more time with the family, she increasingly began to use change meaning interventions to shift their highly blaming attributions and to establish hope. She started the development of themes early in the first session by using such terms as *protection* and *survivors*. Initially, these labels were used in a passing manner and were not developed. However, as the first session was ending, the therapist developed these concepts into a larger relational theme by stating, 'You are a family that feels deeply. All of you are similar in that way. There is an intensity about each of you. I would say that you are fighters. But that is a disservice. Right, Kennet? Yeah, you fight, but that is not who you are. Mother, you yell, but that is not who you are as a mother. There is a fierceness that you all share. You stand up for what you believe. A lot of times that does not work. That is because of the how you guys choose to stand up. You have all been through hell together and none of you has quit. You survived and will continue to do so.' At the very end of the session, the therapist further developed the theme to lock in a relational connection and build hope by saying, 'I said earlier to you mother that you have high expectations of your kids. I think that is not just you. Your kids also have high expectations of you and each other. I think that is part of the gift you gave to them when you refused to allow challenges to destroy your family. You created a strength inside of both of them to never give up, and you taught them to look to each other and you. Yea, life has not been perfect, and there is real pain and loss. Many of these losses have been buried deep by this survivor mode you guys are in. Unfortunately, what comes out is anger and fury, not pain or sadness. At a deep level you are all well connected to the pain and suffering that your family members have been through. Kennet, that is likely why you look out so closely for your sister. It is why mother is so passionate about both of you kids.' This theme was further elaborated on in the second and third sessions. During these sessions, there were significant changes in the nature of the interaction. Mother was less blaming, and there was less conflict between her and Kennet.

The therapist was able to note many strengths and similarities in their styles of communication (e.g., turn-taking, listening) to continue to make it relational and build hope.

With respect to relational assessment, the therapist determined that both Kennet and his mother were autonomous with respect to one another. That is, most of their behaviours served to create some distance or space between them. Kennet's behaviour problems would sometimes lead to an increase in contact (e.g., fighting), but more often than not, his behaviours would create more distance than contact between them. Also, the relationship between them was more symmetrical. That is, they both seemed to have equal levels of influence on one another.

The first behaviour change phase session was focused on building effective negotiation skills. This matched to their relational functions as well as to the development stage of both kids. The therapist chose to go straight to negotiation because the family had many strengths in their communication process (e.g., listening, clarity and directness of communication). A big part of the negotiation skills was helping them to create a 'give something to get something' plan for the family. Kennet had taken on a lot of responsibility for helping to monitor his sister, but this came at an expense for him with respect to time he could spend with his friends. The mother, Kennet and his sister were able to develop daily strategies for both weekdays and weekends that met the need for keeping everyone safe but that also gave Kennet opportunities to spend time with his friends. This was an excellent match to his relational function of being more autonomous with respect to his mother (as well as her relational need for autonomy as well).

Several other skill-building tasks were introduced to the family, such as coping with negative moods and emotion regulation strategies. However, the task that had the biggest impact for all of them was the introduction of *fair fighting rules*. This was a critical piece for all of them, especially Kennet and his mother, who tended to escalate arguments into personal and demeaning attacks. Fighting fair was introduced early and was used to help the family as they progressed through treatment. Examples of the types of risk factors that were addressed in fighting fair were (1) discuss one issue at a time, (2) take a moment to figure out why you are angry, and (3) do not use degrading statements or comments. The second topic (e.g., take a moment) provided an excellent setup for both the coping with negative mood and emotion regulation topics.

During the generalization phase, the therapist helped the family to negotiate the time for them to work together to set a weekly schedule. The therapist also was able to help the family work with the justice system and the school to address concerns about safety and appropriate behaviour at school. Part of the strategy involved a requirement for Kennet to apologize to the teacher he had threatened. The strategies that he learned around negotiation were critical in this process, not so much the skill itself, but rather the ability to take someone else's perspective when determining an appropriate 'give and get'. Kennet was connected to school and had a lot at stake for returning to the placement. As such, he was highly motivated to work with the school. Finally, the therapist developed a plan for anticipating and managing future risky situations. This plan included both formal (e.g., schools) and informal (e.g., extended family, friends) systems.

Summary of the FFT Model and Core Elements

FFT is a relational, family-based and CBT-based model. FFT produces change through a phase-based process: engagement, motivation, relational assessment, behaviour change and generalization. These phases are wrapped in and informed by core concepts of matching, non-blaming relational focus, balanced alliance and respectfulness with all family members.

Since its inception, various theoretical models have informed the development of FFT, but they have been enhanced and integrated in unique and evidence-based ways. FFT recognizes that each perspective, and the processes they assume to be relevant to successful treatment, may be more or less influential or appropriate in any given family or even any particular aspect of a family. FFT thus is an integrative model that allows us to conceptualize families and problem behaviours, as well as family strengths, from various perspectives depending on a number of contextual variables. However, these perspectives must not be mutually exclusive nor represent paradigm shifts or clashes with respect to FFT core principles.

FFT heavily incorporates research-supported CBT strategies, and many of the elements of FFT are consistent with the core competencies outlined by Sburlati et al. [7]. In fact, considerable process research has shed light on how these competencies

operate within the FFT model. For example, research on therapist interpersonal/relational style [4] and balanced alliances [15] contributed to the articulation of specific ways in which general therapist competence is represented in the engagement and motivation phases of FFT. Also, for decades, FFT has included a range of techniques from the clinical research literature on communication and CBT in the behaviour change and generalization phases. CBT techniques are implemented in the context of conjoint sessions to target risk factors at multiple levels (individual family members, family processes and social ecology).

Therapists are trained to be consumers of the extant clinical literature to understand the characteristics of specific populations, the developmental literature for working with a range of children and adolescents and the therapy literature to identify effective strategies. With this in mind, FFT therapists are trained and supervised to be clear about the overall principles and perspective that guides the integrative process. Our default mode is relational and respectful, but it is accommodating enough to use other perspectives as long as they are consistent with the core FFT model and they help the therapist understand and intervene with *this particular family, effectively, at this particular time*. Thus, breadth, not narrowness, of perspective characterizes how the FFT therapist approaches each family. At the same time, however, therapists do not engage in an eclectic stew of concepts and techniques. FFT therapists reach their destination by assessing and constantly incorporating input from diverse sources, integrating such input with their own experience and monitoring the effects of every decision and manoeuvre in which they engage.

FFT a complex and rich intervention. The complexity of FFT matches the complexity of families and the communities in which they reside. Successful treatment requires that our interventions are both relevant and matched to families. Creating lasting change appreciates that the whole is (indeed) more than the sum of the parts. Therapists are tasked with the responsibilities of understanding how each part contributes to the functioning of the whole and for guiding the family in ways that facilitate positive outcomes for all. This is challenging and difficult work, but it is also noble and rewarding.

References

1. Alexander JF, Parsons BV. *Functional Family Therapy: Principles and Procedures*. Carmel, CA: Brooks & Cole, 1982.

2. Alexander JF, Waldron HB, Robbins MS, Neeb A. *Functional Family Therapy for Adolescent Behavior Problems*. Washington, DC: American Psychological Association, 2013.

3. Robbins MA, Alexander JF, Turner CW, Hollimon A. Evolution of functional family therapy as an evidence-based practice for adolescents with disruptive behavior problems. *Family Process* 2016; **55**:543–57.

4. Alexander JF, Barton C, Schiavo RS, Parsons BV. Behavioral intervention with families of delinquents: Therapist characteristics and outcome. *Journal of Clinical Psychology* 1976; **44**:656–64.

5. Alexander JF, Parsons BV. Short term behavioral intervention with delinquent families: Impact on family process and recidivism. *Journal of Abnormal Psychology* 1973; **81**:219–25.

6. Parsons BV, Alexander JF. Short term family intervention: A therapy outcome study. *Journal of Clinical Psychology* 1973; **41**:195–201.

7. Sburlati ES, Schniering CA, Lyneham HJ, Rapee RM. A model of therapist competencies for the empirically supported cognitive behavioral treatment of child and adolescent anxiety and depressive disorders. *Clinical Child and Family Psychology Review* 2011; **14**:89–109.

8. Barton C, Alexander JF, Waldron HB, et al. Generalizing the treatment effects of functional family therapy: Three replications. *American Journal of Family Therapy* 1985; **13**:16–26.

9. Waldron HB, Turner CW. Evidence-based psychosocial treatments for adolescent substance abuse. *Journal of Clinical Child and Adolescent Psychology* 2008; **37**:238–61.

10. Klein N, Alexander JF, Parsons BV. Impact of family systems intervention on recidivism and sibling delinquency: A model of primary prevention and program evaluation. *Journal of Clinical Psychology* 1977; **45**:469–74.

11. Gordon DA, Graves K, Arbuthnot J. The effect of functional family therapy for delinquents on adult criminal behavior. *Criminal Justice Behavior* 1995; **22**:60–73.

12. Gottfredson DC, Kearley G, Thornberry TP, et al. Scaling-up evidence-based programs using a public funding stream: A randomized trial of functional family therapy for court-involved youth. *Prev Sci* 2018; **19**:939–53.

13. Thornberry TO, Kearley B, Gottfredson DC, et al. Reducing crime among youth at risk for gang involvement: A randomized trial. *Criminology and Public Policy* 2018; **17**:953–89.

14. Turner CW, Robbins MK, Winokur Early K, et al. Juvenile justice risk factors and functional family therapy fidelity on felony recidivism. *Criminal Justice and Behavior* 2018; **46**:697–717.

15. Robbins MS, Turner CW, Alexander JF, Perez GA. Alliance and dropout in family therapy for adolescents with behavior problems: Individual and systemic effects. *Journal of Family Psychology* 2003; **17**:534–44.

16. Alexander JF. Defensive and supportive communications in normal and deviant families. *Journal of Clinical Psychology* 1973; **46**, 223–31.

17. Alexander JF, Waldron HB, Barton C, Mas CH. Minimizing blaming attributions and behaviors in delinquent families: Special series on marital and family disorders. *Journal of Clinical Psychology* 1989; **57**:19–24.

18. Barton C, Alexander FK, Turner CW. Defensive communications in normal and delinquent families: The impact of context and family role. *Journal of Family Psychology* 1988; **1**:390–405.

19. Mas CH, Alexander JF, Turner CW. Dispositional attributions and defensive behavior in high- and low-conflict delinquent families. *Journal of Family Psychology* 1991; **5**:176–91.

20. Morris SB, Alexander JF, Turner CW. Do reattributions of delinquent behavior reduce blame? *Journal of Family Psychology* 1991; **5**:192–203.

21. Robbins MS, Alexander JF, Newell RM, Turner CW. The immediate effect of reframing on client attitude in family therapy. *Journal of Family Psychology* 1996; **10**:28–34.

22. Robbins MS, Alexander JF, Turner CW. Disrupting defensive interactions in family therapy with delinquent adolescents. *Journal of Family Psychology* 2000; **14**:688–701.

23. Alexander JF, Waldron HB, Barton CH, Mas CH. Beyond the technology of family therapy: The anatomy of intervention model. In: Craig KD, McMahon J (eds.), *Advances in Clinical Behavior Therapy*. New York: Brunner/Mazel, 1983, pp. 48–73.

24. Watzlawick P, Weakland J, Fisch R. *Change Principles of Problem Formation and Problem Resolution*. New York: W.W. Norton, 1974.

25. Webster-Stratton C. *The Incredible Years: A Trouble-Shooting Guide for Parents of Children Ages 3–8 Years*. Toronto: Umbrella Press, 1992.

Chapter 13

Autism Spectrum Disorders in Young Children
The Early Start Denver Model (ESDM)

Elizabeth A. Fuller and Sally J. Rogers

Children under the age of three years and even younger are increasingly being diagnosed with autism spectrum disorders (ASD). The more widespread use of early screening measures and adaptations to diagnostic tools has led to children being diagnosed with ASD as early as 12–18 months of age [1]. However, children in the 12- to 36-month age ranges have different needs and different learning styles than do preschoolers. Thus, there is an increasing need for early intervention services specifically targeted at very young children with ASD, particularly interventions that are family centred and comprehensive to meet the individualized developmental needs of young children. This is particularly important given the legal requirements of many public laws and policies that require the implementation of services specifically intended for young children, such as Part C of the Individuals with Disabilities Education Act of 2004 (IDEA) in the United States.

The Early Start Denver Model (ESDM) is one of the few evidenced-based family-centred comprehensive interventions designed specifically for the needs of very young children with autism [2]. The ESDM is one of the most studied early interventions and has been shown to be efficacious for children between 12 and 60 months of age. The ESDM relies on teaching strategies from applied behaviour analysis, which has been a well-studied, effective intervention for older children with ASD, as well as on a strong foundation of child development and naturalistic implementation to fit the learning styles of infants and toddlers. Most important, the ESDM was designed to be delivered by parents and caregivers as well as trained interventionists. Because ESDM is delivered in everyday activities and coaches caregivers to use the strategies in daily routines, it is compliant with the recommendations that early interventions use a family-centred approach. Lastly, the ESDM has a strong evidence base, with more than 20 studies showing its effectiveness [3, 4],

including studies that have tested implementation via coached caregivers [5–9].

This chapter describes the background and foundations of the ESDM, describes the strategies used in the intervention as well as those used to coach caregivers, reviews the evidence supporting the ESDM, and finally, review the competencies required for successful delivery. The purpose of this chapter is to assist clinicians, parents, educators and others in their search for evidence to support ASD intervention practices for toddlers.

ESDM as a Naturalistic Developmental Behavioural Intervention

Naturalistic developmental behavioural interventions (NDBIs; [10]) are a class of interventions that were first defined in 2015 but originated in the 1980s. The acronym NDBI describes any intervention that uses strategies involving naturally occurring environments and activities, child-responsive interaction styles and teaching strategies derived from the science of applied behaviour analysis. NDBIs focus on fostering a close relationship between the child and his or her partner as a key component. The ESDM, with its developmental foundations and naturalistic implementation style, falls into this category. However, it also has features that distinguish it from other NDBIs. First, it is one of the few NDBIs that is manualized and published, including its assessment tools, teaching steps and curriculum. It also has a manual specifically written for caregivers that includes a family-friendly description of the strategies [2, 6]. Online or in-person training is available, as well as a complete certification programme. This makes it one of the few NDBIs that is commercially accessible for community providers. The ESDM is also one of the few developmentally comprehensive programmes for ASD; although there is a particular focus on social communication given the known deficits in this area, the ESDM teaches skills across nine developmental domains (receptive communication, expressive communication, social skills, imitation, play skills, cognitive skills, gross motor skills, fine motor skills and adaptive functioning skills). Finally, the ESDM has a clear structure for taking frequent and reliable data and using those data to inform treatment decisions. Using this structure, the intervention is systematically individualized, with a decision-tree framework for troubleshooting when a child is not progressing. Given these strengths, combined with the large body of evidence demonstrating its effectiveness, the ESDM has been established as an efficacious and feasible model of early intervention. Some community-based studies are also beginning to demonstrate its effectiveness [5, 8, 11]. The ESDM is appropriate for children as young as 12 months of age, for whom other evidence-based practices for children with ASD, such as the mass trial instruction of discrete trial training, would not be appropriate.

Foundations

The ESDM grew out of the earlier Denver model [12, 13]. This Denver model was originally implemented in a child with ASD in the 1980s. Several principles of the Denver model were carried into the current ESDM, including the focus on building close relationships, a reliance on developmental science to inform teaching objectives and curriculum, the use of child interests and preferences to drive the interaction, an emphasis on building imitation and social communication skills, a focus on play as a cognitive and social learning platform, the use of an interdisciplinary team to address all areas of development and the inclusion of parents as implementation agents [2].

The ESDM was also influenced by two theories in ASD development: the social motivation hypothesis [14] and Rogers and Pennington's model of interpersonal development in autism [15]. The social motivation hypothesis holds that biological differences underlying ASD results in lowered sensitivity to social reward, which, in turn, results in lower-frequency attention to social attention, social orienting, seeking out social interaction and maintaining social relationships. This reduced frequency of social stimuli then results in reduced social learning opportunities which negatively affect the child's development [16, 17].

For example, consider a child interacting with her father during snack time. The father talks to the child, labelling the food (e.g., 'bananas') and singing a song

about what she's eating. The father then takes a bite of his own banana, says, 'Yummy! I love bananas!', and smiles at her. The child looks at her father and laughs, which encourages the father to continue singing and eating. The child vocalizes ('baba'), perhaps trying to sing along or requesting another bite of snack. The father responds naturally ('Yes! Bananas!') and gives the child more of the snack while continuing to sing the song. Now consider a child who is not as socially motivated by this situation. Perhaps she doesn't make eye contact or laugh, and as a result, the father may not be motivated to sing or to comment on the snack. This then reduces the child's learning opportunities for associating the word with the food, and the reduced language input might make her less likely to vocalize than the first child described, which, in turn, reduces stimuli that lead to additional father language and gestures. In this situation, there is a domino effect of the child's reduced interest in social communication and interaction that has a clear impact on the naturally occurring learning opportunities offered, especially in the area of communication. The ESDM uses several strategies to increase the salience and reward of social stimuli in order to foster socially motivating relationships with communication partners and increase the frequency of learning opportunities.

The second theoretical basis of the ESDM is Rogers and Pennington's model of interpersonal development in autism [15], which stipulates that an early deficit in imitation and bodily synchrony for young children with ASD leads to impairments in the imitative and affective sharing between the infant and caregiver, which, in turn, affects the child's development across developmental domains, but especially in communication. The ESDM addresses this early deficit by emphasizing the role of a responsive and sensitive partner to foster early relationships, to reflect and convey emotional experiences and to focus on developing motor, facial, gestural and verbal reciprocal imitation skills in all activities.

The ESDM also draws on the principles of other evidence-based interventions, specifically of applied behaviour analysis (ABA) and pivotal response training (PRT) to teach within routines. The principles of ABA hold that all behaviours happen within a context: something happens before the behaviour (the antecedent) and something happens after the behaviour (the consequence). Changing the antecedents and/or consequences of a behaviour can either increase or decrease the occurrence of that behaviour. Using these principles, ABA relies on changing the antecedent-behaviour-consequence (ABC) structure to increase the occurrence of positive behaviours and decrease the occurrence of negative behaviours. Originally, this was done using a mass trial instructional format, where many trials (often 10 or more) of the same instruction are delivered in quick succession to allow for rapid practice, typically delivered in a highly structured environment with highly preferred reinforcement (i.e., preferred foods) [18]. PRT differs from this format in that it uses the ABC structure of ABA within engaging routines and activities and with naturally occurring consequences to promote child learning. Consider again the first banana example described earlier. The father and child are enjoying their snack together, singing songs and eating the banana. At one point the father holds up a banana just outside the child's reach and waits. This is the antecedent. The child, wanting another bite, reaches for the banana and vocalizes ('baba'). This is the behaviour. The father responds by giving the child the desired bite of banana and pairs it with positive attention and language ('More banana!'). This is the consequence. The ABC structure is preserved, but it occurs in an everyday routine, and the consequence is naturally occurring. The child's behaviours (requesting for a desired item by reaching and vocalizing) are likely to increase because the behaviours are being reinforced with the delivery of the desired item and positive social attention. In this way, PRT uses the principles of ABA to embed teaching trials into child-initiated activities [19, 20]. The ESDM uses these same principles to embed teaching goals from nine developmental domains.

ESDM Implementation

Agent of Implementation. The ESDM was designed to be implemented by teams that included interventionists and caregivers and is typically implemented in one of two capacities: (1) delivered exclusively by parents, who are coached to use the strategies either in person or, more recently, via telemedicine, or (2) delivered in part by parents and in part directly by therapists. Regardless, the model typically uses an interdisciplinary team of early childhood professionals that might include early childhood special educators, social workers, speech-language pathologists, ABA professionals, occupational therapists and clinical or developmental psychologists. Typically, a team leader is identified. The team lead, with assistance and input from the rest of the team,

completes the assessment, writes treatment objectives, coaches parents and consults with parents to make treatment decisions. Because the ESDM spans many developmental domains, the intervention is best designed by teams within which there is expertise across domains. Additionally, feedback from other professionals (e.g., medical professionals, public health nurses, social workers, child psychiatrists, feeding specialists, etc.) is included as needed on a child-by-child basis. However, it is also a generalist model, with one team member – the team leader – taking the major responsibility for designing and implementing or supervising the treatment team. Other team members serve as consultants to the team leader.

Using Assessment to Write Treatment Objectives. A particular strength of the ESDM is its streamlined model of the assessment-to-treatment transition. The ESDM uses a *curriculum checklist* as a systematic assessment and curriculum tool administered every 12 weeks. It is a criterion-based assessment that examines the child's skills across the following nine domains: receptive communication, expressive communication, social skills, imitation, play skills, cognitive skills, gross motor skills, fine motor skills and adaptive functioning skills. The administration of the checklist generally lasts between 1 and 1.5 hours and is delivered in play- and routine-based interactions with the assessor and the parent or caregiver. Scoring the assessment takes into account input from direct observation (of the child with both the assessor and the parent present) and report from the parent or other persons (e.g., teacher, other caregiver).

A set of 12-week objectives are developed based on the results of the curriculum checklist combined with parents' goals and priorities for the child's short-term progress. Learning objectives are written systematically. Each objective includes the following four components:

1. *The antecedent:* a statement of the stimulus that occurs directly before the desired behaviour.
2. *The behaviour:* a clear statement of the target behaviour.
3. *The mastery criteria:* a specific statement of the criteria that define the mastery criterion of that skill, which may describe a percentage correct, a frequency count, a duration or a specified timing (e.g., at the first opportunity).
4. *The generalization criteria:* A specific statement that defines the mastery criteria across environs, people and materials.

Although all objectives are written using the same four components, objectives that are written for clinician implementation will differ from objectives written for parent implementation. This is because a clinician is present for a finite amount of time (typically between one and three hours), during which he or she records data every 15 minutes. Parents will likely implement the strategies throughout the entire day and would not be expected to record data every 15 minutes throughout the entire day.

Consider the following scenario from an example case. Marc is a 24-month-old with ASD and has received a score of *N*, for not yet acquired, on the following curriculum item: 'combines vocalization and gaze for intentional request (expressive communication, level 1, item 9)'. A 12-week treatment objective to address this skill might be written as follows for a clinician: 'during play activities or in natural opportunities to request (antecedent), Marc will combine vocalization with eye contact to request (behaviour) six or more times per hour (mastery criteria) for four of five consecutive treatment sessions with two or more people and three different activities (generalization criteria)'. The same objective intended to be implemented by a parent would be written as follows: 'during three different activities (snack time, dressing, bath time; antecedent with generalization), Marc will make a sound combined with eye contact (behaviour) several times (mastery criterion) with mom or dad'. Although the goal is the same, the second writing of the objective is more friendly for parents and is more feasible for a parent or caregiver to successfully implement throughout the day. However, both goals use the same consistent framework, which clearly states the behavioural expectations and specifies a level of consistency of performance over multiple days, people, contexts and environments that, when accomplished, indicates a generalized, stable skill.

After a learning objective is written, the team leader breaks each objective into four to six teaching steps. These teachings steps act as a roadmap to get the child from his or her current skill level to the mastered objective. Each of these teaching steps is typically accomplished in one to two weeks. Consider Marc's expressive communication objective again. The following may be teaching steps: during play activities or in natural opportunities to request (e.g., when an adult pauses in a preferred part of the activity):

1. *Current skill:* When an adult says a word or sound (e.g., 'Bubbles!'), Marc will make eye contact to request some of the time.

2. When an adult says a word or sound, Marc will look towards the adult three times per activity.

3. When an adult says a word or sound, Marc will vocalize to request one time per activity.

4. When an adult says a word or sound, Marc will vocalize to request three times per activity.

5. When an adult says a word or sound, Marc with combine eye contact and a vocalization to request three times per activity.

6. *Learning objective:* During play activities or in natural opportunities to request (antecedent), Marc will independently combine vocalization with eye contact to request (behaviour) six or more times per activity (mastery for criteria).

Developing clear teaching steps is crucial for successful implementation. The specific teaching steps outline how the adult will break down the objective into teachable steps, and it maps out how the child will progress to the final objective over a 12-week period. This includes specifying when and what level of prompt should be used to support a child's learning. In the preceding example, a verbal cue to look and vocalize is used in steps 1–5. A different set of teaching steps might change the level of prompt. For example, it might specify moving from a full physical prompt to a partial physical prompt to a gesture prompt as the child progresses through the steps. The teaching steps also specify the mastery criterion for each step. The preceding example moves from requiring the behaviour once per activity to requiring the behaviour six times per activity.

The teaching steps also allow the therapist to record daily data on the progress on the targeted objective by collecting data on the performance of the demonstrated step. Although parents are not expected to collect data, some choose to. Having specified teaching steps allows the parent and therapist to clearly see if the child is stuck on a certain skill so that they can make thoughtful and targeted changes to the teaching programme. For example, if a team leader notices that a child is consistently making slow progress when moving from a physical prompt to an independent response, this may indicate that the child shows prompt dependence, and goals can be reformulated to mitigate prompt dependence.

ESDM Core Strategies

Before implementing these teaching steps, the person implementing the intervention needs to establish a context for teaching. The ESDM focuses on reciprocal relationships and balanced interactions between the adult and the child. This requires that the adult be sensitive and comforting to the child, offering emotional support and positive energy at a level that meets the child's needs in the moment. It also requires that the adult respond to the child's many forms of communication contingently and does his or her best to understand the child's intention. Building a relationship through play and everyday routines allows the adult to target the teaching objectives that have been established for the child naturalistically. This is done using several core strategies.

Step into the Spotlight. Stepping into the spotlight requires the adult to position himself or herself across from the child and at eye level, close to the child's attentional focus, and to maintain objects between the child and adult. This is important for several reasons. First, this positioning helps support child direct eye contact. It also allows the adult to be a more responsive and sensitive partner because he or she is more likely to pick up on and respond to more subtle child communication such as gestures and facial expressions. This is crucial to understanding a child's intentions and preferences.

Become a Play Partner. Becoming a play partner sets the scene for the adult to be an active, supportive and socially motivating partner for the child. This is the essence of the relationship-based approach. The adult can become a play partner by imitating the child. Adult imitation of children's behaviour is a strategy that has been linked with increases in joint attention and responsiveness [21, 22]. By imitating the child's actions, the adult is sharing an interest with the child and creating a dyadic interaction. Imitating the child also gives the adult a role in the interaction and provides him or her with an opportunity to model language by narrating what the pair is doing together. Finally, the adult captures the child's attention by taking a turn with the same materials. The importance of the child's visual attention on the adult cannot be overstated, since attention is the first step for learning. Information cannot be encoded without first being attended to. Thus, ESDM, like discrete trial training (DTT), sets up presses for focused attention on the adult. The ESDM strategies make the adult's presence in the interaction salient and create a clear back-and-forth interaction in a context where relational synchrony can be fostered without requiring that the child inhibit all behaviour on command. By working

within the moment, ESDM techniques result in child-focused attention without the sometimes-challenging process of teaching 'learning to learn' skills outside child-friendly activities. Imitation is also the beginning of turn-taking; one partner acts and then the other partner mimics. Turn-taking is an important part of being a play partner – both partners have choices and opportunities to lead the play. Thus, ESDM is not so much child directed as it is balanced – a balanced relationship of both partners in terms of leading and following the other. The reciprocity that underlies turn-taking is important to learn as children start to play with others and also as they learn language and communication because it is the first step in learning to converse.

Language Modelling. As the adult and child play, the adult narrates and comments on what the he or she and the child are doing together. This allows the adult to model language that is clear and salient to the child. The ESDM follows the 'one word up' rule. If the child typically communicates in gestures or sounds, the adult models language using one- or two-word utterances; if the child uses one-word statements spontaneously, the adult generally models two- or three-word phrases; and so on. By modelling language only slightly above what the child uses spontaneously, it is more likely that the child will understand and imitate the language. This also scaffolds a child to increase his or her mean length of utterance over time. The adult responds to the child's communication, both gestural and verbal, by restating/expanding the child's utterance or the meaning of the gesture. Using restatements rather than generic praise provides additional language input and lets the child know that he or she is heard and understood. The exception to this rule is for children who engage in high amounts of echolalia. For these children, the adult does not use the one-word-up rule on echoed phrases. Rather, he or she bases the modelling language unit on the child's spontaneous phrases and focuses on the child's non-imitative language. The ESDM avoids praise statements such as 'Good talking!'. Instead, the adult models the language that he or she wants the child to learn, focusing on target vocabulary, syntax or target sounds for newer talkers.

Joint Activity Routines. Described in the banana example is the beginning of a four-step *joint activity routine* (JAR), a core feature of the ESDM. The JAR is a long-standing tool used in early learning, first described by Bruner [23]. The JAR is a simple two-person back and forth routine that has clear roles for each person and repeatable steps. For example, in the banana example, the father sings the song, waits for the child to communicate and then gives her a bite of the banana before repeating these three steps several more times. Each person has a role in the activity, and each step can be repeated several times within that activity, as well as in other snack- or meal-time activities throughout the day or week. Bruner originally highlighted the JAR as an important tool for language learning because it provides a context for familiar language, predictable and repeatable steps and clearly delineated roles for each person. In ESDM, the JAR provides an interaction throughout which the adult embeds language and learning objectives that fit naturally into the activity. The four steps of the JAR consist of (1) an opening or setup, (2) the establishment of a theme (a repeatable step or set of steps), (3) one or more elaborations that increase learning opportunities within the routine, and (4) a closing/transition. For example, a JAR might start with taking cuttable fruits and vegetables out of at container (the setup) and cutting them (the theme). Then the adult might model pretending to eat the fruit (the elaboration), which the adult repeats with several fruits before returning the fruits to the container (the closing). In each of the four steps, the adult and the child alternate turns or actions, offering many opportunities for imitation, turn-taking and modelling appropriate language (the one-word-up rule).

Although the routine just described sets out an object-play routine, a JAR does not need to be object based. In fact, JARs known as *sensory social routines* (SSRs) are a key strategy of the ESDM. SSRs include songs and sensory play in which the focus is on the person-to-person dyadic interaction rather than on objects. Games such as airplane, tickle, chase, songs with actions and peekaboo are primary examples. In sensory social games, the turn-taking often takes the form of one partner starting up a game and then stopping and waiting for a cue from the other to continue. This pattern of stop-and-wait for child response distinguishes the use of these routines for learning as opposed to use of these routines just to entertain children. In a successful SSR, the child must be communicating directly with the adult with voice and/or body about the request for the game, maintenance of the game or ending of the game. SSRs are especially important because they foster social orienting, emotion sharing via gaze and facial expressions,

many opportunities for communication, and they are exciting and thus motivating for children. A sensory social routine might be a child choosing a song (setup), the adult and child singing and doing the hand motions of the song together (theme), the adult initiating a new verse of the song and offering new gestures for the child to imitate, which the child does imitate, and finally an indication that the song is done and a transition to a new activity (closing/transition).

In addition to the role that SSRs play in fostering dyadic engagement and directed communication, they have a second important role, which is the regulation of child arousal to optimize the child's readiness to learn. SSRs are used to 'rev up' a passive or lethargic child, to calm down an overly aroused child (through slow, quiet movement patterns and sounds/songs, chants) and to keep children socially engaged with people rather than being focused only on objects. In ESDM, it is common to alternate object-based JARs, which lend themselves so well to working on joint attention and reference and thus sharing ideas or symbols, and SSRs, which lend themselves so well to dyadic face-to-face engagement and experiencing shared joy and pleasure with the partner. Both of these are examples of joint attention – of being on the same wavelength as another, with shared ideas in the former and shared emotions in the latter.

Embedding Teaching Objectives. The framework of the JAR allows for clear and frequent opportunities to embed teaching objectives. The adult embeds objectives during naturally occurring opportunities in the ongoing JAR. These naturally occurring opportunities arise from the parts of the routine that are the most motivating for, or most expected by, the child. Teaching follows the antecedent-behaviour-consequence format of learning/behavioural theory; the antecedent and behaviour to be used in teaching within JARS are those clearly specified in the objective's teaching steps, and the consequence is the naturally occurring reinforcer of the routine and the social pleasure experienced by both. For example, in the case of Marc, consider his objective to point to an object. Marc is currently on teaching step 5, using a combination of eye contact and vocalization in response to an adult's words or sounds three times per hour. Marc and his mother are singing 'Wheels on the Bus', one of Marc's favourite songs. Marc and his mother sing this song regularly, so Marc is familiar with the song. Marc's mother started the activity by offering a choice of songs to sing, and then she sang the first verse while doing the corresponding hand motions. Marc's mother knows that Marc especially loves the verse of the song when the wipers go 'whish whish whish' as she swings her arms back and forth. She begins the verse ('The wipers of the bus go') but pauses just before his favourite part. This is the antecedent, as described in the teaching step. Marc looks at his mother and vocalizes the sound he wants her to make (the behaviour). His mother responds by continuing with his favourite part of the song and swinging her arms (the consequence). They continue with singing the various verses of the song with several more pauses for Marc to vocalize and make eye contact until the song is finished, at which point his mother indicates that the song is over and together they move on to another activity.

In this example, the adult embeds the expressive communication objective while still following the child's lead and capitalizing on his motivation for this activity. However, the adult is not only targeting one objective in this example. She is likely targeting several objectives across multiple domains, including expressive objectives (e.g., producing single words), receptive objectives (e.g., responding to gestures following one-step directions), social skills (e.g., maintaining engagement in a sensory social routine for two minutes) and imitation (e.g., imitating motor actions). A skilled therapist implements a teaching episode every 10–20 seconds. Many repetitions of the key behaviours occur because of the child's desire to repeat the activity rather than the adult's requirement, thus demonstrating how naturalistic teaching can embed many trials without losing child motivation to act on the materials.

Tracking Progress and Troubleshooting. The ESDM data system and troubleshooting decision tree are two of the model's many strengths because they allow the intervention to be highly individualized while also systematically implemented. Session data are recorded for each objective in 15-minute intervals and tallied across the intervals to determine skill progress and performance for a single session. Tallying data across sessions allows one to chart progress and determine mastery. If the child is not progressing at the speed expected, the ESDM provides a decision-making framework on how to make specific adjustments to the teaching plan to better meet the needs of individual learners. Teaching plans are adjusted by re-evaluating the reinforcement, by creating more structure in the teaching environment (e.g., targeting certain objectives during tabletop routines) or by adding visual supports. In some cases, if the child is

not progressing with expressive language, augmentative or alternative communication systems are added. All decisions to adjust teaching plans are made following a review of the data and a discussion with the whole team, including the parents.

Caregiver Coaching

Traditional parent coaching in the ESDM is delivered during weekly 1.5-hour coaching sessions for 12 weeks. Effectively and sensitively coaching caregivers in their daily interactions with their children is a high-level skill and requires an additional level of training that can be obtained through workshops after the therapist has demonstrated mastery of the ESDM delivery. Coaching typically occurs in the clinic or home setting. Following the initial assessment, the therapist will have already asked about home routines and goal priorities and taken these into account while writing objectives. The therapist and parent can then talk together about how to use ESDM strategies (e.g., becoming a responsive play partner, stepping into the spotlight, the joint activity routine, embedding objectives) within ongoing routines.

Typically, the therapist refrains from modelling the strategy directly with the child. In some cases, the therapist might model the strategy to the parent. However, modelling with the child may be counterproductive. If the child responds better to the therapist, it may leave the parents feeling less competent. If the child responds better to the parents than the therapist, it may make the therapist feel inadequate. Rather, the therapist and parents follow each activity with a period of reflection and discussion to support parent learning and child progress. Along the same lines, the therapist tends to refrain from evaluative statements such as praise (e.g., 'Good job!'), instead using reflective statements that closely tie the parents' use of a strategy to the child's behaviour. For example, 'I see him looking at you and smiling a lot in this activity!'. Here the therapist seems to really feedback for parents about the effects of their strategies on the skills they are trying to help their children develop.

Evidence Base

Over 20 studies have demonstrated the effectiveness of ESDM [3, 4], including both single-case design [9] and group-design studies [24–26]. The ESDM has shown evidence for improved language, cognition, adaptive functioning and play skills [11, 25, 27, 28].

In the first randomized, controlled trial [28], 48 children (ages 18–30 months) were randomized to either 20 hours per week of ESDM intervention and biweekly parent coaching for two years or treatment as usual. After two years of treatment, the ESDM group showed significant improvements in Intelligence Quotient (IQ) and adaptive behaviour and a reduction in autism severity. The ESDM group had an average gain of 17.6 points on a standardized measure of IQ (where one standard deviation is 15 points) compared with a 7.0 gain in IQ for the control group. In a multisite intent-to-treat replication trial involving 118 children ages 14–24 months [25], these significant improvements were partially replicated. Following two years of 15 hours per week of intervention and parent coaching, the intervention group showed significantly more growth on language outcomes. However, the previous findings that showed significant group differences in cognition, adaptive functioning and autism diagnosis were not replicated. Instead, both groups made considerable progress, achieving the same or greater improvements than occurred in the 2010 trial.

Another key finding of the ESDM literature is significant changes in brain activity in response to social stimuli. In a follow-up study of the participants in the study by Dawson et al. [28], the children in the ESDM group showed normalized brain activity [29] to social versus non-social photos. The children in the ESDM group showed a shorter latency measured with netcat (nc latency) and increased cortical activation while viewing faces compared to objects, a pattern which is associated with improvements in social behaviour. The ESDM group and a group of typically developing children showed the same pattern, whereas the community group showed the opposite pattern. This indicates that early and intensive exposure to the ESDM could have lasting observable changes in brain activity, which could mean lasting changes in the trajectory of development.

The ESDM has also been used in group settings. In a study of an Australian public day-care centre, the ESDM was adapted to be delivered in the group setting, with group sizes of up to 10 children [30]. Twenty-seven children (ages 18–30 months) with ASD in the ESDM classrooms were compared to 30 well-matched children with ASD in a community-based ASD-specialized setting. Both groups were enrolled in their respective settings for 15–25 hours per week for 12 months. After 12 months, children in the ESDM setting showed significantly greater gains in developmental growth and receptive language than did the comparison group, as seen by significant between-group differences on the Mullen Scales of Early Learning. Further, the ESDM model was demonstrated to be a feasible model to implement in the setting, as indicated by high ratings of fidelity; was considered acceptable in the community, as indicated by a high-demand for enrolment from parents; and was rated by independent auditors as practical and appropriate.

ESDM has been shown to be effectively taught to parents and caregivers [5, 7, 9]. In a recent study, the traditional model with the addition of motivational interviewing, online materials and coaching sessions conducted in the home rather than the clinic setting resulted in greater gains in the use of ESDM strategies than traditional coaching. In this study, children in both groups showed accelerated development from pre-test to post-test, as indicated by significantly higher scores of the modified ESDM curriculum checklist; however, there was a significant relationship between the increase in parent ESDM skill use and an increase in child learning rates, as measured on the curriculum checklist [5]. Researchers continue to pilot novel approaches to parent coaching to make the ESDM increasingly accessible to hard-to-reach populations. This has included coaching via telehealth [31] and online modules [5].

Cost of ESDM

These studies demonstrating the benefit of the ESDM have important implications for dissemination of the ESDM as a cost-effective means to therapy. In a cost-benefit analysis that followed children in an ESDM intervention until age six, researchers found that although *during* the ESDM delivery, costs were higher than the cost of the community services received by the comparison group (by $14,000 per year), for the years *following* this early intensive intervention, the cost of intervention for children who were in the ESDM group averaged $19,000 per child per year *less* than the group that had received community services, thus making up the original cost in under two years [32]. In this analysis, comparison to community-based interventions revealed that the ESDM is a more cost-effective alternative than community services and that the benefits began to accrue by the time children reached school age. This clearly speaks to the economic advantage of the intensive ESDM intervention over the community services available in that community at the time.

Therapist Competencies

General Competencies. Sburlati et al. [33] highlighted four general competencies necessary for the effective implementation of CBT for treatment of children and adolescents: (1) practising professionality, (2) understanding relevant child characteristics, (3) building a positive relationship and (4) conducting a thorough assessment. Although all four of the competencies are also required for successful implementation of the ESDM, the most important of these is the building of a positive relationship between the therapist and the child. Because the ESDM is a relationship-based model, the importance of building a positive relationship between the child and the therapist so that the therapist establishes herself or himself as positive reinforcement is absolutely necessary for all other aspects of the intervention to be successful. This is particularly important for children with ASD, who, according to the social motivation theory [14], show lowered reward in response to social stimuli. Thus, emphasizing this positive social relationship and establishing oneself as a reinforcing communication partner are critical. Often novice therapists underemphasize this skill by placing too much focus on embedded teaching trials. This can make the interaction feel more like mass trial instruction than a routines-based, naturalistic intervention. Too many forced teaching trials can be punishing for the child, who may then disengage from the interaction with the therapist. By focusing on the relationship and interaction first and foremost and embedding teaching opportunities into naturally occurring moments, the therapist can better focus on the dyadic relationship and all the communication and positive engagement that comes along with that relationship.

Theory-Based Competencies. In addition to general competencies, the ESDM requires several theory-based competencies, including an understanding of the theoretical underpinnings of the ESDM but also an understanding of general child development and of ASDs. Autism represents a wide spectrum of both strengths and challenges that can look very different from one child to the next. Therefore, having a deep understanding of the relevant background knowledge will help therapists develop, implement and augment treatment plans as necessary. Because the ESDM is rooted in multiple theories, it is necessary that the therapist have experience and understanding of applied behaviour analysis as well as an understanding of naturalistic interventions.

Specific Evidence-Based Techniques. In addition to the core ESDM strategies just detailed, the therapist needs to be competent in managing behaviours and optimizing engagement. As with any early intervention, this competency often comes with practice and experience but also relies on thoughtful reflection about sessions. ESDM therapists frequently video-record their own sessions and rate their own fidelity in order to reflect on which strategies are effective for a particular child and which strategies need to be changed for more effective implementation. Engaging in reflective practices can be a beneficial tool for therapists of all years of experience.

Additional Competencies for Parent Coaches. As described earlier, becoming an ESDM parent coach requires additional training and experience. This goes along with several additional competencies. An effective parent coach needs to have expertise in communicating and working alongside others in a collaborative way. The parent coach also needs to have a theoretical understanding of adult learning styles to effectively and sensitively coach the caregiver to use the relevant strategies without being overly didactic. ASD has an old history of blaming parents for a child's developmental delays, and despite vast evidence to the contrary, parents can still experience feelings of inadequacy. Thus, it is especially importation that coaches promote a parent's many existing skills and collaborate with the parent to build on those skills in order to further enhance their child's learning opportunities in daily life.

Conclusion

The ESDM is an effective intervention that is appropriate for children with ASD between the ages 12 and 60 months. This model of intervention emphasizes the importance of a responsive and sensitive partner to teach across nine developmental domains during everyday routines using four key strategies: becoming a play partner, stepping into the spotlight, using joint activity routines and embedding teaching objectives. The systematic assessment tool, daily interval-based data and troubleshooting decision tree allow the intervention to be systematically individualized to meet the learning needs of a wide range of learners. Further, the ESDM has ample evidence as an effective intervention for improving language, cognition and adaptive functioning and can be carried out by a wide range of adults, including parents and caregivers. To effectively implement the ESDM, therapists must develop several competencies, including (1) developing positive and reinforcing relationships between themselves and the child, (2) forming a deep understanding of the theoretical underpinnings of the ESDM and ASD and (3) managing behaviours and optimizing engagement. Lastly, therapists need to have expertise in communicating and working alongside parents in a collaborative way so that the ESDM can be implemented daily in the child's natural environment.

References

1. Zwaigenbaum L, Bauman ML, Choueiri R, et al. Early intervention for children with autism spectrum disorder under 3 years of age: recommendations for practice and research. *Pediatrics* 2015; **136**(Supp. 1): S60–81.

2. Rogers SJ, Dawson G. *Early Start Denver Model for Young Children with Autism: Promoting Language, Learning, and Engagement.* New York: Guilford Press, 2010.

3. Waddington H, van der Meer L, Sigafoos J. Effectiveness of the Early Start Denver Model: A systematic review. Review Journal of Autism and Developmental Disorders 2016; **3**(2):93–106.

4. Baril EM, Humphreys BP. An evaluation of the research evidence on the Early Start Denver Model. *Journal of Early Intervention* 2017; **39**(4):321–38.

5. Rogers SJ, Estes A, Vismara L, et al. Enhancing low-intensity coaching in parent implemented Early Start Denver Model intervention for early autism: A randomized comparison treatment trial. *Journal of Autism and Developmental Disorders* 2019; **49** (2):632–46.

6. Rogers SJ, Estes A, Lord C, et al. Effects of a brief Early Start Denver Model (ESDM)–based parent intervention on toddlers at risk for autism spectrum disorders: A randomized controlled trial. *Journal of the American Academy of Child and Adolescent Psychiatry* 2012; **51**(10):1052–65.

7. Vismara LA, Colombi C, Rogers SJ. Can one hour per week of therapy lead to lasting changes in young children with autism? *Autism* 2009; **13**(1):93–115.

8. Vismara LA, McCormick CE, Wagner AL, et al. Telehealth parent training in the Early Start Denver Model: Results from a randomized controlled study. *Focus on Autism and Other Developmental Disabilities* 2018; **33**(2):67–79.

9. Vismara LA, Rogers SJ. The Early Start Denver Model: A case study of an innovative practice. *Journal of Early Intervention* 2008; **31**(1):91–108.

10. Schreibman L, Dawson G, Stahmer AC, et al. Naturalistic developmental behavioral interventions: Empirically validated treatments for autism spectrum disorder. *Journal of Autism and Developmental Disorders* 2015; **45**(8):2411–28.

11. Eapen V, Črnčec R, Walter A. Clinical outcomes of an early intervention program for preschool children with autism spectrum disorder in a community group setting. *BMC Pediatrics* 2013; **13**(1):3.

12. Rogers SJ, Herbison JM, Lewis HC, et al. An approach for enhancing the symbolic, communicative, and interpersonal functioning of young children with autism or severe emotional handicaps. *Journal of the Division for Early Childhood* 1986; **10**(2):135–48.

13. Rogers SJ, Lewis HAL. An effective day treatment model for young children with pervasive developmental disorders. *Journal of the American Academy of Child and Adolescent Psychiatry* 1989; **28** (2):207–14.

14. Dawson G, Meltzoff AN, Osterling J, et al. Children with autism fail to orient to naturally occurring social stimuli. *Journal of Autism and Developmental Disorders* 1998; **28**(6):479–85.

15. Rogers SJ, Pennington BF. A theoretical approach to the deficits in infantile autism. *Development and Psychopathology* 1991; **3**(2):137–62.

16. Dawson G, Toth K, Abbott R, et al. Early social attention impairments in autism: Social orienting, joint attention, and attention to distress. *Developmental Psychology* 2004; **40**(2):271.

17. Mundy P, Sigman M. The theoretical implications of joint-attention deficits in autism. *Development and Psychopathology* 1989; **1**(3):173–83.

18. Lovaas OI. Behavioral treatment and normal educational and intellectual functioning in young autistic children. *Journal of Consulting and Clinical Psychology* 1987; **55**(1):3.

19. Schreibman L, Pierce K. Achieving greater generalization of treatment effects in children with autism: Pivotal response training and self management. *Clinical Psychology* 1993; **46**(4):184–91.

20. Koegel RL. *How to Teach Pivotal Behaviors to Children with Autism: A Training Manual.* Santa Barbara: University of California, 1988.

21. Escalona A, Field T, Nadel J, Lundy B. Brief report: Imitation effects on children with autism. *Journal of Autism and Developmental Disorders* 2002; **32** (2):141–4.

22. Ingersoll B, Schreibman L. Teaching reciprocal imitation skills to young children with autism using a naturalistic behavioral approach: Effects on language, pretend play, and joint attention. *Journal of*

Autism and Developmental Disorders 2006; **36** (4):487–505.

23. Bruner JS. The ontogenesis of speech acts. *Journal of Child Language* 1975; **2**(1):1–19.

24. Rogers SJ, Estes A, Vismara L, et al. Enhancing low-intensity coaching in parent implemented Early Start Denver Model intervention for early autism: A randomized comparison treatment trial. *Journal of Autism and Developmental Disorders* 2019; **49** (2):632–46.

25. Rogers SJ, Estes A, Lord C, et al. A multisite randomized, controlled two-phase trial of the early Start Denver Model compared to treatment as usual. *Journal of the American Academy of Child and Adolescent Psychiatry* 2019; **58**(9):853–65.

26. Colombi C, Narzisi A, Ruta L, et al. Implementation of the Early Start Denver model in an Italian community. *Autism* 2018; **22**(2):126–33.

27. Fulton E, Eapen V, Črnčec R, et al. Reducing maladaptive behaviors in preschool-aged children with autism spectrum disorder using the Early Start Denver Model. *Frontiers in Pediatrics* 2014; **2**:40.

28. Dawson G, Rogers S, Munson J, et al. Randomized, controlled trial of an intervention for toddlers with autism: The Early Start Denver Model. *Pediatrics* 2010; **125**(1):e17–23.

29. Dawson G, Jones EJ, Merkle K, et al. Early behavioral intervention is associated with normalized brain activity in young children with autism. *Journal of the American Academy of Child and Adolescent Psychiatry* 2012; **51**(11):1150–9.

30. Vivanti G, Paynter J, Duncan E, et al. Effectiveness and feasibility of the Early Start Denver Model implemented in a group-based community childcare setting. *Journal of Autism and Developmental Disorders* 2014; **44**(12):3140–53.

31. Vismara LA, Young GS, Rogers SJ. Community dissemination of the Early Start Denver Model: Implications for science and practice. *Topics in Early Childhood Special Education* 2013; **32** (4):223–33.

32. Cidav Z, Munson J, Estes A, et al. Cost offset associated with Early Start Denver Model for children with autism. *Journal of the American Academy of Child and Adolescent Psychiatry* 2017; **56** (9):777–83.

33. Sburlati ES, Schniering CA, Lyneham HJ, Rapee RM. A model of therapist competencies for the empirically supported cognitive behavioral treatment of child and adolescent anxiety and depressive disorders. *Clinical Child and Family Psychology Review* 2011; **14** (1):89–109.

Chapter 14

Family-Based Treatment for Eating Disorders

Sasha Gorrell and Daniel Le Grange

Eating disorders (EDs) are among the most serious and pernicious mental disorders and for many years have posed considerable challenges for young people, caretakers, clinicians and researchers alike. Research evidence has demonstrated devastating consequences associated with EDs, including elevated rates of morbidity and mortality [1], marked distress and impairment [2, 3], elevated suicidality [4, 5], high treatment costs [6] and considerable caregiver burden [7]. Despite evidence that these disorders commonly onset in adolescence and early adulthood [3, 8], with increasing incidence rates of EDs among adolescents [9], relatively little research has focused specifically on these populations. Of those studies which have focused on younger samples, early intervention contributes to the best prognostic outcomes [10]. For example, when treated in adolescence, individuals with anorexia nervosa (AN) experience reduced mortality, improved recovery rates and symptom reduction [1]. As such, increasing research attention has been oriented towards the development of treatment interventions for EDs in adolescence.

Based on the past several decades of investigation, a consensus principally supports the use of family therapy among children and adolescents with EDs [11, 12]. While there are a limited number of randomized, controlled trials (RCTs) for adolescents with EDs, family interventions have been the most frequently tested (e.g., [13–21]). Subsequently, specialty family therapy is currently considered the first choice of treatment for youth with AN and is recommended as the primary treatment for youth with bulimia nervosa (BN) [22]. This chapter describes caregiver involvement in ED treatment and summarizes existing research findings from the study of family-based approaches for the treatment of youth and adolescent EDs. This chapter also highlights core clinician competencies that contribute to treatment outcomes, as well as strategies that expand and adapt current family-based approaches in efforts to improve the breadth

and scope of ED treatment among youth, adolescents and transition-aged youth (i.e., emerging adults).

Caregiver Involvement in ED Treatment

Historically, parents were excluded from ED diagnosis and intervention, as caregivers were errantly considered to be causal factors in the development of the ED [11, 23, 24]. A more recent, evidence-based shift away from an emphasis on family responsibility in ED pathogenesis has allowed for parents to be actively involved in treatment [21, 23] and to be viewed as a potential, vital resource in aiding the youth in the process of recovery [25]. The family-based treatment (FBT) approach to EDs may be characterized by an agnostic stance towards the origin of the illness, along with the overarching tenet that parents are the most influential resource in their offspring's recovery (AN [26], BN [25]). While FBT posits that parents naturally possess the necessary commitment and skills to help their child recover, caretakers are frequently diverted from their instincts by the formidable presence of the ED, which, in turn, can inadvertently result in a level of accommodation to the ED symptoms within the family's structural system [11]. Consequently, treatment is initially focused on empowering parents to mobilize their strengths and resources in subverting the constellation of ED symptoms, in addition to restoring adequate nutrition and weight.

Given the severe nature of medical concerns associated with AN and BN [27], weight restoration, as well as cessation of life-threatening behaviour (e.g., purging) takes precedence over other treatment foci. In so doing, parents are encouraged to exert parental authority in ensuring that all contributing behavioural factors (e.g., dietary restriction, compensatory exercise) are minimized. When families are incorporated into the treatment for adolescents with AN [28], such involvement significantly reduces psychological and medical morbidity, as well as treatment attrition rates [24]. As weight restoration and behavioural symptom resolution are facilitated, less parental authority may be required, and the adolescent is encouraged to demonstrate developmentally appropriate levels of autonomy over eating behaviour. As the child returns to age-appropriate functioning (e.g., eating independently with friends), therapeutic focus can shift to typical adolescent developmental issues that were interrupted by the onset and course of the ED [26].

In the first RCT to include parents in treatment for adolescent AN, findings indicated that for patients with fewer than three years of illness duration, family therapy provided superior outcomes over individual psychotherapy [29]. In the three decades since, FBT continues to demonstrate encouraging treatment outcomes with empirical support from RCTs (e.g., [19]), meta-analyses [30], dismantling (i.e., a study which aims to identify the components of therapy that are responsible for change) [31], dissemination (i.e., a study that attempts to distribute therapeutic intervention more widely) [32], and case-series studies [33]. Reflective of a larger body of literature, family treatment for adolescent AN (Maudsley's FT-AN [15]) and FBT with adolescent treatment manuals correspondent to AN [26] and BN [25] have emerged as the most promising outpatient treatments for medically stable adolescent ED presentations.

Family-Based Treatment for AN

Six RCT's have systematically studied the efficacy of FBT among adolescent samples with AN, collectively providing quite strong support for the use of this manualized treatment format. In the first study using the FBT-AN manual, a two-site RCT, adolescents with AN ($N = 121$) were randomized to one of two treatment arms: FBT or adolescent-focused therapy (AFT) [19]. As in several subsequent FBT RCTs, the primary study outcome was full remission (i.e., reaching 95 per cent of expected body weight [%EBW] and achieving eating disorder examination [EDE] global scores within one standard deviation of community norms [34]). No between-group differences were evidenced at end of treatment (EOT), but patients receiving FBT were significantly more likely to achieve full remission at six-month ($p = .03$) and 12-month ($p = .02$) follow-up than AFT counterparts.

To further investigate specifically how parents may function within FBT, a six-site RCT ($N = 164$) compared FBT with systemic family therapy (SFT) [13]. In SFT, the focus of treatment is on the family system; in this approach, the ED is postulated to arise within relationships, interactions and language contained within it, and normalization of eating and weight is not a specific focus of treatment unless raised by the family. In terms of the primary outcome (%EBW), study results did not reveal any between-group differences at EOT or one-year follow-up. However, those receiving treatment in the FBT arm gained weight significantly more quickly than their SFT counterparts ($p = .003$) and with less time spent in hospital ($p = .02$).

To determine whether the length of a standard course of FBT could be modified, a trial was conducted in which adolescents with AN ($N = 86$) were randomized to either 6 or 12 months of treatment (10 or 20 sessions, respectively) [35]. Primary outcomes at EOT (i.e., one year) were EDE scores and weight gain. Main findings indicated that a shorter course of treatment was comparable in resolving EDE scores and bringing about weight change; follow-up analyses indicated that those with elevated obsessive ED symptoms or those from non-intact or single families benefitted more from the original, longer course of treatment [35].

A trial that evaluated the impact of length of pre-outpatient treatment hospitalization enrolled adolescents with AN ($N = 82$) and randomized patients to either a brief hospital stay for medical stabilization or a longer stay (i.e., until 90% EBW) [20]. In each treatment arm, patients received 20 outpatient FBT sessions following discharge. Findings indicated that early weight gain (i.e., >1.8 kg at session 4) predicted elevated %EBW and remission status at EOT, as well as at 12-month follow-up. Notably, it was this evidence of early weight gain and not treatment arm randomization that predicted these positive outcomes. These results emphasize the importance of early weight gain, as well as suggest that longer hospitalization is not necessary to enhance the effectiveness of outpatient FBT treatment for AN.

In summary, FBT has demonstrated promising treatment outcomes related to weight gain. For example, 50–75 per cent of adolescents are weight restored within one year of beginning FBT treatment [23], with robust maintenance of treatment gains at 6- and 12-month follow-up [19, 30]. Further, FBT treatment has also demonstrated promising capacity for reducing maladaptive cognitive AN symptoms (e.g., drive for thinness, weight and shape concerns) comparable to other adolescent treatment formats [19]. However, 30–50 per cent of patients do not fully remit from symptoms during FBT [36], indicating that there are a considerable number of patients for whom certain individual or familial differences may negatively impact treatment outcomes. Taken together, the trials highlighted here support the use of FBT for AN over and above other forms of psychosocial treatment but also suggest that study of FBT for AN should include adaptations to specifically address moderators that may impact treatment outcomes. Two additional RCTs comparing standard conjoint FBT to a separated version of this treatment (i.e., parent focused therapy [PFT] [18]), as well as to an augmented format [37], are discussed later in this chapter in sections that are specific to treatment moderators.

Family-Based Treatment for BN

Following the emergence of family-based interventions for adolescent AN, corresponding work has also advanced an FBT model for adolescent presentation of BN [25]. Although prevalence estimates for adolescent BN consistently surpass those of adolescent AN [3], there is a comparatively limited amount of research evaluating psychological treatment outcomes in this population [38]. To date, three of four published RCTs for adolescent BN have specifically evaluated the efficacy of family therapy (FT) or FBT. In the first of these studies, adolescents with BN or 'eating disorder not otherwise specified' ($N = 85$) were randomized to FT or to self-guided cognitive behavioural therapy (CBT) [39]. In this trial, the FT approach was an adaptation of family therapy for AN for use with individuals with BN, and CBT-guided self-care was undertaken by the adolescent and supported by a health-care professional. Primary outcomes were abstinence from binge eating and purging following six months of treatment and at a six-month post-treatment follow-up; secondary outcomes included attitudinal bulimic symptoms and treatment cost. Findings indicated that adolescents receiving CBT-guided self-care had significant reductions in binge eating at six months, but these differences were not retained at follow-up. Further, there were no differences between groups at EOT in purging behaviour or attitudinal symptoms. Direct cost

of care was reduced in CBT, but groups did not differ across other cost categories. Despite this cost advantage, primary findings from this study indicate that CBT-guided self-care did not evidence statistical superiority in the main outcome criteria compared with a FT approach at EOT.

In the same year, a manualized approach to FBT for BN (FBT-BN) was used in a study comparing this treatment to individual supportive psychotherapy (SPT) [16]. In this RCT, adolescents ($N = 80$) with a *Diagnostic and Statistical Manual of Mental Disorders*, fourth edition (DSM-IV), diagnosis of BN or partial BN (i.e., those who endorsed binge eating and purge episodes averaging once per week over six months) were randomized to one of these two treatments, each for 20 sessions over six months. As a general, nondirective treatment, SPT does not involve specific active therapeutic elements. The FBT-BN approach shares similar core theoretical tenets with the aforementioned AN model, particularly in centrally leveraging parental involvement to address ED symptoms (e.g., shape and weight concern, restrictive eating). However, FBT-BN is somewhat distinct from AN in that the primary symptoms (i.e., binge eating and purging) are almost universally experienced as distressing and perhaps even ego dystonic (i.e., in conflict with one's self-image). Thus, FBT-BN features a more collaborative stance between the patient and his or her caretakers in collectively strategizing to overcome the distressing behavioural BN symptoms [25]. Results of this trial indicated that FBT-BN had significantly higher rates of abstinence from binge eating and purging episodes (39 versus 18 per cent; $p = .049$) at EOT; the rate of abstinence declined when assessed at 12-month follow-up for both groups (29 and 10 per cent, respectively), although the rate between the two groups remained statistically in favour of FBT-BN ($p = .05$). As the first test of a manualized specialty treatment for BN in a sample of adolescents, this trial demonstrated the clinical and statistical superiority of FBT-BN over non-specialty treatment.

In a more recent trial, FBT-BN was compared with a version of CBT that was adapted for adolescents with BN (CBT-A) [17]. In this study, adolescents ($N = 109$, aged 12–18 years) with a DSM-IV diagnosis of BN or partial BN (as defined previously) were randomized to one of these two treatments, each for 18 sessions over six months. CBT-A is an individual therapy that focuses on reducing dieting and amending maladaptive behaviours and cognitions specifically related to shape and weight [35]. Adaptations to CBT unique to adolescents included exploration of developmental challenges and collateral sessions with parents with a focus on psychoeducation of BN. FBT-BN was delivered with the approach described earlier (see [25]). Findings indicated that abstinence from binge eating and purging for the 28 days prior to EOT was statistically superior for FBT-BN versus CBT-A (39.4 versus 19.7 per cent, respectively; $p = .04$). At six-month follow-up, abstinence rates for both groups continued to improve but remained significantly elevated for FBT-BN (44 and 25.4 per cent respectively; $p = .03$); between-group abstinence rates did not differ statistically at 12-month follow-up, but notably, the study was not powered for these follow-up analyses.

Taken together, these RCTs provide provisional yet robust support for the use of a family-centred approach in the treatment of adolescent BN. In particular, the two trials described here comparing the efficacy of a manualized FBT-BN with another distinct and active treatment (SPT and CBT-A, respectively) suggest the superiority of this intervention over other established treatments. However, as no treatment tested to date demonstrates statistically superior outcomes after 12 months, families who prefer individual treatment or with an adolescent who is unwilling to involve caretakers may find that CBT treatment is a beneficial alternative.

Expanding FBT

Since its emergence, the implementation of FBT has been considerably expanded to address alternate populations, different developmental stages and a wider range of diagnoses. It has also been modified to improve its dissemination. While much of this work is preliminary, what is described in the following sections demonstrates notable expansion efforts, including remote treatment delivery methods, which may greatly improve accessibility to specialty treatment. Detailed next, further recent enhancements of FBT have included intensive and multifamily formatting and adaptation for trans-diagnostic EDs and for patients beyond a traditional adolescent age group.

Remote Delivery of FBT

Because of factors that include a shortage of providers, physical distance, high demands and long waiting lists, gaining access to specialized treatment for EDs is challenging for many individuals and families. In an effort to disseminate access to specialty treatment to a greater number of families, recent work has evaluated the feasibility and preliminary outcomes for adolescents with AN when FBT is delivered via telehealth [40, 41]. In this pilot work ($N = 10$), duration of treatment was six months, over which participants received 20 FBT sessions. Results indicated that participants showed significant increases in per cent median body mass index ($p = .01$) and improved eating pathology ($p = .002$) at EOT, progress that was retained at six-month follow-up ($p = .03$ and .001, respectively). Future confirmation of the success of this particular format in an adequately powered treatment trial may ultimately allow more families to secure access to greatly needed specialty treatment.

Intensive Single-Family and Multifamily Treatment

Moulded from a standard approach to FBT, a short-term intensive family therapy (IFT) format typically consists of a five-day, eight-hour/day treatment week for families of adolescents with AN [42, 43]. This intensive approach may be a particularly helpful alternative for families who cannot regularly access specialty ED care and may also serve as an option for treatment-resistant cases [44]. Including several families in this intensive approach (multifamily therapy [M-IFT]) may hold some benefits over the single-family format (S-IFT). Specifically, a multifamily format supports the idea that bringing families together as groups serves to amplify family resources and support for one another, which may then lead to improved outcomes [15]. The presence of several families working alongside one another in overcoming AN may aid in destigmatizing the illness and allow for the experience of both being helped by and acting as consultants to other families. Together these experiences may further solidify one's self-efficacy and agency [45].

Controlled empirical evidence supporting multifamily therapy for AN remains sparse, but a prospective study of IFT in both S-IFT and M-IFT formats conferred promising outcomes [42]. In this treatment study ($N = 74$), full remission was defined as normal weight (≥95 per cent of expected weight for sex, age and height), EDE global score within one standard deviation of community norms and absence of binge eating or purging behaviours. Partial remission was defined as weight of 85 per cent or more of expected or 95% or more of expected but with elevated eating pathology and the presence of binge eating or purging symptoms (<1/week). Over 30-month follow-up, results showed that nearly 90 per cent of participants achieved full (61 per cent) *plus* partial remission (27 per cent), whereas 12 per cent reported a poor outcome; findings indicated that both formats had comparable outcomes in achieving full or partial remission. Taken together, preliminary evidence suggests that short-term, intensive treatments – in both S-IFT and M-IFT formats – may confer overall positive treatment outcomes and may serve to improve accessibility, increase family support and provide a higher level of care that is comparatively less disruptive.

FBT for Transition-Aged Youth

Whereas a good portion of the extant literature on family interventions for ED has focused on adolescents ages 12–18 years, the definition of adolescence is mutable and, for many, extends into early adulthood. Distinct from both adolescents and more mature adults, transition-aged youth (TAY; 16–25 years old) may reside with their parents, from whom they may also receive substantial financial and emotional support. These family and relational circumstances suggest that adapting FBT for this patient population may yield favourable outcomes. While previous research indicates that FBT-AN might be less effective for older than for younger adolescents [46], a recent feasibility and acceptability trial of FBT for TAY demonstrated that an appropriately modified adaptation of FBT resulted in successful weight restoration in this patient population [47]. Some of the adaptations made in a manualized FBT-TAY approach include asking the young adults to describe the essential features of support they would like from family during mealtimes and increasing the collaborative nature of how their treatment is delivered [48]. Other modifications include strategies for age-appropriate meal accommodations (e.g., eating on a college campus) and how recovery may include more developmentally normative transition issues (e.g., return to living with a partner). In a recent modest-sized open trial of FBT-TAY ($N = 26$), findings indicated significant improvement in overall eating pathology at EOT and three months after treatment ($p < .001$) [49]. Participants also achieved and maintained weight restoration at EOT and three months after treatment when compared to baseline ($p < .001$), suggesting that FBT-TAY is a promising adaptation of FBT for which a larger clinical trial is warranted.

FBT for Other Eating and Weight Disorders

Clinical trials evaluating family-based interventions that include samples with ED diagnoses other than AN and BN are limited, and to date, no large-scale trial has specifically examined the use of FBT for adolescents with binge eating disorder. In response to public health concern regarding obesity among youth and its predictable course of obesity into adulthood, FBT for paediatric obesity (FBT-PO) has been developed and tested in a preliminary case study and trial [50–52]. In FBT-PO, parents are involved at the beginning of treatment to varying degrees depending on the age of the child. As necessary, given the child's developmental maturity, parents initially assume full responsibility for eating- and exercise-related changes in the home; all family-level modifications are health oriented, safe and applicable even for non-overweight family members. As with FBT-AN and FBT-BN, parental control over eating and exercise lessens over the course of treatment [53].

Currently, multiple research sites are engaged in the development and testing of versions of FBT for avoidant resistant food intake disorder (ARFID; e.g., [54]). In FBT for ARFID, psycho-education is provided about the unique features of this ED, including those characteristics which distinguish it from AN. As with FBT-AN and FBT-BN, treatment focus is on empowering parents, restoring weight as necessary, uniting the family against the ED and improving eating behaviours. As research continues to improve understanding of ED diagnoses, including those clarified by DSM-V, adapting FBT for appropriate use in these populations holds promise in addressing a wider array of ED presentations and symptoms across a variety of formats.

Adaptations of FBT Based on Clinical Challenges

Evidence from evaluation of moderators of treatment outcomes for FBT-AN and FBT-BN has led to the development of specific adaptations to the standard intervention protocol. Early weight gain (e.g., [55, 56]), parental criticism (e.g., [14, 57]) and obsessionality (e.g., [35, 46]) have all been identified as moderators that may significantly and negatively impact outcomes. To address each of these in turn, modified versions of FBT have been developed and tested.

Parental Empowerment and Early Weight Gain

Early weight gain (~2.5 kg by the end of one month of manualized FBT) is a robust early predictor of remission [20, 55, 56, 58, 59]. Parental self-efficacy has been proposed as a candidate mediator of FBT treatment outcomes, suggesting that facilitating earlier weight gain may assist parents in becoming more empowered within the context of treatment, thereby improving overall weight gain at EOT [60]. For adolescents with AN who do not restore a sufficient amount of weight (<2.5 kg) after approximately four weeks of manualized FBT (early non-responders), an adaptive treatment approach with intensive parental coaching (IPC) has been developed for these non-responders. In this augmented treatment format, sessions four through six follow a specific protocol with the intent to enhance parental self-efficacy. Session four introduces the adaptive treatment and re-emphasizes the importance of weight gain. Session five is a separated family session whereby parents receive a session alone in an effort to orchestrate a renewed awareness of the severity of illness and reinvigorate a sense of urgency for weight gain. In session six, parents participate with their adolescent in a second family meal (in FBT, the second session consists of a family meal; cf. [26]), with particular attention to specific challenges that persist in refeeding. In a two-site pilot study of this adapted treatment, 45 adolescents with AN were randomized to either FBT (n =10) or FBT-IPC (n =35) if patients did not gain 2.4 kg by session four [37]. As described earlier, in addition to standard FBT, those in the FBT-IPC treatment arm attended three adapted sessions (i.e., sessions 4–6). At EOT, patients receiving FBT-IPC had gained significantly more weight than patients continuing after session four with standard FBT (p = .002). Based on the promise of these preliminary results, a confirmatory treatment trial of this adapted treatment is currently being conducted with a two-site sample of adolescents with AN and their families.

Critical to FBT, as well as to this particular adaptation of this treatment modality, is parental empowerment in the domain of early and sustained weight gain. To demonstrate some key clinical strategies to enhance parental empowerment, a brief case vignette is presented here.

Case Vignette

Genevieve is a 16-year-old girl with a diagnosis of AN. She has been involved in FBT for three weeks but has not met her weight gain targets and continues to exhibit ED symptoms, including food refusal and excessive exercise. At this point in treatment, her parents report high caregiver burnout and feeling like they do not have the skills needed to increase her daily nutritional intake and promote more rapid and sustained weight gain.

In their third FBT session, the therapist voices to the parents her concerns about Genevieve's struggles and the consequent lack of weight gain. The parents recognize that it is a treatment crisis but report that they feel that they do not have the skills necessary to increase Genevieve's nutrition. The therapist asks the parents to identify their primary barriers to refeeding, and the parents state that mealtimes are tense and anxiety inducing (for both Genevieve and the rest of the family) and that Genevieve's distress manifests in screaming, yelling and throwing food or other objects. The therapist helps the parents to identify ways they can cope in those moments in order to remain calm in the face of Genevieve's distress. The therapist also elicits ideas for what the parents can do to set limits for Genevieve around not completing meals. Through extensive problem-solving in session, the parents came up with various strategies to address these behaviours. These include having the parents provide the therapist with a detailed account of exactly what food, types and quantities, they prepare and present to Genevieve. Given this information, it was apparent to the therapist that the daily caloric value was insufficient to promote weight gain in someone quite as underweight as Genevieve. Consequently, the therapist carefully reviewed each meal (breakfast, morning snack, lunch, etc.) with the parents and encouraged them to come up with what they could add to each of these mealtimes. The therapist helped focus the parents to keep to familiar foods, known to them as a family, and in keeping what they used to prepare for Genevieve (and her younger brother) before the onset of the ED. The therapist emphasized that this strategy (parents deciding on and preparing the food for each meal) should be followed meticulously and daily without exception.

Given that Genevieve struggled to complete the meals that were presented to her, the therapist also helped the parents problem-solve around how they encourage their daughter to complete what they present to her and underscored that it is not helpful to argue or debate 'the eating disorder' but that all these decisions are squarely within the parents' domain for now. The therapist discussed with the parents the need for them to work out a schedule, given their various other family and professional commitments, as to who will be sitting with Genevieve at each meal and to communicate deliberately and clearly to their daughter (1) that there are to be no discussions around types or amounts of food, (2) that she will need to finish what is on her plate and (3) that one or both parents will sit with her and support her at each meal until she is able to finish all her food. In addition, not attending school and being able to go out with her friends are not in the cards, as Genevieve is simply not medically fit to engage meaningfully in these activities.

The parents are encouraged to come up with tangible strategies to support one another around feeding, such as Genevieve's father preparing the meals while her mother supervises Genevieve and her mother supervising meals while her father takes care of Genevieve's younger brother. The therapist also reminded the parents that while their daughter is struggling with AN, she is still the same daughter, the one they have been able to feed since she was born; they have the skills and the knowledge necessary to help her but may need to put more structure in place to support the refeeding process.

Minimizing Parental Criticism and Expressed Emotion

Parental criticism towards the unwell adolescent, as measured by expressed emotion (EE), has been shown to negatively impact treatment outcomes when FBT is delivered in a conjoint format rather than a separated format (e.g., parent-focused therapy [PFT]) [14, 57, 61]. To address this issue, a recent RCT compared FBT-AN with PFT, a version of the same treatment that is delivered in a separated format [18]. In PFT, the adolescent is met by a nurse who weighs the patient at the beginning of the session, followed by brief supportive counselling (~10 minutes); the parents are seen on their own by the treating clinician, who devotes the full therapy hour to this meeting. In this study, comparing conjoint FBT to PFT ($N = 107$),

remission rates were higher in PFT than in FBT (43 versus 22 per cent) at EOT. Specifically, rates of remission (i.e., weight restoration at or above 95 per cent of median body mass index *plus* an EDE global score within one standard deviation of community norms) were superior for PFT given a standard course of treatment. However, the treatment groups did not differ statistically at 6- or 12-month follow-up [18]. Taken together, these findings suggest that PFT, a separated format of FBT, can be efficacious in treating adolescents with AN. Further, PFT may be preferred for clinicians who are hesitant to work in a format that includes parents, other caregivers and siblings in addition to the patient. Most notably, though, and regardless of remission rates, reduction in criticism was significantly more likely to occur within the context of PFT compared with FBT.

Following early EE studies [14, 61] that alluded to the possibility that a separated format of FBT is more apt at reducing levels of parental criticism than the conjoint format, Allan et al. [57] showed that compared to conjoint FBT, PFT was associated with a decrease in maternal criticism regardless of adolescent remission. Further, increased maternal criticism was more likely to be observed in conjoint FBT than PFT ($p = .001$), and adolescents of mothers who demonstrated increased EE or remained high in EE were less likely to remit compared with adolescents for whom EE decreased or remained low ($p = .03$); there were no significant effects for paternal EE. The clinical implications of these findings support allocating families with high levels of parental criticism to PFT rather than conjoint FBT. It remains unclear, though, why conjoint FBT seems less effective in supporting high EE families.

How best to help families who are quite critical of their offspring when they have an ED remains a significant challenge. The following brief vignette will attempt to demonstrate some key interventions in this domain.

Case Vignette

Aiden is a 13-year-old boy with a diagnosis of atypical AN. The family has been successful at promoting weight gain, although Aiden is still in phase 1 of FBT with parents supervising all meals and snacks. However, his parents still report that Aiden is acting in a way that they feel is disrespectful, rude and inappropriate, particularly around meals. He has been increasingly mean to his younger sister, especially before and after mealtimes, and has been yelling at his parents, a behaviour he did not exhibit prior to the eating disorder. For instance, he now will often tell his parents that he hates them and that they do not understand him. His parents report that they will engage with Aiden in these situations and that the family is getting into explosive arguments most nights of the week. While they recognize that his nutrition is going well, his other behaviours around eating and interactions with the family are very distressing to his parents and sister. The parents report, in a critical tone, that Aiden needs to pull himself together and show some resolve.

Crucial to helping parents distinguish or separate their child from the ED is to externalize the illness or to separate the ED from the healthy teen. If the parents can make this distinction, it becomes easier for them not to attribute illness behaviours to their son but to the ED instead. This is a delicate intervention on the part of the therapist, as she has to 'match' this intervention with the parents' level of anxiety. Metaphors or analogies can vary from describing the illness as being like an alien – scary – and has overtaken your child (for the parents who show little or no anxiety about the impact of the eating disorder) to equating it with cancer when parents show appropriate levels of concern about the impact of the illness. Finally, the Venn diagram analogy can be used with parents who are 'too' anxious and requires containment via a more academic discussion to understand the difference between their child and the eating disorder. Aiden's parents probably fell into this last group of very anxious parents and in this instance perhaps managed their own anxieties by being critical, particularly of their son.

In session, the therapist shared a discussion of Venn diagrams, explaining to Aiden's parents by gesturing with her hands that 'here we have your healthy son, before the ED came along' and encouraging the parents to elaborate on how Aiden used to behave in the absence of the ED. With her other hand, the therapist makes another diagram, and explains to the parents how the ED has moved towards the healthy Aiden, and like a solar eclipse, the ED has now moved in front of their child, and it is difficult to determine 'who is who'. If the parents are able to keep this separation in their minds, that is, the healthy Aiden on the one hand and the ED on the other, they might be better able to appreciate that many of the uncharacteristic behaviours they now observe,

both ED- and non-ED-related, are probably manifestations of the ED rather than of their son. In addition, the therapist highlights that most of these behaviours started when the ED did and worsen around mealtimes. She encourages the parents to name what healthy parts of their son are still present; they identify that he still enjoys watching movies and playing games with his family, spending time with their pets and going fishing with his dad. The therapist encourages parents to recognize the uncharacteristic behaviours as the ED and asks them to come up with ways to respond to Aiden in these moments that are not reactive or critical towards him but towards the illness. Finally, the therapist also encourages the parents to recognize that, for Aiden, having them currently involved in every aspect of his life may be challenging for him and also for themselves but that this level of involvement is temporary until the ED begins to recede and finally dissipates completely.

Counteracting Obsessive-Compulsive Features of an Eating Disorder

When young people with AN present with elevated obsessive-compulsive features or severity in perseverative ED cognitions, FBT is particularly superior to AFT in achieving weight restoration [46]. This seems to make clinical sense in that the behavioural and parent-oriented approach of FBT might better equip parents to address significant levels of psychopathology presenting in their child compared to individual psychotherapy such as AFT, where the onus largely falls on the adolescent to contain elevated levels of obsessive-compulsive behaviours and thoughts. Along the same lines, and turning to the earlier FBT dose study [62], adolescents with elevated levels of ED-related obsessive-compulsive features required a longer course of FBT (i.e., 20 sessions over 12 months rather than 10 sessions over 6 months). Correspondingly, recent preliminary work suggests that cognitive-remediation therapy is feasible and acceptable to adolescents with AN and could minimize the effects of cognitive inflexibility on treatment outcome [63]. In this study, adolescents with AN ($N = 30$) who also reported perseverative thinking were randomized to FBT-AN plus cognitive remediation or manualized FBT plus art therapy. Results indicated that both groups gained weight and showed improvements in global eating pathology, and as such, it remains unclear whether adding a targeted therapy to FBT aimed at perseverative thinking warrants further study.

Treatment adaptations that have targeted moderators of negative treatment outcome show promise in improving specialty treatment efforts in certain identified populations. Continued study of trans-diagnostic predictors of response to FBT, along with factors that moderate the effects of treatment on outcome, is critical to the development of more precise and tailored treatment. These research efforts are particularly needed in adequately powered trials of treatment for BN, where moderators of outcome have been less studied.

Self-starvation is often 'surrounded' by ED-related (and non-ED-related) obsessions and compulsions such as 'needing' to hide food from parents, engaging in extensive smearing of food on dinner plates or cutting food into several pieces (but not eating), to name but a few. Parents are often at a loss as to how best to intervene when these behaviours are exhibited, and the brief case vignette that follows aims to demonstrate one or two key clinical strategies.

Case Vignette

Lucille is a 14-year-old girl with AN who has been engaged in FBT for two months. While her weight gain is slow, her weight is steadily increasing, but she still engages in many ED rituals, such as smearing food on the plate, cutting it into small bites, eating in a specific order and, occasionally, hiding food in her pockets or feeding it to the family dog under the table. She is completing most of her nutrition orally and will supplement with a nutritional shake if she does not finish her meals but will only complete a meal if she can 'use' ED behaviours during meals. These rituals cause considerable distress for her parents and two younger siblings.

The parents raise concerns about these behaviours during a session with their FBT therapist and ask for specific strategies to help manage these behaviours. The therapist commends them on recognizing that despite their daughter's weight gain and completion of meals and snacks, these behaviours are still indicative of the ED being present. In the session, the therapist encourages the parents to come up with strategies they can use in the moment to disrupt these behaviours when they see them occur. After a while of encouraged back-and-forth between the parents, they came up with specific ideas for either redirecting Lucille's ED behaviours and/or distracting

her (e.g., with games or music) at the table during mealtimes. The therapist also asks what the parents may be able to do before meals to interrupt these behaviours, and the parents agree to pre-cut Lucille's food and not provide her with a knife to continue doing it herself. They also came up with a suggestion to put limits in place around what Lucille can wear, for example, no garment with large, loose pockets at the table, so that she does not have a place to hide her food. The parents also decided to keep the family dog in the other room during meals to eliminate any opportunity to pass the food on to the family pet.

Core Competencies in Delivering FBT

There are several key tenets that set FBT apart from other ED treatment approaches. One of these tenets is the very pragmatic, unwavering initial focus on symptom reduction (and weight restoration). In an effort to reduce long-term damage secondary to malnutrition, the therapist must encourage parents to interrupt patterns of restriction and other ED symptoms. In so doing, the therapist works to increase parental empowerment, considered another key tenet that directly relates to parental self-efficacy [60]. Parents are entrusted with taking charge of the recovery process, and the therapist communicates that he or she has confidence in their ability to beat the ED. There is an accompanying non-authoritarian role that the therapist assumes. With this tenet, the therapist takes an active role in guiding the family through the recovery process. The therapist does not tell the parents how to help their child recover and instead joins the family in helping them to problem-solve the best ways to re-feed their unwell child. Therapists might remind parents that they have historically been able to provide appropriate discipline for their child, outside of the ED, and also emphasize that parents retain expert knowledge of their child. Accordingly, parents can be encouraged to use a particular reward (e.g., allowing their child to participate in a favoured activity) following a meal that will increase the likelihood of meal completion or to provide firm feedback in a consistent and warm manner that will assist in extinguishing problematic behaviour (e.g., letting the young person know that hiding food during a meal will not be tolerated).

Along with the above-mentioned tenets, there are, at minimum, two key components of FBT that have been identified as most predictive of therapeutic outcomes: agnosticism and externalization [64].

Agnosticism can be defined as an approach whereby a clinician encourages the patient and family to join in a stance that refuses to take on the question of aetiology or cause of the ED. This perspective may be particularly challenging to adopt not only for caregivers but also for mental health providers for whom a professional focus has been based on questions of causation or aetiology. Adherence to an agnostic stance is antithetical to any guilt or blame parents may experience related to the origin of the ED. Parents frequently need to be reminded, particularly at the start of treatment, that they are not the reason that their child became ill. It is also helpful to redirect parents to spend less time dwelling on *why* the ED began and to instead shift energy to thinking about how to arrest the ED in its process. Working together with an agnostic stance can therefore interrupt inaction that derives from guilt and instead facilitate parental self-efficacy; as mentioned earlier, caretaker self-efficacy may be critical in bringing about early weight gain in the context of treatment [60].

Externalization is another key assumption in FBT, and compared with agnosticism, it is perhaps an easier intervention and may not require a high degree of clinical subtlety to be most effective. It can be referred to as separating the illness from the adolescent and allows parents to distinguish normal developmental autonomy (i.e., asserting independence) from ED cognitions and behaviours. For the therapist, this may mean reflecting what a parent says regarding their child's behaviour in a way that distinguishes the young person from the disorder. For example, when a parent might say something like 'He just refused to eat', the therapist might respond with something to the effect of, 'It sounds like the ED was really in control there, not allowing your son to do what the healthy side of him wanted'. Depending on the family, the therapist may help the young person and parents to name the ED or to clarify its external identity (e.g., 'that evil thing that possesses me'). In so doing, the parents can fight the illness without fear of harming normal development, and this also serves to reduce blame on the adolescent. Taken together, these identified functions of externalization may also help to reduce parental criticism [46]. Related to all these core tenets, problems associated with the ED that can include depressed mood, anxiety and irritability are not addressed directly in the first phase of FBT. Many of these secondary issues will resolve with the return

of appropriate nutrition and physical health. Further, with its known impact on treatment outcomes, it is essential that the clinician ensures that the focus for the family at the beginning stages of treatment remains on weight restoration.

Future Directions

Systematic review of AN treatment among youth and adult samples indicates that specialty treatments such as FBT are more adept than comparator interventions at achieving weight-based improvement at EOT; however, the same review demonstrated that psychological symptoms relief do not follow a commensurate course [65]. Within FBT for adolescents specifically, weight restoration is an explicit focus; based on evidence that early weight gain in the context of treatment is critical (e.g., [20, 55]), future study of FBT adaptations that increase early weight gain may improve indices of weight restoration at follow-up. To address the latency of psychological symptoms in the context of recovery, improving the implementation of FBT across specific populations for whom standard FBT is less effective may greatly improve treatment response.

Despite mounting empirical evidence that contributes to clinically useful inferences, few RCTs to date have reported potential moderators of outcome in adolescent ED treatment, and even fewer have identified treatment mediators [13, 18, 46, 59, 66], As such, the resulting sparse evidence base has precluded the development of an overarching theoretical framework accounting for the interaction of moderating and mediating variables in the treatment of adolescent EDs. There can be little question as to the ongoing need for greater investigation in this realm.

Another primary aim in improving care for a greater number of adolescents with EDs is increasing the dissemination capacity of empirically based specialty treatments, including FBT. Because there are a limited number of trained providers outside the specific sites where FBT was developed, and even less specialty care outside of urban environs [67], increasing access to FBT training through web-based education and supervision is a priority area of development. Further, while preliminary effectiveness for the delivery of FBT via telehealth [40, 41] and a parental guided self-help treatment format [68] has been established, remote delivery methods require examination across larger, adequately powered trials.

Summary and Conclusions

The last decade has witnessed considerable advances in the development of FBT for adolescent AN, with a more recent, notable initiation in the study of FBT for BN. Taken together, there is a robust body of evidence supporting the efficacy for the treatment of this patient population with a family-based focus. Further investigation is necessary to determine for whom and under what conditions certain types of family involvement might be most effective. Specifically, research efforts ought to develop and test augmentations to treatments oriented towards adolescents with EDs in light of both (1) moderating factors which may identify conditions under which treatment may be less effective and (2) mediating processes which may undermine components of treatment. Finally, the dissemination of specialty treatments for ED such as FBT (i.e., via improved competency training and remote treatment delivery) is crucial to the advancement of mental health care for adolescents.

Acknowledgements

Dr. Gorrell has not commercial relationships to disclose; she is supported by the National Institutes of Health (T32 Grant MH0118261-33). Dr. Le Grange receives royalties from Guilford Press and Routledge and is co-director of the Training Institute for Child and Adolescent Eating Disorders, LLC.

References

1. Steinhausen HC. The outcome of anorexia nervosa in the 20th century. *American Journal of Psychiatry* 2002; **159**(8):1284–93.

2. Schaumberg K, Welch E, Breithaupt L, et al. The science behind the Academy for Eating Disorders' nine truths about eating disorders. *European Eating Disorders Review* 2017; **25**(6):432–50.

3. Swanson SA, Crow SJ, Le Grange D, et al. Prevalence and correlates of eating disorders in adolescents: Results from the national comorbidity survey replication adolescent supplement. *Archives of General Psychiatry* 2011; **68**(7):714–23.

4. Crow S, Eisenberg ME, Story M, Neumark-Sztainer D. Suicidal behavior in adolescents: Relationship to weight status, weight control behaviors, and body dissatisfaction. *International Journal of Eating Disorders* 2008; **41**(1):82–7.

5. Pisetsky EM, Thornton LM, Lichtenstein P, et al. Suicide attempts in women with eating disorders. *Journal of Abnormal Psychology* 2013; **122**(4):1042–56.

6. Agras WS. The consequences and costs of the eating disorders. *Psychiatric Clinics of North America* 2001; **24**(2):371–9.

7. Anastasiadou D, Medina-Pradas C, Sepulveda AR, Treasure J. A systematic review of family caregiving in eating disorders. *Eating Behaviors* 2014; **15** (3):464–77.

8. Kohn M, Golden NH. Eating disorders in children and adolescents. *Paediatric Drugs* 2001; **3**(2):91–9.

9. Smink FR, Van Hoeken D, Hoek HW. Epidemiology of eating disorders: incidence, prevalence and mortality rates. *Current Psychiatry Reports* 2012; **14**(4):406–14.

10. Treasure J, Russell G. The case for early intervention in anorexia nervosa: Theoretical exploration of maintaining factors. *British Journal of Psychiatry* 2011; **199**(1):5–7.

11. Eisler I. The empirical and theoretical base of family therapy and multiple family day therapy for adolescent anorexia nervosa. *Journal of Family Therapy* 2005; **27**(2):104–31.

12. Lock J, Le Grange D. Family-based treatment: Where are we and where should we be going to improve recovery in child and adolescent eating disorders. *International Journal of Eating Disorders* 2018; **52**:481–7.

13. Agras WS, Lock J, Brandt H, et al. Comparison of two family therapies for adolescent anorexia nervosa: A randomized parallel trial. *JAMA Psychiatry* 2014; **71** (11):1279–86.

14. Eisler I, Dare C, Hodes M, et al. Family therapy for adolescent anorexia nervosa: The results of a controlled comparison of two family interventions. *Journal of Child Psychology and Psychiatry and Allied Disciplines* 2000; **41**(6):727–36.

15. Eisler I, Simic M, Hodsoll J, et al. A pragmatic randomised multi-centre trial of multifamily and single family therapy for adolescent anorexia nervosa. *BMC Psychiatry* 2016; **16**(1):422.

16. Le Grange D, Crosby RD, Rathouz PJ, Leventhal BL. A randomized controlled comparison of family-based treatment and supportive psychotherapy for adolescent bulimia nervosa. *Archives of General Psychiatry* 2007; **64**(9):1049–56.

17. Le Grange D, Lock J, Agras WS, et al. Randomized clinical trial of family-based treatment and cognitive-behavioral therapy for adolescent bulimia nervosa. *Journal of the American Academy of Child and Adolescent Psychiatry* 2015; **54**(11):886–94.

18. Le Grange D, Hughes EK, Court A, et al. Randomized clinical trial of parent-focused treatment and family-based treatment for adolescent anorexia nervosa. *Journal of the American Academy of Child and Adolescent Psychiatry* 2016; **55**(8):683–92.

19. Lock J, Le Grange D, Agras WS, et al. Randomized clinical trial comparing family-based treatment with adolescent-focused individual therapy for adolescents with anorexia nervosa. *Archives of General Psychiatry* 2010; **67**(10):1025–32.

20. Madden S, Miskovic-Wheatley J, Wallis A, et al. Early weight gain in family-based treatment predicts greater weight gain and remission at the end of treatment and remission at 12-month follow-up in adolescent anorexia nervosa. *International Journal of Eating Disorders* 2015; **48**(7):919–22.

21. Schmidt U, Treasure J. Anorexia nervosa: Valued and visible. A cognitive-interpersonal maintenance model and its implications for research and practice. *British Journal of Clinical Psychology* 2006; **45**(3):343–66.

22. National Institute for Health and Care Excellence. *Eating Disorders: Recognition and Treatment* (NICE Guideline No. NH69), 2017. Available at www .nice.org.uk/guidance/ng69.

23. Le Grange D, Eisler I. Family interventions in adolescent anorexia nervosa. *Child and Adolescent Psychiatric Clinics of North America* 2009; **18** (1):159–73.

24. Le Grange D, Lock J, Loeb K, Nicholls D. Academy for eating disorders position paper: The role of the family in eating disorders. *International Journal of Eating Disorders* 2010; **43**(1):1–5.

25. Le Grange D, Lock J. *Treating Bulimia in Adolescents: A Family-Based Approach*. New York: Guilford Press, 2009.

26. Lock J, Le Grange D. *Treatment Manual for Anorexia Nervosa: A Family-Based Approach*. New York: Guilford Press, 2015.

27. Westmoreland P, Krantz MJ, Mehler PS. Medical complications of anorexia nervosa and bulimia. *American Journal of Medicine* 2016; **129**(1):30–7.

28. Le Grange D, Lock J. The dearth of psychological treatment studies for anorexia nervosa. *International Journal of Eating Disorders* 2005; **37**(2):79–91.

29. Russell GF, Szmukler GI, Dare C, Eisler I. An evaluation of family therapy in anorexia nervosa and bulimia nervosa. *Archives of General Psychiatry* 1987; **44**(12):1047–56.

30. Couturier J, Kimber M, Szatmari P. Efficacy of family-based treatment for adolescents with eating disorders: A systematic review and meta-analysis. *International Journal of Eating Disorders* 2013; **46**(1):3–11.

31. Ellison R, Rhodes P, Madden S, et al. Do the components of manualized family-based treatment for anorexia nervosa predict weight gain?. *International Journal of Eating Disorders* 2012; **45** (4):609–14.

32. Loeb KL, Walsh BT, Lock J, et al. Open trial of family-based treatment for full and partial anorexia nervosa in adolescence: Evidence of successful dissemination. *Journal of the American Academy of Child and Adolescent Psychiatry* 2007; **46** (7):792–800.

33. Le Grange D, Binford R, Loeb KL. Manualized family-based treatment for anorexia nervosa: A case series. *Journal of the American Academy of Child and Adolescent Psychiatry* 2005; **44**(1):41–6.

34. Fairburn CG, Cooper I. The eating disorder examination. In: Fairburn CG, Wilson GT (eds.), *Binge Eating: Nature, Assessment, and Treatment*,12th ed. New York: Guilford Press, 1993.

35. Lock J. Adjusting cognitive behavior therapy for adolescents with bulimia nervosa: Results of case series. *American Journal of Psychotherapy* 2005; **59** (3):267–81.

36. Fisher CA, Hetrick SE, Rushford N. Family therapy for anorexia nervosa. *Cochrane Database of Systematic Reviews* 2010(4).

37. Lock J, Le Grange D, Agras WS, et al. Can adaptive treatment improve outcomes in family-based therapy for adolescents with anorexia nervosa? Feasibility and treatment effects of a multi-site treatment study. *Behaviour Research and Therapy* 2015;**73**:90–5.

38. Le Grange D, Loeb KL, Van Orman S, Jellar CC. Bulimia nervosa in adolescents: A disorder in evolution?. *Archives of Pediatrics and Adolescent Medicine* 2004; **158**(5):478–82.

39. Schmidt U, Lee S, Beecham J, et al. A randomized, controlled trial of family therapy and cognitive behavior therapy guided self-care for adolescents with bulimia nervosa and related disorders. *American Journal of Psychiatry* 2007; **164**(4):591–8.

40. Anderson KE, Byrne C, Goodyear A, et al. Telemedicine of family-based treatment for adolescent anorexia nervosa: A protocol of a treatment development study. *Journal of Eating Disorders* 2015; **3**(1):25.

41. Anderson KE, Byrne CE, Crosby RD, Le Grange D. Utilizing telehealth to deliver family-based treatment for adolescent anorexia nervosa. *International Journal of Eating Disorders* 2017; **50**(10):1235–8.

42. Marzola E, Knatz S, Murray SB, et al. Short-term intensive family therapy for adolescent eating disorders: 30-month outcome. *European Eating Disorders Review* 2015; **23**(3):210–18.

43. Rockwell RE, Boutelle K, Trunko ME, et al. An innovative short-term, intensive, family-based treatment for adolescent anorexia nervosa: Case series. *European Eating Disorders Review* 2011; **19** (4):362–7.

44. Knatz S, Kaye W, Marzola E, Boutelle K. A brief, intensive application of family based treatment for eating disorders. In: *Family Therapy for Adolescent Eating and Weight Disorders: New Applications.* New York: Routledge, 2015; **27**:72–91.

45. Dare C, Eisler I. A multi-family group day treatment programme for adolescent eating disorder. *European Eating Disorders Review: The Professional Journal of the Eating Disorders Association* 2000; **8**(1):4–18.

46. Le Grange D, Lock J, Agras WS, et al. Moderators and mediators of remission in family-based treatment and adolescent focused therapy for anorexia nervosa. *Behaviour Research and Therapy* 2012; **50**(2), 85–92.

47. Chen EY, Weissman JA, Zeffiro TA, et al. Family-based therapy for young adults with anorexia nervosa restores weight. *International Journal of Eating Disorders* 2016; **49**(7):701–7.

48. Dimitropoulos G, Lock J, Le Grange D, Anderson K. Family therapy for transition youth. In: Loeb KL, Le Grange D, Lock J (eds.), *Family Therapy for Adolescent Eating and Weight Disorders: New Applications.* New York: Routledge/Taylor & Francis Group, 2015, pp. 230–55.

49. Dimitropoulos G, Landers AL, Freeman V, et al. Open trial of family-based treatment of anorexia nervosa for transition age youth. *Journal of the Canadian Academy of Child and Adolescent Psychiatry.* 2018 Jan;**27**(1):50.

50. Loeb KL, Le Grange D, Lock J, editors. Family therapy for adolescent eating and weight disorders: new applications. Routledge; 2015 Mar 27.

51. Loeb K, Le Grange D, Celio Doyle A, et al. Adapting family-based treatment for pediatric obesity: A randomized, controlled pilot trial. *European Eating Disorders Review* 2019; **27**(5):521–30.

52. Stiles-Shields C, Doyle AC, Le Grange D, Loeb KL. Family-based treatment for pediatric obesity: Case study of an adaptation for a non-psychiatric adolescent population. *Journal of Contemporary Psychotherapy* 2018; **49**(2):111–18.

53. Loeb KL, Celio Doyle A, Anderson K, et al. Family-based treatment for child and adolescent overweight and obesity: A transdevelopmental approach. In: Loeb KL, Le Grange D, Lock J (eds.), *Family Therapy for Adolescent Eating and Weight Disorders: New Applications.* New York: Routledge, 2015. pp. 177–229.

54. Fitzpatrick KK, Forsberg SE, Colborn D. Family-based therapy for avoidant restrictive food intake disorder: Families facing food neophobias. In: Loeb KL, Le Grange D, Lock J (eds.), *Family Therapy for Adolescent Eating and Weight Disorders: New Applications.* New York: Routledge, 2015, pp. 256–76.

55. Hughes EK, Sawyer SM, Accurso EC, et al. Predictors of early response in conjoint and separated models of family-based treatment for adolescent anorexia nervosa. *European Eating Disorders Review* 2019; **27**(3):283–94.

56. Le Grange D, Accurso EC, Lock J, et al. Early weight gain predicts outcome in two treatments for adolescent anorexia nervosa. *International Journal of Eating Disorders* 2014; **47**(2):124–9.

57. Allan E, Le Grange D, Sawyer SM, et al. Parental expressed emotion during two forms of family-based treatment for adolescent anorexia nervosa. *European Eating Disorders Review* 2018; **26**(1):46–52.

58. Doyle PM, Le Grange D, Loeb K, et al. Early response to family-based treatment for adolescent anorexia nervosa. *International Journal of Eating Disorders* 2010; **43**(7):659–62.

59. Lock J, Couturier J, Bryson S, Agras S. Predictors of dropout and remission in family therapy for adolescent anorexia nervosa in a randomized clinical trial. *International Journal of Eating Disorders* 2006; **39**(8):639–47.

60. Byrne CE, Accurso EC, Arnow KD, et al. An exploratory examination of patient and parental self-efficacy as predictors of weight gain in adolescents with anorexia nervosa. *International Journal of Eating Disorders* 2015; **48**(7):883–8.

61. Le Grange D, Eisler I, Dare C, Hodes M. Family criticism and self-starvation: A study of expressed emotion. *Journal of Family Therapy* 1992; **14**(2), 177–92.

62. Lock J, Agras WS, Bryson S, Kraemer HC. A comparison of short- and long-term family therapy for adolescent anorexia nervosa. *Journal of the American Academy of Child and Adolescent Psychiatry* 2005; **44**(7):632–9.

63. Lock J, Fitzpatrick KK, Agras WS, et al. Feasibility study combining art therapy or cognitive remediation therapy with family-based treatment for adolescent anorexia nervosa. *European Eating Disorders Review* 2018; **26**(1):62–8.

64. Forsberg S, Fitzpatrick KK, Darcy A, et al. Development and evaluation of a treatment fidelity instrument for family-based treatment of adolescent anorexia nervosa. *International Journal of Eating Disorders* 2015; **48**(1):91–9.

65. Murray SB, Quintana DS, Loeb KL, et al. Treatment outcomes for anorexia nervosa: A systematic review and meta-analysis of randomized controlled trials. *Psychological Medicine* 2019; **49**(4):535–44.

66. Le Grange D, Crosby RD, Lock J. Predictors and moderators of outcome in family-based treatment for adolescent bulimia nervosa. *Journal of the American*

Academy of Child and Adolescent Psychiatry 2008; **47**(4):464–70.

67. Murray SB, Le Grange D. Family therapy for adolescent eating disorders: An update. *Current Psychiatry Reports* 2014; **16**(5):447–553.

68. Lock J, Darcy A, Fitzpatrick KK, et al. Parental guided self-help family based treatment for adolescents with anorexia nervosa: A feasibility study. *International Journal of Eating Disorders* 2017; **50**(9):1104–8.

Sleep Problems

Gabrielle Rigney, Elizabeth Keys, Michelle Johnson,
Jocelyn Paul and Penny Corkum

Sleep is essential for health and wellbeing and plays an important role in development for children and adolescents. Sleep problems are common throughout development, with up to a third of children and two-thirds of adolescents experiencing sleep problems [1]. The most common sleep problems are behavioural in nature, and include difficulties falling asleep, staying asleep and early morning awakenings. This grouping of symptoms, when clinical levels are reached, is known as *insomnia*. We will refer to insomnia/symptoms of insomnia as behaviourally based sleep problems throughout this chapter. Inadequate sleep for both children and adolescents can have deleterious effects on mental health and cognitive functioning (including attention, memory, executive functioning and school performance) and is associated

with increased risk for behavioural problems and physical health problems such as obesity [2, 3]. Sleep problems experienced during childhood and adolescence are important to consider from a family context both in regards to the impact poor sleep in a child or adolescent can have on the rest of the family and in considering the influence the family environment can have on the sleep behaviour of the child or adolescent [4].

It is important to be aware that there is a spectrum from sleep problems through to diagnosed sleep disorders. The *International Classification of Sleep Disorders* (ICSD-3), which was published in 2014, classifies seven major categories of sleep disorders. Please refer to Table 15.1 for a summary description of the classified sleep disorders. This chapter focuses primarily on

Table 15.1 Examples of Sleep Disorders in Children

Sleep Disorder Grouping	Description	Examples
Insomnia disorders	Include a frequent and persistent difficulty initiating or maintain sleep	• Limit-setting disorder • Sleep-association disorder
Sleep-related breathing disorders	Characterized by abnormalities of respiration during sleep (In some of these disorders, respiration is also abnormal during wakefulness.)	• Obstructive sleep apnoea • Central sleep apnoea
Central disorders of hyper-somnolence	The primary complaint in these disorders is daytime sleepiness not caused by disturbed nocturnal sleep.	• Narcolepsy type 1 • Narcolepsy type 2 • Klein-Levin syndrome • Idiopathic hyper-somnolence
Circadian rhythm sleep-wake disorders	Alterations of the circadian time-keeping system, its entrainment mechanisms or a misalignment of the endogenous circadian rhythm and the external environment	• Delayed sleep phase • Advanced sleep phase
Sleep-related movement disorders	Primarily characterized by relatively simple, usually stereotyped movements that disturb sleep or its onset	• Rhythmic movement disorder • Restless leg syndrome • Periodic limb movements in sleep
Parasomnias	Undesirable physical events or experiences that occur during entry into sleep, within sleep or during arousal from sleep	• Nightmares • Sleep terrors • Somnambulism (sleep walking) • Confusional arousals • Somniloquy (sleep talking)

behaviourally based sleep problems, which include insomnia disorder at the extreme end of the spectrum. Insomnia, the most common sleep disorder across the lifespan, is defined as *frequent and chronic* difficulties with falling asleep, staying asleep and early-morning awakenings that *interfere with daily functioning*. Prevalence rates for children and adolescents who have been diagnosed with insomnia disorder are lower than those described as having behaviourally based sleep problems, varying between 9 and 23 per cent [1]. However, many youth experience insomnia symptoms but do not meet full diagnostic criteria for this disorder. While many sleep disorders should be treated by qualified sleep specialists, insomnia and symptoms of insomnia are often treatable by frontline generalist health-care providers with appropriate training.

What Is Sleep and How Is It Regulated?

Sleep is defined as a reversible state of perceptual disengagement from, and unresponsiveness to, the environment [5]. There are two broad states of sleep, known as *rapid eye movement* (REM) and *non–rapid eye movement* (NREM) sleep. REM sleep is associated with the occurrence of story-like dreams, where the brain is highly activated, but the individual experiences muscle atonia and therefore is unable to move most muscles [5]. NREM sleep is divided into three stages (N1–N3) progressing from light sleep (N1) through to deep slow-wave sleep (N3). REM and NREM states cycle throughout a sleep period, with NREM most prominent in sleep cycles that occur earlier in the period, and REM sleep progressively lengthens with each sleep cycle. There are natural brief arousals at the end of each sleep cycle, of which the individual is often not aware [5]. While the exact functions of sleep are not entirely known, both REM and NREM sleep are critical for the restoration of physiological and mental functions [6].

Regulation of sleep involves two physiological processes that work together to ensure optimal alertness during wake periods, and these processes play an important role in the timing, intensity and duration of sleep. These two processes are known as the *circadian system* and the *homeostatic sleep drive* [7]. The circadian system is more commonly known as the *body clock*, which is determined by the endogenous circadian pacemaker located in the brain, and this helps to regulate daily rhythms to an approximate 24-hour

cycle [8]. The circadian process promotes sleep at night and alertness during the day. The homeostatic sleep drive (*sleep pressure*) works with the circadian system; it progressively builds during periods of wakefulness and then decreases throughout a sleep period [7]. Regulation of sleep differs in children and adolescents compared to adults. For example, the circadian system does not stabilize until an infant is approximately six months old and then undergoes changes again during puberty. The build-up of sleep pressure is greater in infants and children, as evidenced by increased napping behaviour and greater sleep durations [9]. These developmental changes will be explained in more detail later in this chapter.

Sleep Assessment Overview

The assessment process will vary depending on the health-care provider's access to measures, as well as the individual's presenting symptoms (for a more detailed overview of assessment, see Table 15.2). Physiological sleep problems (e.g., sleep apnoea) often require measurement of physiological functions (e.g., respiration), whereas behaviourally based sleep problems (e.g., insomnia) often require clinical assessment. Assessment of insomnia symptoms typically begins with an interview with the individual and/or their parent. Following that interview, further information is often gathered using subjective (e.g., sleep questionnaires, sleep diary) and/or objective measurement tools (e.g., actigraphy). Polysomnography is rarely required for the assessment of insomnia, unless there is a differential diagnosis of another physiologically based sleep disorder. Information obtained from subjective and objective measurement tools allow for improved diagnostic accuracy and assists in the development of a treatment plan.

Treatment Principles of Behaviourally Based Sleep Problems in Children

Theoretical Underpinnings. There are both cognitive and behavioural theoretical underpinnings that form the basis of interventions for treating behaviourally based sleep problems, and both are complementary to the success of treatment. The cognitive component addresses parent and/or the individual's cognitions regarding sleep needs, behaviours and responses. Cognitive factors can include level of knowledge and understanding, interpretation, expectations and emotions. Parental

Table 15.2 Description of Sleep Assessment Tools

Assessment Tool	Description
Interviews	Interviews help to guide the clinician's assessment and treatment planning. Parents are the primary informant for children, and it is recommended that they are included in the interview process for adolescents. The interview should explore issues related to both physical and mental health and aim to uncover specific sleep issues. The 4-P model should also be applied throughout the interview.
Questionnaires	Sleep questionnaires can be either parent report or self-report. There are a wide range of published sleep questionnaires to choose from. These include broadband sleep questionnaires, which cover various sleep disorder symptoms, and narrowband sleep questionnaires, which focus on one sleep disorder. Information obtained from sleep questionnaires can be enhanced when additional information is obtained from sleep diary and/or actigraphy data.
Sleep diary	A sleep diary is a subjective tool that allows the recording of information about sleep and wake times, night wakings, daytime naps and other variables of interest. Sleep diaries are typically completed daily for one week to one month in duration, using either parent or self-report.
Actigraphy	Actigraphy is a well-established objective method of assessing sleep patterns, which can be used in the home environment. An actigraph is a watch-like device that is generally worn on the non-dominant wrist for children and adolescents. It collects information about body movements throughout the night. However, actigraphy does not collect information about some aspects of sleep, such as sleep stages and symptoms related to sleep-disordered breathing.
Polysomnography	Polysomnography is classified as the 'gold standard' of objective measurement for sleep. It is an overnight test that monitors multiple body physiology. Electrodes are attached to various parts of the body to monitor brain waves, eye movements, muscle tone, breathing and leg movements. Polysomnography should not be used as a primary assessment tool for behaviourally based sleep problems.

interactions with their child are often based on their cognitive interpretation of their child's sleep behaviour. The cognitive perceptions parents hold towards the treatment for their child's behaviourally based sleep problems can cause strong emotive reactions (e.g., guilt, frustration), which can lead to difficulties in promoting positive changes in parenting behaviour surrounding sleep [10]. In older children and adolescents, the role of cognition is commonly linked with anxiety, resulting in longer time to fall asleep or night arousals [11].

Using a behavioural perspective, common childhood sleep problems, such as trouble settling to sleep and frequent night waking, are related to the association of parental bedtime involvement. The positive feedback children experience from bedtime interactions with parents can be rewarding and can lead to dependence on parents when it comes to sleep behaviours [10]. These associations are often treated using a form of extinction with which the parent is comfortable (see Table 15.3 for descriptions of different forms of extinction).

The combined form of treatment, cognitive behavioural therapy (CBT) is routinely used with adolescents [12]. CBT designed specifically for insomnia, known as *CBT-I*, typically involves weekly sessions with a trained clinician that focus on both cognitive and behavioural interventions used to treat insomnia [13]. Techniques such as cognitive restructuring, where adaptive thoughts substitute common faulty thoughts, as well as implementing relaxation strategies into the bedtime routine, are common components of CBT-I [14]. Recent reviews have demonstrated that CBT-I in school-aged children and adolescents is effective, but further research using the gold standard randomized, controlled trial (RCT) methodology is needed [1, 15].

The 4-P Model. The 4-P model, often used to create clinical case formulations, is helpful to clinicians to systematically classify biopsychosocial factors associated with an individual's sleep problem. Using this method, the clinician typically organizes relevant factors into four primary categories: (1) predisposing, (2) precipitating, (3) perpetuating and (4) protective factors, all of which are relevant to the assessment and treatment of insomnia.

Predisposing factors are relevant factors specific to the individual that likely increased their risk of developing their *current* sleep problem. Additionally, predisposing factors can also be factors that might increase the individual's risk of developing a *future* sleep problem. Examples of predisposing factors for insomnia include familial or hereditary factors, irritable affective temperament and an insecure

Table 15.3 Interventions for Behaviourally Based Sleep Problems

Intervention	Description
Extinction	*Unmodified extinction:* Infant is placed in bed while awake, left alone until asleep and night-wakings are ignored. Infant learns to self-soothe once realizing that night-time crying does not result in parental attention. *Extinction with parent presence:* Parent remains in room during extinction, acting as a reassurance for the child but providing little interaction. *Graduated extinction:* This involves ignoring negative behaviours (i.e., crying) for a given amount of time before checking on the child. The parent gradually increases the amount of time between crying and parental response. Parents provide reassurance through their presence for short durations and with minimal interaction.
Bedtime fading	Operates by delaying bedtime closer to the child's target bedtime. The goal of this treatment is for the child to develop a positive association between being in bed and falling asleep rapidly. Bedtimes can be gradually moved earlier to promote an easier transition to sleep during these earlier bedtimes.
Stimulus control	Making the bedroom/bed a discriminant stimulus for sleep by only using the bedroom/bed for sleep (not play, time-out, etc.)
Reward programmes	Reinforce healthy sleep practices, appropriate time in bed, etc.
Sleep scheduling	Scheduling regular, appropriate sleep and wake times that allow for an adequate sleep opportunity
Sleep restriction	Restrict time in bed to build sleep pressure and gradually lengthen time in bed as sleep efficiency improves. Contraindicated in youth with parasomnias, seizure disorders, obstructive sleep apnoea (OSA), mania
Relaxation training	Teach diaphragmatic (belly) breathing and progressive muscle relation to reduce arousal. Need to practise regularly before introducing at bedtime.

attachment style [16–18]. *Precipitating factors* are best understood as relevant stressful events in the individual's life that likely triggered their *current* sleep problem. Examples of precipitating factors for insomnia might include the use of electronics before bedtime or an inconsistent sleep-wake schedule [19–21].

Perpetuating factors often refer to factors that either sustained the individual's current sleep problem or were unanticipated negative outcomes of past efforts to manage the sleep problem. Examples of perpetuating factors might include poor mental health and persistent detrimental beliefs about sleep health [22, 23]. Finally, *protective factors* are person-specific resilience factors that increase the likelihood that the individual will achieve successful recovery from their sleep problem. Examples of protective factors for insomnia might include healthy sleep practices, parent-set bedtimes and a living environment with minimal interpersonal conflict [24, 25].

Stepwise Approach to Treatment. The stepwise (or staged) approach to treatment of behaviourally based sleep problems consists of four stages: (1) psycho-education, (2) implementation of healthy sleep practices, (3) specific behavioural interventions and (4) medication [26, 27]. Psycho-education is an important first step to treatment, as it allows parents to be educated about the biology of sleep, risk factors that can lead to problematic sleep and the

consequences of inadequate sleep. Although there is currently no evidence to support sleep education on its own as an effective treatment, it does allow for an increased level of motivation and understanding in the following treatment steps and, as such, is thought to be a foundation to treatment. The second stage of treatment is the implementation of healthy sleep practices (previously referred to as *sleep hygiene*). These consist of a range of recommendations for the individual to engage in behaviours that promote healthy sleep and to avoid behaviours that negatively impact sleep behaviour. These healthy sleep practices have been arranged into a mnemonic, the *ABCs of SLEEPING* [28, 29], which stands for *a*ge-appropriate *b*edtimes, wake times, and naps with *c*onsistency, *s*chedule and routines, *l*ocation, no *e*lectronics in the bedroom or before bed, *e*xercise and diet, *p*ositivity and relaxation, *i*ndependence when falling asleep, *n*eeds met during the day, with all of these equalling *g*reat sleep!

The third stage involves applying common psychological strategies within a sleep context. The strategies are based on the cognitive and behavioural theoretical underpinnings described earlier. Table 15.3 provides descriptions of some of the common interventions used to treat behaviourally based sleep problems in children and adolescents. The final stage in this treatment framework is the use of sleep-promoting medication. There is minimal research on the use, efficacy, appropriate dosage and side effects of medications used to treat paediatric behaviourally based sleep problems, and medication should be considered the last step in the treatment hierarchy and only used if the psychological treatments are not successful [30].

Sleep Across Developmental Stages

There are predictable developmental changes that occur in both the quantity and quality of sleep throughout the lifespan, and these changes are particularly evident from infancy through to adolescence. There are predictable developmental changes that occur in both the quantity and quality of sleep throughout the lifespan (Table 15.4). Sleep problems are persistent across child and adolescent development, with problems settling independently at night being common during early childhood and bedtime refusal increasing as children progress through to adolescence. Treatment interventions often vary depending on the age of the child. This next section will provide an overview of sleep behaviour, common sleep problems and recommended treatment strategies for early childhood, school-aged children and adolescents. The role of, and impact on, the family at each stage will also be considered.

Early Childhood. During early childhood (birth through five years of age), children experience one of the largest and most significant changes in their sleep patterns. In particular, sleep and wake behaviours in the first year of life (e.g., total sleep time, night waking, time to fall asleep, wake time and sleep quality) change dramatically [31]. Although specific reference

values vary based on sample size, sleep assessment method and country of report, the typical trend of rapid change in the first six months, followed by a continued but more gradual consolidation of sleep into the night-time period, is widespread for typically developing infants [31]. Both the quantity and quality of sleep during infancy, as well as increasing consolidation of sleep into the night-time hours, appear to positively influence memory, development of language and executive function [32]. Newborn infants may not have the capacity to independently transition to the sleep state; thus, infants may often rely on their parents or caregivers to assist with falling asleep. By three to four months of age, infants have an established circadian rhythm, which helps to shift their sleep patterns into the night-time periods. Parents and caregivers may consider their newborn's or younger infant's sleep to be problematic despite patterns and characteristics within typical parameters.

Sleep problems that present with co-morbid regulatory problems, such as feeding and settling difficulties, as well as sleep problems that persist throughout early childhood, are associated with significant increased psychosocial difficulties up to 10 years of age [33–35]. In children up to four years, there is some evidence that shorter sleep duration is linked to emotional regulation and cognitive development, and it also has been associated with increased obesity [36].

In infants younger than six months of age, sleep difficulties can be interconnected with feeding and settling difficulties [37], and clinicians should assess for difficulties across all three areas. As infants gain awareness of their environment (starting at about four months of age) and develop object permanence (the

Table 15.4 Sleep Duration Ranges by Developmental Stage

Developmental Stage	Recommended Total (24-Hour) Duration[a]	Observed Ranges
Newborn (0–3 months)	14–17 hours	Daytime: 3–6.5 hours Nocturnal: 7–10 hours [67]
Infant (4–11 months)	12–15 hours	Daytime: 1–4 hours Nocturnal: 8–12 hours [67]
Toddler (1–2 years)	11–14 hours	Daytime: 1–3 hours Nocturnal: 9–11.5 hours [101]
Preschool (3–5 years)	10–13 hours	Daytime: 1–3 hours Nocturnal: 9.5–13 hours [102]
School age (6–13 years)	9–11 hours	Daytime: — Nocturnal: 7–12 hours [31]
Adolescence (14–17 years)	8–10 hours	Daytime: — Nocturnal: 7–11 hours [31]

capacity to understand that entities exist without seeing them), they learn to associate certain behaviours and conditions with the process of falling asleep (*sleep associations*). This awareness may result in infants becoming more sensitive to the need for recreating sleep associations that occur on sleep onset. The development of motor and language skills, along with a sense of autonomy and independence, may lead to struggles to gain control and bedtime difficulties.

Continued reliance on parental assistance to fall and stay asleep is often associated with parental perception of problematic sleep during early childhood. Although night-time sleep consolidation typically increases throughout early childhood, with corresponding decreases in night-time awakenings, nocturnal wakefulness and daytime sleep duration, how and when parents respond to night waking can influence the development and perpetuation of early childhood sleep problems [38]. Parental beliefs about infant and child sleep [39–43] and tolerance of crying [44] often shape these parental sleep-related responses and behaviours. Maternal, but not paternal, circadian preference for evenings has been associated with shorter daytime sleep duration, longer sleep latency, later bedtime and parental perceived sleep problems in young children [45]. Paternal involvement and effective co-parenting are associated with improved sleep quality [46–48], as is high maternal emotional availability at bedtime [49–51]. Preschool children in families of racial and cultural minorities may have more irregular sleep habits and shorter night-time sleep duration [52].

Parents play a significant role in the development of children's sleep habits throughout early childhood. While parental education is thought to have positive effects on increasing infant sleep duration [53], interventions that specifically focus on the prevention of infant behaviourally based sleep problems have been assessed with mixed results [54–58]. For this developmental stage, implementing pre-sleep routines (which are part of implementing healthy sleep practices) can improve sleep [59–62] within as few as three days [63]. Psycho-education (i.e., anticipatory guidance on typical infant sleep and education about strategies to manage common sleep concerns) appeared to improve nocturnal sleep duration but not night waking in infants younger than one year of age [64]. Parental consistency in the application of intervention strategies seems to be an important aspect to

improving sleep [65]. Psycho-education and implementing healthy sleep practices (e.g., parental education, advice and support, implementation of bedtime routines) with behavioural sleep interventions (e.g., modified extinction to parental response at bedtime and awakenings, bedtime fading, scheduled awakenings and, in older toddlers and preschool children, the use of positive reinforcement such as charts and rewards) have also been shown to improve sleep-onset latency, the number of night wakings and night waking duration in children from birth to five years of age [12].

School-Aged Children. School age (or latency age) includes children from 5 to approximately 12 years or, more accurately, until the time of mid-puberty, which for girls can range from 10 to 12 years and for boys from 12 to 14 years. During this stage of development, peer relationships become increasingly important to the child, and the child seeks out more opportunities for social engagement with their peers (including increased use of social media). As the child moves through this stage, there are increasing academic demands and expectations for more independence. This developmental stage is also a time of increased anxiety, particularly social anxiety. The child starts to spend increasingly more of their time outside the home engaging in activities with their peers (e.g., socializing, extracurricular activities). These key developmental changes can lead to sleep problems that have the potential to result in insomnia. The child may prioritize time with their peers at the expense of getting a good night's sleep. They may use social media to communicate with peers into the late evening and also engage in extracurricular activities that can impact sleep duration (e.g., playing sports in the evening or early morning). Children may sacrifice sleep to complete homework, especially towards the end of this stage of development. Children in this stage of development may also worry at bedtime, especially about social relationships, often resulting in difficulties falling asleep [66].

It is recommended that latency-aged children sleep for 9–11 hours per night with no naps during the day [67, 68]. They should fall asleep within 20 minutes and not have regular night awakenings [69, 70]. This stage of development is thought to be the 'golden age of sleep' as the sleep regulation mechanisms are stable and fewer sleep problems are experienced compared to early childhood and adolescence. However, sleep problems do occur, and approximately 15 per cent of children this age meet criteria for insomnia [71, 72]. As children approach the end of this stage, sex differences begin to emerge, with girls sleeping a bit longer than boys, and circadian sleep phase preferences (i.e., lark or owl) become more evident [72–4].

Sleep problems can persist from earlier developmental stages or can arise during this development stage [75]. School-aged children with behaviourally based sleep problems experience a wide range of negative consequences, including more difficulties with the skills that they are meant to master during this developmental stage [76]. For example, school-aged children with sleep disorders are more likely to be experiencing social difficulties and academic underachievement. Sleep problems contribute to these challenges through sleep's negative impact on cognitive functioning (e.g., attention, memory) and emotional and behavioural regulation [77, 78]. Poor sleep has also been found to be a moderator between certain life stressors and outcomes. For example, children who live in chaotic home environments have poorer academic outcomes if they have sleep problems [79], and children who are victimized by their peers are more likely to experience internalizing psychopathology if they have sleep problems [80]. Children with sleep problems also experience more negative family relationships with bi-directional influences of family functioning on child sleep [81].

Unlike earlier stages of development, in which the parent is the sole implementer of sleep interventions for behavioural sleep problems, school-aged children play an increasingly active role in the intervention. At earlier ages, they may participate through selecting rewards and practising relaxation skills, whereas older school-aged children may benefit from learning cognitive strategies to counteract maladaptive beliefs about sleep difficulties. They may also be able to be involved in setting goals for their sleep and self-monitor their sleep. Most school-aged children still have active parental involvement in their sleep, which can help with the effectiveness of sleep interventions [13]. Teaching children about healthy sleep practices is important at this stage in order to prepare them for more independence with their sleep routine as they enter adolescence.

Adolescents. Adolescence is a critical time of life, as the child seeks greater independence from their family and begins their transition into adulthood. The 'perfect storm' is a common metaphor used to describe the sleep patterns of adolescents [5]. It is during this developmental stage that a range of biopsychosocial factors have been found to interact and result in reduced sleep quantity and quality. Psychosocial factors commonly encountered during the school-aged developmental period are often intensified during adolescence. These psychosocial factors include the importance of peer relationships, social media use and independence seeking [5], as well as increased academic demands and mental health concerns [82]. During adolescence, it is common for psychosocial factors to be prioritized above sleep, increasing the vulnerability of this age group. In addition, adolescents experience maturational changes to their internal, biological mechanisms that help to regulate sleep [5]. One major change is a phase delay to the circadian timing system, which shifts the timing of sleep to be later. Homeostatic sleep pressure also takes longer to rise during puberty. Both of these physiological changes result in the preference of adolescents to go to bed later, as they do not feel sleepy until later in the evening [5].

It is recommended that adolescents aged between 14 and 17 years obtain 8–10 hours of sleep each night [67, 68]. Of concern is that up to 30 per cent of adolescents are obtaining sleep durations that are *shorter* than the recommended guidelines across all days of the week [83]. The marked delay in sleep timing is particularly strong when sleep is not restricted by the school schedule (i.e., weekends and holidays). Particularly as children get older, the gap between school day (Sunday–Thursday) and non-school day (Friday and Saturday nights) sleep has been found to increase, with adolescents sleeping approximately one hour more on weekends compared to weekdays [83]. Poor sleep in adolescents has been linked to negative effects on daytime functioning, including psychological (e.g., increased rates of mental health disorders), learning (e.g., poorer grades) and physical (e.g., increased rates of metabolic disorders) effects, as well as an increase in risk-taking behaviour [84].

A number of protective factors for adolescent sleep were identified in a recent meta-analytic review [24]. These protective factors include the implementation of healthy sleep practices, having a parent-set bedtime, engaging in physical activity and school bodies considering the impact of early school start times on sleep behaviour and whether a delay in school start times for adolescents is possible [24]. This review also discussed risk factors, along with factors they found to be neither risky nor protective. The family environment was identified as a key risk factor, with a negative environment (e.g., high conflict, chaotic) resulting in short sleep durations and longer sleep-onset times [24]. Evening light and technology use were also listed as potential risk factors. Interestingly, both technology and substance use produced mixed meta-analytic findings regarding their impact on adolescent sleep. Important findings pertaining to technology use were that technological multitasking (i.e., using more than one device at a time) and engaging with interactive forms of technology (e.g., computer, phone, videogames) compared to passive devices (e.g., television) were associated with less sleep [24]. Continuing education regarding the implementation of healthy sleep practices is important for adolescents as a preventative measure so that they are able to make informed decisions about best practices for behaviours within their control that have an impact on their sleep behaviour.

Adolescence is characterized by an increased desire for independence, which needs to be taken into consideration when treating behaviourally based sleep problems in this population. As they progress through adolescence, individuals will begin to limit active parental involvement in their sleep behaviour, choosing to set their own sleep routine and sleep-wake schedule. Although the transitional process from paediatric to adult-oriented care has not been researched widely in relation to the treatment of behaviourally based sleep problems, it has for other health conditions and is applicable in the context of sleep. Throughout the transition process, health-care providers should aim to build trust and strengthen independence in adolescents through encouraging self-management and open communication from childhood, as well as assist in adjustment to changes in the parental role over time [85, 86]. A smooth transition process from paediatric to adult-oriented care will result in a more positive family environment, with lower conflict, which should result in healthier sleep patterns during this vulnerable time.

Role of the Therapist: Core Competencies Approach

The health-care provider has a pivotal role in the continuing care of children with various sleep problems. It is common for children to have regularly scheduled appointments with either a family practice physician or a paediatrician, and as a result, paediatric sleep problems are often discussed with frontline health-care providers. However, a recent review of the literature on sleep in paediatric primary care found that only 10–15 per cent of parents who have concerns about their child's sleep bring this to the attention of their health-care provider [87]. In addition, health-care providers expect that parents will bring any sleep problems to their attention, as opposed to routinely asking about children's sleep [87]. Research indicates that a key barrier to the assessment and treatment of paediatric behaviourally based sleep problems is that health-care providers have low to moderate knowledge in this area [88]. This is due to insufficient time being devoted to the assessment and treatment of paediatric sleep problems within the training curriculum for various health-care provider disciplines. For example, in the United States, only 389 of 175,000 (0.2 per cent) physicians are certified with a subspecialty in sleep [87].

In an effort to address the lack of paediatric sleep-related training in the education of various health-care professionals, Boerner, Coulombe and Corkum [89] employed the Delphi method (a popular research tool designed to achieve consensus on an issue by administering rounds of questionnaires to experts on the subject in question) to determine the core competencies required for health-care professionals providing services in non-sleep-specialist settings. Six core competency areas were identified as being necessary for health-care providers to provide support to parents of children with behaviourally based sleep problems and include the basics of sleep, causes of sleep problems, outcomes of inadequate sleep, assessment and screening, behavioural interventions and supporting parents throughout the insomnia intervention (each of these is described below in greater detail). It should be noted, however, that these specific competencies related to behaviour sleep problems must be used in combination with foundational competencies including generic therapeutic competencies, CBT and other theory-based competencies and specific evidence-based techniques [90].

The Basics of Sleep. Before health-care providers can begin to determine the causes, impacts and specific treatment plan for families of children presenting with behavioural sleep problems, they must first acquire a general understanding of the basics of sleep. These key building blocks of sleep-knowledge include an understanding of sleep across development, sleep needs and concerns in special populations and normal sleep physiology, including knowledge pertaining to sleep stages and cycles, sleep-wake regulation, circadian rhythms and homeostatic processes. Furthermore, an understanding of cultural influences on sleep is vital for creating and implementing effective behavioural sleep interventions specific to the family in need.

Causes of Sleep Problems. In order to provide effective treatment, it is also important for health-care providers to understand what causes behaviourally based sleep problems. Behaviourally based sleep problems can have behavioural, cognitive or emotional causes stemming from either the parent or child, environmental causes (including light, activity, noise, temperature or even bedding) or physiological causes, such as the effects of the child's diet or medications.

Outcomes of Inadequate Sleep. To effectively manage behaviourally based sleep problems, health-care providers must also understand the negative effects that sleep problems can have on both the child and the rest of the family. A lack of sleep can result in problems with behaviour, cognition and affect regulation (e.g., school, social, daytime sleepiness), along with issues pertaining to physical health (e.g., illness, obesity). Furthermore, insomnia can also have negative effects on parenting, parents' sleep and parents' daytime functioning.

Assessment and Screening. Insomnia is both a symptom and a disorder [91], highlighting the importance of the clinician's ability to provide a differential diagnosis of insomnia from other related disorders and non-behavioural insomnia problems of sleep in paediatrics. Furthermore, in order to effectively diagnose and treat insomnia, clinicians must have knowledge of the many ways of measuring behaviourally based sleep problems, such as sleep diaries, screening tools and questionnaires, as well as possessing skills in clinical interview techniques to be used with both the child/adolescent and parents. Finally, it is the responsibility of health-care providers to know when to refer the individual to a sleep specialist.

Behavioural Interventions. To begin treatment, the clinician must have knowledge of various behavioural interventions, including healthy sleep practices, sleep-promoting routines and behaviours, age-appropriate wakefulness, general principles of behaviour change, sleep restriction and bedtime fading and extinction/graduated extinction or extinction with parental presence and an understanding of how to approach them with cultural competence and respect for diversity. They must also understand how cognitions and emotions relate to behavioural interventions.

Supporting Parents Throughout Insomnia Intervention. Finally, it is the clinician's responsibility to support parents throughout behavioural interventions. They must help parents set realistic and age-appropriate goals and expectations, help them to evaluate treatment progress and inform them about what to expect during the treatment process, as well as the common pitfalls of insomnia interventions.

Case Study

The following is a presentation of a case study that involves three children, Taylor aged 30 months, Johnny aged 10 years, and Kate aged 16 years, who are all the biological children of Anne and Rob. They live in a three-bedroom home in an inner-city neighbourhood, next to a busy highway. None of the children have any history of serious physical or mental health concerns; Rob has a history of generalized anxiety disorder. Since age three months, Taylor has been unable to fall asleep without being fed milk to fall asleep and has been waking up four to five times per night, requiring Anne's assistance to fall back asleep. Anne is worried that Taylor will follow in Johnny's footsteps, whose sleep can always be easily 'thrown off' by a cold, toothache or vacation, and he is now taking a long time to fall asleep. Johnny started playing competitive hockey this year, and his ice time is in the evening or early morning. Since then, he no longer wakes up on his own in the morning and resists getting up when his parents wake him. He seems tired and more irritable during the day. His school grades have declined, and his teachers report that he is not paying attention. Anne stated that her oldest child, Kate, seems to have also become increasingly tired and moodier, and she seems to have less patience with her younger siblings. Kate has found it increasingly challenging to wake up in the morning, and she has been late for school at least once a week for the past month. When Kate gets home from school, she often falls asleep on the couch for up to an hour. Anne notes that she often struggles with trouble sleeping and that she and Rob are both night owls and stay up until at least midnight. It is with these concerns that Anne and Rob present for assistance.

Assessment. The therapist collects further information using an interview. Kate sleeps in her own bedroom, whereas Taylor and Johnny share a room. Although Anne and Rob did not initially plan to bedshare and had not done so with their older children, Anne usually ends up bringing Taylor into her bed at some point in the night to prevent waking Johnny. Taylor's bedtime is usually 7:00 pm, but Taylor often does not fall asleep until 9:00 pm. Taylor wakes four to five times per night and has one 60-minute nap per day at day care during the week (no naps at home on the weekend). Johnny's usual bedtime is 8:30 pm, but on nights that he has hockey, it is closer to 10:00 pm. Anne and Rob had believed that Kate was attempting to sleep when she went into her bedroom at their agreed-upon bedtime (10:00 pm). However, they recently realized that when Kate was going into her bedroom, she was staying up until after midnight. Johnny and Kate both need to leave for school at 7:30 am, and Anne and Rob drop off Taylor at day care at 8:30 am on their way to work. On weekdays, everyone is up by 7:00 am. On weekends, the family usually tries to sleep in until at least 9:00 am, except for days when Johnny has an early-morning hockey practice at 6:00 am.

Taylor's bedtime routine consists of a bath, massage with lotion, diaper and pajama change, a story and then a lullaby while being nursed to sleep, before being slipped quietly into the crib. Anne is occasionally able to get Taylor to fall asleep without feeding, but this usually involves holding and/or walking. Johnny usually struggles to fall asleep after an evening

hockey practice and has started taking his iPad to bed to 'de-stress'. He watches YouTube videos, plays puzzle games and talks to friends. His parents have suggested that he read instead of playing on his iPad, but Johnny says that it's the only thing that helps him relax. Most nights after heading to her bedroom at 10:00 pm, Kate usually completes homework on her laptop, chats with friends via social media and text messages and has Netflix on her tablet device in the background.

To encourage healthier sleep behaviours, Anne and Rob have asked Kate and Johnny to leave electronic devices in the kitchen once it is bedtime, and they have been doing the same to set a good example. This has resulted in arguments and tension, as Kate believes that she is old enough to decide what time she should be going to sleep and has refused to remove electronic devices from her bedroom come bedtime. Johnny states that it is not fair that Kate gets to use electronics in her bedroom and not him. The therapist organizes this information according to the four P's (Figure 15.1).

Treatment. The therapist decided to provide a combination of psycho-education on sleep and sleep patterns, implementation of healthy sleep practices and specific behavioural interventions over a series of four sessions over 12 weeks.

Session 1. The therapist discussed basic elements of how sleep works with Anne, Rob, Kate and Johnny. This includes information on recommended and observed sleep durations, the development of sleep patterns (including how sleep consolidates in early

Figure 15.1 Assessment organized using the 4-P model

The 4-P Model

Predisposing Factors
- parental history of generalized anxiety disorder and insomnia (all children)
- circadian preference of parents (all children)
- loud and irregular traffic noise at night (all children)
- expected phase shift during adolescence (Kate)
- early school start time (Kate and Johnny)
- history of difficulty sleeping (Johnny)

Precipitating Factors
- inconsistent sleep-wake schedule from hockey (Johnny & Kate)
- electronics use in evening (Kate & Johnny)
- feeding-to-sleep association (Taylor)

Perpetuating Factors
- sleeping in on weekends (all children)
- fear of disrupting sleep even more, with shared bedroom (Taylor)
- disagreement about autonomy of sleep habits (Kate)

Protective Factors
- parental involvement, motivation, and knowledge of healthy sleep habits (all children)
- no known mental or physical health problems (all children)

childhood, as well as a phase shift during adolescence) and sleep associations. The therapist suggests that Anne and Rob complete sleep diaries for Taylor and Johnny and that Kate completes her own sleep diary. No changes to the family's sleep schedule or habits are recommended at this session.

Session 2. The therapist reviews the sleep diaries with the family, pointing out patterns, such as inconsistent bed and wake times on the weekend and patterns of light exposure from electronics for both Kate and Johnny. The therapist explains how these two things work against the body's natural clock and can cause problems falling asleep, something that both Kate and Johnny are frustrated with. The therapist suggests a two-week trial period of consistent wake times based on the earliest time that the child needs to get up, a 'no screen' time period in the evenings and matching bedtimes to the time of the night when the children are falling asleep. The family brainstorms activities they might do together before bedtime, and they decide on picture and word puzzles. The therapist has the family discuss what rewards they would like to have for successfully completing the two-week trial. Taylor picks pancakes for breakfast, as well as a redeemable sticker chart for a trip to the pool. Johnny decides on a weekly hockey shinny game with his parents, and Kate would like more practice with the car to get her driver's licence. The therapist encourages the family to continue completing their sleep diaries.

Session 3. After reviewing the sleep diaries with the family, both Kate and Johnny are being more consistent with bedtimes and wake times and are limiting use of electronics before bed. However, Taylor's schedule continues to be inconsistent. The therapist suggests that Anne feed Taylor at the start of the routine in the living room during the family's puzzle time and then move to complete a shorter bedtime routine in Taylor's bedroom. The therapist suggests that Rob and Anne gradually move (every three to four nights) from holding Taylor until sleep to sitting next to the bed and finally sitting outside the bedroom and that they add a new reward for nights when Taylor is able to fall asleep more independently. The therapist has Johnny and Kate continue with their previously developed plan to consolidate these positive changes. Sleep diaries continue to be collected. The therapist arranged a check-in phone call between sessions to offer parental support while changing Taylor's schedule.

Session 4. The therapist reviewed the changes in the family's sleep patterns and habits. Anne and Rob stated that sleep had improved greatly in their family. The therapist helped the family identify potential future challenges (e.g., family trips or vacations, changing schools, puberty) and used the ABCs of SLEEPING mnemonic to guide recommendations for the maintenance of healthy sleep practices.

Conclusion

Behaviourally based sleep problems, including insomnia, are highly prevalent across all stages of development and result in significant impacts across developmental domains. These sleep problems arise in the context of the family and impact child and family functioning. There exist evidence-based interventions for behaviourally based sleep problems in typically developing children and adolescents and growing evidence for children/adolescents with special needs [92]. Despite solid evidence for behaviourally based sleep interventions, the majority of youth do not receive evidence-based treatments [93]. A qualitative study of 124 Canadian health-care providers found that the most common barrier to evidence-based care for behaviourally based sleep problems was knowledge, training and education [89]. As such, one of the main ways to address the existing treatment gap is to train more health-care providers.

With some additional training, behavioural sleep problems can be treated by health-care providers without sleep specialist training. Health-care providers already have the foundational competencies and skills but do require additional training to be effective in delivering interventions to treat behavioural sleep problems. This training can be difficult to access, given that it is rarely included in health-care provider educational programme, but rather this often needs to be sought out through professional development (PD) opportunities. Health-care provider professional associations may host these PD opportunities, or they can be accessed through sleep conferences. For example, the International Paediatric Sleep Association Congress and the Biennial Conference on Paediatric Sleep Medicine both host best-practice PD workshops.

These PD workshops prepare health-care providers to provide treatment for behavioural sleep problems in typically developing children and adolescents. However, many children with sleep problems also have other co-morbid conditions such as neurodevelopmental disorders and mental health disorders. Recent research has demonstrated that a transdiagnostic approach to treating behavioural sleep problems is feasible, and some preliminary efficacy data are available [94]. This does not mean that one size fits all but rather that the core treatment components needed to treat behavioural sleep problems in typically children (e.g., psycho-education, healthy sleep practices, behavioural interventions and medication) are the same for children with co-morbid conditions. However, these children may require some modifications to these treatment components (e.g., increased time to learn the new behaviours, more immediate rewards for successful behavioural change, use of visual strategies such as visual schedules and charts). Healthcare providers need to ensure that they have the specialized training needed to treat children with behavioural sleep problems and co-morbid conditions. Seeking out specific PD is necessary to build the competencies needed to work with special populations.

Another way to address the treatment gap is to harness the power of the Internet to deliver evidence-based interventions to treat behavioural sleep problems in children and adolescents. e-Health interventions have been demonstrated to be effective in creating behavioural change in the treatment of a number health and mental health problems (e.g., smoking, nutrition and diet, depression) across all stages of development from young children to seniors [95]. e-Health programmes to treat sleep problems have also been demonstrated to be effective in adults [96]. There have been very few trials examining e-health programmes to treat children and adolescents with behavioural sleep problems, but the few published studies have found promising results with young children [60] and adolescents [97, 98]. There are no published evaluations of e-health programmes for latency-aged children, but we have just completed a pan-Canadian RCT of our e-health programme called 'Better Nights, Better Days' [99]. This programme is for parents of typically developing children with insomnia between the ages of 1 and 10 years (http://betternightsbetterdays.ca/). This programme was recently modified into a trans-diagnostic intervention for children with neurodevelopmental disorders [100] and is now being evaluated through an RCT (http://ndd.betternightsbetterdays.ca/). If these interventions are found to be efficacious, they would provide an important way to address the treatment gap.

In order to address behaviourally based sleep problems in children and adolescents, we will need to increase the training of non-sleep specialist health-care providers and use a range of delivery methods, including face-to-face individual and group interventions as well as e-health interventions. Parents are key to the intervention process for infants to adolescents. With appropriate training, health-care providers can support parents in their efforts to ensure that their children and adolescents are sleeping well so that they can experience optimal daytime functioning. Healthy sleep for children and adolescents translates into better sleep for the whole family and, as such, should be a target of treatment whenever sleep problems are identified in children and adolescents.

References

1. Dewald-Kaufmann J, de Bruin E, Michael G. Cognitive behavioral therapy for insomnia (CBT-I) in school-aged children and adolescents. *Sleep Medicine Clinics* 2019; **14**(2):155–65.

2. Astill RG, Van der Heijden KB, Van Ijzendoorn MH, Van Someren EJ. Sleep, cognition, and behavioral problems in school-age children: A century of research meta-analyzed. *Psychological Bulletin* 2012; **138**(6):1109–38.

3. Owens J. Insufficient sleep in adolescents and young adults: An update on causes and consequences. *Pediatrics* 2014; **134**(3):e921.

4. Dahl RE, El-Sheikh M. Considering sleep in a family context: introduction to the special issue. *Journal of Family Psychology* 2007; **21**(1):1–3.

5. Carskadon M, Dement W. Monitoring and staging human sleep. In: Kryger M, Roth T, Dement C (eds.), *Principles and Practice of Sleep Medicine*, 5th ed. St. Louis: Elsevier Saunders, 2011, pp. 16–26.

6. Dattilo M, Antunes HK, Medeiros A, et al. Sleep and muscle recovery: Endocrinological and molecular basis for a new and promising hypothesis. *Medical Hypotheses* 2011; **77**(2):220–2.

7. Borbely AA. A two process model of sleep regulation. *Human Neurobiology* 1982; **1**(3):195–204.

8. Czeisler C, Duffy J, Shanahan T, et al. Stability, precision, and near-24-hour period of the human circadian pacemaker. *Science* 1999; **284**(5423):2177–81.

9. Jenni OG, Carskadon MA. Sleep behavior and sleep regulation from infancy through adolescence: Normative aspects. *Sleep Medicine Clinics* 2007; **2**(3):321–9.

10. Sadeh A. Cognitive-behavioral treatment for childhood sleep disorders. *Clinical Psychology Review* 2005; **25**(5):612–28.

11. Peterman JS, Carper MM, Elkins RM, et al. The effects of cognitive-behavioral therapy for youth anxiety on sleep problems. *Journal of Anxiety Disorders* 2016; **37**:78–88.

12. Meltzer LJ, Mindell JA. Systematic review and meta-analysis of behavioral interventions for pediatric insomnia. *Journal of Pediatric Psychology* 2014; **39**(8):932–48.

13. Tikotzky L, Sadeh A. The role of cognitive-behavioral therapy in behavioral childhood insomnia. *Sleep Medicine* 2010; **11**(7):686–91.

14. Badin E, Haddad C, Shatkin JP. Insomnia: The sleeping giant of pediatric public health. *Current Psychiatry Reports* 2016; **18**(5):47–55.

15. Blake MJ, Sheeber LB, Youssef GJ, et al. Systematic review and meta-analysis of adolescent cognitive-behavioral sleep interventions. *Clinical Child and Family Psychology Review* 2017; **20**(3):227–49.

16. Lane JM, Jones SE, Dashti HS, et al. Biological and clinical insights from genetics of insomnia symptoms. *Nature Genetics* 2019; **51**(3):387–93.

17. Oniszczenko W, Rzeszutek M, Stanislawiak E. Affective temperaments, mood, and insomnia symptoms in a nonclinical sample. *Behavioral Sleep Medicine* 2019; **17**(3):355–63.

18. Palagini L, Petri E, Novi M, et al. Adult insecure attachment plays a role in hyperarousal and emotion dysregulation in insomnia disorder. *Psychiatry Research* 2018; **262**:162–7.

19. Giannotti F, Cortesi F, Sebastiani T, Ottaviano S. Circadian preference, sleep and daytime behaviour in adolescence. *Journal of Sleep Research* 2002; **11**(3):191–9.

20. Lemola S, Perkinson-Gloor N, Brand S, et al. Adolescents' electronic media use at night, sleep disturbance, and depressive symptoms in the smartphone age. *Journal of Youth and Adolescence* 2015; **44**(2):405–18.

21. Wolfson AR, Carskadon MA. Understanding adolescent's sleep patterns and school performance: A critical appraisal. *Sleep Medicine Reviews* 2003; **7**(6):491–506.

22. Li SX, Chan NY, Man Yu MW, et al. Eveningness chronotype, insomnia symptoms, and emotional and behavioural problems in adolescents. *Sleep Medicine* 2018; **47**:93–9.

23. Sidani S, Ibrahim S, Lok J, et al. Comparing the experience of and factors perpetuating chronic insomnia severity among young, middle-aged, and older adults. *Clinical Nursing Research* 2018; **10**(15):1–24.

24. Bartel KA, Gradisar M, Williamson P. Protective and risk factors for adolescent sleep: A meta-analytic review. *Sleep Medicine Review* 2015; **21**:72–85.

25. Yen CF, Ko CH, Yen JY, Cheng CP. The multidimensional correlates associated with short nocturnal sleep duration and subjective insomnia among Taiwanese adolescents. *Sleep* 2008; **31**(11):1515–25.

26. Morgenthaler T, Owens J, Alessi C, et al. Practice parameters for behavioral treatment of bedtime problems and night wakings in infants and young children. *Sleep* 2006; **29**(10):1277–81.

27. Taylor D, Roane B. Treatment of insomnia in adults and children: A practice-friendly review of research. *Journal of Clinical Psychology* 2010; **66**(11):1137–47.

28. Allen SL, Howlett MD, Coulombe JA, Corkum PV. ABCs of SLEEPING: A review of the evidence behind pediatric sleep practice recommendations. *Sleep Medicine Review* 2016; **29**:1–14.

29. Bessey M, Aimee Coulombe J, Corkum P. Sleep hygiene in children with ADHD: Findings and recommendations. *ADHD Report* 2013; **21**:1–7.

30. Owens JA, Moturi S. Pharmacologic treatment of pediatric insomnia. Child and Adolescent Psychiatric Clinics of North America 2009; **18**(4):1001–16.

31. Dias C, Figeriredo B, Rocha M, Field T. Reference values and changes in infant sleep-wake behaviour during the first 12 months of life: A systematic review. *Journal of Sleep Research* 2018; **27**(5):e12654.

32. Tham E, Schneider N, Broekman B. Infant sleep and its relation with cognition and growth: A narrative review. *Nature and Science of Sleep* 2017; **9**:135–49.

33. Cook F, Giallo R, Hiscock H, et al. Infant regulation and child mental health concerns: A longitudinal study. *Pediatrics* 2019; **143**(3):e20180977.

34. Williams K, Nicholson J, Walker S, Bethelsen D. Early childhood profiles of sleep problems and self-regulation predict later school adjustment. *British Journal of Educational Psychology* 2016; **86**(2):331–50.

35. Winsper C, Wolke D. Infant and toddler crying, sleeping and feeding problems and trajectories of dysregulated behavior across childhood. *Journal of Abnormal Child Psychology* 2014; **42**(5):831–43.

36. Chaput JP, Gray CE, Poitras VJ, et al. Systematic review of the relationships between sleep duration and health indicators in school-aged children and youth. *Applied physiology, nutrition, and metabolism* 2016; 41(6), S266–S282.

37. Cook F, Mensah F, Bayer J, Hiscock H. Prevalence, comorbidity and factors associated with sleeping,

crying and feeding problems at 1 month of age: A community-based survey. *Journal of Paediatrics and Child Health* 2019; **55**(6):644–51.

38. Voltaire S, Teti D. Early nighttime parental interventions and infant sleep regulation across the first year. *Sleep Medicine* 2018; **52**:107–15.

39. Guillory S. Predictors of infant sleep problems: Maternal psychosocial contributions. PhD dissertation, Mills College, Ann Arbor, MI, 2013.

40. Morrell J. The role of maternal cognitions in infant sleep problems as assessed by a new instrument, the Maternal Cognitions About Infant Sleep Questionnaire. *Journal of Child Psychology and Psychiatry* 1999; **40**(2):247–58.

41. Reader J, Teti D, Cleveland M. Cognitions about infant sleep: Interparental differences, trajectories across the first year, and coparenting quality. *Journal of Family Psychology* 2017; **31**(4):453–63.

42. Sadeh A, Flint-Ofir E, Tirosh T, Tikotzky L. Infant sleep and parental sleep-related cognitions. *Journal of Family Psychology* 2007; **21**(1):74–87.

43. Tikotzky L, Sadeh A. Maternal sleep-related cognitions and infant sleep: A longitudinal study from pregnancy through the 1st year. *Child Development* 2009; **80**(3):860–74.

44. Sadeh A, Juda-Hanael M, Livne-Karp E, et al. Low parental tolerance for infant crying: An underlying factor in infant sleep problems? *Journal of Sleep Research* 2016; **25**(5):501–7.

45. Morales-Munoz I, Partonen T, Saarenpaa-Heikkila O, et al. The role of parental circadian preference in the onset of sleep difficulties in early childhood. *Sleep Medicine* 2019; **54**:223–30.

46. Millikovsky-Ayalon M, Atzaba-Poria N, Meiri G. The role of the father in child sleep disturbance: Child, parent, and parent-child relationship. *Infant Mental Health Journal* 2015; **36**(1):114–27.

47. Tikotzky L, Sadeh A, Glickman-Gavrieli T. Infant sleep and paternal involvement in infant caregiving during the first 6 months of life. *Journal of Pediatric Psychology* 2011; **36**(1):36–46.

48. Tikotzky L, Sadeh A, Volkovich E, et al. Infant sleep development from 3 to 6 months postpartum: Links with maternal sleep and paternal involvement. *Monographs of the Society for Research in Child Development* 2015; **80**(1):107–24.

49. Jian N, Teti D. Emotional availability at bedtime, infant temperament, and infant sleep development from one to six months. *Sleep Medicine* 2016; **23**(Supp C):49–58.

50. Kim B, Teti D. Maternal emotional availability during infant bedtime: An ecological framework. *Journal of Family Psychology* 2014; **28**(1):1–11.

51. Teti D, Kim B, Mayer G, Countermine M. Maternal emotional availability at bedtime predicts infant sleep quality. *Journal of Family Psychology* 2010; **24**(3):307–15.

52. Smith J, Hardy S, Hale L, Gazmararian J. Racial disparities and sleep among preschool aged children: A systematic review. *Sleep Health* 2019; **5**(1):49–57.

53. Bryanton J, Beck C, Montelpare W. Postnatal parental education for optimizing infant general health and parent-infant relationships. *Cochrane Database of Systematic Reviews* 2013; **11**:CD004068.

54. Galland B, Sayers R, Cameron S, et al. Anticipatory guidance to prevent infant sleep problems within a randomised controlled trial: Infant, maternal and partner outcomes at 6 months of age. BMJ Open 2017; 7:e014908.

55. Hiscock H, Cook F, Bayer J, et al. Preventing early infant sleep and crying problems and postnatal depression: A randomized trial. *Pediatrics* 2014; **133**(2):e346–54.

56. Nikolopoulo M, St James-Roberts I. Preventing sleeping problems in infants who are at rise of developing them. *Archives of Disease in Childhood* 2003; **88**(2):108–11.

57. Stremler R, Hodnett E, Lee K, et al. A behavioral-educational intervention to promote maternal and infant sleep: A pilot randomized, controlled trial. *Sleep* 2006; **29**(12):1609–15.

58. Stremler R, Hodnett E, Kenton L, et al. Effect of behavioural-educational intervention on sleep for primiparous women and their infants in early postpartum: Multisite randomised controlled trial. *British Medical Journal* 2013; **346**:1164.

59. Covington L, Rogers V, Armstrong B, et al. Toddler bedtime routines and associations with nighttime sleep duration and maternal and household factors. *Journal of Clinical Sleep Medicine* 2019; **15**(6):865–71.

60. Mindell J, Lee C, Leichman E, Rotella K. Massage-based bedtime routine: Impact of sleep and mood in infants and mothers. *Sleep Medicine* 2018; **41**:51–57.

61. Mindell J, Telofski L, Wiegand B, Kurtz E. A nightly bedtime routine: Impact on sleep in young children and maternal mood. *Sleep* 2009; **32**(5):599–606.

62. Staples A, Bates J, Peterson I. Bedtime routines in early childhood: Prevalence, consistency, and associations with nighttime sleep. *Monographs of the Society for Research in Child Development* 2015; **80**(1):141–59.

63. Mindell J, Leichman E, Lee C, et al. Implementation of a nightly bedtime routine: How quickly do things improve?. *Infant Behavior and Development* 2017; **49**:220–7.

64. Kempler L, Sharpe L, Miller CB, Bartlett DJ. Do psychosocial sleep interventions improve infant sleep or maternal mood in the postnatal period? A systematic review and meta-analysis of randomised controlled trials. *Sleep Medicine Reviews* 2016; **29**:15–22.

65. Hatch B, Galland B, Gray A, et al. Consistent use of bedtime parenting strategies mediates the effects of sleep education of child sleep: Secondary findings from an early-life randomized controlled trial. *Sleep Health* 2019; **5**(5):433–43.

66. Vriend J, Corkum P. Clinical management of behavioral insomnia of childhood. *Psychology Research and Behavior Management* 2011; **4**:69–79.

67. Hirshkowitz M, Whiton K, Albert SM, et al. National Sleep Foundation's sleep time duration recommendations: Methodology and results summary. *Sleep Health* 2015; **1**(1):40–43.

68. ParticipACTION. 2018. Available at www.participaction.com/en-ca.

69. Galland BC, Short MA, Terrill P, et al. Establishing normal values for pediatric nighttime sleep measured by actigraphy: A systematic review and meta-analysis. *Sleep* 2018; **41**(4):10.1093/sleep/zsy017.

70. Galland BC, Taylor BJ, Elder DE, Herbison P. Normal sleep patterns in infants and children: A systematic review of observational studies. Sleep Medicine Reviews 2012; **16**(3):213–22.

71. Segura-Jiménez V, Carbonell-Baeza A, Keating XD, et al. Association of sleep patterns with psychological positive health and health complaints in children and adolescents. *Quality of Life Research* 2015; **24**(4):885–95.

72. Liu X, Liu L, Owens JA, Kaplan DL. Sleep patterns and sleep problems among schoolchildren in the United States and China. *Pediatrics* 2005; **115**(Suppl 1):241–9.

73. Crabtree V, Williams N. Normal sleep in children and adolescents. *Child and Adolescent Psychiatric Clinics of North America* 2009; **14**(4):799–811.

74. Liu Y, Zhang J, Li SX, et al. Excessive daytime sleepiness among children and adolescents: Prevalence, correlates, and pubertal effects. *Sleep Medicine* 2019; **53**:1–8.

75. Simola P, Laitalainen E, Liukkonen K, et al. Sleep disturbances in a community sample from preschool to school age. *Child: Care, Health and Development* 2012; **38**(4):572–80.

76. Astill RG, Van der Heijden KB, Van Ijzendoorn MH, Van Someren EJ. Sleep, cognition, and behavioral problems in school-age children: A century of research meta-analyzed. *Psychological Bulletin* 2012; **138**(6):1109–38.

77. Vriend J, Davidson F, Rusak B, Corkum P. Emotional and cognitive impact of sleep restriction in children. *Sleep Medicine Clinics* 2015; **10**(2):107–15.

78. Davidson F, Rusak B, Chambers C, Corkum P. The impact of sleep restriction on daytime functioning in school-age children with and without ADHD: A narrative review of the literature. *Canadian Journal of School Psychology* 2018; **34**(3):188–214.

79. Berger RH, Diaz A, Valiente C, et al. The association between home chaos and academic achievement: The moderating role of sleep. *Journal of Family Psychology* 2019; **33**(8):975–81.

80. Tampke EC, Blossom JB, Fite PJ. The role of sleep quality in associations between peer victimization and internalizing symptoms. *Journal of Psychopathology and Behavioral Assessment* 2019; **41**(1):25–35.

81. El-Sheikh M, Kelly RJ. *Sleep in Children: Links with Marital Conflict and Child Development*. New York: Oxford University Press, 2011, pp. 3–28.

82. Fuligni AJ, Arruda EH, Krull JL, Gonzales NA. Adolescent sleep duration, variability, and peak levels of achievement and mental health. *Child Development* 2018; **89**(2):e18–28.

83. Chaput JP, Janssen I. Sleep duration estimates of Canadian children and adolescents. *Journal of Sleep Research* 2016; **25**(5):541–8.

84. Tarokh L, Saletin JM, Carskadon MA. Sleep in adolescence: Physiology, cognition and mental health. *Neuroscience and Biobehavioral Reviews* 2016; **70**:182–8.

85. Hart LC, Maslow G. The medical transition from pediatric to adult-oriented care: Considerations for child and adolescent psychiatrists. *Child and Adolescent Psychiatric Clinics of North America* 2018; **27**(1):125–32.

86. van Staa AL, Jedeloo S, van Meeteren J, Latour JM. Crossing the transition chasm: Experiences and recommendations for improving transitional care of young adults, parents and providers. *Child: Care, Health and Development* 2019; **37**(6):821–32.

87. Honaker SM, Meltzer LJ. Sleep in pediatric primary care: A review of the literature. *Sleep Medicine Review* 2016; **25**:31–9.

88. Boreman CD, Thomasgard MC, Fernandez SA, Coury DL. Resident training in developmental/behavioral pediatrics: Where do we stand? *Clinical Pediatrics (Philadelphia)* 2007; **46**(2):135–45.

89. Boerner KE, Coulombe JA, Corkum P. Core competencies for health professionals' training in pediatric behavioral sleep care: A Delphi study. *Behavioral Sleep Medicine* 2015; **13**(4):265–84.

90. Sburlati E, Schniering C, Lyneham H, Rapee R. A model of therapist competencies for the empirically supported cognitive behavioral treatment of child and

adolescent anxiety and depressive disorders. *Clinical Child and Family Psychology Review* 2011; **14**:89–109.

91. Saddichha S. Diagnosis and treatment of chronic insomnia. *Annals of Indian Academy of Neurology* 2010; **13**(2):94–102.

92. Meltzer LJ, Mindell JA. Systematic review and meta-analysis of behavioral interventions for pediatric insomnia. *Journal of Pediatric Psychology* 2014; **39**(8):932–48.

93. Corkum P, Weiss S, Hall W, et al. Assessment and treatment of behavioral sleep disorders in Canada. *Sleep Medicine* 2019; **56**:29–37.

94. Rigney G, Ali NS, Corkum PV, et al. A systematic review to explore the feasibility of a behavioural sleep intervention for insomnia in children with neurodevelopmental disorders: A transdiagnostic approach. *Sleep Medicine Reviews* 2018; **41**:244–54.

95. Wantland DJ, Portillo CJ, Holzemer WL, et al. The effectiveness of web-based vs. non-web-based interventions: A meta-analysis of behavioral change outcomes. *Journal of Medical Internet Research* 2004; **6**(4):e40.

96. Zachariae R, Lyby MS, Ritterband LM, O'Toole MS. Efficacy of internet-delivered cognitive-behavioral therapy for insomnia: A systematic review and meta-analysis of randomized controlled trials. *Sleep Medicine Reviews* 2016; **30**:1–10.

97. Werner-Seidler A, Wong Q, Johnston L, et al. Pilot evaluation of the Sleep Ninja: A smartphone application for adolescent insomnia symptoms. *BMJ Open* 2019; **9**(5):e026502.

98. de Bruin E, Bogels F, Oort F, Meijer A. Improvements of adolescent psychopathology after insomnia treatment: Results from a randomized controlled trial over 1 year. *Journal of Child Psychology and Psychiatry* 2018; **59**(5):509–22.

99. Corkum PV, Reid GJ, Hall WA, et al. Evaluation of an internet-based behavioral intervention to improve psychosocial health outcomes in children with insomnia (Better Nights, Better Days): Protocol for a randomized controlled trial. *JMIR Research Protocols* 2018;7(3):e76.

100. Ali N, Rigney G, Weiss SK, et al. Optimizing an eHealth insomnia intervention for children with neurodevelopmental disorders: A Delphi study. *Sleep Health* 2018; **4**(2):224–34.

101. Sadeh A, Mindell J, Luedtke K, Wiegand B. Sleep and sleep ecology in the first 3 years: A web-based study. *Journal of Sleep Research* 2009; **18**:60–73.

102. Iglowstein I, Jenni O, Molinari L, Largo R. Sleep duration from infancy to adolescence: Reference values and generational trends. *Pediatrics* 2003; **111**(2):302–7.

Chapter

16

Working with Parents with Depression in Family Intervention

Emma A. Archibald, Sarah H. Gladstone and Tracy R. G. Gladstone

Major depressive disorder (MDD) is among the most prevalent mental illnesses in the United States, with approximately 7.1 per cent of adults and 13.3 per cent of adolescents experiencing an episode of major depression in 2017 [1]. A report by the Institute of Medicine (2009) indicates that approximately 7.5 million adults with depression are parents to a child under the age of 18, and 15 million children in the United States live with at least one depressed parent [2]. Children with a depressed parent are at an increased risk of developing mental illnesses themselves. Specifically, these children are three to four times more likely to be diagnosed with major depression compared to their peers without a depressed parent [3–6]. Given the elevated risk for depression that these children face, prevention efforts are becoming an increasingly popular option for families hoping to reduce this risk.

In addition to the increased risk of developing depression, children with a depressed parent are at risk for poor outcomes in other areas of life. Within the family, parental depression is associated with ineffectual parenting and increased family conflict and misunderstanding [7, 8]. In addition, children of depressed parents are at greater risk for poor academic, social and developmental outcomes [9–11]. Clinicians address these associated issues in family-based preventive interventions by working individually with the identified at-risk child and other family members and with the family as a whole.

To date, most family-based preventive interventions targeting children of depressed parents have focused on children during toddlerhood, middle childhood and adolescence, with the majority of programmes targeting children ages 8–17 years. This chapter describes the impact of parental depression on children and families, risk and protective factors that are targeted through preventive efforts, the state of the field of prevention science and then the preventive interventions available to families with

a depressed parent, including a case study and review of the clinician skills and competencies needed to deliver effective interventions to this population.

Effects of Parental Depression on Children and Adolescents

Parental depression impacts children and families across multiple domains, including the cognitive and academic, socio-emotional and psychological health domains. Children are affected by their parents' depressive symptoms starting in infancy, and these effects may persist even after their parent's depression is in remission [12]. Fortunately, over the past two decades, researchers have found evidence that remission of parental depression is associated with improved outcomes in children [13, 14].

Cognitive and Academic Outcomes

The extant literature shows that children with a depressed parent are at significant risk for impairments in cognitive development, including in the areas of learning, language and academics. A 2001 study from Cardiff University found that children with postnatally depressed mothers (at child age three months) had significantly lower Intelligence Quotient (IQ) scores and increased difficulties with attentional and mathematical reasoning at age 11 years compared to children without postnatally depressed mothers [15]. Letourneau et al. [16] studied the role of maternal depression on children in the early years of development and found that children whose mothers experienced symptoms of postpartum depression were significantly more likely to show inattention and low receptive vocabulary than children whose mothers were not depressed. This was especially true for children whose mothers experienced chronic depression throughout the child's first five years of life. In fact, maternal depression predicted child academic performance at ages four and five years, with increased depressive symptoms being related to decreased academic, cognitive and behavioural outcomes. This relation is seen also in paternal depression. For example, Leinonen, Solantaus and Punanmäki [17] explored the role of parenting behaviours in explaining the relation between parental depressive symptoms and school performance. Overall, children with a depressed parent had impaired school outcomes. However, non-punitive fathering was related to better school motivation and performance outcomes in both sons and daughters, and involved mothering was related to better outcomes in sons. In addition, results of a Swedish cohort study indicate that maternal and paternal depressions were associated with lower academic performance at 16 years of age, and outcomes were especially poor for daughters with depressed mothers [18]. Taken together, this literature suggests that parental depression affects children's cognitive and academic functioning throughout development regardless of child or parent gender.

Socio-emotional Outcomes

Children with a depressed parent experience deficits in social and emotional outcomes as well. There is evidence that these children experience internalizing and externalizing symptoms at a higher rate than children without depressed mothers and that this increase is related to social and emotional dysfunction throughout development. According to a study by Murray et al. [19], when children at age five years were approached in a friendly manner by others, those whose mothers had been postnatally depressed were more likely to respond negatively than those whose mothers had not been depressed. Similar findings have emerged from studies with adolescents. For example, Hay et al. [20] found that adolescent children in Britain whose mothers were depressed during pregnancy were almost twice as likely to exhibit antisocial behaviour and four times as likely to be violent than children whose mothers had not been depressed during pregnancy.

Emotional development is also impaired by parental depression and is often directly associated with social dysfunction. Evidence for a sensitive period in socio-emotional outcomes was found by Maughan et al. [21]. Their study found that children whose mothers experienced depression before the child reached the age of 21 months experienced dysregulated emotion patterns on witnessing anger at age four

years and were more likely to report low social acceptance one year later. This result was not replicated for children whose mothers had depression after the child was aged 21 months. In the case of paternal depression, researchers have demonstrated an association between paternal depressive symptoms during the postnatal period and emotional, conduct and hyperactivity problems in preschool age children [22]. Moreover, there is evidence to show that the effects of postnatal parental depression on the young child persist into adolescence. For example, female adolescents whose mothers had postnatal depression showed heightened emotional sensitivity at age 13 compared to adolescents whose mothers did not have postnatal depression [23]; in the presence of an insecure maternal attachment, adolescent boys showed decreased social maturity, but there was no effect of maternal attachment on social maturity for adolescent girls [23]. Furthermore, the risk of poor emotional and behavioural outcomes is reduced in the presence of a parent without symptoms of a mood or anxiety disorder such that these healthy parents may buffer their children against the effects of parental mood or anxiety concerns [24, 25].

Psychological Outcomes

Over and above the heightened risk for socio-emotional difficulties, parental depression is associated with an increased risk of mental illness symptoms and disorders in offspring [3]. Children with a depressed parent are at heightened risk for the development of both internalizing and externalizing disorders. Many prevention programmes targeting this population aim to ameliorate the risk of developing internalizing disorders, namely major depression. According to Lieb et al. [26], parental major depression is associated with an increased risk of affective disorder (i.e., major depression, dysthymia and bipolar I/II), substance use disorder (i.e., alcohol abuse, nicotine dependence, illicit drug abuse/dependence, substance use disorder) and anxiety disorder (i.e., panic disorder, specific phobia, generalized anxiety disorder, obsessive-compulsive disorder, posttraumatic stress disorder) diagnoses in offspring. Externalizing behaviours such as behavioural problems are also cited in the literature. For example, at ages three and four, children with a depressed and/or anxious mother experience emotional dysregulation and behavioural problems (i.e., oppositional defiant disorder) at a higher rate than children with a non-depressed/non-anxious mother [27, 28]. The available literature indicates that both paternal and maternal depressive symptoms are related to children's externalizing problems [29]. Overall, children with a depressed parent are more likely than children without a depressed parent to have mental health problems, especially depression, anxiety and behavioural issues.

Risk Factors, Protective Factors and Resiliency

Risk and protective factors are associated with the likelihood that an individual will become depressed. In the context of parental depression, there are both individual and environmental factors that influence the cognitive, academic, socio-emotional and psychological outcomes described earlier. Characteristics of the parent (i.e., parenting behaviours and overall functioning), of the child (i.e., age, gender and temperament) and of the environment (i.e., poverty and a lack of social support) moderate the relation between parental depression and child outcomes. Building resiliency, or the ability to thrive and adapt despite experiencing stress or challenges, is an important component of depression prevention programmes [30–32]. Family-based depression prevention interventions work with the child and family – together, separately or in parallel – to improve parent, child and family outcomes by reducing risk factors and increasing protective factors [30–32]. In working with the child and family to develop resiliency, clinicians should evaluate and target the parent, child and environmental risk and protective factors in a child's life.

Parent Factors

Most parent and child depression studies focus on the mother-child relationship; until recently, it was thought that paternal depression did not have a great negative effect on children's development or functioning [22]. Not only has there been a lack of focus on the role of fathers in child mental illness, but also historically, mothers have been blamed for their child's psychopathology [33]. A recent study on the role of paternal depressive symptoms in child depressive symptoms, however, shows that adolescents with fathers with depressive symptoms are just as likely as adolescents with mothers with depressive symptoms to experience depressive symptoms themselves [34].

Lieb et al. [26] found no difference in the genetic inheritance of maternal and paternal depression such that approximately 26 per cent of adolescents with one parent diagnosed with MDD reported experiencing at least one episode of major depression, and this did not differ by parent gender. This finding suggests that family-based depression prevention programmes must address both maternal *and* paternal depressive symptoms when identifying potential risk factors.

Over and above an increased genetic risk for the development of depression, children with a depressed parent are likely to be put at risk via exposure to impaired parenting behaviours. In a meta-analysis examining the connection between parental depression and parenting behaviours, Lovejoy et al. [35] found that compared to non-depressed mothers, currently depressed mothers were more likely to exhibit negative parenting behaviours such as coercive tactics, hostility, disengagement and irritability, and this was especially true for mothers with young children. Others have suggested that there is a cumulative and bidirectional relationship between mother and child, meaning that a child's behavioural issues could contribute to the mother's depressive symptoms, and vice versa [36, 37]. This relationship, if not addressed, could lead to a cycle of maladaptive interaction in the family and across other social relationships. Although these same parenting behaviours have not been widely researched in father-child dyads, clinicians should address both parents' parenting behaviours when implementing family-based depression prevention programmes. Behavioural alteration will support children in receiving more appropriate emotional and social cues from their parents.

The chronicity and severity of parental depressive symptoms also have been found to influence a child's risk for the development of depression, perhaps because, in severe cases of parental depression, a parent may struggle to meet the needs of their child, which can lead to complex risk and poor child outcomes. According to Hammen and Brennan [38], children whose mothers experienced mild depression for 12 or more months or moderate to severe depression for one to two months had similar rates of depression. Moreover, using data from the Sequenced Treatment Alternatives to Relieve Depression (STAR*D) study, Foster et al. [39] found that children (mean age 11.5 years) whose mothers had prolonged current depressive episodes had greater internalizing and externalizing problems than children whose mothers had shorter current major depressive episodes (MDEs). These findings suggest that children with mothers who have severe or chronic depressive symptoms are more likely to experience symptoms of psychopathology themselves compared to children with mothers who have mild or intermittent depressive symptoms. Clinicians therefore should take an accurate report of the parents' depressive symptoms, including severity, timing and current functioning.

Child Factors

Although the majority of the depression prevention literature is focused on adolescents, there is evidence to show that children experience the effects of their parent's depression long before they reach adolescence. For example, Barker et al. [36] suggested that exposure to significant risk factors associated with maternal depression before age two is related to increased rates of externalizing and internalizing diagnoses at age 7.5 years. Moreover, Bagner et al. [40] recruited 175 mothers from the Oregon Adolescent Depression Project to assess outcomes throughout childhood and found that children whose mothers were depressed in the child's first 12 months had higher levels of internalizing problems and higher overall scores on the Child Behaviour Checklist at age five years than children whose mothers were depressed prior to or during pregnancy. Child age at exposure to maternal depression appears to be a significant risk factor for increased internalizing and externalizing symptoms, with exposure in the first two years of life being associated with the most negative long-term outcomes.

In addition, the depression gender gap is widely cited in the depression literature. Starting around adolescence (i.e., age 14), girls and women are approximately twice as likely as boys and men to report an episode of depression [41, 42]. Recently, Mason et al. [43] surveyed parents with depressive symptoms at child age 11 years to explore the role of gender in child depressive symptoms at ages 11, 18 and 21 years. They found a direct effect of maternal depressive symptoms on adolescent girls' symptoms at age 18 but no such effect emerged for adolescent boys. No direct effects of paternal depressive symptoms emerged for girls or boys, although indirect effects of paternal depression were noted for young adults of both genders. Although future studies will need to replicate this finding, it seems that girls are at

greater risk than boys for developing depressive symptoms if their parent is depressed, especially if their mother is depressed.

Another, albeit less commonly discussed, risk factor is child temperament. Jessee et al. [44] studied the role of child temperament in moderating the effect of parental depressive symptoms on child behaviour problems. They found that children high in parent-reported and observed surgency (a temperamental trait associated with increased levels of activity and approach) had more behaviour problems when their mother had elevated symptoms of depression than children with low surgency. The same pattern emerged for children with negative affect and for children with high observed incongruous negative emotionality. Depressive symptoms in fathers were associated with more child behavioural problems only when children were high on parent-reported surgency. Difficult temperament, as a risk factor, is also associated with increased sensitivity to negative parenting behaviours such as authoritarian control and hostility, as well as with increased sensitivity to positive parenting behaviours, such as authoritative control and warmth [45]. Parents with depression therefore should be aware of how their parenting strategies affect their children, especially if their child has a difficult temperament. Because temperament, by definition, is a relatively stable trait, clinicians implementing depression prevention programmes should focus their efforts on decreasing negative parenting behaviours and increasing positive ones instead of attempting to alter the child's temperamental style.

Environmental Factors

Environmental factors, such as poverty and a lack of social support, also have been found to increase risk for children with a depressed parent. Although these factors pose a risk to all children regardless of parental mental health status, they may be especially harmful for children and adolescents with a depressed parent [46, 47]. In a longitudinal study, Spence et al. [46] found that children who were exposed to chronic poverty in infancy and at age five years experienced elevated symptoms of depression and anxiety in early adolescence compared to children who were not exposed to chronic poverty, although they did not find the effects of poverty to be changed in the presence of maternal depressive symptoms. Kiernan and Huerta [47], however, used structural equation modelling to elucidate the connection between maternal depression, poverty and child outcomes and found that maternal depression mediated the relation between poverty and child behaviour problems, with maternal depression diagnoses relating to increased child internalizing and externalizing problems at age three years. These findings suggest that poverty acts as a risk factor for the development of internalizing and externalizing behaviours and that maternal depression may act as a cumulative risk factor. Although it often is not possible to target poverty through family-based depression prevention programmes, clinicians should be aware of the increased need for such programmes in low-income areas.

The protective role of social support against depression has long been acknowledged [48, 49]. Maternal social support has been found to mediate (both directly and indirectly) the relation between maternal depressive symptoms and child internalizing behaviours. For example, Herwig, Wirtz and Bengel [50] found that maternal social support was strongly related to maternal depressive symptoms ($r = -.47$), maternal depressive symptoms were strongly related to parenting ($r = .62$) and parenting was strongly related to child internalizing behaviours ($\beta = .46$). This pathway suggests an indirect mediating relationship: a lack of maternal social support is related to dysfunctional parenting, which, in turn, is related to increased child internalizing behaviours. McCarty and McMahon [51] found that social support satisfaction mediates the relation between maternal depressive symptoms and children's internalizing disorders. The authors reasoned that mothers could be modelling social dysfunction or that children could be prompted to provide inappropriate caregiving to their mothers as a result of maternal dysfunction. Regardless of the mechanisms behind this relation, it is clear that social dysfunction or a lack of social support as a result of maternal depressive symptoms is a risk factor for increased child internalizing behaviours. Likewise, children's social support may affect their responses to parental depression. For example, in a review of resilience in families with a depressed parent, Chen and Kovacs [52] noted that for children living with a depressed parent, the presence of non-parental adults and prosocial peers may provide benefit, although the effects of such forms of social support may vary by, among other factors, ethnic group, child gender and the nature of the distress children are experiencing (i.e., supportive peers may not buffer children from the negative effects of parental depression, although they may provide support to children in managing social and school-related stress). Overall, the literature suggests that family social support, including support provided to both parents and children, may affect child outcomes when a parent is depressed.

Cumulative Risk

The literature shows that both individual and environmental factors put a child at risk for developing depressive symptoms when a parent has depression. Parental depression is a risk factor in and of itself; therefore, the addition of other risk factors puts children at heightened risk for developing depressive symptoms [36, 53, 54]. The additive effect of risk is well cited and is the basis for the idea behind cumulative risk [36, 53, 54]. The AVON Longitudinal Study of Parents and Children [36] examined the association between risk factors and child outcomes in the presence of a depressed mother and developed a cumulative risk index of environmental, family and maternal lifestyle risk factors that, with each risk factor exposure up to age two years, children were 20 per cent more likely to be diagnosed with an internalizing or externalizing disorder at age 7.5 years. In addition, Beardslee, Gladstone and O'Connor [55] described how other risk factors, such as exposure to stressful life events, subsyndromal depressive symptoms and skill deficits in interpersonal functioning, problem-solving skills or cognitive style make children more vulnerable to their parent's depression. Both specific risk factors, which are linked directly to depression, such as parental depression and gender, and non-specific risk factors, such as poverty and stressful life experiences, influence a child's resiliency. Furthermore, as Barker et al. [36] described, it is the additive nature of risk that is most detrimental to children who have a depressed parent. It is essential, therefore, that families and clinicians understand the importance of increasing protective factors and reducing risk factors whenever possible.

Prevention Science in the Context of Parental Depression

Prevention programmes aim to decrease risk factors and increase protective factors in order to promote resiliency, whereas treatment programmes generally provide intervention to individuals who have already been diagnosed with a disorder. Preventive intervention programmes for children of depressed parents focus on the specific risk factor of parental depression but also target other risk factors such as child temperament and family conflict [36, 55]. Clinicians work with children and their families to increase protective factors that encourage a developmentally supportive environment for the child in order to reduce the likelihood that depression will onset. An ancillary goal of these programmes is to increase general functioning and reduce associated negative outcomes.

Prevention science has become increasingly popular in the field of psychology, especially over the past few decades. Prevention efforts reduce the economic and public health burden of illness by intervening before symptoms arise and have been used in public health efforts to reduce the risk of obesity, heart disease, diabetes and so on. Mental illness is the primary source of disability in children and adolescents worldwide [56], making depression and other mental disorders the most recent focus of public health efforts. There is a substantial economic and public health cost of illness for child and adolescent depression, with Dutch scientists estimating that the mean cost per family with a clinically depressed adolescent in the Netherlands is approximately $16,600 [57]. An investigation conducted in the United States by Dieleman et al. [58] approximates that in 2013, 7.1 per cent of the $71.1 billion of personal health-care spending for depressive disorders went towards individuals under the age of 20 years. This amount, which comes to just over $5 billion, does not include economic burden expenditures, such as labour and productivity loss within the family. Cost-effectiveness analyses of depression prevention programmes suggest that such interventions may actually be cost-effective and ultimately may help reduce the economic burden of mental illness [59, 60].

As a rising number of prevention studies show a reduction in child and adolescent depressive symptoms and diagnoses [61–63], it has become clear that prevention programmes are an effective tool for combatting major depression. Preventive intervention programmes that are selective (i.e., target populations with a known risk for disorder) and indicated (i.e., target populations with symptoms) have been shown to be moderately effective in reducing symptoms of depression in children and adolescents [63]. Compared to universal screening programmes, which target all

members of a population, selective programmes have been found to be more effective both immediately after intervention and at follow-up [63]. Clinicians therefore should be familiar with the core competencies necessary for the effective implementation of selective prevention intervention programmes. The following section will describe several depression prevention programmes for children, adolescents and families who have a parent diagnosed with depression.

Depression Prevention Interventions

Interventions for Adolescents with a Parent Component

This section describes three prevention programmes for adolescents with a depressed parent that include a parent component. Parents are not active participants in these programmes; instead, they attend informational sessions or learn about the programme through some other format. In this way, parents are aware of their teenager's involvement in the programme and may provide them with support.

Coping with Stress

Clarke et al. [64] developed a cognitive therapy prevention programme that was tested against a usual-care condition in a randomized, controlled trial. The programme, called 'Coping with Stress', is an abbreviated version of a longer programme, called the 'Adolescent Coping with Depression Course' (CWD). The intervention was designed for children ages 13–18 years who had sub-syndromal symptoms of depression (but no current MDE) and a parent with either current major depression or dysthymia. The programme implemented cognitive restructuring techniques in 15 group-based sessions where adolescents learned to identify and challenge negative thoughts, with a focus on content related to their parent's depression. Parents participated in three separate informational meetings throughout the programme, where they discussed the skills taught to their children. In this prevention programme, the parent's diagnosis of major depression or dysthymia was not discussed with the parent, and the adolescents and their parents did not meet as a family. When compared to the usual-care condition, adolescents in the experimental condition reported significantly fewer symptoms of depression at the conclusion of the trial and significantly fewer MDEs at 14 months follow-up. Preventive effects decreased at 24-month follow-up. The authors identified this as a limitation and suggested that booster sessions might sustain the preventive effects. Their results indicate that this cognitive therapy programme may reduce the risk for depressive episodes and symptoms in teens that are at risk because of their parent's depression.

Prevention of Depression

Garber et al. [65] aimed to replicate the findings of the Coping with Stress study in a second, multisite randomized, controlled trial called the 'Prevention of Depression' (POD) study. In addition to determining depressive symptom and episode outcomes, the authors sought to understand how baseline eligibility criteria moderated depressive outcomes. Participants included 316 adolescents between the ages of 13 and 17 years who had at least one parent with a history of depression and who had sub-syndromal symptoms of depression and/or a history of depressive disorder that was in remission. The experimental condition included eight weekly 90-minute sessions, supplemented by six monthly 90-minute booster sessions. Adolescents attended the sessions in groups of up to 10 that were led by a master's-level therapist to learn cognitive restructuring techniques and problem-solving skills. In the booster sessions, adolescents reviewed previously learned material and learned new skills such as behavioural activation and relaxation. Parents attended information sessions at the start and conclusion of the intervention programme. Adolescents in the intervention group reported significantly fewer diagnoses and symptoms of depression at follow-up compared to the adolescents in the usual-care condition, and depressive symptoms decreased at a higher rate for children in the intervention condition. However, moderator analyses indicated that the intervention was not more likely to reduce the risk of MDEs than usual care when parents were currently depressed at baseline. The authors concluded that combined parent-child intervention programmes should be explored when a parent is currently depressed. Versions of the Coping with Depression (CWD) course (i.e., Coping with Stress, Prevention of Depression) have been disseminated worldwide over the past several decades; a meta-analysis of outcomes from this intervention approach suggests that it is efficacious both in preventing new cases of depression and in treating current depressive disorders [66].

Survivalkid

Youth depression prevention programmes are challenged by a lack of retention and attendance, shame and guilt surrounding mental illness, a lack of trust in the clinician-patient relationship, a desire for autonomy and parental discouragement [67]. To address these barriers, Drost, Cuijpers and Schippers [67] from the Netherlands developed Survivalkid, an interactive website for adolescents with a mentally ill parent, which includes interactive psycho-educational activities for adolescents and young adults ages 12–24 years. Survivalkid provides information about parental mental illness, teaches coping skills, allows opportunities for mutual understanding and provides information about ways to contact a staff member, if desired. Adolescents may participate in either private or group chat sessions, which are monitored and facilitated by trained clinicians. Users are encouraged to respond to surveys on the group platform feature and to answer questionnaires about their psychosocial development and use of the group sessions. Similar to the face-to-face programmes described earlier, the website offers parents an explanation and demonstration of the programme but does not actively involve the parents. Over a two-year period, the website received 10,000 hits, with 397 adolescents creating accounts and 237 adolescents visiting several times. The majority of users were female (82.1 per cent) and had parent(s) who were diagnosed with depression. Future studies will be necessary to determine health and health-care outcomes, as well as the role of parents, if any, in the programme's efficacy.

The Coping with Stress, Prevention of Depression and Survivalkid depression prevention programmes seem to reduce the symptoms of depression in adolescents whose parents are diagnosed with depression. The programmes make use of psycho-educational and cognitive behavioural techniques to inform and challenge thoughts and emotions associated with parental depression. Without the direct involvement of the parents, however, children may fail to understand the impact of their parent's depression on the family and their ill parent's perspective on the challenges that the family may face.

Family-Based Interventions

This section describes six intervention programmes that actively involve the parent(s). These family-based depression prevention programmes often include a child component, a parent component and a family component. Together and in parallel, family members learn about the effects of parental depression on the family and learn coping skills that promote resilience.

Preventive Intervention Project and Family Talk

The Preventive Intervention Project (PIP) aims to promote resilience in children who are at increased risk for depression as a result of living with a depressed parent [30, 68, 69]. This project introduces a clinician-based prevention programme that uses a narrative model of therapy with the goal of creating intimate and meaningful family conversations around parental affective illness. The intervention consists of six to eight sessions, including two preliminary sessions with the parents to discuss their mental health history, individual sessions with each child, a planning session, a family meeting and a final session with the parents. In the preliminary parent sessions, the clinician completes a clinical assessment, provides psycho-educational materials and teaches about risk and resilience in children. Parents build a narrative of their experience and make personal connections to the psycho-educational materials. A similar process occurs with the children, whereby the clinician provides developmentally appropriate psycho-educational materials and discusses the child's experience with their parent's affective disorder.

This clinician-based intervention was compared to a lecture-based programme that presented similar psycho-educational materials to parents without connecting those materials to the family's illness experience and without involving the children. Both programmes were associated with positive changes in parents' child-related behaviours and attitudes, and children in both groups reported heightened understanding of parental illness, fewer internalizing problems after the intervention and improved parent-child relationships. However, parents in the clinician-facilitated group reported more behavioural and attitudinal changes associated with their illness and their children's experiences than parents in the lecture group. Moreover, Beardslee et al. [30] found a positive association between the degree of change children reported regarding their understanding of parental illness and the number of changes parents reported regarding child-related behaviours and attitudes. Intervention effects were sustained for 4.5 years

[69]. The PIP suggests the benefits of including both children and parents in efforts to prevent mental illness in children of depressed parents and shows the benefits of tailoring an intervention to each family's individual needs.

The PIP, also known as 'Family Talk', has been adapted for use in several countries. Solantaus et al. [70, 71] developed Finland's Effective Child and Family Programme in 2001 based in part on Family Talk, following a mandate from the Finnish Child Welfare Act requiring increased care for children whose parents receive services for mental health or substance abuse problems. In a feasibility study, Solantaus et al. [70] compared a one- or two-session discussion with parents to a family intervention involving the entire family; they found that both children and parents reported intervention benefits from both conditions, but parents reported a preference for the family-based approach. The authors concluded that both intervention approaches are feasible public health tools that can be widely implemented for support families with a depressed parent.

Likewise, with government funding, researchers in Australia have introduced a national initiative, Children of Parents with a Mental Illness (COPMI), to address the effects of parental mental illness on children [72]. The COPMI initiative generally targets children ages 8–13 years who do not themselves exhibit symptoms of mental illness; COPMI efforts focus on providing children with access to peer support, information about mental illness, coping strategies, a break from caretaking, fun activities and support in building resilience. As part of the COPMI programme and using the Family Talk intervention as a model, Marston et al. [73] developed the Family Focus DVD to present an abbreviated (one-hour) version of the clinician-facilitated Family Talk programme; they conducted a preliminary evaluation of the DVD with parents who were receiving treatment for a diagnosis of anxiety or depression and a child aged 8–12 years. Results indicated that parents who watched the DVD reported changes in their awareness of how their mental illness affected their children and in how they talked about mental illness to their children, although it did not seem to help children and partners talk to the parent with mental illness. A qualitative analysis of parental responses to the Family Focus DVD revealed that many parents felt that their children were happy to now have new information about their parent's mental illness and also described feeling relieved that they now could interact more openly about their mental health concerns [73]. Further research is required to determine whether the DVD had positive clinical effects.

Family Group Cognitive Behavioural (FGCB) Preventive Intervention

The Family Group Cognitive Behavioural (FGCB) preventive intervention aimed to address stressful parent-child interactions that often accompany parental depression and to teach children secondary coping skills to manage stress caused by parents' depression using a small family group format [74]. In a randomized, controlled trial of this programme, Compas et al. [74] enrolled 111 parents with a history of MDD in their child's lifetime and their children aged 9–15 years. Families were randomized into either the family intervention treatment condition or the written information control condition. The family intervention programme used cognitive behavioural techniques in eight weekly and four monthly sessions with groups of up to four families led by two facilitators. In the first three weekly sessions, families were educated on depression and introduced to coping skills; in the next five weekly sessions, parents were taught parenting skills, and children were taught secondary coping skills from separate facilitators. Additionally, in four monthly booster sessions, families practised parenting and coping skills by applying them to challenges the family faced at home. Homework was used throughout the intervention to practise and apply the skills learned during the sessions. In the written information self-study condition, parents and their children were mailed materials on depression and were asked to read them on a schedule that parallelled the eight weekly family intervention sessions [74].

The FGCB preventive intervention has shown clinically significant outcomes at follow-up [74]. Specifically, at 12 months, the family intervention programme was associated with child self-reports of reduced depressive and internalizing symptoms and parent self-reports of reduced depressive symptoms relative to written information; the effect of the family intervention on children's depressive diagnoses was marginally significant [74]. Likewise, at 18 months, there was a significant decrease in self-reported anxiety and depressive symptoms, internalizing symptoms and externalizing symptoms for children in the family intervention programme relative to children in the written information programme; at 24 months, there was a significant group effect on children's depressive diagnoses favouring the family intervention programme [61]. These results indicate that the FGCB preventive intervention effectively reduced both symptoms and diagnoses of depression in children whose parents had a diagnosis of MDD.

Keeping Families Strong

Child and family functioning are the targets of the Keeping Families Strong (KFS) programme, an intervention developed by Valdez et al. [31] for depressed mothers, their partners and their children. Rooted in the family stress and strengths-based models, KFS uses a multifamily group format and a series of separate parent and child sessions to teach and practice cognitive behavioural and solutions-focused techniques with low- and middle-income mothers currently in treatment for depression and their partners and children (aged 9–16 years). Valdez et al. [31] enrolled 17 families into a pilot study of this programme; 10 families attended more than 90 per cent of the sessions and completed the post-intervention assessment. Overall, the goal of the intervention was to encourage conversation among and between families about depression and to teach families cognitive behavioural techniques to manage symptoms and family challenges.

As a result of the intervention, mothers reported improvement in several categories of family life, including large improvements in family togetherness, modest improvements in couple togetherness and small improvements in family management and participation in mealtimes and family chores. Mothers cited improvements in their own symptoms of depression and anxiety and reported small decreases in children's internalizing symptoms and behaviour problems. In addition, children reported an increase in coping and support-seeking strategies and parental acceptance and a decrease in parental rejection [31]. A second pilot study [75], called 'Fortalezas Familiares' ('Family Strengths'), used an adaptation of KFS with Latina mothers and showed large improvements in mothers' perceptions of child hyperactivity, inattention and conduct problems, as well as small improvements in child-reported conflict behaviour, conduct problems, emotional symptoms and prosocial behaviour. In order to determine these programmes' effectiveness, future studies will need to demonstrate significant positive results with a larger sample size and compare the programmes to a control condition.

Family Options

Family Options, a community-based intervention programme centred in Marlborough, Massachusetts, provides support to mothers with serious mental illnesses and their children (ages 18 months–16 years) [32]. The programme aims to build resilience and connect families with professional and peer support to address family-identified needs (e.g., family relationships, transportation, child behaviour management) by pairing families with a family coach who provides support to the family at home, in the community and on the phone on a weekly basis over 12–18 months. A pilot study of the Family Options programme enrolled 22 mothers and their children. Mothers reported diagnoses of MDD, post-traumatic stress disorder, bipolar disorder, anxiety disorder and psychotic disorder, as well as significant trauma histories and other risk factors, including homelessness and drug use. Six-month outcomes indicated significant improvement in maternal trauma symptom severity, mental health status, social support and number of needed services. This programme failed to measure child symptoms, diagnoses and functioning at baseline, and therefore, its impact on children cannot be adequately assessed. However, the goals (i.e., increasing family support and resilience) and method (i.e., connecting families with resources) of the programme are key tenants of effective preventive interventions. The family coaching model may provide insight into the clinical competencies needed to deliver such interventions. In order to determine the effectiveness of the Family Options programme, future studies will need to compare the intervention to a control condition.

EFFEKT-E

EFFEKT-E, a family-based depression programme for depressed mothers and their four- to seven-year-old children, was implemented in a mother-child rehabilitation centre in Germany [76]. The programme sought to improve parenting behaviours and child problem-solving skills and decrease children's risk of developing internalizing and externalizing symptoms. The parenting module (six biweekly sessions) included positive parenting and psycho-educational components that aimed to decrease depressive thoughts surrounding parenting. Mothers also learned effective discipline strategies, coping skills and how to seek out social support. The children's training focused on enhancing problem-solving skills to overcome challenges associated with their mother's depression. In a quasi-experimental study conducted in 13 mother-child clinics in Germany, depressed mothers and their children were enrolled into either the EFFEKT-E experimental group or a control group. After six months, mothers who received the experimental condition reported satisfaction with the programme and noted a significantly increased sense of competence. Positive intervention effects also emerged for children's emotional problems, hyperactivity and inattentiveness, and fewer disturbed mother-child interactions were noted for families in the EFFEKT-E group versus the control group. Future investigations of this intervention approach need to include direct evaluation of the children rather than relying solely on maternal reports of child outcomes, and long-term efficacy data are needed.

Home-Visiting Intervention for Depressed Mothers

Karin van Doesum et al. [77] developed a home-visiting intervention to improve maternal sensitivity in depressed mothers towards their infant children. The goal of the programme – to prevent relationship problems in the mother-infant dyad – is achieved through individualized parent training with a focus on improving mother-infant interaction, attachment security and infant socio-emotional functioning following a video analysis of the mother's parenting behaviours. Video feedback and individual tailoring allow mothers to identify maladaptive communications and interactions and to subsequently learn more adaptive parenting strategies.

In this study [77] comparing this intervention to a telephone coaching control condition, mothers and their infants participated in 8–10 home visits (60–90 minutes) over the course of three to four months. The study measured the effect of the intervention on the quality of the mother-child interaction, child attachment security and infant socio-emotional functioning. Compared to the control group, mother-child dyads in the experimental group were observed to show more maternal sensitivity, maternal structuring, child responsiveness and child involvement at six-month follow-up. Additionally, infants in the experimental condition were found to have more attachment security than infants in the control group. Unfortunately, no measures of children's socio-emotional functioning were taken at baseline; at six-month follow-up, children in the experimental condition were found to have higher competence than children in the control group, but no group differences emerged in externalizing, internalizing or dysregulation scores. All mothers were receiving treatment for their depression during the course of this study, and level of depression decreased for mothers in both the experimental and control groups. Although these results indicate that family-based interventions may improve the mother-infant relationship in families with a depressed mother, more research is needed to examine the role of such family-based interventions on children's mental health outcomes.

Many of the family-based depression prevention interventions described here report positive results across multiple domains, including family functioning, quality of the parent-child relationship and emotional, behavioural and psychological child outcomes. By working with the whole family, clinicians are able to address specific challenges faced in the family context and develop greater interpersonal understanding and collaboration. Future randomized, controlled trials are needed to continue to evaluate the effectiveness of these programmes.

Case Study

In this section, we present the case of Adin Young as an illustration of one of the family-based interventions introduced earlier, Family Talk.[1] Adin is a 42-year-old European-American husband and father of three who presented with his wife, Celia, to address the effects of his depressive illness on Celia and their three daughters, eight-year-old Penny and six-year-old twins Josie and Jill. Adin has no significant medical history, but since college, he has struggled with chronic depressive illness for which he takes antidepressant medication and has worked with a range of individual therapists without relief. Celia worries about the family's financial security because of Adin's unstable work performance, and she worries about Penny's recent difficulties sleeping and being away from her parents. Adin and Celia sought treatment with a therapist who specialized in Family Talk, and

here we trace the progression of their work using this intervention approach.

Module 1

In the first session, the clinician met with Adin and Celia together and expressed admiration for their decision to engage in the Family Talk intervention. She explained the intervention approach, which involves meetings with the parents, individual meetings with the children, planning and conducting a family meeting and planning for the future.

The parents were asked to identify family strengths and also concerns. Adin noted that he and Celia generally have a warm, supportive relationship, although he acknowledged that they have been arguing more frequently now as his depressive symptoms have worsened. He highlighted their strong family network, with two sets of parents nearby, and also reported that the girls were thriving socially and in school. Celia reported more concerns about her relationship with Adin since he has been missing more days of work and has been spending more time at home, doing nothing, while she runs around to take care of the children and the household. Celia also reported that Penny has turned down recent play dates because she doesn't want to be away from the house in the afternoons.

During the first meeting, the clinician encouraged each parent to share their experience of Adin's depression. Adin reported that for the past few months, he has been having difficulty getting out of bed in the morning, and he has found himself dozing at work and feeling unable to focus. He said that when he comes home from work, he goes directly to bed and feels little interest in engaging with the girls. Although he works weekly with a therapist and takes antidepressant medication, his symptoms persist, and he feels that his therapist has run out of ideas to help him. The clinician explored with both parents the possibility that Adin would benefit from meeting with a new psychiatrist who could approach his symptoms with fresh eyes, and she provided some referral information. Celia reported that Adin has been withdrawing from the family more and more and that she feels frustrated and inadequate because she is unable to make him happy.

Finally, the clinician asked the parents to describe their children and to consider the effects of Adin's depressive illness on them. Adin reported that the girls are thriving, and he does not think they notice

---

[1] This character's story is a composite of several cases we have seen using the Family Talk approach.

his depression. Celia insisted that all three girls are affected by Adin's withdrawal from the family. In particular, she expressed concerns that Penny's clingy behaviour represents her worries about Adin.

Together the clinician and the Youngs agreed on some goals for the intervention, including (1) talking with the girls about Adin's depression and (2) increasing healthy family interactions.

Module 2

During this meeting, the clinician provided Adin and Celia with general information about depression. Specifically, she began by asking them what they knew about depression and learned that while they knew Adin's diagnosis, they knew little about the range of symptoms associated with this disorder and about the varied possibilities for treatment. The clinician thus reviewed the common symptoms of depression, risk factors, resiliency and evidence-based treatments.

Also during this meeting, the clinician worked with Adin and Celia to plan individual meetings with Penny, Josie and Jill, which were scheduled for the following week. The clinician explained that the goal of these meetings would be to learn about the children's perspectives on their father's symptoms and how those symptoms might be affecting them individually and as a family. The clinician asked Adin and Celia to mention these meetings to the girls ahead of time. They discussed their sense that none of the girls would feel concerned or uncomfortable about such a meeting, given that Penny meets already with an individual therapist and the twins always enjoy talking to kind adults.

Module 3

During the third meeting with the Young family, the clinician met individually with Penny, Josie and Jill. Penny was a shy, reserved child, but she allowed herself to be drawn into conversation, and she presented as bright, engaging and slightly anxious. After just a few minutes of introduction, she spoke openly about her concerns for her father, who she viewed as fragile and distant, and she also expressed worries about her parents' marriage dissolving. She also expressed concern that if her father got fired from work, they would not have enough money to visit their grandparents in Florida that winter.

Josie was a bouncy little girl who eagerly took the crayons the clinician offered and then sat down to draw while chatting about her school and her friends. The clinician asked Josie about her family, and aside from complaining that Penny is bossy during their walks to school, Josie expressed no concerns at all. She described her mother as always busy and a great cook, and she noted that she spends very little time with her father, who likes to sleep a lot after work. In an individual meeting with Jill, the therapist learned that the little girl was determined to advance to the next-level swim class and that her mother was bringing her to the pool early so that she could practise for the swim test next week. Jill said that she had no worries about her father, who she described as 'always busy'.

At the conclusion of the individual child meetings, the clinician said that she looked forward to meeting with the entire family soon to talk about how things work in their home and to address family members' worries and concerns.

Module 4

During this meeting between the clinician, Adin and Celia, the clinician thanked both parents for allowing her to meet with the children and expressed how delightful she found each girl to be. She highlighted Penny's inquisitive nature and her insight regarding her family's strengths, she spoke with admiration about Josie's enthusiasm and energy and she applauded Jill's determination and persistence.

Together the clinician and parents planned the family meeting. They decided that Adin would tell his children about his struggle with depression and would clearly explain that depression is an illness and that he is getting treatment for his symptoms. Celia agreed to help Adin with this discussion and also noted that she could help provide reassurance that he will be okay and that the girls are not responsible for caring for him. They also planned to give each child the opportunity to share her perception of Adin's illness and also to address the effects of Adin's illness on the family's functioning, including planning ways that the family can enjoy some fun activities together.

Module 5

The clinician opened the family meeting and quickly set some ground rules around confidentiality and taking turns to speak, and then she immediately turned the meeting over to Adin, who was prepared to share with his daughters his long-term struggles with depression. As planned, Celia jumped in to support Adin in this discussion, displaying the unity that they agreed would help Penny to feel less fearful about her parents' arguing.

The parents then invited the children to share their worries. In response to Penny's concerns about the family's finances, the parents assured all three girls that Adin was not in danger of losing his job and that they had the resources they needed to manage family expenses long term, even if he would not be able to work for some time. Celia also explained to Penny that she did not need to worry about her parents when she was not home because they were working with doctors to treat Adin's illness, and Celia would make sure that he was cared for at all times. When Josie and Jill expressed that they missed Adin because he goes right to his room after work, the parents explained that Adin's depression means that he often needs some 'break' time when he gets home from work. They did, however, talk as a family about building in some family fun time each week and together generated a list of activities they could plan for each week that were not too expensive, felt manageable to Adin and would strengthen family connections. They concluded by planning another family meeting in one month, when they could connect again about Adin's depression and also check in on how their family fun time was going.

Module 6

During this session, the clinician congratulated Adin and Celia on a successful family meeting and invited each parent to share their impressions of it. Adin noted that prior to the meeting, he was worried about how it would go but soon found that he felt some relief in openly talking about his depression with his daughters. Celia expressed relief that Penny readily accepted their reassurances and that all three girls were so eager to plan some fun family activities. They reported that just the previous evening, the family had made popcorn and watched a movie together and that they were hoping the weather would hold so that they could go on a hike together on Saturday afternoon, allowing Adin time in the morning to sleep late and prepare mentally for the activity. They discussed plans for the next family meeting, now just over two weeks away.

Module 7

Six months later, the therapist met again with Adin and Celia for a follow-up. They reported that Adin has been working with a new psychiatrist, Dr. Plough, who prescribed a different medication. While Adin still struggles during the afternoons at work, he has less difficulty getting himself to the office each day, and Dr. Plough has helped him to develop strategies that enable him to have more energy for his daughters when he returns home each evening. They reported that Penny continues to meet biweekly with her individual therapist for support but that she has been more willing to go to friends' houses after school since the start of the new school year. They agreed that Josie remained her cheerful self and really seems to enjoy the family's midweek movie nights, which have continued since their first family meeting in the spring; they shared that Jill did pass her swim test and felt proud of being more accomplished than her twin in this area. Both parents reported that they have found monthly family meetings to be an important way for all family members to check in about how things are going and to keep lines of communication open.

Conclusions

This case illustrates the strengths-based Family Talk approach to intervention with families when a parent is depressed. This approach is often combined with other forms of treatment for family members, such as individual therapy for Adin and Penny and, ultimately, couples therapy for Adin and Celia. The overall goal of the Family Talk approach is to help families create a narrative about parental depression and to encourage shifts in parenting behaviours and attitudes to support healthy child development. It is indeed a preventive approach that aims to reduce risk factors associated with psychopathology in children of parents with depression.

Conclusions: Clinical Competencies Associated with the Delivery of Depression Prevention Interventions

In order to deliver effective depression prevention interventions to families with a depressed parent, clinicians must be competent in several domains. It is important for clinicians to follow implementation guidelines for evidence-based interventions, especially when these programmes are not highly manualized. Doing so will ensure that clinician-facilitated programmes provide accurate and equal prevention to all participants regardless of who is implementing the programme. To support successful outcomes through family-based depression prevention programmes, clinicians must exhibit both generic and specific therapeutic competencies [78]. Essential generic competencies include the ability to establish a therapeutic alliance and uphold ethical principles, familiarity with child and adolescent development principles and cultural humility [79]; specific competencies include skills surrounding the techniques associated with cognitive and behavioural interventions given that these approaches are most commonly employed in family-based depression prevention interventions.

Generic therapeutic competencies are integral to delivering any type of prevention or intervention programme [78]. Such competencies, including the ability to establish a therapeutic alliance while maintaining ethical principles, ensure that the clinician is creating an appropriate relationship with families. Clinicians must respect parents' privacy by establishing what details of the parent's illness and treatment will be shared with the child, receiving parental consent to discuss the parent's illness with the child and to ask children about their own experiences or symptoms and maintaining family confidentiality. Another component of creating an appropriate and ethical relationship with the family is establishing that the parents are the most knowledgeable informants when it comes to their children; clinicians should respect the parent-child dyad and parental role and should partner with parents in supporting children's healthy development.

A second essential generic therapeutic competency is knowledge of the principles of development. Clinicians who work with families need to be able to work effectively with both adults and children and need to be able to understand the developmental competencies of children and adolescents. Clinicians need to consider how parental depression influences child outcomes and what factors make children more or less vulnerable to their parent's depression across development. For example, clinicians need to understand that play therapy may be most appropriate when interacting with young children about parental depression, whereas more direct and empathic language may be more appropriate when speaking with adolescents. Similarly, a focus on the concrete effects of parental depression (e.g., parents not being able to help with homework) may resonate more with younger children, whereas it may be more appropriate to focus on the emotional effects of parental unavailability with adolescents.

A third generic therapeutic competency involves the idea of practising with cultural humility [79]. Clinicians must be aware that factors such as race, ethnicity and culture may affect their approach to working with families around the effects of parental depression and that different cultural groups may hold different beliefs about mental illness and parenting roles. Clinicians must be careful to refrain from imposing their own cultural values and environmental experiences on their clients and must work to adapt intervention approaches to a family's cultural values.

In addition to generic therapeutic competencies, clinicians should be adept at specific preventive intervention techniques, including those related to cognitive behavioural therapy and interpersonal therapy approaches, and must understand which prevention programmes are likely to be most effective for particular families. Although prevention programmes make use of varying techniques (e.g., cognitive restructuring, communication skills), clinicians should be familiar with the theories behind commonly used programmes, including theories related to cognitive behavioural therapy, interpersonal therapy and mindfulness approaches. Family characteristics should also be taken into consideration. Timing of parental depression, for example, may play a role in the effectiveness of family-based prevention programmes such that families with a currently depressed parent may not benefit from family-based depression prevention interventions until current depressive symptoms have been treated or are in remission [65]. Depression prevention interventions seem to be better delivered at times of relative wellness for parents [80]. In addition to knowledge of the target population served by the intervention, familiarity with the programme's theories, goals and techniques will support clinicians in providing appropriate preventative care to the families they serve.

Children who have a depressed parent are at an increased risk for developing depressive symptoms themselves and for exhibiting deficits in cognitive, social, emotional and academic domains [15–36]. Risk for these children is heightened by factors related to the child, parent and environment, but risk may be reduced in the presence of resilient characteristics. Family-based depression prevention interventions aim to reduce the likelihood that depressive symptoms and episodes will onset. In such programmes, clinicians work with the family to decrease risk factors, increase protective factors and bolster resilient characteristics by identifying what supports the family already has in place and by teaching effective parenting and coping skills. There is evidence to suggest that family-based depression prevention programmes may reduce the likelihood that children will develop depressive symptoms or episodes [13, 14, 64]. Further research is needed to expand upon pilot-study programmes, assess child outcomes from baseline and compare interventions to control conditions [31, 32, 67, 76]. As nations continue to recognize the public health burden of depression and need for preventive programming, clinicians must be willing and able to accommodate families seeking depression prevention intervention.

References

1. Substance Abuse and Mental Health Services Administration (SAMHSA). *Key Substance Use and Mental Health Indicators in The United States: Results from the 2017 National Survey on Drug Use and Health.* Rockville, MD: Center for Behavioral Health Statistics and Quality, Substance Abuse and Mental Health Services Administration, 2018.

2. Institute of Medicine (IOM). *Depression in Parents, Parenting, and Children: Opportunities to Improve Identification, Treatment, and Prevention.* Washington, DC: National Research Council (US) and Institute of Medicine (US), 2009.

3. Beardslee WR, Versage EM, Gladstone TR. Children of affectively ill parents: A review of the past 10 years. *Journal of the American Academy of Child and Adolescent Psychiatry* 1998; 37(11):1134–41.

4. Weissman MM, Wickramaratne P, Nomura Y, et al. Offspring of depressed parents: 20 years later. *American Journal of Psychiatry* 2006; 163(6):1001–8.

5. Murray L, Arteche A, Fearon P, et al. Maternal postnatal depression and the development of depression in offspring up to 16 years of age. *Journal of the American Academy of Child and Adolescent Psychiatry* 2011; 50(5):460–70.

6. Hammen C, Burge D, Burney E, Adrian C. Longitudinal study of diagnoses in children of women with unipolar and bipolar affective disorder. *Archives of General Psychiatry* 1990; 47(12):1112–17.

7. Cummings EM, Keller PS, Davies PT. Towards a family process model of maternal and paternal depressive symptoms: exploring multiple relations with child and family functioning. *Journal of Child Psychology and Psychiatry* 2005; 46(5):479–89.

8. Smith M. Parental mental health: disruptions to parenting and outcomes for children. *Child and Family Social Work* 2004; 9(1):3–11.

9. Luoma I, Tamminen T, Kaukonen P, et al. Longitudinal study of maternal depressive symptoms and child well-being. *Journal of the American Academy of Child and Adolescent Psychiatry* 2001; 40(12):1367–74.

10. Beardslee WR, Solantaus TS, Morgan BS, et al. Preventive interventions for children of parents with depression: International perspectives. *Medical Journal of Australia* 2013; 199(Suppl 3):S23–5.

11. Gladstone TR, Beardslee WR. Treatment, intervention, and prevention with children of depressed parents: A developmental perspective. In: Goodman SH, Gotlib H (eds.), *Children of Depressed Parents: Mechanisms of Risk and Implications for Treatment.* Washington, DC: American Psychological Association, 2002, pp. 277–305.

12. Goodman SH, Gotlib IH. Transmission of risk to children of depressed parents: Integration and conclusions. *Psychological Review* 1999; 106(3):458–90.

13. Garber J, Ciesla JA, McCauley E, et al. Remission of depression in parents: Links to healthy functioning in their children. *Child Development* 2011; 82(1):226–43.

14. Foster CE, Webster MC, Weissman MM, et al. Remission of maternal depression: Relations to family functioning and youth internalizing and externalizing symptoms. *Journal of Clinical Child and Adolescent Psychology* 2008; 37(4):714–24.

15. Hay DF, Pawlby S, Sharp D, et al. Intellectual problems shown by 11-year-old children whose mothers had postnatal depression. *Journal of Child Psychology and Psychiatry* 2001; 42(7):871–89.

16. Letourneau NL, Tramonte L, Willms JD. Maternal depression, family functioning and children's longitudinal development. *Journal of Pediatric Nursing* 2013; 28(3):223–34.

17. Leinonen JA, Solantaus TS, Punamaki RL. Parental mental health and children's adjustment: The quality of marital interaction and parenting as mediating factors. *Journal of Child Psychology and Psychiatry* 2003; 44(2):227–41.

18. Shen H, Magnusson C, Rai D, et al. Associations of parental depression with child school performance at age 16 years in Sweden. *JAMA Psychiatry* 2016; 73(3):239–46.

19. Murray L, Sinclair D, Cooper P, et al. The socioemotional development of 5-year-old children of postnatally depressed mothers. *Journal of Child Psychology and Psychiatry* 1999; **40**(8):1259–71.

20. Hay DF, Pawlby S, Waters CS, et al. Mothers' antenatal depression and their children's antisocial outcomes. *Child Development* 2010; **81**(1):149–65.

21. Maughan A, Cicchetti D, Toth SL, Rogosch FA. Early-occurring maternal depression and maternal negativity in predicting young children's emotion regulation and socioemotional difficulties. *Journal of Abnormal Child Psychology* 2007; **35**(5):685–703.

22. Ramchandani P, Stein A, Evans J, O'Connor TG, Team AS. Paternal depression in the postnatal period and child development: A prospective population study. *Lancet* 2005; **365**(9478):2201–5.

23. Murray L, Halligan SL, Adams G, et al. Socioemotional development in adolescents at risk for depression: The role of maternal depression and attachment style. *Developmental Psychopathology* 2006; **18**(2):489–516.

24. Kahn RS, Brandt D, Whitaker RC. Combined effect of mothers' and fathers' mental health symptoms on children's behavioral and emotional well-being. *Archives of Pediatrics and Adolescent Medicine* 2004; **158**(8):721–9.

25. Foley DL, Pickles A, Simonoff E, et al. Parental concordance and comorbidity for psychiatric disorder and associate risks for current psychiatric symptoms and disorders in a community sample of juvenile twins. *Journal of Child Psychology and Psychiatry* 2001; **42**(3):381–94.

26. Lieb R, Isensee B, Hofler M, et al. Parental major depression and the risk of depression and other mental disorders in offspring: A prospective longitudinal community study. *Archives of General Psychiatry* 2002; **59**(4):365–74.

27. Hoffman C, Crnic KA, Baker JK. Maternal depression and parenting: Implications for children's emergent emotion regulation and behavioral functioning. *Parenting: Science and Practice* 2006; **6**(4):271–95.

28. Meadows SO, McLanahan SS, Brooks-Gunn J. Parental depression and anxiety and early childhood behavior problems across family types. *Journal of Marriage and Family* 2007; **69**(5):1162–77.

29. Middleton M, Scott SL, Renk K. Parental depression, parenting behaviours, and behaviour problems in young children. *Infant and Child Development: An International Journal of Research and Practice* 2009; **18**(4):323–6.

30. Beardslee WR, Gladstone TR, Wright EJ, Cooper AB. A family-based approach to the prevention of depressive symptoms in children at risk: Evidence of parental and child change. *Pediatrics* 2003; **112**(2): e119–31.

31. Valdez CR, Mills CL, Barrueco S, et al. A pilot study of a family-focused intervention for children and families affected by maternal depression. *Journal of Family Therapy* 2011; **33**(1):3–19.

32. Nicholson J, Albert K, Gershenson B, et al. Family options for parents with mental illnesses: A developmental, mixed methods pilot study. *Psychiatric Rehabilitation Journal* 2009; **33**(2):106–14.

33. Jackson D, Mannix J. Giving voice to the burden of blame: A feminist study of mothers' experiences of mother blaming. *International Journal of Nursing Practice* 2004; **10**(4):150–8.

34. Lewis G, Neary M, Polek E, et al. The association between paternal and adolescent depressive symptoms: Evidence from two population-based cohorts. *Lancet Psychiatry* 2017; **4**(12):920–6.

35. Lovejoy MC, Graczyk PA, O'Hare E, Neuman G. Maternal depression and parenting behavior: A meta-analytic review. *Clinical Psychology Review* 2000; **20**(5):561–92.

36. Barker ED, Copeland W, Maughan B, et al. Relative impact of maternal depression and associated risk factors on offspring psychopathology. *British Journal of Psychiatry* 2012; **200**(2):124–9.

37. Gross HE, Shaw DS, Moilanen KL. Reciprocal associations between boys' externalizing problems and mothers' depressive symptoms. *Journal of Abnormal Child Psychology* 2008; **36**(5):693–709.

38. Hammen C, Brennan PA. Severity, chronicity, and timing of maternal depression and risk for adolescent offspring diagnoses in a community sample. *Archives of General Psychiatry* 2003; **60**(3):253–8.

39. Foster CE, Webster MC, Weissman MM, et al. Course and severity of maternal depression: Associations with family functioning and child adjustment. *Journal of Youth and Adolescence* 2008; **37**(8):906–16.

40. Bagner DM, Pettit JW, Lewinsohn PM, Seeley JR. Effect of maternal depression on child behavior: A sensitive period? *Journal of the American Academy of Child and Adolescent Psychiatry* 2010; **49** (7):699–707.

41. Van de Velde S, Bracke P, Levecque K. Gender differences in depression in 23 European countries: Cross-national variation in the gender gap in depression. *Social Science and Medicine* 2010; **71** (2):305–13.

42. Wade TJ, Cairney J, Pevalin DJ. Emergence of gender differences in depression during adolescence: National panel results from three countries. *Journal of the American Academy of Child and Adolescent Psychiatry* 2002; **41**(2):190–8.

43. Mason WA, Chmelka MB, Trudeau L, Spoth RL. Gender moderation of the intergenerational transmission and stability of depressive symptoms from early adolescence to early adulthood. *Journal of Youth and Adolescence* 2017; **46** (1):248–60.

44. Jessee AD, Mangelsdorf SC, Shigeto A, Wong MS. Temperament as a moderator of the effects of parental depressive symptoms on child behavior problems. *Social Development* 2012; **21**(6):610–27.

45. Slagt M, Dubas JS, Dekovic M, van Aken MA. Differences in sensitivity to parenting depending on child temperament: A meta-analysis. *Psychology Bulletin* 2016; **142**(10):1068–110.

46. Spence SH, Najman JM, Bor W, et al. Maternal anxiety and depression, poverty and marital relationship factors during early childhood as predictors of anxiety and depressive symptoms in adolescence. *Journal of Child Psychology and Psychiatry* 2002; **43**(4):457–69.

47. Kiernan KE, Huerta MC. Economic deprivation, maternal depression, parenting and children's cognitive and emotional development in early childhood. *British Journal of Sociology* 2008; **59** (4):783–806.

48. Dumont A, Provost M. Resilience in adolescents: Protective role of social support, coping strategies, self-esteem, and social activities on experience of stress and depression. *Journal of Youth and Adolescence* 1999; **28**(3):343–63.

49. Surkan PJ, Peterson KE, Hughes MD, Gottlieb BR. The role of social networks and support in postpartum women's depression: A multiethnic urban sample. *Maternal and Child Health Journal* 2006; **10**(4):375–83.

50. Herwig JE, Wirtz M, Bengel J. Depression, partnership, social support, and parenting: interaction of maternal factors with behavioral problems of the child. *Journal of Affective Disorders* 2004; **80**(2–3):199–208.

51. McCarty CA, McMahon RJ, Conduct Problems Prevention Research Group. Mediators of the relation between maternal depressive symptoms and child internalizing and disruptive behavior disorders. *Journal of Family Psychology* 2003; **17** (4):545–56.

52. Chen HJ, Kovacs PJ. Working with families in which a parent has depression: A resilience perspective. *Families in Society: The Journal of Contemporary Social Services* 2013; **94**(2):114–20.

53. Chapman DP, Whitfield CL, Felitti VJ, et al. Adverse childhood experiences and the risk of depressive disorders in adulthood. *Journal of Affective Disorders* 2004; **82**(2):217–25.

54. Evans GW, Li D, Whipple SS. Cumulative risk and child development. *Psychology Bulletin* 2013; **139** (6):1342–96.

55. Beardslee WR, Gladstone TR, O'Connor EE. Transmission and prevention of mood disorders among children of affectively ill parents: A review. *Journal of the American Academy of Child and Adolescent Psychiatry* 2011; **50**(11):1098–109.

56. Erskine HE, Moffitt TE, Copeland WE, et al. A heavy burden on young minds: The global burden of mental and substance use disorders in children and youth. *Psychological Medicine* 2015; **45**(7):1551–63.

57. Bodden DHM, Stikkelbroek Y, Dirksen CD. Societal burden of adolescent depression: An overview and cost-of-illness study. *Journal of Affective Disorders* 2018; **241**:256–62.

58. Dieleman JL, Baral R, Birger M, et al. US spending on personal health care and public health, 1996–2013. *Journal of the American Medical Association* 2016; **316** (24):2627–46.

59. Lynch FL, Hornbrook M, Clarke GN, et al. Cost-effectiveness of an intervention to prevent depression in at-risk teens. *Archives of General Psychiatry* 2005; **62**(11):1241–8.

60. Lynch FL, Dickerson JF, Clarke GN, et al. Cost-effectiveness of preventing depression among at-risk youths: Postintervention and 2-year follow-up. *Psychiatric Services* 2019; **70**(1):279–86.

61. Compas BE, Forehand R, Thigpen JC, et al. Family group cognitive-behavioral preventive intervention for families of depressed parents: 18- and 24-month outcomes. *Journal of Consulting and Clinical Psychology* 2011; **79**(4):488–99.

62. Merry SN, Hetrick SE, Cox GR, et al. Psychological and educational interventions for preventing depression in children and adolescents. *Cochrane Database of Systematic Reviews* 2011:(12):CD003380.

63. Horowitz JL, Garber J. The prevention of depressive symptoms in children and adolescents: A meta-analytic review. *Journal of Consulting and Clinical Psychology* 2006; **74**(3):401–15.

64. Clarke GN, Hornbrook M, Lynch F, et al. A randomized trial of a group cognitive intervention for preventing depression in adolescent offspring of depressed parents. *Archives of General Psychiatry* 2001; **58**(12):1127–34.

65. Garber J, Clarke GN, Weersing VR, et al. Prevention of depression in at-risk adolescents: A randomized controlled trial. *Journal of the American Medical Association* 2009; **301**(21):2215–24.

66. Cuijpers P, Munoz RF, Clarke GN, Lewinsohn PM. Psychoeducational treatment and prevention of depression: The 'Coping with Depression' course

thirty years later. *Clinical Psychology Review* 2009; **29** (5):449–58.

67. Drost LM, Cuijpers P, Schippers GM. Developing an interactive website for adolescents with a mentally ill family member. *Clinical Child Psychology and Psychiatry* 2011; **16**(3):351–64.

68. Focht L, Beardslee WR. 'Speech after Long Silence': The use of narrative therapy in a preventive intervention for children of parents with affective disorder. *Family Process* 1996; **35**(4):407–22.

69. Beardslee WR, Gladstone TRG, Wright EJ, Forbes P. Long-term effects from a randomized trial of two public health preventive interventions for parental depression. *Journal of Family Psychology* 2007; **21** (4):703–13.

70. Solantaus T, Toikka S, Alasuutari M, et al. Safety, feasibility and family experiences of preventive interventions for children and families with parental depression. *International Journal of Mental Health Promotion* 2009; **11**(4): 15–24.

71. Solantaus TS, Toikka S. The effective family programme: Preventative services for the children of mentally ill parents in Finland. *International Journal of Mental Health Promotion* 2006; **8** (3):37–44.

72. Reupert AE, Maybery DJ. A 'snapshot' of Australian programs to support children and adolescents whose parents have a mental illness. *Psychiatric Rehabilitation Journal* 2009; **33**(2):125–32.

73. Marston N, Maybery D, Reupert A. Empowering families where a parent has a mental illness: A preliminary evaluation of the 'Family Focus' DVD. *Advances in Mental Health* 2014; **12** (2):136–46.

74. Compas BE, Forehand R, Keller G, et al. Randomized controlled trial of a family cognitive-behavioral preventive intervention for children of depressed parents. *Journal of Consulting and Clinical Psychology* 2009; **77**(6):1007–20.

75. Valdez CR, Padilla B, Moore SM, Magana S. Feasibility, acceptability, and preliminary outcomes of the Fortalezas Familiares intervention for Latino families facing maternal depression. *Family Process* 2013; **52**(3):394–410.

76. Bühler A, Kötter C, Jaursch S, Lösel F. Prevention of familial transmission of depression: EFFEKT-E, a selective program for emotionally burdened families. *Journal of Public Health* 2011; **19**:321–7.

77. van Doesum KT, Riksen-Walraven JM, Hosman CM, Hoefnagels C. A randomized controlled trial of a home-visiting intervention aimed at preventing relationship problems in depressed mothers and their infants. *Child Development* 2008; **79**(3):547–61.

78. Sburlati ES, Schniering CA, Lyneham HJ, Rapee RM. A model of therapist competencies for the empirically supported cognitive behavioral treatment of child and adolescent anxiety and depressive disorders. *Clinical Child and Family Psychology Review* 2011; **14** (1):89–109.

79. Beardslee WR. Master clinician review: Parental depression and family health and wellness: What clinicians can do and reflections on opportunities for the future. *Journal of American Academy of Child and Adolescent Psychiatry* (in press).

80. Gladstone TRG, Diehl A, Thomann LO, Beardslee WR. The association between parental depression and child psychosocial intervention outcomes: Directions for future research. *Harvard Review of Psychiatry*; **58**(8):759–67.

Working with Parents with Anxiety in Family Intervention

Sisi Guo and Tara S. Peris

Over one-quarter of adults in the general population meet diagnostic criteria for an anxiety disorder (AD) [1, 2]. As one of the most common mental disorders, AD are also among the most disabling conditions; it is associated with a range of negative outcomes, including poorer physical health, lower quality of life and reduced workplace productivity [3, 4]. Increasingly, researchers are interested in how anxiety hinders parenting functions [5, 6]. Although the rates of AD among caregivers is not yet well established, there is growing evidence that parental anxiety plays an important role in both the development and treatment of a range of childhood disorders (e.g., [7–10]). In this chapter, we review the extant literature on caregivers with anxiety or AD in order to (1) define the problem, (2) identify treatment approaches that may be of use for offsetting its impact on youth psychopathology and (3) develop a set of clinical competencies for working with this particular population in the context of treatment for child and adolescent psychopathology. In doing so, we document both advancements and challenges in the development of effective treatments for complex families and highlight important future directions in family-based interventions.

Nature of the Problem

The theory of multifinality posits that a single risk factor such as parental psychopathology can predict a wide range of negative outcomes [11]. Indeed, children of parents with a mental health condition assume greater family responsibilities, experience lower academic achievement and social functioning and are at higher risk for mental disorders of their own [12, 13]. In addition, children of parents with a mental disorder are less likely to access care and receive the necessary treatment compared to children from families not affected by parental psychopathology [14]. Building on this robust field of research, scholars have begun to examine youth adjustment in the context of specific parental psychopathologies (e.g., parental depression, substance abuse and anxiety) [15–17].

The research linking parent and child AD is particularly robust [18–21]. Both top-down and bottom-up studies show that AD tends to run in families [7, 22]. Compared to the general population, rates of AD are higher among family members of affected individuals. Up to 60 per cent of parents with an AD have an anxious child, and more than 80 per cent of children with an AD have an anxious parent [19, 23–8]. Children of anxious parents have a four-fold risk of AD compared to children of healthy parents and a two-fold risk compared to children of parents with other psychiatric diagnoses [29]. The risk for AD also increases if the child has more than one parent with an AD [18, 20]. Finally, there appears to be specificity in the transmission of certain ADs. In particular, panic disorder, social anxiety disorder and specific phobias are three subtypes with high rates of transmission between parents and children [30–3].

In contrast, the association between parental anxiety and other child and adolescent mental health outcomes is less clear. In terms of internalizing problems, recent meta-analyses found that children of anxious parents are more likely to develop depressive disorders than children of healthy parents [29, 34]. This is the case whether parents have or do not have co-morbid mood disorders. However, the risk of developing depressive disorders disappears when children of anxious parents are compared to children of parents with other psychiatric diagnoses. In terms of externalizing problems, research has produced largely inconsistent results. Some studies found that parental anxiety confers greater risk for behavioural problems [19, 35–8]. However, others have found no association between parental anxiety and externalizing behaviours [18–21, 39]. In fact, one study found that parental anxiety attenuated the link between externalizing symptoms between parents and children [39].

Taken together, research to date provides partial support for the theory of multifinality, with children of anxious parents being at the greatest risk of developing an AD of their own. This raises the question of how anxiety is passed down from parents to children. Twin and adoption studies estimate that genetics account for up to one-third of the variability in AD [22]. In order to understand what other factors contribute to the intergenerational transmission of anxiety, researchers have turned to the shared environment between parents and children, paying particular attention to the *parenting behaviours* of anxious caregivers. Here it is important to note the difference between parenting styles and behaviours. Parenting *styles* are the global parental attitudes and parenting patterns, whereas parenting *behaviours* are the specific kinds of interactions parents have with children in specific situations [40]. Earlier studies of anxious parenting relied largely on self-report measures to identify parenting styles of parents with anxiety or AD. This line of research raised the methodological issue of retrospective and potentially biased recall from anxious individuals about broad patterns of parental attitudes and behaviours [41, 42]. Recent studies have shifted towards observational or experimental designs to examine in real time parenting behaviours of parents with and without anxiety during interactions with their children in unstructured and structured tasks.

Observational and experimental studies have found notable differences in parenting behaviours between anxious and non-anxious parents. Compared to control parents, parents with AD or elevated symptoms of anxiety tend to be more critical, grant less autonomy, display less warmth and positivity, use more catastrophic thinking and disengage or withdraw more during interactions with their children [43–45]. Moreover, anxious parents are more likely than non-anxious parents to transfer information concerning threat and model anxious responses for their children [46–48]. Of note, context and anxiety subtypes appear to be important factors to consider in distinguishing the behaviours of anxious and non-anxious parents. Though the two groups of parents may behave similarly in non-stressful situations, differences are more likely to emerge when the situation is perceived as challenging and relates to the parent's specific anxiety [6, 49, 50].

Many of the parenting behaviours seen commonly but not exclusively in anxious parents may help to explain the transmission of anxiety within families. Labelled as *anxiety-enhancing behaviours*, the parenting practices that have been most implicated in the development of child AD are parental control and negativity [8, 10]. It is theorized that when parents excessively regulate their children's behaviours by preventing them from facing threat, encouraging avoidance and discouraging independence, they are communicating to their children that the world is dangerous and uncontrollable and deterring them from developing new coping strategies to face age-appropriate challenges. As a result, children do not achieve a sense of control over feared situations and are unable to gather evidence that can contradict a biased view of the world [51, 52]. Parental control as a mechanism of transmission has received extensive support from cross-sectional and experimental studies (e.g., [40, 53, 54]). Similarly, it is theorized that when parents are negative and critical in their interactions with their children, they are communicating to their children that the world is hostile and threatening. Finally, others have also posited that when children receive such feedback from their parents, they are more likely to experience low self-worth and competence and expect greater negative outcomes in their environment, all of which are associated with anxiety [55, 56], a hypothesis that has received less consistent support from empirical research [53].

Scholars contend that parents are likely to pass down their anxious thinking and behaviours to their children through modelling and information transfer. Indeed, a number of studies have found that parents' expression of anxiety predicted fearful behaviours in their children at a later point [47, 48, 57–9]. There is also some empirical support that parents' communication of threat and negative information predicted children's anxiety at a later time [46, 60, 61]. Consistent with social learning theory, children who observe their parents act or communicate in an anxious manner are likely to act and think in a similar fashion, perpetuating catastrophic thinking and avoidant behaviours rather than developing effective coping strategies [8].

In their influential model of intergenerational transmission of depression, Goodman and Gotlib [62] pointed to the important interactions between parent and child characteristics. This model appears to be apt for the transmission of anxiety as well [44, 46, 48, 55, 63–5]. Recent aetiological models of anxiety posit that just as anxious caregivers can promote anxiety in their children through anxiety-enhancing behaviours, anxious children can also elicit anxious parenting behaviours from their caregivers. There is growing support for the bidirectional transfer of anxiety within families. In one longitudinal study, researchers not only found that youth's perception of anxious maternal behaviours predicted youth anxiety after one year, but they also found that maternal perception of youth anxiety at baseline predicted anxious maternal behaviours later [66]. In experimental studies, parents' and children's anxious behaviours actively influenced each other. Hudson and Doyle [67] found that mothers displayed more anxious behaviours during interactions with anxious children than non-anxious children, regardless of whether they had a child with an AD. In dyads of children and parents with and without anxiety, anxious dyads responded to each other more negatively and engaged in less productive behaviours related to a laboratory task. In contrast, non-anxious dyads responded to each other with more warmth and showed more productive behaviours in order to complete the assigned task [68, 69]. The reciprocal relationship between parent and child anxiety has also been documented in treatment research; treatment of childhood anxiety not only decreased rates of youth and parental anxiety, but the reduction in youth anxiety preceded improvement in negative parenting behaviours and parental anxiety [63, 70, 71].

Treatment Approaches

The last several decades have seen a rapid growth in empirically supported interventions for child and adolescent disorders [72]. In particular, cognitive behavioural therapy (CBT) has garnered extensive support from efficacy and effectiveness trials as an evidence-based treatment (EBT) for a range of disorders, including anxiety, depression and behaviour problems [73–6]. Despite the strong evidence base, many children do not respond to CBT [7, 77], which in its most investigated form has been child focused with limited involvement from parents [8]. Recognizing the limits of individually focused treatments, researchers and clinicians are increasingly interested in parent-involved and family-based interventions to address systemic issues such as parent

psychopathology and parent-child conflict that may impede treatment [78].

Indeed, there is growing evidence that parental psychopathology such as AD is not only a risk factor for negative child outcomes but also a deterrent in the treatment of child problems. Most of the research examining the negative effect of parental anxiety have centred on child AD treatment (e.g., [79–85]). Children of anxious parents show less favourable treatment outcomes than those of non-anxious parents. This is particularly true if the child is young [79] or has parents with clinical levels of anxiety (e.g., [82, 83, 86]). Findings are more mixed when parental anxiety is considered along a continuum (e.g., [87]) and for adolescents (e.g., [79]).

Given the negative association between parental anxiety and symptom improvement, researchers and clinicians have begun to explore how treatments can be enhanced to address parental anxiety and, more broadly, anxiety-enhancing parenting behaviours. In 2007, the American Academy of Child and Adolescent Psychiatry arrived at a set of clinical guidelines for working with families in child treatment. The guidelines advise clinicians (1) to pay attention to the role of parental anxiety in modelling anxious behaviour, along with the quality of parent-child interactions and communication, and (2) to increase parental skill in supporting the child's use of coping skills learned in treatment [88]. In theory, child treatment can be enhanced if parents are able to learn new and more adaptive ways of thinking and behaving. This is the principle behind parenting programmes for externalizing disorders, which have received extensive empirical support (for a review, see Michelson et al. [89]); there is also parallel evidence emerging in child anxiety [90] and obsessive-compulsive disorder (OCD) [91]. By identifying and modifying parents' maladaptive cognitions and actions, parent-involved interventions can (1) address parental factors that contribute to the maintenance of childhood problems and (2) facilitate the successful transfer, generalization and maintenance of new skills that children learn in treatment [8, 9]. A prominent theoretical model of change for parent-involved and family-based interventions is the *transfer of control* [92, 93]. Scholars posit that by actively involving parents in child treatment, knowledge and skills for coping are first communicated and transferred from the clinician to the parents and eventually to the child.

To date, no treatment protocol has been designed exclusively for parents with AD. Rather, parenting programmes have been developed to target anxiety-enhancing behaviours that can interfere in the treatment of various childhood disorders. Among these family-based interventions, family CBT for child AD stands out in its treatment approach for working with parents, many of whom experience anxiety or AD of their own. In family CBT, parents either join the child in treatment sessions or have individual meetings with the clinician. The general goals of these parent sessions are to (1) remove reinforcement of child's anxious behaviours, (2) model appropriate behaviours and (3) reduce family conflict [9]. Parents are taught to reinforce brave behaviours with praise and reward and extinguish avoidant behaviours and expressions of fear with compassionate responses initially and planned ignoring if maladaptive behaviours persist. To model adaptive coping skills, clinicians work with parents to recognize their own anxious responses in stressful situations and modify their anxious and maladaptive thinking and actions. Finally, parents learn techniques to decrease conflict and improve family communication in order to foster a more positive parent-child relationship. To achieve these broad parenting goals, family CBT for child AD can be further distilled into the following specific treatment components: (1) psycho-education about the aetiology of anxiety, with an emphasis on the role of family, (2) parent training to promote positive parenting behaviours (e.g., decreasing parental control and granting more autonomy to the child), (3) parental modelling of useful coping skills during stressful situations, (4) contingency management to increase adaptive child behaviours (e.g., decreasing avoidance and increasing brave behaviours), (5) cognitive restructuring to replace maladaptive parental beliefs about their children and the environment, (6) parental anxiety management by teaching parents cognitive behavioural skills to decrease anxiety or seek additional support, (7) collaborative problem-solving to reduce parent-child conflict and increase effective solutions to problems, (8) communication skills to promote positive interactions among family members and (9) relapse prevention to sustain treatment gains [7, 94].

A number of randomized, controlled trials (RCTs) have assessed the efficacy of family CBT for child and adolescent AD. In general, family CBT outperforms waiting-list controls in reducing youth anxiety (e.g.,

[55, 95–7]). A few studies have found that family CBT is better than child-focused CBT alone in the treatment of youth anxiety [54, 98, 99]. However, other studies have not found the added value of family involvement over treatment of the child alone [7, 90, 97]. Methodological differences appear to explain some of the mixed findings [9]. The RCTs included a broad range of anxiety symptoms and diagnoses, age and parent psychopathology. Further, the degree of parent involvement also varied in format (i.e., joint versus independent parent sessions), number of parent/family sessions and the role of the parents (e.g., co-therapist, co-client or collaborators). Some scholars argue that it is too premature to draw conclusion about the enhanced benefits of parental involvement [7, 9]. Instead, the decision to include parents in treatment should be personalized based on the child's age, primary diagnosis and parent psychopathology. For example, the involvement of parents as co-clients appears to have added benefit over individual treatment when children are younger, the presenting problem involves the parent, such as separation anxiety, and parents have high levels of anxiety [83, 97, 98, 100].

Beyond methodological differences, there are a number of limitations in the development and assessment of family-based interventions that may reduce their treatment efficacy relative to child-focused CBT. First, few interventions have systematically targeted the parenting behaviours that are associated with the development and maintenance of child anxiety (e.g., [101]). In the rare instances where treatment addressed specific anxiety-enhancing behaviours (e.g., teaching parents to reinforce non-anxious behaviours and modifying maladaptive parental cognitions and assumptions), family CBT has produced more favourable outcomes relative to individual treatment (e.g., [98, 102]). Second, most family-based interventions are not based on an explicit model of change [7, 8]. Although studies have actively incorporated parents in treatment, they often fail to describe or test the underlying theoretical principle of how parental involvement can lead to changes in the child's behaviours (e.g., parent facilitating transfer of control from clinician to the child; e.g., [103–5]). Third, few studies have examined outcomes beyond the core symptoms of the child. Without knowing how variables such as parent psychopathology and parenting behaviours change from pre- to post-treatment, it would be difficult to draw conclusions about the success of parent involvement in treatment. Finally, studies often lack focus by targeting too many parental factors at once without devoting time to any specific maladaptive parenting behaviours [8]. A recent meta-analysis examining the active ingredients in family CBT found that transfer of control and parental anxiety management were specific treatment components that predicted the child's improved functioning. In contrast, contingency management and communication skills did not have added benefit over individual CBT for youth anxiety outcomes [106]. This suggests that it may be more beneficial to concentrate efforts on a few maladaptive parenting behaviours than dilute treatment to cover an expansive set of negative parent/family components.

A recent RCT comparing parent-only treatment with standard CBT for anxiety addressed several of these design and assessment limitations. Specifically, the study (1) targeted a specific maladaptive parenting behaviour that has been linked to child anxiety through empirical research (i.e., *family accommodation*, or the ways in which parents modify their behaviours to help the child avoid or reduce anxiety-related distress), (2) described a model of change (i.e., parental reduction of accommodation will increase adaptive coping in the child) and (3) tested the model by measuring both child and parent outcomes. The researchers found that the parent-only programme was comparable to standard CBT in reducing child anxiety. Moreover, the theorized mechanism of change of family accommodation was reduced more in the parent-only treatment arm, specifying the added value of parent involvement in anxiety treatment [90].

In addition to child AD, treatment programmes for child OCD have also made a concerted effort to incorporate parents, many of whom report high levels of anxiety and parental distress [107]. Although there are far fewer RCTs focused on family interventions for OCD, research thus far suggests that parent involvement in treatment aids in the reduction of child OCD symptoms [108, 109]. However, findings are mixed on whether family interventions have added benefit over individual treatment [110]. Family therapy for OCD has a number of treatment components in common with family CBT for AD, but it also offers some innovative approaches to working with highly distressed or anxious parents. Similar to the aetiology of AD, family appears to play a large role in the development and maintenance of OCD in

children. Adverse family factors that have been implicated in child OCD include negative parenting styles and, relatedly, expressed emotions such as over-involvement, criticism and hostility, family conflict and lack of cohesion, and family accommodations [107, 110–13]. Among these risk factors, family accommodation has received the most attention as a maladaptive parenting behaviour to target in family-based interventions [114–16]. In order to reduce family accommodation, the goals of parent sessions include (1) psycho-education about accommodation and its role in the maintenance of OCD, (2) identification of alternative and adaptive parenting behaviours to support the child during times of distress, (3) mapping of a hierarchy of family accommodations and (4) systematic reduction of accommodation behaviours, including a detailed plan for how to communicate, implement and troubleshoot the accommodation-reduction plan [117].

Emerging research points out that the level of accommodation is related to negative parenting emotions of anxiety and distress [91, 118, 119]. Families with high anxiety and conflict have difficulty resisting accommodations [107], conferring worse outcomes in treatment (e.g., [120]). Following this line of research, family-based interventions for child OCD have begun to target parents' negative emotional responses in addition to their maladaptive behaviours in order to decrease accommodation within the family. A recent RCT showed that family treatment that teaches OCD-related emotion regulation and problem-solving outperformed traditional exposure and response prevention (ERP) with family psycho-education alone [121]. In this particular study, parents were taught to (1) regulate their own emotions, (2) solve problems collaboratively with their children and (3) manage and model appropriate affect for their children in order to decrease the negative emotions associated with family accommodations. Specifically, clinicians worked with parents to normalize the range of parental emotional responses to OCD while teaching them to regulate their emotions through labelling, monitoring and early intervention (e.g., encouraging walking away from difficult and often emotionally charged OCD episodes to prevent escalation and teaching self-soothing skills to the parent and child). As a way to promote cohesion, which is often low in OCD-affected families, parents also learned to engage in positive and collaborative communication with their children to resolve family problems and conflict. And lastly, treatment taught parents to tolerate their own distress related to OCD and ERP treatment by recognizing their own anxious responses in these stressful situations and replacing them with a more calm and neutral stance as a model of emotion regulation.

Case Study

In this section, we present the case study of Brian to illustrate some of the key treatment approaches discussed earlier for working with parents who have anxiety in the context of a family-based intervention for child OCD. Brian was an eight-year-old European-American boy who came to our specialty intensive outpatient programme for treatment of severe OCD. Brian lived with his mother, father and five-year-old brother. He had no significant medical history and met all his developmental milestones within normal limits.

Assessment and Case Conceptualization

At the intake evaluation, the therapist met with Brian and his parents to obtain information about his presenting problems. According to the family, Brian had nearly constant obsessions and compulsions across multiple symptom clusters that led to significant impairment at home and school. Specifically, Brian experienced frequent intrusive thoughts of hurting his family (e.g., obtaining a gun to kill them), himself (e.g., electrocuting himself) and others (e.g., causing something 'terrible' to occur). To relieve distress related to these obsessions, Brian would repeatedly ask his parents if he has hurt others or confess to them that he had already caused harm (e.g., 'I know I hurt someone'). The parents stated that they would always reassure Brian that he has not or will ever hurt anyone, but their responses provided only temporary relief, and Brian would resume his questioning and confessions, up to hundreds of times a day. Brian also presented with symptoms in the moral/scrupulosity cluster, expressing excessive concerns about stealing, lying and cheating. Related compulsions include responding with 'maybe' to yes/no questions from his parents and others, asking his parents whether he is still 'the same person' or a 'good person' and involving his parents in checking behaviours (e.g., returning to a store to make sure that they paid for their purchases). Lastly, Brian had contamination obsessions and compulsions. Fearing he would become ill, Brian washed his hands excessively,

developed a routine around toileting and showering and avoided touching perceived contaminants. To ensure that he was not contaminated or ill, Brian would frequently ask his parents whether he had cleaned himself properly and instruct them to measure his temperature.

In addition to information gathering, the therapist also used the intake to build rapport with the family, gain trust and buy-in, provide psycho-education and assess family factors that may facilitate or interfere with treatment (e.g., co-morbidities, motivation and insight and concerns/distress related to upcoming treatment). At Brian's intake, the therapist used the Children's Yale-Brown Obsessive-Compulsive Scale (CY-BOCS [122]) to systematically gather the preceding information about Brian's OCD symptoms, paying close attention to the degree of family accommodation, the level of impairment to the child and family, each family member's insight into the irrational nature of OCD symptoms and the family's motivation to improve. Over the course of the CY-BOCS administration, it became increasingly apparent to the therapist and the parents that (1) the family was heavily involved in Brian's compulsions, (2) the parental accommodations caused significant interference to the family's daily functioning (e.g., delays or changes in daily routines because of the excessive reassurance seeking) and (3) the family involvement provided only temporary relief to Brian's distress. In this manner, the CY-BOCS served both the purpose of gathering information and increasing the family's insight/motivation towards change.

Lastly, the therapist used the intake to observe how the parents and Brian interacted in a relatively novel and potentially challenging situation, as discussion about a child's presenting problems is likely to elicit stress from the family. In Brian's case, the parents' anxiety and distress were notable on several occasions. At the outset, the therapist asked Brian to describe in his own words what his worries were. Brian appeared nervous and quickly turned to his parents for answers. After this exchange, Brian's parents proceeded to answer nearly all the therapist's questions, even when they were unsure about the nature of Brian's specific obsessions. In addition, the parents repeatedly described Brian as a 'sensitive' child who was 'easily overcome with emotions'. Indeed, Brian became tearful when his parents talked about some of his challenging OCD behaviours. Seeing such reaction from Brian, Brian's father requested to finish the interview alone with the therapist while Brian and his mother waited outside the interview room. He believed that a separate meeting would be particularly helpful when discussing some of Brian's more 'troubling' symptoms (e.g., harm obsessions). The therapist acknowledged the difficulty of sharing 'scary worries', assured the family that Brian's symptoms are common to OCD and that she has treated them in the past and emphasized the value of having both the parents' and Brian's input about his symptoms. Interestingly, Brian quickly recovered with these words of encouragement and validation. He took a short break but was able to return to the interview room to complete the intake. By the end of the meeting, he even voluntarily disclosed some symptoms that his parents did not know about.

In addition to expressing concerns about Brian's ability to share information, the parents also reported worry about the efficacy of treatment. After the therapist provided psycho-education to the family about the standard of care for moderate to severe OCD as ERP with medication support [123], the parents had many questions about the appropriateness of such treatment for their child. Specifically, they expressed concern that given Brian's young age and 'sensitivity', he would have difficulty understanding, tolerating and ultimately responding positively to treatment that involves exposure to anxiety-inducing stimuli. The therapist validated the parents' concerns but provided a firm rationale for the recommended treatment. At the same time, the therapist recognized the need for ongoing discussions with the family about their concerns. Further, the therapist believed that greater parent involvement would help address some of the parenting behaviours that were maintaining Brian's OCD and anxiety. During the intake, both parents described themselves as 'rule followers' who try to raise their children with a clear sense of right and wrong. Their household rules include never lying or cheating, sharing everything openly with each other and adhering to 'proper hygiene' (e.g., always washing hands before dinner, never sitting near a sick person in the waiting area).

Taken together, the therapist viewed Brian as an eight-year-old with severe OCD characterized by obsessions and compulsions related to harm/aggression, contamination and moral/scrupulosity (CY-BOCS score = 34). The parents were not only heavily involved in Brian's current compulsions, but they also engaged in a number of parenting practices that were

likely maintaining or exacerbating his symptoms. Relatedly, the parents exhibited an elevated degree of anxiety and distress that likely modelled and reinforced Brian's maladaptive thinking, behaviours and affect regulation. Given Brian's young age, significant family accommodation and elevated parental anxiety, the therapist formulated a treatment plan that combined standard ERP with active parent participation in treatment. In doing so, the therapist aimed to decrease Brian's OCD and address family risk factors that may maintain his symptoms and interfere with treatment progression.

Treatment Plan and Execution

The therapist formulated the treatment plan to include (1) child-focused ERP sessions to decrease obsessions and compulsions, (2) parent sessions to reduce family accommodations and parental anxiety and (3) joint family meetings to generalize adaptive coping skills across family members and settings. Reduction of family accommodation and anxious parenting behaviours was theorized as the model of change.

The first part of treatment focused on psycho-education about OCD and the goals of treatment. In the child session, Brian learned that (1) obsessions and compulsions feed into each other in a negative cycle, (2) obsessions can go away on their own without compulsions and (3) treatment will teach him to tolerate the distress from obsessions without doing a compulsion. In the parent session, the therapist provided similar psycho-education about the OCD cycle and the rationale for exposure-based CBT. This traditional psycho-education was enhanced by further teaching the parents that (1) accommodation is a part of the OCD cycle and one that serves a similar function as compulsions, providing only temporary relief and maintaining the OCD, (2) a goal of treatment is to refrain from accommodation and support exposure-based approaches, (3) this requires parents to be able to monitor and manage the emotions that come up in treatment and (4) accordingly, treatment will teach them emotion regulation and problem-solving skills to support disengagement from accommodation. Through psycho-education, the therapist helped the family recognize that while compulsions and accommodations were initially performed to help with Brian's distress, they had become harmful over time and must be changed to improve Brian's and the family's functioning.

231

The second part of treatment focused on emotion regulation skills. Given that both Brian and his parents displayed elevated levels of anxiety at intake, the therapist selected this treatment module to provide the family with some adaptive coping skills that would be consistently reinforced throughout the rest of treatment. Specifically, the therapist introduced the concept of affect labelling to help Brian and his parents become aware of their emotional responses to OCD and identify them in the moment. Parallelling the use of the feelings thermometer in individual child sessions, Brian's parents also learned to use the feelings thermometer to label and monitor the intensity of their emotions, particularly the feeling of anxiety/distress in the context of OCD treatment (e.g., when resisting a compulsion or refraining from accommodating to the symptoms). Finally, the therapist taught Brian and his parents self-soothing skills that they can use when they notice their anxiety rising on the feelings thermometer but prior to the moment that they are 'overcome with emotions', as the parents described during the intake. Specific strategies included relaxation (e.g., deep breathing, progressive muscle relaxation) and mindfulness/grounding techniques (e.g., using all five senses to observe your surroundings). The goal of this treatment module was to provide Brian and his parents with a common language to communicate their feelings and identify moments when they can engage in adaptive coping in order to reduce distress and respond to difficult situations more effectively. The parents thus were encouraged to recognize and monitor their emotions in a way that parallelled Brian's distress ratings in the upcoming exposure sessions.

In the third stage of family treatment, the therapist worked with Brian and his parents to develop a hierarchy for disengaging from symptom accommodation. This hierarchy was viewed as somewhat separate from the hierarchy developed in individual sessions because it required both parents and child to be ready to try new ways of responding to OCD. For each item on the hierarchy, the parents rated how hard it would be for them to disengage, and Brian rated how hard it would be for him if his parents did not provide accommodation. This strategy allowed the therapist to gauge each person's readiness for change without the influence of other family members and to process differences in their ratings. It provided a springboard for highlighting cases in which Brian's parents were more anxious than he was (or where they

anticipated a potentially worse outcome than he did). The goal of the hierarchy development was to teach the family about a gradual stepwise approach to taking on appropriate new challenges that would maximize the chance of successful practice. For the parents, the symptom hierarchy was also a good model for teaching the concept of scaffolding. Specifically, Brian's parents were taught to use the feelings thermometer to identify situations or modify exposures to be sufficiently challenging so that Brian has the opportunity to learn without becoming overwhelmed. For Brian's parents, the ability to label and compare distress ratings was particularly useful, as they saw over time that their expectations of Brian's reaction did not always match with Brian's own experience. Moreover, the anticipated distress ratings from both the parents and Brian often exceeded the actual experience of distress in the moment.

Using the symptom hierarchy as a guide, the therapist and Brian began to complete exposures in session to target his fears of contamination (e.g., touching public surfaces such as drinking fountains and elevator buttons, eating food with 'dirty' hands and sitting in hospital waiting areas without washing or cleaning), harming self and others (e.g., plugging in electrical appliances, sitting next to 'dangerous' objects such as knives and lighters, interacting with people he worries he could hurt, such as children and people with physical disabilities, without checking or seeking reassurance from the therapist and his parents), and wrongdoing (e.g., taking samples from stores without asking, wasting food, littering, giving definitive responses to questions regardless of whether he knows the answer or not and taking tests while having access to the answer key without checking or confessing to the therapist and his parents).

In the parent sessions, the therapist collaborated with Brian's parents to reduce their accommodations at home. Since Brian was asking questions and making confessions hundreds of times a day, a plan was created to gradually decrease the frequency and kinds of reassurances the parents were providing. When designing this stepwise plan, the therapist took into consideration the distress that both Brian and his parents may experience when preparing and making changes to their family routine. First, the parents agreed that if Brian asked the same question or made the same confession multiple times, they would provide reassurance once and, if needed, repeat that response verbatim (i.e., reducing the frequency of the accommodation). Once this goal was achieved, the parents agreed that Brian could write down his questions or confessions and they would answer them during specific times of the day (e.g., at bedtime), that is, delaying the behaviour and tolerating the corresponding distress. Next, Brian could answer some of his own questions or confessions and, if needed, confirm his response with his parents (further reduction in accommodation). Finally, the parents agreed that Brian could answer all his own questions without any validation from them (i.e., removal of the behaviour altogether).

Although parental anxiety was not the focus of Brian's treatment, it was a notable factor that required ongoing attention. In the early phase of treatment, the parents reiterated their concern that Brian would have difficulty understanding the basic principles of ERP and tolerating distress associated with the exposures. Relatedly, the parents worried that Brian may be coerced into doing exposures that he was not ready to do and feared that he would be excessively triggered. To rectify the parents' concerns, the therapist encouraged Brian to share information with his parents about exposures he completed and how each activity related back to his obsessions or compulsions. Using Brian's own words to explain the purpose of exposures allowed the parents to see his grasp of ERP and reinforced his learning. The therapist also invited the parents to shadow the child sessions as she guided Brian through different exposures. The goal of shadowing was to help parents (1) recognize that exposures are completed through the process of scaffolding, (2) observe Brian's ability to tolerate distress with repeated and graduated practice, (3) practise managing their own emotions during exposure and (4) facilitate the parents' ability to support ERP at home.

The parents also expressed some concerns over specific exposures completed in session. Although they were educated about the rationale for ERP, they believed that some exposures defied common parenting practices, including their own (e.g., sitting near sick people, keeping secrets from parents). Here it was important for the therapist to balance her expertise in OCD with collaborative discussions with the family. The therapist provided further psycho-education about the purpose of exposures, including the concept of over-learning (i.e., completing relatively extreme exposures that challenge the child beyond the limits of normal day-to-day life) to achieve mastery in a newly acquired skill. At the same time, the therapist invited the parents to modify the exposures to be more applicable to their home setting. Finally, it was important to provide cognitive behavioural tools to help parents label and manage their anxiety in the context of Brian's treatment.

In addition to the emotion regulation tools discussed earlier, the therapist focused on helping parents identify their negative and, at times, catastrophic thinking (e.g., Brian would not understand treatment concepts or tolerate distress) as well as the consequences of such thinking on their emotions and behaviours (e.g., feeling nervous and guilty about putting Brian in a stressful situation and encouraging avoidance of exposures). The therapist had extensive discussions with the parents about the effect of their anxiety on the child, highlighting the important role they played in modelling and reinforcement. As such, the parents were taught ways to challenge their anxious thoughts, face their own fears (e.g., seeing their child in distress) and practise self-soothing skills. Additionally, they were encouraged to validate Brian's distress but give him time to recover on his own. On this point, the therapist provided extensive psycho-education to the parents that such parenting approach was not dismissing the child's emotions; instead, the parents were teaching their child that they have confidence in his ability to cope, which, in turn, helps the child gain a sense of efficacy and mastery over stressful situations.

Over the course of treatment, Brian and his parents made significant improvement in reducing OCD-related compulsions and accommodations. By the end of treatment, Brian was rarely seeking reassurance from parents. In fact, when his parents challenged him with his worries (e.g., 'Did you hurt your brother?' or 'You may have taken something'), he was able to confidently refute their comments. Such interaction highlighted both Brian's and his parents' progress in treatment. Brian was able to respond calmly to an intrusive thought, and his parents were able to purposefully challenge him to face his fear, a task that would have caused the parents significant distress at the outset of treatment. Indeed, each family member's ability to tolerate distress improved significantly over time. Although Brian still experienced obsessions, he was generally able to resist the urge to perform a compulsion or purposefully challenge his OCD with an exposure. Similarly, although parents had their own set of parenting practices, they were increasingly open to doing exposures that bend the household rules (e.g., not washing hands at every meal), recognizing that Brian's willingness to complete these exercises did not mean that he was acquiring a bad habit or challenging family values. In supporting Brian in daily exposures, the parents were also sending the positive message to Brian that he is capable of handling distress; rather than helping him escape from challenging events, they were modelling and reinforcing his courageous behaviours of confronting his fears, labelling his emotions and using adaptive coping tools to self-sooth. Taken together, Brian had made significant improvement and was ready to transition from our intensive outpatient programme to weekly outpatient therapy (CY-BOCS score = 17).

Summary and Future Directions

Parental anxiety is a strong risk factor for child AD, although more research is needed to understand its role in the aetiology of other psychosocial outcomes. Parents are likely to promote and maintain anxiety in their children through negative parenting behaviours (i.e., parental control and negativity), along with the modelling and reinforcement of anxious responses. Conversely, anxious children can also elicit anxiety-enhancing behaviours from their parents, underscoring the bidirectional transmission of anxiety within families. In the treatment of childhood disorders, parental anxiety has also been linked to inferior treatment outcomes. To address this treatment barrier within the family, parental anxiety and anxiety-enhancing parenting behaviours have been increasingly targeted in family-based interventions with encouraging results. However, efforts to address negative parenting factors have been variable and fragmented, limiting the efficacy of parent-based interventions relative to traditional child-focused treatment for disorders such as AD and OCD.

Future Directions in Research

The limited support for parenting programmes that target parental anxiety and anxiety-enhancing behaviours is in stark contrast to the robust evidence base for behavioural parent training for disruptive behaviours is in part, the difference stems from how the two branches of parenting programmes are developed. In behavioural parent training, negative parenting behaviours are recognized and targeted as the core

intervention for youth outcomes. In contrast, management of parental anxiety has been primarily an 'add-on' to child-directed interventions for anxiety and related disorders [124]. As a result of this conceptualization, few studies have paid close attention to empirically derived parenting factors associated with negative youth outcomes (e.g., parental control and negativity) [7, 69, 125]. Similarly, without a clear theoretical model of change in mind, research examining the efficacy of parenting programmes for anxiety has traditionally not included any parenting measures, restricting our understanding of the possible mechanisms of change. To overcome these limitations, scholars stress the importance of accurate and effective assessment of parental and family factors that are relevant to childhood problems. Routine monitoring of systems-level variables (e.g., parental anxiety, maladaptive parenting behaviours and parent-child conflict) can help identify specific family factors to target in treatment and potential mechanisms of change just as the treatment research on behavioural parenting programmes has done [7].

In order to understand whether family-based interventions provide additional benefits over individual treatment, more research is needed to examine the long-term effects of treatments that target negative parenting factors such as anxiety. Theoretically, the inclusion of a parenting component should help generalize skills and extend treatment gains in the treatment of child problems [124]. Another future direction in research is how to individualize family treatment. There is some evidence that parent-involved treatment is more beneficial for certain groups, such as younger children and families with higher parental distress and anxiety [8]. Following this line of research, it is possible that the degree of parental involvement depends on factors such as gender of the child, structure of the family and family cultural background and values. Lastly, although there is extensive research linking parent and child AD, few studies have examined the role of parental anxiety in the development and treatment of other childhood disorders. This is problematic as co-morbidities are common among treatment-seeking youth [126, 127]. An important next step in research is to determine how parental anxiety and anxiety-enhancing parenting behaviours can be targeted in the treatment of different disorders. To date, studies suggest that certain parenting behaviours are unique to a problem cluster, whereas other behaviours are common across problem clusters. For example, parental control appears to be high for child AD but low for disruptive behaviours. In contrast, parental warmth and high hostility are associated with both internalizing and externalizing behaviours [124, 128]. How could these common and unique parenting behaviours be targeted in the treatment of youth with complex presentations?

Future Directions in Treatment and Training

In recent years, competency models have gained popularity as a way to translate EBTs into routine clinical settings. For clinicians who are working with families characterized by high levels of parental stress or anxiety, we recommend the adoption of a common-factors approach by flexibly using conceptualizations and techniques from multiple empirically supported protocols. Specifically, we recommend that clinicians gain competency in the following categories as outlined by Sburlati et al. [72].

In terms of generic competencies, it is important for clinicians working with anxious parents to examine the impact that systems-level factors such as family structure, parent-child relationships and parenting behaviours has on the child's behaviours. This can be achieved by conducting a thorough evaluation and gathering relevant data using evidence-based measures. Another generic competency that can enhance treatment outcomes is the building of a positive relationship with different family members. Given the important role of parental anxiety in the maintenance and treatment of child outcomes, it is important to build rapport and trust with the parents as well as the child when establishing care. In terms of CBT competencies, we recommend that clinicians pay close attention to the specific parenting behaviours that contribute to negative child outcomes (e.g., intrusiveness, overprotection, criticism) and how negative outcomes are transferred between family members (e.g., modelling, information transfer, reinforcement). It is also important that clinicians are able to design, execute and adapt a CBT formulation and treatment plan. When working with a family high on parental anxiety and stress, outcomes are likely to be enhanced if clinicians can tailor the degree of parental involvement in treatment based on the family's functioning, parent-child relationship and parents' willingness and ability to assist. Again, this may require returning to the generic competency of conducting a comprehensive evaluation at the outset of treatment. Finally, in terms of specific CBT techniques, we recommend that clinicians target maladaptive parenting factors that have been linked to negative child outcomes in empirical research. These include parent training to promote positive parenting behaviours (e.g., decreasing parental control and granting more autonomy to the child), management of parental anxiety using cognitive behavioural skills (e.g., cognitive restructuring, relaxation) and contingency management to promote courageous child behaviours.

For beginning clinicians, several factors are important to keep in mind when working with a complex family system: (1) the reciprocal relationship between parents and children, (2) establishment of a therapeutic alliance with all family members without overly identifying with any particular individual, (3) comprehensive assessment of relevant systems-level factors that could affect treatment and (4) individualization of treatment based on those family variables. For new clinicians, it is also important to know that parents who experience high levels of anxiety or distress may not readily disclose their fears and worries. Rather, their distress may manifest in the form of subtle changes to treatment goals or avoidance of planned treatment activities. Once again, a thorough assessment of the family environment, establishment of positive rapport and open communication are crucial to identifying and managing parental anxiety over the course of treatment.

In order to move towards the clinical competencies just outlined, it is also important to take a competency-based approach to training. Specifically, we recommend clinical training programmes to educate future clinicians about common factors that inform the change process in family interventions. Students not only should gain exposure to a variety of empirically supported protocols but also should recognize the overarching approach and techniques that are relevant to multiple evidence-based practices [129]. Moreover, students should receive training to analyse findings from empirical studies, select evidence-based measurement tools and adapt evidence-based protocols for real-world settings in order to translate EBTs into their daily clinical practice [78].

References

1. Kessler RC, Petukhova M, Sampson NA, et al. Twelve-month and lifetime prevalence and lifetime morbid risk of anxiety and mood disorders in the United States. *International Journal of Methods in Psychiatric Research* 2012; **21**(3):169–84.

2. Kessler RC, Wai TC, Demler O, Walters EE. Prevalence, severity, and comorbidity of 12-month DSM-IV disorders in the National Comorbidity Survey Replication. *Archives of General Psychiatry* 2005; **62**(6):617–27.

3. Barrera TL, Norton PJ. Quality of life impairment in generalized anxiety disorder, social phobia, and panic disorder. *Journal of Anxiety Disorders* 2009; **23**(8):1086–90.

4. Stein MB, Roy-Byrne PP, Craske MG, et al. Functional impact and health utility of anxiety disorders in primary care outpatients. *Medical Care* 2005; **43**(12):1164–70.

5. Chavira DA, Drahota A, Garland AF, et al. Feasibility of two modes of treatment delivery for child anxiety in primary care. *Behaviour Research and Therapy* 2014; **60**:60–6.

6. Murray L, Lau PY, Arteche A, et al. Parenting by anxious mothers: Effects of disorder subtype, context and child characteristics. *Journal of Child Psychology and Psychiatry and Allied Disciplines* 2012; **53**(2):188–96.

7. Wei C, Kendall PC. Parental involvement: Contribution to childhood anxiety and its treatment. *Clinical Child and Family Psychology Review* 2014; **17**(4):319–39.

8. Breinholst S, Esbjørn BH, Reinholdt-Dunne ML, Stallard P. CBT for the treatment of child anxiety disorders: A review of why parental involvement has not enhanced outcomes. *Journal of Anxiety Disorders* 2012; **26**(3):416–24.

9. Barmish AJ, Kendall PC. Should parents be co-clients in cognitive-behavioural therapy for anxious youth? *Journal of Clinical Child and Adolescent Psychology* 2005; **34**(3):569–81.

10. Creswell C, Cooper P, Murray L. Parents with anxiety disorders. Parental psychiatric disorder: Distressed parents and their families. In: Reupert A, Maybery D, Nicolson J, et al. (eds.), *Parental Psychiatric Disorder: Distressed Parents and Their Families*, 3rd ed. Cambridge, UK: Cambridge University Press, 2015, pp. 127–37.

11. Cicchetti D, Rogosch FA. Equifinality and multifinality in developmental psychopathology. *Developmental Psychopathology* 1996; **8**(4):597–600.

12. Reupert AE, J Maybery D, Kowalenko NM. Children whose parents have a mental illness: prevalence, need and treatment. *Medical Journal of Australia* 2013; **199**(3):S7–9.

13. Rasic D, Hajek T, Alda M, Uher R. Risk of mental illness in offspring of parents with schizophrenia, bipolar disorder, and major depressive disorder: A meta-analysis of family high-risk studies. *Schizophrenia Bulletin* 2014; **40**(1):28–38.

14. Suveg C, Shaffer A, Morelen D, Thomassin K. Links between maternal and child psychopathology symptoms: Mediation through child emotion regulation and moderation through maternal behaviour. *Child Psychiatry and Human Development* 2011; **42**(5):507.

15. Tompson MC, Pierre CB, Boger KD, et al. Maternal depression, maternal expressed emotion, and youth psychopathology. *Journal of Abnormal Child Psychology* 2010; **38**(1):105–17.

16. Schleider JL, Ginsburg GS, Keeton CP, et al. Parental psychopathology and treatment outcome for anxious youth: Roles of family functioning and caregiver strain. *Journal of Consulting and Clinical Psychology* 2015; **83**(1):213.

17. Burstein M, Stanger C, Dumenci L. Relations between parent psychopathology family functioning and adolescent problems in substance-abusing families: Disaggregating the effects of parent gender. *Child Psychiatry and Human Development* 2012; **43**(4):631–47.

18. Beidel DC, Turner SM. At risk for anxiety: I. Psychopathology in the offspring of anxious parents. *Journal of the American Academy of Child and Adolescent Psychiatry* 1997; **36**(7):918–24.

19. Biederman J, Petty C, Faraone SV, et al. Effects of parental anxiety disorders in children at high risk for panic disorder: A controlled study. *Journal of Affective Disorders* 2006; **94**(1–3):191–97.

20. Merikangas KR, Avenevoli S, Dierker L, Grillon C. Vulnerability factors among children at risk for anxiety disorders. *Biological Psychiatry*. 1999; **46**(11):1523–35.

21. Merikangas KR, Mehta RL, Molnar BE, et al. Comorbidity of substance use disorders with mood and anxiety disorders: Results of the International Consortium in Psychiatric Epidemiology. *Addictive Behaviours*. 1998; **23**(6):893–907.

22. Telman LGE, van Steensel FJA, Maric M, Bögels SM. What are the odds of anxiety disorders running in families? A family study of anxiety disorders in mothers, fathers, and siblings of children with anxiety disorders. *European Child and Adolescent Psychiatry* 2018; **27**(5):615–24.

23. Fisak B, Grills-Taquechel AE. Parental modeling, reinforcement, and information transfer: Risk factors in the development of child anxiety? *Clinical Child and Family Psychology Review* 2007; **10**(3):213–31.

24. Schreier A, Wittchen HU, Höfler M, Lieb R. Anxiety disorders in mothers and their children: Prospective

longitudinal community study. *British Journal of Psychiatry* 2008; **192**(4):308–9.

25. Steinhausen HC, Foldager L, Perto G, Munk-Jørgensen P. Family aggregation of mental disorders in the nationwide Danish three generation study. *European Archives of Psychiatry and Clinical Neuroscience* 2009; **259**(5):270–7.

26. Li X, Sundquist J, Sundquist K. Age-specific familial risks of anxiety: A nation-wide epidemiological study from Sweden. *European Archives of Psychiatry and Clinical Neuroscience* 2008; **42**(10):808–14.

27. Ginsburg GS, Schlossberg MC. Family-based treatment of childhood anxiety disorders. *International Review of Psychiatry* 2002; **14**(2):143–54.

28. Hughes AA, Furr JM, Sood ED, et al. Anxiety, mood, and substance use disorders in parents of children with anxiety disorders. *Child Psychiatry and Human Development* 2009; **40**(3):405–19.

29. Micco JA, Henin A, Mick E, et al. Anxiety and depressive disorders in offspring at high risk for anxiety: A meta-analysis. *Journal of Anxiety Disorders* 2009; **23**(8):1158–64.

30. Biederman J, Hirshfeld-Becker DR, Rosenbaum JF, et al. Further evidence of association between behavioural inhibition and social anxiety in children. *American Journal of Psychiatry* 2001; **158**(10):1673–9.

31. Biederman J, Monuteaux MC, Faraone S V, et al. Does referral bias impact findings in high-risk offspring for anxiety disorders? A controlled study of high-risk children of non-referred parents with panic disorder/agoraphobia and major depression. *Journal of Affective Disorders* 2004; **82**(2):209–16.

32. Lieb R, Wittchen HU, Höfler M, et al. Parental psychopathology, parenting styles, and the risk of social phobia in offspring: A prospective-longitudinal community study. *Archives of General Psychiatry* 2000; **57**(9):859–66.

33. Unnewehr S, Schneider S, Florin I, Margraf J. Psychopathology in children of patients with panic disorder or animal phobia. *Psychopathology* 1998; **31**(2):69–84.

34. Lawrence PJ, Murayama K, Creswell C. Systematic review and meta-analysis: Anxiety and depressive disorders in offspring of parents with anxiety disorders. *Journal of the American Academy of Child and Adolescent Psychiatry* 2019; **58**(1):46–60.

35. Meadows SO, McLanahan SS, Brooks-Gunn J. Parental depression and anxiety and early childhood behaviour problems across family types. *Journal of Marriage and Family* 2007; **69**(5):1162–77.

36. Biederman J, Newcorn J, Sprich S. Comorbidity of attention deficit hyperactivity disorder with conduct, depressive, anxiety, and other disorders. *American Journal of Psychiatry* 1991; **148**(5):564–77.

37. Silverman WK, Cerny JA, Nelles WB, Burke AE. Behaviour problems in children of parents with anxiety disorders. *Journal of the American Academy of Child and Adolescent Psychiatry* 1988; **27**(6):779–84.

38. Turner SM, Beidel DC, Costello A. Psychopathology in the offspring of anxiety disorders patients. *Journal of Consulting and Clinical Psychology* 1987; **55**(2):229.

39. Burstein M, Ginsburg GS, Tein JY. Parental anxiety and child symptomatology: An examination of additive and interactive effects of parent psychopathology. *Journal of Abnormal Child Psychology* 2010; **38**(7):897–909.

40. Wood JJ, McLeod BD, Sigman M, et al. Parenting and childhood anxiety: Theory, empirical findings, and future directions. *Journal of Child Psychology and Psychiatry and Allied Disciplines* 2003; **44**(1):134–51.

41. Masia CL, Morris TL. Parental factors associated with social anxiety: Methodological limitations and suggestions for integrated behavioural research. *Clinical Psychology: Science and Practice* 1998; **5**(2):211–28.

42. Rapee RM, Heimberg RG. A cognitive-behavioural model of anxiety in social phobia. Behaviour Research and Therapy. 1997; **35**(8):741–56.

43. Hirshfeld DR, Biederman J, Brody L, et al. Expressed emotion toward children with behavioural inhibition: Associations with maternal anxiety disorder. *Journal of the American Academy of Child and Adolescent Psychiatry* 1997; **36**(7):910–17.

44. Whaley SE, Pinto A, Sigman M. Characterizing interactions between anxious mothers and their children. *Journal of Consulting and Clinical Psychology* 1999; **67**(6):826.

45. Woodruff-Borden J, Morrow C, Bourland S, Cambron S. The behaviour of anxious parents: Examining mechanisms of transmission of anxiety from parent to child. *Journal of Clinical Child and Adolescent Psychology* 2002; **31**(3):364–74.

46. Moore PS, Whaley SE, Sigman M. Interactions between mothers and children: Impacts of maternal and child anxiety. *Journal of Abnormal Psychology* 2004; **113**(3):471.

47. Murray L, Cooper P, Creswell C, et al. The effects of maternal social phobia on mother-infant interactions and infant social responsiveness. *Journal of Child Psychology and Psychiatry and Allied Disciplines* 2007; **48**(1):45–52.

48. Murray L, Creswell C, Cooper PJ. The development of anxiety disorders in childhood: An integrative review. *Psychological Medicine* 2009; **39**(9):1413–23.

237

49. Caron A, Weiss B, Harris V, Catron T. Parenting behaviour dimensions and child psychopathology: Specificity, task dependency, and interactive relations. *Journal of Clinical Child and Adolescent Psychology* 2006; **35**(1):34–45.

50. Ginsburg GS, Grover RL, Cord JJ, Ialongo N. Observational measures of parenting in anxious and nonanxious mothers: Does type of task matter? *Journal of Clinical Child and Adolescent Psychology* 2006; **35**(2):323–8.

51. Chorpita BF. The developmental psychopathology of anxiety. In: Vasey MW, Dadds MR (eds.), *The Developmental Psychopathology of Anxiety*. New York: Oxford University Press, 2001, pp. 112–42.

52. Chorpita BF, Barlow DH. The development of anxiety: The role of control in the early environment. *Psychological Bulletin* 1998; **124**(1):3–21.

53. McLeod BD, Weisz JR, Wood JJ. Examining the association between parenting and childhood depression: A meta-analysis. *Clinical Psychology Review* 2007; **27**(8):986–1003.

54. Wood JJ, Piacentini JC, Southam-Gerow M, Chu BC, Sigman M. Family cognitive behavioural therapy for child anxiety disorders. *Journal of the American Academy of Child and Adolescent Psychiatry* 2006; **45**(3):314–21.

55. Bögels SM, Brechman-Toussaint ML. Family issues in child anxiety: Attachment, family functioning, parental rearing and beliefs. *Clinical Psychology Review* 2006; **26**(7):834–56.

56. Parker G. *Parental Overprotection: A Risk Factor in Psychosocial Development*. New York: Grune & Stratton, 1983.

57. de Rosnay M, Cooper PJ, Tsigaras N, Murray L. Transmission of social anxiety from mother to infant: An experimental study using a social referencing paradigm. *Behaviour Research and Therapy* 2006; **44**(8):1165–75.

58. Gerull FC, Rapee RM. Mother knows best: Effects of maternal modelling on the acquisition of fear and avoidance behaviour in toddlers. *Behaviour Research and Therapy* 2002; **40**(3):279–87.

59. Aktar E, Majdandžić M, De Vente W, Bögels SM. Parental social anxiety disorder prospectively predicts toddlers' fear/avoidance in a social referencing paradigm. *Journal of Child Psychology and Psychiatry and Allied Disciplines* 2014; **55**(1):77–87.

60. Hadwin JA, Garner M, Perez-Olivas G. The development of information processing biases in childhood anxiety: A review and exploration of its origins in parenting. *Clinical Psychology Review* 2006; **26**(7):876–94.

61. Chorpita BF, Albano AM, Heimberg RG, Barlow DH. A systematic replication of the prescriptive treatment of school refusal behaviour in a single subject. *Journal of Behavior Therapy and Experimental Psychiatry* 1996; **27**(3):281–90.

62. Gotlib IH, Goodman SH. Children of parents with depression. In: Silverman WK, Ollendick TH (eds.), *Developmental Issues in the Clinical Treatment of Children*. Needham Heights, MA: Allyn & Bacon, 1999, pp. 415–32.

63. Silverman WK, Kurtines WM, Jaccard J, Pina AA. Directionality of change in youth anxiety treatment involving parents: An initial examination. *Journal of Consulting and Clinical Psychology* 2009; **77**(3):474–85.

64. Brooker RJ, Neiderhiser JM, Leve LD, et al. Associations between infant negative affect and parent anxiety symptoms are bidirectional: Evidence from mothers and fathers. *Frontiers in Psychology* 2015; **6**:1875.

65. Creswell C, Murray L, Stacey J, Cooper P. Parenting and child anxiety. In: Silverman, WK, Field AP (eds.), *Anxiety Disorders in Children and Adolescents*. Cambridge, UK: Cambridge University Press, 2011, pp. 299–322.

66. Rapee RM. Early adolescents' perceptions of their mother's anxious parenting as a predictor of anxiety symptoms 12 months later. *Journal of Abnormal Child Psychology* 2009; **37**(8):1103–12.

67. Hudson JL, Doyle AM, Gar N. Child and maternal influence on parenting behaviour in clinically anxious children. *Journal of Clinical Child and Adolescent Psychology* 2009; **38**(2):256–62.

68. Schrock M, Woodruff-Borden J. Parent-child interactions in anxious families. *Child and Family Behavior Therapy* 2010; **32**(4):291–310.

69. Williams SR, Kertz SJ, Schrock MD, Woodruff-Borden J. A sequential analysis of parent-child interactions in anxious and nonanxious families. *Journal of Clinical Child and Adolescent Psychology* 2012; **41**(1):64–74.

70. Settipani CA, O'Neil KA, Podell JL, et al. Youth anxiety and parent factors over time: Directionality of change among youth treated for anxiety. *Journal of Clinical Child and Adolescent Psychology* 2013; **42**(1):9–21.

71. Simon E, Bögels SM, Voncken JM. Efficacy of child-focused and parent-focused interventions in a child anxiety prevention study. *Journal of Clinical Child and Adolescent Psychology* 2011; **40**(2):204–19.

72. Sburlati ES, Schniering CA, Lyneham HJ, Rapee RM. A model of therapist competencies for the empirically supported cognitive behavioural treatment of child

and adolescent anxiety and depressive disorders. *Clinical Child and Family Psychology Review* 2011; **14**(1):89–109.

73. Ogundele MO. Behavioural and emotional disorders in childhood: A brief overview for paediatricians. *World Journal of Clinical Pediatrics* 2018; **7**(1):9–26.

74. Spirito A, Esposito-Smythers C, Wolff J, Uhl K. Cognitive-behavioural therapy for adolescent depression and suicidality. *Child and Adolescent Psychiatric Clinics of North America* 2011; **20**(2):191–204.

75. Seligman LD, Ollendick TH. Cognitive-behavioural therapy for anxiety disorders in youth. *Child and Adolescent Psychiatric Clinics of North America* 2011; **20**(2):217–38.

76. Lochman JE, Powell NP, Boxmeyer CL, Jimenez-Camargo L. Cognitive-behavioural therapy for externalizing disorders in children and adolescents. *Child and Adolescent Psychiatric Clinics of North America* 2011; **20**(2):305–18.

77. Hudson JL, Rapee RM, Lyneham HJ, et al. Comparing outcomes for children with different anxiety disorders following cognitive behavioural therapy. *Behaviour Research and Therapy* 2015; **72**:30–7.

78. Kaslow NJ, Broth MR, Smith CO, Collins MH. Family-based interventions for child and adolescent disorders. *Journal of Marital and Family Therapy* 2012; **38**(1):82–100.

79. Berman SL, Weems CF, Silverman WK, Kurtines WM. Predictors of outcome in exposure-based cognitive and behavioral treatments for phobic and anxiety disorders in children. *Behavior Therapy* 2000; **31**(4):713–31.

80. Crawford AM, Manassis K. Familial predictors of treatment outcome in childhood anxiety disorders. *Journal of the American Academy of Child and Adolescent Psychiatry* 2001; **40**(10):1182–9.

81. Rapee RM. Group treatment of children with anxiety disorders: Outcome and predictors of treatment response. *Australian Journal of Psychology* 2000; **52**(3):125–9.

82. Bodden DHM, Bögels SM, Nauta MH, et al. Child versus family cognitive-behavioral therapy in clinically anxious youth: An efficacy and partial effectiveness study. *Journal of the American Academy of Child and Adolescent Psychiatry* 2008; **47**(12):1384–94.

83. Cobham VE, Spence SH, Dadds MR. The role of parental anxiety in the treatment of childhood anxiety. *Journal of Consulting and Clinical Psychology* 1998; **66**(6):893–905.

84. Cooper PJ, Gallop C, Willetts L, Creswell C. Treatment response in child anxiety is differentially related to the form of maternal anxiety disorder. *Behavioural Cognitive Psychotherapy* 2008; **36**(1):41–8.

85. Compton SN, Peris TS, Almirall D, et al. Predictors and moderators of treatment response in childhood anxiety disorders: Results from the CAMS trial. *Journal of Consulting and Clinical Psychology* 2014; **82**(2):212.

86. Hudson JL, Newall C, Rapee RM, et al. The Impact of Brief Parental Anxiety management on child anxiety treatment outcomes: A controlled trial. *Journal of Clinical Child and Adolescent Psychology* 2014; **43**(3):370–80.

87. Lundkvist-Houndoumadi I, Hougaard E, Thastum M. Pre-treatment child and family characteristics as predictors of outcome in cognitive behavioural therapy for youth anxiety disorders. *Nordic Journal of Psychiatry* 2014; **68**(8):524–35.

88. Connolly SD, Bernstein GA. Practice parameter for the assessment and treatment of children and adolescents with anxiety disorders. *Journal of the American Academy of Child and Adolescent Psychiatry* 2007; **46**(2):267–83.

89. Michelson D, Davenport C, Dretzke J, et al. Do evidence-based interventions work when tested in the 'real world?' A systematic review and meta-analysis of parent management training for the treatment of child disruptive behaviour. *Clinical Child and Family Psychology Review* 2013; **16**(1):18–34.

90. Lebowitz ER, Marin C, Martino A, et al. Parent-based treatment as efficacious as cognitive behavioral therapy for childhood anxiety: A randomized noninferiority study of supportive parenting for anxious childhood emotions. *Journal of the American Academy of Child and Adolescent Psychiatry* 2020; **59**(3):362–72.

91. Peris TS, Yadegar M, Asarnow JR, Piacentini J. Pediatric obsessive compulsive disorder: Family climate as a predictor of treatment outcome. *Journal of Obsessive-Compulsive and Related Disorders* 2012; **1**(4):267–73.

92. Ginsburg GS, Silverman WK, Kurtines WK. Family involvement in treating children with phobic and anxiety disorders: A look ahead. *Clinical Psychology Review* 1995; **15**(5):457–73.

93. Silverman WK, Kurtines WM. *Anxiety and Phobic Disorders: A Pragmatic Approach*. Miami: Springer Science and Business Media, 1996.

94. Drake KL, Ginsburg GS. Family factors in the development, treatment, and prevention of childhood anxiety disorders. *Clinical Child and Family Psychology Review* 2012; **15**(2):144–62.

95. Rapee RM, Abbott MJ, Lyneham HJ. Bibliotherapy for children with anxiety disorders using written materials for parents: A randomized controlled trial. *Journal of Consulting and Clinical Psychology* 2006; **74**(3):436–44.

96. Shortt AL, Barrett PM, Fox TL. Evaluating the FRIENDS Program: A cognitive-behavioural group treatment for anxious children and their parents. *Journal of Clinical Child and Adolescent Psychology* 2001; **30**(4):525–35.

97. Kendall PC, Gosch E, Furr JM, Sood E. Flexibility within fidelity. *Journal of the American Academy of Child and Adolescent Psychiatry* 2008; **47**(9):987–93

98. Barrett PM, Rapee RM, Dadds MR. Family treatment of childhood anxiety: A controlled trial. *Journal of Consulting and Clinical Psychology* 1996; **64**(2):333–42.

99. Wood JJ, McLeod BD, Piacentini JC, Sigman M. One-year follow-up of family versus child CBT for anxiety disorders: Exploring the roles of child age and parental intrusiveness. *Child Psychiatry and Human Development* 2009; **40**(2):301–16.

100. Meichenbaum DL, Fabiano GA, Fincham F. Communication in relationships with adolescents. In: Patterson T (ed.), *Comprehensive Handbook of Psychotherapy: Cognitive-Behavioural Approaches,* Vol. **2**. Hoboken. NJ: Wiley, 2002.

101. Mendlowitz SL, Manassis K, Bradley S, et al. Cognitive-behavioral group treatments in childhood anxiety disorders: The role of parental involvement. *Journal of the American Academy of Child and Adolescent Psychiatry* 1999; **38**(10):1223–9.

102. Barrett PM, Duffy AL, Dadds MR, Rapee RM. Cognitive-behavioural treatment of anxiety disorders in children: Long-term (6-year) follow-up. *Journal of Consulting and Clinical Psychology* 2001; **69**(1):135–41.

103. Heyne D, King NJ, Tonge BJ, et al. Evaluation of child therapy and caregiver training in the treatment of school refusal. *Journal of the American Academy of Child and Adolescent Psychiatry* 2002; **41**(6):687–95.

104. Nauta MH, Scholing A, Emmelkamp PMG, Minderaa RB. Cognitive-behavioural therapy for anxiety disordered children in a clinical setting: Does additional cognitive parent training enhance treatment effectiveness?, *Clinical Psychology and Psychotherapy* 2001; **8**(5):330–40.

105. Nauta MH, Scholing A, Emmelkamp PMG, Minderaa RB. Cognitive-behavioral therapy for children with anxiety disorders in a clinical setting: No additional effect of a cognitive parent training. *Journal of the American Academy of Child and Adolescent Psychiatry* 2003; **42**(11):1270–8.

106. Khanna MS, Kendall PC. Exploring the role of parent training in the treatment of childhood anxiety. *Journal of Consulting and Clinical Psychology* 2009; **77**(5):981–86.

107. Peris TS, Sugar CA, Lindsey Bergman R, et al. Family factors predict treatment outcome for pediatric obsessive-compulsive disorder. *Journal of Consulting and Clinical Psychology* 2012; **80**(2):255–63.

108. Peris TS, Piacentini J. Optimizing treatment for complex cases of childhood obsessive compulsive disorder: A preliminary trial. *Journal of Clinical Child and Adolescent Psychology* 2013; **42**(1):1–8.

109. Merlo LJ, Lehmkuhl HD, Geffken GR, Storch EA. Decreased family accommodation associated with improved therapy outcome in pediatric obsessive-compulsive disorder. *Journal of Consulting and Clinical Psychology* 2009; **77**(2):355–60.

110. Turner C, Krebs G, Destro J. Family-based conceptualization and treatment of obsessive-compulsive disorder. In: Abramowitz JS, McKay D, Storch EA (eds.), *Wiley Handbook of Obsessive-Compulsive Disorders*. Hoboken, NJ: Wiley, 2017, pp. 614–31.

111. Murphy YE, Flessner CA. Family functioning in paediatric obsessive compulsive and related disorders. *British Journal of Clinical Psychology* 2015; **54**(4):414–34.

112. Storch EA, Geffken GR, Merlo LJ, et al. Family accommodation in pediatric obsessive-compulsive disorder. *Journal of Clinical Child and Adolescent Psychology* 2007; **36**(2):207–16.

113. Przeworski A, Zoellner LA, Franklin ME, et al. Maternal and child expressed emotion as predictors of treatment response in pediatric obsessive-compulsive disorder. *Child Psychiatry and Human Development* 2012; **43**(3):337–53.

114. Thompson-Hollands J, Abramovitch A, Tompson MC, Barlow DH. A randomized clinical trial of a brief family intervention to reduce accommodation in obsessive-compulsive disorder: A preliminary study. *Behavior Therapy* 2015; **46**(2):218–29.

115. Piacentini J, Bergman RL, Chang S, et al. Controlled comparison of family cognitive behavioural therapy and psychoeducation/relaxation training for child obsessive-compulsive disorder. *Journal of the American Academy of Child and Adolescent Psychiatry* 2011; **50**(11):1149–61.

116. Wu MS, Lewin AB, Murphy TK, et al. Phenomenological considerations of family accommodation: Related clinical characteristics and family factors in pediatric obsessive-compulsive disorder. *Journal of Obsessive-Compulsive and Related Disorders* 2014; **3**(3):228–35.

117. Lebowitz ER. Treatment of extreme family accommodation in a youth with obsessive-compulsive disorder. In: Storch EA, Lewin AB (eds.), *Clinical Handbook of Obsessive-Compulsive and Related Disorders: A Case-Based Approach to Treating Pediatric and Adult Populations*. New York: Springer International Publishing, 2015.

118. Settipani CA, Kendall PC. The effect of child distress on accommodation of anxiety: Relations with maternal beliefs, empathy, and anxiety. *Journal of Clinical Child and Adolescent Psychology* 2017; **46** (6):810–23.

119. Vreeland A, Peris TS. Involving family members of children with OCD in CBT. In: Storch EA, McGuire JF, McKay D (eds.), *The Clinician's Guide to Cognitive-Behavioural Therapy for Childhood Obsessive-Compulsive Disorder*. London: Academic Press, 2018.

120. Garcia AM, Sapyta JJ, Moore PS, et al. Predictors and moderators of treatment outcome in the pediatric obsessive compulsive treatment study (POTS I). *Journal of the American Academy of Child and Adolescent Psychiatry* 2010; **49**(10):1024–33.

121. Peris TS, Rozenman MS, Sugar CA, et al. Targeted family intervention for complex cases of pediatric obsessive-compulsive disorder: A randomized controlled trial. *Journal of the American Academy of Child and Adolescent Psychiatry* 2017; **56** (12):1034–42.

122. Scahill L, Riddle MA, McSwiggin-Hardin M, et al. Children's Yale-Brown Obsessive Compulsive Scale: Reliability and validity. *Journal of the American Academy of Child and Adolescent Psychiatry* 1997; **36** (6):844–52.

123. Geller DA, March J. Practice parameter for the assessment and treatment of children and adolescents with obsessive-compulsive disorder. *Journal of the American Academy of Child and Adolescent Psychiatry* 2012; **51** (1):98–113.

124. Forehand R, Jones DJ, Parent J. Behavioural parenting interventions for child disruptive behaviours and anxiety: What's different and what's the same. *Clinical Psychology Review* 2013; **33** (1):133–45.

125. Schwartz OS, Dudgeon P, Sheeber LB, et al. Parental behaviours during family interactions predict changes in depression and anxiety symptoms during adolescence. *Journal of Abnormal Child Psychology* 2012; **40**(1):59–71.

126. Bearman SK, Weisz JR. Review: Comprehensive treatments for youth comorbidity: Evidence-guided approaches to a complicated problem. *Child and Adolescent Mental Health* 2015; **20**(3):131–41.

127. Garber J, Weersing VR. Comorbidity of anxiety and depression in youth: Implications for treatment and prevention. *Clinical Psychology: Science and Practice* 2010; **17** (4):293–306.

128. McKee L, Colletti C, Rakow A, et al. Parenting and child externalizing behaviours: Are the associations specific or diffuse? *Aggression and Violent Behaviour* 2008; **13**(3):201–15.

129. Karam EA, Sprenkle DH. The research-informed clinician: A guide to training the next-generation MFT. *Journal of Marital and Family Therapy* 2010; **36**(3):307–19.

Chapter 18

Working with Families of Children Who Have Experienced Maltreatment

Dave S. Pasalich and Nicola Palfrey

Child maltreatment is a public health concern around the globe, with prevalence rates ranging from less than 1 per cent to one third of children [1]. Many experiences of abuse and neglect involve a serious failure of or disruption in the caregiver-child relationship and may seriously undermine an individual's health and wellbeing across their life [2]. By contrast, families can provide a crucial source of support and healing for children exposed to trauma. In this light, the family is central to both risk and resilience for child maltreatment.

Using a competency-based framework, this chapter aims to provide a state-of-the-art description of scientific principles and evidence-informed strategies that underpin effective practice with families of children at risk for or exposed to maltreatment. Drawing from general competencies in child psychology [3], we outline core knowledge, skills and attitudes necessary for competent practice with these families (see Table 18.1). The competency domains in this model are integrated in practice and should not be considered separately. Notably, clinicians will always have to consider and manage *diversity issues* and therapeutic *relationships* at all stages of their work with families.

For their safety and wellbeing, children exposed to severe abuse and neglect may be removed from their birth parents and placed in out-of-home care (OOHC). Thus, in this chapter, *parent* refers to any adult who has primary responsibility for the care of a child (e.g., birth, kinship and foster parents). We use *children* to refer to children and adolescents; however, the focus of this chapter is on early-middle childhood, when children are more vulnerable to maltreatment and more likely to be involved with child welfare services [4].

Conceptualizing Child Maltreatment

Developmental Impact of Child Maltreatment

Knowledge of child maltreatment and its impact on development is fundamental for effectively supporting families of maltreated children. The World Health Organization defines *maltreatment* as all forms of abuse and/or neglect that inflict actual or potential harm to children's development and welfare and occur in a relationship of responsibility, trust or power [5]. Abuse involves acts of *commission*, including engaging a child in sexual activities (e.g., sexual contact or exposure to sexual acts or materials) that are inappropriate for their age or developmental level (sexual abuse), physically harming a child (physical abuse) and repeatedly scolding, degrading or threatening a child in a way that undermines their self-esteem or security (emotional abuse). Emotional abuse may also include exposure to severe family violence. By contrast, neglect involves the persistent *omission* of care that fails to meet the child's basic physical, psychological and/or supervisory needs and jeopardizes developmental and health outcomes (e.g., failing to provide medical care or stable housing). Perpetration of these forms of maltreatment may be intentional or unintentional, though not accidental. Neglect is more prevalent than abuse, but most children experience more than one maltreatment type [6].

Trauma and Development. Without appropriate support, the traumatic stress caused by maltreatment may have enduring consequences on an individual's functioning. Children experience trauma when they feel overwhelmed or helpless by intense events or adversities, particularly those which threaten or harm their actual or perceived safety and security. Trauma can significantly affect a wide range of

Table 18.1 Model of Clinician Competencies for Working with Families of Children Exposed to Maltreatment

Competency Domain	Domain-Specific Competencies
Conceptualizing child maltreatment	• Developmental impact of child maltreatment • Child and family assessment • Diversity issues
Promoting wellbeing in families of children at risk for or exposed to maltreatment	• Treatment strategies • Prevention and family support • Relationships • Role of multiple disciplines and service delivery systems • Consultation and liaison roles
Scientific and professional issues	• Scientific knowledge and methods • Professional, ethical and legal issues • Reflective practice and self-assessment

biological, cognitive and social-emotional processes across development. For instance, it can shape children's brain development, particularly the organization of the limbic system that is involved in behavioural and emotional reactions, and cause heightened amygdala reactivity to fear [7]. Moreover, trauma can lead to toxic stress: excessive and prolonged activation of the physiological stress response systems that undermines the body's ability to cope with stress [8]. Regarding cognitive functioning, repeated trauma influences how children process their surroundings, creating a bias towards attending to socially threatening information (e.g., angry voices) and seeing hostile intentions in people's behaviour [9, 10]. In other words, trauma can cause a child to overestimate the likelihood of danger and oversee threat in their environment. Over time, some children learn to cope with traumatic stress by dissociating, or disconnecting, from mental states and surroundings [11]. Finally, in part as a result of these biological and cognitive changes, trauma has detrimental effects on social-emotional outcomes, including difficulties in children's ability to recognize and regulate emotions [12], and impairments in empathy because of heightened personal distress or emotional numbing [13]. These impairments, in turn, may contribute to disruptions in peer and family relationships.

It is also important for practice that clinicians understand developmental mechanisms regarding *how* child traumatic stress may increase the risk for poor psychosocial health. As discussed earlier, the impact of trauma on children's physiological reactivity, threat perception and emotion dysregulation may, in turn, contribute to the emergence of externalizing (e.g., aggression and hyperactivity) and internalizing (e.g., withdrawn and depressed mood) problems and symptoms of post-traumatic stress [12, 14]. Developmental outcomes associated with a severe course of maltreatment are varied and complicated and may not be adequately captured by current psychiatric nosology. Accordingly, *complex trauma* is a term used to describe chronic exposure to multiple and repeated forms of maltreatment within the primary caregiving system, often across different stages of development [15]. It may result in dysregulated and impaired intra- and interpersonal functioning, which can continue to impact families in the successive generation. Complex trauma is very concerning because it typically involves an early-onset course of maltreatment embedded in a relationship where the attachment figure is the source of harm and fear.

Trauma and Attachment. Considering the major focus on relational interventions for maltreatment, clinicians must know how trauma impacts the parent-child attachment relationship. In a secure attachment, children feel confident that their most important emotional needs – such as comfort and protection when sad or scared – will be met by their caregiver, who is sensitively attuned and responsive to their inner experiences [16]. However, a caregiver who is the perpetrator of maltreatment abdicates their parenting role by becoming a source of both distress and fear and protection for the child [17]. As a result of this attachment paradox, children are at risk for developing a disorganized attachment characterized by the absence of any coherent strategy for seeking proximity to the caregiver to alleviate their distress [18]. Disorganized attachment exacerbates rather than mitigates stress and is meta-analytically associated with externalizing problems [19]. Maltreatment also predisposes risk for the formation of other insecure yet organized attachment strategies, namely avoidant and ambivalent patterns of attachment involving the deactivation/minimization or escalation of attachment needs, respectively [20]. Moreover, attachment insecurity is linked with negative internal working models of how children understand themselves (e.g., 'I'm unlovable'), others (e.g., 'People can't be trusted') and the world (e.g., 'The world is unsafe') that can undermine their self-esteem and weaken trust in future relationships [16].

Children who have experienced an extreme pattern of severely disrupted care, such as chronic trauma and loss in caregiving relationships because of multiple foster care placements, are vulnerable to developing more pervasive difficulties in forming selective attachments. Attachment disorders are considered to lie at the most extreme end of the continuum of attachment-related behaviour and are manifested by withdrawn behaviour and a lack of attachment behaviours (reactive attachment disorder) or indiscriminate social behaviour and non-selective attachments (disinhibited social engagement disorder) [21]. As disorganized attachment is more prevalent than attachment disorders in children with maltreatment histories, clinicians need to be cognizant of not pathologizing every attachment injury given the over-diagnosis of attachment disorders in this field [22].

Attachment theory also guides thinking about how the responses of non-perpetrating parents to children's exposure to trauma affects their child's ability to cope with stress. Caregiver sensitivity provides a secure base for children following exposure to maltreatment that can play a crucial protective role in mitigating fear and distress and alleviating trauma [17]. On the contrary, parents may react to their child's maltreatment by denying, ignoring or minimizing their experience, which often exacerbates traumatic stress. This may be because parents are co-victims of the maltreatment (e.g., family violence) and/or carry their own history of maltreatment and are triggered by their child's trauma experience or reactions. When triggered, parents with unresolved trauma may act in a frightening or frightened manner towards their child, increasing the risk for disorganized attachment [18]. Furthermore, non-interpersonal traumatic events, such as a home fire or natural disaster, may increase the risk for maltreatment if the event has a severe impact on the stability of the family system [23].

Developmental Psychopathology Framework. A developmental psychopathology framework helps conceptualize the unique developmental trajectories of children who experience maltreatment. From this theoretical perspective, children are differentially impacted by trauma depending on the severity, chronicity and form(s) of the maltreatment but also its developmental timing and cascading effects across other developmental domains [24]. For instance, a severe disruption in caregiving – including a prolonged separation from, or loss of, a primary caregiver – may have a greater effect on social-emotional development in a toddler than an adolescent, as young children rely more heavily on their attachment figure for support in regulating emotions and forming a positive self-concept. Moreover, although maltreatment heightens the risk for various negative developmental outcomes, many children and their families demonstrate resilient functioning. Resilience can be understood as 'competent adaptation despite exposure to significant adversity or prolonged trauma' [25, p. 17]. A comprehensive approach to resilience is necessary considering that a child may be resilient in one domain of functioning (e.g., academic) or developmental stage but not in another [24].

From the standpoint of developmental psychopathology, children's responses to the trauma of abuse and neglect are best viewed as adaptive, or safety promoting, in the maltreating/dangerous environment. They may become maladaptive in other, less dangerous contexts, however, where maltreatment is no longer occurring, yet the child remains affected by trauma. As discussed earlier, hyper-vigilance to real or perceived threats following chronic exposure to maltreatment activates fear and attachment systems. Children develop strategies to cope with constant danger and unpredictability in order to survive and gain a sense of control over their circumstances. To illustrate, hoarding food may help a child feel safe and secure in a neglectful home where meals are inconsistent, but this behaviour might be misunderstood and reprimanded in a new foster home where ample food is provided. It is vital that clinicians appreciate the function of children's behaviour in light of both their past and present circumstances and the prior and ongoing effects of trauma.

Given that children exposed to maltreatment may demonstrate a range of positive and negative outcomes, it is important to consider broader contextual factors that may influence these outcomes. Within the developmental psychopathology perspective, an ecological-transactional model [26] aids in conceptualizing the various factors and systems that contribute to and prevent the negative sequelae of child maltreatment. The ecological-transactional model suggests that risk and protective factors interact across individual, familial, school and broader community levels to influence adaptive and maladaptive outcomes. For example, exposure to community violence may compound the reciprocal effects between a parent's severe physical punishment and their child's behaviour problems. A natural mentor at high school (e.g., a teacher or sports coach), however, may help buffer against stressors by supporting the child as they navigate new developmental tasks in adolescence. From this viewpoint, the contribution of family processes to risk and resilience in children is best understood in terms of the ongoing interplay between children's characteristics and their broader environment [24, 26].

Child and Family Assessment

A thorough understanding of the developmental impact of maltreatment is imperative for developing a comprehensive and tailored case formulation that will help guide intervention. Core knowledge and skills necessary for assessing families of children at risk for or exposed to maltreatment are discussed next. Although the focus here is on selected features of family-based assessment, it is essential in practice to evaluate aspects of the child's broader environment (e.g., school functioning, peer relationships).

Safety and Risk Assessment. When working with families of maltreated children, it is vital to ensure that the child is currently living in a safe and secure environment. When there is reasonable cause to suspect that a child is being maltreated, child protection services (CPS) or the statutory agency may conduct a safety and risk assessment with the child's family to determine their support needs and the level of risk. Given that many cases of maltreatment are not reported to CPS [27], clinicians working with distressed families should always be vigilant to suspected child abuse or neglect. Assessment of potential exposure to maltreatment entails having knowledge of

physical and psychological symptoms of abuse and neglect across different ages (see guidelines from UK National Institute for Health and Care Excellence [28] for further information) and the ability to interview the child without biasing their responses (e.g., by asking open-ended questions; see Saywitz, Lyon and Goodman [29] for a review). It is also important to evaluate whether a child may be at risk for future abuse and neglect based on known risk factors for maltreatment perpetration (e.g., parental anger/hyper-reactivity, parental perception of the child as a problem) [30]. Moreover, assessing children's risk of harm to themselves and others is essential, considering the elevated levels of self-harming and suicidal behaviour in maltreated children [31].

Assessment of the History and Outcomes of Maltreatment. Rather than focus on what is wrong with a child who has been maltreated, we should consider what has happened to the child in order to properly appreciate their current functioning. This requires conducting a thorough assessment of the child's trauma history, typically in the context of taking a developmental history. Clinicians should be willing to directly and sensitively ask parents about their own and their child's trauma histories given that some individuals may not be able to identify or recognize the importance of traumatic exposure or might avoid discussing those events [32]. If the child is not too young or traumatized, they may be able to share their perspective of traumatic events they have witnessed or experienced in an individual interview that prioritizes safety and rapport with the child (e.g., does not pressure a child to discuss trauma when they are in denial). However, a history of investigative interviews may impact children's trust and willingness in telling their story to new professionals. Other important positive and negative life events in families and less obvious experiences of trauma (e.g., intergenerational trauma) should also be carefully evaluated.

Maltreatment predicts diverse outcomes for children and their families [2]. There are several core topics to consider in assessing the sequelae of abuse and neglect in a family context. First, the child's cognitive, behavioural and social-emotional functioning both pre- and post-trauma should be evaluated with respect to developmental competencies for the child's age. Often maltreated children will function at a developmental stage that is lower than their chronological age because of the disrupted care they have received (including prenatally) and use of maladaptive coping strategies [24]. Second, the quality and pattern of family interactions should be assessed, including attachment relationships to birth and foster/kinship parents, relationships between parents (e.g., marital relationship, relationship between birth and foster parents) and sibling interactions. Siblings provide positive support for some maltreated children [33], but siblings are sometimes separated when they enter out-of-home care (OOHC), which can exacerbate grief and loss. Finally, clinicians should evaluate aspects of parents' functioning, such as their mental health, social support, caregiving behaviour and attributions/attitudes regarding their child. It is especially important to assess parents' responses to their child's maltreatment, including their own distress or trauma. Moreover, motivational enhancement strategies may be needed in the assessment phase to engage a resistant or defensive parent [34], such as a perpetrating parent who lacks insight into the impact of their parenting behaviour but has good intentions for their child. Overall, both strengths and difficulties should be identified across multiple areas of child and family functioning.

Using multiple informants and methods in a trauma-informed assessment helps clinicians develop a holistic perspective on the child's development and adjustment across different settings. Various reporters are able to provide unique insight into the functioning of a maltreated child and their family, including children, birth and foster/kinship parents, caseworkers or agency staff and school teachers. For instance, children provide a vital perspective on their own mental states, including their desires, anxieties and perceived threats, whereas caseworkers are knowledgeable about contextual factors – such as placement changes and contact visits – that may affect children and their caregivers. Regarding assessment methods, children and parents ideally should be interviewed both individually and together as a family to assess personal, parenting and systemic issues. Semi-structured interviews are available for assessing trauma-related symptoms [35] but are time and labour consuming. Questionnaires are more easily administered, and a number of standardized tools to assess child and family exposure to trauma and outcomes are reviewed by the National Child Traumatic Stress Network [36]. Observations of family interaction can complement data collected via informant reports and help generate and test hypotheses regarding parenting behaviour and family dynamics. There are often opportunities for naturalistic or unstructured observations of parent-child interactions (e.g., attachment-related behaviour [37]) in home, agency or clinic settings.

Case Formulation and Diagnostic Considerations. Clinicians require the ability to integrate the assessment data with theory and research evidence to generate hypotheses about the pattern of strengths and difficulties in the child and their family [38]. The case formulation should focus on how the child has learned to adapt to stressors (in terms of both healthy and maladaptive outcomes), how the trauma has impacted the family more broadly, the level of family and other support available for the child and the role of other contextual characteristics (e.g., cultural beliefs, CPS involvement). A particular focus should be on identifying potential trauma triggers for the child (e.g., perceived lack of control, yelling at home) that are maintaining difficulties. Children's fight, flight or freeze reactions to these triggers and perceived threats typically manifest through different forms of dysregulated affect and behaviour [15]. For example, explosive anger might be underpinned by hyper-arousal, and dazed and withdrawn behaviour can be linked with dissociative responding.

These physiological and behavioural responses to trauma may overlap with criteria for a variety of internalizing and externalizing disorders (e.g., conduct disorder, depression), as well as post-traumatic stress disorder (PTSD) [39]. Core PTSD symptoms include re-experiencing/remembering trauma (may be shown in children's play), avoiding trauma reminders, negative cognitions and mood and alterations in arousal. Children's trauma responses can also be camouflaged by various disorders if not understood properly [40]. For example, a trauma-impacted child may be (mis)diagnosed with attention deficit hyperactivity disorder (ADHD) because he or she is observed to be fidgety, hyperactive and inattentive in class. On further assessment, these symptoms might appear most salient in the presence of trauma triggers and fluctuate with the child's mood. Furthermore, children exposed to maltreatment, particularly experiences of complex trauma, do not always meet criteria for psychological disorders, even though they exhibit significant distress and impairments in their development [40]. In this light, a trauma-informed case formulation that hypothesizes underlying causes of difficulties is more meaningful for identifying intervention targets than a diagnostic approach that presents a symptom-focused account of the child's mental health.

It is recommended that the case formulation be developed in collaboration with the family by sharing a simplified account of the child and family's functioning with the parents and child (when appropriate) and eliciting their feedback and suggestions. This approach is also empowering to families that have been impacted by trauma and may increase their buy-in and engagement in therapy. Families should also be informed that the case formulation is ongoing and often revised when new information comes to light, including later disclosures of trauma and the family's response to intervention.

Diversity Issues

Clinicians should have an ongoing commitment to enhancing their awareness, knowledge and skills for working with diversity in a family context. With the rise in international migrants and refugees, families are becoming increasingly multicultural. What constitutes abuse and neglect varies across cultures; thus, the cultural norms of clinicians and their clients impact how they view caregiving and child development and their interpretation of traumatic events and experiences [41]. For example, corporal punishment that increases risk for physical abuse is normative in some cultural groups and may be considered an important component of childrearing according to religious beliefs or ingrained family or community practices [42]. Important aspects of cultural competence for working with families regarding parenting practices that are potentially abusive include (1) clinician cultural self-awareness (e.g., impact of stereotypes and biases), (2) understanding the sociocultural context for parents' behaviour and, if necessary, (3) suggesting alternative parenting practices that are consistent with the family's values, beliefs and goals.

Key to understanding the sociocultural and historical context of families is recognizing that trauma may be experienced at an individual level as well as collectively in a cultural or ethnic group. Many Indigenous peoples have endured lasting effects of historical trauma originating from colonization and compounded by policies [43]. For instance, government policies between the late 1800s and 1970s in Canada and Australia forcibly removed young children from their birth parents (referred to as the 'Stolen Generations'). The unresolved trauma, grief and loss associated with these past events have been transmitted to successive generations through impaired parenting; fractured family, kinship and community relations; and loss of cultural identity. This intergenerational trauma provides a backdrop for understanding the over-representation of Indigenous children in CPS today and the critical need to preserve their family and cultural connections in OOHC. A culturally sensitive approach to working with families exposed to historical trauma involves adopting a holistic perspective and understanding how trauma impacts the social, emotional, spiritual and cultural wellbeing of individuals and their communities across generations [44]. The collective resilience of Indigenous cultures should also be appreciated.

Promoting Wellbeing in Families of Children At Risk for or Exposed to Maltreatment

A trauma-informed case formulation is critical for developing an effective intervention plan. In this section, we discuss several different family-based intervention approaches that are commonly employed for children at risk for or exposed to maltreatment: cognitive behavioural therapy (CBT), relational interventions and a components-based intervention framework to *treat* the sequelae of child maltreatment and reduce its reoccurrence, and parent management training to *prevent* the perpetration of abuse and neglect. Decisions about implementing a particular approach should be informed by the primary intervention goals and targets (e.g., treating child traumatic stress versus preventing abusive parenting), CPS case plan goals (e.g., family reunification) and other child and family factors (e.g., child age, complex needs, family preferences). Here we delineate competencies for delivering common components for each of these empirically supported approaches and briefly refer to example intervention models (see the California Evidence-Based Clearinghouse for Child Welfare [45] for a comprehensive list of programmes).

Treatment Strategies

Cognitive Behavioural Therapy. CBT-based programmes have demonstrated effectiveness for treating traumatic stress and other trauma-related symptoms in children (3–17 years of age) who have experienced abuse [46]. They aim to help children cope with past traumatic events through promoting more adaptive cognitive appraisals of and behavioural responses to memories and reminders of the trauma while also supporting parents in managing their own and their child's trauma responses. Common components of this intervention approach include psycho-education about trauma, training in emotion regulation skills (e.g., relaxation strategies), cognitive processing (e.g., challenging inaccurate or unhelpful cognitions about the trauma), imaginal and in vivo exposure to overcome generalized avoidance of trauma reminders and problem-solving [46].

Trauma-focused CBT (TF-CBT [47]) has the strongest empirical support in this family of treatment models and is delivered across 12–15 weekly sessions in three sequential phases: (1) stabilization and skill building, (2) trauma narration and processing and (3) integration and consolidation. Parents and children are mainly seen separately in the first two treatment phases to work on the components in parallel, and conjoint parent-child sessions are used in the final phase to promote parent-child communication. Parents are also taught skills in responding to children's dysregulated behaviour and affect (e.g., praise, time-out). Only non-perpetrating parents participate in TF-CBT, but other CBT models have been developed to include maltreating parents and their child(ren).

Combined parent-child CBT (CPC-CBT [48]) is based on the TF-CBT model and aims to concurrently reduce the reoccurrence of physical abuse in offending parents and support children's recovery from trauma following the abuse. CPC-CBT includes most of the components listed earlier to treat child traumatic stress, along with additional components delivered to the at-risk/perpetrating parent individually or together with their child. These are focused on enhancing parents' empathy towards their children, strengthening parents' adaptive coping skills and positive parenting and promoting family safety [48]. There may be advantages in having the same therapist work with both the child and offending parent (versus referring them to separate services) in terms of more effective monitoring of risk and progress in the family and determining opportunities to improve the parent-child relationship through conjoint sessions.

Clinicians need to consider and manage important parent and child processes when implementing CBT programmes with families of trauma-impacted children. Parent involvement is a chief principle of most of these treatment models, but how parents engage in the treatment may moderate child outcomes in different ways. Research findings suggest that parents' responses to children's trauma or symptoms during TF-CBT sessions may impact programme effectiveness. Specifically, parents' avoidance and blame of the child might worsen child symptomatology in treatment, whereas parents' cognitive-emotional processing (e.g., making meaning of trauma-related material and changing their emotional response to it) and support of the child improve child symptomatology [49]. Furthermore, TF-CBT may improve parents' own mental health, which, in turn, increases treatment gains for children [50]. Together these findings highlight the importance of splitting CBT sessions equally between children and parents when delivering individual parallel sessions to ensure that there is enough time to complete components with parents.

Clinicians should also know how to tailor a CBT programme to the child's experience of past trauma and their current functioning. For instance, in vivo exposure is an optional component in TF-CBT and should only be implemented when a child is avoiding innocuous situations or cues (e.g., their bedroom) that remind them of the trauma, and this avoidance is impacting their adaptive functioning [47]. There is some evidence to suggest that explicit exposure to trauma reminders may not be necessary and that the gradual exposure to trauma-related themes across the other components might be sufficient for reducing trauma-related anxiety [46]. TF-CBT can also be adapted for children who have experienced complex trauma. For example, more time may be spent building coping skills in the initial treatment phase if the child is severely dysregulated and has difficulties across multiple domains of functioning [47]. Furthermore, the therapist should sensitively collaborate with the child regarding how they might share their trauma narrative with their parent (e.g., foster carer) if they are reluctant to do so and, if necessary, respect their decision not to share in order to preserve the therapeutic relationship.

Relational Interventions. Relational interventions have received empirical support for improving child emotional and behavioural regulation following maltreatment [51]. These interventions are largely informed by attachment theory and aim to strengthen caregiver sensitivity and, in turn, promote attachment security and child adjustment. Most relational interventions have been designed for parents of children five years of age or younger and may be delivered in parent groups or individually in the service setting or family's home. Evidence is also emerging for relational programmes designed for parents of older children and teens (e.g., Connect [52]). Common components of this intervention approach include promoting caregiver sensitivity (e.g., provision of a safe haven and secure base support), enhancing parents' reflective functioning (e.g., recognizing attachment needs underlying children's behaviour) and educating parents about healthy and maladaptive development from an attachment perspective (e.g., 'miscuing' of emotional needs in maltreated children) [51].

Attachment and bio-behavioural catch-up (ABC) [53] and Promoting First Relationships (PFR) [53] are brief models of relational intervention for infants/toddlers which have been supported through randomized trials with CPS-involved families [55, 56]. They are delivered in 10 joint parent-child sessions in the home and can be implemented with high-risk birth parents and other caregivers (e.g., foster parents). Reflective video feedback is a key component in these models and includes using taped episodes of caregiver-child interactions wherein the clinician guides discussion concentrating on parenting strengths and interpretation of the child's cues through an attachment lens. Moreover, 'in-the-moment comments' regarding parents' behaviour (e.g., noting how the parent is following the child's lead or providing nurturance) are considered an active ingredient of these programmes [53]. In fact, frequent and high-quality (i.e., informative and on-target) use of in-the-moment comments during ABC sessions predicts greater post-treatment gains in parental sensitivity [57]. ABC and PFR also include reflective comments and questions to help parents understand how their own attachment experiences might influence their automatic reactions to their child. Importantly, research suggests that PFR improves sensitivity in parents with their own history of child abuse [58].

Child-parent psychotherapy (CPP [60]) is an example of an intensive model of relational intervention that is delivered to parent-child dyads in weekly sessions over one year. Strategies to enhance caregiver sensitivity are less directive than those used in the brief models, with a primary aim of achieving change at the representational level of caregiving. More time in therapy is devoted to helping parents process and link their own childhood experiences (including trauma) to current caregiving representations and behaviour using the therapeutic relationship to provide a corrective emotional experience for the parent. Although meta-analytic findings suggest that briefer relational interventions with a behavioural focus may have stronger effects on caregiver sensitivity and attachment security [60], CPP has also shown positive outcomes in these domains [61].

Relationally based interventions may be most effectively implemented by clinicians who are both skilled in manualized strategies to promote caregiver sensitivity (e.g., providing video-based and in vivo feedback) and have a secure state of mind regarding attachment [53]. The latter is partly indicated by the capacity to openly and coherently reflect on one's own history of relationship experiences in a non-defensive manner. An attitude that is valuing of attachment experiences underpins clinicians' ability to form an emotionally supportive and empathic therapeutic relationship that can provide a secure base for parents to explore new ways of understanding and relating to their child. Relatedly, clinicians require the ability to regulate their own reactions to hearing about a family's trauma so that they can remain attuned and responsive to their client's needs [59].

Attachment, Regulation and Competency: A Core-Components Approach. For some complex trauma cases, the flexible delivery of core intervention components may be a more suitable approach to tailoring and personalizing treatment than following a manualized protocol. Attachment, Regulation and Competency (ARC [62]) is an intervention framework for working with trauma-exposed children (up to 18 years of age) and their caregiving systems that incorporates research-informed treatment principles based on attachment and traumatic stress theories. This components-based model identifies eight treatment targets structured according to three core domains of intervention: attachment (e.g., fostering caregiver attunement), regulation (e.g., promoting children's understanding and modulation of internal experiences) and competency (e.g., strengthening children's adaptive functioning skills). Treatment is individualized by selecting a set of strategies from a menu of treatment goals described in the ARC guidebook. There is growing research support for the effects of ARC-informed intervention on reducing traumatized children's PTSD symptoms and externalizing and internalizing problems [63]. We illustrate how the ARC framework can be applied to working with families with complex needs in the case study at the end of this chapter.

Prevention and Family Support

Parent Management Training. Parent management training (PMT) is a well-established treatment for child externalizing problems and supports parents in developing more positive parenting strategies that strengthen the parent-child relationship [64]. There is growing evidence for the promise of PMT in preventing child maltreatment given that it targets major risk factors for abuse and neglect, such as coercive parenting and poor knowledge regarding child development and child behaviour problems, while strengthening protective factors, including parental self-efficacy and family support [65]. Common components of PMT for reducing risk for maltreatment in school-aged children include coaching parents in using non-coercive and positive parenting practices (e.g., time-out, praise), strengthening family communication and interactions and promoting emotion regulation [66].

Using a population-based strategy, PMT may effectively prevent maltreatment-related outcomes (e.g., substantiated child maltreatment, OOHC placements) when delivered widely to families in the community [67]. Alongside core competencies for conducting PMT with individual families (see Chapter 10), additional skills and knowledge are necessary for implementing PMT on a community level using a public health initiative for maltreatment prevention. For example, clinicians need to collaborate with parents as consumers and be able to disseminate the parenting programme in a destigmatizing way to maximize its reach and uptake in the community [68]. Moreover, delivering community-wide parenting support requires skills in implementation science, such as designing systematic strategies to promote fidelity and building a supportive organizational climate [67].

Relationships

The ability to forge safe and strong therapeutic relationships with maltreatment-impacted families is a fundamental competency for clinicians and a prerequisite for effective therapy. Building positive alliances with distressed families first requires understanding how children's and parents' past trauma and adverse relational experiences may shape their

perceptions of and reactions to the therapeutic relationship. To illustrate, maltreatment in a caregiving relationship involves a serious attachment injury that damages children's trust in adults. Following maltreatment, some children experience additional relational stressors when they are separated from their birth parents and then experience multiple placements in OOHC. In care, children may feel a sense of loyalty conflict towards birth and foster/kinship parents which further strains and confuses their attachment system. They also tend to cycle through different caseworkers because of high turnover among child welfare professionals. These unpredictable and disorganizing relational experiences can lead to fear, anxiety, anger, distress and mistrust that is generalized to new relationships and interferes with children's ability to connect with their therapist [69]. Maltreated children might experience the therapeutic relationship itself as a trauma reminder because it involves being vulnerable again, receiving empathy and building trust [47]. Moreover, children's maladaptive strategies for coping with traumatic stress, such as dissociation and denial, also have potential to complicate relational dynamics in therapy.

Non-perpetrating parents may experience the therapeutic relationship in similar ways given that they sometimes carry their own maltreatment history, have been co-victims of the child maltreatment and/or have been impacted by intergenerational trauma. They can have difficulties acknowledging their child's maltreatment because they feel guilty or overwhelmed, which presents a significant barrier to parent-child communication during conjoint sessions in treatment. In regards to service systems and support agencies, parents sometimes feel threatened by or are suspicious of professionals because of past adversities, including historical trauma.

Clinicians need skills in using this trauma-informed understanding to develop strategies to help navigate challenges in fostering a curative therapeutic relationship [32]. Although there is not a one-size-fits-all approach to forming positive alliances with distressed families, several key principles should be considered. First, empathy, open communication and transparency are crucial for building trust and safety with families who may be fearful and suspicious in therapy. Second, to empower children and parents and decrease their sense of vulnerability, families should be collaboratively engaged in decision-making. Third, consistency and routines in and across sessions (e.g., playing the same warm-up activity at the start of each session with children) should be used to enhance predictability. Fourth, adopting a strengths-based approach helps promote resilience in maltreated children and may improve low self-efficacy in parents who can feel threatened by negative feedback regarding their caregiving. Finally, clinicians require the reflective capacity to be aware of their own reactions to their clients in therapy, taking care not to respond in ways that could strengthen a parent's or child's insecurity [70]. For example, children may test therapists' commitment to the relationship by using challenging or non-compliant behaviour, and parents may distract from sharing their feelings about the trauma. Clinicians should be curious about the meaning of their client's behaviour in therapy and sensitively respond to their needs in a manner that will gradually challenge, rather than reinforce, negative expectations that children and parents bring into the therapeutic relationship (e.g., that the therapist is untrustworthy or unsupportive).

Role of Multiple Disciplines and Service Delivery Systems

Families of maltreated children are typically engaged with multiple systems and services, including health, education, legal and child welfare services. Clinicians should understand these systems' purposes, roles and responsibilities so that they can support families in navigating issues they encounter with different agencies and better integrate interventions across services. This can be challenging, however, as these systems often have distinct priorities and ways of operating [6]. Inter-professional practice across different services is crucial for safeguarding children who may be highly vulnerable [71]. For instance, reviews of maltreatment-related deaths highlight the lack of communication and effective collaboration across agencies as being instrumental in children's welfare and safety 'slipping through the cracks' [72]. Although knowledge about different disciplines (e.g., social work, paediatrics, law) involved in supporting maltreated children provides a basis for inter-professional practice, it is imperative that clinicians engage in multidisciplinary teamwork to develop collaborative competencies [71]. These experiences foster clinicians' ability to work inter-professionally, focusing on the complementary roles of each member of the group rather than on comparative involvement while shaping a collective approach in consultation with the family. Parallel to therapeutic alliances, building strong working alliances with professionals in multidisciplinary teams is integral to promoting intervention outcomes for families.

Consultation and Liaison Roles

Inter-professional practice is foundational for providing consultation with different professionals in regards to a client's needs or goals. Because of the significant impact of maltreatment on children's development, relationships and learning [73], consultation and liaison with schools constitute a significant role for clinicians. Clinicians working with families can enable a shared understanding of the impacts of trauma on a child across the family and school, allowing for consistent and appropriate supports to be put in place. This may involve personalized learning and behaviour plans developed in collaboration with the child, family and educators. These plans provide consistent and clear protocols for supporting children's engagement in school, with information regarding known trauma triggers, as well as strategies for managing distress or escalations [74]. The use of shared language and strategies can reduce stress for both children and educators. Clinicians should also be skilled in facilitating relationships between parents and educators. Many parents themselves have had negative experiences within the school system and can be reluctant to engage and share information for fear of judgement or other negative consequences.

Consultation may also involve advocating for a child's needs at school and in other institutional settings. If families are involved with CPS, clinicians are often asked to make recommendations regarding visitation or placement (e.g., reunification) decisions that have significant implications for children's well-being across development [75]. Advocacy in this regard requires the ability to make inferences about children's needs based on in-depth understanding of the child and their family system and knowledge of important policies, procedures and constraints in child welfare services.

Scientific and Professional Issues

Scientific Knowledge and Methods

From an evidence-based practice framework, at the very least, clinicians should be informed consumers of research so that they can use the best available scientific knowledge to inform their work with children and families. This requires understanding research design and methodology, psychometrics and statistical tests to have the ability to critically evaluate the quality of relevant research and assessment tools. Beyond testing main effects, research is increasingly examining *how* and for *whom* family-based interventions for children exposed to maltreatment may be effective in improving outcomes [76]. These findings help inform case conceptualization and tailoring of interventions.

Professional, Ethical and Legal Issues

It is essential that clinicians working with maltreated children and their parents possess the ability to monitor and manage professional, legal and ethical issues that arise in their practice, particularly in regards to confidentiality and mandated reporting. Clinicians are responsible for understanding the boundaries of confidentiality between children and therapists, as well as their legislated or mandated requirements for reporting, as these legal and ethical guidelines differ across jurisdictions and disciplines. Common issues faced by clinicians in this field include uncertainty about when to disclose confidential information about a child to their parents (e.g., regarding teen sexual behaviour) and concerns about thresholds for CPS notification and the ramifications of reporting for the therapeutic relationship. However, these need to be balanced against the risks to the child of failure to act in terms of both ongoing harm and prevention of the activation of support for the child and family [77].

In our experience supervising novice therapists, the process of making a report to CPS concerning suspected child maltreatment or harmful behaviour is often considered in isolation from the therapeutic relationship. When reporting, clinicians should first decide whether or not to inform the parent that they will be making a report. There are some special circumstances where the child could be placed in greater danger by informing the parent (e.g., if there is suspicion that the adult might disappear with the child). If this is not the case, there are potential benefits of informing parents of the need to make a notification. Openly discussing the clinician's concerns regarding the child and therefore the need to report, as well as the parent's concerns and questions about the process, demonstrates the clinician's

transparency and may prevent a rupture in the therapeutic relationship [78]. Parents' emotional responses – such as fear, anger, distress or despair – should also be empathically responded to. Furthermore, if appropriate, parents can be asked if they would like to contact CPS themselves during the session or perhaps make a report together with the clinician. This collaborative approach can be empowering to parents and may reduce re-traumatization in individuals with prior CPS involvement. Alongside the clinician's ethical and legal duty to report, parents should also be informed of the goal of contacting CPS to access additional support services for the family. If clinicians are in doubt about reporting, they are advised to consult with colleagues or contact CPS to discuss the issues [77].

Reflective Practice and Self-Assessment

Capacity for and skills in reflective practice and self-assessment are essential when working with families of maltreated children in terms of both clinician efficacy and their ethical responsibility for self-care. Left unchecked, ongoing indirect exposure to families' trauma can result in clinicians experiencing secondary traumatic stress (PTSD-related symptoms) or vicarious trauma (changes in worldview) that have a personal and professional toll [79]. This trauma can be manifested in clinicians by cynicism and despair about systems, society or the families with whom they are working and compassion fatigue and burnout [80]. Clinicians also need to be self-aware of the desire to 'rescue' families, which can lead to boundary violations and disempowerment of the clients they are seeking to support, disrupting or undermining family dynamics [79].

In addition to recognizing their own traumatic reactions, clinicians should be open and willing to access support to review their practices and inner experiences of their work. Therapists may sometimes feel ashamed of feelings of being overwhelmed or hopeless and deny their existence to supervisors and peers. Reflective supervision should be used to explore clinicians' emotional reactions in the context of their values and the meaning of the work in which they are engaging to help contextualize experiences and responses. While signs of secondary and vicarious trauma should be monitored, it is also beneficial to acknowledge the 'vicarious hope' that clinicians can experience when they are positively affected by the strength and resilience demonstrated by children and families exposed to adversities.

Tailoring Family-Based Intervention for Complex Trauma: A Case Illustration

Jack was eight years old and lived with his mother, Ava, and five-year-old sister. Ava had an extensive history of drug use and prostitution; CPS placed her first daughter in kinship care with Ava's mother eight years before Jack's birth. When Jack was three, he experienced a prolonged separation (six months) from Ava, as she was unwell and unexpectedly left the family. Ava was still using drugs until Jack was five, when she and her two young children fled their home and entered a women's shelter. This was precipitated by severe family violence, mainly involving Jack's father assaulting Ava. At initial assessment, Jack presented with severely dysregulated behaviour and emotions (e.g., aggressive and angry outbursts, impulsivity) and other trauma-related symptoms (e.g., dissociation, avoidance of trauma reminders). Although he partially met criteria for PTSD, Jack's disturbances in self-regulatory competencies were best understood as sequelae of complex trauma [15], given his early exposure to chronic and severe emotional neglect and abuse (e.g., witnessing family violence) in the context of fractured attachments. His strengths included his kindness and humour, but he struggled to make friends because of his interpersonal difficulties.

The family was supported by a comprehensive multimodal intervention. Jack had a history of absconding from school and was suspended after he threatened staff with a knife. Following the suspension, a specialist school engagement team implemented an intervention to gradually reintegrate Jack back into his class. This involved individual therapy with Jack to improve his social-emotional adjustment. The goal of our therapy was to provide family support in the context of working with the multidisciplinary school team supporting Jack. Given the family's complex needs and Jack's ongoing therapy at school, we decided to implement a tailored components-based intervention using the ARC framework. Ava's poor distress tolerance and initial denial of Jack's trauma (because of her guilt linked with the maltreatment and avoidance of her own trauma triggers) also warranted a more flexible approach to treatment.

Although Jack attended some family assessment sessions, as he was currently participating in therapy, we only worked directly with Ava. In collaboration with Ava, we established intervention goals to promote the parent-child relationship and Jack's regulatory competencies and implemented ARC-informed core components in three treatment phases. First, treatment focused on strengthening *attachment* by helping Ava understand the impact of trauma on her family and becoming more attuned and responsive to both her own and Jack's emotional needs. Second, we worked with Ava to complement the school-based therapy Jack was receiving in strengthening his *regulation* by improving her skills in recognizing, discussing and responding to Jack's distress and arousal levels at home. This involved in-session rehearsal of emotion-focused and other positive parenting (e.g., praise) strategies to increase Jack's modulation of his physiological and emotional experiences. Third, parallel to the school-based intervention, Jack's social-emotional *competency* was targeted via strategies to enhance his relational and school connectedness and positive self-concept. For example, Ava created opportunities (e.g., playdates) for Jack to practise his social skills with support from adults. Finally, throughout the intervention, we augmented *trauma experience integration* by encouraging Ava to have regular check-ins with Jack (as well as establish other family rituals) to reflect on and process past and new experiences together and support his formation of a coherent self-narrative.

At the end of our intervention, Ava and the school support team reported improvements in Ava's parental self-efficacy and relationship with Jack and in Jack's self-regulation. However, Jack still struggled academically, and his school-based intervention continued. Several important process factors were vital for these positive outcomes. For example, the therapeutic relationship was tested early on when we had to make a CPS report regarding Jack's behaviour. This was a trauma trigger for Ava as she lost the care of her first daughter before Jack was born. Notwithstanding this, we were able to maintain a strong and safe alliance with Ava by being empathic, transparent, collaborative and strengths based. Moreover, our close working relationship with the school team directly caring for Jack ensured that we could effectively liaise with them and consult in regards to the ARC-informed treatment principles. This facilitated consistency across the interventions at home and school, ultimately helping steer Jack's family onto a longer-term path of healing and resilience.

Summary

This chapter reviewed clinician competencies that underpin effective practice with families of children at risk for or exposed to maltreatment. Scientific knowledge of the impact of trauma on development and attachment is vital for informing family-based approaches to assessment and intervention for child maltreatment. Beyond being knowledgeable about assessment and intervention content, clinicians should aspire to be competent in recognizing and responding to trauma-related processes in therapy that influence family outcomes. The cornerstone of competent practice with maltreatment-impacted families is the ability to build and maintain strong and safe working relationships with children and parents, as well as professionals in external systems. These relational skills are best learned experientially in supervised practice. Moreover, given the rise in multiculturalism, clinicians must have competence in diversity and be sensitive to culturally relevant issues affecting families, such as the intergenerational impact of historical trauma. Finally, clinicians should aim to developmentally progress along a continuum of mastery – from basic to expert – regarding the various competencies outlined in this chapter. Expertise may be attained when a clinician is able to effectively integrate the competencies in their work and flexibly adapt their evidence-informed practice to meet the individual needs and preferences of families [3]. To deliver optimal therapeutic care for families with complex needs, it is important that we continually advance our competencies through staying abreast of the scientific literature, engaging in self-reflective practice and supervision and pursuing additional education and training.

References

1. Stoltenborgh M, Bakermans-Kranenburg MJ, Alink LR, van IJzendoorn MH. The prevalence of child maltreatment across the globe: Review of a series of meta-analyses. *Child Abuse Review* 2014, **24**(1): 37–50.

2. Carr A, Duff H, Craddock E. A systematic review of reviews of the outcome of noninstitutional child maltreatment. *Trauma, Violence and Abuse* 2020; **21**(4):828–43.

3. Hupp SD, Jewell JD, Reitman D, LeBlanc M. Competencies in child clinical psychology. In: Thomas JC, Hersen M (eds.), *Handbook of Clinical Psychology Competencies*. New York: Springer, 2010, pp. 43–72.

4. US Department of Health and Human Services, Administration for Children and Families, Administration on Children, Youth and Families, Children's Bureau. *Child Maltreatment, 2017*. Available at www.acf.hhs.gov/cb/resource/child-maltreatment-2017 (accessed 6 May 2019).

5. Butchart A, Phinney Harvey A, Mian M, et al. *Preventing Child Maltreatment: A Guide to Taking Action and Generating Evidence*. Geneva: World Health Organization and International Society for Prevention of Child Abuse and Neglect, 2006.

6. Zeanah CH, Humphreys KL. Child abuse and neglect. *Journal of the American Academy of Child and Adolescent Psychiatry* 2018; **57**(9):637–44.

7. Hein TC, Monk CS. Research review: Neural response to threat in children, adolescents, and adults after child maltreatment: A quantitative meta-analysis. *Journal of Child Psychology and Psychiatry* 2017; **58**(3):222–30.

8. Shonkoff JP, Garner AS, Siegel BS, et al. The lifelong effects of early childhood adversity and toxic stress. *Pediatrics* 2012; **129**(1):e232–46.

9. Dodge KA, Pettit GS, Bates JE, Valente E. Social information-processing patterns partially mediate the effect of early physical abuse on later conduct problems. *Journal of Abnormal Psychology* 1995; **104**:632–43.

10. Shackman JE, Shackman AJ, Pollak SD. Physical abuse amplifies attention to threat and increases anxiety in children. *Emotion* 2007; **7**:838–52.

11. Putnam FW. *Dissociation in Children and Adolescents: A Developmental Perspective*. New York: Guilford Press, 1997.

12. Jaffee SR. Child maltreatment and risk for psychopathology in childhood and adulthood. *Annual Review of Clinical Psychology* 2017; **13**:525–51.

13. Kerig PK, Bennett DC, Thompson M, Becker SP. 'Nothing really matters': Emotional numbing as a link between trauma exposure and callousness in delinquent youth. *Journal of Traumatic Stress* 2012; **25**:272–9.

14. McLaughlin KA, Lambert HK. Child trauma exposure and psychopathology: Mechanisms of risk and resilience. *Current Opinion in Psychology* 2017, **14**:29–34.

15. Cook A, Spinazzola J, Ford J, et al. Complex trauma in children and adolescents. *Psychiatric Annals* 2005; **35**:390–8.

16. Bowlby J. *Attachment and Loss*, Vol. 1: *Attachment*, 2nd ed. New York: Basic Books, 1982.

17. George C, Solomon J. The caregiving system: A behavioral systems approach to parenting. In: Cassidy J, Shaver PR (eds.), *Handbook of Attachment: Theory, Research, and Clinical Applications*, 2nd ed. New York: Guilford Press, 2008, pp. 833–56.

18. Lyons-Ruth K, Bronfman E, Parsons E. Atypical attachment in infancy and early childhood among children at developmental risk. *Monographs of the Society for Research in Child Development* 1999; **64**:67–96.

19. Fearon RP, Bakermans-Kranenburg MJ, van IJzendoorn MH, et al. The significance of insecure attachment and disorganization in the development of children's externalizing behavior: A meta-analytic study. *Child Development* 2010; **81**:435–56.

20. Cyr C, Euser EM, Bakermans-Kranenburg MJ, van IJzendoorn, MH. Attachment security and disorganization in maltreating and high-risk families: A series of meta-analyses. *Development and Psychopathology* 2010; **22**:87–108.

21. Zeanah CH, Gleason MM. Annual research review: Attachment disorders in early childhood: Clinical presentation, causes, correlates, and treatment. *Journal of Child Psychology and Psychiatry* 2015; **56** (3):207–22.

22. Woolgar M, Scott S. The negative consequences of over-diagnosing attachment disorders in adopted children: The importance of comprehensive formulations. *Clinical Child Psychology and Psychiatry* 2014; **19**(3):355–66.

23. Curtis T, Miller BC, Berry EH. Changes in reports and incidence of child abuse following natural disasters. *Child Abuse and Neglect* 2000; **24**(9):1151–62.

24. Cicchetti D. Socioemotional, personality, and biological development: Illustrations from a multilevel developmental psychopathology perspective on child maltreatment. *Annual Review of Psychology* 2016; **67**:187–211.

25. Cicchetti D, Toth SL. The past achievements and future promises of developmental psychopathology: The coming of age of a discipline. *Journal of Child Psychology and Psychiatry* 2009; **50**:16–25.

26. Cicchetti D, Lynch M. Toward an ecological/transactional model of community violence and child maltreatment: Consequences for children's development. *Psychiatry* 1993; **56**(1):96–118.

27. Gilbert R, Kemp A, Thoburn J, et al. Recognising and responding to child maltreatment. *Lancet* 2009; **373**:167–80.

28. National Institute for Health and Care Excellence. *Child Maltreatment: When to Suspect Maltreatment in Under 18s.* London: NICE, 2017. Available at www .nice.org.uk/guidance/cg89 (accessed 4 November 2019).

29. Saywitz KJ, Lyon TD, Goodman GS. When interviewing children: A review and update. In: Klika B, Conte J (eds.), *APSAC Handbook on Child Maltreatment.* Newbury Park, CA: SAGE Publishing, 2018, pp. 310–29.

30. Stith SM, Liu T, Davies LC, et al. Risk factors in child maltreatment: A meta-analytic review of the literature. *Aggression and Violent Behavior* 2009; **14**:13–29.

31. Miller AB, Esposito-Smythers C, Weismoore JT, Renshaw KD. The relation between child maltreatment and adolescent suicidal behavior: A systematic review and critical examination of the literature. *Clinical Child and Family Psychology Review* 2013; **16**:146–72.

32. Cook JM, Newman E. A consensus statement on trauma mental health: The New Haven Competency Conference process and major findings. *Psychological Trauma: Theory, Research, Practice, and Policy* 2014; **6**:300–7.

33. Whelan D. Using attachment theory when placing siblings in foster care. *Child and Adolescent Social Work Journal* 2003; **20**:21–36.

34. Forrester D, Westlake D, Glynn G. Parental resistance and social worker skills: Towards a theory of motivational social work. *Child and Family Social Work* 2012; **17**(2):118–29.

35. Hawkins SS, Radcliffe J. Current measures of PTSD for children and adolescents. *Journal of Pediatric Psychology* 2006; **31**:420–30.

36. National Child Traumatic Stress Network. 2019. Available at www.nctsn.org/ (accessed 5 November 2019).

37. McLaughlin A, Espie C, Minnis H. Development of a brief waiting room observation for behaviours typical of reactive attachment disorder. *Child and Adolescent Mental Health* 2010; **15**(2):73–79.

38. Havighurst SS, Downey L. Clinical reasoning for child and adolescent mental health practitioners: The mindful formulation. *Clinical Child Psychology and Psychiatry* 2009; **14**(2):251–71.

39. Copeland WE, Keeler G, Angold A, Costello EJ. Traumatic events and posttraumatic stress in childhood. *Archives of General Psychiatry* 2007; **64** (5):577–84.

40. D'Andrea W, Ford J, Stolbach B, et al. Understanding interpersonal trauma in children: Why we need a developmentally appropriate trauma diagnosis. *American Journal of Orthopsychiatry* 2012; **82**(2):187.

41. Raman S, Hodes D. Cultural issues in child maltreatment. *Journal of Paediatrics and Child Health* 2012; **48**(1):30–7.

42. Durrant JE. Physical punishment, culture, and rights: Current issues for professionals. *Journal of*

Developmental and Behavioral Pediatrics 2008; **29** (1):55–66.

43. Gone JP, Hartmann WE, Pomerville A, et al. The impact of historical trauma on health outcomes for indigenous populations in the USA and Canada: A systematic review. *American Psychologist* 2019; **74** (1):20–35.

44. Atkinson J, Nelson J, Brooks R, et al. Addressing individual trauma and transgenerational trauma. In: Dudgeon P, Milroy H, Walker R (eds.), *Working Together: Aboriginal and Torres Strait Islander Mental Health and Wellbeing Principles and Practice*, 2nd ed. Canberra: Commonwealth of Australia, 2014, pp. 289–306.

45. California Evidence-Based Clearinghouse for Child Welfare. 2019. Available at www.cebc4cw.org/ (accessed 5 November 2019).

46. Dorsey S, McLaughlin KA, Kerns SE, et al. Evidence base update for psychosocial treatments for children and adolescents exposed to traumatic events. *Journal of Clinical Child and Adolescent Psychology* 2017; **46** (3):303–30.

47. Cohen JA, Mannarino AP, Deblinger E. *Treating Trauma and Traumatic Grief in Children and Adolescents*, 2nd ed. New York: Guilford Press, 2017.

48. Runyon MK, Deblinger E. *Combined Parent-Child Cognitive Behavioral Therapy: An Approach to Empower Families At-Risk for Child Physical Abuse.* New York: Oxford University Press, 2014.

49. Yasinski C, Hayes A, Ready B, et al. In-session caregiver behavior predicts symptom change in youth receiving trauma-focused cognitive behavioral therapy (TF-CBT). *Journal of Consulting and Clinical Psychology* 2016; **84**(12):1066–77.

50. Martin CG, Everett Y, Skowron EA, Zalewski M. The role of caregiver psychopathology in the treatment of childhood trauma with trauma-focused cognitive behavioral therapy: A systematic review. *Clinical Child and Family Psychology Review* (in press).

51. Valentino K. Relational interventions for maltreated children. *Child Development* 2017; **88**:359–67.

52. Moretti MM, Pasalich DS, O'Donnell KA. Connect: An attachment-based program for parents of teens. In Steele H, Steele M (eds.), *Handbook of Attachment-Based Interventions*. New York: Guilford Press, 2018, pp. 375–401.

53. Dozier M, Bernard K, Roben CKP. Attachment and biobehavioral catch-up. In: Steele H, Steele M (eds.), *Handbook of Attachment-Based Interventions*. New York: Guilford Press, 2018, pp. 27–49.

54. Kelly JF, Sandoval D, Zuckerman T, Buehlman K. *Promoting First Relationships: A Program for Service Providers to Help Parents and Other Caregivers Nurture*

Young Children's Social and Emotional Development, 2nd ed. Seattle, WA: NCAST Programs, 2008.

55. Bernard K, Dozier M, Bick J, et al. Enhancing attachment organization among maltreated children: Results of a randomized clinical trial. *Child Development* 2012; **83**:623–36.

56. Spieker SJ, Oxford ML, Kelly JF, et al. Promoting first relationships: Randomized trial of a relationship-based intervention for toddlers in child welfare. *Child Maltreatment* 2012; **17**:271–86.

57. Caron E, Bernard K, Dozier M. In vivo feedback predicts parent behavior change in the attachment and biobehavioral catch-up intervention. *Journal of Clinical Child and Adolescent Psychology* 2016; **47** (Suppl 1):S35–46.

58. Pasalich DS, Fleming CB, Spieker SJ, et al. Does parents' own history of child abuse moderate the effectiveness of the Promoting First Relationships intervention in child welfare? *Child Maltreatment* 2019; **24**:56–65.

59. Lieberman AF, Ghosh Ippen C, Van Horn P. *'Don't Hit My Mommy!': A Manual for Child–Parent Psychotherapy with Young Children Exposed to Violence and Other Trauma*, 2nd ed. Washington, DC: Zero to Three, 2015.

60. Bakermans-Kranenburg MJ, van IJzendoorn MH, Juffer F. Less is more: Meta-analyses of sensitivity and attachment interventions in early childhood. *Psychology Bulletin* 2003; **129**:195–215.

61. Cicchetti D, Rogosch FA, Toth SL. Fostering secure attachment in maltreating families through preventive interventions. *Development and Psychopathology* 2006; **18**:623–50.

62. Blaustein M, Kinniburgh K. *Treating Traumatic Stress in Children and Adolescents: How to Foster Resilience Through Attachment, Self-Regulation, and Competency*, 2nd ed. New York: Guilford Press, 2019.

63. Hodgdon H, Kinniburgh K, Gabowitz D, et al. Development and implementation of trauma-informed programming in youth residential treatment centers using the ARC framework. *Journal of Family Violence* 2013; **28**:679–92.

64. McMahon RJ, Pasalich, DS. Parenting and family intervention in treatment. In: Sanders M, Morawska A (eds.), *Handbook of Parenting and Child Development Across the Lifespan*. New York: Springer, 2018, pp. 745–73.

65. Chen M, Chan KL. Effects of parenting programs on child maltreatment prevention: A meta-analysis. *Trauma, Violence and Abuse* 2016; **17**(1):88–104.

66. Temcheff CE, Letarte MJ, Boutin S, Marcil K. Common components of evidence-based parenting

programs for preventing maltreatment of school-age children. *Child Abuse and Neglect* 2018; **80**:226–37.

67. Prinz RJ, Sanders MR, Shapiro CJ, et al. Addendum to Population-based prevention of child maltreatment: The US triple P system population trial. *Prevention Science* 2016; **17**(3):410–16.

68. Sanders MR, Pickering JA. The prevention of child maltreatment: The case for a public health approach to behavioural parenting intervention. In: Dixon L, Perkins DF, Hamilton-Giachritis C, Craig LA (eds.), *The Wiley Handbook of What Works in Child Maltreatment: An Evidence Based Approach to Assessment and Protection in Child Protection.* Hoboken, NJ: Wiley Blackwell, 2017, pp. 163–75.

69. Eltz MJ, Shirk SR, Sarlin N. Alliance formation and treatment outcome among maltreated adolescents. *Child Abuse and Neglect* 1995; **19**(4):419–31.

70. Dozier M, Bates BC. Attachment state of mind and the treatment relationship. In: Atkinson L, Goldberg S (eds.), *Attachment Issues in Psychopathology and Intervention.* London: Lawrence Erlbaum Associates, 2004, pp. 167–80.

71. Hood R, Gillespie J, Davies J. A conceptual review of interprofessional expertise in child safeguarding, *Journal of Interprofessional Care* 2016; **30**(4):493–8.

72. Reder P, Duncan S. Making the most of the Victoria Climbié inquiry report. *Child Abuse Review* 2004; **13**:95–114.

73. Romano E, Babchishin L, Marquis R, Fréchette S. Childhood maltreatment and educational outcomes. *Trauma, Violence and Abuse* 2015; **16**(4):418–37.

74. Cole SF, O'Brien JG, Gadd MG, et al. *Helping Traumatized Children Learn: Supportive School Environments for Children Traumatized by Family Violence.* Boston: Massachusetts Advocates for Children, 2005.

75. Tarren-Sweeney M. It's time to re-think mental health services for children in care, and those adopted from care. *Clinical Child Psychology and Psychiatry* 2010; **15**(4):613–26.

76. Pasalich DS, Fleming CB, Oxford ML, et al. Can parenting intervention prevent cascading effects from placement instability to insecure attachment to externalizing problems in maltreated toddlers? *Child Maltreatment* 2016; **21**:175–85.

77. Kenny MC, Abreu RL, Marchena MT, et al. Legal and clinical guidelines for making a child maltreatment report. *Professional Psychology Research and Practice* 2017; **48**(6):469–80.

78. Pietrantonio AM, Wright E, Gibson K, et al. Mandatory reporting of child abuse and neglect: Crafting a positive process for health professionals and caregivers. *Child Abuse and Neglect* 2013; **37**:102–9.

79. Canfield J. Secondary traumatization, burnout, and vicarious traumatization. *Smith College Studies in Social Work* 2005; **75**(2):81–101.

80. Craig CD, Sprang G. Compassion satisfaction, compassion fatigue, and burnout in a national sample of trauma treatment therapists. *Anxiety, Stress and Coping* 2010; **23**(3): 319–39.

Chapter 19

Working with Families and Children Exposed to Intimate Partner Violence

Caitlin Rancher, Renee McDonald, Helena Draxler and Ernest N. Jouriles

Every year, millions of children are exposed to parental intimate partner violence (IPV) and physical child maltreatment [1–3]. Many children exposed to these forms of family violence develop significant mental health problems [4–5]. Project Support is an efficacious treatment designed to improve parenting in families in which IPV or child maltreatment has occurred and to address behavioural problems among the children in the family.

Overview of Project Support

Project Support is a theory-driven, empirically based parenting intervention that was originally designed to reduce behaviour problems among children three to nine years of age who have been exposed to parental IPV or physical child maltreatment. Initial iterations of Project Support targeted families (mothers and their children) seeking shelter following severe IPV [6–8], and it was subsequently evaluated among families referred to child welfare services because of physical child maltreatment [9–10] and to families referred to Swedish social services agencies because of IPV [11]. Although Project Support was initially designed for mothers who were leaving a violent relationship, it has been used successfully to address child behaviour problems and parenting difficulties more generally with other important caregivers (e.g., grandparents, fathers). Thus, in this chapter, we use *parents* and *parenting* as opposed to referring exclusively to *mothers* and *mothering*.

The foundation for Project Support is Patterson's theory and research on the development and maintenance of child conduct problems, such as aggression and noncompliance, and literature on children's exposure to frequent and severe IPV [12]. Patterson's theory [12, 13] and social cognitive theory [14] hold that parents and other adults function as role models for children. Parental aggression and maladaptive expressions of anger can unintentionally teach children, via modelling and observational

learning, how to behave aggressively and that aggressive and defiant behaviour is permissible and perhaps even a desirable means to reach certain ends. In addition, Patterson's theory [12, 13] proposes that parents sometimes inadvertently reinforce aggressive and defiant child behaviour by withdrawing or failing to follow through on requests or instructions for compliance. For example, in response to IPV and the stressors it introduces, caregivers' emotional and attentional resources can become diminished, which can alter their ability to respond effectively to their children's behaviour. This can result in parents reinforcing problematic child behaviour and also missing opportunities to reinforce desirable child behaviour. It can also reduce caregivers' ability to be warm and caring towards their children in general [15].

Warm and responsive parenting is theorized to promote improvements in child adjustment by rewarding prosocial behaviour with positive parental attention [14]; however, frequent and severe IPV is associated with harsh and inconsistent parenting [10]. Theory and research converge to suggest that harsh and inconsistent parenting, and an absence of reinforcement for prosocial behaviour, are associated with the development and maintenance of children's conduct problems [12, 16]. Furthermore, the challenges of parenting a child with significant behaviour problems can, over time, alter the dynamics of parenting in ways that end up sustaining rather than ameliorating the child's misbehaviour. For example, parents may feel that they have to be stricter or harsher to get a child's behaviour under control or, after trying a number of different things to address the problem, may resign themselves to the situation and give up trying to improve it. Whereas theory and research suggest that developing a positive parent-child relationship by enhancing supportive and responsive parenting can improve the parent-child relationship and reduce child and parent psychological distress [17–19].

Project Support provides parents with instrumental and emotional support (i.e., intensive casework) to help reduce the stress and emotional distress that often accompany IPV and can interfere with optimal parenting. In addition, Project Support was designed to decrease harsh and inconsistent parenting and increase positive parenting by providing parents with effective child behaviour management skills. To address child behaviour problems and improve the parent-child relationship, Project Support provides parents with a specific set of skills, with each skill building on the previous ones. For each skill, parents learn its purpose, the circumstances under which it can be used to good effect and how to use it correctly. Historically, skills-based approaches have been criticized for potentially downplaying previous experiences or ignoring other psychological issues. However, the goals of Project Support are consistent with intervention research suggesting that addressing broad family stressors [20] and teaching parents more effective child management skills [21, 22] are effective ways to reduce children's conduct problems. Attending to the parent's socio-emotional needs and increasing the frequency of positive parent-child interactions can change the child's behaviour and potentially challenge previously held maladaptive beliefs about family relationships or parenting. In this way, learning the skills creates opportunities to address other important issues.

Key Components of Project Support

As noted earlier, Project Support involves two primary components: (1) providing instrumental and emotional support and (2) teaching parents a set of parenting skills. Project Support was initially evaluated with mothers and children experiencing multiple significant stressors (e.g., families departing from a domestic violence shelter or families referred to the child welfare system), so services were typically provided in the family's home to address logistical or transportation barriers to participation, but it has also been provided in agency settings. Similar to advocacy interventions [23], the instrumental and emotional support component involves providing parents with attentive, unconditional positive regard and tangible assistance, such as facilitating access to services and resources available in the community. This support can also involve teaching problem-solving and

decision-making skills so that the parent can feel more confident in their ability to manage everyday problems as they arise.

The parenting skills component involves teaching parents a structured sequence of skills. Relationship enhancement and positive reinforcement skills are taught first, followed by skills to address misbehaviour. The relationship enhancement and positive reinforcement skills include active listening and attending to the child's behaviour and praising and rewarding successes or prosocial behaviours. These skills increase the child's sense of feeling heard, loved and important to their mother, and they shape the dynamics of the parent-child relationship. Consistent with social learning theory [14], these positive parenting skills provide a prosocial model for the child to observe and help promote improvements in child behaviour by rewarding prosocial behaviours with attention and affection. Improving the parent-child relationship in this way is sometimes sufficient to significantly reduce child behaviour problems and to foster a warmer, more rewarding relationship between parents and their children [17, 18].

The process for teaching the skills involves a sequence of steps: providing information and instruction about the skill, discussing the parents' experiences and thoughts about the skill and how it might (or might not) work for the family, demonstrating use of the skill via a brief role play, providing opportunities for the parent to practise the skill (with the clinician, in role play), providing feedback and gradually helping the parent master the skill, in vivo practice with the child in the session and then having the parent begin using the skill at home. The skills are cumulative, with later skills building on earlier ones; thus a parent must demonstrate mastery of a skill before progressing to the next one.

Evidence of Project Support's Effectiveness

Several randomized, controlled trials have provided evidence for the efficacy of Project Support in reducing children's behavioural problems and improving parenting competencies [6, 8, 24, 25], and research in Sweden has found similar efficacious effects [11]. Specifically, Project Support has been found to reduce children's conduct problems and sustain these changes in follow-up studies two years after the treatment services ended [8]. Project Support results in moderate effect sizes for reducing children's externalizing problems, with one evaluation reporting $d = .66$ immediately after treatment and $d = .63$ one year later [6]. Project Support also decreases harsh and inconsistent parenting, increases parents' confidence in their parenting and reduces parents' psychological distress [6, 11, 25, 26]. Furthermore, parents who received Project Support after departing a domestic violence shelter were less likely than parents in the control condition to experience subsequent incidents of IPV during participation in the study [6, 8, 27], and families who received Project Support after a referral to the child welfare system because of physical maltreatment were less likely than those in the control group to be re-referred over the following year.

Core Competencies for Project Support Clinicians

General Clinical Skills

As others have noted [28, 29], certain general clinical skills are common to all psychotherapy and interventions. These are also required for optimally delivering Project Support. The skills include what are traditionally considered *soft skills*, such as the ability to establish and maintain rapport and the therapeutic alliance, using open body language and appropriately engaging the client in sessions. The general clinical skills also include awareness of and adherence to the professional, ethical and legal standards for working with clients. Relevant to the provision of Project Support and working with children and families exposed to family violence, the clinician should know how to assess and manage risks, including the potential for self-harm or suicide and for new or previously unreported incidents of IPV or child abuse. Clinicians should be familiar with the symptoms of psychopathology that commonly occur in the context of family violence, such as anxiety, trauma and depression. They should also have a working knowledge of the clinical presentations of serious mental illness and addiction disorders in part because individuals with active psychosis or substance abuse may not be able to participate in and benefit from Project Support until the mental health problems have abated. Clinicians should also be aware and respectful of cultural values and differences, including how their own identity and assumptions may mesh with those of

their clients over the course of treatment and may affect outcomes.

Clinicians administering Project Support should also have knowledge of normal child development and of how exposure to family violence can affect parents and children, as well as an understanding of behavioural and social cognitive learning principles. Such knowledge helps ensure that Project Support skills are taught systematically and correctly, in a way that makes sense to the families, and allows the therapist to help build client understanding and acceptance for the intervention. This can involve helping parents understand that children can learn aggressive or defiant behaviours by observing others' behaviours (e.g., a parent's violence) and helping parents reframe beliefs that they are a 'bad parent' or are solely to blame for their child's behaviour problems. Clinicians may need to help parents understand that it is common to feel stressed, hurt, depressed, irritable or withdrawn in the context of family violence and that such distress can, at times, disrupt the parent-child relationship and influence how the child behaves. It can be important to help parents understand how what has happened may affect them as an individual and as a parent.

Instrumental Support

When providing Project Support to families in dire financial circumstances, it is vital to help them navigate social and government service agencies to identify and obtain the resources for which they are eligible. Successful implementation of Project Support requires clinicians to identify and respond adaptively to the family's particular needs, priorities and capabilities for meeting those needs. During the initial sessions, the clinician should help assess and prioritize the family's tangible needs, gauge the parents' ability to navigate and advocate for their family in locating resources and help the parents decrease the urgency to 'fix' all the family problems at once. A core clinical competency is the ability to target the social and instrumental support to those aspects of the family's circumstances that are most critical. For example, some parents may need help with safety planning in the event that a violent partner returns, others may need assistance in obtaining food or other basic necessities, whereas others may need help finding work, an apartment or suitable child care. Prioritizing and targeting such needs appropriately, while not losing sight of (and progress in) the parenting skills training, can be challenging for clinicians helping families who do not have adequate resources for self-sufficiency.

Project Support was originally designed to help mothers and children departing domestic violence shelters. Many such families have few financial resources and lack access to personal transportation. To best help these families, clinicians need to be familiar with local social services and aware of the available community resources. Keeping abreast of donation centres where families can readily obtain clothing and household items; organizations that assist with job training, education or employment; and organizations that provide rental, utilities or transportation assistance is critical. Through the course of the intervention, parents learn how to obtain resources and services independently, but it is important for clinicians to facilitate access to such supports when needed. This is important not only for family stability but also because it helps the parents recognize that the family's welfare in general – not just parenting – matters to the clinician.

Engaging the Family and Instilling Hope

Clinicians need to be aware of motivational factors that influence engagement in Project Support. Parents differ in their emotional resources, readiness and motivation to attempt to change their parenting. They can sometimes feel that they need to be very stern or harsh in response to child misbehaviour or believe that their child will not respond to 'regular' parenting approaches. Alternatively, some parents may feel overwhelmed and withdraw or 'give up' on trying to manage their child's behaviour after having tried unsuccessfully for quite some time. Clinicians need to help parents believe that they can help their child. For example, clinicians can help explain that just as it took time for the child's problems to develop, it will take time for new relationship patterns to take hold and reverse the problems. It is important to instil hope that the child's behaviour can be improved and help the parent feel confident and capable to help their child.

Another component of engaging the family involves being clinically sensitive to the child. Although much of the intervention consists of the clinician and parent working together, there are times when parents will practise newly learned skills in interactions with the child, with the clinician observing. For this reason, it is important that the clinician, together with the parent, explain the situation to the child. For example,

> Your family has been having some hard times lately. Your mom wants to improve things for the two of you and wants to learn new ways of being together. Sometimes we'll ask you to come in the room and join us because your mother has learned something new that she wants to do together with you. Are you okay with this? . . . If you have any questions, just let us know.

It is important to adapt the information to the child's age and level of development and to give the child the opportunity to ask questions. Children want to be informed on matters that concern them, and it is important to provide accurate information so that they do not get false impressions about what is happening or think that they are not allowed to talk about it.

Teaching the Parenting Skills: Behavioural Practice and Skill Mastery

Project Support differs from many parenting interventions in two important ways: (1) the teaching of the parenting skills includes practice role plays with clinician feedback, with the goal of achieving incremental steps in mastering the skills (as a result, the amount of time spent in skills practice and feedback is typically greater in Project Support than in other parenting interventions), and (2) parents must *demonstrate mastery* of one skill before moving on to the next. Parents who try to use a skill with their child before they have mastered it can become disappointed or blame themselves if it does not work as they had hoped. It is important for the clinician to balance building a parent's confidence in learning the skills and letting the parent know that if the skills are used incorrectly or inconsistently, they are less likely to work. Therefore, a core competency of administering Project Support is teaching the parenting skills well, by demonstrating the skill, accurately gauging the parent's ability in correctly performing the skill and incrementally engaging the parent in practising the skills until mastery is achieved.

Teaching the parenting skills involves tailoring the pacing of the programme to meet the parent's abilities. This flexibility may involve moving slowly at times – spending several weeks to teach certain more complex skills. This can be difficult for parents dealing with an especially difficult child; they are eager to move quickly to solve the problem, which they often think will involve focusing primarily on how to respond when the child misbehaves. It is important that clinicians know the theories on which Project Support is based so that they can help the parent understand the value and importance of increasing warmth and positive interaction with the child before turning to skills that address misbehaviour. Clinicians should also explain that the introductory skills themselves do reduce, and sometimes eliminate, problem behaviours. It is not uncommon for parents to truly engage once they see how the dynamics of their relationship with their child improves simply by using the initial skills. However, until then, they are sometimes resistant or doubtful that the skills will work with their child.

During the initial stage of teaching each parenting skill, clinicians engage parents in behavioural practice. The clinician demonstrates the skill via role play, with the clinician taking the role of the parent and the parent taking the role of the child. During this role play, the clinician observes how the parent portrays the child's behaviour so that when the parent practices the skill in subsequent role plays, the clinician can realistically take on the role of the child. This requires clinicians to have a high level of proficiency in the specific parenting skill they are teaching, as well monitoring what the parent is doing. These preliminary role plays also offer important opportunities for the parent to voice concerns (e.g., 'My child will think this is weird!') and to adapt the skill for situations the parent sees as particularly challenging.

After demonstrating the skill, the clinician and parent change roles in the behavioural practice, where the role of the parents is to play themselves, and the clinician acts as the child. As the parent demonstrates the skills in the practice sessions, the clinician makes mental note of what the parent is doing well, as well as noting areas in need of further development or strengthening. Helping the parent make successive, incremental steps towards mastering a skill is done via brief check-in conversations after practice attempts, where the clinician and parent revisit the goals and behaviours for a given skill. For example, with listening skills, parents are instructed to engage in certain nonverbal (e.g., eye contact, nodding) and verbal responses (e.g., 'What happened next?') to both encourage the child to talk and feel as though their parent is listening. While using the listening skills, parents are discouraged from lecturing, criticizing or telling the child what to do. During a check-in conversation, after highlighting aspects of the skill that the parent executed well, the clinician might ask the parents to reflect on their performance and areas where they could use more practice or guidance. The clinician can then suggest, 'Let's try it again, then, and this time try _____'.

The in-session practice can be challenging for parents initially, and performance anxiety is common. Parents may worry about performing poorly or being judged negatively by the clinician. It is very important for feedback to be grounded in encouragement and praise. For example, for a parent who performed the rudimentary aspects of a skill correctly but needs to alter the frequency or quality of the skill, a clinician may provide feedback such as:

> I really liked the way you commented on (attended to, praised) _____ when your child _____. Let's do that same thing again, and this time, see if you can add in maybe three or four more of those kinds of comments. Let's think of some in advance so that you can be ready. You can write them down if you want to, in case you can't remember them easily in the moment.

The purpose of feedback is to provide positive reinforcement for something the parent performed well and to guide the pacing and direction of further practice. The clinician provides feedback in incremental steps to help facilitate the parents' success in acquiring the skill and to make the process a positive one. Another example of feedback for parents who could benefit from modulating or showing emotion in their tone of voice might involve the following:

> You really noticed that your child was excited about playing the game with you, and you let him know you were aware of that. That's great! So, now, let's check in on where we are with this skill. ... Hmm, you clearly gave your child your full attention, and you reflected his emotion back to him. What about inflection – do you think your child could tell by your tone of voice that you were happy he was excited to play with you and that you were having fun, too? ... So, okay, let's do it again, and this time see if you can change your tone of voice a bit to communicate that you're having fun, too. The idea is for him to really know that you're enjoying the activity with him.

When the parent demonstrates mastery of the skill in practice with the clinician, the child can be brought into the session, and the parent uses the skill in an interaction (set up by the clinician) with the child. During this in vivo practice, the clinician assesses the parent's use of the skill with the child and the child's response. Following this practice, the clinician provides additional feedback and helps the parent continue to work towards mastering the skill with the child and beginning to use the skill regularly at home.

Organizational Structure That Facilitates Project Support Sessions

Project Support largely involves the parent and clinician, with the child involved in parts of some sessions. This means that unless the parent has someone to watch the children, two people may need to work together with a family, one who delivers the intervention and the other who takes care of the child (or children). The person taking care of the child should be proficient in positive child management skills, in part, to model effective child management practices for the parent. The benefit to this approach includes providing a context in which the parent can receive emotional support and can learn and practise the parenting skills with reduced distraction.

This approach can also provide benefits to the clinician, helping to ensure the safety of project staff (e.g., during visits to client homes). Although clinicians are encouraged to trust their client's sense of danger and need for a family safety plan, project staff can help support each other and check in on their own comfort and safety while conducting visits in clients' homes. For example, project staff might develop safety signals and response plans should an unanticipated risk arise during a session. A team approach to delivering Project Support can have both direct and indirect benefits to the family and project staff. It can also provide opportunities for post-session self-care, social support and opportunities to discuss how to handle specific situations before meeting with families. When beginning to learn to deliver Project Support, clinicians also need organizational support from their employer, including adequate time to learn to administer the intervention correctly, close clinical supervision of initial cases and flexibility in scheduling sessions to meet families' needs.

Responding to Crises

Families leaving from a domestic violence shelter or those receiving child welfare services are likely to have many immediate stressors and competing priorities.

Participating in a programme focused on improving the parent-child relationship and child adjustment is seldom a top priority. A core competency for Project Support clinicians is the ability to be sensitive and responsive to the parent's individual needs and any ongoing or newly emerging crises but still managing session time to ensure that steady progress is made on the parenting skills. This can be challenging, but waiting 'until things have calmed down' is seldom the answer. For many families, things won't calm down for a long time, and the need to parent well is even more important for children *during* difficult family times. Nor will the child's difficulties disappear by themselves. It is therefore important to have a strategy to prioritize both responding to the crisis and making progress on the parenting skills.

Project Support clinicians typically explain to the parent, right from the start, that part of each session (up to half, if needed) will focus on the parent's needs and how they are doing, and part will be spent on the children and the parent-child relationship. Sometimes parents have a lot on their mind, and clinicians can become overwhelmed by all the things that have happened in the family. Both parties may find it hard to 'shift gears' midway through a session. In such instances, the clinician needs to be comfortable validating the parent's needs and helping change the focus, saying something like:

> Boy, you've had a really rough week. But I'm glad we've come up with some ideas for what to do to, such as _____, and hopefully that will make it a little easier for you. Let's see how it goes for you over this next week. Right now, we're about halfway through our time together today, so it is about time to shift topics, so let me ask, 'How are things going with you and the children?'

If this is done consistently, parents grow accustomed to the rhythm of sessions structured in this way, and they feel that both their own needs and the needs of the children are considered. When done skilfully, shifting topics feels seamless in the conversation. Both the parenting skills and the social and emotional support components of Project Support are important; this division helps the family in the best way, as neither component should be prioritized at the expense of the other.

There may be times, of course, when a crisis occurs that does require the need to alter the structure of the session. For example, if the family has just been evicted from their apartment and has nowhere to go, the parent is unlikely to be able to truly participate or benefit from learning new parenting skills in that moment. In some instances, there may be a temporary need to provide additional sessions to support the parent effectively. Short of truly life-altering crises, however, it is important to work steadily in each session on the parenting skills. Clinicians may also need to recognize when a family needs outside referrals to best manage care.

Treatment Considerations

Developmental Considerations

The parenting skills are theorized to be most effective with children aged three to nine years old. To benefit from Project Support, both the parent and the child need a certain level of cognitive abilities, receptive and expressive language capabilities and the ability to actively engage in treatment. Therefore, a three-year-old who has not yet developed language skills or a child or parent with significant developmental delay may not be able to fully benefit from this intervention. Adolescents may require alternative services, such as their own individual treatment or family psychotherapy, depending on the clinical presentation. A competency for delivering Project Support requires understanding the developmental and clinical considerations that influence the likelihood that the intervention can be effective for a given family and either tailoring the intervention accordingly or providing alternative referrals as warranted.

Co-morbid Psychopathology

As noted previously, Project Support was originally designed for women and children leaving a domestic violence shelter, understanding that these women, at least initially, often have some ongoing distress. They often also recognize that their children have suffered because of the violence in the family. One strength of Project Support is that it allows parents to be the major agents of change in their children's adjustment in the aftermath of violence. This sense of agency often helps parents feel better about themselves and, over time, can help alleviate feelings of guilt about what their children experienced. Nonetheless, the clinician needs to carefully assess the parent's level of overall distress and psychological symptoms to help determine whether the parent is likely to be able to fully engage in and benefit from the intervention.

Specifically, parents must be able and willing to learn the skills and use them with their children. Parents with significant impairments, such as symptoms of psychosis (e.g., delusions, hallucinations) or active substance abuse, or parents suffering from serious, debilitating illnesses, whether physical or psychological (e.g., severe depression), may not be able to engage or participate fully in the sessions or follow through between sessions.

In some cases, such problems may not be apparent or may emerge after services have already begun. For example, a mother may have downplayed or not fully recognized the extent of her own traumatic stress symptoms or may have a substance abuse relapse midway through the intervention. As before, the primary consideration is whether the family can meaningfully participate and be expected to benefit from the programme. This may involve ongoing monitoring of the parent's symptoms and collaborative discussions concerning the need for additional or alternative resources or referrals.

Children also need to be able to understand and respond to the parent's use of new parenting skills. Children experiencing symptoms of serious mental illness, autism, sequelae to significant head injury or acute trauma or depressive symptoms may need additional or alternative interventions.

Risk of Family Violence

Protection from threats and violence and safety in everyday life should not be taken for granted in families with a history of family violence. In cases where there is a risk of continued violence in the family, it is crucial to discuss the family's safety during initial sessions. This planning needs to include consideration of the safety of the child as well as the parent. For example, responses to circumstances such as a violent parent unexpectedly contacting the child at school, or rules about keeping doors and windows locked, or what the children should do if a risky situation emerges should be discussed.

It is also not unusual for a parent to reunite with their previous partner or start a new intimate relationship during treatment. Some romantic partners may therefore remain in the home or be present during in-home sessions. Clinicians should work collaboratively with their clients to determine their sense of safety and their preference for including the partner. Some parents may desire to include their partner in services, and some may request to continue meeting with the clinician outside the home, keeping the partner unaware of the services. It is critical for the clinician to be flexible and to remain aware of their own safety in these situations. Project Support is suitable for both single parents and their partners (or other important supporting family members) to participate in together; however, it is not couples therapy, and the inclusion of an additional partner should not alter the content or goals of the programme.

Case Study

Maria was a 32-year-old white woman living with her five-year-old daughter, Lisa, and her seven-year-old son, Billy, in a two-bedroom apartment provided by social services for women and children seeking shelter following domestic violence. Maria had experienced severe physical and psychological abuse during her relationship with her children's father, and although she tried to end her relationship with him in the past, each time they ended up getting back together. At the time Maria began participating in Project Support, she had fled her home and was seeking social and legal assistance so that she could permanently leave her abusive partner. At her first appointment, Maria said that she felt very afraid of her partner and not very confident in her ability to keep her children safe and take of care them well as a single mom. She also admitted that she had left her job as a home health aide because of her fear of her partner and her anxiety about being able to properly care for her children.

Maria reported that Lisa had significant behavioural problems, including tantrums, aggression, fighting and yelling at other children and adults. Maria also indicated that Lisa was 'very clingy', to the point that Maria could not leave the room without taking Lisa with her or Lisa would scream and cry. Maria tried to manage Lisa's difficult behaviour by using physical punishment or restraining her, but this frequently resulted in Lisa scratching, kicking and fighting back – at times injuring them both.

A Project Support two-person team met with Maria and her children in their home. While one provider worked with Maria, the other engaged with Billy and Lisa and modelled positive child management skills. A primary concern was being sensitive to Maria's acute crisis and the potential for the recurrence of violence. The Project Support clinician helped Maria develop a safety plan for her family, including installing an entry alarm in her apartment. The clinician also helped Maria obtain and complete

the paperwork to file a restraining order against her partner and petition for sole custody of her children. This support helped Maria feel more confident that she could keep her children safe and more hopeful that she could be a better parent. The knowledge that she could turn to her Project Support team for such things, as well as for emotional support and help with her parenting, helped Maria feel more confident that she had support to sustain her family without having to return to her partner.

After addressing the immediate safety concerns, the clinician began teaching Maria how to improve her relationship with Lisa, including how to better manage Lisa's behaviour and help her feel less afraid when separated from her mother. Since Maria´s other parenting methods had not worked, she believed that she needed to be harsh with Lisa to get her behaviour under control. Thus, while helping Maria learn to interact more positively with Lisa, it was important to also reassure her that these skills would help alleviate Lisa's misbehaviours and would improve the quality of Maria and Lisa's relationship overall. Although she was reluctant at first, Maria reported that she really enjoyed the practice with the therapists; she noted that practising the skills in session made the situations feel real and helped her see how she could use these skills at home with Lisa. Over time, as Maria learned and mastered the various skills and was interacting differently with Lisa, Maria told her clinician, 'This is fun and amazingly good. All parents should be doing this, even if they have never experienced violence, because I think, in turn, their children will be better.' Learning the skills also helped Maria feel that she had agency and abilities to help her child, 'It is not just that I'm a bad mom.' Maria described feeling so good about Lisa's progress and her own ability to contribute to it that she started sharing and encouraging her friends to use the parenting skills she was learning.

Over time, Maria reported changes in Lisa's behaviour. Lisa's tantrums became shorter and less intense. Maria also described changes in their parent-child interactions, as Lisa began to mimic Maria's use of certain relationship enhancement skills, such as praising each other's behaviours. Eventually, Maria transitioned to living in her own home and returned to work. The Project Support team continued to meet with Maria and her family in their home for 21 sessions over the course of one year. Maria did not return to her violent partner throughout the duration of Project Support and reported feeling confident that she would never return, even after the programme ended. As Maria continued to use the parenting skills she had learned, Lisa's behaviour problems diminished further, and Maria and Lisa's interactions became warmer and more positive. Lisa also became less fearful, she began separating from her mother more comfortably, and by the end of treatment, Lisa was able routinely to have fun playing outside with her brother.

Conclusion

Project Support is an empirically supported intervention that reduces behaviour problems among school-aged children who have been exposed to family violence. The success of the intervention relies on clinicians demonstrating competencies in broad terms of both their soft skills and familiarity with behaviour theory and their specific knowledge of the needs of families recovering from violence and the didactic instruction of the Project Support parenting skills. We believe that it is the fluid combination of these competencies that in part drives Project Support's success in helping families recover and thrive.

References

1. Finkelhor D, Turner H, Ormond R, et al. Juvenile justice bulletin: National survey of children's exposure to violence 2009. Available at www.ncjrs.gov/pdffiles1/ojjdp/227744.pdf (accessed 12 May 2019).

2. McDonald R, Jouriles EN, Ramisetty-Mikler S, et al. Estimating the number of American children living in partner-violent families. *Journal of Family Psychology* 2006; **20**(1):137–42.

3. Stoltenborgh M, Bakermans-Kranenburg MJ, Alink LRA, van Ijzendoorn MH. The prevalence of child maltreatment across the globe: Review of a series of meta-analyses. *Child Abuse Review* 2014; **24**(1):37–50.

4. Norman RE, Byambaa M, De R, et al. The long-term health consequences of child physical abuse, emotional abuse, and neglect: A systematic review and meta-analysis. *PLOS Medicine* 2012; **9**(11):e1001349.

5. Vu NL, Jouriles EN, McDonald R, Rosenfield D. Children's exposure to intimate partner violence: A meta-analysis of longitudinal associations with child adjustment problems. *Clinical Psychology Review* 2016; **46**:25–33.

6. Jouriles EN, McDonald R, Rosenfield D, et al. Reducing conduct problems among children exposed to intimate partner violence: A randomized clinical trial examining effects of Project Support. *Journal of Consulting and Clinical Psychology* 2009; **77**:705–17.

7. Jouriles EN, McDonald R, Stephens N, et al. Breaking the cycle of violence: Helping families departing from battered women's shelters. In: Holden GW, Geffner R, Jouriles EN (eds.), *Children Exposed to Marital Violence: Theory, Research, and Applied Issues* (APA Science Volumes). Washington, DC: American Psychological Association, 1998, pp. 337–69.

8. McDonald R, Jouriles EN, Skopp NA. Reducing conduct problems among children brought to women's shelters: Intervention effects 24 months following termination of services. *Journal of Family Psychology* 2006; **20**:127–36.

9. Appel AE, Holden GW. The co-occurrence of spouse and physical child abuse: A review and appraisal. *Journal of Family Psychology* 1998; **12**:578–99.

10. Jouriles EN, McDonald R, Slep AMS, et al. Child abuse in the context of domestic violence: Prevalence, explanations, and practice implications. *Violence and Victims* 2008; **23**(2):221–35.

11. Draxler H, Hjärthag F, Almqvist K. Replicability of effect when transferring a supportive programme for parents exposed to intimate partner violence and their children from the US to Sweden. *Child Care in Practice* 2019; **25**(4):367–82.

12. Patterson GR. *Coercive Family Process*. Eugene, OR: Castalia, 1982.

13. Patterson GR, Reid JB, Dishion TJ. *Antisocial Boys*. Eugene, OR: Castalia, 1992.

14. Bandura A. *Aggression: A Social Learning Analysis*. Oxford, UK: Prentice-Hall, 1973.

15. Holden GW, Ritchie KL. Linking extreme marital discord, child rearing, and child behavior problems: Evidence from battered women. *Child Development* 1991; **6**:311–27.

16. Salari R, Wells MB, Sarkadi A. Child behaviour problems, parenting behaviours and parental adjustment in mothers and fathers in Sweden. *Scandinavian Journal of Public Health* 2014; **42**(7):547–53.

17. Boughton KL, Lumley MN. Parent prediction of child mood and emotional resilience: The role of parental responsiveness and psychological control. *Depression Research and Treatment* 2011; **2011**:375398.

18. Bowlby J. *Attachment and Loss*, Vol. I: *Attachment*. London: Hogarth Press and the Institute of Psycho-Analysis, 1969.

19. Wong JJ, Gonzales NA, Montaño Z, et al. Parenting intervention effects on parental depressive symptoms: Examining the role of parenting and child behavior. *Journal of Family Psychology* 2014; **28**(3):267–77.

20. Miller GE, Prinz RJ. Enhancement of social learning family interventions for childhood conduct disorder. *Psychological Bulletin* 1990; **108**(2):291–307.

21. Kazdin AE. Parent management training: Evidence, outcomes, and issues. *Journal of the American Academy of Child and Adolescent Psychiatry* 1997; **36**:1349–56.

22. Kazdin AE, Weisz JR. Identifying and developing empirically supported child and adolescent treatments. *Journal of Consulting and Clinical Psychology* 1998; **66**:19–36.

23. Sullivan CM, Bybee DI. Reducing violence using community-based advocacy for women with abusive partners. *Journal of Consulting and Clinical Psychology* 1999; **67**(1):43–53.

24. Jouriles EN, McDonald R, Spiller L, et al. Reducing conduct problems among children of battered women. *Journal of Consulting and Clinical Psychology* 2001; **69**:774–85.

25. Jouriles EN, McDonald R, Rosenfield D, et al. Improving parenting in families referred for child maltreatment: A randomized controlled trial examining effects of Project Support. *Journal of Family Psychology* 2010 **24**:328–38.

26. McDonald R, Dodson MC, Rosenfield D, Jouriles EN. Effects of a parenting intervention on features of psychopathy in children. *Journal of Abnormal Child Psychology* 2011; **39**(7):1013–23.

27. Jouriles EN, Rosenfield D, McDonald R, et al. Children exposed to intimate partner violence: Conduct problems, interventions, and partner contact with the child. *Journal of Clinical Child and Adolescent Psychology* 2018; **47**(3):397–409.

28. Roth AD, Pilling S. Using an evidence-based methodology to identify the competences required to deliver effective cognitive and behavioural therapy for depression and anxiety disorders. *Behavioural and Cognitive Psychotherapy* 2008; **36**(2):129–47.

29. Sburlati ES, Schniering CA, Lyneham HJ, Rapee RM. A model of therapist competencies for the empirically supported cognitive behavioral treatment of child and adolescent anxiety and depressive disorders. *Clinical Child and Family Psychology Review* 2011; **14**(1):89–109.

Tuning in to Kids: An Emotion Coaching Approach to Working with Parents

Sophie S. Havighurst and Christiane E. Kehoe

Emotions are often intense and challenging for many families, especially those attending child and adolescent mental health services. Clinicians working within this system will regularly need to assist parents and carers with both how to manage their own emotions and also how to respond to their children's emotions. This seemingly simple task is not an easy one. How can we assist parents to respond supportively and calmly to anger when they themselves have often had frightening and painful childhood experiences with this emotion? Or what about the parent who is so detached from their own emotions that identifying and responding in an attuned, empathic way is nearly impossible for them?

Parenting has been a significant focus in treatment of child and adolescent mental health problems [1, 2], and research has identified a number of modifiable parenting factors as potential targets of intervention to help reduce child mental health problems [3, 4]. Recently, we have learned that parents' emotional competence, that is, their ability to identify, understand and regulate their own and their children's emotions, may be an important target when working with parents [5, 6]. Addressing these aspects of parenting is an important focus for those working with prevention and intervention of child mental health problems because when parents are able to notice, accept and validate children's emotions, they facilitate close connection within an emotionally secure relationship – a process also referred to as an *emotion coaching communication style* [7].

In this chapter, we outline how an emotion coaching approach to working with parents and carers (hereafter referred to as *parents*) can be used in child and adolescent mental health work. In particular, we describe the theory and empirical research in relation to parent emotion socialization (i.e., parent emotion regulation, reactions to children's emotions and emotion coaching) and how our team have used this theory in an evidence-based intervention called

Tuning in to Kids (TIK). Then, using our TIK approach to teaching emotion coaching, we provide detail about how components or steps of emotion coaching can be used in clinical work, explore some of barriers and challenges that are often encountered in using these, and outline a case study to illustrate the main principles. A discussion is also included about addressing the emotion competence of parents in a parallel process that is important to include alongside the parenting skills. Lastly, we discuss how factors both within the clinician and the service system contribute to effective application of this emotion-focused approach to parenting intervention.

Theory and Empirical Foundation

The way parents manage emotions and respond to their children's emotions plays an important role in shaping children's emotional development [8]. Children's emotional competence consists of three main components: emotional expressiveness (initially determined by temperament influencing patterns of emotional intensity), emotion understanding (such as identification and knowledge about their own and other people's emotions, understanding social display rules and understanding having mixed emotions) and emotion regulation (a combination of biologically determined aspects of attention control and behavioural inhibition as well as learned strategies). These different components determine how a child will react in any given situation where emotions occur. Some children are more emotionally reactive, anxious and/ or have poorer emotion regulation than others from early in life, and these qualities can be challenging for parents to manage.

Considerable focus has been given to how emotional competence is socialized through relationships with parents, carers, teachers, siblings, peers and others within the child's ecological system [8, 9]. Parent emotion socialization processes, including how parents manage their emotions around their child, how they respond to the child's emotions and whether they teach or coach their child in learning about emotions, all play a role in the development of children's emotional competence during childhood and adolescence. When parents are able to regulate their emotions, they provide an important model for their children about how to display and manage emotions. Parent emotion regulation also impacts the emotional climate around the child, creating a family environment that can be either calm, safe and holding or, conversely, stressful, chaotic and non-supportive [8]. If a parent is regularly emotionally overwhelmed, reactive, dysregulated and unaware of their emotions, this provides a poor model for children but also creates significant stress and emotional tension that can contribute to emotional dysregulation in the child [6].

The way parents respond to children's emotions is also important and may prevent or allow a child to share their emotional experience. If parents respond supportively (i.e., communicate acceptance of emotions, empathize and help the child with their emotions), the messages a child receives are that emotions are acceptable, they can be understood and resolved and they provide important information about a situation and can assist in problem-solving. Conversely, if parents respond unsupportively (e.g., with criticism, avoidance, minimization of their child's feelings or their own intense emotional reactivity), the child receives the message that emotions are unacceptable, scary and a sign of something wrong within them or that looking out for the parents' emotional needs is the priority. This, in turn, can lead to children either detaching from, suppressing or reacting intensely or destructively when they experience emotions [8, 9].

Parents' responses to their own and their child's emotions depend on their meta-emotion philosophy (MEP) – their thoughts and feelings about experiencing and expressing emotions [7]. Family of origin, culture and social context all influence parents' beliefs about emotions and therefore how they react to their children's emotions [10]. Automatic reactions to emotions that are emotionally dismissive, critical or avoidant tend to occur when parents hold an MEP that is not supportive of emotions. If the social or cultural context is one where emotions should not be shared or talked about, this can influence parents' views and practices surrounding suppressing or avoiding emotions. In addition, the way in which an individual's own parents/carers expressed emotions and how they responded to their child will have conveyed messages about whether emotions were acceptable and how (or how not to) express emotions. Family-of-origin experiences often vary according to the emotion, the gender of the child/parent, the birth order and the temperament of the child: for some families, sadness was acceptable for girls but not for boys; for others, anger was acceptable at low levels (such as a child with a calm temperament) but not acceptable at high levels (such as a child with high negative reactivity), resulting in punishment. In some families, emotions were viewed as acceptable and important, and individuals grew up more comfortable with experiencing and expressing emotions, maximizing the likelihood of developing emotional competence [7].

If a parent has an MEP that views emotions in a positive functional light, they are more likely to respond to their child's emotions using emotion coaching. This way of responding outlined by Gottman and DeClaire [11] involves five steps, where (1) a parent notices the child's emotions, (2) views emotions as an opportunity for connection and teaching, (3) communicates empathy and acceptance of the child's feelings, (4) helps the child to name or reflect the emotion and (5) assists the child to solve problems or put in limits around behaviour (if necessary). In a longitudinal study conducted by Gottman, Katz and Hooven [7], emotion coaching parenting was found to be related to better child emotional competence, behaviour and social, academic and physical functioning. Conversely, when parents were emotionally dismissive, children had poorer outcomes. A number of studies have further validated these aspects of emotion coaching and emotion dismissing and their contribution to child outcomes [12, 13].

When this research on emotion coaching first emerged in the late 1990s, Sophie Havighurst and Ann Harley [14, 15] developed a parenting programme, Tuning in to Kids (TIK), that would facilitate parents' ability to respond in an emotion coaching way, thereby improving family relationships and children's emotion competence, and reducing behaviour problems. This way of working was developed as a contrast to the dominant theoretical approach of the time, which focused primarily on teaching parents behaviour management. Instead, TIK was fashioned as a trans-diagnostic approach where intervention targeted a number of core aspects

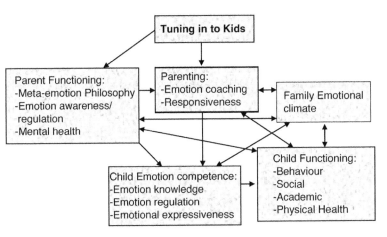

Figure 20.1 Tuning in to Kids: impacts on parent functioning, parenting and child functioning

of parent, child and family emotional functioning that had been found to underlie mental health difficulties. Figure 20.1 provides a model of how the programme aims to influence children's functioning.

We have undertaken a number of randomized, controlled trials (RCTs) to establish the evidence for the TIK programme as well as the other variants of the programme: Dads Tuning in to Kids, Tuning in to Teens and Tuning in to Toddlers. These programmes have been evaluated in community and clinical settings.

In community settings, the TIK programme has been evaluated in efficacy and effectiveness trials with parents of preschool children. An RCT of TIK was carried out with a community sample of 216 parents of preschoolers using parent and teacher reports on questionnaires as well as observation measures [16] and showed greater improvements in parents' ability to respond supportively and less critically to their children's emotions if parents took part in TIK. Parents and teachers also reported that children in the TIK condition had significantly greater reductions in behaviour problems compared to control children. A real-world trial of the programme with 120 parents of preschoolers, where TIK was delivered by community practitioners, replicated these findings [17], as did an RCT with 150 fathers of preschool children [18]. Fathers who took part in the father-specific seven-session version of Dads TIK reported significantly greater increases in empathy and emotion coaching, had greater parenting satisfaction and efficacy and saw reductions in their children's difficult behaviours when compared to waiting-list control

fathers. Their non-participating partners also reported reduced emotion dismissing and less psychological distress.

Trials of TIK have also been conducted with children with behaviour problems in clinical settings. An RCT with 56 children presenting with behaviour problems to the Melbourne Royal Children's Hospital compared six weekly group sessions of the TIK programme with standard paediatric care [19]. Though there were improvements for participants in both conditions, parents in the TIK condition were observed to use and reported using more emotion coaching, greater empathy and less emotion dismissing of their children's emotions. Parents in both conditions reported significantly improved child behaviour, but teachers reported significant improvements in children's behaviour only for those in the TIK condition.

TIK has also been used in an RCT effectiveness trial for primary-school-aged children with emerging conduct problems delivered by child and adolescent mental health service clinicians/education staff [20, 21]. The trial randomized 300 families into either control or one of two intervention conditions that included screening for behaviour problems, universal prevention (the PATHS programme, or professional development for teachers about behaviour problems), a child social-emotional programme, a parenting programme (either a behavioural parenting programme: Triple P or TIK) and a tertiary referral service (for those who require more intervention after group programmes). Findings from this study showed that both intervention conditions (Triple P and TIK) significantly and equally improved children's behaviour problems compared to control children, who did not improve. Further, those in the TIK condition made greater change than those in Triple P if the parent also had their own psychological difficulties.

Other variants of TIK, such as Tuning in to Teens [22, 23] and Tuning in to Toddlers [24, 25], have also been evaluated in RCTs, with results showing improvements in emotion socialization and reductions in child internalizing and externalizing problems for families who took part in the programme.

Key Components of TIK: Using Emotion Coaching in Parent Work

The five steps of emotion coaching are simple, and when they are described to parents, they often make sense. However, putting emotion coaching into practice is much harder than it would outwardly seem. In this section, we outline the five steps of emotion coaching established by Gottman and DeClaire [11] and describe tools to teach these skills while also addressing the challenges that frequently emerge in applying these tools to clinical work.

Step 1: Notice Emotions

Paying attention and noticing emotions constitute the first step of emotion coaching. In TIK, we encourage parents to look for emotions 'behind' the child's verbal expressions, behaviours or situations. In trying to identify the child's emotions, parents are able to be present with their child and can reorient their behaviour to a more child-focused response. At the beginning of the work, we encourage parents to start by noticing lower-intensity emotions when children (and parents) are not flooded by intense arousal. Parents often have difficulty identifying early signs of emotional arousal in their children and do not respond until the child's emotions have escalated. We encourage parents to attend to the cues on a child's face, their body language, their non-verbal sounds or the words they are using. Noticing the context is part of this and linking the situation with the cues of emotion in the child – for example, a child has come home quiet and withdrawn from school; there are increased squawks as the Lego does not fit together; the child is moving much faster than usual before heading out for his football game; the child's face is downcast while the other children are playing together; the child appears frozen as she approaches another child's house for a birthday party. We help

parents notice these cues and then take the next steps of emotion coaching.

We also want parents to start noticing patterns in their child with regards to emotions. How is their child when angry, worried, disappointed, jealous, excited, calm? What are the situations that typically lead to this emotional response? Helping parents to notice the unique and typical patterns of emotion expression allows them to better understand their child and helps them to prepare for how to respond. Parents are then less likely to be susceptible to emotion contagion or be triggered by their child's emotions. Siblings often have very different patterns of responding with emotions, and helping parents notice these contrasts is important for determining individual responses that work for each child. If it is not clear what the emotion is, this step might require finding out more information by asking questions: 'I wonder if school was hard today?' or 'Sounds like it's been difficult with the other kids at school?'.

Challenges to Step 1

Noticing emotions in children sounds simple, but it is often difficult for parents. This may be because they are unable to identify emotions in themselves or their children. Developmentally, children first need to be able to identify their own basic emotions before they develop accuracy in identifying other people's emotions. Many adults have not had this developmental experience in their own childhoods and may have been raised in families where no one talked about emotions. For others, emotions may have been intense and destructive in their family of origin, and they may have learned to detach from or avoid emotions, or they may experience emotions as an uncontrollable rush of emotion without insight, control or awareness. Family-of-origin experiences therefore provide a template for parents in being able to notice their children's emotions: change requires examining what the impact of their family-of-origin experience has been and then learning emotional identification skills.

Some children may be 'hard to read' or quickly escalate to intense anger or distress, making it difficult to notice lower-intensity emotions. Some parents say, 'My child goes from 0 to 100 in one second!'. This may be because the child has a quick and intense emotional rise, and it can be hard to see cues for emotional arousal. This is when noticing the patterns in their child with regards to emotions can help, such as knowing typical triggers that result in this rapid rise – for example, situations such as when the child has low blood sugar after school, when a child feels jealous at perceived inequality or when a child is told off in front of others. Parents can then enter these situations with greater sensitivity and awareness or engage in emotion coaching conversations with the child proactively ahead of the event to prepare and plan (e.g., muesli bar in pocket, checking in about what classes a child will attend that day) for how the child might regulate his or her emotions.

Parents may also miss emotional cues in their children when they are themselves emotionally overwhelmed. This requires teaching parents emotion regulation strategies early in the programme because their dysregulation inhibits their capacity to learn emotion coaching. Moving away before they react, breathing slowly, stretching their body and counting to ten are all examples of how to help a parent first regulate so that they can reduce their emotional arousal, enabling them to then start to notice what their child is experiencing.

Helping parents with this first step often requires that the clinician work with the parent to identify what emotions they experience when their child is emotional. Do they become very irritated with their child while the child tries to build a block tower? Do they experience overwhelming hopelessness when their child talks of being bullied and left out of school activities? While the parent's own emotional activation may be partly a parent re-experiencing emotions from their own history, often it will be an important symbiotic connection or attunement with their child, and the parent may want to use this information to assist in exploring the child's emotion. For example, if a parent notices heaviness in their own body when connecting with their child, he or she might ask, 'I wonder if you are feeling a little sad?'.

Step 2: Viewing Emotions as an Opportunity for Connection and Teaching

The second step of emotion coaching occurs after emotions have been noticed. This involves viewing the child's emotion as an opportunity to connect and teach rather than something to stop or fix. Parents are encouraged to see that challenging behaviours signal that the child is 'acting out' emotions and needs help with managing his or her feelings. Emotions may have been generated because of unmet needs or the child lacking skills to meet expectations. This is a functionalist view of emotions that comes from the evolutionary concept that emotions are central to survival and can provide us with important information regarding our needs. Shifting parents' beliefs about emotions is crucial so that they view challenging behaviours as an opportunity for emotion coaching. Negative attitudes towards emotions often underpin avoiding, ignoring or hoping the emotion will go away and can lead to reprimanding the child for their emotions and behaviour. Step 2 acts as a cognitive reappraisal process that allows a parent to move from self-focused responding (e.g., my child is driving me crazy/the child is are out of control/ doing this deliberately) to child-focused responding (e.g., my child needs help).

Facilitating a parent's ability to connect with their child when emotions occur is a central component of a responsive attachment relationship [26]. Repeated pairing of emotional activation in a child and supportive, responsive parenting to assist with regulation provide security and contribute (over time) to an internal experience of 'felt security' and internalization of emotion regulation by the child. In connecting with the child when the child is emotional, a parent's ability to name and 'sit with' emotions using empathy soothes and calms the child. This experience of being co-regulated creates opportunities to experience intimacy and closeness. Experiencing understanding, love and acceptance is key to achieving a secure responsive attachment relationship and provides a message to the child that his or her parents are there for the child even when the child is at his or her worst. Children are able to remain authentic in their emotional experience and do not have to compromise authenticity in order to maintain connection to their parent.

Challenges to Step 2

To connect, be close and communicate at times when a child is emotional can be challenging for many parents, especially if they view the child's behaviour as deliberate. If parents have had painful family-of-origin experiences where emotions were destructive or co-occurred with punishment, hurt and rejection, it may be difficult for them to connect with their child when emotions occur. A shift in MEP is necessary for many parents so that they view emotions as opportunities for closeness and that they are capable of connecting with their child at these times. If parents hold beliefs that emotions should be avoided, that their child's emotional expressions are about 'attention seeking' or 'weakness' or that the child's emotions are in some way manipulative, connection is often difficult. Parents can be reminded (either consciously or unconsciously) of past experiences where others have been overwhelming, rejecting or frightening when they are emotional, and this can activate parents' defences. These responses can interfere with the capacity to connect with a child during emotional encounters, and emotion coaching (even with guidance) can be difficult. Instead, these automatic reactions may result in emotionally dismissive responses to children.

We address negative/dismissive MEPs and automatic reactions to emotions in two ways. The first way is to help parents explore their family-of-origin experiences with emotions in order for them to understand their beliefs about emotions, where these have originated and how they affect their automatic responses to their children's emotions. We start by exploring the social and cultural context in which the parents have grown up: how did their culture typically respond to sadness/grief, anger, jealousy, fear, excitement, happiness, pride? Then, in subsequent sessions, we explore parents' family experiences, addressing a different emotion in each session so that parents can consider similarities and differences across the emotions: in some families, sadness might have been acceptable but anger not; for others, all emotions were allowed; in some families, no emotion was tolerated. In this exploration, we ask about the messages their parents had

communicated to them about expressing and managing emotions. This reflection on family-of-origin experiences with emotions plays a pivotal role in helping parents shift in their beliefs about their own children's emotions and to start being less dismissive.

The second main way we address negative MEPs is to teach parents specific skills to inhibit automatic reactions during emotional moments so that new skills and learning can be applied. Automatic scripts for emotional responses are frequently well ingrained, and non-cognitive strategies need to be employed by the parent to enable the change process to occur. Building in a pause (see Figure 20.2) and helping parents reduce emotional arousal are therefore necessary to use new skills in emotion coaching (which requires cognitive capacities). We advocate for use of both bottom-up and top-down approaches for parents to regulate their emotions during emotional encounters, the first being more effective for regulating high-intensity emotions. Bottom-up techniques involve engaging the body to regulate emotions, including one's reflexes, and attending to the senses to reduce emotional arousal, requiring less frontal lobe functioning. Conversely, top-down approaches require cognitive strategies such as reappraisal of a situation or acceptance of one's emotional reaction. We recognize that when parents are emotionally activated, cognitive strategies are harder to employ. For this reason, when parents are emotionally activated, strategies to build in a pause are essential.

Figure 20.2 Strategies for building in a pause

Building in a pause might include:

- Telling oneself to, 'Stop!' or visualizing a red traffic light

- Breathing slowly and deeply

- Counting slowly to ten (or counting backwards)

- Holding a necklace, bracelet or car keys as a way of bringing attention to here and now.

   How does the object feel? How does it look?

- Focusing on the senses: attending to colours, sounds, tastes, smells, the sensation of touch

- Feeling one's feet on the floor

- Running one's hands under cold water, having a cold drink, or sucking on ice

- Stepping outside or going to the toilet to have 'five seconds' space

- Walking, swinging, stretching, moving

Step 3: Empathy and Acceptance

The third step of emotion coaching is to help parents empathize and validate their child's emotions so that the child feels accepted and understood. Empathy is to 'understand and share' or 'feel with' the feelings of another person [27, 28]. Validation occurs when an empathic response communicates acceptance of emotions. Empathy involves perspective taking (the cognitive part of empathy) and responding with care (the affective part of empathy) to comprehend another's emotional experience without judgement [28]. To engage in an empathic response requires parents' emotion awareness and an emotion vocabulary, as well as the ability to remain calm. Many parents see their child's emotional situation as not being worthy of an emotional reaction. They may not understand why their child has these feelings and can minimize their child's response. Part of helping parents develop empathy is to find ways of helping parents 'step into the shoes' of their child in order to identify, connect and communicate an understanding of their child's emotions. We use a concrete exercise called 'The Emotion Detective'. This involves a series of typical emotionally evocative events for a child where parents are asked to identify an adult equivalent situation and consider feelings they might have in that situation. For example, with a child's experience of the 'birth of a sibling', a parent might consider their own partner coming home with a new boyfriend/girlfriend and telling them that this person is to share their life/bed and we will love them like we love each other. A parent might imagine that their own feelings in this context might be fear, jealousy, anger, rage, confusion, rejection, loss, hurt and/or betrayal. After reflecting on these feelings, a parent might draw on this awareness to consider their child's feelings when interacting with a new sibling. Empathy can then be communicated verbally or non-verbally. Pre-planning empathic responses often creates a significant shift for parents in engaging with their child's emotional world in a more connected way. This technique can then be used whenever a parent is having difficulty empathizing with their child.

Simple words and acknowledgement with verbal empathy can be practised. In addition, low, soft tone of voice, closer proximity, being at the same level as the child (not standing over), touch (holding a hand, gentle stroking, an arm around, a hug, picking up and holding), or rocking, soothing rhythmic responses are all non-verbal ways of communicating empathy that facilitate connection and help the child regulate his or her emotions.

Challenges to Step 3

For some parents, empathy is a very difficult parenting (or relational) skill. There may have been very little empathy shown to them as a child, or they may have poor emotional awareness, making it difficult to identify their child's emotion and 'step into their child's shoes'. An insecure attachment history and low parental reflective functioning (the capacity to consider one's own or another's internal world) can make empathy difficult [27, 28]. We have found under these circumstances that we can still assist parents with a set of 'emotion coaching rules' to follow if empathy does not come naturally. The approach of pre-planning in 'typical situations' can prepare a parent for how their child might be feeling and provide them with scripts of a response of what to do. Addressing a parent's family-of-origin experiences and the lack of empathy they might have experienced can also assist them in understanding their automatic reactions and assist them with learning this skill with their child.

Step 4: Naming and Reflecting Emotions

The fourth step of emotion coaching is to reflect the child's emotion and/or help the child to name his or her emotions. This step can alternate with the third step of empathy – they often work interchangeably, and a parent may move back and forward between steps 3 and 4. Sometimes a parent may name what they think the child is feeling even if they are not certain: 'I wonder if you are a little sad that your friend has gone away?', or this step might involve asking, 'I wonder how you are feeling while Sally is away from school?'. Naming emotions can be regulating for the child and is especially useful with younger children, whereas a combination of naming and exploring emotions with further questions can be helpful as children get older. Some children struggle to put words to their emotions, especially when emotionally aroused. It may not be necessary for them to say how they feel, but hearing a parent reflect, 'I can see that is so frustrating!', can help a child to calm and understand their own response.

It can also be helpful to pair emotion labels with pictures of emotions while exploring with the child a typical situation (for them) that might result in this emotion. We use 'feeling faces' posters (with basic emotions for toddlers and more complex emotions for older children) to assist in this process and suggest that parents place a poster on their fridge or on the bedroom wall to be accessed easily. Then, when a child is emotional, parents can ask the child to point to the emotion he or she is feeling (or if this is not possible, parents can point to the feeling face they think the child is having). This process helps the child to start making conceptual links between the experience of emotion, words to describe the feeling and understanding the link between a situation and an emotion. Emotion identification and understanding form the basis for self-talk to regulate emotions and can assist with engaging a parent in assisting with support and soothing.

Surface emotions, such as fear of a monster under the bed or anger about not getting a special toy, are at times the way children express core emotions that lie 'underneath the iceberg'. Parents may start by naming these emotions and empathizing, but the emotion stays elevated and does not seem to resolve: this may be because there are other larger, significant emotions behind what is presented as the problem. Parents often focus on the surface emotion but do not get the full story and the core emotion. For example, the monster under the bed might reflect a fear the child will die and never see his or her mother again, or jealousy that one's sister gets a special toy might be a fear that one is not loved as much as a sibling. Especially when working with families in mental health services, children may be unable to share their core fears and worries, and assisting parents to see surface emotions as clues for deeper feelings is an important part of the therapeutic work.

Some children cope better with talking and naming emotions after the event, especially those who experience very high levels of emotional activation. These children may prefer simple noticing, connection and empathy rather than verbalizing in the moment. Then, at a later time, when the child is calm, the parent can use all five steps of emotion coaching, especially naming emotions. Helping parents to identify the timing and methods used in emotion coaching is important.

When children are young, they experience emotions (often intensely) in their body and are aware of these sensations. Helping children develop an emotion vocabulary and creating a link between their emotions, situations, language and physiological cues can aid in building skills in emotion awareness and understanding. Emotions have a physiological component to them (such as cortisol production readying to fight, flee or freeze and the corresponding tightening in the muscles and shortening of breath). While these can feel uncomfortable, it is helpful to assist children to notice where an emotion is felt in their body and help them make these links. Relaxation and meditation using a script read by a parent or an online app, tense and release (robot/rag doll) exercises in the moment of intense emotion and body scans where the child notices each part of his or her body in turn and perhaps shakes it to release tension and then relaxes – can assist in relieving emotional and physiological activation by increasing awareness of emotions and regulating them.

Challenges with Step 4

For many children who attend mental health services, speech and language skills may be limited, and they may have considerable difficulty putting words to their feelings. This may be the result of a physical cause (e.g., 'glue ear' or otitis media), a multisystemic factor (e.g., trauma and family stressors) that contributes to both speech/language and emotional delays or because there has been very little talk in the child's life about emotions. Speech/language assessment and corresponding treatment are vital in such situations and important parallels to an emotion coaching intervention.

Parents may also lack the verbal skills to name emotions, and it is important to never assume that parents have a comprehensive emotional vocabulary. Provision of a list of emotion words and working through their corresponding meaning can be helpful for parents' own emotional literacy. This may also be important if English is a second language or if the country of origin of a parent has a limited number of emotion words.

Parents may also fear putting emotion words 'into their child's mouth', or the parents may be concerned that they cannot correctly identify the child's emotion. We encourage parents to make an attempt to guess at their child's emotion, and many children will automatically correct a parent if they are wrong. In cases where children are uncertain about their emotions, the parent can give them a choice and then ask where the emotion is experienced in their body. Sometimes establishing whether the emotions lie in the stomach (common in fear/worry) or in the arms/chest and head (common in anger) can help parent and child determine what emotions are being experienced.

Step 5: Problem-Solving and Limit-Setting

We consider step five of emotion coaching as an opportunity to guide the child in how to regulate emotions, make choices about how to resolve emotionally evocative events, solve problems and, when necessary, provide limits around behaviour. Often, however, the first four steps have resulted in a reduction of the child's emotional arousal, and then there is no longer a problem or the child is able to work out what to do. The first four steps provide a scaffold for the child to be able to resolve his or her own problems, and parents are guides rather than problem-solvers. Sometimes parents find this confronting because their automatic response is to rescue and 'fix' their child's problems. It is important for the clinician to name and validate these desires and help parents 'sit with' their child's emotions.

Talking with children about ways to regulate emotions and behaviour is an important part of the fifth step that can occur after emotions have calmed or when anticipating an emotion-evoking event. Once a child has been able to talk about his or her worry about separation from the parent, his or her fear of being judged or his or her concern that he or she will forget the lines in a speech, parents then need to help the child with strategies for how to manage his or her emotions and face fears or manage behaviour. Facing fears while managing the corresponding emotional arousal is a key component of working through anxiety and preventing avoidance [29]. Parents can plan strategies with their child that might assist, such as reducing arousal prior to the experience using relaxation, in situ slow breathing, tense and release, grounding using a necklace or other tactile object to connect with an attachment figure (i.e., a photo of the parent, a special 'stone' from a necklace to hold, a teddy bear), coping statements and facing challenges using a graded hierarchy. Emotion coaching after facing feared events can also help the child process the event and corresponding emotions, while facilitating a narrative about being able to cope with challenges and regulate his or her emotions.

With anger, helping the child learn skills that will be used to manage their emotion and behaviour is important to do ahead of time. Plans and strategies to regulate anger and behaviour might include determining whether a child wants/needs closeness or for their parent to be across the room when the child is very angry; use of physical release strategies such as hitting a pillow or punching bag, kicking a ball, ripping up newspaper or running around outside the house; calming activities such as breathing slowly, swinging on a swing or tense and release exercises; or imaginary strategies such as visualizing oneself as a turtle and crawling into one's shell while breathing slowly. Later, once the anger has reduced, talking through the event and the emotions that occurred can be helpful. Repairing when one has behaved in ways that are destructive and hurtful is important, and learning to apologize and take responsibility for one's behaviour is an important learning goal. This last step should happen once the child has calmed, and parent and child can talk about how to remedy what has occurred.

A significant but often unrecognized feature of emotion coaching is that the sequencing and timing of the steps need to be congruent with the emotional arousal of the child. Parents often need to hold or 'sit with' their child's emotions so that they reduce in intensity before attempting the last step of problem-solving or limit-setting. In practice, this means that when a child is emotional, a parent notices and connects (steps 1 and 2). The parent being with and 'holding space' for the child's emotions help the child regulate his or her emotion through the attachment relationship and the parent communicating non-verbal acceptance. Sometimes, however, parents are too quick at putting words to the child's experience, asking questions, giving explanations or limit-setting. Instead, they may need to 'zip up their mouth and sit on their hands' when encountering emotions in their child. Rather than action, the parent needs to be still – providing a model of regulation, security and calm. Breathing slowly, lowering eye contact and, if necessary, using proximity, connection or touch may be helpful and/or necessary, whereas at other times closeness without talking is all that is required.

A useful visual to help parents understand the importance of timing is Dan Siegel's *hand model of the brain* [30], which can be used to highlight the impact of emotion intensity on the brain and the need to align the emotion coaching steps with the level of emotional arousal in the child. This simple visual model uses the hand in a fist to illustrate the components of the brain: wrist and palm match the brain stem and midbrain, thumb touching palm of hand represents the limbic system or emotional centre and four fingers curled

277

over top of the thumb matches with the frontal lobes or the thinking part of the brain. When an individual is calm, all parts of the brain are well connected: thinking about one's emotions and deciding what to do can occur in a regulated and reasoned way. In contrast, a 'flipped lid' is where the four fingers are now pointing straight up, representing what occurs in an individual's brain under high levels of emotional arousal: there is now a disconnect between the thinking brain and the emotional brain. Therefore, a parent first must tune into the emotional brain (using the first four steps of emotions coaching), using empathy and naming the feeling to calm and reconnect, before targeting the thinking brain (step 5 of emotion coaching). Explaining this model to parents can be a useful way to help them understand that talking (i.e., giving lots of information or suggestions), questions (i.e., 'what are you feeling?', 'What made you do that?'), problem-solving (i.e., 'you need to say sorry to your sister and work out how you can fix her broken scooter') and limit-setting with family rules or values (i.e., 'it is not okay to speak to people that way – treating people with respect is important') are better reserved for when a child (or adult) is calmer: then the child is more likely to be able to access the thinking brain.

The literature on emotion-focused therapies with individuals, couples and families places an emphasis on therapist-assisted holding and 'sitting with' people's emotions so that they move through feelings while being supported and validated by a 'safe' other [31, 32]. Through this process, new understanding can occur, the strong emotional hold over memories often abates and symptoms reduce. Applying emotion coaching is a very similar process. Emotion coaching works when the timing of the steps is right. By a parent 'sitting with' the emotion as a child describes an experience of rejection or a transgression in behaviour, the child moves through the associated emotions within the context of the supportive attachment relationship. If a parent moves to problem-solving or limit-setting too quickly, the child's emotion is still too elevated for them to 'think through' what to do. Step 5 needs to occur when the emotion has de-escalated and the child feels 'held and accepted' in his or her emotions, even if the behaviour is not accepted. In this way, emotional experience can be processed and even allow other underlying emotions (perhaps jealousy with a sibling, fear of abandonment, sadness at parental separation) to be unearthed and explored. These emotions and thoughts can often be

the distal factors underlying triggers for anger and anxiety in more immediate contexts.

Sitting with emotions is not the same as being permissive about inappropriate behaviour. Children need clear limits around behaviours that are destructive or hurtful, although they often continue to learn best about these when the conversation occurs at a calmer moment (talking through after an incident is often when children are more receptive to thinking about what to do in the future).

Challenges to Step 5

The most common challenge to step 5 is that parents jump to it too fast. Getting the timing right and sitting with emotions are not always easy for parents (or anyone), and emotion coaching often gets sidetracked or fails when parents think they have done the first four steps and proceed with limit-setting or problem-solving when the child is still too emotionally aroused. This process requires the parent to remain relatively quiet but in proximity to the child while the child is emotionally activated. It may result in holding the child close, rocking the child or holding the child in a more therapeutic hold (provided that the parent is not angry or at risk of hurting the child) if the child is at risk of losing control of his or her behaviour. However, for many parents we see in the mental health system, the child's intense emotion can activate their own automatic reaction or fight, flight or freeze response. Working with parents ahead of time to prepare them and to explore potential triggers that may be activated or defences that may ensue is important. At the same time, if the parents are not able to sit with the emotions of the child because of their own emotional activation, they need to ensure that the child is safe but also regulate their own emotions and behaviour. Working with the parents over a period of time to explore these automatic reactions might be an important ongoing part of the parents' work. Helping the parents to learn how to sit with their child's emotions might require therapist-assisted practice with the child in the room. A number of dyadic relational therapies can assist in this process (see, e.g., [33]).

Other challenges with this step are that a parent often wants to punish the child or is angry with the child, and their response is driven by their own emotion (i.e., embarrassment at their child's behaviour, concern that their child is disrespectful). Assisting parents to communicate their values about their child's behaviour at times when the child has not 'flipped his or her lid' is important.

Role-Play Practice

We have found that one of the most important ways that parents learn the five steps of emotion coaching is by practising them in session (group or one-on-one) with the clinician to guide this process. We use demonstration role plays, video examples of emotion coaching and scripted role plays where we contrast emotion coaching with emotion-dismissing responses. We then move to scaffolded unscripted role plays to help the parent start using the language of emotion coaching with their own examples. Powerful insight can be gained by being on the receiving end of emotion-dismissing responses; therefore, parents are often encouraged to play their child. Role-play practice also helps parents learn to sit with emotions with their child rather than proceeding to problem-solving or limit-setting too quickly. This level of instructional input by a clinician is often found in cognitive behaviour therapy (CBT), where skills are learned with therapist assistance.

Parallel Processes for Parents

In order to teach parents how to emotion coach their child, it is equally important to work with parents' own emotion awareness and regulation and explore their family-of-origin experiences with emotions. We have found that parents may not come to treatment for their own emotional difficulties, but if the focus is on their child, they are more open and willing to consider their own emotional challenges. It can be useful from the beginning of treatment to outline to parents that they will have the most influence on their child's emotional development. Parents provide important role models for children about managing emotions, and this includes how to repair relationships when interactions go badly.

Half the work in teaching parents emotion coaching is assisting them in their own competence with emotions. This can be part of ongoing parent/individual therapy, but it can also be woven into the parenting skills. This includes

- Psycho-education about emotions and the value of attending to them;
- Increasing parents' emotion vocabulary and awareness of their own emotions (use of emotion lists, feeling faces posters, regular emotional check-ins);
- Making connections between emotions and awareness of where these are experienced in the body (this might involve exercises such as 'Stop at any given moment in a day. How are you feeling? Where do you feel this in your body?');
- Guided relaxation/meditation to increase emotional awareness and reduce arousal;
- Building in a pause to prevent automatic reactions to emotions, which is the time when the parents may engage in emotionally dismissive responses;
- Letting off steam with exercise and tense and release for in situ emotion reduction;
- Self-care and calming techniques to proactively reduce stress and emotional arousal;
- Family-of-origin exploration to help parents develop awareness of their automatic reactions to emotions and where these might have been learned; and
- Reflection on similarities and differences to one's partner (if co-parenting) about how each responds to the children's emotions and (ideally) working with both parents so that similar responses to children's emotions occur.

Case Study

Karl was an eight-year-old boy presenting with chronic health difficulties of asthma and food allergies, separation anxiety, school refusal and parent-child relationship difficulties. He lived with his mother, Julie, and 10-year-old brother, Henry, who had a diagnosis of autism spectrum disorder (ASD). Karl had no current contact with his father, Morris. His parents had separated when Karl was one year old, after a difficult and conflictual relationship. Julie suffered from depression, which was partly treated with medication. The following outlines the parenting sessions that focused on emotion coaching. In addition (but not discussed here), two family therapy sessions with Julie and the boys occurred midway through the parent sessions, and Julie was referred for individual therapy to assist with her depression.

The emotion-focused parent work began with psycho-education, providing Julie with information about children's emotional development and building a rationale for helping Karl to develop skills in understanding and regulating emotions. Exploring how parenting could facilitate this and how it interacted with her son's behaviourally inhibited temperament was important. Julie said that Karl had always been more timid about new people, situations and change and that in recent years this had led to more tantrums with her. She said that the tantrums made her stressed and that she was at a loss with how to stop them. Detail was provided about the five steps of emotion coaching, and role-play scripts were used so that Julie could experience what it felt like to contrast emotion coaching and emotion-dismissing responses. Brief links were also made with Julie's upbringing, which was to 'not show any emotions' and a family where children who whined or got angry would usually get 'the belt' or be sent to their bedroom. She reported feeling overwhelmed and sometimes scared of her children's emotions, and her main reaction was to walk away when her boys got emotional.

Session two consisted of helping Julie notice emotions in Karl and to use emotional reflection. This was not an easy process because Julie often became overwhelmed by her son's refusal to attend school and the conflict they had around this, and she often missed primary emotions that were occurring when Karl was angry. Use of the 'iceberg metaphor' was helpful: seeing anger on the surface but recognizing that feelings underneath included fear, uncertainty, sadness, times of loneliness and worry. Role plays helped Julie practice responding to school refusal by emotion coaching these primary feelings rather than being dismissive. In this session, Julie's own anxiety was explored, especially surrounding her fear of Karl having an asthma attack and dying or of something happening to her and there being no one to care for the boys.

Session three explored comparable adult scenarios to emotional experiences Karl encountered. This exercise was a helpful turning point for Julie. In particular, she was able to see that her son's fear of going to school was very like her fear of walking down the road, going to new places or when people looked at her. Julie reported that prior to session three, she had tried to ask Karl if he was scared (when he was angry), but this had resulted in angry retorts by her son and a refusal to talk any more. During the week, Julie tried a number of times to have this conversation and often became angry with Karl because he wouldn't talk to her. In role plays, Julie was able to practise emotion coaching, using her new understanding of what it might be like for her son, which helped Julie to name Karl's feelings with more genuine empathy.

In session four, Julie's anxiety was explored more, and she was assisted in finding suitable tools to help manage her own emotions, including a daily 10-minute meditation through a phone app, slow breathing and anxiety-management strategies to reduce sensory and emotional arousal. Strategies for building in a pause to inhibit automatic reactions of withdrawal were also explored, and Julie settled on slow breathing and having a drink of water. This session and session five included further exploration of her family-of-origin experiences with emotions. This approach, parallel with her past and how she handled emotions now, was very helpful for Julie, and she expressed sadness and anger towards her own parents during these conversations. She also made an important and significant link that her own strategy of withdrawal was due to fearing others' responses to her emotions. She also identified that leaving her children increased their anxiety, and they felt as lost as she had felt when her parents were harsh with her as a child. From this stage in the therapy, Julie became much more aware of her automatic reactions to her children's emotions. At times, she could use her 'build in a pause' strategies and 'sit with' their emotions longer. She was often surprised that staying connected when Karl was angry, worried or sad, rather than resulting in escalation, emotion coaching allowed him to cry, express his worries or sadness and helped him to calm down – shortly after, he would want to cuddle up to her.

Sessions six and seven focused on anger both in Julie's own family of origin and in how she managed her own and her children's anger. She identified that she did not feel like she got angry, just sad and depressed. Responding to her children's anger was a more challenging topic. She remained physiologically aroused with anxiety and anger when her children were angry, and this was the most difficult emotion for her to tolerate. At times, she would still leave the room, and this often resulted in Karl escalating his behaviour. Strategies of building in a pause to help her remain present, rather than leaving, were again explored.

The last session involved continued practising of the emotion coaching skills, especially reflection and sitting with emotions, plus using the problem-solving question with her children of 'what do you think would help?'. The session also included reflecting on what Julie felt she had learned (she said that anger might not always be scary, that she was no longer avoiding emotional moments with her boys, that she recognized that when she was coping better, she was more aware of her boys' emotions and could respond to these). She still struggled with sitting with the emotions, predominantly anger, and at times still avoided talking about fears and worries. She reported that Karl was talking more with her and occasionally shared when he was worried about things at school, his asthma or when he thought Henry was getting more attention. In turn, Julie reported that she was better at seeing the jealousy in these moments and that while she still often missed the emotion, she could return to talking about these experiences and use emotion coaching later. Lastly, she reported that while Karl still had some difficult days going to school, these had decreased significantly, and she now felt better able to support him through his fears rather than succumbing to his desire to stay home.

Clinician Competencies and Challenges

Focusing on emotions in parent work can be challenging for clinicians and requires professional training and development, ongoing clinical supervision and service system support to ensure that the work can be delivered effectively. Helping parents shift their ways of responding to their children's emotions (and behaviours) can elicit clinicians' own reactions, and it is important that they have an awareness of their MEP. We advocate that clinicians use time to explore their own family-of-origin experiences with emotions so that they understand their automatic reactions (see Figure 20.3 for reflective questions). It is difficult to do emotion-focused parent work unless the clinician has first explored these issues for themselves. For some,

this might occur during professional training (such as a Tuning in to Kids professional training), workshops on emotion-focused therapy, meeting with colleagues to explore how this work can be applied or undertaking one's own therapy. Regular peer or clinical supervision is also important. Emotions in parents can evoke emotions in clinicians – especially when working with parents who may remind clinicians of someone in their own life. Many parents get stuck, have critical and emotionally dismissive attitudes, and their actions towards their children can be painful to hear or witness: this can also be emotionally stressful for clinicians. Having a way of working through individual reactions is important. When more than one clinician works in an emotion-focused way, there is often greater opportunity for sharing experiences and supporting one another.

Challenges for the clinician in emotion-focused parent work are that, for many, the helping profession is in and of itself about solving people's problems. Emotion coaching involves a dual process for clinicians where they have to teach the ideas while also acting as emotion coaching role models. There is a tension between giving advice to parents about how to implement the five steps of emotion coaching while also emotion coaching them during this learning. If clinicians always jump to giving suggestions about what a parent should do in an emotional event, they mismatch with the process, and it can leave parents feeling unheard. The clinician needs to first notice the feelings of the parent, connect, empathize

Figure 20.3 Reflective questions for clinicians: what is your meta-emotion philosophy (MEP)?

- What were the cultural attitudes and practices about expressing sadness, anger, fear and happiness when you were growing up?
- How did those raising you express emotions?
- What were the responses of those raising you to emotions such as sadness, anger, fear, joy, jealousy, pride? What message did this communicate to you about these emotions?
- What are your automatic reactions now when you or others are emotional?
- Are there any emotions that you find more difficult to express or experience in others?
- What is it like when someone else is angry, sad, worried or happy? Are you able to 'sit with' these emotions in someone else? Do you jump to rescuing, problem solving, limit setting or avoidance when others are emotional?
- What would you like to change (if anything) about how you respond to emotions?

and even name the emotion. Then strategies for how to respond can be explored.

Support within one's clinical service or work setting is also important. If a workplace is emotionally dismissive of a worker's reactions to decisions, employment conditions, work stress, sadness/distress/anger about clinical work, this can make the environment non-optimal for this type of clinical work. However, for many practitioners, the workplace is affected by limitations in funding, services, supervision, time and staff, and yet people continue to be emotionally supportive to children, parents and families. Helping clinicians to find relevant peer support either face-to-face or through online interest groups, accessing emotion-focused supervision and ongoing professional development can assist in helping clinicians to improve their capacity to be emotion coaching in their work.

Conclusion

Working with families in the mental health system often requires providing intervention with parents to help them understand and regulate their own emotions as well as assisting them in how to respond to their children in ways that promote emotional competence and reduce mental health difficulties. This chapter has outlined a way of applying the theory about emotion socialization and emotion coaching to parent work. Complex families often require comprehensive therapeutic approaches that target a range of risk processes, and helping parents with emotion coaching can be highly beneficial to children and families when used in combination with other components of intervention.

References

1. Hoagwood KE, Cavaler MA, Burns BJ, et al. Family support in children's mental health: A review and synthesis. *Clinical Child and Family Psychology Review* 2010; **13**:1–45.

2. Ryan R, O'Farrelly C, Ramchandania P. Parenting and child mental health. London Journal of Primary Care. 2017; **9**:86–94.

3. Kaminski JW, Valle LA, Filene JH, Boyle CL. A meta-analytic review of components associated with parent training program effectiveness. *Journal of Abnormal Child Psychology* 2008; **36**(4):567–89.

4. Dretzke J, Davenport C, Frew E, et al. The clinical effectiveness of different parenting programmes for children with conduct problems: A systematic review of randomised controlled trials. *Child and Adolescent Mental Health* 2009; **3**:1753–2000.

5. Maliken AC, Katz LF. Exploring the impact of parental psychopathology and emotion regulation on evidence-based parenting interventions: A transdiagnostic approach to improving treatment effectiveness. *Clinical Child and Family Psychology Review* 2013; **16**(2):173–86.

6. Havighurst SS, Kehoe CE. The role of parental emotion regulation in parent emotion socialization: Implications for intervention. In: Deater-Deckard K, Panneton R (eds.), *Parental Stress and Early Child Development: Adaptive and Maladaptive Outcomes.* Cham: Springer International, 2017, pp. 285–307.

7. Gottman JM, Katz LF, Hooven C. *Meta-Emotion: How Families Communicate Emotionally.* Mahway, NJ: Erlbaum Associates, 1997.

8. Morris AS, Silk JS, Steinberg L, et al. The role of the family context in the development of emotion regulation. *Social Development* 2007; **16**(2):361–88.

9. Eisenberg N, Cumberland A, Spinrad TL. Parental socialization of emotion. *Psychological Inquiry* 1998; **9**:241–73.

10. Brown GL, Craig AB, Halberstadt AG. Parent gender differences in emotion socialization behaviors vary by ethnicity and child gender. *Parenting: Science and Practice* 2015; **15**(3):135–57.

11. Gottman JM, DeClaire J. *The Heart of Parenting: How to Raise an Emotionally Intelligent Child.* London: Bloomsbury, 1997.

12. Johnson AM, Hawes DJ, Eisenberg N, et al. Emotion socialization and child conduct problems: A comprehensive review and meta-analysis. Clinical Psychology Review 2017; **54**:65–80.

13. Lunkenheimer ES, Shields AM, Cortina KS. Parental emotion coaching and dismissing in family interaction. *Social Development* 2007; **16**:232–48.

14. Havighurst SS, Harley A, Prior M. Building preschool children's emotional competence: A parenting program. *Early Education and Development* 2004; **15**(4):423–48.

15. Havighurst SS, Harley A. *Tuning in to Kids: Emotionally Intelligent Parenting Program Manual.* Melbourne: University of Melbourne, 2007.

16. Havighurst SS, Wilson KR, Harley AE, et al. Tuning in to Kids: Improving emotion socialization practices in parents of preschool children – findings from a community trial. *Journal of Child Psychology and Psychiatry* 2010; **51**:1342–50.

17. Wilson KR, Havighurst SS, Harley AE. Tuning in to Kids: An effectiveness trial of a parenting program targeting emotion socialization of preschoolers. *Journal of Family Psychology* 2012; **26**:56–65.

18. Havighurst SS, Harley AE, Wilson K, Kehoe CE. Dads Tuning in to Kids: A randomized controlled trial of

an emotion socialization parenting program for fathers. *Social Development* 2019; **28**(4):979–97.

19. Havighurst SS, Wilson KR, Harley AE, et al. 'Tuning into Kids': Reducing young children's behavior problems using an emotion coaching parenting program. *Child Psychiatry and Human Development* 2013; **44**(2):247–64.

20. Duncombe ME, Havighurst SS, Kehoe CE, et al. Comparing an emotion – and a behavior-focused parenting program – as part of a multi-systemic intervention for child conduct problems. *Journal of Clinical Child and Adolescent Psychology* 2016; **45** (3):320–34.

21. Havighurst SS, Duncombe ME, Frankling EJ, et al. An emotion-focused early intervention for children with emerging conduct problems. *Journal of Abnormal Child Psychology* 2015; **43**(4):749–60.

22. Kehoe CE, Havighurst SS, Harley AE. Examining the efficacy of an emotion-focused parenting intervention in reducing pre-adolescents' internalising and externalising problems. Presented at the 28th International Congress of Applied Psychology, Paris, 2014.

23. Havighurst SS, Kehoe CE, Harley AE. Tuning in to Teens: Improving parental responses to anger and reducing youth externalizing behavior problems. *Journal of Adolescence* 2015; **42**:148–58.

24. Lauw MSM, Havighurst SS, Wilson KR, et al. Improving parenting of toddlers' emotions using an emotion coaching parenting program: A pilot study of Tuning in to Toddlers. *Journal of Community Psychology* 2014; **42**:169–75.

25. Havighurst SS, Kehoe CE, Harley AE, et al. Tuning in to Toddlers: Research protocol and recruitment for evaluation of an emotion socialization program for

parents of toddlers. *Frontiers of Psychology* 2019; **10**:1–13.

26. van der Voort A, Juffer F, Bakermans-Kranenburg MJ. Sensitive parenting is the foundation for secure attachment relationships and positive social-emotional development of children. *Journal of Child Services* 2014; **9**:165–76.

27. Decety J, Morigochi Y. The empathic brain and its dysfunction in psychiatric populations: Implications for intervention across different clinical conditions. *Biopsychosocial Medicine* 2007; **1**:22.

28. Wispé L. The distinction between sympathy and empathy: To call forth a concept, a word is needed. *Journal of Personality and Social Psychology* 1986; **50**:314–21.

29. Kehoe CE, Havighurst SS. Treating emotion dysregulation in internalizing disorders. In: Beauchaine TP, Crowell SE (eds.), *The Oxford Handbook of Emotion Dysregulation*. Oxford, UK: Oxford University Press, 2018.

30. Siegel DJ, Bryson TP. The Whole-Brain Child: 12 Revolutionary Strategies to Nurture Your Child's Developing Mind, Survive Everyday Parenting Struggles, and Help Your Family Thrive. New York: Delacorte Press, 2011.

31. Greenberg LS. Emotions, the great captains of our lives: their role in the process of change in psychotherapy. *American Psychologist* 2012; **67**:697–707.

32. Johnson SM, Greenman PS. The path to a secure bond: Emotionally focused couple therapy. *Journal of Clinical Psychology* 2006; **62**:597–609.

33. Hughes DA. Attachment-Focused Parenting: Effective Strategies to Care for Children. New York: Norton, 2009.

Emotion Coaching in the Context of Intimate Partner Violence

Lynn Fainsilber Katz and Kyrill Gurtovenko

The importance of parenting practices for children's long-term psychological adjustment has been a central tenet in developmental, child clinical and family psychology. Parents play a vital role in shaping child development, and emotion socialization specifically describes the process by which parents support children in attaining emotional competence [1–5]. Emotion coaching (EC) is an emotion socialization construct that has been shown to be predictive of a range of positive developmental outcomes for pre-schoolers, elementary school-age children and adolescents [6–9]. EC is broadly characterized by parents' capacity to be accepting of their own and their child's emotions, their skill at acknowledging and validating child emotion, and their ability to coach their children in effectively understanding, expressing, and regulating emotion [10]. In this chapter, we review the historical background and empirical research on EC. We also discuss the relevance of an emotion-focused intervention for families exposed to intimate partner violence (IPV), provide an overview of a 12-session EC intervention developed for this at-risk population and provide a clinical case example to illustrate the EC treatment principles and process. Finally, we identify several core competencies that we believe enhance delivery and outcomes of the EC intervention and consider potential directions for future work on EC.

Historical Background on EC

Historically, psychological research and theory have placed little attention on examining parents' feelings and cognitions about their own and their child's affect or on how parents respond and socialize children's affective experience and expression. Much of the early developmental research on parenting focused on parental affect and discipline, studying variables such as warmth, control and responsiveness [11, 12]. In the 1990s, the role of parents in the socialization of child understanding, expression and regulation of emotion emerged as an important parenting dimension. Three social learning mechanisms involved in parental socialization of children's emotion-related skills were identified, including (1) parents' own expression and regulation of emotion, (2) parents' reactions to children's expression of emotion and (3) parents' coaching and discussion of children's emotions [1, 13].

In 1996, Gottman, Katz and Hooven [14] introduced a new parenting concept called *parental meta-emotion philosophy* (PMEP), which refers to an organized set of feelings and thoughts that parents have about their own and their children's emotions. Early empirical studies of PMEP suggested that parents varied in the degree to which they had an emotion coaching or emotion dismissing meta-emotion philosophy. Parents who had a PMEP that was high in emotion coaching were aware of low-intensity emotions in themselves and their children, viewed children's negative emotion as an opportunity for intimacy or teaching, validated and labelled their children's emotion and discussed goals and strategies for dealing with the situation that led to the emotion. Parents who had a PMEP that was dismissive of emotions tended to deny or ignore emotion, viewed their job as needing to change negative emotions quickly, conveyed to their children that emotions are not very important and hoped that the dismissing strategy would make the emotion go away quickly.

In our initial studies, we found that when parents were emotion coaching, their children showed fewer behaviour problems, higher academic achievement, greater attentional abilities, less negative and more positive peer relations, fewer stress-related illnesses and greater physiological regulatory abilities [14, 15]. We also determined that emotion coaching was not the same as parental warmth, as very concerned and generally warm parents can be oblivious to the world of emotion [14]. The concept of emotion coaching is now central to studies of emotion socialization [16] and has been examined in families with children varying in age from toddlers to adolescents [9, 17–19].

Emotion coaching has also been studied in families with various risk conditions, including eating disorders [20–2], anxiety disorders [23, 24], conduct-related problems [10, 25–31], attention deficit hyperactivity disorder (ADHD) [32], autism spectrum disorders and other developmental disabilities [33, 34], substance use issues [35, 36], depression [6, 37], suicide ideation [38], trauma [39], maltreatment [8], military families facing deployment [40], mothers reuniting with children after prison [41], adoptive families [42] and low-income families [43, 44]. In addition to largely Caucasian American and Canadian samples, emotion coaching has been examined in African-American families [45] and families from Mexico [46], Taiwan [47], India [48, 49], Australia [26], Iran [50] and Korea [51, 52].

The concept of PMEP advanced our understanding of emotion socialization in several ways. First, it highlighted the idea that parents' thoughts and feelings about their *own* emotions are related to their thoughts and feelings about their *children's* emotions. Previous studies of emotion socialization had focused largely on parenting behaviours and responses to children's feelings but had not examined parents' thoughts and feelings about their own feelings as important contributors to how they respond to child affect.

Second, a core principle underlying PMEP's conceptual framework is the idea that parents' beliefs, thoughts and attitudes about emotion guide their emotion socialization behaviours. According to the meta-emotion framework, PMEP was an underlying basis for parents' expression and regulation of their own emotions, reactions to children's emotions and coaching of children's emotions. In support of this notion, we found that PMEP relates to parenting behaviours such as emotional scaffolding, praising, validation and self-disclosure [14, 53, 54].

Third, findings indicating that PMEP is distinct from parental warmth suggested that PMEP reflects a unique parenting dimension that had not been previously identified [15]. Sheeber et al. [55] reported that PMEP is not only distinct from warmth but also explains variance in child adjustment over and above parenting qualities such as warmth or harshness [55]. This 'value-added' effect highlights the unique contribution of PMEP to children's socio-emotional adjustment.

Fourth, at the centre of our conceptual model is the idea that emotion coaching impacts children's ability to regulate emotion. Theoretical discussions of factors relating to children's emotional development support the idea that children learn how to express and regulate their emotions within the course of parent-child interactions [1, 56–60]. In our early studies, we found that parental meta-emotion was strongly related to parenting during a laboratory teaching interaction and to the child's physiological regulatory abilities (vagal tone and the suppression of vagal tone). Vagal tone or respiratory sinus arrhythmia (RSA) has been conceptualized as an index of the child's ability to self-soothe when upset and is associated with better emotion regulation and attentional abilities. Gottman, Katz and Hooven [14, 58] found that children whose parents were emotion coaching had higher vagal tone and greater ability to suppress vagal tone when engaging in tasks that demand impulse control and mental effort. Physiological regulatory abilities at age five predicted children's ability to down-regulate their own negative affect at age eight, and both abilities, in turn, predicted child outcomes reflecting behavioural and physical health. A considerable amount of research has found that children's ability to regulate emotion has important downstream consequences. Children who are able to regulate emotion show better psychosocial adjustment and peer relations [14, 16, 61].

Given that PMEP and emotion coaching were associated with a range of markers of child and family functioning and adaptation, work in this area began to shift towards developing practical and useful interventions based on these empirical foundations. We also began considering which at-risk populations might benefit most from an emotion coaching intervention.

Targeting Emotion Regulation in Families Exposed to Intimate Partner Violence

Children exposed to IPV exhibit higher levels of a variety of mental health problems than comparison children. Exposed children are at increased risk for difficulties with anxiety [62], depression [63, 64], self-esteem [65] and externalizing problems [66–8]. Children exposed to IPV also have greater difficulty with peers when compared to other children [69, 70]. They are less likely to have a best friend, show a diminished degree of depth and connectedness in their friendships, exhibit higher levels of school loneliness and have more conflict with a best friend [71,

72]. They are also more likely to bite, hit and slap others without provocation and to insult or call other children names [73]. IPV also sets children at risk for poor long-term outcomes. Exposure to IPV as a child predicts later dating violence among college students [74], spouse abuse [75], adult criminal activity [76], and depression and low self-esteem in adulthood [77, 78].

Increasing evidence suggests that emotion regulation is a critical mechanism that explains the heightened risk for psychopathology in IPV-exposed children. There is growing evidence that IPV-exposed children show disturbances in affective awareness, expression and regulation [79–81]. Graham-Bermann and Levendosky [73] reported that emotional expression in children exposed to IPV was significantly more negative and dysphoric than a in comparison group. Children exposed to IPV had higher rates of sadness, depression, worry, anger and frustration than their peers. Their ability to regulate emotion was also less well developed. They were less likely to show appropriate emotions to events and more readily expressed their negative feelings. In a longitudinal study, Katz, Hessler and Annest [80] found that IPV when children were five years of age was associated with lower levels of emotional awareness and poorer ability to regulate emotional arousal at age nine. Exposure to IPV in childhood is also associated with anger-related dysregulation in adulthood [82]. Children's emotion regulation also mediates links between IPV exposure and children's internalizing and externalizing difficulties [83–85].

The ability to regulate negative affect may be an especially important skill for children exposed to IPV. When a stressful situation is controllable, problem-solving or active coping methods are associated with positive adjustment in children [86]. However, children exposed to IPV are often powerless to stop the violence they witness at home. Compas et al. [86] suggest that when a stressful situation is uncontrollable, emotion-focused coping may be a superior strategy. Thus, interventions that help children exposed to IPV learn appropriate strategies for managing their strong negative affect may function to increase their feelings of control and self-efficacy in face of an uncontrollable stressor.

Similarly, mothers' emotion regulation is emerging as an important predictor of both child adjustment and parenting outcomes following IPV exposure [87–90] and may be a factor that predicts

the intergenerational transmission of violence [87]. Emotion dysregulation is also a significant correlate and predictor of IPV and abusive behaviour in adulthood [91] and mediates the impact of early maltreatment on IPV [92].

Since both mother and child emotion regulation is a factor predicting child adjustment following IPV exposure and is associated with a range of negative long-term outcomes, interventions aimed at reducing risk among IPV-exposed families may benefit from including techniques to target emotion regulation skills.

IPV, Maternal Emotion Regulation and EC

Research on the effectiveness of intervention programmes for children exposed to IPV is still very much in its infancy. Although most shelters and community-based IPV agencies across the United States offer intervention programmes aimed at helping children exposed to IPV, few studies have directly assessed the efficacy of these interventions. Interventions for children exposed to IPV largely include advocacy and support services for battered women [93, 94] and treatment groups for children that focus on educating children about family violence, improving coping skills and/or reducing problem behaviours [94–100].

Only three interventions developed for IPV survivors include a parenting component. Based in an attachment framework, Lieberman and Van Horn [101] developed the 52-week child-parent psychotherapy (CPP) programme for preschoolers exposed to IPV. The goals of CPP include creating a joint trauma narrative for mother and child, increasing maternal responsiveness, addressing non-aggressive parenting and developmentally appropriate interactions and decreasing maladaptive behaviours. A second intervention, Kid's Club [102, 103], is designed to enhance the social and emotional adjustment of mothers who experienced IPV through strengthening coping and social support, community resources and parenting skills. A third intervention, Project SUPPORT [93], includes weekly behavioural parenting training and social and instrumental support. Of these programmes, only one addresses emotion awareness and regulation, and discussions occur during group-based sessions only with children [104]. No current interventions for IPV-exposed families specifically target the development of mother or child emotion regulation within the context of parenting.

The ability of mothers to regulate emotion is a critical part of effective parenting in both high- and low-risk families [105]. In IPV-exposed families in particular, the mother's emotion regulation is an important mechanism and risk factor related to both parenting and child adjustment outcomes. For example, higher maternal post-traumatic stress symptoms are related to more negative emotion socialization parenting following IPV exposure, but only for mothers who show poor emotion regulation abilities [89]. There is also evidence that the mother's emotion regulation mediates relations between maternal post-traumatic stress symptoms (PTSS) and positive emotion socialization parenting practices [89], as well as child internalizing and externalizing problems [88]. How parents talk to children about emotion may be particularly important for IPV-exposed families, as children are exposed to hostile and threatening interactions that can be highly emotionally arousing, and children can benefit from parenting that helps them learn to manage strong arousal. Not surprisingly, children's emotion regulation is a protective factor that supports child adjustment following IPV exposure [88, 106].

EC has protective effects for children exposed to IPV. Katz and Windecker-Nelson [7] reported that EC moderates relations between IPV and child adjustment. This study showed that for children whose parents were low in EC, there was a significant relationship between IPV and child maladjustment. However, for children whose parents were high in EC, there was no relationship between IPV and child maladjustment. Using a clinical sample, Shipman et al. [107] reported that maltreating mothers were less EC than non-maltreating mothers and that EC mediated the effects of maltreatment on child adjustment. Given the overlap between maltreatment and IPV [108–111], these data suggest that EC can buffer children from the negative effects of IPV and underscore the importance of turning these basic research findings into a viable parenting intervention for IPV-exposed families.

Description of the EC Parenting Intervention

The EC intervention was developed to reflect the main theoretical notions inherent in the work of Gottman, Katz and Hooven [14] on EC. It was also designed to address central concerns in IPV-exposed groups (e.g., dealing with anger, talking about the abuse) while also being easily modifiable for use with other at-risk

populations. A group-based intervention delivery model was used to maximize cost-effectiveness and to parallel the group structure common in support groups for IPV survivors. The 12-week skills-based EC programme targeted mothers' awareness of emotion in themselves and their children, emotion regulation abilities, emotion coaching abilities and responding to anger and talking about the abuse. The intervention was administered in groups consisting of approximately five to eight mothers. Four sessions of the EC module occurred with both mother and child to allow for in vivo training and feedback. The intervention relied on didactic presentations, vignettes or case studies; modelling and role playing; and discussions. Videotapes demonstrating EC behaviour (e.g., validation, feeling talk, emotional scaffolding) and parental derogation (i.e., criticism, derisive humour, minimizing/punishing) were used to illustrate behaviours the intervention was targeting.

Introduction (Session 1).

This session focused on introductions, establishing group rules, providing psycho-education about IPV and the purpose of the programme and setting goals.

Mother's Awareness of Emotion (Sessions 2 and 3).

This segment targeted four component skills: (1) paying attention to bodily cues and cognitive processes associated with different emotional states, (2) differentiating between different negative emotions (e.g., anger, sadness, fear) in themselves and their child, (3) increasing sensitivity to low-intensity emotion in themselves and in their child and (4) understanding the cause of negative emotions in themselves and in their child. Homework exercises included use of a diary to increase attention to bodily sensations and cognitions associated with specific emotions and creation of a personal emotional barometer to increase sensitivity to different levels of emotional intensity. Session 2 focused on awareness of one's own emotion, and Session 3 focused on awareness of child emotion.

Mother's Own Emotion Regulation Abilities (Sessions 4 and 5).

Borrowing select elements on emotion regulation from Dialectical Behavior Therapy [112], mothers were taught to (1) increase mindfulness to current emotions through acceptance of painful feelings, (2) apply distress tolerance techniques to tolerate negative emotions without impulsive actions, (3) apply emotion regulation techniques when their emotional barometers escalate beyond a low set point, (4) use proximal strategies to self-soothe (e.g., taking deep breaths, stopping/inhibiting action) and (5) use distal strategies to self-soothe (e.g., take a bath, talk to friend, listen to music, watch a funny movie).

Emotion Coaching (Sessions 6–9).

Eight component skills were targeted to teach mothers to (1) view emotional moments as an opportunity for intimacy and teaching, (2) increase active listening skills (e.g., eye contact, nodding, saying 'um-hum'), (3) increase their use of emotion language with the child, (4) pay attention to the emotion behind the child's words, (5) validate the child's expression of feelings, (6) use 'feeling talk' and story-telling to contextualize the child's emotional experience, (7) increase emotional scaffolding by letting the child come up with solutions and (8) decrease parental minimizing, punishing and invalidation of emotion.

Responding to Anger and Talking About the Abuse (Sessions 10 and 11).

This segment of the programme focused on psychoeducation about trauma and anger, teaching mothers how to accept intense trauma-related emotions, set limits and define appropriate child behaviours and talk to their children about the abuse and the abuser.

Summary and Planning (Session 12).

A final session focused on reviewing the programme content, assessing progress and discussing plans for maintaining and expanding support of their child past the end of the intervention.

Intervention Findings

Results from an initial pilot study of the EC intervention for survivors of IPV are encouraging [113]. Relative to mothers in the waiting-list group, mothers in the intervention group showed (1) improvements in their awareness of emotion and emotion coaching, (2) increases in emotion regulation as assessed by baseline RSA, (3) increased use of validation and decreased use of sermonizing/lecturing/scolding during parent-child interaction and (4) an increased sense of parenting competence. Relative to children of mothers in the waiting-list group, children of mothers in the intervention group showed (1) increases in emotion regulation as measured by parent report and baseline RSA, (2) decreases in negativity during parent-child interaction and (3) decreases

in depressive symptoms. These findings highlight the potential usefulness of an EC parenting intervention for populations at risk for emotion regulation and parenting difficulties, although further studies are needed to replicate these findings and to better understand the efficacy and effectiveness of the EC intervention for families exposed to IPV and other at-risk groups.

Clinical Case Example

To illustrate EC components and principles and highlight some of the common barriers to treatment and strategies for overcoming them, we present the following clinical case example. We focus here on the delivery of EC in an individual therapy context as opposed to a group context to more succinctly and effectively portray the experience of the family and the therapist during the course of EC treatment.

Janette, a 38-year-old Chinese-American woman, and her eight-year-old son, Christopher, presented for treatment after Christopher was referred for a mental health evaluation by the family's primary care provider. Specifically, Christopher was referred because of Janette's report of recent increased behavioural difficulties and 'mood swings' at home and at school. During the evaluation, Janette noted several recent family stressors, including leaving an abusive relationship three months prior, moving to a new city and home and Christopher entering a new school for third grade. These recent stressors have caused Janette to feel increasingly less confident as a parent, and she is frequently becoming overwhelmed by her painful emotions about her abusive ex-partner as well as her deteriorating relationship with Christopher. Janette reports experiencing intense guilt, sadness, anger and frustration at the way things have been going. She notices that her extreme emotions lead her to be more reactive as a parent lately, oscillating between angry outbursts and becoming overwhelmed with sadness and anxiety and avoiding interacting with Christopher altogether when they are both upset. Given these recent patterns of interaction, Janette understandably presents with significant worries and hopelessness about the future of Christopher's well-being and their relationship. With his mother working more often now and all the demands of adjusting to a new place to live and a new school, Christopher is also showing significant challenges with regulation of his emotions and behaviours. He is frequently crying, experiencing behaviourally dysregulated temper tantrums, not complying with requests made by Janette, more frequently arguing with and yelling at his mom and sometimes blaming her for 'making us move away from dad and my friends'. At school, Christopher is having some of the same challenges with noncompliance and rule breaking and appears to be struggling to make friends – he reports that 'I hate my new school; I want to go back to my old school'.

This brief background illustrates one type of parent-child dyad for which EC would be an appropriate intervention. A case conceptualization informed by an EC lens would highlight the clear recent challenges in the parent-child relationship which are causing distress in both Janette and Christopher. Both Janette and Christopher are likely struggling with learning to regulate their heightened negative emotions following their recent stressors. In addition, their individual dysregulated emotion is spilling over into their patterns of interaction with one another. Janette is understandably overwhelmed with adjusting to all their recent life changes, and she needs some extra support to effectively manage her emotions and harnessing her parenting skills so that she can both get her relationship with Christopher back on a positive trajectory and help Christopher learn to regulate his emotions.

In the first session, the EC therapist presents the above-mentioned conceptualization, accepts elaborations and corrections from Janette and ties the conceptualization into a discussion of the rationale of the EC programme. The therapist generates hope by emphasizing how different skills and elements of the EC intervention will be helpful in improving the quality of Janette and Christopher's interactions and how the EC skills will support Christopher's current and future adjustment. Janette leaves the first session already experiencing some relief, having received the message that the family's current challenges are understandable given their recent stressors (and are not a sign of her being a flawed parent or their relationship being broken) and that fine-tuning Janette's skills in interacting with her son will increase her sense of competence and confidence in effective parenting.

Sessions 2 and 3 are spent teaching and practising skills (both in session and in between sessions) to increase Janette's awareness of her own and Christopher's emotions. At this stage, Janette's processing and discussion of her emotion diary tracking homework helps increase her awareness and understanding of how painful emotions about her prior relationship have been affecting her behaviour at work and interactions with Christopher. During this phase, Janette also increases her ability to notice that more subtle expressions of fear and sadness tend to make Christopher more vulnerable to angry outbursts, which increases her compassion for her son and decreases her negative judgement of his misbehaviour.

With Janette's increasing ability to be aware of what she is feeling and why, sessions 4 and 5 are focused on helping her respond most effectively to her emotions. Janette is taught a variety of techniques that can support her in 'not getting hijacked' by her emotions. Given that 'no one size fits all', she is encouraged to practise a variety of strategies in a variety of contexts and to evaluate their effectiveness. The EC therapist focuses on teaching Janette evidence-based emotion regulation strategies (e.g., mindfulness skills, acceptance, cognitive restructuring, problem-solving, etc.) and also aims to foster Janette's regulatory flexibility – that is, Janette's ability to grow her repertoire of emotion regulation strategies and her ability to mindfully select, implement, evaluate and modify them across a variety of contexts as needed [114].

In the next several sessions, the EC therapist taught and practised the core EC skills with Janette and Christopher. For Janette, making behavioural changes in her ability to (1) decrease her leaping in with problem-solving, which Christopher frequently experienced as emotion dismissing, and (2) increase her ability to actively listen and provide validation, which had a huge positive impact on the quality of their interactions. At this stage of treatment, Christopher regularly attended sessions with Janette, and much of the sessions were dedicated to modelling and role plays with feedback. Although Janette and Christopher were both initially hesitant to interact while being observed by the therapist, the role plays and practice activities became more natural and enjoyable for everyone after the first practice-heavy session.

Following Janette's treatment gains in her improved abilities to monitor and regulate day-to-day emotions, the EC therapist moved into targeting Janette's awareness, processing and managing of higher-intensity emotions and thoughts about her abusive relationship. Janette and the EC therapist specifically narrowed in on better understanding how Janette's trauma-related thoughts and emotions impacted her parenting attitudes and behaviours when interacting with Christopher. Relying on psycho-education and heavy doses of validation, she and the EC therapist collaborated on exploring ways to balance setting clear behavioural expectations for Christopher's tantrums and anger outbursts while also applying EC strategies to help the dyad connect and process Christopher's feelings about their recent life changes. Most importantly, during this phase of treatment, Janette learned how to more skilfully respond to Christopher's blaming comments towards her, balancing validation of his emotions with effective and developmentally appropriate discussions of why they no longer lived with Christopher's father. Janette relied on her emotion regulation strategies during discussions with Christopher so that she would not personalize his negative comments and could stay focused on using EC skills with Christopher.

In the final session, the EC therapist elicited, highlighted and praised Janette's and Christopher's progress during treatment. Janette was asked to identify specific skills that she felt she had a good handle on, as well as specific EC skills or contexts in which she would commit to continuing to practise. To foster skills consolidation and generalization, the therapist presented a few mock parenting scenarios that Janette might encounter in the future and asked Janette to brainstorm how she might apply skills and principles learned in the programme to tackle these challenges. This strategy was used to help Janette end treatment with a longer-term vision for how she was now equipped to effectively support her own and Christopher's emotional functioning, wellbeing and relationship.

So far we have described a brief example of how the EC treatment generally progresses with a specific family. Next, we discuss core competencies of EC and continue our discussion of the clinical case example with discussion of several treatment barriers and core competency–based approaches to overcoming them.

Core Competencies

We believe that EC is a relatively flexible and intuitive clinical intervention that can be delivered successfully by therapists with a wide range of backgrounds and experience. Despite this, there are several characteristics, or core competencies, that we have consistently

identified as enhancing effective delivery of EC. In parallel to the model of Sburlati et al. [115] of therapist competencies of cognitive behavioural treatments for children and adolescents, we divide core competencies for the EC intervention into two broad domains: (1) generic therapeutic competencies and (2) EC competencies. Generic therapeutic competencies include competencies which are needed for successfully delivering any evidence-based or evidence-informed treatment for children, adolescents and their families. EC competencies are clinical competencies and clinician characteristics that we believe are useful to successfully implement the EC intervention in particular. We have implemented and studied EC conducted in a group-based format (as described earlier), as well as in individual therapy settings. The competencies we describe are relevant for both modes of delivery, and we also illustrate examples of how each competency played a role in the treatment process for our case example.

Generic Therapeutic Competencies

Several generic therapeutic competencies are necessary for effectively delivering an EC intervention. All the generic competencies identified by Sburlati et al. [115], such as the ability to practise professionally; understanding clinically relevant child and adolescent characteristics; competence at building positive therapeutic relationships with children, adolescents and their caregivers; and clinical assessment skills, are needed for EC. We identify and elaborate on three further generic therapeutic competencies here that we believe are useful for the EC intervention, as well as most other evidence-based treatments for children and adolescents.

Orientation Towards Evidence Based Treatments. Although clinicians with a range of theoretical orientations are capable of successfully delivering the EC intervention, they should have some experience and comfort with delivering evidence-based interventions. Clinicians should demonstrate a willingness to follow a relatively structured programme that proceeds in a specifically designed sequence from session to session. This programme also calls for ease and flexibility in using handouts, worksheets, practice activities and role plays strategically, often in sessions with both the child and parent. Evidence-based treatments for children, adolescents and families are often highly structured and time limited [116], and the same is true of EC. Delivering the EC intervention also requires a relatively directive (rather than passive) clinical style, similar to other evidence-based treatments. The EC intervention calls for clinicians to come to sessions prepared with all the necessary materials as well as with a clear yet flexible outline of goals for each session.

An effective EC therapist acts as both a caring, validating and empathic listener and a dynamic and engaging expert, teacher and coach. It should be noted that 'manualized' and 'evidence-based treatment' should not be mistaken for a rigid, robotic and inflexible treatment approach [117]. The EC intervention has room to accommodate a wide range of clinical styles and strengths. Some EC therapists will inevitably make modifications to intervention delivery with the aim of meeting the needs of each unique client. Nonetheless, we believe that such modifications should be driven by case conceptualization and assessment of treatment progress and typically should be made after the standard 'by the book' approach has been attempted or strongly considered. Clinicians with prior experience using evidence-based treatments or those well oriented to the structure, pace and process of evidence-based treatments will be most skilled in effectively matching the essential ingredients of EC with the client's needs and treatment goals, as well as with their own personal clinical style.

Janette had a history of seeing several different therapists since she was an adolescent. She described past therapy experiences as 'somewhat helpful', and she saw prior therapists on an as-needed basis with no consistently specified treatment goals or length. Thus, the time-limited nature of EC and the heavy emphasis on behavioural skills practice and between-session homework were new for her. To increase Janette's commitment and buy-in to the treatment, the EC therapist had to confidently highlight the advantages of a targeted evidence-based approach, briefly discuss research support for such treatment approaches and convincingly link the specific components and process of EC to Janette's current goals. Despite the EC therapist's best efforts, Janette left the first session stating, 'I believe that this treatment is helpful for people, but I'm still not sure if I will be able to keep up with the homework.' The EC therapist commended Janette for her honesty and willingness to try a new therapeutic approach and suggested that they 'try it out' for a few weeks and regularly check in on whether Janette is finding EC feasible and helpful to her and her son as it progresses. Over time, and

with consistent troubleshooting and problem-solving from the therapist, Janette came to appreciate the practical and skills-based focus of the treatment and was relieved that she and Christopher would not have to be in therapy 'for years' to make tangible improvements in their lives.

Prioritizing, Monitoring and Strengthening Treatment Engagement. If a client drops out of treatment or is only partially engaged in treatment (including in-session engagement as well as out-of-session engagement such as homework and practice), the EC intervention will not work. Given the high rates of treatment dropouts for IPV populations [118], it is particularly important for the clinician to be skilled at monitoring and attending to client engagement throughout the course of treatment. Similar to dialectical behaviour therapy, wherein a client's treatment-interfering behaviours are highly prioritized treatment targets [112], a competent EC therapist knows when treatment engagement needs to be strengthened before proceeding to the next treatment steps. This involves consistent and transparent assessment of attendance, homework completion and other important markers of treatment engagement. If and when client engagement wavers, the EC clinician should prioritize increasing engagement as a treatment target to address as they are proceeding with the intervention. This involves collaborative and culturally sensitive assessment, solution generating and troubleshooting of strategies aimed to increase treatment engagement week to week [119]. Another useful strategy to this end is continually emphasizing to clients how their consistency and hard work will help them reach their personal treatment goals.

In the case of Janette and Christopher, the EC therapist noticed that after they took a week off from therapy for a family vacation, Janette began attending more sporadically and would call to reschedule appointments about every other week. After a few such occurrences, the EC therapist non-judgementally highlighted this pattern by stating

Janette, it's great to see you today. I'm really glad you made it. Before we catch up on how things have been going and start talking about this week's skills, I wanted to check in about how our treatment process is going. I have noticed that since we took a break during your vacation, it has been challenging for us to keep up with weekly meetings. Can you tell me a little more about how that's going for you? What's getting in the way of being able to make it weekly?

This question led the therapist and Janette to have an open conversation about treatment attendance, to consider the potential impact attendance has on treatment progress and to engage in collaborative problem-solving around this issue. In Janette's case, helping her notice how variable attendance has potentially slowed down the course of tangible progress towards her goals and re-scheduling to a more feasible time and day of the week for weekly sessions helped her re-establish consistent attendance. The therapist relied on principles of motivational interviewing, dialectical behaviour therapy commitment strategies and other therapeutic methods as needed to increase Janette's commitment and engagement.

Alignment with the Importance of Parenting. Parenting is one of the most powerful proximal factors shaping children's healthy development [120], as well as their adjustment following the stress of IPV exposure [7, 121]. Teaching and fostering effective parenting skills are at the core of many of our currently most well-established treatments for children, such as parent management training (PMT) interventions [122, 123]. Similarly, positively shaping how parents experience, relate to and respond to their own and their child's emotions is at the heart of EC. Effective EC clinicians are prepared to explain how and why a parent's reactions to their child are one of the most powerful mechanisms of change and socialization and emphasize that the EC therapist's role is to support parents finding and harnessing their parenting skill set. The importance of parenting should be strategically emphasized in the early stages of treatment, given that many parents may not want to be part of the intervention but instead want the therapist to treat only the child. In these circumstances especially, it is useful to orient the parent to the importance of their role in the treatment and their child's wellbeing. It is common for parents in treatment to experience stigma, guilt and shame about seeking mental health support for their child. Thus, it is essential that the emphasis on parenting and working on parental skills is delivered in a non-judgemental and validating manner. Cultural values are also associated with shame, guilt and embarrassment that parents experience in the context of their child's treatment [124], and it is important for the EC therapist to be aware, flexible and culturally competent in empowering parents in shaping their child's healthy development.

Like many parents, Janette presented to treatment expecting the EC therapist to spend most of their time working directly with Christopher to help him change his behaviours and 'get better'. Thus, in their first session, when discussing the EC programme and rationale, the therapist had to make specific efforts to 'sell' Janette on why a parenting skills–focused approach would be useful. The therapist suggested that although Janette's parenting has not *caused* Christopher's current challenges (decreasing parental guilt and shame), fine-tuning Janette's responses to her son could have very powerful and long-lasting effects in supporting his behaviour change, as well as improving the quality of their relationship. This also served to deeply validate the central importance of Janette in Christopher's ongoing healthy development, which also helped to increase her buy-in and commitment to this treatment. The ability to discuss and learn skills for more effectively managing her own emotions (not just those related to her role as a parent) was also an appealing and unexpected perk of EC for Janette.

EC Core Competencies

Several EC competencies are needed for successfully delivering the EC intervention. These are competencies required for planning, implementing and flexibly adapting specific EC content and techniques with the individual child and their caregivers.

Comfort with In-Session Practice. Like many parenting-based interventions [125–127], the EC intervention relies heavily on within-session exercises and practice of the skills. The general sequence of skills teaching in the EC intervention typically begins with psycho-education and the rationale for the session's skill or content. Next, the therapist proceeds to demonstrate the skill in action using a within-session practice exercise. Once the therapist demonstration has been debriefed with the parent and the parent demonstrates adequate understanding of the skill, the parent is asked to practise the skill themselves in session. If the child is present in session, inclusion of the child in role plays and exercises is ideal. If and when the child is not in attendance, the EC therapist gets creative and flexible and may ask the parent to role play the child's part and role play the child themselves during the parent's practice. In-session exercises can bring up emotion and hesitation for both parents and therapists alike. Skilled EC therapists are those who can validate the momentary 'awkwardness' of in-session exercises while still emphasizing the importance and value of collaborative practice. In our experience, in-session practice can be the most revealing assessment of a parent's pattern of strengths and weaknesses. Reinforcing moments of skillful behaviour and using principles of shaping in the context of in-session practice are a most powerful means of supporting parents' skills acquisition and refinement. The EC therapist who recognizes the importance of within-session practice and prioritizes this therapeutic technique will be most adept at delivering the EC intervention.

In Janette's case, both Janette and the therapist were pleased with how quickly Janette reported her increasing awareness of Christopher's emotions and her growing interest in approaching emotional moments as opportunities for connection with her son. When the EC therapist scheduled an in-session practice with Janette and Christopher in the fourth session, it revealed that Janette's positive intentions for being more EC were significantly limited by her behavioural skills deficits in parent-child interactions. Specifically, the EC therapist noticed that Janette appeared hesitant to praise Christopher, often missed opportunities for providing validation of low-level emotions and had a style of delivering validating comments (e.g., voice tone, exaggerated facial expressions) that may not have consistently been experienced as authentically validating by others. It took several sessions of repeated discussion, modelling and practice for the therapist to provide corrective feedback and for Janette to make behavioural changes in these interactions. During these sessions, the therapist always led feedback with genuine praise for the things that Janette did well, such as her good eye contact with Christopher and her energy and enthusiasm in role plays, before suggesting specific ways that Janette could make the EC interactions even better. Although Janette was initially very embarrassed about her performance in role plays, over time she came to appreciate the therapist's willingness to give such precise and close care and attention to her and Christopher's interactions.

Therapist's Meta-Emotion Philosophy. EC therapists should examine their own attitudes and beliefs about emotion and work towards developing an EC (rather than emotion-dismissing) philosophy themselves. Clinicians with an EC philosophy are sensitive to and aware and accepting of both high- and low-intensity levels of emotion in themselves and their clients. Being aware of emotion is especially relevant during in-session practice and feedback to parents,

during which clinicians rely heavily on their own in-the-moment perceptions for highlighting, modelling and shaping effective EC skills. For example, in order to support a parent in learning to better recognize and acknowledge emotion in their child, the therapist should be relatively skilled at identifying child emotion and providing genuine and effective validation to the child himself or herself (in session as a teaching demonstration, for example). Therapists who are themselves high in EC are also those who view negative emotion in the session as a potential opportunity for teaching or applying the EC skills. If and when clients experience negative emotion about their life circumstances or even about the intervention or therapeutic relationship, such in-session interactions can be important opportunities for making the EC skills immediately relevant. Clinicians who recognize such moments as opportunities to relate the content of the intervention and even practice labelling, validating and managing emotions in the moment are likely to have more success delivering the intervention. In contrast, clinicians who are prone to avoid, deny or dismiss negative emotion that arises in session may be modelling behaviour that directly conflicts with the very skills being taught. To our knowledge, there has not been research on how EC versus Emotion-dismissing philosophies in therapists are associated with treatment outcomes. Despite this, characteristics of EC therapists overlap with well-studied common factors of psychotherapy, which are known to be strong predictors of treatment outcome [128–130]. That is, we believe that EC (versus emotion-dismissing) therapists are more likely to bring genuine empathy, warmth, validation and congruence to the therapeutic relationship. These qualities, which are well aligned with an EC philosophy, are essential for a strong therapeutic alliance leading to positive treatment outcomes.

When working with Janette and Christopher, the EC therapist's own meta-emotion philosophy and comfort with this construct came into play in several ways. Early in treatment, the EC therapist picked up on Janette's discomfort around acknowledging negative emotions in herself and Christopher. Because Janette initially preferred to avoid talking about negative' emotions (i.e., fear, sadness, anger), as well as her thoughts, feelings and beliefs about negative emotions (meta-emotion), the therapist had to be gently persistent in helping Janette explore her own emotions and meta-emotion philosophy. In teaching these concepts, the therapist used her own upbringing to model how her own individual background shaped her attitudes about her own emotions, with emphasis on when this worked well and when it didn't. This discussion helped Janette be more open and willing to explore her own family history and how it shaped her meta-emotion philosophy. Janette noted that emotional restraint was valued in her family growing up and that expressing negative emotion was frowned upon and even taken as a sign of poor character. Janette could see that some of these attitudes may have been culturally ingrained in her more traditional Chinese-American family upbringing and likely worked well for her family most of the time. The EC therapist helped Janette explore and consider alternative attitudes and interpretations of negative emotions and their role in Janette and Christopher's life now while balancing validation of Janette's own developmental and cultural background. Over time, this freed Janette to intentionally choose which of her family's values and attitudes about emotion she wanted to pass on and model for Christopher, as well as expanding on them to include approaches to emotion that worked well for supporting their relationship.

Understanding Relevant Affective Science Theory and Research. Another unique core competency of an effective EC clinician is some knowledge and familiarity with affective science, the scientific study of emotion. Theory and research about the role of emotion in a clinical context have often proceeded independently from basic affective science research [131]. Despite this, we believe that incorporating affective science research into clinical science and practice can greatly enhance treatment efforts. For example, integrating affective science to enhance the treatment of clinical problems has long been used in dialectical behaviour therapy, particularly within its emotion regulation skills module (see Linehan [132]). We recommend a similar approach when delivering an EC intervention, given that EC, like dialectical behaviour therapy, also targets emotional expression and regulation as core intervention components. For example, understanding and being able to teach and discuss the functional and multifaceted aspects of specific emotions can help facilitate clients' awareness and acceptance of emotion. This is an important step towards teaching them how to listen to and respond to their own and their children's emotions most effectively, which is a central goal of an EC intervention. A clinician who has basic knowledge of affective

science will be more likely to deliver an EC intervention with confidence and expertise. In Janette's case, experiencing the EC therapist as an 'expert' on emotion was highly beneficial to her taking the EC treatment skills seriously. Moreover, learning some of the scientific ideas about emotions increased Janette's confidence in talking about emotions with Christopher.

Familiarity with Other Effective Parenting Techniques and Principles. Another EC competency is the clinician's ability to flexibly draw on a variety of other parenting techniques and principles. A range of parenting skills is needed for effectively responding to child behaviour and for building and maintaining a positive parent-child relationship. This includes skills such as positive interaction techniques, use of differential attention, effective use of consequences and communication and problem-solving skills [133]. Although not all families receiving an EC intervention will need support with other non-EC parenting skills, a consistently positive parent-child relationship that is not overburdened by chronically conflicted and coercive interactions is one that will most readily benefit from an EC intervention. Thus, clinicians should be prepared to identify and teach a range of essential parenting skills in conjunction with EC skills as needed.

In Janette's case, interactions between her and Christopher were so consistently fraught with frustration that it was challenging for Janette to engage Christopher in EC moments. Both Janette and Christopher were wary of spending extended periods of time together because their interactions would often erupt into emotionally laden arguments. Thus, the EC therapist prioritized teaching and asking Janette to regularly practise child-directed play and positive attention and praise skills. Over time, this made both Christopher and Janette more effective at spending genuinely positive time together and created a context in which Janette could now practise EC skills. Towards the end of the treatment, it also became apparent that Janette had some difficulties with implementing consistent rewards and consequences for supporting Christopher's effective behaviours. The EC therapist paired teaching emotion regulation strategies with parallel teaching of contingency management strategies. This significantly decreased Janette's use of reactive and emotionally driven consequences and gave her more proactive skills for consistently using appropriate and effective rewards to support Christopher's behavioural functioning.

Familiarity with Cognitive Behavioural Techniques and Principles. Another EC competency is having familiarity with principles of cognitive behavioural therapy (CBT). The EC intervention relies on parents and children gaining better awareness and control over their thoughts, behaviours and emotions, which is a central component of CBT [134]. CBT competencies are further broken down to include the understanding of CBT theory and research, CBT case formulation and treatment planning, conducting sessions collaboratively and a range of other specific CBT techniques [115]. For further discussion of CBT-specific competencies for working with children, adolescents and families, we direct readers to Sburlati et al. [115]. Janette found it particularly helpful to disentangle and better understand how her trauma-related thoughts (such as 'it's my fault that Christopher was exposed to all of our fighting') were connected to how she felt ('guilty, ashamed, sad') and how these emotions were driving her avoidance of conversations with Christopher about his father.

Familiarity with Mindfulness-Based Techniques and Principles. The EC intervention targets increased parent awareness and acceptance of their own as well as their child's emotions. We believe that mindfulness skills training and practice are key mechanisms for reaching this goal. Mindfulness is increasingly recognized as a useful intervention for a wide range of problems [135], as well as being important for effective parenting practices [136]. Mindfulness skills can support parents in staying with the present moment and controlling their attention and emotion in stressful parenting situations [137]. Thus, practical use of mindfulness in parenting can be thought of as a prerequisite for parental mastery of EC skills. Furthermore, the EC intervention includes components aimed at building and practising effective emotion regulation and distress tolerance skills for parents and children and draws on specific skills and processes outlined in dialectical behavioural therapy to accomplish these treatment goals (for further details on adaptations of dialectical behavioural therapy for parents, see Ben-Porath [137]). Some familiarity and comfort with mindfulness-based cognitive behavioural treatment approaches such as Dialectical Behavior Therapy [112] and Acceptance and Commitment Therapy (ACT [138]) is a considerable strength for the EC therapist.

For Janette, increasing her ability to non-judgementally observe her painful thoughts about the past and learning to mindfully describe (rather than avoid or impulsively react to) her emotions helped her to decrease reactive parenting behaviours, such as yelling or dismissing/minimizing the cause of Christopher's emotions. The daily practice of mindfully pausing for a few seconds before responding to Christopher, particularly when he was misbehaving, helped Janette to stay more calm and regulated during interactions and supported her in choosing the most effective parenting response in each situation.

Future Directions

Despite the growing research base on EC interventions [17, 32, 139], as well as the increased study and application of EC as a critical emotion socialization process, there are still several important directions for future work in this area.

EC as a Modular Treatment. EC has been tested and shown to be an important buffer against negative outcomes in a diverse range of populations [140]. One potential next step in this work is to use and study EC as a modular treatment. Modularity in treatment can be used to separate functions of an intervention into independent modules which contain active ingredients needed to reach one specific aspect of a desired treatment outcome [141]. The EC intervention can be thought of as a modular approach on two levels. First, the full EC intervention we have described can be used in conjunction with other treatments or treatment modules. For example, the intervention has been successfully delivered in conjunction with a parent management training (PMT) approach [32, 142, 143]. Second, because many EC intervention sessions have their own clear treatment targets, individual EC session components/skills may also be clinically useful as standalone strategies in the context of a broader treatment. For example, if a parent's lack of awareness of their own and others' emotions is significantly limiting effective communication and connection at home, the clinician may spend one or two sessions in the context of a broader family-based treatment delivering EC sessions and skills matched to these specific treatment targets. There are many potential treatment contexts in which using either the full EC treatment or EC modules may be clinically useful. Future research testing the efficacy and effectiveness of using EC as a modular approach may expand on the clinical utility and flexibility of this treatment approach.

Adaptations for Other Populations and Settings. Although we have described the EC intervention as tailored specifically for families exposed to IPV in this chapter, another future direction is adaptations of EC for use with other populations. The intervention may be especially well suited for clinical populations which may be at risk of difficulties with parenting, emotion regulation and emotional functioning in general. For example, a study is currently in progress evaluating the effectiveness of EC adapted for children with behavioural difficulties and callous-unemotional traits [142, 143]. As noted earlier in this chapter, there may be many other populations for whom EC may be helpful.

Another future direction is extending the current clinic-based treatment delivery model to other settings where it has the potential to reach more families. There are many treatment barriers to receiving family-focused outpatient mental health services [144]. Adapting EC to be delivered in schools or other community settings may be one important way to increase overall treatment attendance and engagement, as well as expand the intervention reach to high-risk families. A recent pilot study of EC in a rural disadvantaged area of England showed promising outcomes for school practitioners and the children they work with in school settings [145]. Tele-mental health, or the use of telemedicine to provide psychological services, is also increasingly shown to be an effective model for service delivery [146]. Developing and testing adaptations of the EC intervention to this delivery method has the potential to exponentially increase access to care, particularly for families who live in areas underserved by mental health professionals, those with physical limitations restricting their access to traditional care or families whose work schedules and other responsibilities pose significant barriers to treatment [147].

Conclusion

We have described the development of an EC intervention for families who have experienced IPV, discussed the core competencies that support effective implementation and outcomes of the intervention and illustrated some of the treatment principles and components using a clinical case example. Within the category of generic therapeutic competencies, which we believe support effective delivery of most evidence-based treatments for children, adolescents and families, we have emphasized and elaborated on three aspects in particular: (1) orientation towards evidence-based treatments, (2) prioritizing, monitoring and strengthening treatment engagement and (3) alignment with the importance of parenting. Of these, we believe that the competency around fostering and maintaining treatment engagement is particularly important given the high rate of attrition for IPV populations [118] and in family-based treatments in general [148]. Keeping clients motivated to attend and stay engaged in the intervention is critical, and we refer readers to articles such as Snell-Johns, Mendez and Smith [148] for discussion of evidence-based strategies which support families' engagement in treatment. A therapist's positive attitude and orientation towards the use of evidence-based treatments is also extremely important for effective delivery of EC. Organizational climate and culture are other factors that are associated with the implementation of evidence-based treatments [115, 149, 150], and we have experienced this to be the case with the EC intervention as well. More research is needed to better identify and define organization-level factors and competencies that support the effective adoption and delivery of the intervention.

We also discussed several core competencies specific to the EC intervention, including (1) comfort with in-session practice, (2) therapist's own meta-emotion philosophy, (3) understanding relevant affective science theory and research, (4) familiarity with other effective parenting techniques and principles, (5) familiarity with CBT techniques and principles and (6) familiarity with mindfulness-based techniques and principles. We believe all of these EC competencies work in tandem to support the skilled delivery of an EC intervention. Attaining all these competencies may seem like a daunting task to the new clinician interested in EC. Despite this, we encourage interested therapists to consider using the EC intervention with families exposed to IPV or other at-risk families, even if they have not yet attained all the core competencies we have described. Most importantly, we believe that a clinician's awareness of his or her own strengths and gaps in knowledge, as well as his or her willingness to seek appropriate resources, training, supervision and consultation as needed during the course of treatment, is enough to aid that therapist in reaching a high level of skill with the EC intervention.

EC is based on clear theoretical considerations and informed by a trans-diagnostic perspective, underscoring the utility of Luthar and Eisenberg's [151] recommendations to build interventions that target mechanisms with the potential to effect change across multiple domains of functioning. With the potential downstream effects of changes to emotion regulation and parenting on many areas of both child and parent psychosocial functioning, an EC intervention may be an effective mechanism to alleviate adverse outcomes for families in a variety of stressful or adverse contexts.

References

1. Eisenberg N, Cumberland A, Spinrad TL. Parent socialization of emotion. *Psychological Inquiry* 1998; **9** (4):241–73.

2. Morris AS, Silk JS, Steinberg L, et al. The role of the family context in the development of emotion regulation. *Social Development* 2007; **16**(2):361–88.

3. Oppenheimer CW, Ladouceur CD, Waller JM, et al. Emotion socialization in anxious youth: Parenting buffers emotional reactivity to peer negative events. *Journal of Abnormal Child Psychology* 2016; **44** (7):1267–78.

4. Saarni C. Emotional competence: A developmental perspective. In: James DA (ed.), *The Handbook of Emotional Intelligence: Theory, Development, Assessment, and Application at Home, School, and in the Workplace.* San Francisco: Jossey-Bass, 2000, pp. 68–91.

5. Silk JS, Shaw DS, Prout JT, et al. Socialization of emotion and offspring internalizing symptoms in mothers with childhood-onset depression. *Journal of Applied Developmental Psychology* 2011; **32** (3):127–36.

6. Katz LF, Hunter EC. Maternal meta-emotion philosophy and adolescent depressive symptomatology. *Social Development* 2007; **16** (2):343–60.

7. Katz LF, Windecker-Nelson B. Domestic violence, emotion coaching, and child adjustment. *Journal of Family Psychology* 2006; **20**(1):55–67.

8. Shipman KL, Schneider R, Fitzgerald MM, et al. Maternal emotion socialization in maltreating and non-maltreating families: Implications for children's emotion regulation. *Social Development* 2007; **16** (2):268–85.

9. Stocker CM, Richmond MK, Rhoades GK, Kiang L. Family emotional processes and adolescents' adjustment. *Social Development* 2007; **16** (2):310–25.

10. Dunsmore JC, Booker JA, Ollendick TH. Parental emotion coaching and child emotion regulation as protective factors for children with oppositional defiant disorder. *Social Development* 2013; **22** (3):444–64.

11. Baumrind D. Current patterns of parental authority. *Developmental Psychology* 1971; 4(1, Pt. 2):1–103.

12. Grusec JE, Hastings PD. *Handbook of Socialization: Theory and Research*, 2nd ed. New York: Guilford Press, 2015.

13. Halberstadt AG. Toward an ecology of expressiveness: Family socialization in particular and a model in general. In: Feldman RS, Rimé B (eds.), *Studies in Emotion and Social Interaction: Fundamentals of Nonverbal Behavior.* New York: Cambridge University Press, 1991, pp. 106–60.

14. Gottman JM, Katz LF, Hooven C. Parental meta-emotion philosophy and the emotional life of families: Theoretical models and preliminary data. *Journal of Family Psychology* 1996; **10**(3):243–68.

15. Katz LF, Gottman JM, Hooven C. Meta-emotion philosophy and family functioning: Reply to Cowan (1996) and Eisenberg (1996). *Journal of Family Psychology* 1996; **10**(3):284–91.

16. Katz LF, Maliken AC, Settler NM. Parental meta-emotion philosophy: A review of research and theoretical framework. *Child Development Perspectives* 2012; **6**(4):417–22.

17. Lauw MS, Havighurst SS, Wilson KR, Harley AE. Improving parenting of toddlers' emotions using an emotion coaching parenting program: A pilot study of Tuning in to Toddlers. *Journal of Community Psychology* 2014; **42**(2):169–75.

18. Silkenbeumer JR, Schiller EM, Kartner J. Co- and self-regulation of emotions in the preschool setting. *Early Childhood Research Quarterly* 2018; **44**:72–81.

19. Yap MB, Allen NB, Leve C, Katz LF. Maternal meta-emotion philosophy and socialization of adolescent affect: The moderating role of adolescent temperament. *Journal of Family Psychology* 2008; **22** (5):688–700.

20. Dolhanty J, Lafrance A. Emotion-focused family therapy for eating disorders. In: Greenberg LS, Goldman RN (eds.), *Clinical Handbook of Emotion-Focused Therapy.* Washington, DC: American Psychological Association, 2019, pp. 403–23.

21. Peterson CM, Fischer S, Loiselle K, Schaffer A. FBT with adjunctive parent emotion coaching in an adolescent male with anorexia nervosa. *Clinical Case Studies* 2016; **15**(5):409–23.

22. Lafrance AR, Dolhanty J, Stillar A, et al. Emotion-focused family therapy for eating disorders across the lifespan: A pilot study of a 2-day transdiagnostic

intervention for parents. *Clinical Psychology and Psychotherapy* 2016; **23**(1):14–23.

23. Hurrell KE, Houwing FL, Hudson JL. Parental meta-emotion philosophy and emotion coaching in families of children and adolescents with an anxiety disorder. *Journal of Abnormal Child Psychology* 2017; **45**(3):569–82.

24. Remmes CS, Ehrenreich-May J. Parental emotion regulation strategy use and responses to youth negative affect. *Journal of Cognitive Psychotherapy* 2014; **28**(1):34–47.

25. Havighurst SS, Kehoe CE, Harley AE. Tuning in to teens: Improving parental responses to anger and reducing youth externalizing behavior problems. *Journal of Adolescence* 2015; **42**:148–58.

26. Havighurst SS, Duncombe M, Frankling E, et al. An emotion-focused early intervention for children with emerging conduct problems. *Journal of Abnormal Child Psychology* 2015; **43**(4):749–60.

27. Katz LF, Windecker-Nelson B. Parental meta-emotion philosophy in families with conduct-problem children: Links with peer relations. *Journal of Abnormal Child Psychology* 2004; **32** (4):385–98.

28. Loop L, Mouton B, Stievenart M, Roskam I. One or many? Which and how many parenting variables should be targeted in interventions to reduce children's externalizing behavior? *Behaviour Research and Therapy* 2017; **92**:11–23.

29. Dunsmore JC, Booker JA, Ollendick TH, Greene RW. Emotion socialization in the context of risk and psychopathology: Maternal emotion coaching predicts better treatment outcomes for emotionally labile children with oppositional defiant disorder. *Social Development* 2016; **25**(1):8–26.

30. Ramsden SR, Hubbard JA. Family expressiveness and parental emotion coaching: Their role in children's emotion regulation and aggression. *Journal of Abnormal Child Psychology* 2002; **30**(6):657–67.

31. Wilson BJ, Petaja H, Yun J, et al. Parental emotion coaching: Associations with self-regulation in aggressive/rejected and low aggressive/popular children. *Child and Family Behavior Therapy* 2014; **36**(2):81–106.

32. Chronis-Tuscano A, Lewis-Morrarty E, Woods KE, et al. Parent-child interaction therapy with emotion coaching for preschoolers with attention deficit hyperactivity disorder. *Cognitive and Behavioral Practice* 2016; **23**(1):62–78.

33. Paterson AD, Babb KA, Camodeca AS, et al. Emotion-related parenting styles (ERPS): A short form for measuring parental meta-emotion philosophy. *Early Education and Development* 2012; **23**(4):583–602.

34. Wilson BJ, Berg JL, Zurawski ME, King KA. Autism and externalizing behaviors: Buffering effects of parental emotion coaching. *Research in Autism Spectrum Disorders* 2013; **7**(6):767–76.

35. Hersh MA, Hussong AM. The association between observed parental emotion socialization and adolescent self-medication. *Journal of Abnormal Child Psychology* 2009; **37**(4):493–506.

36. Shadur JM, Hussong AM. Conceptualization and measurement of parent emotion socialization among mothers in substance abuse treatment. *Journal of Child and Family Studies* 2018; **28**(2):325–42.

37. Schwartz OS, Rowell VJ, Whittle S, et al. Family meta-emotion and the onset of major depressive disorder in adolescence: A prospective longitudinal study. *Social Development* 2018; **27**(3):526–42.

38. Machell KA, Rallis BA, Esposito-Smythers C. Family environment as a moderator of the association between anxiety and suicidal ideation. *Journal of Anxiety Disorders* 2016; **40**:1–7.

39. Colegrove VM, Havighurst SS, Kehoe CE, Jacobsen SL. Pilot randomized controlled trial of tuning relationships with music: Intervention for parents with a trauma history with their adolescent. *Child Abuse and Neglect* 2018; **79**:259–68.

40. Rossetto KR. Developing conceptual definitions and theoretical models of coping in military families during deployment. *Journal of Family Communication* 2015; **15**(3):249–68.

41. Shortt JW, Eddy MJ, Sheeber L, Davis B. Project home: A pilot evaluation of an emotion-focused intervention for mothers reuniting with children after prison. *Psychological Services* 2014; **11**(1):1–9.

42. Merchant EK. An exploration of the impact of attachment, parental meta-emotion and emotion regulation in adoptive families. Doctoral dissertation University of North Carolina, Greensboro, 2018.

43. Brophy-Herb HE, Schiffman RF, Bocknek EL, et al. Toddlers' social-emotional competence in the contexts of maternal emotion socialization and contingent responsiveness in a low-income sample. *Social Development* 2011; **20**(1):73–92.

44. Criss MM, Morris AS, Ponce-Garcia E, et al. Pathway to adaptive emotion regulation among adolescents from low-income families. *Family Relations* 2016; **65** (3):517–29.

45. Bowie BH, Carrere S, Cooke C, et al. The role of culture in parents' socialization of children's emotional development. *Western Journal of Nursing Research* 2013; **35**(4):514–33.

46. Cervantes CA. Early mother-child emotion talk in Mexican-descent families. Doctoral dissertation, University of California Santa Cruz, 1998.

47. Shyu LY, Tu CH, Yeh CB. The problem of emotion regulation and its association with family context in children with attention deficit hyperactivity disorder. *Chinese Journal of Psychology* 2017; **59**(1):45–62.

48. Daga SS, Raval VV, Raj SP. Maternal meta-emotion and child socioemotional functioning in immigrant Indian and White American families. *Asian American Journal of Psychology* 2015; **6**(3):233–41.

49. Karkhanis DG, Winsler A. Temperament, gender, and cultural differences in maternal emotion socialization of anxiety, somatization and anger. *Psychological Studies* 2016; **61**(3):137–58.

50. Edrissi F, Havighurst SS, Aghebati A, et al. A pilot study of the Tuning in to Kids parenting program in Iran for reducing preschool children's anxiety. *Journal of Child and Family Studies* 2019; **28**(6):1695–702.

51. Nahm EY. A cross-cultural comparison of Korean American and European American parental meta-emotion philosophy and its relationship to parent-child interaction. Doctoral dissertation, University of Washington, Seattle, 2006.

52. Ryu S. The relationship between Korean mothers' communication practices with their children and children's deliberation-relevant communication abilities: Emotional regulation capacity and social cognitive development. Doctoral dissertation Ohio State University, Columbus, 2006.

53. Cleary R, Katz LF. Family-level emotion socialization and children's comfort with emotional expressivity. *Family Psychology* 2008; **24**:6–13.

54. Gurtovenko K, Stettler N, Kawamura J, Katz LF. Parent meta-emotion philosophy, emotion regulation, and parent-child interaction in survivors of intimate partner violence. Poster symposium presentation at the Annual Meeting of the Society for Research in Child Development, Philadelphia, March 2014.

55. Sheeber L, Shortt JW, Low S, Katz LF. Emotion coaching as a unique predictor of adolescent internalizing problems. Poster presentation at the Annual Meeting of the Society for Research in Psychopathology, Seattle, WA, October 2010.

56. Eisenberg N, Fabes RA, Murphy BC. Parents' reactions to children's negative emotions: Relations to children's social competence and comforting behavior. *Child Development* 1996; **67**(5):2227–47.

57. Cole PM, Kaslow NJ. Interaction and cognitive strategies for affect regulation: Developmental perspective on childhood depression. In: Alloy LB (ed.), *Cognitive Processes in Depression*. New York: Guilford Press, 1988, pp. 310–43.

58. Gottman JM, Katz LF, Hooven C. *Meta-Emotion: How Families Communicate Emotionally*. Hillsdale, NJ: Erlbaum Associates, 1997.

59. Thompson RA. Emotion and regulation. In: Thompson RA (ed.), *Current Theory and Research in Motivation*, Vol. 36: *Nebraska Symposium on Motivation, 1988: Socioemotional Development*. Lincoln, NE: University of Nebraska Press, 1990, pp. 367–467.

60. Thompson RA. Emotional regulation and emotional development. *Educational Psychology Review* 1991; **3**(4):269–307.

61. Lunkenheimer ES, Shields AM, Cortina KS. Parental emotion coaching and dismissing in family interaction. *Social Development* 2007; **16**(2):232–48.

62. Graham-Bermann SA. Family worries: Assessment of interpersonal anxiety in children from violent and nonviolent families. *Journal of Clinical Child Psychology* 1996; **25**(3):280–7.

63. Spaccarelli S, Sandler IN, Roosa M. History of spouse violence against mother: Correlated risks and unique effects in child mental health. *Journal of Family Violence* 1994; **9**(1):79–98.

64. Sternberg KJ, Lamb ME, Greenbaum C, et al. Effects of domestic violence on children's behavior problems and depression. *Developmental Psychology* 1993; **29**(1):44–52.

65. Reynolds MW, Wallace J, Hill TF, et al. The relationship between gender, depression, and self-esteem in children who have witnessed domestic violence. *Child Abuse and Neglect* 2001; **25**(9):1201–1206.

66. Fantuzzo JW, DePaola LM, Lambert L, et al. Effects of interparental violence on the psychological adjustment and competencies of young children. *Journal of Consulting and Clinical Psychology* 1991; **59**(2):258–65.

67. Jouriles EN, Norwood WD, McDonald R, Peters B. Domestic violence and child adjustment. In: Grych JH, Fincham FD (eds.), *Interparental Conflict and Child Development: Theory, Research, and Applications*. New York: Cambridge University Press, 2001, pp. 315–36.

68. Wolfe DA, Korsch B. Dimensions of child maltreatment and their relationship to adolescent adjustment. *Developmental Psychopathology* 1994; **6**(1):165–81.

69. Jaffe P, Wolfe D, Wilson S, Zak L. Similarities in behavioral and social maladjustment among child victims and witnesses to family violence. *Am J Orthopsychiat.* 1986 Jan;**56**(1):142–46.

70. Wolfe DA, Jaffe P, Wilson SK, Zak L. Children of battered women: The relation of child behavior to

family violence and maternal stress. *Journal of Consulting and Clinical Psychology* 1985; **53** (5):657–65.

71. McCloskey LA, Stuewig J. The quality of peer relationships among children exposed to family violence. *Development and Psychopathology* 2001; **13** (1):83–96.

72. Graham-Bermann, SA, Levendosky, AA. The social functioning of preschool-age children whose mothers are emotionally and physically abused. *Journal of Emotional Abuse* 2004; **1**(1): 59–84.

73. Graham-Bermann SA, Levendosky AA. Traumatic stress symptoms in children of battered women. *Journal of Interpersonal Violence* 1998; **13**(1):111–28.

74. Foo L, Margolin G. A multivariate investigation of dating aggression. *Journal of Family Violence* 1995; **10** (4):351–77.

75. Hotaling GT, Sugarman DB. An analysis of risk markers in husband to wife violence: The current state of knowledge. *Violence and Victims* 1986; **1** (2):101–24.

76. McCord J. Some child-rearing antecedents of criminal behavior in adult men. *Journal of Personality and Social Psychology* 1979; **37**(9):1477–86.

77. Forsstrom-Cohen B, Rosenbaum A. The effects of parental marital violence on young adults: An exploratory investigation. *Journal of Marriage and Family* 1985; **47**(2):467–72.

78. Henning K, Leitenberg H, Coffey P, et al. Long-term psychological and social impact of witnessing physical conflict between parents. *Journal of Interpersonal Violence* 1996; **11**(1):35–51.

79. Graham-Bermann SA. The impact of woman abuse on children's social development: Research and theoretical perspectives. In: Holden GW, Geffner R, Jouriles EN (eds.), *Children Exposed to Marital Violence: Theory, Research, and Applied Issues* (APA Science Vols.).Washington, DC: American Psychological Association, 1998, pp. 21–54.

80. Katz LF, Hessler DM, Annest A. Domestic violence, children's emotional competence and peer relations. *Social Development* 2007; **16**:513–38.

81. Lee C. *Women's Health: What Do We Know? What Do We Need to Know?* Brisbane, AU:Australian Academic Press, 2001.

82. Iverson KM, McLaughlin KA, Adair KC, Monson CM. Anger dysregulation as a factor linking childhood physical abuse and interparental violence with intimate partner violence experience. *Violence and Victims* 2014; **29**(4):564–78.

83. Harding HG, Morelen D, Thomassin K, et al. Exposure to maternal- and paternal-perpetrated intimate partner violence, emotion regulation, and child outcomes. *Journal of Family Violence* 2013; **28** (1):63–72.

84. Katz LF, Hessler DM, Annest A. Domestic violence, emotional competence, and child adjustment. Social Development 2007; **16**(3):513–38.

85. Zarling AL, Taber-Thomas S, Murray A, et al. Internalizing and externalizing symptoms in young children exposed to intimate partner violence: Examining intervening processes. *Journal of Family Psychology* 2013; **27**(6):945–55.

86. Compas BE, Connor-Smith JK, Saltzman H, et al. Coping with stress during childhood and adolescence: Problems, progress, and potential in theory and research. *Psychology Bulletin* 2001; **127**(1):87–127.

87. Ahonen L, Loeber R. Dating violence in teenage girls: Parental emotion regulation and racial differences. *Criminal Behaviour and Mental Health* 2016; **26** (4):240–50.

88. Katz LF, Gurtovenko K. Posttraumatic stress and emotion regulation in survivors of intimate partner violence. *Journal of Family Psychology* 2015; **29** (4):528–36.

89. Gurtovenko K, Katz LF. Post-traumatic stress, mother's emotion regulation, and parenting in survivors of intimate partner violence. *Journal of Interpersonal Violence* 2017; **35**(3–4).

90. Katz LF, Gurtovenko K, Maliken A, et al. An emotion coaching parenting intervention for families exposed to intimate partner violence. *Developmental Psychology* 2020; **56**(3):638.

91. Boeckel MG, Wagner A, Grassi-Oliveira R. The effects of intimate partner violence exposure on the maternal bond and PTSD symptoms of children. *Journal of Interpersonal Violence*. 2015; **32** (7):1127–42.

92. Smyth EJ, Gardner FL, Marks DR, Moore ZE. An exploration of the mediators between childhood maltreatment and intimate partner violence. *Violence and Victims* 2017; **32**(4):567–83.

93. Jouriles, EN, McDonald R, Rosenfield D, et al. Reducing conduct problems among children exposed to intimate partner violence: A randomized clinical trial examining effects of Project Support. *Journal of Consulting and Clinical Psychology* 2009; **77**:705–17.

94. Graham-Bermann SA. Preschool Kids' Club: A preventive intervention for young children exposed to violence. Department of Psychology, University of Michigan, Ann Arbor, 2020.

95. Hughes HM. Brief interventions with children in a battered women's shelter: A model preventive program. *Family Relations* 1982; **31**(4):495–502.

96. Hughes HM, Barad SJ. Psychological functioning of children in a battered women's shelter: A preliminary

investigation. *American Journal of Orthopsychiatry* 1983; **53**(3):525–31.

97. Wagar JM, Rodway MR. An evaluation of a group treatment approach for children who have witnessed wife abuse. *Journal of Family Violence* 1995; **10** (3):295–306.

98. Peled E, Davis D. *Interpersonal Violence: The Practice Series,* Vol. 10: *Groupwork with Children of Battered Women: A Practitioner's Manual.* Thousand Oaks, CA: Sage Publications, 1995.

99. Tutty LM, Wagar J. The evolution of a group for young children who have witnessed family violence. *Social Work Groups* 1994; **17**(1–2):89–104.

100. Ragg DM, Sultana M, Miller D. Decreasing aggression in child witnesses of domestic violence. Paper presented at the Program Evaluation and Family Violence Research Conference, Durham, NC, July 1998.

101. Lieberman AF, Van Horn P. *'Don't Hit My Mommy!': A Manual for Child-Parent Psychotherapy with Young Witnesses of Family Violence,* 2nd ed. Washington, DC: Zero to Three Press, 2005.

102. Graham-Bermann SA. Preschool Kids' Club: A preventive intervention for young children exposed to violence. Department of Psychology, University of Michigan, Ann Arbor, 2020.

103. Graham-Bermann SA, Lynch S, Banyard V, et al. Community-based intervention for children exposed to intimate partner violence: An efficacy trial. *Journal of Consulting and Clinical Psychology* 2007; **75**(2):199–209.

104. Graham-Bermann SA, Hughes H. Intervention for children exposed to interparental violence (IPV): Assessment of needs and research priorities. *Clinical Child and Family Psychology Review* 2003; **6** (3):189–204.

105. Crandall A, Deater-Deckard K, Riley AW. Maternal emotion and cognitive control capacities and parenting: A conceptual framework. *Developmental Review* 2015; **36**:105–26.

106. Katz LF, Stettler N, Gurtovenko K. Traumatic stress symptoms in children exposed to intimate partner violence: The role of parent emotion socialization and children's emotion regulation abilities. *Social Development* 2015; **25**(1):47–65.

107. Shipman K, Schneider R, Sims C. Emotion socialization in maltreating and nonmaltreating mother-child dyads: Implications for children's adjustment. *Journal of Clinical Child and Adolescent Psychology* 2005; **34**(3):590–6.

108. Appel AE, Holden GW. The co-occurrence of spouse and physical child abuse: A review and appraisal. *Journal of Family Psychology* 1998; **12** (4):578–99.

109. Edleson JL. Children's witnessing of adult domestic violence. *Journal of Interpersonal Violence* 1999; **14** (8):839–70.

110. O'Leary KD, Slep AM, O'Leary SG. Co-occurrence of partner and parent aggression: Research and treatment implications. *Behavior Therapy* 2000; **31** (4):631–48.

111. McGuigan WM, Pratt CC. The predictive impact of domestic violence on three types of child maltreatment. *Child Abuse and Neglect* 2001; **25** (7):869–83.

112. Linehan MM. *Cognitive-Behavior Treatment of Borderline Personality Disorder.* New York: Guilford Press, 1993.

113. Katz LF, Gurtovenko K, Maliken A, et al. An emotion coaching parenting intervention for families exposed to intimate partner violence. *Developmental Psychology* 2020; **56**(3):638.

114. Bonnano GA, Burton CL. Regulatory flexibility: An individual differences perspective on coping and emotion regulation. Perspectives in Psychological Science 2013; **8**(6):591–612.

115. Sburlati ES, Schniering CA, Lyneham HJ, Rapee RM. A model of therapist competencies for the empirically supported cognitive behavioral treatment of child and adolescent anxiety and depressive disorders. *Clinical Child and Family Psychology Review* 2011; **14**(1):89–109.

116. Weisz JR, Kasdin AE. *Evidence-Based Psychotherapies for Children and Adolescents,* 3rd ed. New York: Guilford Press, 2017.

117. Kendall PC, Hayes C, Nauta M. Breathing life into a manual: Flexibility and creativity with manual-based treatments. *Cognitive and Behavioral Practice* 1998; **5**(2):177–98.

118. Graham-Bermann SA, Miller-Graff L. Community-based intervention for women exposed to intimate partner violence: A randomized control trial. *Journal of Family Psychology* 2015; **29**(4):537–47.

119. Swartz HA, Zuckoff A, Grote NK, et al. Engaging depressed patients in psychotherapy: Integrating techniques from motivational interviewing and ethnographic interviewing to improve treatment participation. *Professional Psychology Research and Practice* 2007; **38**(4):430–9.

120. Hutchings J, Lane E. Parenting and the development and prevention of child mental health problems. *Current Opinion in Psychiatry* 2005; **18**(4):386–91.

121. Levendosky AA, Leahy KL, Bogat GA, et al. Domestic violence, maternal parenting, maternal

mental health, and infant externalizing. *Journal of Family Psychology* 2006; **20**(4):544–52.

122. Lee P, Niew W, Yang H, et al. A meta-analysis of behavioral parent training for children with attention deficit hyperactivity disorder. *Research in Developmental Disabilities* 2012; **33**(6):2040–9.

123. Serketich WK, Dumas JE. The effectiveness of behavioral parent training to modify antisocial behavior in children: A meta-analysis. *Behavior Therapy* 1996; **27**(2):171–86.

124. Lau A, Takeuchi D. Cultural factors in help-seeking for child behavior problems: Value orientation, affective responding, and severity appraisals among Chinese-American parents. *Journal of Community Psychology* 2001; **29**(6):675–91.

125. McMahon RJ, Forehand R. *Helping the Noncompliant Child: Family-Based Treatment for Oppositional Behavior*, 2nd ed. New York: Guilford Press, 2003.

126. Sanders MR. Triple p-positive parenting program: Towards an empirically validated multilevel family support strategy for the prevention of behavior and emotional problems in children. *Clinical Child and Family Psychology Review* 1999; **2**(2):71–90.

127. Zisser A, Eyberg SM. Parent-child interaction therapy and the treatment of disruptive behavior disorders. In: Weisz JR, Kazdin AE (eds.), *Evidence-Based Psychotherapies for Children and Adolescents*. New York: Guilford Press, 2010, pp. 179–93.

128. Lambert MJ, Barley DE. Research summary on the therapeutic relationship and psychotherapy outcome. *Psychotherapy* 2001; **38**(4):357–61.

129. Shirk SR, Karver M. Prediction of treatment outcome from relationship variables in child and adolescent therapy: A meta-analytic review. *Journal of Consulting and Clinical Psychology* 2003; **71**(3):452–64.

130. Shirk SR, Karver M. Alliance in child and adolescent therapy. In: Norcross JC (ed.), *Psychotherapy Relationships That Work: Evidence-Based Responsiveness*, 2nd ed. New York: Oxford University Press, 2011, pp. 70–91.

131. Tracy JL, Klonksy ED, Proudfit GH. How affective science can inform clinical science: An introduction to the special series on emotions and psychopathology. *Clinical Psychological Science* 2014; **2**(4):371–86.

132. Linehan MM. *DBT Skills Training Manual*, 2nd ed. New York: Guilford Press, 2015.

133. Kaminski JW, Valle LL, Filene JH, Byle CL. A meta-analytic review of components associated with parent training program effectiveness. *Journal of Abnormal Child Psychology* 2008; **36**(4):567–89.

134. Beck JS. *Cognitive Therapy: Basics and Beyond*, 2nd ed. New York: Guilford Press, 2011.

135. Creswell DJ. Mindfulness interventions. *Annual Review of Psychology* 2017; **68**(1):491–516.

136. Duncan LG, Coatsworth JD, Greenberg MT. A model of mindful parenting: Implications for parent-child relationships and prevention research. *Clinical Child and Family Psychology Review* 2009; **12**(3):255–70.

137. Ben-Porath D. Dialectical Behavior Therapy applied to parent skills training: Adjunctive treatment for parents with difficulties in affect regulation. *Cognitive and Behavioral Practice* 2010; **17**(4):458–65.

138. Hayes SC, Strosahl K, Wilson KG. *Acceptance and Commitment Therapy: An Experiential Approach to Behavior Change*, 2nd ed. New York: Guilford Press, 2017.

139. Havighurst SS, Wilson KR, Harley AE, et al. 'Tuning into Kids': Reducing young children's behavior problems using an emotion coaching parenting program. *Child Psychiatry and Human Development* 2013; **44**(2):247–64.

140. Katz LF, Maliken AC, Stettler NM. Parental meta-emotion philosophy: A review of research and theoretical framework. *Child Development Perspectives* 2012; **6**(4):417–22.

141. Lungu A, Linehan MM. Dialectical Behavior Therapy: A comprehensive multi- and transdiagnostic intervention. In: Nezu CM, Nezu AM (eds.), *The Oxford Handbook of Cognitive and Behavioral Therapies*. New York: Oxford University Press, 2015, pp. 200–14.

142. Katz LF, McMahon RJ, Kerns, S, et al. Emotion coaching and parent management training for children with callous-unemotional traits: A treatment development study. Paper presented at the Annual Meeting of the Society for Research in Child Development, Austin, TX, April 2017.

143. McMahon RJ, Katz LF, Kerns SE, et al. Parent management training and emotion coaching for children with callous-unemotional traits: Initial outcomes. Paper presented at the Annual Meeting of the Society for the Scientific Study of Psychopathy, Las Vegas, NV, May 2017.

144. Baker-Ericzen M, Jenkins MM, Haine-Schlagel R. Therapist, parent, and youth perspectives of treatment barriers to family-focused community outpatient mental health services. *Journal of Child and Family Studies* 2013; **22**(6):854–68.

145. Rose J, McGuire-Snieckus R, Gilbert L. Emotion coaching – A strategy for promoting behavioral self-regulation in children/young people in schools:

A pilot study. *European Journal of Social and Behavioural Sciences* 2015; **13**(159):1766–90.

146. Hilty DM, Ferrer DC, Parish MB, et al. The effectiveness of telemental health: A 2013 review. *Telemedicine Journal and e-Health* 2013; **19** (6):444–54.

147. Aboujaoude E, Salame W, Naim L. Telemental health: A status update. *World Psychiatry* 2015; **14** (2):223–30.

148. Snell-Johns J, Smith BH, Mendez JL. Evidence-based solutions for overcoming access barriers, decreasing attrition, and promoting change with underserved families. *Journal of Family Psychology* 2004; **18** (1):19–35.

149. Aarons GA, Sawitzky AC. Organizational culture and climate and mental health provider attitudes toward evidence-based practice. *Psychological Services* 2006; **3**(1):61–72.

150. Mendel P, Meredith LS, Schoenbaum M, et al. Interventions in organizational and community context: A framework for building evidence on dissemination and implementation in health services research. *Administration and Policy in Mental Health* 2008; **35**(1–2):21–37.

151. Luthar SS, Eisenberg N. Resilient adaptation among at-risk children: Harnessing science toward maximizing salutary environments. *Child Development* 2017; **88**(2):337–49.

Index